# GENERAL MOTORS | ASTRO/SAFARI
## 1985-96 REPAIR MANUAL

Covers all U.S. and Canadian models of Chevrolet Astro and GMC Safari; including rear and all wheel drive models

by Kevin M. G. Maher, A.S.E.

## CHILTON Automotive Books

PUBLISHED BY HAYNES NORTH AMERICA, Inc.

Manufactured in USA
© 1997 Haynes North America, Inc.
ISBN 0-8019-8826-8
Library of Congress Catalog Card No. 94-069429
8901234567  9876543210

**Haynes Publishing Group**
Sparkford Nr Yeovil
Somerset BA22 7JJ England

**Haynes North America, Inc**
861 Lawrence Drive
Newbury Park
California 91320 USA

ABCDE
FGHIJ
K

# Contents

# Contents

**DRIVE TRAIN 7**

**SUSPENSION AND STEERING 8**

**BRAKES 9**

**BODY & TRIM 10**

**GLOSSARY**

**MASTER INDEX**

## SAFETY NOTICE

Proper service and repair procedures are vital to the safe, reliable operation of all motor vehicles, as well as the personal safety of those performing repairs. This manual outlines procedures for servicing and repairing vehicles using safe, effective methods. The procedures contain many NOTES, CAUTIONS and WARNINGS which should be followed, along with standard procedures to eliminate the possibility of personal injury or improper service which could damage the vehicle or compromise its safety.

It is important to note that repair procedures and techniques, tools and parts for servicing motor vehicles, as well as the skill and experience of the individual performing the work vary widely. It is not possible to anticipate all of the conceivable ways or conditions under which vehicles may be serviced, or to provide cautions as to all possible hazards that may result. Standard and accepted safety precautions and equipment should be used when handling toxic or flammable fluids, and safety goggles or other protection should be used during cutting, grinding, chiseling, prying, or any other process that can cause material removal or projectiles.

Some procedures require the use of tools specially designed for a specific purpose. Before substituting another tool or procedure, you must be completely satisfied that neither your personal safety, nor the performance of the vehicle will be endangered.

Although information in this manual is based on industry sources and is complete as possible at the time of publication, the possibility exists that some car manufacturers made later changes which could not be included here. While striving for total accuracy, the authors or publishers cannot assume responsibility for any errors, changes or omissions that may occur in the compilation of this data.

## PART NUMBERS

Part numbers listed in this reference are not recommendations by Haynes North America, Inc. for any product brand name. They are references that can be used with interchange manuals and aftermarket supplier catalogs to locate each brand supplier's discrete part number.

## SPECIAL TOOLS

Special tools are recommended by the vehicle manufacturer to perform their specific job. Use has been kept to a minimum, but where absolutely necessary, they are referred to in the text by the part number of the tool manufacturer. These tools can be purchased, under the appropriate part number, from your local dealer or regional distributor, or an equivalent tool can be purchased locally from a tool supplier or parts outlet. Before substituting any tool for the one recommended, read the SAFETY NOTICE at the top of this page.

## ACKNOWLEDGMENTS

Portions of materials contained herein have been reprinted with the permission of General Motors Corporation, Service Technology Group.

# 1

# ROUTINE MAINTENANCE & TUNE-UP

## HOW TO USE THIS BOOK

This Chilton's Total Car Care manual for the Chevrolet Astro and GMC Safari Vans is intended to help you learn more about the inner workings of your vehicle while saving you money on its upkeep and operation.

The beginning of the book will likely be referred to the most, since that is where you will find information for maintenance and tune-up. The other sections deal with the more complex systems of your vehicle. Systems (from engine through brakes) are covered to the extent that the average do-it-yourselfer can attempt. This book will not explain such things as rebuilding a differential because the expertise required and the special tools necessary make this uneconomical. It will, however, give you detailed instructions to help you change your own brake pads and shoes, replace spark plugs, and perform many more jobs that can save you money and help avoid expensive problems.

A secondary purpose of this book is a reference for owners who want to understand their vehicle and/or their mechanics better.

### Where to Begin

Before removing any bolts, read through the entire procedure. This will give you the overall view of what tools and supplies will be required. So read ahead and plan ahead. Each operation should be approached logically and all procedures thoroughly understood before attempting any work.

If repair of a component is not considered practical, we tell you how to remove the part and then how to install the new or rebuilt replacement. In this way, you at least save labor costs.

### Avoiding Trouble

Many procedures in this book require you to "label and disconnect . . . " a group of lines, hoses or wires. Don't be think you can remember where everything goes—you won't. If you hook up vacuum or fuel lines incorrectly, the vehicle may run poorly, if at all. If you hook up electrical wiring incorrectly, you may instantly learn a very expensive lesson.

You don't need to know the proper name for each hose or line. A piece of masking tape on the hose and a piece on its fitting will allow you to assign your own label. As long as you remember your own code, the lines can be reconnected by matching your tags. Remember that tape will dissolve in gasoline or solvents; if a part is to be washed or cleaned, use another method of identification. A permanent felt-tipped marker or a metal scribe can be very handy for marking metal parts. Remove any tape or paper labels after assembly.

### Maintenance or Repair?

Maintenance includes routine inspections, adjustments, and replacement of parts which show signs of normal wear. Maintenance compensates for wear or deterioration. Repair implies that something has broken or is not working. A need for a repair is often caused by lack of maintenance. for example: draining and refilling automatic transmission fluid is maintenance recommended at specific intervals. Failure to do this can shorten the life of the transmission/transaxle, requiring very expensive repairs. While no maintenance program can prevent items from eventually breaking or wearing out, a general rule is true: MAINTENANCE IS CHEAPER THAN REPAIR.

Two basic mechanic's rules should be mentioned here. First, whenever the left side of the vehicle or engine is referred to, it means the driver's side. Conversely, the right side of the vehicle means the passenger's side. Second, screws and bolts are removed by turning counterclockwise, and tightened by turning clockwise unless specifically noted.

Safety is always the most important rule. Constantly be aware of the dangers involved in working on an automobile and take the proper precautions. Please refer to the information in this section regarding SERVICING YOUR VEHICLE SAFELY and the SAFETY NOTICE on the acknowledgment page.

### Avoiding the Most Common Mistakes

Pay attention to the instructions provided. There are 3 common mistakes in mechanical work:

1. Incorrect order of assembly, disassembly or adjustment. When taking something apart or putting it together, performing steps in the wrong order usually just costs you extra time; however, it CAN break something. Read the entire procedure before beginning. Perform everything in the order in which the instructions say you should, even if you can't see a reason for it. When you're taking apart something that is very intricate, you might want to draw a picture of how it looks when assembled in order to make sure you get everything back in its proper position. When making adjustments, perform them in the proper order. One adjustment possibly will affect another.

2. Overtorquing (or undertorquing). While it is more common for overtorquing to cause damage, undertorquing may allow a fastener to vibrate loose causing serious damage. Especially when dealing with aluminum parts, pay attention to torque specifications and utilize a torque wrench in assembly. If a torque figure is not available, remember that if you are using the right tool to perform the job, you will probably not have to strain yourself to get a fastener tight enough. The pitch of most threads is so slight that the tension you put on the wrench will be multiplied many times in actual force on what you are tightening.

There are many commercial products available for ensuring that fasteners won't come loose, even if they are not torqued just right (a very common brand is Loctite®). If you're worried about getting something together tight enough to hold, but loose enough to avoid mechanical damage during assembly, one of these products might offer substantial insurance. Before choosing a threadlocking compound, read the label on the package and make sure the product is compatible with the materials, fluids, etc. involved.

3. Crossthreading. This occurs when a part such as a bolt is screwed into a nut or casting at the wrong angle and forced. Crossthreading is more likely to occur if access is difficult. It helps to clean and lubricate fasteners, then to start threading the bolt, spark plug, etc. with your fingers. If you encounter resistance, unscrew the part and start over again at a different angle until it can be inserted and turned several times without much effort. Keep in mind that many parts have tapered threads, so that gentle turning will automatically bring the part you're threading to the proper angle. Don't put a wrench on the part until it's been tightened a couple of turns by hand. If you suddenly encounter resistance, and the part has not seated fully, don't force it. Pull it back out to make sure it's clean and threading properly.

Be sure to take your time and be patient, and always plan ahead. Allow yourself ample time to perform repairs and maintenance.

## TOOLS AND EQUIPMENT

▶ **See Figures 1 thru 15**

Without the proper tools and equipment it is impossible to properly service your vehicle. It would be virtually impossible to catalog every tool that you would need to perform all of the operations in this book. It would be unwise for the amateur to rush out and buy an expensive set of tools on the theory that he/she may need one or more of them at some time.

The best approach is to proceed slowly, gathering a good quality set of those tools that are used most frequently. Don't be misled by the low cost of bargain tools. It is far better to spend a little more for better quality. Forged wrenches, 6 or 12-point sockets and fine tooth ratchets are by far preferable to their less expensive counterparts. As any good mechanic can tell you, there are few worse

experiences than trying to work on a vehicle with bad tools. Your monetary savings will be far outweighed by frustration and mangled knuckles.

Begin accumulating those tools that are used most frequently: those associated with routine maintenance and tune-up. In addition to the normal assortment of screwdrivers and pliers, you should have the following tools:

• Wrenches/sockets and combination open end/box end wrenches in sizes 1/8–3/4 in. and/or 3mm–19mm 13/16 in. or 5/8 in. spark plug socket (depending on plug type).

➡ **If possible, buy various length socket drive extensions. Universal-joint and wobble extensions can be extremely useful, but be careful when using them, as they can change the amount of torque applied to the socket.**

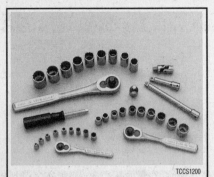

**Fig. 1 All but the most basic procedures will require an assortment of ratchets and sockets**

TCCS1200

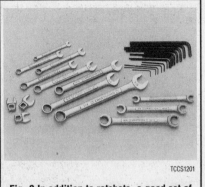

**Fig. 2 In addition to ratchets, a good set of wrenches and hex keys will be necessary**

TCCS1201

**Fig. 3 A hydraulic floor jack and a set of jackstands are essential for lifting and supporting the vehicle**

TCCS1202

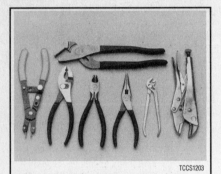

**Fig. 4 An assortment of pliers, grippers and cutters will be handy for old rusted parts and stripped bolt heads**

TCCS1203

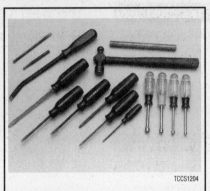

**Fig. 5 Various drivers, chisels and prybars are great tools to have in your toolbox**

TCCS1204

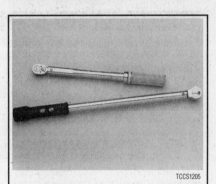

**Fig. 6 Many repairs will require the use of a torque wrench to assure the components are properly fastened**

TCCS1205

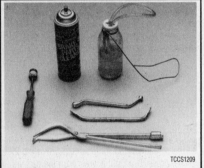

**Fig. 7 Although not always necessary, using specialized brake tools will save time**

TCCS1209

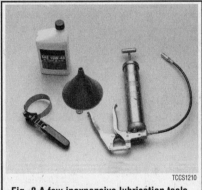

**Fig. 8 A few inexpensive lubrication tools will make maintenance easier**

TCCS1210

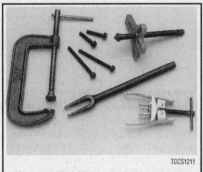

**Fig. 9 Various pullers, clamps and separator tools are needed for many larger, more complicated repairs**

TCCS1211

**Fig. 10 A variety of tools and gauges should be used for spark plug gapping and installation**

TCCS1212

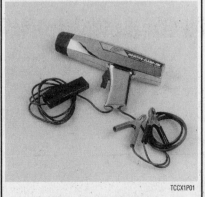

**Fig. 11 Inductive type timing light**

TCCX1P01

**Fig. 12 A screw-in type compression gauge is recommended for compression testing**

TCCX1P02

**Fig. 13 A vacuum/pressure tester is necessary for many testing procedures**

TCCX1P03

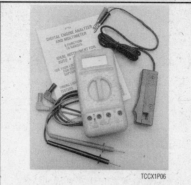

**Fig. 14 Most modern automotive multimeters incorporate many helpful features**

TCCX1P06

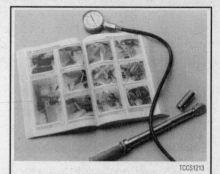

**Fig. 15 Proper information is vital, so always have a Chilton Total Car Care manual handy**

TCCS1213

- Jackstands for support.
- Oil filter wrench.
- Spout or funnel for pouring fluids.
- Grease gun for chassis lubrication (unless your vehicle is not equipped with any grease fittings)
- Hydrometer for checking the battery (unless equipped with a sealed, maintenance-free battery).
- A container for draining oil and other fluids.
- Rags for wiping up the inevitable mess.

In addition to the above items there are several others that are not absolutely necessary, but handy to have around. These include an equivalent oil absorbent gravel, like cat litter, and the usual supply of lubricants, antifreeze and fluids. This is a basic list for routine maintenance, but only your personal needs and desire can accurately determine your list of tools.

After performing a few projects on the vehicle, you'll be amazed at the other tools and non-tools on your workbench. Some useful household items are: a large turkey baster or siphon, empty coffee cans and ice trays (to store parts), a ball of twine, electrical tape for wiring, small rolls of colored tape for tagging lines or hoses, markers and pens, a note pad, golf tees (for plugging vacuum lines), metal coat hangers or a roll of mechanic's wire (to hold things out of the way), dental pick or similar long, pointed probe, a strong magnet, and a small mirror (to see into recesses and under manifolds).

A more advanced set of tools, suitable for tune-up work, can be drawn up easily. While the tools are slightly more sophisticated, they need not be outrageously expensive. There are several inexpensive tach/dwell meters on the market that are every bit as good for the average mechanic as a professional model. Just be sure that it goes to a least 1200–1500 rpm on the tach scale and that it works on 4, 6 and 8-cylinder engines. The key to these purchases is to make them with an eye towards adaptability and wide range. A basic list of tune-up tools could include:

- Tach/dwell meter.
- Spark plug wrench and gapping tool.
- Feeler gauges for valve adjustment.
- Timing light.

The choice of a timing light should be made carefully. A light which works on the DC current supplied by the vehicle's battery is the best choice; it should have a xenon tube for brightness. On any vehicle with an electronic ignition system, a timing light with an inductive pickup that clamps around the No. 1 spark plug cable is preferred.

In addition to these basic tools, there are several other tools and gauges you may find useful. These include:

- Compression gauge. The screw-in type is slower to use, but eliminates the possibility of a faulty reading due to escaping pressure.
- Manifold vacuum gauge.
- 12V test light.
- A combination volt/ohmmeter
- Induction Ammeter. This is used for determining whether or not there is current in a wire. These are handy for use if a wire is broken somewhere in a wiring harness.

As a final note, you will probably find a torque wrench necessary for all but the most basic work. The beam type models are perfectly adequate, although the newer click types (breakaway) are easier to use. The click type torque wrenches tend to be more expensive. Also keep in mind that all types of torque wrenches should be periodically checked and/or recalibrated. You will have to decide for yourself which better fits your pocketbook, and purpose.

## Special Tools

Normally, the use of special factory tools is avoided for repair procedures, since these are not readily available for the do-it-yourself mechanic. When it is possible to perform the job with more commonly available tools, it will be pointed out, but occasionally, a special tool was designed to perform a specific function and should be used. Before substituting another tool, you should be convinced that neither your safety nor the performance of the vehicle will be compromised.

Special tools can usually be purchased from an automotive parts store or from your dealer. In some cases special tools may be available directly from the tool manufacturer.

## SERVICING YOUR VEHICLE SAFELY

▶ **See Figures 16, 17 and 18**

It is virtually impossible to anticipate all of the hazards involved with automotive maintenance and service, but care and common sense will prevent most accidents.

The rules of safety for mechanics range from "don't smoke around gasoline," to "use the proper tool(s) for the job." The trick to avoiding injuries is to develop safe work habits and to take every possible precaution.

### Do's

- Do keep a fire extinguisher and first aid kit handy.
- Do wear safety glasses or goggles when cutting, drilling, grinding or prying, even if you have 20–20 vision. If you wear glasses for the sake of vision, wear safety goggles over your regular glasses.

- Do shield your eyes whenever you work around the battery. Batteries contain sulfuric acid. In case of contact with, flush the area with water or a mixture of water and baking soda, then seek immediate medical attention.
- Do use safety stands (jackstands) for any undervehicle service. Jacks are for raising vehicles; jackstands are for making sure the vehicle stays raised until you want it to come down.
- Do use adequate ventilation when working with any chemicals or hazardous materials. Like carbon monoxide, the asbestos dust resulting from some brake lining wear can be hazardous in sufficient quantities.
- Do disconnect the negative battery cable when working on the electrical system. The secondary ignition system contains EXTREMELY HIGH VOLTAGE. In some cases it can even exceed 50,000 volts.
- Do follow manufacturer's directions whenever working with potentially hazardous materials. Most chemicals and fluids are poisonous.
- Do properly maintain your tools. Loose hammerheads, mushroomed

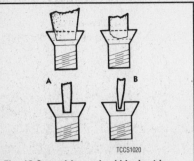

**Fig. 16 Screwdrivers should be kept in good condition to prevent injury or damage which could result if the blade slips from the screw**

**Fig. 17 Using the correct size wrench will help prevent the possibility of rounding off a nut**

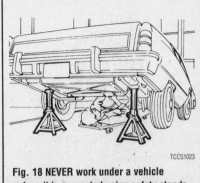

**Fig. 18 NEVER work under a vehicle unless it is supported using safety stands (jackstands)**

punches and chisels, frayed or poorly grounded electrical cords, excessively worn screwdrivers, spread wrenches (open end), cracked sockets, slipping ratchets, or faulty droplight sockets can cause accidents.

• Likewise, keep your tools clean; a greasy wrench can slip off a bolt head, ruining the bolt and often harming your knuckles in the process.

• Do use the proper size and type of tool for the job at hand. Do select a wrench or socket that fits the nut or bolt. The wrench or socket should sit straight, not cocked.

• Do, when possible, pull on a wrench handle rather than push on it, and adjust your stance to prevent a fall.

• Do be sure that adjustable wrenches are tightly closed on the nut or bolt and pulled so that the force is on the side of the fixed jaw.

• Do strike squarely with a hammer; avoid glancing blows.

• Do set the parking brake and block the drive wheels if the work requires a running engine.

## Don'ts

• Don't run the engine in a garage or anywhere else without proper ventilation—EVER! Carbon monoxide is poisonous; it takes a long time to leave the human body and you can build up a deadly supply of it in your system by simply breathing in a little at a time. You may not realize you are slowly poisoning yourself. Always use power vents, windows, fans and/or open the garage door.

• Don't work around moving parts while wearing loose clothing. Short sleeves are much safer than long, loose sleeves. Hard-toed shoes with neoprene soles protect your toes and give a better grip on slippery surfaces. Watches and jewelry is not safe working around a vehicle. Long hair should be tied back under a hat or cap.

• Don't use pockets for toolboxes. A fall or bump can drive a screwdriver deep into your body. Even a rag hanging from your back pocket can wrap around a spinning shaft or fan.

• Don't smoke when working around gasoline, cleaning solvent or other flammable material.

• Don't smoke when working around the battery. When the battery is being charged, it gives off explosive hydrogen gas.

• Don't use gasoline to wash your hands; there are excellent soaps available. Gasoline contains dangerous additives which can enter the body through a cut or through your pores. Gasoline also removes all the natural oils from the skin so that bone dry hands will suck up oil and grease.

• Don't service the air conditioning system unless you are equipped with the necessary tools and training. When liquid or compressed gas refrigerant is released to atmospheric pressure it will absorb heat from whatever it contacts. This will chill or freeze anything it touches.

• Don't use screwdrivers for anything other than driving screws! A screwdriver used as an prying tool can snap when you least expect it, causing injuries. At the very least, you'll ruin a good screwdriver.

• Don't use an emergency jack (that little ratchet, scissors, or pantograph jack supplied with the vehicle) for anything other than changing a flat! These jacks are only intended for emergency use out on the road; they are NOT designed as a maintenance tool. If you are serious about maintaining your vehicle yourself, invest in a hydraulic floor jack of at least a 1½ ton capacity, and at least two sturdy jackstands.

# FASTENERS, MEASUREMENTS AND CONVERSIONS

## Bolts, Nuts and Other Threaded Retainers

▶ **See Figures 19 and 20**

Although there are a great variety of fasteners found in the modern car or truck, the most commonly used retainer is the threaded fastener (nuts, bolts, screws, studs, etc.). Most threaded retainers may be reused, provided that they are not damaged in use or during the repair. Some retainers (such as stretch bolts or torque prevailing nuts) are designed to deform when tightened or in use and should not be reinstalled.

Whenever possible, we will note any special retainers which should be replaced during a procedure. But you should always inspect the condition of a retainer when it is removed and replace any that show signs of damage. Check all threads for rust or corrosion which can increase the torque necessary to achieve the desired clamp load for which that fastener was originally selected. Additionally, be sure that the driver surface of the fastener has not been compromised by rounding or other damage. In some cases a driver surface may become only partially rounded, allowing the driver to catch in only one direction. In many of these occurrences, a fastener may be installed and tightened, but the driver would not be able to grip and loosen the fastener again.

If you must replace a fastener, whether due to design or damage, you must ALWAYS be sure to use the proper replacement. In all cases, a retainer of the

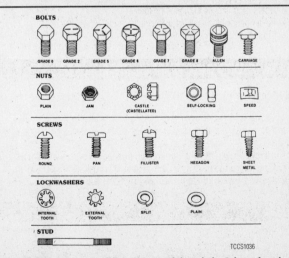

**Fig. 19 There are many different types of threaded retainers found on vehicles**

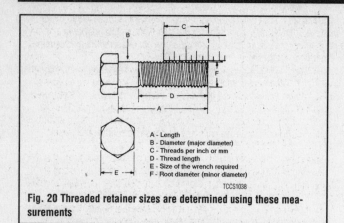

**Fig. 20 Threaded retainer sizes are determined using these measurements**

A - Length
B - Diameter (major diameter)
C - Threads per inch or mm
D - Thread length
E - Size of the wrench required
F - Root diameter (minor diameter)

TCCS1038

same design, material and strength should be used. Markings on the heads of most bolts will help determine the proper strength of the fastener. The same material, thread and pitch must be selected to assure proper installation and safe operation of the vehicle afterwards.

Thread gauges are available to help measure a bolt or stud's thread. Most automotive and hardware stores keep gauges available to help you select the proper size. In a pinch, you can use another nut or bolt for a thread gauge. If the bolt you are replacing is not too badly damaged, you can select a match by finding another bolt which will thread in its place. If you find a nut which threads properly onto the damaged bolt, then use that nut to help select the replacement bolt.

### ❊❊ WARNING

**Be aware that when you find a bolt with damaged threads, you may also find the nut or drilled hole it was threaded into has also been damaged. If this is the case, you may have to drill and tap the hole, replace the nut or otherwise repair the threads. NEVER try to force a replacement bolt to fit into the damaged threads.**

## Torque

Torque is defined as the measurement of resistance to turning or rotating. It tends to twist a body about an axis of rotation. A common example of this would be tightening a threaded retainer such as a nut, bolt or screw. Measuring torque is one of the most common ways to help assure that a threaded retainer has been properly fastened.

When tightening a threaded fastener, torque is applied in three distinct areas, the head, the bearing surface and the clamp load. About 50 percent of the measured torque is used in overcoming bearing friction. This is the friction between the bearing surface of the bolt head, screw head or nut face and the base material or washer (the surface on which the fastener is rotating). Approximately 40 percent of the applied torque is used in overcoming thread friction. This leaves only about 10 percent of the applied torque to develop a useful clamp load (the force which holds a joint together). This means that friction can account for as much as 90 percent of the applied torque on a fastener.

### TORQUE WRENCHES

#### ♦ See Figure 21

In most applications, a torque wrench can be used to assure proper installation of a fastener. Torque wrenches come in various designs and most automotive supply stores will carry a variety to suit your needs. A torque wrench should be used any time we supply a specific torque value for a fastener. Again, the general rule of "if you are using the right tool for the job, you should not have to strain to tighten a fastener" applies here.

#### Beam Type

The beam type torque wrench is one of the most popular types. It consists of a pointer attached to the head that runs the length of the flexible beam (shaft) to a scale located near the handle. As the wrench is pulled, the beam bends and the pointer indicates the torque using the scale.

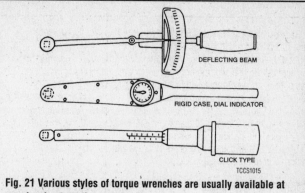

**Fig. 21 Various styles of torque wrenches are usually available at your local automotive supply store**

DEFLECTING BEAM

RIGID CASE, DIAL INDICATOR

CLICK TYPE

TCCS1015

#### Click (Breakaway) Type

Another popular design of torque wrench is the click type. To use the click type wrench you pre-adjust it to a torque setting. Once the torque is reached, the wrench has a reflex signaling feature that causes a momentary breakaway of the torque wrench body, sending an impulse to the operator's hand.

#### Pivot Head Type

#### ♦ See Figure 22

Some torque wrenches (usually of the click type) may be equipped with a pivot head which can allow it to be used in areas of limited access. BUT, it must be used properly. To hold a pivot head wrench, grasp the handle lightly, and as you pull on the handle, it should be floated on the pivot point. If the handle comes in contact with the yoke extension during the process of pulling, there is a very good chance the torque readings will be inaccurate because this could alter the wrench loading point. The design of the handle is usually such as to make it inconvenient to deliberately misuse the wrench.

➡ **It should be mentioned that the use of any U-joint, wobble or extension will have an effect on the torque readings, no matter what type of wrench you are using. For the most accurate readings, install the socket directly on the wrench driver. If necessary, straight extensions (which hold a socket directly under the wrench driver) will have the least effect on the torque reading. Avoid any extension that alters the length of the wrench from the handle to the head/driving point (such as a crow's foot). U-joint or wobble extensions can greatly affect the readings; avoid their use at all times.**

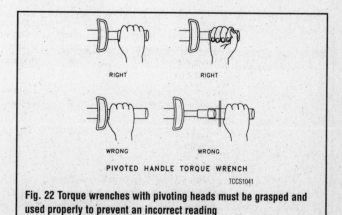

RIGHT

RIGHT

WRONG

WRONG

PIVOTED HANDLE TORQUE WRENCH

TCCS1041

**Fig. 22 Torque wrenches with pivoting heads must be grasped and used properly to prevent an incorrect reading**

#### Rigid Case (Direct Reading)

A rigid case or direct reading torque wrench is equipped with a dial indicator to show torque values. One advantage of these wrenches is that they can be held at any position on the wrench without affecting accuracy. These wrenches are often preferred because they tend to be compact, easy to read and have a great degree of accuracy.

## TORQUE ANGLE METERS

Because the frictional characteristics of each fastener or threaded hole will vary, clamp loads which are based strictly on torque will vary as well. In most applications, this variance is not significant enough to cause worry. But, in certain applications, a manufacturer's engineers may determine that more precise clamp loads are necessary (such is the case with many aluminum cylinder heads). In these cases, a torque angle method of installation would be specified. When installing fasteners which are torque angle tightened, a predetermined seating torque and standard torque wrench are usually used first to remove any compliance from the joint. The fastener is then tightened the specified additional portion of a turn measured in degrees. A torque angle gauge (mechanical protractor) is used for these applications.

## Standard and Metric Measurements

◆ See Figure 23

Throughout this manual, specifications are given to help you determine the condition of various components on your vehicle, or to assist you in their installation. Some of the most common measurements include length (in. or cm/mm), torque (ft. lbs., inch lbs. or Nm) and pressure (psi, in. Hg, kPa or mm Hg). In most cases, we strive to provide the proper measurement as determined by the manufacturer's engineers.

Though, in some cases, that value may not be conveniently measured with what is available in your toolbox. Luckily, many of the measuring devices which are available today will have two scales so the Standard or Metric measurements may easily be taken. If any of the various measuring tools which are available to you do not contain the same scale as listed in the specifications, use the accompanying conversion factors to determine the proper value.

The conversion factor chart is used by taking the given specification and multiplying it by the necessary conversion factor. For instance, looking at the first line, if you have a measurement in inches such as "free-play should be 2 in." but your ruler reads only in millimeters, multiply 2 in. by the conversion factor of 25.4 to get the metric equivalent of 50.8mm. Likewise, if the specification was given only in a Metric measurement, for example in Newton Meters (Nm), then look at the center column first. If the measurement is 100 Nm, multiply it by the conversion factor of 0.738 to get 73.8 ft. lbs.

---

## CONVERSION FACTORS

**LENGTH–DISTANCE**

| | | | | |
|---|---|---|---|---|
| Inches (in.) | x 25.4 | = Millimeters (mm) | x .0394 | = Inches |
| Feet (ft.) | x .305 | = Meters (m) | x 3.281 | = Feet |
| Miles | x 1.609 | = Kilometers (km) | x .0621 | = Miles |

**VOLUME**

| | | | | |
|---|---|---|---|---|
| Cubic Inches (in3) | x 16.387 | = Cubic Centimeters | x .061 | = in3 |
| IMP Pints (IMP pt.) | x .568 | = Liters (L) | x 1.76 | = IMP pt. |
| IMP Quarts (IMP qt.) | x 1.137 | = Liters (L) | x .88 | = IMP qt. |
| IMP Gallons (IMP gal.) | x 4.546 | = Liters (L) | x .22 | = IMP gal. |
| IMP Quarts (IMP qt.) | x 1.201 | = US Quarts (US qt.) | x .833 | = IMP qt. |
| IMP Gallons (IMP gal.) | x 1.201 | = US Gallons (US gal.) | x .833 | = IMP gal. |
| Fl. Ounces | x 29.573 | = Milliliters | x .034 | = Ounces |
| US Pints (US pt.) | x .473 | = Liters (L) | x 2.113 | = Pints |
| US Quarts (US qt.) | x .946 | = Liters (L) | x 1.057 | = Quarts |
| US Gallons (US gal.) | x 3.785 | = Liters (L) | x .264 | = Gallons |

**MASS–WEIGHT**

| | | | | |
|---|---|---|---|---|
| Ounces (oz.) | x 28.35 | = Grams (g) | x .035 | = Ounces |
| Pounds (lb.) | x .454 | = Kilograms (kg) | x 2.205 | = Pounds |

**PRESSURE**

| | | | | |
|---|---|---|---|---|
| Pounds Per Sq. In. (psi) | x 6.895 | = Kilopascals (kPa) | x .145 | = psi |
| Inches of Mercury (Hg) | x .4912 | = psi | x 2.036 | = Hg |
| Inches of Mercury (Hg) | x 3.377 | = Kilopascals (kPa) | x .2961 | = Hg |
| Inches of Water ($H_2O$) | x .07355 | = Inches of Mercury | x 13.783 | = $H_2O$ |
| Inches of Water ($H_2O$) | x .03613 | = psi | x 27.684 | = $H_2O$ |
| Inches of Water ($H_2O$) | x .248 | = Kilopascals (kPa) | x 4.026 | = $H_2O$ |

**TORQUE**

| | | | | |
|---|---|---|---|---|
| Pounds–Force Inches (in–lb) | x .113 | = Newton Meters (N·m) | x 8.85 | = in–lb |
| Pounds–Force Feet (ft–lb) | x 1.356 | = Newton Meters (N·m) | x .738 | = ft–lb |

**VELOCITY**

| | | | | |
|---|---|---|---|---|
| Miles Per Hour (MPH) | x 1.609 | = Kilometers Per Hour (KPH) | x .621 | = MPH |

**POWER**

| | | | | |
|---|---|---|---|---|
| Horsepower (Hp) | x .745 | = Kilowatts | x 1.34 | = Horsepower |

**FUEL CONSUMPTION***

| | | | |
|---|---|---|---|
| Miles Per Gallon IMP (MPG) | x .354 | = Kilometers Per Liter (Km/L) | |
| Kilometers Per Liter (Km/L) | x 2.352 | = IMP MPG | |
| Miles Per Gallon US (MPG) | x .425 | = Kilometers Per Liter (Km/L) | |
| Kilometers Per Liter (Km/L) | x 2.352 | = US MPG | |

*It is common to covert from miles per gallon (mpg) to liters/100 kilometers (1/100 km), where mpg (IMP) x 1/100 km = 282 and mpg (US) x 1/100 km = 235.

**TEMPERATURE**

| | |
|---|---|
| Degree Fahrenheit (°F) | = (°C x 1.8) + 32 |
| Degree Celsius (°C) | = (°F – 32) x .56 |

TCCS1044

**Fig. 23 Standard and metric conversion factors chart**

## SERIAL NUMBER IDENTIFICATION

### Vehicle

▶ See Figures 24 and 25

The Vehicle Identification Number (VIN) is found on various anti-theft labels, but the most important is the vehicle serial number plate located on the top left side of the instrument panel (it can be viewed through the windshield). The VIN identifies the body style, model year, assembly plant, engine usage and production number.

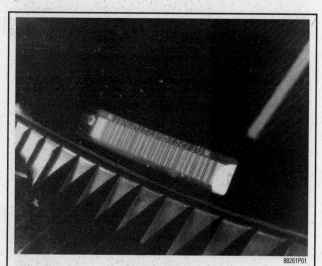

Fig. 24 The VIN is on a plate attached to the dash and visible through the driver's side of the windshield

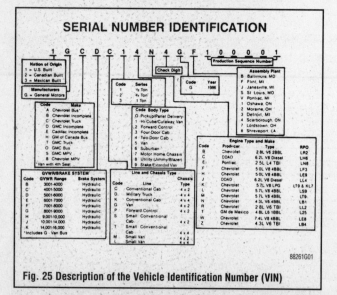

Fig. 25 Description of the Vehicle Identification Number (VIN)

### Engine

▶ See Figures 26, 27 and 28

Your first stop in engine identification is the VIN which will supply you with a code to identify the engine with which the vehicle was originally equipped. If you believe the engine is not original equipment for your vehicle, identification can be a little more difficult. Check the labels found on about the engine compartment (radiator shroud, power steering pump reservoir, air cleaner) for more clues. Your last resort is the often difficult to interpret engine codes.

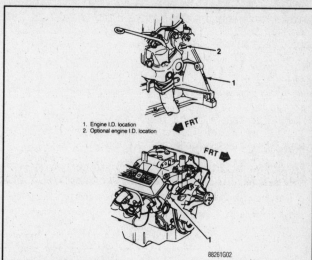

Fig. 26 Engine identification number location—early-model engines (2.5L top, 4.3L bottom)

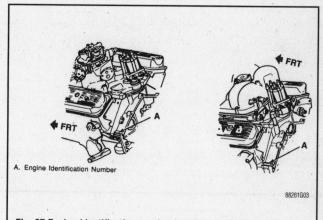

Fig. 27 Engine identification number locations—1990-93 4.3L engines

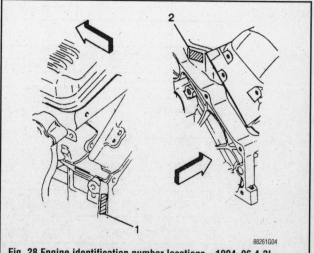

Fig. 28 Engine identification number locations—1994-96 4.3L engines

All engines will have some engine build code attached on a label and usually stamped or laser cut into a portion of the block. The 2.5L engine identification numbers are stamped on the left side of the rear engine block flange. All of the early-model (1985–89) and many of the later (1990–93) 4.3L engine identification numbers are stamped on a pad of the engine block which is located at the lower front edge of the right side cylinder head. On these vehicles the eighth digit of the serial number identifies the engine used in the vehicle.

Many of the later model engines relocated the identification numbers. On some 1990–93 4.3L engines, the number can be found at the rear left of the block, just above the oil filter adapter. The left rear location is also used on many of the 1994–96 engines covered by this manual. The balance of late-model engine codes are found on the upper right, rear of the block. On late-model 4.3L engines, the number is a 8 digit code which includes, a source code, month of build, date of build and broadcast code. See your dealer's parts department for translation of these codes.

## Manual Transmission

The transmission serial numbers are located on the front right side of the main housing.

## Automatic Transmission

The Turbo Hydra-Matic 700-R4 (also known as the 4L60 on models through 1992) and their electronically controlled cousin the 4L60-E (1993–96) 4-spd automatic transmission serial numbers are located on the rear right side of the transmission case, above the oil pan.

## Drive Axle

All Astro and Safari Vans have the drive axle serial number located on the forward side of the right axle tube. The 2 or 3 letter prefix in the serial number identifies the drive axle gear ratio.

## Transfer Case

The All Wheel Drive transfer case identification is located on a tag bolted to the bottom of the front output flange.

### VEHICLE IDENTIFICATION

| Engine Code | | | | | | | Model Year | |
|---|---|---|---|---|---|---|---|---|
| Code | Liters | Cu. In. (cc) | Cyl. | Fuel Sys. | Eng. Mfg. | | Code | Year |
| E | 2.5 | 151 (2474) | 4 | TBI | Pontiac/CPC | | F | 1985 |
| N | 4.3 | 263 (4293) | 6 | 4BC | Chevrolet | | G | 1986 |
| B | 4.3 | 263 (4293) | 6 | TBI | CPC | | H | 1987 |
| W | 4.3 | 263 (4293) | 6 | CMFI/CSFI 1 | CPC | | J | 1988 |
| Z | 4.3 | 263 (4293) | 6 | TBI | Chevrolet/CPC | | K | 1989 |
| | | | | | | | L | 1990 |
| | | | | | | | M | 1991 |
| | | | | | | | N | 1992 |
| | | | | | | | P | 1993 |
| | | | | | | | R | 1994 |
| | | | | | | | S | 1995 |
| | | | | | | | T | 1996 |

BC - Barrel carburetor
CMFI - Central multi-port fuel injection
CPC - Chevrolet/Pontiac/Canada
CSFI - Central sequential fuel injection
TBI - Throttle body fuel injection
1 1992-95: CMFI
1996: CSFI

88261C01

### ENGINE IDENTIFICATION
All measurements are given in inches.

| Year | Model | Engine Displacement Liters (cc) | Engine Series (ID/VIN) | Fuel System | No. of Cylinders | Engine Type |
|---|---|---|---|---|---|---|
| 1985 | Astro/Safari | 2.5 (2474) | E | TBI | 4 | OHV |
| | Astro/Safari | 4.3 (4293) | N | 4BC | 6 | OHV |
| 1986 | Astro/Safari | 2.5 (2474) | E | TBI | 4 | OHV |
| | Astro/Safari | 4.3 (4293) | Z | TBI | 6 | OHV |
| 1987 | Astro/Safari | 2.5 (2474) | E | TBI | 4 | OHV |
| | Astro/Safari | 4.3 (4293) | Z | TBI | 6 | OHV |
| 1988 | Astro/Safari | 2.5 (2474) | E | TBI | 4 | OHV |
| | Astro/Safari | 4.3 (4293) | Z | TBI | 6 | OHV |
| 1989 | Astro/Safari | 2.5 (2474) | E | TBI | 4 | OHV |
| | Astro/Safari | 4.3 (4293) | Z | TBI | 6 | OHV |
| 1990 | Astro/Safari | 2.5 (2474) | E | TBI | 4 | OHV |
| | Astro/Safari | 4.3 (4293) | B | TBI | 6 | OHV |
| | Astro/Safari | 4.3 (4293) | Z | TBI | 6 | OHV |
| 1991 | Astro/Safari | 4.3 (4293) | B | TBI | 6 | OHV |
| | Astro/Safari | 4.3 (4293) | Z | TBI | 6 | OHV |
| 1992 | Astro/Safari | 4.3 (4293) | W | CMFI | 6 | OHV |
| | Astro/Safari | 4.3 (4293) | Z | TBI | 6 | OHV |
| 1993 | Astro/Safari | 4.3 (4293) | W | CMFI | 6 | OHV |
| | Astro/Safari | 4.3 (4293) | Z | TBI | 6 | OHV |
| 1994 | Astro/Safari | 4.3 (4293) | W | CMFI | 6 | OHV |
| | Astro/Safari | 4.3 (4293) | Z | TBI | 6 | OHV |
| 1995 | Astro/Safari | 4.3 (4293) | W | CMFI | 6 | OHV |
| 1996 | Astro/Safari | 4.3 (4293) | W | CSFI | 6 | OHV |

BC - Barrel carburetor
CMFI - Central multi-port fuel injection
CSFI - Central sequential fuel injection
TBI - Throttle body fuel injection
OHV - Overhead valve

88261C02

**ROUTINE MAINTENANCE AND TUNE-UP**

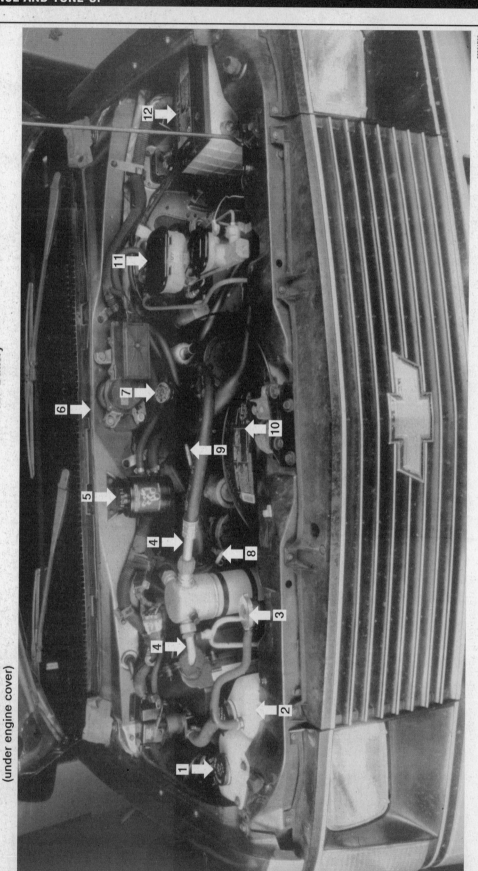

UNDERHOOD MAINTENANCE COMPONENTS & LOCATIONS - EARLY MODEL (CARBURETED AND TBI) ENGINES

1. Windshield washer fluid reservoir
2. Engine coolant reservoir
3. Radiator cap
4. A/C lines - CAUTION-
5. Power steering pump reservoir/dipstick
6. Air cleaner/distributor (under engine cover)
7. Engine oil filler cap/tube
8. Engine oil dipstick
9. Automatic transmission fluid dipstick
10. Vehicle emission control information label
11. Brake master cylinder reservoir
12. Battery

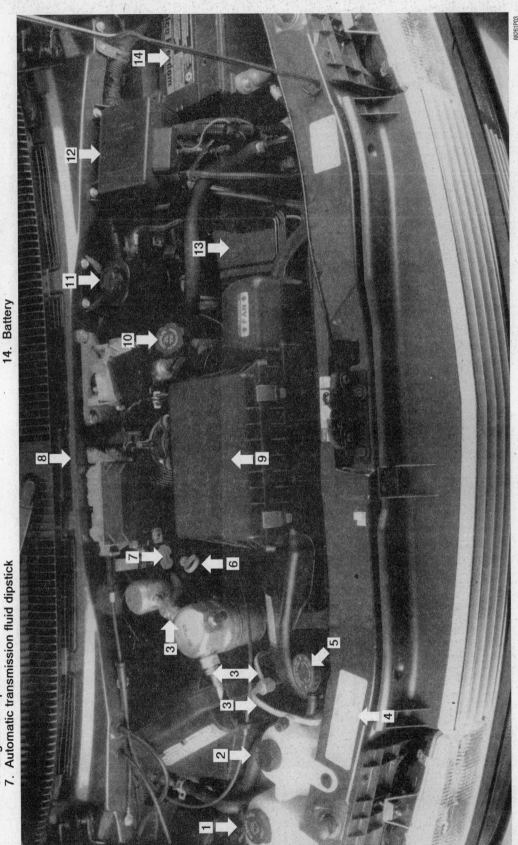

**UNDERHOOD MAINTENANCE COMPONENTS AND LOCATIONS - LATE-MODEL (CMFI AND CSFI VORTEC) ENGINES**

1. Windshield washer fluid reservoir
2. Engine coolant reservoir
3. A/C lines -CAUTION-
4. Vehicle emission control information label
5. Radiator cap
6. Engine oil dipstick
7. Automatic transmission fluid dipstick
8. Distributor/HVS (under engine cover)
9. Air cleaner element housing
10. Engine oil filler cap/tube
11. Power steering pump reservoir/dipstick
12. Underhood fuse and relay box
13. Brake master cylinder reservoir
14. Battery

88261P03

Proper maintenance and tune-up is the key to long and trouble-free vehicle life. Studies have shown that a properly tuned and maintained vehicle can achieve better gas mileage than an out-of-tune vehicle. As a conscientious owner and driver, set aside a Saturday morning, say once a month, to check or replace items which could cause major problems later. Keep your own personal log to jot down which services you performed, how much the parts cost you, the date, and the exact odometer reading at the time. Keep all receipts for such items as engine oil and filters, so that they may be referred to in case of related problems or to determine operating expenses. As a do-it-yourselfer, these receipts are the only proof you have that the required maintenance was performed. In the event of a warranty problem, these receipts will be invaluable.

The literature provided with your vehicle when it was originally delivered includes the factory recommended maintenance schedule. If you no longer have this literature, replacement copies are usually available from the dealer.

## Engine Cover

Many of the components on your van are serviced in the same way that most conventional passenger cars or trucks are repaired. Raising the hood (to expose the engine compartment), or raising and supporting the vehicle (to expose the underbody) will allow you access to most of the components. However, because of the inherent space-saving design of a van (which moves the dash forward in the chassis (over the motor), some parts of the engine simply cannot be accessed from underhood or under the engine. Many of the mid-to-rear mounted engine components such as the distributor, spark plugs and even the air cleaner (on all carbureted and TBI models) must be accessed in a different way. Some components can be reached through access panels in the wheel wells, but in most cases your will have to remove the Engine Cover from the center of the dash in the passenger compartment. A procedure is provided for engine cover removal in this section, as it is assumed that if you are to properly maintain your vehicle, it is something you will become quite familiar with over time.

### REMOVAL & INSTALLATION

**1985–89 Vehicles**

▶ **See Figures 29, 30, 31 and 32**

1. Open the hood and disconnect the negative battery cable for safety.
2. With a long-handled screwdriver, loosen the upper left and upper right cover retaining screws at the rear of the engine compartment. Turn the screws counterclockwise until they release the cover, but keep in mind that the screws are not designed to come out of the bracket assembly which is attached to the engine compartment opening.

➡ **On some vehicles, the air cleaner intake snorkel will interfere with access to the cover retaining screws. On these vehicles, remove the snorkel buy carefully, but firmly, grasping it and pulling it away from the air cleaner, then by pulling it from the front air intake duct.**

3. Walk around the vehicle to the passenger compartment, then slide both front seats to their furthest back positions in order to give yourself more working space.
4. Remove the instrument panel extension housing retainers. There are 2 bolts at the top of the housing (which are accessed by opening the glove box) and there are 2 nuts at the bottom of the housing.
5. Carefully pull the extension housing outward and disengage any wiring connectors, such as the cigarette lighter. Remove the extension housing and position aside, being careful not to scratch the plastic trim.
6. Release the 2 latches at the bottom of the engine cover, then pull the straps off the studs.
7. Remove the engine cover by carefully sliding it backwards, then rotating the top of the cover to the rear and upward. Again, be careful not to damage any of the decorative plastic trim pieces and be careful not to catch any edges on the interior fabric.
8. Inspect the engine cover rubber seal for wear or damage. The seal MUST be replaced if there are any sings of damage which would prevent a proper seal between the engine and passenger compartments.

**To install:**

9. Lift the engine cover into the vehicle, rotate it backwards and then carefully slide it all the way forward making sure to keep the straps attached to the upper instrument panel bracket clear.

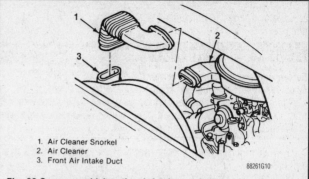

1. Air Cleaner Snorkel
2. Air Cleaner
3. Front Air Intake Duct

88261G10

**Fig. 29 On some vehicles, the air intake snorkel must be removed for access to the engine cover retaining screws**

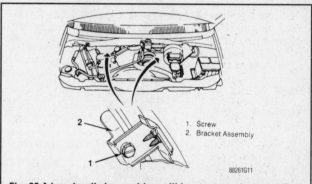

1. Screw
2. Bracket Assembly

88261G11

**Fig. 30 A long-handled screwdriver will be necessary to access the 2 upper engine compartment-to-engine cover retaining screws**

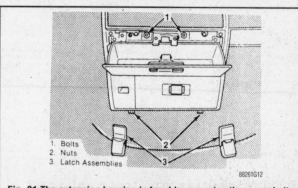

1. Bolts
2. Nuts
3. Latch Assemblies

88261G12

**Fig. 31 The extension housing is freed by removing the upper bolts and lower nuts, then the cover latches can be released**

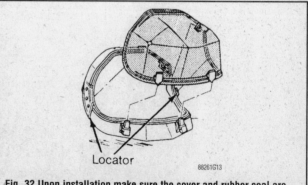

Locator

88261G13

**Fig. 32 Upon installation make sure the cover and rubber seal are properly positioned to isolate the engine compartment**

10.   Place the cover between the engine cover locators (as shown in the accompanying illustration), then install the 2 screws from the engine compartment.

### ✳✳ WARNING

**Before tightening the engine compartment screws or setting the cover latches, make sure the cover's rubber seal is in place. The seal is necessary to keep harmful fumes (as well as engine heat) from the passenger compartment. It should be replaced if any signs of damage or improper sealing are evident.**

11.   With the rubber seal in position over the latches, secure latches at the base of the cover.

12.   Install the 2 straps that are attached to the upper instrument panel bracket. Be sure to pull each strap tight before attaching the bracket to the engine cover stud.

13.   Position the instrument panel extension, then engage any necessary electrical connectors.

14.   Install the extension by carefully spreading and holding the sides while sliding it into position on the 4 locators. Secure the extension using the nuts and bolts removed earlier.

15.   If removed earlier, install the air cleaner intake snorkel.

16.   Connect the negative battery cable.

### 1990–96 Vehicles

▶ **See Figures 33 thru 49**

1.   Open the hood and disconnect the negative battery cable for safety.

2.   Slide both front seats to their furthest back positions in order to give yourself more working space.

3.   Remove the instrument panel extension housing retainers. There are 2 bolts at the top sides of the housing and there are 2 nuts at the bottom of the housing.

4.   Carefully grasp the extension housing at the bottom, then rotate it upward and outward for access. Disengage any wiring connectors, such as the cigarette lighter, then remove the extension housing and position aside, being careful not to scratch the plastic trim.

5.   Remove the engine cover heating and air duct:

a.   For 1990–95 vehicles, grasp the duct at the top and firmly, but gently, pull downward to release it from the dash and the engine cover studs.

b.   Disconnect the engine cover heating and air duct from the air distributor (at the top of the duct). If equipped, remove the nuts retaining the duct to the floor studs and/or disconnect the air outlet from the rear seat ducts. Position the cover heater and air duct aside.

6.   Remove the bolt and loosen the nut on each of the 2 engine cover brackets, then rotate the brackets out of the way.

7.   Release the 2 latches at the bottom of the engine cover.

8.   Using a long-handled screwdriver to loosen the 2 engine cover-to-cowl screws (at the sides of the engine cover).

➡ **The screw on each side of the engine cover is NOT designed to come out of the engine cover. Simply loosen the screw until the cover is free from the cowl.**

9.   Remove the engine cover by grasping the bottom and carefully sliding it backwards, then rotating the top of the cover to the rear and upward. Again, be careful not to damage any of the decorative plastic trim pieces and be careful not to catch any edges on the interior fabric.

### ✳✳ WARNING

**Because the engine cover-to-cowl screws remain attached to the engine cover, take extra care during cover removal to make sure they do not scratch and damage the rest of the instrument panel.**

10.   Inspect the engine cover rubber seal for wear or damage. The seal MUST be replaced if there are any sings of damage which would prevent a proper seal between the engine and passenger compartments.

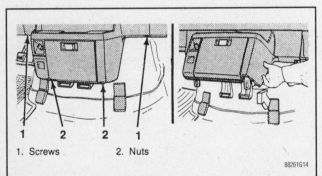

1. Screws       2. Nuts

88261G14

**Fig. 33 The instrument panel extension housing is retained by 2 nuts and 2 bolts—1990–95 shown (1996 similar)**

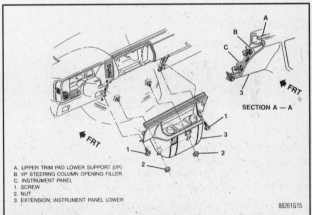

A. UPPER TRIM PAD LOWER SUPPORT (I/P)
B. I/P STEERING COLUMN OPENING FILLER
C. INSTRUMENT PANEL
1. SCREW
2. NUT
3. EXTENSION, INSTRUMENT PANEL LOWER

88261G15

**Fig. 34 Exploded view of the instrument panel extension housing— 1990–95 vehicles**

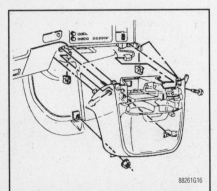

88261G16

**Fig. 35 Exploded view of the instrument panel extension housing—1996 vehicles**

88261P04

**Fig. 36 Loosen and remove the instrument panel extension housing upper retaining bolts . . .**

88261P05

**Fig. 37 . . . then remove the extension housing lower retaining nuts**

Fig. 38 Carefully pull the extension housing forward, disengage the wiring and remove it from the vehicle

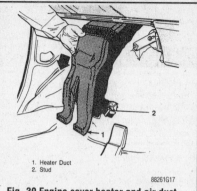

1. Heater Duct
2. Stud

Fig. 39 Engine cover heater and air duct mounting—1990–95 vehicles

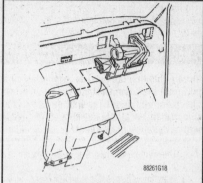

Fig. 40 Engine cover heater and air duct mounting—1996 vehicles

Fig. 41 On 1990–95 vehicles, the cover heater and air duct is removed by pulling it gently downward

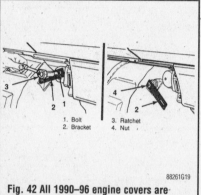

1. Bolt
2. Bracket
3. Ratchet
4. Nut

Fig. 42 All 1990–96 engine covers are retained by upper brackets

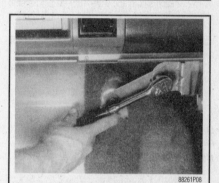

Fig. 43 Remove the bolt and loosen the nut from each cover bracket, then rotate the brackets out of the way

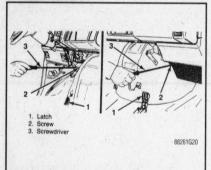

1. Latch
2. Screw
3. Screwdriver

Fig. 44 The upper cover-to-cowl screws and latches are the final retainers securing the engine cover

Fig. 45 Release the engine cover latches

Fig. 46 Loosen the captive engine cover-to-cowl retaining screws . . .

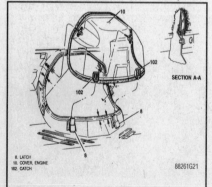

SECTION A-A

8. LATCH
10. COVER, ENGINE
102. CATCH

Fig. 47 Exploded view of the engine cover mounting

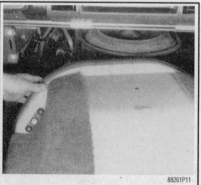

Fig. 48 . . . then carefully pull the cover back and remove it from the vehicle

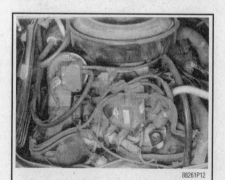

Fig. 49 With the cover removed you have access to almost all of the upper engine components

**To install:**

11. Lift the engine cover into the vehicle, then carefully slide it all the way forward making sure the rubber seal is positioned over the latches.

### ✳✳ WARNING

**Before tightening the cowl screws or setting the cover latches, make sure the cover's rubber seal is in place. The seal is necessary to keep harmful fumes (as well as engine heat) from the passenger compartment. It should be replaced if any signs of damage or improper sealing are evident.**

12. Thread the 2 engine cover-to-cowl retaining screws, but do not tighten fully at this time.

13. With the rubber seal in position over the latches, press downward on each of the 2 latch assemblies and secure latches at the base of the cover.

14. Tighten the engine cover-to-cowl screws.

15. At each side of the cover, turn the bracket into position, then install the bolt and tighten the nut at the other end of the bracket.

16. Install the engine cover heater and air duct.

17. Position the instrument panel extension, then engage any necessary electrical connectors.

18. Grasp the bottom of the instrument panel extension then install the top into the groove first and push the bottom into place. Secure the extension using the nuts and bolts removed earlier.

19. Connect the negative battery cable.

## Air Cleaner (Element)

▶ See Figures 50 and 51

An air cleaner is used to keep airborne dirt and dust out of the air flowing through the engine. This material, if allowed to enter the engine, would form an abrasive compound in conjunction with the engine oil and drastically shorten engine life. For this reason, you should never run the engine without the air cleaner in place (except possibly for a very brief period in when you are diagnosing a problem). You should also be sure to use the proper replacement part to avoid poor fit and consequent air leakage.

Proper maintenance is important since a clogged air filter will not allow the proper amount of air to enter the engine causing reduced power and fuel economy. It is even possible that a clogged filter could contribute to an overly rich fuel mixture on early-model vehicles equipped with a carburetor. Rich fuel mixtures can wreak havoc with the life span of a catalytic converter.

The air cleaner on carbureted or TBI engines consists of a metal housing with a replaceable paper filter and the necessary hoses connecting it to the crankcase ventilation system. The air cleaner cover is held down by 1 or 2 nuts on all models. Unfortunately, the housing is mounted directly on top of the carburetor or throttle body assembly, so access is almost always impossible without first removing the engine cover from the passenger compartment.

The air cleaner assembly on CMFI or CSFI engines is a composite plastic housing placed inline between the fresh air intake ducts and the throttle body

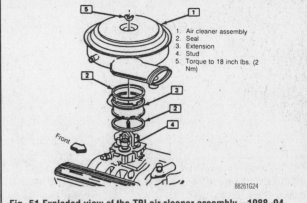

1. Air cleaner assembly
2. Seal
3. Extension
4. Stud
5. Torque to 18 inch lbs. (2 Nm)

Front

88261G24

**Fig. 51 Exploded view of the TBI air cleaner assembly—1988–94 engines shown, early models similar**

assembly. The nice part about this setup for you is that unlike the metal housing on older engines, the plastic inline housing can be accessed by simply raising the hood.

No matter which type of housing and filter you have, the factory recommends that the filter be replaced at least once every 30,000 miles (48,000 km). Inspection and replacement should come more often when the vehicle is operated under dusty conditions. To check the effectiveness of your paper element, remove the air cleaner assembly, if the idle speed increases noticeably, the element is restricting airflow and should be replaced.

### REMOVAL & INSTALLATION

#### Carbureted and TBI Engines

▶ See Figures 52, 53 and 54

1. Remove the engine cover from the passenger compartment for access to the air cleaner housing assembly. For details, please refer to the procedure earlier in this section.

2. Remove the air cleaner top nut(s) and lift off the top to expose the element.

3. Remove the filter from inside the filter housing.

4. Clean any accumulated dirt, dust or oil from the inside of the air cleaner housing using a rag.

**To install:**

5. Position the new filter element in the housing, making sure it has the proper fit.

6. Install the housing cover and secure using the retaining nut(s). Tighten the nuts firmly, but do not crack or deform the cover.

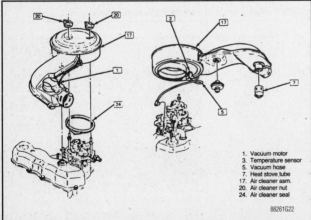

1. Vacuum motor
3. Temperature sensor
5. Vacuum hose
7. Heat stove tube
17. Air cleaner asm.
20. Air cleaner nut
24. Air cleaner seal

88261G22

**Fig. 50 Exploded view of the air cleaner assembly—1985 2.5L engines**

88261P13

**Fig. 52 Remove the nut(s) from the top of the air cleaner housing—1992 4.3L engine shown**

Fig. 53 With the nut(s) removed, lift the cover from the air cleaner housing . . .

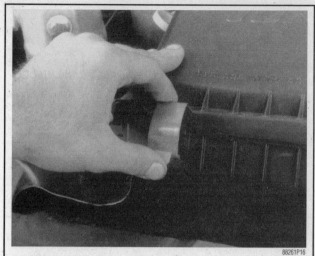

Fig. 55 On these vehicles, simply release the hold-down clamps and lift up on the cover . . .

Fig. 54 . . . then remove the element

Fig. 56 . . . then remove the air cleaner element from the housing

7. Install the engine cover (or, as long as it is off, perform any other necessary maintenance such as checking the distributor cap, rotor and wires).

### CMFI and CSFI Engines

▶ See Figures 55 and 56

1. Raise the hood (and support using the prop rod).
2. Locate the plastic air cleaner housing at the front center of the engine compartment.
3. Release the hold-down clamps at the front of the housing.
4. Lift the air cleaner cover sufficiently to expose the housing, but be careful not to damage any attached components (duct work, wiring).
5. Note the positioning of the filter element, then lift and remove the element from the housing.
6. Clean any accumulated dirt or dust from the inside of the air cleaner housing using a rag.
7. Installation is the reverse of the removal procedure.

### Fuel Filter

There are 3 types of fuel filters used: The internal (1985 4.3L carbureted models), the inline (TBI, CMFI and CSFI) and the in-tank.

---

### ✷✷ CAUTION

**Before removing any component of the fuel system on fuel injected models, be sure to properly release the system pressure. For details on fuel system pressure release procedures and related safety precautions, please refer to Section 5 of this manual.**

The internal carburetor filter and the inline fuel filter should be replaced at least every 30,000 miles (48,000 km) to help assure a clean and trouble-free fuel delivery system. The intank filter should not require replacement unless it becomes clogged. If a vehicle is purchased used and the last fuel filter service is not documented, it is probably a good idea to replace the internal or inline filter anyway to be sure of its condition.

### REMOVAL & INSTALLATION

#### Internal (Carbureted Models)

▶ See Figure 57

1. Disconnect the negative battery cable for safety.
2. At the carburetor, disconnect the fuel line connection from the fuel inlet filter nut.

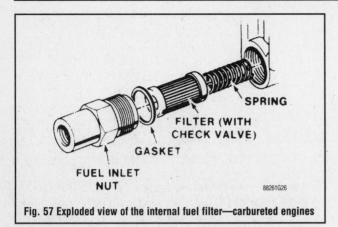

**Fig. 57 Exploded view of the internal fuel filter—carbureted engines**

3. Remove the fuel inlet filter nut from the carburetor.

4. Remove the filter and the spring, then discard the old filter.

**To install:**

➠A check valve MUST be installed in the filter to meet the Motor Vehicle Safety Standards for roll-over. When installing a new filter, pay attention to the direction the fuel must flow through it; it MUST be installed with the check valve end facing the fuel line. The new filter is equipped with ribs on the closed end to ensure that it will not be installed incorrectly unless it is forced.

5. Install the spring and the new filter/check valve assembly into the carburetor inlet, followed by the fuel inlet nut.

6. Tighten the fuel inlet nut to 18 ft. lbs. (25 Nm).

7. Install the fuel line and tighten the connection.

8. Connect the negative battery cable, then start the engine and check for leaks.

### Inline

♦ See Figures 58 thru 63

The location of the inline fuel filter varies depending upon the year and model of the vehicle. On most models, the filter can be found along one of the vehicle's frame rails (usually the left side, towards the front of the vehicle). But, on some later versions of the 2.5L engine, the filter may be found under the engine cover, at the rear of the engine. To save you the trouble of removing the engine cover, we recommend that no matter which engine your van uses, that you check along the frame rails first. If necessary, follow the fuel lines from the tank at the rear of the vehicle, forward until you either find the filter, or the line disappear into the engine cavity.

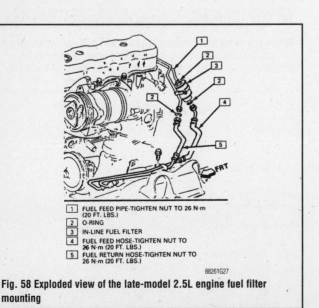

1. FUEL FEED PIPE-TIGHTEN NUT TO 26 N·m (20 FT. LBS.)
2. O-RING
3. IN-LINE FUEL FILTER
4. FUEL FEED HOSE-TIGHTEN NUT TO 26 N·m (20 FT. LBS.)
5. FUEL RETURN HOSE-TIGHTEN NUT TO 26 N·m (20 FT. LBS.)

**Fig. 58 Exploded view of the late-model 2.5L engine fuel filter mounting**

A. Front
B. Frame Rail
1. Fuel Fitting
2. In-Line Filter
3. Bracket
4. Fuel Fitting
5. Bolt

**Fig. 59 Most vehicles covered by this manual use a fuel filter which is mounted vertically along the frame rail**

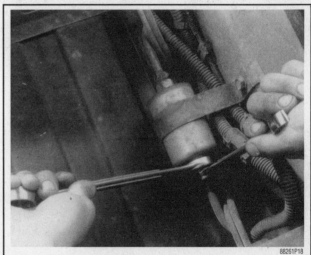

**Fig. 60 A backup wrench is used to keep the filter from twisting (damaging the other fuel line if still attached)**

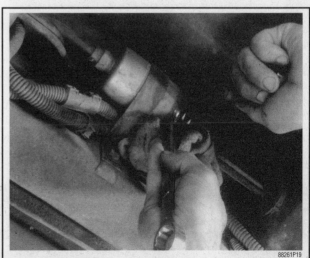

**Fig. 61 Before loosening the fitting completely, position a rag to catch any remaining fuel which may spill**

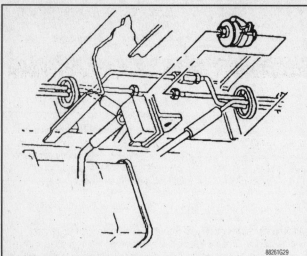

**Fig. 62 The fuel filter on some late-model vehicles is mounted horizontally along the frame rail**

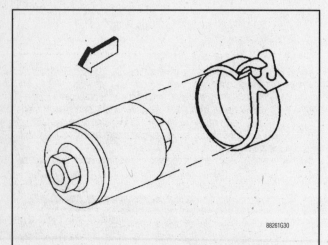

**Fig. 63 Once the filter and clamp assembly is removed (on late-model vehicles) the filter should be separated and discarded (but retain the clamp for the new filter)**

1. Properly relieve the fuel system pressure, then disconnect the negative battery cable.

➡️**When relieving the fuel system pressure, remember to loosen the fuel tank filler cap. If the tank pressure is not released, fuel could be forced through the lines and out the opening, as soon as the fuel fittings are loosened.**

2. Locate the filter along the frame rail or under the engine cover. As necessary for access, either raise and support the vehicle using jackstands or remove the engine cover.

3. Using 2 wrenches (one for backup on the filter itself to keep it from spinning), loosen and remove the fuel lines from the filter. On models where the filter is mounted vertically along the frame rail, it may be easier to loosen the upper fitting first, then the lower fitting.

➡️**Fittings which are stuck to the filter with corrosion may be very difficult to loosen. ALWAYS use the proper size wrench (a line wrench is preferable to a standard open-end tool) or you will risk rounding off the fuel line fittings. Also, spraying the fitting with penetrating oil prior to loosening may help to loosen the corrosion and free the fitting.**

4. Note the direction which the filter is mounted for installation purposes (there may still be a visible arrow on the side of the old filter, or the filter ends may be different). Loosen the filter or filter clamp-to-bracket bolt (as applicable),

then remove the filter and discard it. If the filter and clamp come of the bracket as an assembly, retain the clamp for installation on the new filter.

**To install:**

➡️**When installing a new filter, be sure to install it facing the proper direction. Normally an arrow is found on the side of the filter housing to show proper direction of flow (toward the engine). If no arrow is present, position it in the same way as you noted during removal of the old filter.**

5. If the clamp was removed with the old filter, position it over the replacement.

6. Install the new filter into the bracket and thread, but do not tighten, the retaining bolt.

➡️**If O-rings are used on the threaded fittings, they should be replaced to assure a proper seal.**

7. Connect the fuel lines and tighten using a backup wrench to keep the filter from spinning.

8. Tighten the fuel filter retaining bolt.

9. Connect the negative battery cable, then pressurize the fuel system (by cycling the ignition or cranking the engine) and check for leaks.

10. Either remove the jackstands and carefully lower the vehicle, or install the engine cover, as applicable.

### Intank

The intank filter (also know as the strainer) is usually constructed of woven plastic and is located on the lower end of the fuel pickup tube in the fuel tank. The filter prevents dirt and discourages water from entering the fuel system; though water will enter the system if the filter becomes completely submerged in the water. The filter is normally self cleaning and requires no periodic maintenance; should this filter become clogged, the fuel tank must be flushed.

1. Remove the fuel pump or sending unit from the vehicle, as applicable. For details, please refer to Section 5 of this manual.

2. Carefully remove the fuel filter (strainer) from the fuel pump and clean or replace it, as necessary.

➡️**When installing the intank fuel filter, be careful not to fold or twist it for this may restrict the flow.**

3. Install the strainer, then install the fuel pump or sending unit.

## Positive Crankcase Ventilation (PCV)

The Positive Crankcase Ventilation (PCV) system is used to vent pressure which builds in the crankcase during engine operation. Fresh air is inducted to the crankcase through the ventilation system (which may include a separate filter in the air cleaner on some models) and is then drawn to the engine intake air system so it can be burned. The PCV valve may be the most important part of the system since it regulates the flow of the vapors during engine operation. If the valve becomes stuck open it could allow vapors to enter the intake at the wrong time (causing poor driveability). If is becomes stuck closed or clogged, it could allow excessive crankcase pressure to cause gasket leaks and/or the buildup of damaging sludge in the crankcase oil. In any case, it is an inexpensive part which should NOT be overlooked for periodic inspection and replacement.

The PCV valve is usually attached to a valve cover by a rubber grommet and connected to the intake manifold through a ventilation hose. Replace the PCV valve and the PCV filter (located in the air cleaner on TBI and carbureted models so equipped) every 30,000 miles (48,000 km).

### REMOVAL & INSTALLATION

▸ **See Figures 64 and 65**

1. Open the hood to see if access is possible without removing the engine cover. Depending on your model (and the length of your arms) you may be able to reach the valve for replacement. If not, SORRY, but you will have to remove the engine cover for better access.

2. Pull the PCV from the valve cover grommet and disconnect it from the ventilation hose(s).

3. You can inspect the valve for operation: (1) Shake it to see if the valve is

free; (2) Blow through it (air will pass in one direction only). If you have removed the engine cover, take this opportunity to also check the condition of the vacuum hose and, if applicable, the filter in the air cleaner housing and replace any damaged or worn component.

➡ **When replacing the PCV valve, it is recommended to use a new one. It is usually an inexpensive part, but it performs a very important function for the life of your engine's gaskets and oil.**

4. Upon installation, be sure the valve seats properly in the valve cover grommet and that the vacuum hose is tight on the valve fitting.

## Evaporative Canister

To limit gasoline vapor discharge into the atmosphere, this system is designed to trap fuel vapors, which normally escape from the fuel tank and the intake manifold. Vapor arrest is accomplished through the use of the charcoal canister. This canister absorbs fuel vapors and stores them until they can be removed to be burned in the engine. Removal of the vapors from the canister to the engine is accomplished by various means, depending upon the emission systems on your van. For more details about the operation and components of the evaporative emission system, please refer to Section 4 of this manual.

In addition to the modifications necessary to the fuel system of evaporative emission equipped engines and the addition of a canister, the fuel tank requires a non-vented gas cap. The domed fuel tank positions a vent high enough above the fuel to keep the vent pipe in the vapor at all times. The single vent pipe is routed directly to the canister. From the canister, the vapors are routed to the intake system, where they will be burned during normal combustion.

### SERVICING

▶ **See Figure 66**

The only maintenance necessary to this system on most vehicles covered by this manual is a periodic check to make sure the lines and components are intact and still holding (or routing) vapors. Every 30,000 miles (48,000 km) or 24 months, check all fuel, vapor lines and hoses for proper hookup, routing and condition. If equipped, check that the bowl vent and purge valves work properly. Remove the canister and check for cracks or damage, then replace (if necessary). Some early model vehicles will be equipped with a canister that uses a replaceable filter. You should be able to tell by inspecting the bottom of the canister once it is removed for your maintenance inspection. If your canister is equipped, the filter should be visible. Most vehicles covered by this manual use a sealed canister that does not utilize a replaceable filter.

### FILTER REPLACEMENT

On early model vehicles, the replaceable filter is in the bottom of the carbon canister located in the engine compartment. It should be replaced every 30,000 miles (48,000 km) or 24 months.
1. Disconnect and mark the charcoal canister vent hoses.
2. Remove the canister-to-bracket bolt.
3. Lift the canister from the bracket.

4. At the bottom of the canister, grasp the filter with your fingers and pull it out.
5. To install, use a new filter and reverse the removal procedures.

## Battery

### PRECAUTIONS

Always use caution when working on or near the battery. Never allow a tool to bridge the gap between the negative and positive battery terminals. Also, be careful not to allow a tool to provide a ground between the positive cable/terminal and any metal component on the vehicle. Either of these conditions will cause a short circuit, leading to sparks and possible personal injury.

Do not smoke or all open flames/sparks near a battery; the gases contained in the battery are very explosive and, if ignited, could cause severe injury or death.

All batteries, regardless of type, should be carefully secured by a battery hold-down device. If not, the terminals or casing may crack from stress during vehicle operation. A battery which is not secured may allow acid to leak, making it discharge faster. The acid can also eat away at components under the hood.

Always inspect the battery case for cracks, leakage and corrosion. A white corrosive substance on the battery case or on nearby components would indicate a leaking or cracked battery. If the battery is cracked, it should be replaced immediately.

### GENERAL MAINTENANCE

Always keep the battery cables and terminals free of corrosion. Check and clean these components about once a year.

Keep the top of the battery clean, as a film of dirt can help discharge a battery that is not used for long periods. A solution of baking soda and water may be used for cleaning, but be careful to flush this off with clear water. DO NOT let any of the solution into the filler holes. Baking soda neutralizes battery acid and will de-activate a battery cell.

Batteries in vehicles which are not operated on a regular basis can fall victim to parasitic loads (small current drains which are constantly drawing current from the battery). Normal parasitic loads may drain a battery on a vehicle that is in storage and not used for 6–8 weeks. Vehicles that have additional accessories such as a phone or an alarm system may discharge a battery sooner. If the vehicle is to be stored for longer periods in a secure area and the alarm system is not necessary, the negative battery cable should be disconnected to protect the battery.

Remember that constantly deep cycling a battery (completely discharging and recharging it) will shorten battery life.

### BATTERY FLUID

▶ **See Figure 67**

Check the battery electrolyte level at least once a month, or more often in hot weather or during periods of extended vehicle operation. On non-sealed batteries, the level can be checked either through the case (if translucent) or by

**Fig. 64 The PCV valve is normally fitted to a rubber grommet in the valve cover**

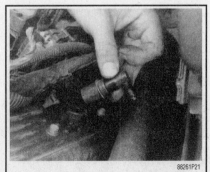

**Fig. 65 Once it is removed from the grommet, carefully pull it free of the vacuum hose**

**Fig. 66 Periodically check the evaporative canister, lines and fittings for leaks**

removing the cell caps. The electrolyte level in each cell should be kept filled to the split ring inside each cell, or the line marked on the outside of the case.

If the level is low, add only distilled water through the opening until the level is correct. Each cell must be checked and filled individually. Distilled water should be used, because the chemicals and minerals found in most drinking water are harmful to the battery and could significantly shorten its life.

If water is added in freezing weather, the vehicle should be driven several miles to allow the water to mix with the electrolyte. Otherwise, the battery could freeze.

Although some maintenance-free batteries have removable cell caps, the electrolyte condition and level on all sealed maintenance-free batteries must be checked using the built-in hydrometer "eye." The exact type of eye will vary. But, most battery manufacturers, apply a sticker to the battery itself explaining the readings.

➡**Although the readings from built-in hydrometers will vary, a green eye usually indicates a properly charged battery with sufficient fluid level. A dark eye is normally an indicator of a battery with sufficient fluid, but which is low in charge. A light or yellow eye usually indicates that electrolyte has dropped below the necessary level. In this last case, sealed batteries with an insufficient electrolyte must usually be discarded.**

### Checking the Specific Gravity

▶ **See Figures 68, 69 and 70**

A hydrometer is required to check the specific gravity on all batteries that are not maintenance-free. On batteries that are maintenance-free, the specific gravity is checked by observing the built-in hydrometer "eye" on the top of the battery case.

### ❊❊ CAUTION

**Battery electrolyte contains sulfuric acid. If you should splash any on your skin or in your eyes, flush the affected area with plenty of clear water. If it lands in your eyes, get medical help immediately.**

The fluid (sulfuric acid solution) contained in the battery cells will tell you many things about the condition of the battery. Because the cell plates must be kept submerged below the fluid level in order to operate, the fluid level is extremely important. And, because the specific gravity of the acid is an indication of electrical charge, testing the fluid can be an aid in determining if the battery must be replaced. A battery in a vehicle with a properly operating charging system should require little maintenance, but careful, periodic inspection should reveal problems before they leave you stranded.

At least once a year, check the specific gravity of the battery. It should be between 1.20 and 1.26 on the gravity scale. Most auto stores carry a variety of inexpensive battery hydrometers. These can be used on any non-sealed battery to test the specific gravity in each cell.

The battery testing hydrometer has a squeeze bulb at one end and a nozzle at the other. Battery electrolyte is sucked into the hydrometer until the float is lifted from its seat. The specific gravity is then read by noting the position of the float. If gravity is low in one or more cells, the battery should be slowly charged and checked again to see if the gravity has come up. Generally, if after charging, the specific gravity between any two cells varies more than 50 points (0.50), the battery should be replaced, as it can no longer produce sufficient voltage to guarantee proper operation.

### CABLES

▶ **See Figures 71 thru 76**

Once a year (or as necessary), the battery terminals and the cable clamps should be cleaned. Loosen the clamps and remove the cables, negative cable first. On top post batteries, the use of a puller specially made for this purpose is recommended. These are inexpensive and available in most parts stores. Side terminal battery cables are secured with a small bolt.

Clean the cable clamps and the battery terminal with a wire brush, until all corrosion, grease, etc., is removed and the metal is shiny. It is especially important to clean the inside of the clamp thoroughly (an old knife is useful here), since a small deposit of oxidation there will prevent a sound connection and inhibit starting or charging. Special tools are available for cleaning these parts,

Fig. 67 Maintenance-free batteries usually contain a built-in hydrometer to check fluid level

Fig. 68 On non-sealed batteries, the fluid level can be checked by removing the cell caps

Fig. 69 If the fluid level is low, add only distilled water until the level is correct

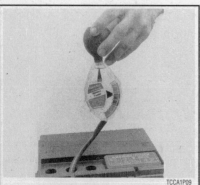

Fig. 70 Check the specific gravity of the battery's electrolyte with a hydrometer

Fig. 71 Loosen the battery cable retaining nut . . .

Fig. 72 . . . then disconnect the cable from the battery

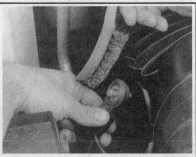

**Fig. 73 A wire brush may be used to clean any corrosion or foreign material from the cable**

**Fig. 74 The wire brush can also be used to remove any corrosion or dirt from the battery terminal**

**Fig. 75 The battery terminal can also be cleaned using a solution of baking soda and water**

**Fig. 76 Before connecting the cables, it's a good idea to coat the terminals with a small amount of dielectric grease**

one type for conventional top post batteries and another type for side terminal batteries. It is also a good idea to apply some dielectric grease to the terminal, as this will aid in the prevention of corrosion.

After the clamps and terminals are clean, reinstall the cables, negative cable last; DO NOT hammer the clamps onto battery posts. Tighten the clamps securely, but do not distort them. Give the clamps and terminals a thin external coating of grease after installation, to retard corrosion.

Check the cables at the same time that the terminals are cleaned. If the cable insulation is cracked or broken, or if the ends are frayed, the cable should be replaced with a new cable of the same length and gauge.

## CHARGING

### ❊❊ CAUTION

**The chemical reaction which takes place in all batteries generates explosive hydrogen gas. A spark can cause the battery to explode and splash acid. To avoid personal injury, be sure there is proper ventilation and take appropriate fire safety precautions when working with or near a battery.**

A battery should be charged at a slow rate to keep the plates inside from getting too hot. However, if some maintenance-free batteries are allowed to discharge until they are almost "dead," they may have to be charged at a high rate to bring them back to "life." Always follow the charger manufacturer's instructions on charging the battery.

## REPLACEMENT

When it becomes necessary to replace the battery, select one with an amperage rating equal to or greater than the battery originally installed. Deterioration and just plain aging of the battery cables, starter motor, and associated wires makes the battery's job harder in successive years. This makes it prudent to install a new battery with a greater capacity than the old.

## Belts

### INSPECTION

▶ **See Figures 77, 78, 79, 80 and 81**

**V-Belts**

➡ **The 1985–86 vehicles covered by this manual utilize 1 or more V-belts to drive engine accessories (such as the alternator, water pump, power steering pump or A/C compressor off the crankshaft.**

Check the drive belt(s) every 15,000 miles/12 months (heavy usage) or 30,000 miles/24 months (light usage) for evidence of wear such as cracking, fraying and incorrect tension. Determine the belt tension at a point halfway between the pulleys by pressing on the belt with moderate thumb pressure. The belt should deflect about ¼ in. (6mm) over a 7–10 in. (178–254mm) span, or ½ in. (13mm) over a 13–16 in. (330–406mm) span, at this point. If the deflection is found to be too much or too little, perform the tension adjustments.

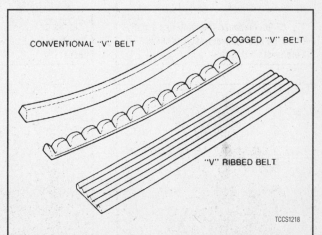

**Fig. 77 There are typically 3 types of accessory drive belts found on vehicles today**

Fig. 78 An example of a healthy drive belt

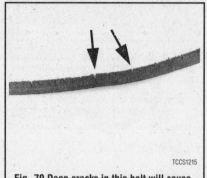

Fig. 79 Deep cracks in this belt will cause flex, building up heat that will eventually lead to belt failure

Fig. 80 The cover of this belt is worn, exposing the critical reinforcing cords to excessive wear

Fig. 81 Installing too wide a belt can result in serious belt wear and/or breakage

## Serpentine Belts

**▶ See Figures 82 and 83**

➡All 1987 and later vehicles covered by this manual utilize a single, ribbed, serpentine belts to drive engine accessories (such as the alternator, water pump, power steering pump or A/C compressor off the crankshaft.

The serpentine belt and pulleys should be inspected every 15,000 miles/12 months (heavy usage) or 30,000 miles/24 months (light usage) for evidence of wear such as cracking, fraying, incorrect alignment and incorrect tension. Proper maintenance of the belt and pulleys can extend normal belt life.

### ✳✳ WARNING

DO NOT use belt dressings in an attempt to extend belt life. Belt dressing will soften the serpentine belt, causing deterioration. Oil

or grease contamination on the belt or pulleys will have the same effect. Keep the drive belt system clear of oil, grease, coolant or other contaminants.

### PULLEY INSPECTION

**▶ See Figure 84**

➡Pulley inspection is most easily accomplished with the drive belt removed so you can freely turn the pulleys and to provide an unobstructed view of each pulley.

1. Visually inspect each of the pulleys for chips, nicks, cracks, tool marks, bent sidewalls, severe corrosion or other damage. Replace any pulley showing these signs as they will eventually lead to belt failure.
2. Place a straightedge or position a length of string across any 2 pulleys making sure it touches all points. When using string, be sure it is straight and not bent at one spot in order to contact all points on the pulley.

➡An assistant is helpful to hold the straightedge or string during the next steps.

3. Turn each pulley ½ revolution and recheck with the straightedge or string.
4. Full contact must be made at all points checked. If contact is not made at all of the points, the pulley may be warped or the shaft may be bent. Replace any damaged parts to assure proper belt life.

### BELT INSPECTION

**▶ See Figure 85**

1. Visually check the belt for signs of damage. Routine inspection may reveal cracks in the belt ribs. These cracks will not impair belt performance and are NOT a basis for belt replacement. HOWEVER, if your inspection reveals that sections of the belt are missing, the belt must be replaced to avoid a possible failure.
2. Visually check the belt for proper routing (when compared with the

Fig. 82 Serpentine drive belts require little attention other than periodic inspection or replacement

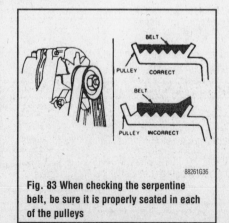

Fig. 83 When checking the serpentine belt, be sure it is properly seated in each of the pulleys

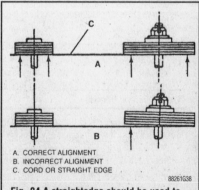

A. CORRECT ALIGNMENT
B. INCORRECT ALIGNMENT
C. CORD OR STRAIGHT EDGE

Fig. 84 A straightedge should be used to check pulley alignment

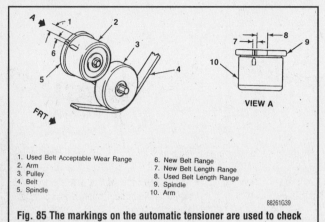

1. Used Belt Acceptable Wear Range
2. Arm
3. Pulley
4. Belt
5. Spindle
6. New Belt Range
7. New Belt Length Range
8. Used Belt Length Range
9. Spindle
10. Arm

88261G39

**Fig. 85 The markings on the automatic tensioner are used to check serpentine belt wear**

engine compartment label or the diagrams in this section). Make sure the belt is fully seated on all pulleys.

3. Check the automatic drive belt tensioner. The belt is considered serviceable if no wear or damage was found in the previous visual inspections and if the arrow on the tensioner assembly is pointing within the acceptable used belt length range on the tensioner spindle.

### ADJUSTING TENSION

#### V-belts

♦ See Figure 86

➡The following procedures require the use of GM Belt Tension Gauge No. BT–33–95-ACBN (regular V-belts) or BT–33–97M (poly V-belts).

If a belt tension gauge is not available, you can adjust tension using the deflection measurements, but this is not as exact. Keep in mind that too tight or too loose an adjustment can damage the components which the belt drives. Too tight will increase preload on the bearings, leading to early failure, while too loose could cause slippage or jerky movements. Of the 2 possibilities, you would prefer the belt to be a little loose, rather than a little tight. The belt should deflect about ¼ in. (6mm) over a 7–10 in. (178–254mm) span, or ½ in. (13mm) over a 13–16 in. (330–406mm) span, at this point.

If a belt tension gauge is available:

1. If the belt is cold, operate the engine (at idle speed) for 15 minutes; the belt will seat itself in the pulleys allowing the belt fibers to relax or stretch. If the belt is hot, allow it to cool, until it is warm to the touch.

➡A used belt is one that has been rotated at least one complete revolution on the pulleys. This begins the belt seating process and it must never be tensioned to the new belt specifications.

2. Disconnect the negative battery cable for safety.
3. Loosen the component-to-mounting bracket bolts.
4. Using a GM Belt Tension Gauge No. BT–33–95–ACBN (standard V–belts) or BT–33–97M (poly V-belts), place the tension gauge at the center of the belt between the longest span.

5. Applying belt tension pressure on the component, adjust the drive belt tension to the correct specifications.
6. While holding the correct tension on the component, tighten the component-to-mounting bracket bolt.
7. When the belt tension is correct, remove the tension gauge and connect the negative battery cable.

#### Serpentine Belts

All 1987–96 Astro and Safari vans are equipped with a single serpentine belt and spring loaded tensioner. The proper belt adjustment is automatically maintained by the tensioner, therefore, no periodic adjustment is needed until the pointer is past the scale on the tensioner. For more information, please refer to the information on serpentine belt and pulley inspection found earlier in this section.

### DRIVE BELT ROUTING

♦ See Figures 87 thru 94

A label is normally provided in the engine compartment which details the proper belt routing for the original engine installed in that vehicle. Check the

88261P24

**Fig. 87 Belt routing can be found on labels such as this one on the power steering reservoir . . .**

88261P25

**Fig. 88 . . . or like this one on a 1996 Astro vehicle emission control information label**

## BELT TENSION SPECIFICATIONS

| Years | Engine | Tensioning | Alternator | Power Steering | Air Cond. | A.I.R. Pump |
|-------|--------|-----------|------------|----------------|-----------|-------------|
| 1985–86 | 2.5L | Before Operating The Engine (New Belt) | ② | 146 Lb. | 169 Lb. | — |
| | | After Operating The Engine (Old Belt) ① | | 67 Lb. | 90 Lb. | |
| | 4.3L | Before Operating The Engine (New Belt) | 135 Lb. | 146 Lb. | 169 Lb. | 146 Lb. |
| | | After Operating The Engine (Old Belt) ① | 67 Lb. | 67 Lb. | 90 Lb. | 67 Lb. |

88261G37

**Fig. 86 A tension gauge is necessary to properly adjust tension on V-belt equipped engines**

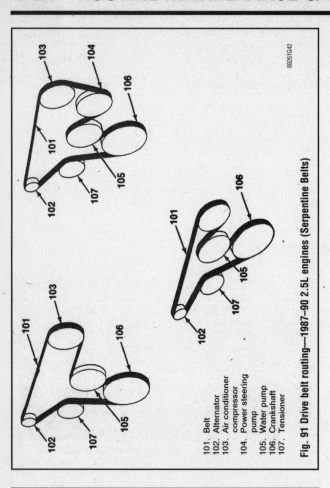

101. Belt
102. Alternator
103. Air conditioner compressor
104. Power steering pump
105. Water pump
106. Crankshaft
107. Tensioner

**Fig. 91 Drive belt routing—1987–90 2.5L engines (Serpentine Belts)**

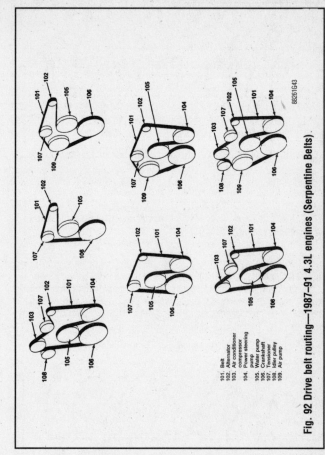

101. Belt
102. Alternator
103. Air conditioner compressor
104. Power steering pump
105. Water pump
106. Crankshaft
107. Tensioner
108. Idler pulley
109. Air pump

**Fig. 92 Drive belt routing—1987–91 4.3L engines (Serpentine Belts)**

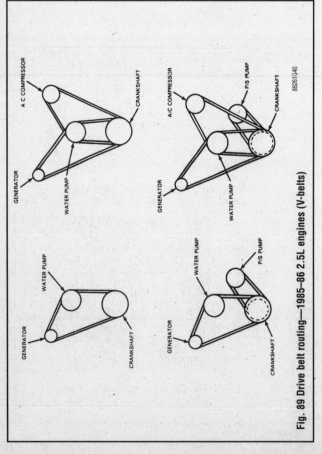

**Fig. 89 Drive belt routing—1985–86 2.5L engines (V-belts)**

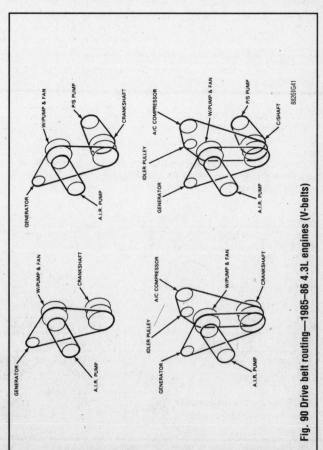

**Fig. 90 Drive belt routing—1985–86 4.3L engines (V-belts)**

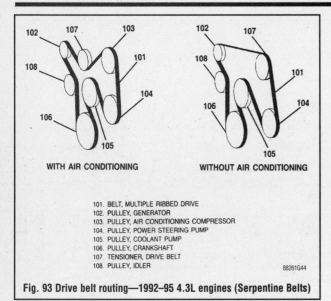

**WITH AIR CONDITIONING**          **WITHOUT AIR CONDITIONING**

101. BELT, MULTIPLE RIBBED DRIVE
102. PULLEY, GENERATOR
103. PULLEY, AIR CONDITIONING COMPRESSOR
104. PULLEY, POWER STEERING PUMP
105. PULLEY, COOLANT PUMP
106. PULLEY, CRANKSHAFT
107. TENSIONER, DRIVE BELT
108. PULLEY, IDLER

88261G44

**Fig. 93 Drive belt routing—1992–95 4.3L engines (Serpentine Belts)**

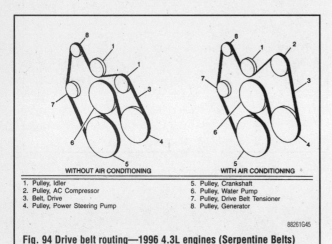

**WITHOUT AIR CONDITIONING**          **WITH AIR CONDITIONING**

1. Pulley, Idler
2. Pulley, AC Compressor
3. Belt, Drive
4. Pulley, Power Steering Pump
5. Pulley, Crankshaft
6. Pulley, Water Pump
7. Pulley, Drive Belt Tensioner
8. Pulley, Generator

88261G45

**Fig. 94 Drive belt routing—1996 4.3L engines (Serpentine Belts)**

routing label (or vehicle emission control information label) for an illustration which resembles your motor first. If no label is present or if the label does not match your engine (perhaps an engine swap was performed on older vehicles before you were the owner) refer to the routing diagrams found in this section. In cases where engine swaps were made, determine the year or the engine using year codes, or visually match the accessories to the diagrams provided.

## REMOVAL & INSTALLATION

### V-belts

#### ◆ See Figures 95 and 96

1. Disconnect the negative battery cable for safety.
2. Loosen the component-to-mounting bracket bolts.
3. Rotate the component to relieve the tension on the drive belt.
4. Slip the drive belt from the component pulley and remove it from the engine.

➡**If the engine uses more than one belt, it may be necessary to remove other belts that are in front of the one being removed.**

5. To install, reverse the removal procedures. Adjust the component drive belt tension to specifications.

### Serpentine Belts

#### ◆ See Figure 97

Belt replacement is a relatively simple matter rotating the tensioner off the belt (to relieve tension) and holding the tensioner in this position as the belt is slipped from its pulley. Depending on the engine and year of production, there are various methods of rotating the tensioner, but all require a breaker bar, large ratchet or wrench. Most early models use a tensioner which has a machined receiver which directly accepts a ½ in. driver. Most later models (through 1995) require that you use a large socket or wrench (usually 16mm or ⅝ in.) over the tensioner pulley bolt. A change was made to the part again in 1996, so the tensioner arm contains a machined receiver for a ⅜ in. driver from a ratchet or breaker bar.

1. Before you begin, visually confirm the belt routing to the engine compartment label (if present) or to the appropriate diagram in this section (if the label is not present). If you cannot make a match (perhaps it is not the original motor for this van), scribble your own diagram on a page in this book before proceeding.
2. Disconnect the negative battery cable for safety.
3. Install the appropriate sized breaker bar, wrench, or socket to the tensioner arm or pulley, as applicable.
4. Rotate the tensioner to the left (counterclockwise) and slip the belt from the tensioner pulley.
5. Once the belt is free from the tensioner, CAREFULLY rotate the tensioner back into position. DO NOT allow the tensioner to suddenly snap into place or damage could occur to the assembly.
6. Slip the belt from the remaining pulleys (this can get difficult is there is little room between the radiator/fan assembly and the accessory pulleys. Work slowly and be patient.
7. Once the belt is free, remove it from the engine compartment.
   **To install:**
8. Route the belt over all the pulleys except the water pump and/or the tensioner. Refer to the routing illustration that you identified as a match before beginning.
9. Rotate the tensioner pulley to the left (counterclockwise) and hold it

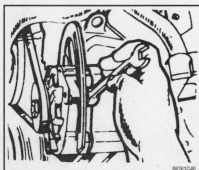

88261G46

**Fig. 95 To adjust or replace belts, first loosen the component mounting and adjusting bolts . . .**

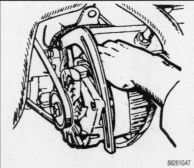

88261G47

**Fig. 96 . . . the pivot the component inward to remove the belt or outward to increase tension**

88261P26

**Fig. 97 On this 4.3L engine, a large wrench (16mm) was used to pivot the belt tensioner and free the belt**

while you finish slipping the belt into position. Slowly allow the tensioner into contact with the belt.

10. Check to see if the correct V-groove tracking is around each pulley.

### ⁕ WARNING

**Improper V-groove tracking will cause the belt to fail in a short period of time.**

11. Connect the negative battery cable.

### Hoses

#### INSPECTION

▶ **See Figures 98, 99, 100 and 101**

Upper and lower radiator hoses along with the heater hoses should be checked for deterioration, leaks and loose hose clamps at least every 15,000 miles (24,000 km) or 12 months. It is also wise to check the hoses periodically in early spring and at the beginning of the fall or winter when you are performing other maintenance. A quick visual inspection could discover a weakened hose which might have left you stranded if it had remained unrepaired.

Whenever you are checking the hoses, make sure the engine and cooling system are both cold. Visually inspect for cracking, rotting or collapsed hoses, and replace as necessary. Run your hand along the length of the hose. If a weak or swollen spot is noted when squeezing the hose wall, the hose should be replaced.

#### REMOVAL & INSTALLATION

1. Disconnect the negative battery cable for safety.
2. Drain the cooling system to a level below the hose which is being

removed. The entire system must be drained if the lower radiator hose is being disconnected from the radiator or engine.

3. Loosen the hose clamps at each end of the hose.
4. Working the hose back and forth, slide it off its connection.

➡**When replacing the heater hoses, maintain a 1½ in. (38mm) clearance between the hose clip-to-upper control arm and between the rear overhead heater core lines-to-exhaust pipe.**

5. To install, reverse the removal procedures.

➡**Draw the hoses tight to prevent sagging or rubbing against other components; route the hoses through the clamps as installed originally. Always make sure the hose clamps are beyond the component bead and placed in the center of the clamping surface before tightening them.**

### CV-Boots

#### INSPECTION

▶ **See Figures 102 and 103**

The front halfshafts on All Wheel Drive (AWD) vehicles use CV (Constant Velocity) joints to transmit power from the differential to the front wheels, while still allowing for suspension travel. The joints are protected by CV-boots which should be checked for damage each time the oil is changed and any other time the vehicle is raised for service. These boots keep water, grime, dirt and other damaging matter from entering the CV-joints. Any of these could cause early CV-joint failure which can be expensive to repair. Heavy grease thrown around the inside of the front wheel(s) and on the brake caliper/drum can be an indication of a torn boot. Thoroughly check the boots for missing clamps and tears. If the boot is damaged, it should be replaced immediately. Please refer to Section 7 for procedures.

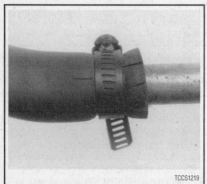

TCCS1219

**Fig. 98 The cracks developing along this hose are a result of age-related hardening**

TCCS1220

**Fig. 99 A hose clamp that is too tight can cause older hoses to separate and tear on either side of the clamp**

TCCS1221

**Fig. 100 A soft spongy hose (identifiable by the swollen section) will eventually burst and should be replaced**

TCCS1222

**Fig. 101 Hoses are likely to deteriorate from the inside if the cooling system is not periodically flushed**

TCCS1011

**Fig. 102 CV-boots must be inspected periodically for damage**

TCCS1010

**Fig. 103 A torn boot should be replaced immediately**

## Spark Plugs

♦ **See Figure 104**

A typical spark plug consists of a metal shell surrounding a ceramic insulator. A metal electrode extends downward through the center of the insulator and protrudes a small distance. Located at the end of the plug and attached to the side of the outer metal shell is the side electrode. The side electrode bends in at a 90 degrees angle so its tip is just past and parallel to the tip of the center electrode. The distance between these 2 electrodes (measured in thousandths of an inch or hundredths of a millimeter) is called the spark plug gap.

The spark plug does not produce a spark but instead provides a gap across which the current can arc. The coil produces anywhere from 20,000–50,000 volts (depending on the type and application) which travels through the wires to the spark plugs. The current passes along the center electrode and jumps the gap to the side electrode, and in doing so, ignites the air/fuel mixture in the combustion chamber.

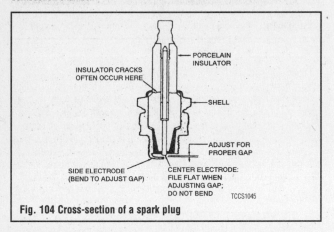

**Fig. 104 Cross-section of a spark plug**

## SPARK PLUG HEAT RANGE

♦ **See Figure 105**

Spark plug heat range is the ability of the plug to dissipate heat. The longer the insulator (or the farther it extends into the engine), the hotter the plug will operate; the shorter the insulator (the closer the electrode is to the block's cooling passages) the cooler it will operate. A plug that absorbs little heat and remains too cool will quickly accumulate deposits of oil and carbon since it is not hot enough to burn them off. This leads to plug fouling and consequently to misfiring. A plug that absorbs too much heat will have no deposits but, due to the excessive heat, the electrodes will burn away quickly and might possibly lead to preignition or other ignition problems. Preignition takes place when plug tips get so hot that they glow sufficiently to ignite the air/fuel mixture before the actual spark occurs. This early ignition will usually cause a pinging during low speeds and heavy loads.

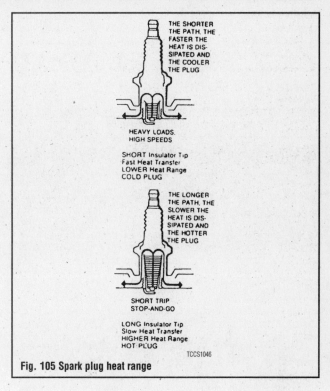

**Fig. 105 Spark plug heat range**

The general rule of thumb for choosing the correct heat range when picking a spark plug is: if most of your driving is long distance, high speed travel, use a colder plug; if most of your driving is stop and go, use a hotter plug. Original equipment plugs are generally a good compromise between the 2 styles and most people never have the need to change their plugs from the factory-recommended heat range.

## REMOVAL

♦ **See Figures 106, 107, 108, 109 and 110**

A set of spark plugs usually requires replacement after about 20,000–30,000 miles (32,000–48,000 km), depending on your style of driving. In normal operation plug gap increases about 0.001 in. (0.025mm) for every 2500 miles (4000 km). As the gap increases, the plug's voltage requirement also increases. It requires a greater voltage to jump the wider gap and about 2 to 3 times as much voltage to fire the plug at high speeds than at idle. The improved air/fuel ratio control of modern fuel injection combined with the higher voltage output of modern ignition systems will often allow an engine to run significantly longer on a set of standard spark plugs, but keep in mind that efficiency will drop as the gap widens (along with fuel economy and power).

**Fig. 106 Access to the spark plugs is through the wheel-well on most Astro and Safari vans**

**Fig. 107 Disconnect the spark plug wire by pulling on the BOOT, NOT THE WIRE**

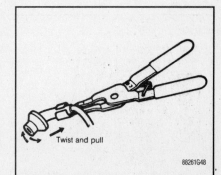

**Fig. 108 A spark plug wire removal tool is recommended to prevent wire damage (and to make it easier)**

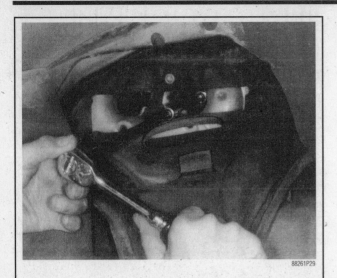

Fig. 109 Loosen the spark plug using a ratchet and extension . . .

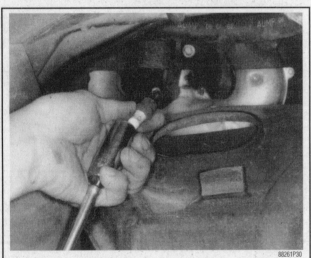

Fig. 110 . . . then carefully unthread and remove the plug from the cylinder head

➡All 1996 models were originally equipped with platinum-tip spark plugs which can be used for as-long-as 100,000 miles (161,000 km). This holds true unless internal engine wear or damage and/or improperly operating emissions controls cause plug fouling. If you suspect this, you may wish to remove and inspect the platinum plugs before the recommended mileage. Most platinum plugs should not be cleaned or regapped. If you find their condition unsuitable, they should be replaced.

**When removing the spark plugs, work on 1 at a time.** Don't start by removing the plug wires all at once because unless you number them, they're going to get mixed up. On some models though, it will be more convenient for you to remove all of the wires before you start to work on the plugs. If this is necessary, take a minute before you begin and number the wires with tape before you take them off. The time you spend here will pay off later.

1. Disconnect the negative battery cable, and if the vehicle has been run recently, allow the engine to thoroughly cool. Attempting to remove plugs from a hot cylinder head could cause the plugs to seize and damage the threads in the cylinder head.

2. Check for access to the plugs on your vehicle. The wheel wells of most vans covered by this manual are designed to allow access to the sides of the engine. A rubber cover may be draped over the opening, and it may require removal of 1 or more plastic body snap-fasteners (which are carefully pried loose using a special C-shaped tool) before you can move it aside for clearance.

If this is your best access point, raise and support the vehicle safely using jackstands, then remove the front tire and wheel assemblies.

➡**On some models, the engine cover may be removed to provide additional access to the spark plugs. This will be necessary if you also plan to check the spark plug wires at this time anyway.**

3. Carefully twist the spark plug wire boot to loosen it, then pull upward and remove the boot from the plug. Be sure to pull on the boot and not on the wire, otherwise the connector located inside the boot may become separated.

➡**A spark plug wire removal tool is recommended as it will make removal easier and help prevent damage to the boot and wire assembly.**

4. Using compressed air (and SAFETY GLASSES), blow any water or debris from the spark plug well to assure that no harmful contaminants are allowed to enter the combustion chamber when the spark plug is removed. If compressed air is not available, use a rag or a brush to clean the area.

➡**Remove the spark plugs when the engine is cold, if possible, to prevent damage to the threads. If plug removal is difficult, apply a few drops of penetrating oil or silicone spray to the area around the base of the plug, and allow it a few minutes to work.**

5. Using a spark plug socket (usually a ⅝ in. socket on these engines) that is equipped with a rubber insert to properly hold the plug, turn the spark plug counterclockwise to loosen and remove the spark plug from the bore.

**✳✳ WARNING**

AVOID the use of a flexible extension on the socket. Use of a flexible extension may allow a shear force to be applied to the plug. A shear force could break the plug off in the cylinder head, leading to costly and frustrating repairs.

**INSPECTION & GAPPING**

▸ **See Figures 111, 112, 113 and 114**

➡**If the specifications on the underhood tune-up sticker in the engine compartment disagree with the Tune-Up Specifications chart in this Section, the figures on the sticker must be used. The sticker often reflects changes made during the production run.**

Check the plugs for deposits and wear. If they are not going to be replaced, clean the plugs thoroughly. Remember that any kind of deposit will decrease the efficiency of the plug. Plugs can be cleaned on a spark plug cleaning machine, which can sometimes be found in service stations, or you can do an acceptable job of cleaning with a stiff brush. If the plugs are cleaned, the electrodes must be filed flat. Use an ignition points file, not an emery board or the like, which will leave deposits. The electrodes must be filed perfectly flat with sharp edges; rounded edges reduce the spark plug voltage by as much as 50%.

➡**All 1996 models were originally equipped with platinum-tip spark plugs which can be used for as-long-as 100,000 miles (161,000 km). This holds true unless internal engine wear or damage and/or improperly operating emissions controls cause plug fouling. If you suspect this, you may wish to remove and inspect the platinum plugs before the recommended mileage. Most platinum plugs should not be cleaned or regapped. If you find their condition unsuitable, they should be replaced.**

Check spark plug gap before installation. The ground electrode (the L-shaped one connected to the body of the plug) must be parallel to the center electrode and the specified size wire gauge (please refer to the Tune-Up Specifications chart for details) must pass between the electrodes with a slight drag.

➡**NEVER adjust the gap on a used platinum type spark plug.**

Always check the gap on new plugs as they are not always set correctly at the factory. Do not use a flat feeler gauge when measuring the gap on a used plug, because the reading may be inaccurate. A round-wire type gapping tool is the best way to check the gap. The correct gauge should pass through the electrode gap with a slight drag. If you're in doubt, try 1 size smaller and 1 larger. The smaller gauge should go through easily, while the larger 1 shouldn't go through at all. Wire gapping tools usually have a bending tool attached. Use that to

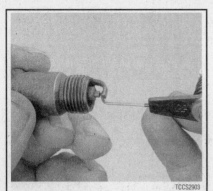

**Fig. 111 Checking the spark plug gap with a feeler gauge**

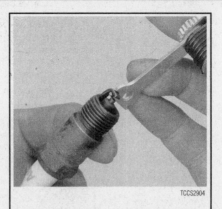

**Fig. 112 Adjusting the spark plug gap**

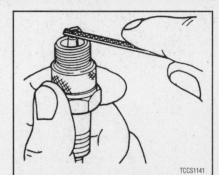

**Fig. 113 If the standard plug is in good condition, the electrode may be filed flat—WARNING: do not file platinum plugs**

A normally worn spark plug should have light tan or gray deposits on the firing tip.

A carbon fouled plug, identified by soft, sooty, black deposits, may indicate an improperly tuned vehicle. Check the air cleaner, ignition components and engine control system.

This spark plug has been left in the engine too long, as evidenced by the extreme gap- Plugs with such an extreme gap can cause misfiring and stumbling accompanied by a noticeable lack of power.

An oil fouled spark plug indicates an engine with worn poston rings and/or bad valve seals allowing excessive oil to enter the chamber.

A physically damaged spark plug may be evidence of severe detonation in that cylinder. Watch that cylinder carefully between services, as a continued detonation will not only damage the plug, but could also damage the engine.

A bridged or almost bridged spark plug, identified by a build-up between the electrodes caused by excessive carbon or oil build-up on the plug.

**Fig. 114 Inspect the spark plug to determine engine running conditions**

adjust the side electrode until the proper distance is obtained. Absolutely never attempt to bend the center electrode. Also, be careful not to bend the side electrode too far or too often as it may weaken and break off within the engine, requiring removal of the cylinder head to retrieve it.

## INSTALLATION

1. Inspect the spark plug boot for tears or damage. If a damaged boot is found, the spark plug wire must be replaced. As mentioned earlier, this is an excellent time to check each of the spark plug wires for proper resistance and/or for damage.

2. Using a wire feeler gauge, check and adjust the spark plug gap. When using a gauge, the proper size should pass between the electrodes with a slight drag. The next larger size should not be able to pass while the next smaller size should pass freely.

3. Carefully thread the plug into the bore by hand. If resistance is felt before the plug is almost completely threaded, back the plug out and begin threading again. In small, hard to reach areas, an old spark plug wire and boot could be used as a threading tool. The boot will hold the plug while you twist the end of the wire and the wire is supple enough to twist before it would allow the plug to crossthread.

### ✳✳ WARNING

**Do not use the spark plug socket to thread the plugs. Always carefully thread the plug by hand or using an old plug wire to prevent the possibility of crossthreading and damaging the cylinder head bore.**

4. Carefully tighten the spark plug. If the plug you are installing is equipped with a crush washer, seat the plug, then tighten about ¼ turn to crush the washer. If you are installing a tapered seat plug, tighten the plug to 11 ft. lbs. (14 Nm) for all engines except 1996 models. On 1996 model engines, tighten the plug to 14 ft. lbs. (20 Nm) on used cylinder heads or to 22 ft. lbs. (30 Nm) on new cylinder heads.

5. Apply a small amount of silicone dielectric compound to the end of the spark plug lead or inside the spark plug boot to prevent sticking, then install the boot to the spark plug and push until it clicks into place. The click may be felt or heard, then gently pull back on the boot to assure proper contact.

### Spark Plug Wires

**▶ See Figures 115 and 116**

At every tune-up/inspection, visually check the spark plug cables for burns cuts, or breaks in the insulation. Check the boots and the nipples on the distributor cap and/or coil. Replace any damaged wiring.

**➡If the spark plug wires have become unserviceable due to time and wear, it is probably a good idea to replace the distributor cap and rotor as well.**

Every 30,000 miles (48,000 km) or so, the resistance of the wires should be checked with an ohmmeter. Wires with excessive resistance will cause misfiring

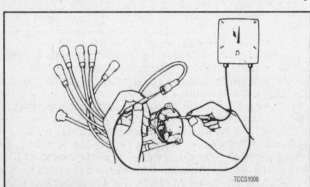

Fig. 115 Checking plug wire resistance through the distributor cap with an ohmmeter

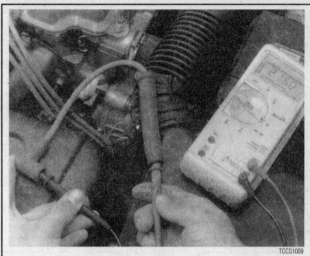

Fig. 116 Checking individual plug wire resistance with a digital ohmmeter

and may make the engine difficult to start in damp weather. Generally, the useful life of the cables is 30,000–45,000 miles (48,000–72,000 km), though some late-model vehicles (such as 1996 Astro or Safari equipped with platinum-tip plugs) use newer long-life wires which could last up to 100,000 (161,000 km) miles in some circumstances.

To check the resistance, remove the distributor cap (you'll have to remove the engine cover for access), leaving the wires in place. Connect 1 lead of an ohmmeter to an electrode within the cap; connect the other lead to the corresponding spark plug terminal (remove it from the spark plug for this test). Replace any wire which shows a resistance over 30,000 ohms or which fluctuates value if the wire is moved/bent slightly.

It should be remembered that resistance is also a function of length; the longer the wire the greater the resistance. If the wire resistance is below 30,000 ohms, then compare the ohmmeter reading to the appropriate specification for that wire's length. Replace any wire which exceeds the appropriate resistance for its length:

- 0–15 in. (0–38 cm)—3000–10,000 ohms
- 15–25 in. (38–64 cm)—4000–15,000 ohms
- 25–35 in. (64–89 cm)—6000–20,000 ohms
- Over 35 in. (89 cm)—5000–10,000 ohms per 12 in. (30 cm)

When installing a new set of spark plug wires, replace the wires 1 at a time so there will be no mix-up. Start by replacing the longest cable first. Install the boot firmly over the spark plug. Route the wire exactly the same as the original. Insert the distributor end of the wire firmly into the distributor cap tower, then seat the boot over the tower. Repeat the process for each wire.

### Distributor Cap and Rotor

At every tune-up/inspection, visually check the distributor cap and rotor for damage, burns or corrosion. Check the spark plug towers and their terminals under the cap to make sure they are free of corrosion which would inhibit proper spark distribution. Replace any damaged or worn components.

**➡If the spark plug wires have become unserviceable due to time and wear, it is probably a good idea to replace the cap and rotor as well.**

#### REMOVAL & INSTALLATION

**▶ See Figures 117, 118, 119, 120 and 121**

1. Disconnect the negative battery cable for safety.
2. Remove the engine cover from the passenger compartment.

**➡Some late-model vehicles, such as 1996 engines with the HVS system, use spark plug wires and distributor caps which are already numbered for ease of service, BUT double-check this before disconnecting any wires.**

Fig. 117 Tag all spark plug wires and matching cap terminals before removal

Fig. 118 Release the distributor cap hold-down bolts

Fig. 119 Remove the cap for inspection, replacement or access to the rotor

Fig. 120 Carefully pull the rotor from the distributor shaft—note this type does NOT use retaining screws

➡If the cap is just being removed for inspection or for access to the rotor, it may be possible to remove the cap without disconnecting any/all of the wires and position it aside. Just remember that if you change your mind and disconnect 2 or more wires you MUST stop and tag them before proceeding.

4. Release the distributor cap retainers. For most vehicles covered by this manual, there should be 2 retaining screws (one on either side of the cap), though some models may use spring loaded cap retainers which are simply twisted ¼–½ turn to release.

5. Remove the cap from the distributor assembly.

6. If you are replacing or inspecting the rotor, check for any retaining screws and remove, if present. Most vans covered by this manual utilize keyed rotor which is mounted to the distributor shaft with a gentle interference fit. Grasp the rotor and gently pull upward to remove it from the shaft.

7. Check the distributor cap and rotor for wear or damage and replace, if necessary.

**To install:**

8. If removed, install the rotor to the top of the distributor shaft.

9. Install the cap to the distributor assembly. Some early models may utilize an internal-coil type distributor cap. Obviously, the old coil must be transferred to the new cap if you are replacing the cap on these models.

10. As tagged, connect any spark plug wires which were removed.

11. Install the engine cover.

12. Connect the negative battery cable.

## Ignition Timing

### GENERAL INFORMATION

Ignition timing is the measurement, in degrees of crankshaft rotation, of the point at which the spark plugs fire in each of the cylinders. It is measured in degrees before or after Top Dead Center (TDC) of the compression stroke.

Because it takes a fraction of a second for the spark plug to ignite the mixture in the cylinder, the spark plug must fire a little before the piston reaches TDC. Otherwise, the mixture will not be completely ignited as the piston passes TDC and the full power of the explosion will not be used by the engine.

The timing measurement is given in degrees of crankshaft rotation before the piston reaches TDC (BTDC). If the setting for the ignition timing is 5° BTDC, the spark plug must fire 5° before each piston reaches TDC. This only holds true, however, when the engine is at idle speed.

As the engine speed increases, the pistons go faster. The spark plugs have to ignite the fuel even sooner if it is to be completely ignited when the piston reaches TDC. To do this, distributors have various means of advancing the spark timing as the engine speed increases. On older vehicles (before the vans covered by this manual), this was accomplished by centrifugal weights within the distributor along with a vacuum diaphragm mounted on the side of the distributor. Later vehicles (such as the Astro and Safari vans are equipped with an electronic spark timing system in which no vacuum or mechanical advance is used, instead all timing changes electronically based on signals from various sensors.

Fig. 121 Some early-model distributors may have the ignition coil mounted to the distributor cap.

3. If the cap is being completely removed (for replacement or for engine service) TAG all of the spark plug wires and matching terminals on the cap, then disconnect the wires.

If the ignition is set too far advanced (BTDC), the ignition and expansion of the fuel in the cylinder will occur too soon and tend to force the piston down while it is still traveling up. This causes engine ping. If the ignition spark is set too far retarded, after TDC (ATDC), the piston will have already passed TDC and started on its way down when the fuel is ignited. This will cause the piston to be forced down for only a portion of its travel. This will result in poor engine performance and lack of power.

Timing marks usually consist of a notch on the rim of the crankshaft pulley and a scale of degrees attached to the front of the engine (often on the engine front cover). The notch corresponds to the position of the piston in the No. 1 cylinder. A stroboscopic (dynamic) timing light is used, which is hooked into the circuit of the No. 1 cylinder spark plug. Every time the spark plug fires, the timing light flashes. By aiming the timing light at the timing marks while the engine is running, the exact position of the piston within the cylinder can be easily read since the stroboscopic flash makes the mark on the pulley appear to be standing still. Proper timing is indicated when the notch is aligned with the correct number on the scale.

➡**Never pierce a spark plug wire in order to attach a timing light or perform tests. The pierced insulation will eventually lead to an electrical arc and related ignition troubles.**

Since your van has electronic ignition, you should use a timing light with an inductive pickup. This pickup simply clamps onto the No. 1 spark plug wire, eliminating the adapter. It is not susceptible to cross-firing or false triggering, which may occur with a conventional light, due to the greater voltages produced by electronic ignition.

### SERVICE PRECAUTIONS

**✳✳ WARNING**

**Some electronic diagnostic equipment and service tachometers may not be compatible with the HEI system, consult your manufacturer before using such equipment.**

1. Before making compression checks, disconnect the engine control switch feed wire at the distributor. To disconnect the connector from the distributor, release the locking tab and pull the connector body downward; NEVER use a metal tool to release the locking tab, for the tab may break off.
2. The distributor needs no periodic lubrication, for the engine lubrication system lubricates the lower bushing and an oil reservoir lubricates the upper bushing.
3. The tachometer (TACH) terminal is located next to the engine control switch (BAT) connector on the distributor cap.

**✳✳ WARNING**

**NEVER allow the tachometer terminal to touch ground, for damage to the module, ECM and/or the coil may result.**

4. Since there are no points in the ignition system, NO manual dwell adjustment is necessary or possible.
5. The material used in the construction of the spark plug wires is very soft

and pliable. These wires can withstand high heat and carry a higher voltage. It is very important that the wires be routed correctly, for they are highly susceptible to scuffing and/or cutting.

➡**When removing a spark plug wire, be sure to twist the boot and then pull on it to remove it. Do NOT pull on the wire to remove it.**

### ADJUSTMENT

▶ **See Figures 122, 123 and 124**

➡**Ignition timing on these engines is controlled by the electronic engine control system and does NOT need to be periodically checked and adjusted. If the distributor has been removed for engine service or if all other causes of a driveability problem have been resolved and the timing is suspect, the initial (base) timing may be checked and adjusted. Also note that although the HVS ignition system used on 1996 engines utilizes a distributor assembly, it is NOT a traditional distributor ignition system (the HVS assembly is keyed for installation in ONLY one position as it is completely electronically controlled) and timing CANNOT be adjusted at all.**

The following procedure requires the use of a distributor wrench and a timing light. When using a timing light, be sure to consult the manufacturer's recommendations for installation and usage.

1. Refer to the ignition timing specifications, listed on the Vehicle Emissions Control Information (VECI) label, located on the radiator support panel and follow the instructions. If the label is missing you MUST obtain the correct replacement in order to assure the proper timing procedures are being followed for YOUR engine.
2. Start and run the engine until it reaches normal operating temperature.

**✳✳ CAUTION**

**NEVER run the engine in a sealed garage. Open all doors and windows, and if possible, use vents or fans to provide further ventilation. Carbon Monoxide which is prevalent in exhaust gas can quickly build-up in your blood, preventing oxygen from reaching your brain. This can cause serious injury or even DEATH.**

3. Disable the electronic ignition advance system (usually known as Ignition Control or IC) by disconnecting the "Set Timing" connector. This connector is in a single wire (tan/black) that breaks out of the engine wiring harness, adjacent to the distributor assembly. On early-model vehicles covered by this manual, you should be able to find the connector by tracing the wire back from the 4-terminal EST connector at the distributor assembly.
4. Connect a timing light to the motor:
   a. If using a non-inductive type, connect an adapter between the No. 1 spark plug and the spark plug wire; DO NOT puncture the spark plug wire, for this will allow arching which will cause engine mis-firing.
   b. If using an inductive type, clamp it around the No. 1 spark plug wire.
   c. If using a magnetic type, place the probe in the connector located near the damper pulley; this type must be used with special electronic timing equipment.

**Fig. 122 Timing marks are found on the crankshaft damper (balancer) and engine front cover—late-model 4.3L engine shown**

| | |
|---|---|
| 1 | BALANCER TIMING GROOVE |
| 2 | TIMING TAB |

4.3L (M/L)

88261G49

**Fig. 123 View of a typical timing mark scale**

88261G51

**Fig. 124 Aim the timing light at the crankshaft damper timing mark, but WATCH OUT for moving engine parts**

88261P35

5. Start the engine and allow it to idle at normal operating temperature. Aim the timing light at the timing mark on the damper pulley (be careful because the strobe affect of the timing light will make moving engine parts appear to be standing still); a line on the damper pulley will align the timing mark. If necessary (to adjust the timing), loosen the distributor hold-down clamp and slowly turn the distributor slightly to align the marks. When the alignment is correct, tighten the hold-down bolt, then re-check the timing with the light to make sure it did not change while you were tightening the distributor bolt.

6. Turn the engine **OFF**, remove the timing light and reconnect the "Set Timing" connector.

## Valve Lash

Valve lash adjustment determines how far the valves enter the cylinder and how long they stay open and/or closed.

➡**While all valve adjustments must be made as accurately as possible, it is better to have the valve adjustment slightly loose than slightly tight, as a burned valve may result from overly tight adjustments.**

All of the engines covered by this manual utilize hydraulic valve lifters. The purpose of hydraulic lifters is to automatically maintain zero valve lash, therefore no periodic adjustments are required on engines equipped with them. However, many of the vehicles utilize rocker arms which are retained by adjusting nuts. If the rocker arms and nuts are loosened or removed, they must be properly adjusted upon installation in order for the lifters to work. For adjustment procedures, please refer to Section 3 of this manual.

## Idle Speed and Mixture Adjustments

### CARBURETED ENGINES

The different combinations of emission systems application on the various available engines have resulted in a great variety of tune-up specifications. All vehicles covered by this manual should have a decal conspicuously placed in the engine compartment giving tune-up specifications.

Because the 4.3L carbureted engine utilizes an electronically controlled feedback carburetor there are no periodic mixture adjustments are necessary or possible. Slow (curb) idle speed can be set using the speed screw at the throttle valve on the carburetor. When setting the curb idle speed, make sure the engine is at normal operating temperature and that all of the conditions on the vehicle emission control information label have been met.

### FUEL INJECTED ENGINES

Engines covered by this manual may be equipped with a variety of fuel injection systems including: Throttle Body Injection (TBI), Central Multi-Port Fuel Injection (CMFI) and Central Sequential Fuel Injection (CSFI). Although each of these systems contain some of their own unique engine control components, what they all share is full computer control of the idle air supply and of all fuel delivery. The fuel injection computer module regulates idle speeds and supplies the correct amount of fuel during all engine operating conditions. No periodic

## GASOLINE ENGINE TUNE-UP SPECIFICATIONS

| Year | Engine ID/VIN | Engine Displacement Liters (cc) | Spark Plugs Gap (in.) | | Ignition Timing (deg.) MT | Ignition Timing (deg.) AT | Fuel Pump (psi) | | Idle Speed (rpm) MT | Idle Speed (rpm) AT | Valve Clearance In. | Valve Clearance Ex. |
|---|---|---|---|---|---|---|---|---|---|---|---|---|
| 1985 | E | 2.5 (2474) | 0.060 | 1 | 4 | 4 | 9-13 | | 4 | 4 | HYD | HYD |
| | N | 4.3 (4293) | 0.040 | 1 | 4 | 4 | 4-6.5 | | 4 | 4 | HYD | HYD |
| 1986 | E | 2.5 (2474) | 0.060 | 1 | 4 | 4 | 9-13 | | 4 | 4 | HYD | HYD |
| | Z | 4.3 (4293) | 0.040 | 1 | 4 | 4 | 9-13 | | 4 | 4 | HYD | HYD |
| 1987 | E | 2.5 (2474) | 0.060 | 1 | 4 | 4 | 9-13 | | 4 | 4 | HYD | HYD |
| | Z | 4.3 (4293) | 0.040 | 1 | 4 | 4 | 9-13 | | 4 | 4 | HYD | HYD |
| 1988 | E | 2.5 (2474) | 0.060 | 1 | 4 | 4 | 9-13 | | 4 | 4 | HYD | HYD |
| | Z | 4.3 (4293) | 0.040 | 1 | 4 | 4 | 9-13 | | 4 | 4 | HYD | HYD |
| 1989 | E | 2.5 (2474) | 0.060 | 1 | 4 | 4 | 9-13 | | 4 | 4 | HYD | HYD |
| | Z | 4.3 (4293) | 0.035 | 1 | 4 | 4 | 9-13 | | 4 | 4 | HYD | HYD |
| 1990 | E | 2.5 (2474) | 0.060 | 1 | - | 4 | 9-13 | | - | 4 | HYD | HYD |
| | B | 4.3 (4293) | 0.035 | 1 | - | 4 | 9-13 | | - | 4 | HYD | HYD |
| | Z | 4.3 (4293) | 0.035 | 1 | - | 4 | 9-13 | | - | 4 | HYD | HYD |
| 1991 | B | 4.3 (4293) | 0.035 | 1 | - | 4 | 9-13 | | - | 4 | HYD | HYD |
| | Z | 4.3 (4293) | 0.035 | 1 | - | 4 | 9-13 | | - | 4 | HYD | HYD |
| 1992 | W | 4.3 (4293) | 0.045 | 1 | - | 4 | 55-61 | 2 | - | 4 | HYD | HYD |
| | Z | 4.3 (4293) | 0.035 | 1 | - | 4 | 9-13 | | - | 4 | HYD | HYD |
| 1993 | W | 4.3 (4293) | 0.045 | 1 | - | 4 | 55-61 | 2 | - | 4 | HYD | HYD |
| | Z | 4.3 (4293) | 0.035 | 1 | - | 4 | 9-13 | | - | 4 | HYD | HYD |
| 1994 | W | 4.3 (4293) | 0.045 | 1 | - | 4 | 55-61 | 2 | - | 4 | HYD | HYD |
| | Z | 4.3 (4293) | 0.035 | 1 | - | 4 | 9-13 | | - | 4 | HYD | HYD |
| 1995 | W | 4.3 (4293) | 0.045 | 1 | - | 3 | 55-61 | 2 | - | 4 | HYD | HYD |
| 1996 | W | 4.3 (4293) | 0.060 | 1 | - | 3 | 58-64 | 2 | - | 4 | HYD | HYD |

NOTE: The Vehicle Emission Control Information label often reflects specification changes made during production. The label figures must be used if they differ from those in this chart.

HYD - Hydraulic

1 Remember that calibrations may vary. Use the value on the underhood label if it differs from this specification

2 With key on and engine off

3 Ignition timing is not adjustable

4 Refer to Vehicle Emission Control Information label

88261C03

adjustments are necessary or possible. If the engine is suspected of maintaining an incorrect idle speed, refer to Section 4 of this manual for information regarding the self-diagnostic features of the computer engine and emission control systems and to Section 5 for information regarding the throttle body and fuel delivery systems.

## Air Conditioning

### SYSTEM SERVICE & REPAIR

♦ **See Figure 125**

➤It is recommended that the A/C system be serviced by an EPA Section 609 certified automotive technician utilizing a refrigerant recovery/recycling machine.

Fig. 125 This label warns technicians to use R-134a refrigerant (R-12 would damage this system)

The do-it-yourselfer should not service his/her own vehicle's A/C system for many reasons, including legal concerns, personal injury, environmental damage and cost.

According to the U.S. Clean Air Act, it is a federal crime to service or repair (involving the refrigerant) a Motor Vehicle Air Conditioning (MVAC) system for money without being EPA certified. It is also illegal to vent R-12 and R-134a refrigerants into the atmosphere. State and/or local laws may be more strict than the federal regulations, so be sure to check with your state and/or local authorities for further information.

➤**Federal law dictates that a fine of up to $25,000 may be levied on people convicted of venting refrigerant into the atmosphere.**

When servicing an A/C system you run the risk of handling or coming in contact with refrigerant, which may result in skin or eye irritation or frostbite. Although low in toxicity (due to chemical stability), inhalation of concentrated refrigerant fumes is dangerous and can result in death; cases of fatal cardiac arrhythmia have been reported in people accidentally subjected to high levels of refrigerant. Some early symptoms include loss of concentration and drowsiness.

➤**Generally, the limit for exposure is lower for R-134a than it is for R-12. Exceptional care must be practiced when handling R-134a.**

Also, some refrigerants can decompose at high temperatures (near gas heaters or open flame), which may result in hydrofluoric acid, hydrochloric acid and phosgene (a fatal nerve gas).

It is usually more economically feasible to have a certified MVAC automotive technician perform A/C system service on your vehicle.

### R-12 Refrigerant Conversion

If your vehicle still uses R-12 refrigerant, one way to save A/C system costs down the road is to investigate the possibility of having your system converted to R-134a. The older R-12 systems can be easily converted to R-134a refrigerant by a certified automotive technician by installing a few new components and changing the system oil.

The cost of R-12 is steadily rising and will continue to increase, because it is no longer imported or manufactured in the United States. Therefore, it is often possible to have an R-12 system converted to R-134a and recharged for less than it would cost to just charge the system with R-12.

If you are interested in having your system converted, contact local automotive service stations for more details and information.

### PREVENTIVE MAINTENANCE

Although the A/C system should not be serviced by the do-it-yourselfer, preventive maintenance should be practiced to help maintain the efficiency of the vehicle's A/C system. Be sure to perform the following:

- The easiest and most important preventive maintenance for your A/C system is to be sure that it is used on a regular basis. Running the system for five minutes each month (no matter what the season) will help ensure that the seals and all internal components remain lubricated.

➤**Some vehicles automatically operate the A/C system compressor whenever the windshield defroster is activated. Therefore, the A/C system would not need to be operated each month if the defroster was used.**

- In order to prevent heater core freeze-up during A/C operation, it is necessary to maintain proper antifreeze protection. Be sure to properly maintain the engine cooling system.
- Any obstruction of or damage to the condenser configuration will restrict air flow which is essential to its efficient operation. Keep this unit clean and in proper physical shape.

➤**Bug screens which are mounted in front of the condenser (unless they are original equipment) are regarded as obstructions.**

- The condensation drain tube expels any water which accumulates on the bottom of the evaporator housing into the engine compartment. If this tube is obstructed, the air conditioning performance can be restricted and condensation buildup can spill over onto the vehicle's floor.

### SYSTEM INSPECTION

Although the A/C system should not be serviced by the do-it-yourselfer, system inspections should be performed to help maintain the efficiency of the vehicle's A/C system. Be sure to perform the following:

The easiest and often most important check for the air conditioning system consists of a visual inspection of the system components. Visually inspect the system for refrigerant leaks, damaged compressor clutch, abnormal compressor drive belt tension and/or condition, plugged evaporator drain tube, blocked condenser fins, disconnected or broken wires, blown fuses, corroded connections and poor insulation.

A refrigerant leak will usually appear as an oily residue at the leakage point in the system. The oily residue soon picks up dust or dirt particles from the surrounding air and appears greasy. Through time, this will build up and appear to be a heavy dirt impregnated grease.

For a thorough visual and operational inspection, check the following:

- Check the surface of the radiator and condenser for dirt, leaves or other material which might block air flow.
- Check for kinks in hoses and lines. Check the system for leaks.
- Make sure the drive belt is properly tensioned. During operation, make sure the belt is free of noise or slippage.
- Make sure the blower motor operates at all appropriate positions, then check for distribution of the air from all outlets.

➤**Remember that in high humidity, air discharged from the vents may not feel as cold as expected, even if the system is working properly. This is because moisture in humid air retains heat more effectively than dry air, thereby making humid air more difficult to cool.**

## Windshield Wipers

➡**Intense heat from the sun, snow and ice, road oils and the chemicals used in windshield washer solvents combine to deteriorate the rubber wiper refills. The refills should be replaced about twice a year or whenever the blades begin to streak or chatter.**

### ELEMENT (REFILL) CARE & REPLACEMENT

◆ **See Figures 126, 127 and 128**

For maximum effectiveness and longest element life, the windshield and wiper blades should be kept clean. Dirt, tree sap, road tar and so on will cause streaking, smearing and blade deterioration if left on the glass. It is advisable to wash the windshield carefully with a commercial glass cleaner at least once a month. Wipe off the rubber blades with the wet rag afterwards. Do not attempt to move wipers across the windshield by hand; damage to the motor and drive mechanism will result.

To inspect and/or replace the wiper blade elements, place the wiper switch in the **LOW** speed position and the ignition switch in the **ACC** position. When the wiper blades are approximately vertical on the windshield, turn the ignition switch to **OFF**.

Examine the wiper blade elements. If they are found to be cracked, broken or torn, they should be replaced immediately. Replacement intervals will vary with usage, although ozone deterioration usually limits element life to about one year. If the wiper pattern is smeared or streaked, or if the blade chatters across the glass, the elements should be replaced. It is easiest and most sensible to replace the elements in pairs.

If your vehicle is equipped with aftermarket blades, there are several different types of refills and your vehicle might have any kind. Aftermarket blades and arms rarely use the exact same type blade or refill as the original equipment.

Regardless of the type of refill used, be sure to follow the part manufacturer's instructions closely. Make sure that all of the frame jaws are engaged as the refill is pushed into place and locked. If the metal blade holder and frame are allowed to touch the glass during wiper operation, the glass will be scratched.

## Tires and Wheels

◆ **See Figure 129**

Common sense and good driving habits will afford maximum tire life. Make sure that you don't overload the vehicle or run with incorrect pressure in the tires. Either of these will increase tread wear. Fast starts, sudden stops and sharp cornering are hard on tires and will shorten their useful life span.

➡**For optimum tire life, keep the tires properly inflated, rotate them often and have the wheel alignment checked periodically.**

Inspect your tires frequently. Be especially careful to watch for bubbles in the tread or sidewall, deep cuts or underinflation. Replace any tires with bubbles in the sidewall. If cuts are so deep that they penetrate to the cords, discard the tire. Any cut in the sidewall of a radial tire renders it unsafe. Also look for uneven tread wear patterns that may indicate the front end is out of alignment or that the tires are out of balance.

### TIRE ROTATION

◆ **See Figure 130**

Tires must be rotated periodically to equalize wear patterns that vary with a tire's position on the vehicle. Tires will also wear in an uneven way as the front steering/suspension system wears to the point where the alignment should be reset.

Rotating the tires will ensure maximum life for the tires as a set, so you will not have to discard a tire early due to wear on only part of the tread. Regular rotation is required to equalize wear.

When rotating "unidirectional tires," make sure that they always roll in the same direction. This means that a tire used on the left side of the vehicle must not be switched to the right side and vice-versa. Such tires should only be rotated front-to-rear or rear-to-front, while always remaining on the same side of the vehicle. These tires are marked on the sidewall as to the direction of rotation; observe the marks when reinstalling the tire(s).

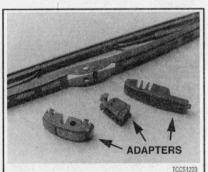

**Fig. 126 Most aftermarket blades are available with multiple adapters to fit different vehicles**

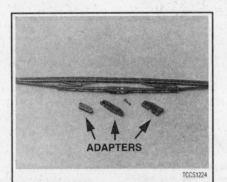

**Fig. 127 Choose a blade which will fit your vehicle, and that will be readily available next time you need blades**

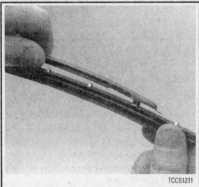

**Fig. 128 When installed, be certain the blade is fully inserted into the backing**

**Fig. 129 This label (usually found on a door or jamb) gives the proper tire inflation pressures for your vehicle**

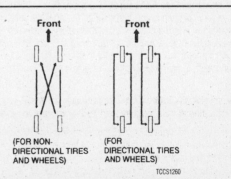

**Fig. 130 Compact spare tires must NEVER be used in the rotation pattern**

Some styled or "mag" wheels may have different offsets front to rear. In these cases, the rear wheels must not be used up front and vice-versa. Furthermore, if these wheels are equipped with unidirectional tires, they cannot be rotated unless the tire is remounted for the proper direction of rotation.

➡**The compact or space-saver spare is strictly for emergency use. It must never be included in the tire rotation or placed on the vehicle for everyday use.**

## TIRE DESIGN

♦ **See Figure 131**

For maximum satisfaction, tires should be used in sets of four. Mixing of different brands or types (radial, bias-belted, fiberglass belted) should be avoided. In most cases, the vehicle manufacturer has designated a type of tire on which the vehicle will perform best. Your first choice when replacing tires should be to use the same type of tire that the manufacturer recommends.

When radial tires are used, tire sizes and wheel diameters should be selected to maintain ground clearance and tire load capacity equivalent to the original specified tire. Radial tires should always be used in sets of four.

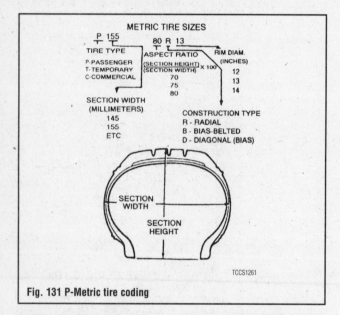

**Fig. 131 P-Metric tire coding**

### ✳✳ CAUTION

**Radial tires should never be used on only the front axle.**

When selecting tires, pay attention to the original size as marked on the tire. Most tires are described using an industry size code sometimes referred to as P-Metric. This allows the exact identification of the tire specifications, regardless of the manufacturer. If selecting a different tire size or brand, remember to check the installed tire for any sign of interference with the body or suspension while the vehicle is stopping, turning sharply or heavily loaded.

### Snow Tires

Good radial tires can produce a big advantage in slippery weather, but in snow, a street radial tire does not have sufficient tread to provide traction and control. The small grooves of a street tire quickly pack with snow and the tire behaves like a billiard ball on a marble floor. The more open, chunky tread of a snow tire will self-clean as the tire turns, providing much better grip on snowy surfaces.

To satisfy municipalities requiring snow tires during weather emergencies, most snow tires carry either an M + S designation after the tire size stamped on the sidewall, or the designation "all-season." In general, no change in tire size is necessary when buying snow tires.

Most manufacturers strongly recommend the use of 4 snow tires on their vehicles for reasons of stability. If snow tires are fitted only to the drive wheels, the opposite end of the vehicle may become very unstable when braking or

turning on slippery surfaces. This instability can lead to unpleasant endings if the driver can't counteract the slide in time.

Note that snow tires, whether 2 or 4, will affect vehicle handling in all non-snow situations. The stiffer, heavier snow tires will noticeably change the turning and braking characteristics of the vehicle. Once the snow tires are installed, you must re-learn the behavior of the vehicle and drive accordingly.

➡**Consider buying extra wheels on which to mount the snow tires. Once done, the "snow wheels" can be installed and removed as needed. This eliminates the potential damage to tires or wheels from seasonal removal and installation. Even if your vehicle has styled wheels, see if inexpensive steel wheels are available. Although the look of the vehicle will change, the expensive wheels will be protected from salt, curb hits and pothole damage.**

## TIRE STORAGE

If they are mounted on wheels, store the tires at proper inflation pressure. All tires should be kept in a cool, dry place. If they are stored in the garage or basement, do not let them stand on a concrete floor; set them on strips of wood, a mat or a large stack of newspaper. Keeping them away from direct moisture is of paramount importance. Tires should not be stored upright, but in a flat position.

## INFLATION & INSPECTION

♦ **See Figures 132 thru 137**

The importance of proper tire inflation cannot be overemphasized. A tire employs air as part of its structure. It is designed around the supporting strength of the air at a specified pressure. For this reason, improper inflation

**Fig. 132 Tires with deep cuts, or cuts which bulge, should be replaced immediately**

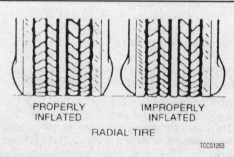

**Fig. 133 Radial tires have a characteristic sidewall bulge; don't try to measure pressure by looking at the tire. Use a quality air pressure gauge**

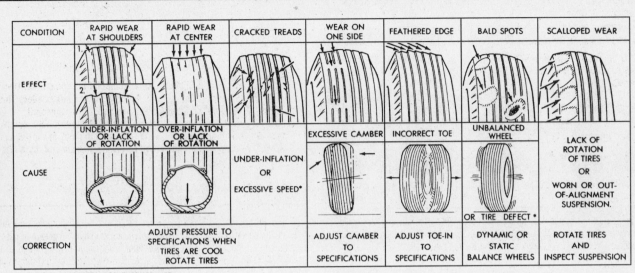

| CONDITION | RAPID WEAR AT SHOULDERS | RAPID WEAR AT CENTER | CRACKED TREADS | WEAR ON ONE SIDE | FEATHERED EDGE | BALD SPOTS | SCALLOPED WEAR |
|---|---|---|---|---|---|---|---|
| EFFECT | | | | | | | |
| CAUSE | UNDER-INFLATION OR LACK OF ROTATION | OVER-INFLATION OR LACK OF ROTATION | UNDER-INFLATION OR EXCESSIVE SPEED* | EXCESSIVE CAMBER | INCORRECT TOE | UNBALANCED WHEEL OR TIRE DEFECT* | LACK OF ROTATION OF TIRES OR WORN OR OUT-OF-ALIGNMENT SUSPENSION. |
| CORRECTION | | ADJUST PRESSURE TO SPECIFICATIONS WHEN TIRES ARE COOL ROTATE TIRES | | ADJUST CAMBER TO SPECIFICATIONS | ADJUST TOE-IN TO SPECIFICATIONS | DYNAMIC OR STATIC BALANCE WHEELS | ROTATE TIRES AND INSPECT SUSPENSION |

*HAVE TIRE INSPECTED FOR FURTHER USE.

TCCS1267

**Fig. 134 Common tire wear patterns and causes**

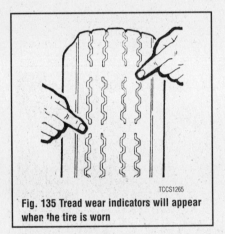

**Fig. 135 Tread wear indicators will appear when the tire is worn**

TCCS1265

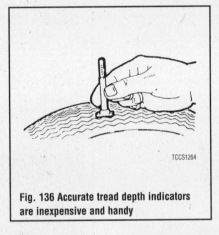

TCCS1264

**Fig. 136 Accurate tread depth indicators are inexpensive and handy**

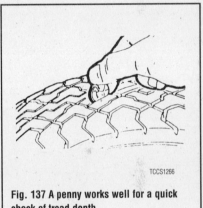

TCCS1266

**Fig. 137 A penny works well for a quick check of tread depth**

drastically reduces the tire's ability to perform as intended. A tire will lose some air in day-to-day use; having to add a few pounds of air periodically is not necessarily a sign of a leaking tire.

Two items should be a permanent fixture in every glove compartment: an accurate tire pressure gauge and a tread depth gauge. Check the tire pressure (including the spare) regularly with a pocket type gauge. Too often, the gauge on the end of the air hose at your corner garage is not accurate because it suffers too much abuse. Always check tire pressure when the tires are cold, as pressure increases with temperature. If you must move the vehicle to check the tire inflation, do not drive more than a mile before checking. A cold tire is generally one that has not been driven for more than three hours.

A plate or sticker is normally provided somewhere in the vehicle (door post, hood, tailgate or trunk lid) which shows the proper pressure for the tires. Never counteract excessive pressure build-up by bleeding off air pressure (letting some air out). This will cause the tire to run hotter and wear quicker.

### ✱✱ CAUTION

**Never exceed the maximum tire pressure embossed on the tire! This is the pressure to be used when the tire is at maximum loading, but it is rarely the correct pressure for everyday driving. Consult the owner's manual or the tire pressure sticker for the correct tire pressure.**

Once you've maintained the correct tire pressures for several weeks, you'll be familiar with the vehicle's braking and handling personality. Slight adjustments in tire pressures can fine-tune these characteristics, but never change the cold pressure specification by more than 2 psi. A slightly softer tire pressure will give a softer ride but also yield lower fuel mileage. A slightly harder tire will give crisper dry road handling but can cause skidding on wet surfaces. Unless you're fully attuned to the vehicle, stick to the recommended inflation pressures.

All automotive tires have built-in tread wear indicator bars that show up as ½ in. (13mm) wide smooth bands across the tire when 1/16 in. (1.5mm) of tread remains. The appearance of tread wear indicators means that the tires should be replaced. In fact, many states have laws prohibiting the use of tires with less than this amount of tread.

You can check your own tread depth with an inexpensive gauge or by using a Lincoln head penny. Slip the Lincoln penny (with Lincoln's head upside-down) into several tread grooves. If you can see the top of Lincoln's head in 2 adjacent grooves, the tire has less than 1/16 in. (1.5mm) tread left and should be replaced. You can measure snow tires in the same manner by using the "tails" side of the Lincoln penny. If you can see the top of the Lincoln memorial, it's time to replace the snow tire(s).

## FLUIDS AND LUBRICANTS

### Fluid Disposal

Used fluids such as engine oil, transmission fluid, antifreeze and brake fluid are hazardous wastes and must be disposed of properly. Before draining any fluids, consult with your local authorities; in many areas waste oil, etc. is being accepted as a part of recycling programs. A number of service stations and auto parts stores are also accepting waste fluids for recycling.

Be sure of the recycling center's policies before draining any fluids, as many will not accept different fluids that have been mixed together.

### Fuel and Engine Oil Recommendations

FUEL

All vehicles covered by this manual are equipped with emission control systems that would be severely damaged or destroyed by the use of leaded fuels or additives. NEVER put any gasoline in your tank that could contain lead or you will likely void your warranty.

### ✳✳ WARNING

**Some fuel additives contain chemicals that can damage the catalytic converter and/or oxygen sensor. Read all of the labels carefully before using any additive in the engine or fuel system.**

Fuel should be selected for the brand and octane which performs best with your engine. Judge a gasoline by its ability to prevent pinging, it's engine starting capabilities (cold and hot) and general all weather performance. As far as the octane rating is concerned, all of the engines covered by this manual are capable of running fine on a high-quality 87 octane gasoline (usually this is a mid or low grade in the U.S.). If necessary at high altitudes, most engines can also run on lower octanes, down to even 85. BUT, when you are working your van hard, such as towing or hauling a full contingent of passengers with luggage, it is recommended that higher octane will help maximize power while preventing damaging engine knock. If your van has the 4.3L (VIN W) CMFI or CSFI engine, it is recommended that you use a minimum of 91 octane gasoline whenever you are towing or hauling heavy loads.

➡ **Your van's engine fuel requirement can change with time, due to carbon buildup, which changes the compression ratio. If your van's engine knocks, pings or runs on, switch to a higher grade of fuel (if possible) and check the ignition timing. Sometimes changing brands of gasoline will cure the problem. If it is necessary to retard the timing from specifications, don't change it more than a 2 degrees. Retarded timing will reduce the power output and the fuel mileage, plus it will increase the engine temperature.**

The vehicles covered by manual are capable of running on various types of blended gasolines as well. Blended gas containing any ONE of the following blends are allowed if they contain no more than 15 percent MTBE (Methyl Tertiary-Butyl Ether), 10 percent Ethanol (Ethyl or grain alcohol) or 5 percent Methanol (wood alcohol).

### ✳✳ WARNING

**Gasolines that contain MORE THAN 5 PERCENT METHANOL are BAD for your engine. It can corrode metal parts in your fuel system while also damaging plastic and rubber parts. Even at 5 percent mixtures make sure there are COSOLVENTS and corrosion preventers in this fuel or AVOID IT.**

OIL

▶ **See Figures 138 and 139**

Use ONLY SG/CC, SG/CD, SH/CC or SH/CD rated oils of the recommended viscosity. Under the classification system developed by the American Petroleum Institute (API), the SH rating (or latest superseding alpha-rating) designates the highest quality oil for use in passenger vehicles. In addition, Chevrolet recom-

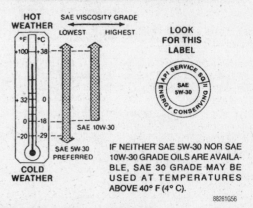

Fig. 138 Engine oil viscosity recommendations

Fig. 139 Look for the API oil identification label when choosing your engine oil

mends the use of an SH/Energy Conserving oil. Oils labeled Energy Conserving (or Saving), Fuel (Gas or Gasoline) Saving, etc. are recommended due to their superior lubricating qualities (less friction—easier engine operation) and fuel saving characteristics. Pick your oil viscosity with regard to the anticipated temperatures during the period before your next oil change. Using the accompanying chart, choose the oil viscosity for the lowest expected temperature. You will be assured of easy cold starting and sufficient engine protection.

➡ **For the first few years of production (1985–88) GM's preferred recommendation was the use of 10W-30 in the 4.3L engine, but only if ambient temperatures did not drop below 0°F (-18°C). During these years 5W-30 was recommended for use, but only in ambient temperatures below 60°F (16°C). It does not seem like any significant changes were made to the bottom end of this engine, but for 1989 and later models, the recommendations changed to prefer 5W-30 for all ambient temperatures.**

The mileage figures given in your owner's manual are the Chevrolet recommended intervals for oil and filter changes assuming average driving. If your Astro or Safari Van is being used under dusty, polluted or off-road conditions, change the oil and filter sooner than specified. The same thing goes for vehicles driven in stop-and-go traffic, used for only for short distances or used in heavy hauling such as trailering or filled with passengers and luggage.

Always drain the oil after the engine has been running long enough to bring it to operating temperature. Hot oil will flow easier and more contaminants will be removed along with the oil than if it were drained cold. You will need a large capacity drain pan, which you can purchase at any store that sells automotive parts. Another necessity is a container for the used oil. You will find that plastic bottles, such as those used for bleach or fabric softener, make excellent storage jugs.

➡**Dispose of used oil ONLY by finding a service station or facility which accepts used oil for recycling.**

Although GM recommends changing both the oil and filter during the first oil change, they then usually permit that the filter be replaced only every other oil change thereafter. For the small price of an oil filter, its cheap insurance to replace the filter at every oil change. Chilton recommends that you change both the oil and filter together at each service. One of the larger filter manufacturers points out in it's advertisements that not changing the filter leaves 1 quart of dirty oil in the engine. This claim is true and should be kept in mind when changing your oil.

### Synthetic Oils

There are excellent synthetic and fuel-efficient oils available that, under the right circumstances, can help provide better fuel mileage and better engine protection. However, these advantages come at a price, which can be 3 or 4 times the cost per quart of conventional motor oils.

Before pouring any synthetic oils into your vehicle's engine, you should consider the condition of the engine and the type of driving you do. Also, check the manufacturer's warranty conditions regarding the use of synthetics.

Generally, it is best to avoid the use of synthetic oil in both brand new and older, high mileage engines. New engines require a proper break-in, and the synthetics are so slippery that they can prevent this. Most manufacturers recommend that you wait at least 5000 miles (8000 km) before switching to a synthetic oil. Conversely, older engines are looser and tend to loose more oil.

Synthetics will slip past worn parts more readily than regular oil. If your van already leaks oil (due to bad seals or gaskets), it will probably leak more with a slippery synthetic inside.

Consider your type of driving. If most of your accumulated mileage is on the highway at higher, steadier speeds, a synthetic oil will reduce friction and probably help deliver fuel mileage. Under such ideal highway conditions, the oil change interval can be extended, as long as the oil filter will operate effectively for the extended life of the oil. If the filter can't do its job for this extended period, dirt and sludge will build up in your engine's crankcase, sump, oil pump and lines, no matter what type of oil is used. If using synthetic oil in this manner, you should continue to change the oil filter at the recommended intervals.

Vans used under harder, stop-and-go, short hop circumstances should always be serviced more frequently, and for these trucks, synthetic oil may not be a wise investment. Because of the necessary shorter change interval needed for this type of driving, you cannot take advantage of the long recommended change interval of most synthetic oils.

## Engine

### OIL LEVEL CHECK

◆ **See Figures 140 thru 145**

Every time you stop for fuel, check the engine oil making sure the engine has fully warmed and the vehicle is parked on a level surface. If the van is used for trailer towing or for heavy-duty use, it is recommended to check the oil more frequently. Because it takes a few minutes for all the oil to drain back to the oil pan, you should wait a few minutes before checking the oil. If you are doing this at a fuel stop, first fill the fuel tank, then open the hood and check the oil, but don't get so carried away as to forget to pay for the fuel. Most station attendants won't believe that you forgot.

1. Make sure the van is parked on level ground.
2. When checking the oil level it is best for the engine to be a normal operating temperature, although checking the oil immediately after stopping will lead

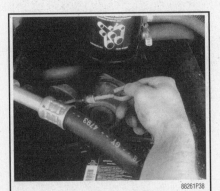

Fig. 140 To check engine oil, start by locating and withdrawing the oil dipstick

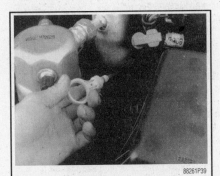

Fig. 141 On late-model vans with automatics, the engine dipstick is usually right below the A/T dipstick

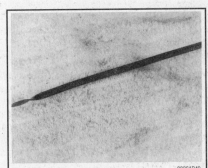

Fig. 142 After the dipstick is cleaned, inserted and withdrawn, read the level using the stick's markings

Fig. 143 If additional oil is necessary, remove the cap from the filler tube . . .

Fig. 144 . . . the recommended viscosity oil may be found on many of the tube caps

Fig. 145 A funnel will help prevent a mess when you are pouring oil into the filler tube

to a false reading. Wait a few minutes after turning OFF the engine to allow the oil to drain back into the crankcase.

3. Open the hood and locate the dipstick which will be in a guide tube mounted in the upper engine block, just below the cylinder head mating surface. On most Astro and Safari vans, the dipstick is found on the passenger side of the engine, about mid-way back in the engine compartment. On late-model vehicles with automatic transmissions, it will probably be right below the A/T dipstick.

4. Pull the dipstick from its tube, wipe all traces of oil from it (using a clean, lint free rag) and then reinsert it into the guide tube. To make sure you get a correct reading, be sure the dipstick is fully seated in the tube and pause for a second.

5. Pull the dipstick out again and, holding it horizontally, read the oil level. The oil should be in the cross-hatched area that represents the OPERATING RANGE (above the ADD mark) on the dipstick. If the oil is below the ADD mark, add oil of the proper viscosity through the capped opening in the oil filler tube. See the fuel and oil recommendations listed earlier in this section for the proper viscosity and rating of oil to use.

6. Insert the dipstick and check the oil level again after adding any oil. Approximately 1 quart of oil will raise the level from the ADD mark to the FULL mark. Be sure not to overfill the crankcase and waste the oil. Excess oil will generally be consumed at an accelerated rate.

**✳✳ CAUTION**

**DO NOT overfill the crankcase. It may result in oil-fouled spark plugs, oil leaks caused by oil seal failure or engine damage due to foaming of the oil.**

## OIL & FILTER CHANGE

♦ **See Figures 146, 147, 148, 149 and 150**

If the vehicle is operated on a daily or semi-daily basis and most trips are for several miles (allowing the engine to properly warm-up), the oil should be changed a minimum of every 12 months or 7500 miles (12,000 km) whichever comes first.

If however, the vehicle is used to tow a trailer, is made to idle for extended periods of time such as in heavy daily traffic or if used as a service vehicle (delivery) or the vehicle is used for only short trips in below freezing temperature, the oil change interval should be shortened. Likewise, if your vehicle is used under dusty, polluted or off-road conditions, the oil should be changed more frequently. Under these circumstances oil has a greater chance of building up sludge and contaminants which could damage your engine. If your vehicle use fits into these circumstance, as most do, it is suggested that the oil and filter be changed every 3000 miles (5000 km) or 3 months, whichever comes first.

Under certain circumstances, Chevrolet and GMC recommend changing both the oil and filter during the first oil change and then only replacing the filter every other oil change thereafter. For the small price of an oil filter, it's cheap insurance to replace the filter at every oil change.

Oil should always be changed after the engine has been running long enough to bring it up to normal operating temperature. Hot oil will flow easier and more contaminants will be removed along with the oil than if it were drained cold. The oil drain plug is located on the bottom of the oil pan (bottom of the engine, underneath the van). The oil filter is usually located on the left side of the engine and in some cases may be easier to reach through the plastic access flap in the wheel well.

You should have available a container that will hold a minimum of 6 quarts

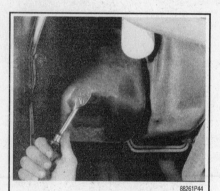

Fig. 146 Loosen the drain plug using a rachet and socket (shown) or a box wrench

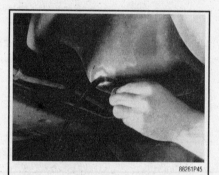

Fig. 147 Unthread the plug, then withdraw it (and your hand) quickly to keep from getting burned by hot oil

Fig. 148 A filter strap wrench is helpful, but it can be tricky in tight places . . .

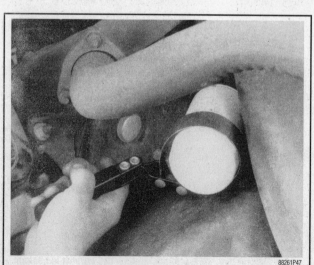

Fig. 149 . . . be sure to maneuver the wrench so your hand stays clear of the HOT exhaust pipe

Fig. 150 Before installing a new oil filter, lightly coat the rubber gasket with clean oil

of liquid (to help prevent spilling the oil even after it is drained), a wrench to fit the drain plug, a spout for pouring in new oil and a rag or two, which you will always need. If the filter is being replaced, you will also need a band wrench or a filter wrench that fits the end of the filter.

➡If the engine is equipped with an oil cooler, this should be drained also, if it is equipped with a drain plug. Be sure to add enough oil to fill the cooler in addition to the engine.

1. Run the engine until it reaches normal operating temperature, then shut the engine OFF, make sure the parking brake is firmly set and block the drive wheels.

2. Clearance may be sufficient to access the drain plug without raising the vehicle. If the van must be lifted, be sure to support it safely with jackstands and be sure to position the drain plug at a low point under the vehicle (this will help assure fast and complete draining of the old oil.

3. Slide a drain pan of a least 6 quarts capacity under the oil pan. Wipe the drain plug and surrounding area clean using an old rag.

### ❈❈ CAUTION

**The EPA warns that prolonged contact with used engine oil may cause a number of skin disorders, including cancer! You should make every effort to minimize your exposure to used engine oil. Protective gloves should be worn when changing the oil. Wash your hands and any other exposed skin areas as soon as possible after exposure to used engine oil. Soap and water, or waterless hand cleaner should be used.**

4. Loosen the drain plug using a ratchet, short extension and socket or a box-wrench. Turn the plug out by hand, using a rag to shield your fingers from the hot oil. By keeping an inward pressure on the plug as you unscrew it, oil won't escape past the threads and you can remove it without being burned by hot oil.

5. Quickly withdraw the plug and move your hands out of the way, but be careful not to drop the plug into the drain pan as fishing it out can be an unpleasant mess. Allow the oil to drain completely in the pan, then install and carefully tighten the drain plug. Be careful not to overtighten the drain plug, otherwise you'll be buying a new pan or a trick replacement plug for stripped threads.

➡Although some manufacturers have at times recommended changing the oil filter every other oil change, we recommend the filter be changed each time you change your oil. The added benefit of clean oil is quickly lost if the old filter is clogged and the added protection to the heart of your engine far outweighs the few dollars saved by using a old filter.

6. Move the drain pan under the oil filter. Use a strap-type or cap-type filter wrench to loosen the oil filter. Cover your hand with a rag and spin the filter off by hand; turn it slowly. Keep in mind that it's holding about 1 quart of dirty, hot oil.

### ❈❈ CAUTION

**On many Chevrolet/GMC engines, especially the V6s, the oil filter is next to the exhaust pipes. Stay clear of these, since even a passing contact can result in a painful burn. ALSO, since all of these vans are equipped with catalytic converters, it advisable to remind you to stay clear of the converter. The outside temperature of a hot catalytic converter can approach 1200°F.**

7. Empty the old filter into the drain pan and properly dispose of the filter.

8. Using a clean rag, wipe off the filter adapter on the engine block. Be sure the rag doesn't leave any lint which could clog an oil passage.

➡To help prevent oil leaks, always check to make sure the threaded nipple or the adapter base bolt(s) are properly tightened.

9. Coat the rubber gasket on the filter with fresh oil, then spin it onto the engine by hand; when the gasket touches the adapter surface, give it another ½–1 turn. No more, or you might squash the gasket causing it to leak.

10. If raised for access, remove the jackstands and carefully lower the van.

11. IMMEDIATELY refill the engine with the correct amount of fresh oil.

Don't risk someone trying to start a dry motor, fill it up right away. For approximate capacities, please refer to the chart at the end of this section.

12. If you fill the engine the first time according to the chart, it is normal for the level to be a bit above the full mark. This is fine, if after having warmed the engine and filled the empty oil filter, the level comes down to normal. It is probably a better idea to fill the engine to a point within 1 quart of total capacity, then check the oil level on the dipstick. The engine can then be run to normal operating temperature, shut OFF, then rechecked and topped off.

13. Start the engine and allow it to idle for a few minutes.

### ❈❈ WARNING

**Do not run the engine above idle speed until it has built up oil pressure, as indicated when the oil light goes out.**

14. Shut OFF the engine and allow the oil to flow back to the crankcase for a minute, then recheck the oil level. Check around the filter and drain plug for any leaks, and correct as necessary.

When you have finished this job, you will notice that you now possess 4–5 quarts of dirty oil. The best thing to do with it is to pour it into plastic jugs, such as milk or antifreeze containers. Then, locate a service station or automotive parts store where you can pour it into their used oil tank for recycling.

## Manual Transmission

### FLUID RECOMMENDATIONS

Fill the main transmission housing with API GL5 SAE-80W90 Multipurpose Gear Oil for the 4-speed transmission. All of the 5-speed transmissions require the use of Dexron®II (or latest superseding) automatic transmission fluid.

### LEVEL CHECK

◗ See Figure 151

Remove the filler plug from the passenger's side of the transmission (the upper plug if the transmission has 2 plugs). The oil should be level with the bottom edge of the filler hole. This should be checked at least once every 6000 miles (9700 km) and more often if any leakage or seepage is observed.

➡When checking the fluid, the vehicle must be level. If it was necessary to raise and support the vehicle to access the filler plug, the vehicle must be supported at sufficient points (all wheels or 4 points on the frame) so it is sitting level and is not tilted forward/backward or to one side.

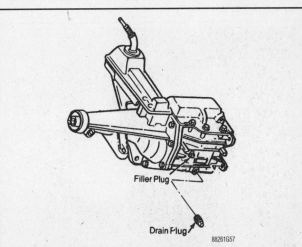

Fig. 151 The filler plug is normally found about mid-way up the side of the transmission, while drain plugs are found towards the bottom of the housing (for hopefully obvious reasons)

### DRAIN & REFILL

◆ **See Figure 151**

Under normal conditions, the transmission fluid should not need to be changed. However, if you purchase a used vehicle, it is usually a good idea to get a clean start with all of the fluids. Also, if the vehicle is operated in high water (up to the level of the transmission) it is definitely a good idea to change the fluid.

1. Drive the vehicle for a few miles to warm the fluid (so it will flow better).
2. Raise and support the vehicle safely using jackstands.
3. Place a fluid catch pan under the transmission.
4. Remove the bottom plug and drain the fluid.
5. Install the bottom plug and refill the transmission housing.

## Automatic Transmission

### FLUID RECOMMENDATIONS

When adding fluid or refilling the transmission, use Dexron®II (or the latest superseding) automatic transmission fluid for 1985–95 models or Dexron®III for 1996 models. The newer Dexron®III supersedes Dexron®II and may be used in all automatic transmissions covered by this manual.

### LEVEL CHECK

◆ **See Figures 152, 153, 154, 155 and 156**

Before checking the fluid level of the transmission, drive the vehicle for at least 15 miles to warm the fluid. Conversely, if the vehicle has just been driven at high speed for at least the past ½ hour, or was just pulling a trailer, let the fluid cool down (back toward the center of normal operating range) before checking the fluid.

1. Place the vehicle on a level surface, then firmly apply the parking brake.
2. Start the engine and move the selector through each range, then place it in **P**.

➡**When moving the selector through each range, DO NOT race the engine.**

3. With the engine running at a low idle (and the GEAR SELECTOR STILL IN **P**), remove the transmission's dipstick to check the fluid level.

➡**Some late-model vehicles utilize a locking, hinged dipstick. To remove these, simply pull upward on the outer portion of the hinge (straightening out the handle). This will release the dipstick from the guide/filler tube.**

4. The level should be at the Full Hot mark of the dipstick. If not, add fluid using a funnel (to prevent a real mess and possible fire hazard) through the dipstick guide/filler tube. One pint raises the level from Add to Full.

### ✴✴ CAUTION

**Add fluid SLOWLY. DO NOT overfill the transmission, damage to the seals could occur. Overfilling the transmission could also cause small amounts of fluid to be forced back up and out of the tube. Automatic transmission fluid could then be expelled onto hot engine parts, possibly even causing a fire.**

Fig. 152 Most transmission fluid dipsticks on later-model vehicles are labeled . . .

Fig. 153 . . . and a few are hinged (locking into place to seal the guide/filler tube)

Fig. 154 As with any dipstick, make sure the fluid level is within the given range(s)

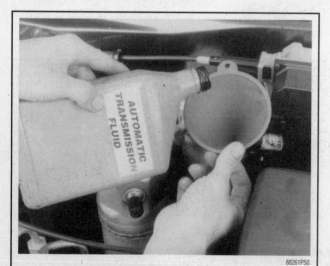

Fig. 155 Fluid is added through the dipstick guide/filler tube . . .

Fig. 156 . . . making a funnel mandatory on most models

➡ The dipstick on some vehicles may have 2 cross-hatched zones (one for HOT and the other for COLD). It is still advisable to check the transmission hot most of the time (it more accurately reflects the level when it matters most), but the COLD zone can be used for an early morning check or as the first refill level during a fluid change.

## DRAIN & REFILL

▶ **See Figures 157 thru 163**

The vehicle should be driven 15 miles to warm the transmission fluid before the pan is removed.

➡ **The fluid should be drained while the transmission is warm. Fluid which is at normal operating temperature will flow better, removing more contaminants or impurities than cold fluid.**

1. Raise and support the front of vehicle using jackstands.
2. Place a drain pan under the transmission pan.
3. If necessary, remove the crossmember from the rear of the transmission.
4. Remove the pan bolts from the front and the sides, then loosen the rear bolts 4 turns.
5. Using a small prybar, carefully separate the front of the pan from the transmission. This will allow the pan to partially drain. DO NOT use excessive force when attempting to break the gasket seal. DO NOT bend or otherwise damage the pan and the gasket mating surfaces. If necessary, loosen the bolts a few more turns to allow the pan more play without stressing the flange.
6. Remove the remaining pan bolts and lower the pan from the transmission. Again, be CAREFUL as the pan still contains a decent amount of HOT and MESSY transmission fluid. This is very slimy stuff and if you spill it on yourself (besides possibly being burned) you will feel slimy for days no matter how much you wash.

➡ **If the transmission fluid is dark or has a burnt smell, transmission damage is indicated. Have the transmission checked professionally.**

7. Empty the pan, remove the gasket material and clean with a solvent. If you use putty knife to clean the gasket surfaces, be very careful not to score or damage them. Most late-model vehicles utilize a rubber-seal that comes off the pan, with relative ease.
8. As-long-as you've gone through the trouble to drop the pan, you might as well replace the filter. Changing the automatic transmission fluid and filter are the MOST important things you can do to help assure a long, trouble-free transmission life. Well, that and avoiding trying to pull tree stumps on a regular basis.
9. To install the oil pan, use a new gasket and sealant, then reverse the removal procedures. GM recommends that you use Transjel® sealant on the new gasket. Tighten the pan bolts to 97 inch lbs. (11 Nm) in a crisscross pattern.
10. Refill the transmission through the dipstick guide/filler tube. Please refer to the capacities chart later in this section to determine the proper amount of fluid to be added.

⁂⁂ **CAUTION**

Add fluid SLOWLY. DO NOT overfill the transmission, damage to the seals could occur. Overfilling the transmission could also cause small amounts of fluid to be forced back up and out of the tube. Automatic transmission fluid could then be expelled onto hot engine parts, possibly even causing a fire.

11. With the gearshift lever in **P**, start the engine and let it idle. DO NOT race the engine.
12. Apply the parking brake and move the gearshift lever through each position. Return the lever to **P** and check the fluid level with the engine idling. The level should be between the 2 dimples on the dipstick, about ¼ in. (6mm) below the ADD mark. On dipsticks that are so marked, the fluid should remain in the COLD zone until the transmission has fully warmed. Add fluid, if necessary.
13. Check the fluid level after the vehicle has been driven enough to thoroughly warm the transmission.

## PAN & FILTER SERVICE

▶ **See Figures 157 thru 163**

1. Remove the transmission oil pan. For details, refer to the drain and refill procedures in this section.
2. Remove the screen and the filter from the valve body.

➡ **When removing the filter from the valve body, be sure the old O-ring is removed with the filter. Sometimes it remains stuck in the pump.**

3. Install a new filter using a new gasket or O-ring.

➡ **If the transmission uses a filter having a fully exposed screen, it may be cleaned and reused.**

4. To install the oil pan, use a new gasket and sealant, then reverse the removal procedures. Tighten the pan bolts to 87 inch lbs. (11 Nm) in a crisscross pattern. Refill the transmission.

## Drive Axle (Front and Rear)

Several axle ratios are available with the various powertrain applications.

## FLUID RECOMMENDATIONS

**Standard Axle**

GM recommends you use SAE 80W–90 GL5 gear or an equivalent lubricant that meets the standards of their part No. 1052271. In cold climates, GM recommends the use of SAE 80W gear oil for some applications. Refer to your owners manual for more details.

You should drain and refill the rear differential at first oil change, then it should be checked at every other oil change. Periodic fluid replacement should

Fig. 157 Loosen all of the transmission pan retaining bolts . . .

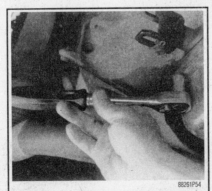
Fig. 158 . . . then remove all but a few at the very rear of the pan

Fig. 159 Once most of the fluid has drained, carefully lower the pan from the transmission

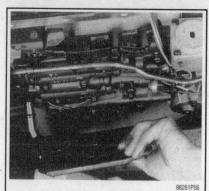

Fig. 160 Remove the filter for inspection and replacement

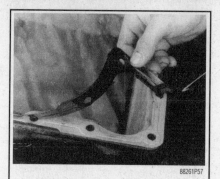

Fig. 161 The gasket (or rubber seal, depending on the application) must be replaced no matter how good it looks

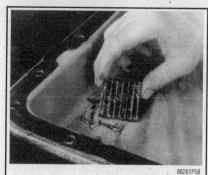

Fig. 162 The magnet at the bottom of the pan should be thoroughly cleaned of all metal particles

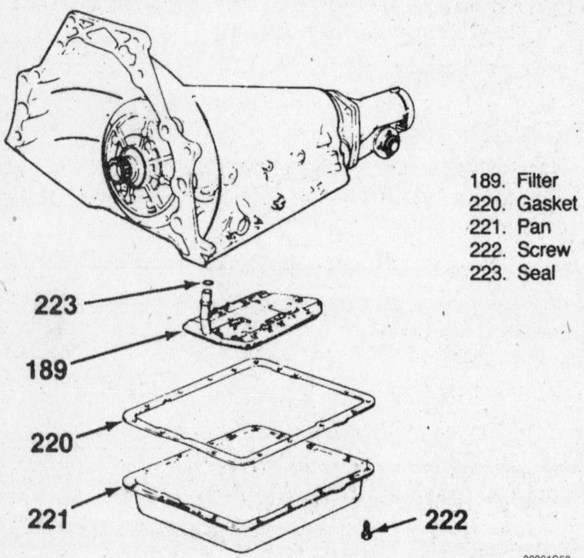

189. Filter
220. Gasket
221. Pan
222. Screw
223. Seal

223
189
220
221
222

Fig. 163 Exploded view of the automatic transmission fluid pan and filter

not be necessary under normal service, but the fluid should be changed if the vehicle is operated in water which is as deep as the axles. Change the fluid at every other engine oil change if the van is used in severe service, such as trailer towing or severely dusty conditions.

Changing the front drive axle fluid on these vehicles usually requires its removal and partial disassembly. The fluid in the front drive axle should not need to be changed unless the axle is removed for repair. It should however, be checked at each engine oil change.

## Locking Axle

Always use GM Rear Axle Fluid No. 1052271 or equivalent SAE 80W–90 GL5 lubricant. Check with your owners manual or parts supplier, on a few earlier models covered by this manual it may be necessary to add 4 ounces of GM Fluid No. 1052358 (limit-slip additive) before refilling. BUT GM SPECIFICALLY WARNS AGAINST using limited slip additive on 1996 locking differentials and does not mention its use for many of the late-model vehicles covered by this manual.

You should drain and refill the rear differential at first oil change, then it should be checked at every other oil change. Periodic fluid replacement should not be necessary under normal service, but the fluid should be changed if the vehicle is operated in water which is as deep as the axles. Change the fluid at every other engine oil change if the van is used in severe service, such as trailer towing or severely dusty conditions.

Changing the front drive axle fluid on these vehicles usually requires its removal and partial disassembly. The fluid in the front drive axle should not

need to be changed unless the axle is removed for repair. It should however, be checked at each engine oil change.

## LEVEL CHECK

▶ **See Figures 164 and 165**

➡**When checking the fluid, the vehicle must be level. If it was necessary to raise and support the vehicle to access the filler plug, the vehicle must be supported at sufficient points (all wheels or 4 points on the frame) so it is sitting level and is not tilted forward/backward or to one side.**

The lubricant level should be checked at each chassis lubrication and maintained at the bottom of the filler plug hole.

1. If necessary for access, raise and support the vehicle on jackstands; BUT be sure the vehicle is level.

2. Remove the filler plug, located at the passenger side of the differential carrier. Most plugs are designed to accept the driver from a ⅜ in. ratchet, breaker bar or extension.

3. Check the fluid level, it should be level with the bottom of the filler plug hole, add fluid (if necessary).

### ✳✳ CAUTION

**Watch for sharp threads in the filler plug opening. When present, they can give you a nasty cut.**

4. When you are finished, install the filler plug and tighten to 26 ft. lbs. (35 Nm).

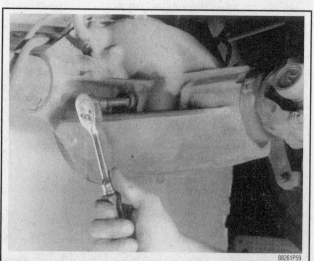

Fig. 164 Use a ratchet and extension to remove the filler plug and check the axle fluid

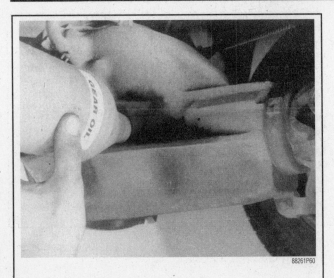

**Fig. 165 Gear oil can be added using a pump or a squeeze bottle**

## DRAIN & REFILL

### Rear Axle Assembly

▶ **See Figures 166 thru 171**

Refer to Fluid Recommendations in this section for information on when to change the fluid.

1. Drive the vehicle until the lubricant reaches operating temperature. Warm fluid flows better, removing more impurities with the oil.

2. Raise and support the rear of the vehicle on jackstands; BUT be sure the vehicle is level (for refilling purposes and to help assure proper draining of the axle housing).

3. Use a wire brush to clean the area around the differential. This will help prevent dirt from contaminating the differential housing while the cover is removed.

4. Position a drain pan under the rear axle.

5. Unscrew the retaining bolts and remove the rear cover. When removing the cover, a small prytool may be used at the base of the cover to gently pry it back from the axle housing, breaking the gasket seal and allowing the lubricant to drain out into the container. You may wish to leave 1 of the cover bolts, loosely installed, to keep the cover from falling suddenly (creating quite a mess) once the seal is broken. Be careful not to use excessive force and damage the cover or housing.

**To install:**

6. Carefully clean the gasket mating surfaces of the cover and axle housing of any remaining gasket or sealer. A putty knife is a good tool to use for this.

7. Install the rear cover using a new gasket and sealant. Tighten the retaining bolts using a crosswise pattern to 20 ft. lbs. (27 Nm).

➡ **Make sure the vehicle is level before attempting to add fluid to the rear axle or an incorrect fluid level will result.**

8. Refill the rear axle housing using the proper grade and quantity of lubricant as detailed earlier in this section. Install the filler plug, operate the vehicle and check for any leaks.

## Transfer Case

### FLUID RECOMMENDATIONS

When adding fluid to the transfer case, use Dexron®II (or the latest superseding) automatic transmission fluid for 1985–95 models or Dexron®III for 1996 models. The newer Dexron®III us the supersedes Dexron®II and may be used in all transfer cases covered by this manual. Inspect the transfer case level at your first oil change, then at every other oil change.

**Fig. 166 Begin by cleaning loose dirt from around the cover to prevent contamination when it is removed**

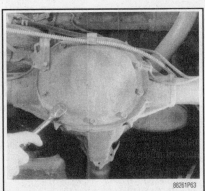

**Fig. 167 Loosen and remove the cover bolts, then . . .**

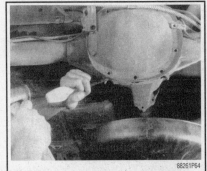

**Fig. 168 . . . carefully break the gasket seal at the housing (DO NOT damage the cover/housing)**

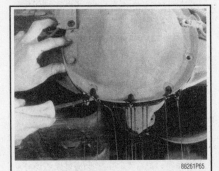

**Fig. 169 With the gasket seal broken, pull the cover back at the bottom allowing the fluid to drain**

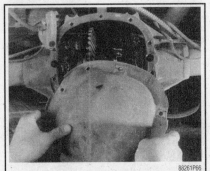

**Fig. 170 Once most of the fluid has been emptied into the drain pan, remove the cover from the housing**

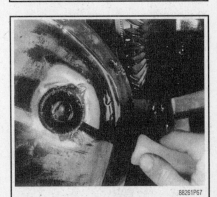

**Fig. 171 If equipped, the magnet should be cleaned of metal particles**

## LEVEL CHECK

▶ **See Figure 172**

The fluid level should be checked at least annually and more often if any leakage or seepage is observed.

➡ **When checking the fluid, the vehicle must be level. If it was necessary to raise and support the vehicle to access the filler plug, the vehicle must be supported at sufficient points (all wheels or 4 points on the frame) so it is sitting level and is not tilted forward/backward or to one side.**

1. If necessary for access to the filler plug, raise and support the vehicle safely using jackstands, but make sure the vehicle is level.
2. Remove the filler plug (upper plug of the 2) from the rear-side of the transfer case.
3. Using your finger, check the fluid level, it should be level with the bottom of the filler hole.

### ❄❄ CAUTION

**Watch for sharp threads in the filler plug opening. When present, they can give you a nasty cut.**

4. If the fluid level is low, add fluid to bring the level up to the filler hole. Most parts stores will carry a small, hand operated pump which will greatly ease the task of adding fluid to the transfer case.
5. Install and tighten the filler plug.

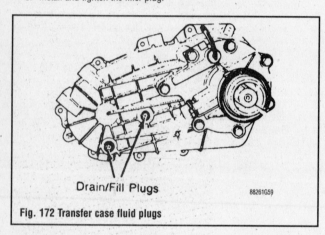

Drain/Fill Plugs

88261G59

**Fig. 172 Transfer case fluid plugs**

## DRAIN & REFILL

▶ **See Figure 172**

Under normal conditions, the transfer case fluid should not need to be changed. However, if you purchase a used vehicle, it is usually a good idea to get a clean start with all of the fluids. Also, if the vehicle is operated in high water (up to the level of the transmission) it is definitely a good idea to change the fluid.

1. Operate the vehicle in 4 wheel drive in order to warm the fluid to normal operating temperature.
2. If necessary for access to the drain and filler plugs, raise and support the vehicle safely using jackstands. Support the truck so it is level; this is necessary to assure the proper fluid level is maintained when the case is refilled.
3. Position drain pan under transfer case.
4. Remove drain and fill plugs, then drain the lubricant into the drain pan.
5. Install and tighten the drain plug.
6. Remove the drain pan and dump the fluid into a used transmission fluid storage tank, for recycling purposes.
7. Fill transfer case to the edge of fill plug opening. Refer to the fluid recommendations found earlier in this section to determine the proper type of fluid.
8. Install and tighten the fill plug.
9. Remove the jackstands and carefully lower the vehicle, then check for proper operation of the transfer case.

## Cooling System

▶ **See Figure 173**

For most of the vehicles covered by this manual (except 1996 which use a different type of coolant) you should inspect, flush and refill the engine cooling system with fresh coolant (antifreeze) at least once every 2 years or 30,000 miles (48,000 km). If the coolant is left in the system too long, it loses its ability to prevent rust and corrosion. If the coolant has too much water, it won't protect against freezing and it can boil-over in the summer.

The cooling systems on all 1996 vehicles were originally filled with silicate-free DEX-COOL® coolant meeting GM specification 6277M. The fluid is easily identified because of its orange color (instead of the green we have come to expect from most types of ethylene glycol antifreeze). If your cooling system is filled with DEX-COOL®, then no periodic service is required, other than fluid level checks, for 100,000 miles (161,000 km) or 5 years, whichever comes first. BUT if you add a silicated coolant to the system (even in small amounts) premature engine, heater core or radiator corrosion may result. In addition, the coolant will have to be changed sooner (30,000 miles/48,000 km or 2 years, just like other vehicles not using DEX-COOL®).

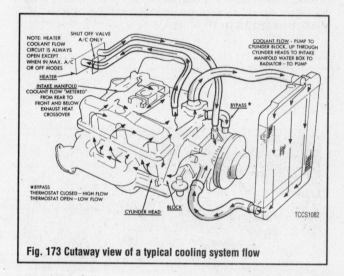

**Fig. 173 Cutaway view of a typical cooling system flow**

## FLUID RECOMMENDATIONS

▶ **See Figure 174**

For 1985–95 vehicles use a good quality ethylene glycol antifreeze (one that will not effect aluminum), mixed with water until a 50–50 antifreeze solution is attained. Colder climates require more antifreeze to prevent freezing. Refer to the chart on the back of the antifreeze container.

**Fig. 174 On 1996 models, labels in the engine compartment warn you that special coolant is used**

➡In addition to the coolant, 1995 vehicles require the addition of 2 sealant pellets (GMSPO No. 3634621) whenever the entire system has been drained and is being refilled with fresh coolant.

As mentioned earlier in this manual, 1996 vehicles were originally equipped with GM DEX-COOL® silicate-free coolant. GM does not recommended any other type of coolant for these vehicles. It is easily identified by its orange color.

➡In all instances, you should premix your coolant and water solution, to be sure you will get the proper ratio of coolant to water. Also, distilled water is preferred as tap water may contain minerals or additives that could be harmful to the cooling system.

## LEVEL CHECK

▶ **See Figures 175 and 176**

The coolant level should be checked EVERY TIME you open the hood.

➡**When checking the coolant level, the radiator cap does not have to be removed, simply check the coolant recovery tank (normally found on the passenger's side of the engine compartment, next to the windshield wiper/washer fluid bottle).**

Check the coolant recovery bottle (see through plastic bottle). With the engine Cold, the coolant should be at the ADD or COLD mark (recovery tank about ¼ full). With the engine warm, the coolant should be at the FULL or HOT mark (recovery tank about ½ full). If necessary, add fluid to the recovery bottle.

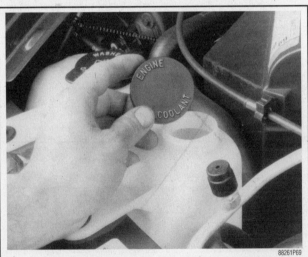

Fig. 175 On all models, the coolant level should be checked through the coolant recovery tank . . .

## COOLING SYSTEM INSPECTION

▶ **See Figures 177 and 178**

**✳✳ CAUTION**

**Never remove the radiator cap under any conditions while the engine is hot! Failure to follow these instructions could result in damage to the cooling system, engine and/or personal injury. To avoid having scalding hot coolant or steam blow out of the radiator, use extreme care whenever you are removing the radiator cap. Wait until the engine has cooled, then wrap a thick cloth around the radiator cap and turn it slowly to the first stop. Step back while the pressure is released from the cooling system. When you are sure the pressure has been released, press down on the radiator cap (still have the cloth in position) turn and remove the radiator cap.**

Dealing with the cooling system can be a dangerous matter unless the proper precautions are observed. It is best to check the coolant level in the radiator when the engine is cold. All vehicles covered by this manual should be equipped with a coolant recovery tank which can be checked hot or cold (refer to the level check information earlier in this section). Always be certain that the filler caps on both the radiator and the recovery tank are closed tightly.

**✳✳ WARNING**

**Never add coolant to a hot engine unless it is running. If it is not running you run the risk of cracking the engine block.**

It is wise to pressure check the cooling system at least once per year. If the coolant level is chronically low or rusty, the system should be thoroughly checked for leaks.

A simple and inexpensive hydrometer should be available in most parts stores to help you test the antifreeze in your system. It will tell you the boiling and freezing points of ethylene glycol antifreeze based on specific gravity. Although this is good in helping to determine the temperature protection it will give your engine, it does NOT tell you how old the coolant it. Even if it tests good for temperature protection, the coolant may no longer be providing corrosion protection and should be changed if you are unsure of its age. Again, the rules on DEX-COOL® are a little different (considering how much longer it lasts and that the ethylene glycol hydrometer readings may not apply) BUT, the principle is the same. If you suspect the coolant in a 1996 vehicle is older than the manufacturer recommends, OR if you think silicate-based coolant may have been added to it, you should probably drain, flush and refill the system.

The pressure cap should be examined for signs of age or deterioration. The fan belt and other drive belts (if equipped) should be inspected and adjusted to the proper tension. (See the information on drive belts earlier in this section.)

Hose clamps should be tightened, and soft or cracked hoses replaced. Damp spots, or accumulations of rust or dye near hoses, water pump or other areas, indicate possible leakage, which must be corrected before filling the system with fresh coolant. (For more information, please refer to Hoses, earlier in this section.)

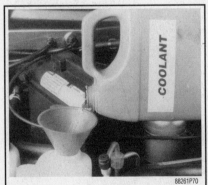

Fig. 176 . . . and if coolant is needed, it should be added to the tank

Fig. 177 Cooling systems should be pressure tested for leaks periodically

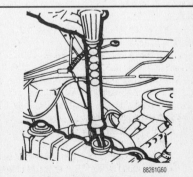

Fig. 178 The freezing/boiling points of your coolant can be checked using a simple, inexpensive antifreeze hydrometer

### Checking the Radiator Cap Seal

▶ **See Figure 179**

While you are checking the cooling system, check the radiator cap for a worn or cracked gasket. It the cap doesn't seal properly, fluid will be lost and the engine will overheat.

Worn caps should be replaced with a new one.

### Checking the Radiator for Debris

▶ **See Figure 180**

Periodically clean any debris — leaves, paper, insects, etc. — from the radiator fins. Pick the large pieces off by hand. The smaller pieces can be washed away with water pressure from a hose.

Carefully straighten any bent radiator fins with a pair of needle-nose pliers. Be careful — the fins are very soft. Don't wiggle the fins back and forth too much. Straighten them once and try not to move them again.

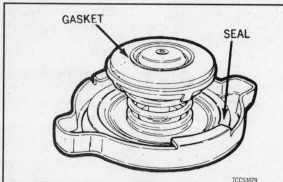

Fig. 179 Be sure the rubber gasket on the radiator cap has a tight seal

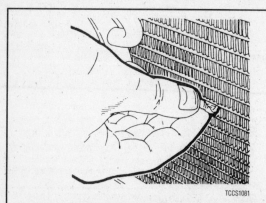

Fig. 180 Periodically remove all debris from the radiator fins

## DRAIN & REFILL

▶ **See Figures 181, 182 and 183**

### ✳✳ CAUTION

**When draining the coolant, keep in mind that cats and dogs are attracted by ethylene glycol antifreeze, and are quite likely to drink any that is left in an uncovered container or in puddles on the ground. This will prove fatal in sufficient quantity. Always drain the coolant into a sealable container. Coolant should be reused unless it is contaminated or several years old. To avoid injuries from scalding fluid and steam, DO NOT remove the radiator cap while the engine and radiator are still HOT.**

1. When the engine is cool, remove the radiator cap using the following procedures.
   a. Slowly rotate the cap counterclockwise to the detent.
   b. If any residual pressure is present, WAIT until the hissing noise stops.
   c. After the hissing noise has ceased, press down on the cap and continue rotating it counterclockwise to remove it.
2. Place a fluid catch pan under the radiator, open the radiator drain valve and, if access is possible, remove the engine drain plugs, then drain the coolant.

➡ **To help prevent a mess when coolant splashes over everything and drips from all points at the front of the vehicle, try placing a short rubber tube over the radiator petcock before opening it. The route the tube down from the vehicle to the drain pan.**

3. Close the drain valve and, if removed, install the engine drain plugs.
4. Empty the coolant reservoir and flush it.
5. Using the correct mixture (AND TYPE, refer to the fluid recommendations earlier in this section if you are unsure) of antifreeze, fill the radiator to about ½ in. (13mm) from the bottom of the filler neck.
6. Start the engine and allow it to idle as the engine warms-up. As the thermostat is opened, air which was trapped in the engine should be expelled, causing the fluid level in the radiator to drop. Add fresh coolant/water mixture until the level reaches the at the bottom of the filler neck.
7. For 1995 vehicles, add 2 sealant pellets (GMSPO part No. 3634621) to coolant mixture in the radiator. This MUST be done to prevent premature water pump leakage. DO NOT add the pellets to the recovery bottle since this might prevent the coolant system from operating properly.
8. Add some of the coolant/water mixture to the coolant tank, but don't go above the ADD or COLD mark at this time.
9. Install the radiator cap (make sure the arrows align with the overflow tube).
10. Run the engine until it reaches the operating temperatures, then check the recovery tank and add fluid (if necessary).

## FLUSHING & CLEANING THE SYSTEM

There are various methods to flush the cooling system, including power flushing equipment or adapters to attach your garden hose. If special equipment is to be used (such as a back flusher), follow the equipment manufacturer's instructions

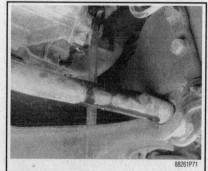

Fig. 181 To prevent a mess when draining the radiator, place a plastic tube over the radiator petcock

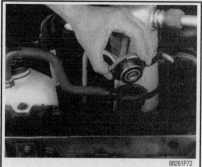

Fig. 182 When refilling the system, pour coolant directly into the radiator, then . . .

Fig. 183 . . . top off using the recovery tank (once the sealed radiator is at normal operating temperature)

closely. Also, carefully read the bottle of any flushing solution, to make sure it is compatible with your cooling system components and the type of antifreeze used.

Most flushing compounds attack metals and SHOULD NOT remain in the cooling system for more than a few minutes. Be sure to use a neutralizer in the cooling system IMMEDIATELY after a descaling solvent has been used. Keep in mind that for extremely hard, stubborn coatings, such as lime scale, a stronger solution may be necessary. BUT, the corrosive action of the stronger solution will affect the thin metals of the radiator, thereby reducing its operating life. A COMPLETE flushing and rinsing is mandatory if this is attempted.

1. Refer to the Drain and Refill procedures in this section, then drain the cooling system.

2. Close the drain valve and install the engine drain plugs, then add sufficient water to the cooling system.

3. Run the engine, then drain and refill the system. Perform this procedure several times, until the fluid (drained from the system) is clear.

4. Empty the coolant reservoir and flush it.

5. Properly refill the engine cooling system with the correct type and mixture of coolant for your vehicle. Refer to the fluid recommendations and the fluid refill procedures found earlier in this section.

## Master Cylinder

♦ See Figures 184, 185, 186, 187 and 188

FLUID RECOMMENDATIONS

### ✳✳ WARNING

**BRAKE FLUID EATS PAINT. Do not allow it to spill, splash or otherwise contact painted surfaces of your vehicle (or at least ones that you care about). If an accident should occur, don't panic, just immediately flush the area with plenty of clean water.**

Use only heavy-duty DOT-3 brake fluid. BUT JUST AS IMPORTANTLY, use ONLY fresh fluid from a sealed container. Brake fluid attracts and absorbs moisture from the atmosphere, which can significantly lower its boiling point. Should fluid boil during heavy use (towing a trailer or hauling passengers and luggage) the fluid will turn to a gas and all/most braking ability could be lost almost instantly. Although the most manufacturers do not require a periodic fluid change for their brake systems, it is a good idea to fill the system with fresh fluid, bleeding out all of the old brake fluid through the wheel bleeders, at least every few years. Keep in mind that over time moisture will even enter a sealed system lowering the brake fluid's boiling point and causing internal corrosion to brake components.

➡ If you decide to change the brake fluid, you will save a LOT of time by removing MOST of the old fluid from the master cylinder reservoirs, before you begin. Replacing the old fluid with fresh before you begin the bleeding procedure will simply require you to bleed a smaller amount of fluid completely through the system before the fresh fluid reaches all bleeding points. For more details on brake bleeding procedures, please refer to Section 9 of this manual.

LEVEL CHECK

The brake fluid level should be checked EVERY TIME YOU OPEN THE HOOD. At the very minimum, a thorough inspection of all fluid level and all components should be conducted every 6 months.

Fig. 184 Many of the earlier models covered by this manual utilize 2 completely separate reservoirs . . .

Fig. 185 . . . remove the cover ONLY from the side that requires fluid

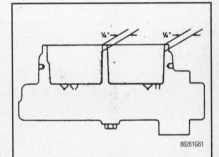

Fig. 186 If there are no markings on the reservoir, keep the fluid approximately ¼ in. (6mm) from the top

Fig. 187 Late-model vehicle, such as this 1996 Astro, use a 1-piece reservoir assembly . . .

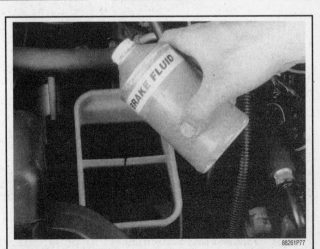

Fig. 188 . . . but fluid is added in the same manner, clean the cover, remove and pour

## ⁂ CAUTION

Before opening the master cylinder reservoir ALWAYS use a clean rag thoroughly clean the reservoir cover and immediate surrounding area. Failure to do this could allow contaminants to fall into the fluid when the cover is removed. These contaminants, if forced through the system by the master cylinder, could destroy seals, leaking to leaks, repairs and possibly even brake failures.

1. Most vehicles covered by this manual use translucent plastic reservoirs, so the cover does NOT need to be removed in order to check the level. Also, most reservoirs will have fill marks or lines on the plastic. The fluid should be about ¼ in. (6mm) from top of the reservoir.

2. If the level is low, thoroughly clean the reservoir and cap(s), then remove the caps to add fluid. Some early-models may have a separate rubber diaphragm seal under the cap. If it is not removed with the cap, it should be carefully removed before fluid is added.

➡Remember to ONLY use fresh fluid from a sealed container.

3. When you are finished, be sure the cap (and separate rubber seal on some early-models) is properly seated.

## Hydraulic Clutch

➡The clutch master cylinder is mounted on the firewall next to the brake master cylinder.

FLUID RECOMMENDATIONS

## ⁂ CAUTION

Before opening the clutch master cylinder reservoir ALWAYS use a clean rag thoroughly clean the reservoir cover and immediate surrounding area. Failure to do this could allow contaminants to fall into the fluid when the cover is removed. These contaminants, if forced through the system by the master cylinder, could destroy seals, leaking to leaks, repairs and possibly even hydraulic clutch failures.

Use only FRESH heavy duty DOT-3 brake fluid from a SEALED container. For more information on DOT-3 fluid and for tips on safe handling, please refer to the brake master cylinder information earlier in this section. Information there includes, the tendency for DOT-3 fluid to absorb moisture and the ability of it to EAT PAINT. Proper care must be used in handling the fluid to prevent vehicle or system damage.

LEVEL CHECK

The hydraulic clutch reservoir should be checked at least every 6 months. As with the brake master cylinder reservoir, you normally check the fluid level through the translucent plastic body of the reservoir. Fill to the line on the reservoir.

➡Although the level should drop slowly with clutch wear, the need to constantly add large amounts of fluid points to the probability of a leak. If a leak is suspected the system should be thoroughly inspected to prevent a hydraulic failure which would leave you stranded.

## Power Steering Pump

▶ See Figures 189, 190, 191, 192 and 193

The power steering pump reservoir is located at the front left or right side of the engine (depending on the year and model. The reservoir is usually mounted to the top of the cowl, remote from the power steering pump, for ease of service.

FLUID RECOMMENDATIONS

Use GM Power Steering Fluid No. 1050017 (1985–95 vehicles), No. 1052884 (1996 vehicles), or a suitable equivalent.

➡Avoid using automatic transmission fluid in the power steering unit, it is not usually a directly compatible substitute any more.

LEVEL CHECK

The power steering fluid should be checked at least every 6 months. There is a Cold and a Hot mark on the dipstick. The fluid should be checked when the engine is warm and turned OFF. If necessary, add fluid to the power steering pump reservoir.

## Chassis Greasing

▶ See Figure 194

Chassis greasing should be performed every 6 months or 7500 miles (12,000 km), it can be performed with a commercial pressurized grease gun or at home by using a hand operated grease gun. Wipe the grease fittings clean before greasing in order to prevent the possibility of forcing any dirt into the component. Just add enough fresh grease to fill (and thereby swell the rubber seal). DO NOT add grease until it pours from the seal, as this means the SEAL can no longer properly protect the grease from moisture or dirt.

## Body Lubrication

HOOD LATCH & HINGES

Clean the latch surfaces and apply clean engine oil to the latch pilot bolts and the spring anchor. Use the engine oil to lubricate the hood hinges as well. Use a chassis grease to lubricate all the pivot points in the latch release mechanism.

Fig. 189 The power steering fluid level is checked using the reservoir cap/dipstick . . .

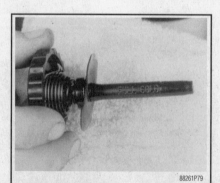

Fig. 190 . . . hold the cap sideways, making sure the fluid level is within the operating range

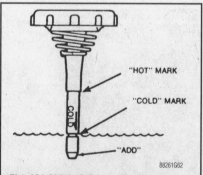

Fig. 191 Although 2 operating ranges are provided, it is preferable to check the level HOT

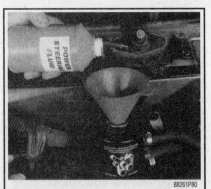

**Fig. 192 If necessary, fluid should be added (and as usual, a funnel is handy)**

**Fig. 193 Late model reservoirs are also mounted to the cowl, just on the other side of the engine**

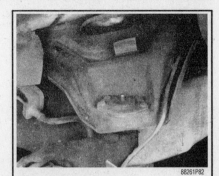

**Fig. 194 Grease fittings, such as the one pictured, should be cleaned before the grease gun is attached**

## DOOR HINGES & LOCKS

The gas tank filler door, the front doors and rear door hinges should be wiped clean and lubricated with clean engine oil. Silicone spray also works well on these parts but must be applied more often. The door lock cylinders can be lubricated easily with a shot of GM silicone spray No. 1052276 or 1 of the many dry penetrating lubricants commercially available.

## PARKING BRAKE LINKAGE

Use chassis grease on the parking brake cable where it contacts the guides, links, levers and pulleys. The grease should be a water resistant one for durability under the vehicle.

## ACCELERATOR LINKAGE

Lubricate the throttle body lever, the cable and the accelerator pedal lever (at the support inside the vehicle) with clean engine oil.

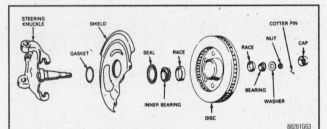

**Fig. 195 Exploded view of the front wheel hub and bearing assembly—2-wheel drive without ABS shown (ABS similar but with a speed sensor assembly on the shield and a reluctor ring on the back of the hub)**

## TRANSMISSION SHIFT LINKAGE

Lubricate the manual transmission shift linkage with water resistant chassis grease which meets GM specification No. 6031M or equivalent. Automatic transmission shift linkage should be lubricated with clean engine oil.

## Wheel Bearings

Once every 30,000 miles (48,000 km) the non-sealed front wheel bearings of rear wheel drive vehicles should be cleaned and repacked with a GM Wheel Bearing Grease No. 1051344 or equivalent. Use only enough grease to completely coat the rollers. Remove any excess grease from the exposed surface of the hub and seal.

## REPACKING & ADJUSTMENT

**2-Wheel Drive**

◆ **See Figures 195 thru 214**

Before handling the bearings, there are a few things that you should remember to do and not to do.

**Remember to DO the following:**
- Remove all outside dirt from the housing before exposing the bearing.
- Treat a used bearing as gently as you would a new one.
- Work with clean tools in clean surroundings.
- Use clean, dry canvas or plastic gloves.
- Clean solvents and flushing fluids are a must.
- Use clean paper when laying out the bearings to dry.
- Protect disassembled bearings from rust and dirt. Cover them up.
- Use clean rags to wipe bearings.
- Keep the bearings in oil-proof paper when they are to be stored or are not in use.
- Clean the inside of the housing before replacing the bearing.

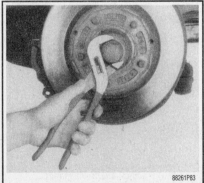

**Fig. 196 Remove the dust cap from the center of the hub and disc assembly**

**Fig. 197 If the cap is stuck use a thin chisel to drive it away from the disc . . .**

**Fig. 198 . . . then pry the cap free, but be careful not to deform and ruin the cap**

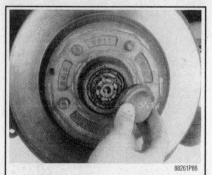

Fig. 199 Once loosened, remove the cap for access to the bearing retainer (cotter pin, washer and nut)

Fig. 200 Bend the ends outward and pull or lever the cotter pin from the spindle . . .

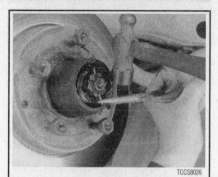

Fig. 201 If difficulty is encountered, gently tap on the pliers with a hammer to help free the cotter pin

Fig. 202 . . . then loosen and remove the castellated spindle nut

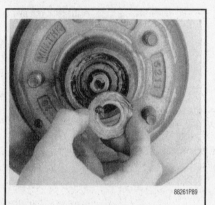

Fig. 203 Withdraw the thrust washer . . .

Fig. 204 . . . then remove the outer bearing, freeing the hub and disc assembly

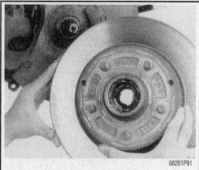

Fig. 205 Pull the hub/disc assembly from the spindle and face downward on a clean working surface

Fig. 206 Remove the inner wheel bearing seal using a seal puller (this really makes the job easier) . . .

Fig. 207 On ABS equipped vehicles a puller removes the seal WITHOUT damaging the reluctor ring (the visible teeth)

Fig. 208 With the seal removed, the inner wheel bearing may be lifted from the back of the hub

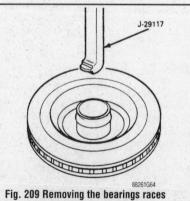

Fig. 209 Removing the bearings races from the hub and disc assembly

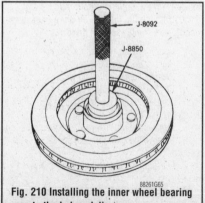

Fig. 210 Installing the inner wheel bearing race to the hub and disc

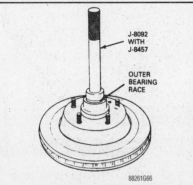

Fig. 211 Installing the outer wheel bearing race to the hub and disc

Fig. 212 Thoroughly pack the bearing with fresh, high temperature wheel-bearing grease before installation

Fig. 213 Apply a thin coat of fresh grease to the new inner bearing seal lip

Fig. 214 Though a driver is preferred, any circular tool (pipe or socket) of similar size can install the seal

**Do NOT do the following:**
- Don't work in dirty surroundings.
- Don't use dirty, chipped or damaged tools.
- Try not to work on wooden work benches or use wooden mallets.
- Don't handle bearings with dirty or moist hands.
- Do not use gasoline for cleaning; use a safe solvent.
- Do not spin-dry bearings with compressed air. They will be damaged.
- Do not spin dirty bearings.
- Avoid using cotton waste or dirty cloths to wipe bearings.
- Try not to scratch or nick bearing surfaces.
- Do not allow the bearing to come in contact with dirt or rust at any time.

➡The following procedures are made easier with the use of GM tools No. J–29117, J–8092, J–8850, J–8457 and J–9746–02 or their equivalents. Although the job can be done using a prybar, some a few LARGE sockets and some assorted drivers.

1. Loosen the lug nuts on the front wheels.
2. Raise and support the front of the vehicle safely using jackstands.
3. Remove the front tire and wheel assemblies.
4. Remove the caliper-to-steering knuckle bolts and the caliper from the steering knuckle. Using a wire, support the caliper from the vehicle; DO NOT disconnect the brake line.
5. Remove the dust cap at the center of the hub and disc assembly.
6. Remove the cotter pin, the spindle nut, the thrust washer and the outer bearing.
7. Grasping the hub and disc assembly firmly, pull the assembly from the axle spindle.
8. Using a small prybar or an inexpensive seal removal tool, pry the grease seal from the rear of the hub/disc assembly, then remove the inner bearing.

➡DO NOT remove the bearing races from the hub, unless they show signs of damage.

9. If it is necessary to remove the wheel bearing races, use the GM front bearing race removal tool No. J–29117 to drive the races from the hub and disc assembly. If the tool is not available, you can use a prybar (if you take care not to damage the hub and disc assembly) or you can use a blunt drift from behind (the other side of the assembly).

➡Wheel bearings and races which have been in service MUST remain together as matched sets. DO NOT switch bearings from side-to-side. ALSO, if the bearings are replaced, new races MUST be installed to insure the proper bearing operating life of the replacement parts.

10. Using solvent, clean the grease from all of the parts, then blow them dry with compressed air.

➡DO NOT spin the dry bearings with the compressed air or damage will likely occur. If compressed air is not available, place the bearings on a clean, dry surface (clean, lint free rag or a plastic bag) and allow them to air dry.

11. Inspect all of the parts for scoring, pitting or cracking, replace the parts (if necessary).

**To install:**
12. If the bearing races were removed, perform the following procedures to the install the replacements:
a. Using grease, lightly lubricate the inside of the hub/disc assembly.
b. Using the GM seal installation tools No. J–8092 and J–8850, drive the inner bearing race into the hub/disc assembly until it seats.

➡When installing the bearing races, be sure to support the hub/disc assembly with GM tool No. J–9746–02.

c. Using the GM seal installation tools No. J–8092 and J–8457, drive the outer race into the hub/disc assembly until it seats.
13. Using wheel bearing grease, lubricate the bearings, the races and the spindle; be sure to place a gob of grease (inside the hub/disc assembly) between the races to provide an ample supply of lubricant.

➡To lubricate each bearing, place a gob of grease in the palm of the hand, then scoop the bearing through the grease to force grease between the rollers and cage. Be sure to thoroughly fill the bearing around the entire circumference from the top and bottom of the assembly, then roll the bearing through the grease to assure it is well lubricated.

14. Place the inner wheel bearing into the hub/disc assembly. Using a smooth flat driver, length of pipe or a large socket, drive the new grease seal into the rear of the hub and disc assembly until it is flush with the outer surface.
15. Position the hub and disc assembly onto the spindle, then install the outer bearing, thrust washer and the hub nut.
16. While turning the wheel, torque the hub nut to 12 ft. lbs. (16 Nm) until the bearings seat. Back off the nut to the "just loose" position, then retighten it by hand. Back the nut off until the nearest nut slot aligns with the spindle hole. The nut should not be turned back more than ½ of a nut flat.
17. Install a new cotter pin through the nut and the spindle, then bend the ends and cut off the excess pin (one outward over the end of the spindle, and the other downward around the spindle). Install the grease cap.

18. If possible, use a dial indicator to the check the rotor end-play. The end-play should be 0.001–0.005 in. (0.03–0.13mm) when the bearings are properly adjusted. If not, readjust the hub/disc assembly.
19. Install the caliper onto the steering knuckle.
20. Install the tire and wheel assembly.
21. Remove the jackstands, then carefully lower the vehicle.
22. Tighten the lug nuts, then road test the vehicle.

## TRAILER TOWING

♦ See Figure 215

### General Recommendations

Your vehicle was primarily designed to carry passengers and cargo. It is important to remember that towing a trailer will place additional loads on your vehicle's engine, drive train, steering, braking and other systems. However, if you decide to tow a trailer, using the proper equipment is a must.

Local laws may require specific equipment such as trailer brakes or fender mounted mirrors. Check your local laws.

### Trailer Weight

The weight of the trailer is the most important factor. A good weight-to-horsepower ratio is about 35:1, 35 lbs. of Gross Combined Weight (GCW) for every horsepower your engine develops. Multiply the engine's rated horsepower by 35 and subtract the weight of the vehicle passengers and luggage. The number remaining is the approximate ideal maximum weight you should tow, although a numerically higher axle ratio can help compensate for heavier weight.

### Hitch (Tongue) Weight

Calculate the hitch weight in order to select a proper hitch. The weight of the hitch is usually 9–11% of the trailer gross weight and should be measured with the trailer loaded. Hitches fall into various categories: those that mount on the frame and rear bumper, the bolt-on type, or the weld-on distribution type used for larger trailers. Axle mounted or clamp-on bumper hitches should never be used.

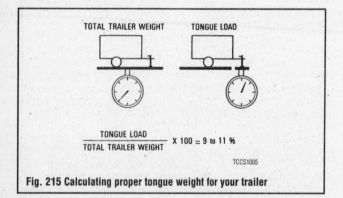

**Fig. 215 Calculating proper tongue weight for your trailer**

Check the gross weight rating of your trailer. Tongue weight is usually figured as 10% of gross trailer weight. Therefore, a trailer with a maximum gross weight of 2000 lbs. will have a maximum tongue weight of 200 lbs. Class I trailers fall into this category. Class II trailers are those with a gross weight rating of 2000–3000 lbs., while Class III trailers fall into the 3500–6000 lbs. category. Class IV trailers are those over 6000 lbs. and are for use with fifth wheel trucks, only.

When you've determined the hitch that you'll need, follow the manufacturer's installation instructions, exactly, especially when it comes to fastener torques. The hitch will subjected to a lot of stress and good hitches come with hardened bolts. Never substitute an inferior bolt for a hardened bolt.

### All Wheel Drive

The all wheel drive front wheel bearings are the sealed type that require no periodic adjusting or repacking. The bearing and hub is a 1 piece assembly requiring replacement if the bearings are defective. Refer to the "Front Wheel Bearing" section in Section 8 for bearing procedures.

## Cooling

### ENGINE

#### Overflow Tank

One of the most common, if not THE most common, problems associated with trailer towing is engine overheating. If you have a cooling system without an expansion tank, you'll definitely need to get an aftermarket expansion tank kit, preferably one with at least a 2 quart capacity. These kits are easily installed on the radiator's overflow hose, and come with a pressure cap designed for expansion tanks.

#### Flex Fan

Another helpful accessory for vehicles using a belt-driven radiator fan is a flex fan. These fans are large diameter units designed to provide more airflow at low speeds, by using fan blades that have deeply cupped surfaces. The blades then flex, or flatten out, at high speed, when less cooling air is needed. These fans are far lighter in weight than stock fans, requiring less horsepower to drive them. Also, they are far quieter than stock fans. If you do decide to replace your stock fan with a flex fan, note that if your vehicle has a fan clutch, a spacer will be needed between the flex fan and water pump hub.

#### Oil Cooler

Aftermarket engine oil coolers are helpful for prolonging engine oil life and reducing overall engine temperatures. Both of these factors increase engine life. While not absolutely necessary in towing Class I and some Class II trailers, they are recommended for heavier Class II and all Class III towing. Engine oil cooler systems usually consist of an adapter, screwed on in place of the oil filter, a remote filter mounting and a multi-tube, finned heat exchanger, which is mounted in front of the radiator or air conditioning condenser.

➡**Depending on the model and accessories originally installed on your vehicle, an integral oil cooler may already be installed in your radiator with lines leading back to your oil filter adapter.**

### TRANSMISSION

An automatic transmission is usually recommended for trailer towing. Modern automatics have proven reliable and, of course, easy to operate, in trailer towing. The increased load of a trailer, however, causes an increase in the temperature of the automatic transmission fluid. Heat is the worst enemy of an automatic transmission. As the temperature of the fluid increases, the life of the fluid decreases.

It is essential, therefore, that you install an automatic transmission cooler. The cooler, which consists of a multi-tube, finned heat exchanger, is usually installed in front of the radiator or air conditioning compressor, and hooked in-line with the transmission cooler tank inlet line. Follow the cooler manufacturer's installation instructions.

Select a cooler of at least adequate capacity, based upon the combined gross weights of the vehicle and trailer.

Cooler manufacturers recommend that you use an aftermarket cooler in addition to, and not instead of, the present cooling tank in your radiator. If you do want to use it in place of the radiator cooling tank, get a cooler at least 2 sizes larger than normally necessary.

➡A transmission cooler can, sometimes, cause slow or harsh shifting in the transmission during cold weather, until the fluid has a chance to come up to normal operating temperature. Some coolers can be purchased with or retrofitted with a temperature bypass valve which will allow fluid flow through the cooler only when the fluid has reached above a certain operating temperature.

## JUMP STARTING A DEAD BATTERY

▶ **See Figure 216**

Whenever a vehicle is jump started, precautions must be followed in order to prevent the possibility of personal injury. Remember that batteries contain a small amount of explosive hydrogen gas which is a by-product of battery charging. Sparks should always be avoided when working around batteries, especially when attaching jumper cables. To minimize the possibility of accidental sparks, follow the procedure carefully.

### ✳✳ CAUTION

**NEVER hook the batteries up in a series circuit or the entire electrical system will go up in smoke, including the starter!**

Vehicles equipped with a diesel engine may utilize two 12 volt batteries. If so, the batteries are connected in a parallel circuit (positive terminal to positive terminal, negative terminal to negative terminal). Hooking the batteries up in parallel circuit increases battery cranking power without increasing total battery voltage output. Output remains at 12 volts. On the other hand, hooking two 12 volt batteries up in a series circuit (positive terminal to negative terminal, positive terminal to negative terminal) increases total battery output to 24 volts (12 volts plus 12 volts).

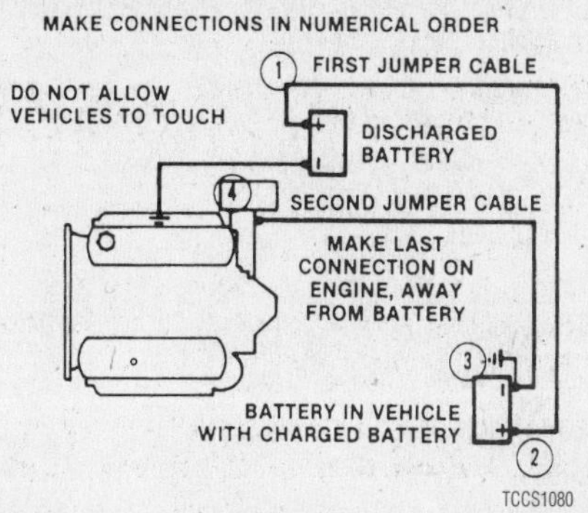

### Jump Starting Precautions

- Be sure both batteries are of the same voltage. Vehicles covered by this manual and most vehicles on the road today utilize a 12 volt charging system.
- Be sure both batteries are of the same polarity (have the same terminal, in most cases NEGATIVE grounded).
- Be sure the vehicles are not touching or a short could occur.
- On serviceable batteries, be sure the vent cap holes are not obstructed.
- Do not smoke or allow sparks anywhere near the batteries.
- In cold weather, make sure the battery electrolyte is not frozen. This can occur more readily in a battery that has been in a state of discharge.
- Do not allow electrolyte to contact your skin or clothing.

### Jump Starting Procedure

1. Make sure the voltages of the 2 batteries are the same. Most batteries and charging systems are of the 12 volt variety.
2. Pull the jumping vehicle (with the good battery) into a position so the jumper cables can reach the dead battery and that vehicle's engine. Make sure the vehicles do NOT touch.
3. Place the transmissions/transaxles of both vehicles in **Neutral** (MT) or **P** (AT), as applicable, then firmly set their parking brakes.

➡**If necessary for safety reasons, the hazard lights on both vehicles may be operated throughout the entire procedure without significantly increasing the difficulty of jumping the dead battery.**

4. Turn all lights and accessories OFF on both vehicles. Make sure the ignition switches on both vehicles are turned to the **OFF** position.
5. Cover the battery cell caps with a rag, but do not cover the terminals.
6. Make sure the terminals on both batteries are clean and free of corrosion or proper electrical connection will be impeded. If necessary, clean the battery terminals before proceeding.

## Handling A Trailer

Towing a trailer with ease and safety requires a certain amount of experience. It's a good idea to learn the feel of a trailer by practicing turning, stopping and backing in an open area such as an empty parking lot.

**Fig. 216 Connect the jumper cables to the batteries and engine in the order shown**

7. Identify the positive (+) and negative (−) terminals on both batteries.
8. Connect the first jumper cable to the positive (+) terminal of the dead battery, then connect the other end of that cable to the positive (+) terminal of the booster (good) battery.
9. Connect 1 end of the other jumper cable to the negative (−) terminal on the booster battery and the final cable clamp to an engine bolt head, alternator bracket or other solid, metallic point on the engine with the dead battery. Try to pick a ground on the engine that is positioned away from the battery in order to minimize the possibility of the 2 clamps touching should 1 loosen during the procedure. DO NOT connect this clamp to the negative (−) terminal of the bad battery.

### ✳✳ CAUTION

**Be very careful to keep the jumper cables away from moving parts (cooling fan, belts, etc.) on both engines.**

10. Check to make sure the cables are routed away from any moving parts, then start the donor vehicle's engine. Run the engine at moderate speed for several minutes to allow the dead battery a chance to receive some initial charge.
11. With the donor vehicle's engine still running slightly above idle, try to start the vehicle with the dead battery. Crank the engine for no more than 10 seconds at a time and let the starter cool for at least 20 seconds between tries. If the vehicle does not start in 3 tries, it is likely that something else is also wrong or that the battery needs additional time to charge.
12. Once the vehicle is started, allow it to run at idle for a few seconds to make sure it is operating properly.
13. Turn ON the headlights, heater blower and, if equipped, the rear defroster of both vehicles in order to reduce the severity of voltage spikes and subsequent risk of damage to the vehicles' electrical systems when the cables are disconnected. This step is especially important to any vehicle equipped with computer control modules.
14. Carefully disconnect the cables in the reverse order of connection. Start with the negative cable that is attached to the engine ground, then the negative cable on the donor battery. Disconnect the positive cable from the donor battery and finally, disconnect the positive cable from the formerly dead battery. Be careful when disconnecting the cables from the positive terminals not to allow the alligator clips to touch any metal on either vehicle or a short and sparks will occur.

## JACKING

▶ **See Figures 217 thru 223**

The jack supplied with the Astro and Safari van is meant for changing tires during emergency roadside operations. No jack is not meant to support a vehicle while you crawl under it and work. Whenever it is necessary to get under a vehicle to perform service operations, always be sure it is adequately supported, preferably by jackstands at the proper points. Always block the wheels when changing tires.

If the van is equipped with a Positraction® (locking differential) rear axle, DO NOT run the engine for any reason with 1 rear wheel off the ground. Power will be transmitted through the rear wheel remaining on the ground, possibly causing the vehicle to drive itself off the jack.

Some of the service operations in this book require that 1 or both ends of the vehicle be raised and supported safely. The best arrangement for this, of course, is a grease pit or a vehicle lift but these items are seldom found in the home garage. However, small hydraulic, screw or scissors jacks are satisfactory for raising the vehicle. If you are serious about home maintenance and repair, do yourself a favor and buy a quality floor jack, the convenience will pay for itself in the long run.

Heavy wooden blocks or adjustable jackstands should be used to support the vehicle while it is being worked on. Drive-on trestles or ramps are also a handy and a safe way to raise the vehicle, assuming their capacity is adequate and that there are no clearance problems with low body panels/skirts or air dams. These can be bought or constructed from suitable heavy timbers or steel.

In any case, it is always best to spend a little extra time to make sure your van is lifted and supported safely.

## ✳✳ CAUTION

**Concrete blocks are not recommended. They may crumble if the load is not evenly distributed. Boxes and milk crates of any description MUST not be used. WE ARE TALKING ABOUT YOUR LIFE HERE! Once the vehicle is on the ramps or jackstands, shake it a few times to make sure the jackstands/ramps are securely supporting the weight before crawling under.**

Before using any jack, read the manufacturer's instructions. This includes the emergency jack provided with your vehicle. When using floor jacks and jackstands, be sure they are positioned on structural components and not on body or floor panels which were not designed to support the vehicle weight (and which will just deform or break once this force is applied). Generally frame rails, differential housings and certain specified suspension components are good jacking points. For more detail, please refer to the accompanying illustrations.

Fig. 217 Floor jacks can be used on frame rails (such as this front crossmember) to raise the vehicle . . .

Fig. 218 . . . but jackstands must be used to support it (note this stand is placed under a frame pad)

Fig. 219 The rear differential is another jacking point (you can get both rear wheels off the ground at once)

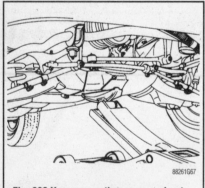

Fig. 220 You can use the crossmember to lift the front of the vehicle

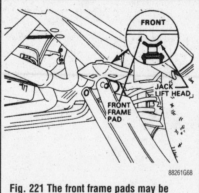

Fig. 221 The front frame pads may be used to lift 1 side of the vehicle

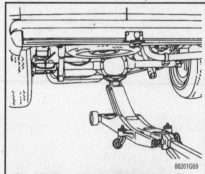

Fig. 222 The rear axle can be used to lift (floor jack pictured) or support (jackstands) the vehicle

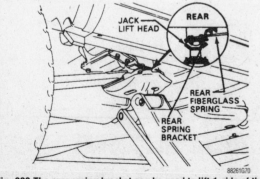

Fig. 223 The rear spring bracket can be used to lift 1 side of the vehicle

## Jacking Precautions

The following safety points cannot be overemphasized:
• Always block the opposite wheel or wheels to keep the vehicle from rolling off the jack.
• When raising the front of the vehicle, firmly apply the parking brake.
• When the drive wheels are to remain on the ground, leave the vehicle in gear to help prevent it from rolling.
• Always use jackstands to support the vehicle when you are working underneath. Place the stands beneath the vehicle's jacking brackets. Before climbing underneath, rock the vehicle a bit to make sure it is firmly supported.

## CAPACITIES

| Year | Model | Engine ID/VIN | Engine Displacement Liters (cc) | Engine Oil with Filter (qts.) | Transmission (pts.) | | | Transfer Case (pts.) | Drive Axle | | Fuel Tank (gal.) | Cooling System (qts.) |
|------|-------|---------------|----------------------------------|-------------------------------|--------|--------|-------|---------------------|------------|-----------|------------------|----------------------|
| | | | | | 4-Spd | 5-Spd | Auto. | | Front (pts.) | Rear (pts.) | | |
| 1985 | Astro/Safari | E | 2.5 (2474) | 3.0 | 5.0 [1] | 4.4 [1] | 10.0 [1] | - | - | 4.0 | 17.0 [2] | 10.0 [3] |
| | Astro/Safari | N | 4.3 (4309) | 5.0 | 5.0 [1] | 4.4 [1] | 10.0 [1] | - | - | 4.0 | 17.0 [2] | 13.5 [4] |
| 1986 | Astro/Safari | E | 2.5 (2474) | 3.0 | 5.0 [1] | 4.4 [1] | 10.0 [1] | - | - | 4.0 | 17.0 [2] | 10.0 [3] |
| | Astro/Safari | Z | 4.3 (4293) | 5.0 | 5.0 [1] | 4.4 [1] | 10.0 [1] | - | - | 4.0 | 17.0 [2] | 13.5 [4] |
| 1987 | Astro/Safari | E | 2.5 (2474) | 3.0 | - | 4.4 [1] | 10.0 [1] | - | - | 4.0 | 17.0 [2] | 10.0 [3] |
| | Astro/Safari | Z | 4.3 (4293) | 5.0 | - | 4.4 [1] | 10.0 [1] | - | - | 4.0 | 17.0 [2] | 13.5 [4] |
| 1988 | Astro/Safari | E | 2.5 (2474) | 3.0 | - | 4.4 [1] | 10.0 [1] | - | - | 4.0 | 17.0 [2] | 10.0 [3] |
| | Astro/Safari | Z | 4.3 (4293) | 5.0 | - | 4.4 [1] | 10.0 [1] | - | - | 4.0 | 17.0 [2] | 13.5 [4] |
| 1989 | Astro/Safari | E | 2.5 (2474) | 3.5 | - | 4.4 [1] | 10.0 [1] | - | - | 4.0 | 17.0 [2] | 10.0 [3] |
| | Astro/Safari | Z | 4.3 (4293) | 5.0 | - | 4.4 [1] | 10.0 [1] | - | - | 4.0 | 17.0 [2] | 13.5 [4] |
| 1990 | Astro/Safari | E | 2.5 (2474) | 3.5 | - | - | 10.0 [1] | - | - | 4.0 | 27.0 | 10.0 [3] |
| | Astro/Safari | B | 4.3 (4293) | 5.0 | - | - | 10.0 [1] | 3.2 | 2.6 | 4.0 | 27.0 | 13.5 [4] |
| | Astro/Safari | Z | 4.3 (4293) | 5.0 | - | - | 10.0 [1] | 3.2 | 2.6 | 4.0 | 27.0 | 13.5 [4] |
| 1991 | Astro/Safari | B | 4.3 (4293) | 5.0 | - | - | 10.0 [1] | 3.2 | 2.6 | 4.0 | 27.0 | 13.5 [4] |
| | Astro/Safari | Z | 4.3 (4293) | 5.0 | - | - | 10.0 [1] | 3.2 | 2.6 | 4.0 | 27.0 | 13.5 [4] |
| 1992 | Astro/Safari | W | 4.3 (4293) | 4.5 | - | - | 10.0 [1] | 3.2 | 2.6 | 4.0 | 27.0 | 13.5 [4] |
| | Astro/Safari | Z | 4.3 (4293) | 4.5 | - | - | 10.0 [1] | 3.2 | 2.6 | 4.0 | 27.0 | 13.5 [4] |
| 1993 | Astro/Safari | W | 4.3 (4293) | 4.5 | - | - | 10.0 [1] | 3.0 | 2.6 | 4.0 | 27.0 | 13.5 [4] |
| | Astro/Safari | Z | 4.3 (4293) | 4.5 | - | - | 10.0 [1] | 3.0 | 2.6 | 4.0 | 27.0 | 13.5 [4] |
| 1994 | Astro/Safari | W | 4.3 (4293) | 4.5 | - | - | 10.0 [1] | 3.0 | 2.6 | 4.0 | 27.0 | 13.5 [4] |
| | Astro/Safari | Z | 4.3 (4293) | 4.5 | - | - | 10.0 [1] | 3.0 | 2.6 | 4.0 | 27.0 | 13.5 [4] |
| 1995 | Astro/Safari | W | 4.3 (4293) | 4.5 | - | - | 10.0 [1] | 3.0 | 2.6 | 4.0 | 27.0 | 13.5 [4] |
| 1996 | Astro/Safari | W | 4.3 (4293) | 4.5 | - | - | 10.0 [1] | 3.0 | 2.6 | 4.0 | 27.0 | 14.3 [4] |

NOTE: All capacities are approximate. Always add fluids gradually, checking the level often.

1　Specification is for drain and refill. Overhaul is usually at least double that capacity

2　Available with optional 27 gallon tank

3　13 qts. with rear heater

4　16.5 qts. with rear heater

88261C04

## Maintenance Intervals
### Schedule I ①

| Item No. | To Be Serviced | When to Perform Miles or Months, Whichever Occurs First Miles (000) | The services shown in this schedule up to 48,000 miles are to be performed after 48,000 miles at the same intervals | | | | | | | | | | | | | | |
|---|---|---|---|---|---|---|---|---|---|---|---|---|---|---|---|---|---|
| | | | 3 | 6 | 9 | 12 | 15 | 18 | 21 | 24 | 27 | 30 | 33 | 36 | 39 | 42 | 45 | 48 |
| 1 | Engine Oil and Oil filter Change | Every 3,000 Miles or 3 Months | ● | ● | ● | ● | ● | ● | ● | ● | ● | ● | ● | ● | ● | ● | ● | ● |
| 2 | Chassis Lubrication | Every oil change | ● | ● | ● | ● | ● | ● | ● | ● | ● | ● | ● | ● | ● | ● | ● | ● |
| 3 | Carburetor Choke and Hose Inspection | At 6,000 Miles, then at 30,000 Miles | | ● | | | | | | | | ● | | | | | ● | |
| 4 | Carburetor or T.B.I. Mounting Bolt Torque Check | | | ● | | | | | | | | ● | | | | | | |
| 5 | Engine Idle Speed Adjustment | | | ● | | | | | | | | ● | | | | | | |
| 6 | Engine Accessory Drive Belts Inspection | Every 12 Months or 15,000 Miles | | | | | ● | | | | | ● | | | | | ● | |
| 7 | Cooling System Service | Every 24 Months or 30,000 Miles | | | | | | | | | | ● | | | | | | |
| 8 | Front Wheel Bearing Repack | Every 15,000 Miles | | | | | ● | | | | | ● | | | | | | |
| 9 | Transmission Service | 15,000 Miles | | | | | ● | | | | | ● | | | | | | |
| 10 | Vacuum Advance System Inspection | Check at 6,000 Miles, then at 30,000 Miles, and at 45,000 Miles | | ● | | | | | | | | ● | | | | | ● | |
| 11 | Spark Plugs and Wire Service | Every 30,000 Miles | | | | | | | | | | ● | | | | | | |
| 12 | PCV System Inspection | Every 30,000 Miles | | | | | | | | | | ● | | | | | | |
| 13 | EGR System Check | Every 30,000 Miles | | | | | | | | | | ● | | | | | | |
| 14 | Air Cleaner and PCV Filter Replacement | Every 30,000 Miles | | | | | | | | | | ● | | | | | | |
| 15 | Engine Timing Check | Every 30,000 Miles | | | | | | | | | | ● | | | | | | |
| 16 | Fuel Tank, Cap and Lines Inspection | Every 12 Months or 15,000 Miles | | | | | ● | | | | | ● | | | | | ● | |
| 17 | Early Fuel Evaporation System Inspection | At 6,000 Miles then at 30,000 Miles | | ● | | | | | | | | ● | | | | | | |
| 18 | Evaporative Control System Inspection | At 30,000 Miles | | | | | | | | | | ● | | | | | | |
| 19 | Fuel Filter Replacement | Every 15,000 Miles | | | | | ● | | | | | ● | | | | | ● | |
| 20 | Valve Lash Adjustment | Every 15,000 Miles | | | | | ● | | | | | ● | | | | | ● | |
| 21 | Thermostatically Controlled Air Cleaner Inspection | Every 30,000 Miles | | | | | | | | | | ● | | | | | | |

Maintenance interval – schedule I

88261C05

## Maintenance Intervals (cont.)
### Schedule II ②

| Item No. | To Be Serviced | When to Perform Miles or Months, Whichever Occurs First Miles (000) | The services shown in this schedule up to 60,000 miles are to be performed after 60,000 miles at the same intervals | | | | | | | |
|---|---|---|---|---|---|---|---|---|---|---|
| | | | 7.5 | 15 | 22.5 | 30 | 37.5 | 45 | 52.5 | 60 |
| 1 | Engine Oil Change | Every 7,500 Miles or 12 Months | ● | ● | ● | ● | ● | ● | ● | ● |
| | Oil Filter Change | At First and Every Other Oil Change or 12 Months | ● | | ● | | ● | | ● | |
| 2 | Chassis Lubrication | Every oil change | ● | ● | ● | ● | ● | ● | ● | ● |
| 3 | Carburetor Choke and Hoses Inspection | At 6 Months or 7,500 Miles and at 60,000 Miles | ● | | | | | | | ● |
| 4 | Carburetor or T.B.I. Mounting Bolt Torque Check | At 6 Months or 7,500 Miles and at 60,000 Miles | ● | | | | | | | ● |
| 5 | Engine Idle Speed Adjustment | At 6 Months or 7,500 Miles and at 60,000 Miles | ● | | | | | | | ● |
| 6 | Engine Accessory Drive Belts Inspection | Every 24 Months or 30,000 Miles | | | | ● | | | | ● |
| 7 | Cooling System Service | Every 24 Months or 30,000 Miles | | | | ● | | | | ● |
| 8 | Front Wheel Bearing Repack | Every 30,000 Miles | | | | ● | | | | ● |
| 9 | Transmission Service | 30,000 miles | | | | ● | | | | ● |
| 10 | Vacuum Advance System Inspection | Check at 6 Months or 7,500 Miles, then at 30,000 Miles, and then at 15,000 Mile intervals. | ● | | | ● | | ● | | ● |
| 11 | Spark Plugs and Wire Service | Every 30,000 Miles | | | | ● | | | | ● |
| 12 | PCV System Inspection | Every 30,000 Miles | | | | ● | | | | ● |
| 13 | EGR System Check | Every 30,000 Miles | | | | ● | | | | ● |
| 14 | Air Cleaner and PCV Filter Replacement | Every 30,000 Miles | | | | ● | | | | ● |
| 15 | Engine Timing Check | Every 30,000 Miles | | | | ● | | | | ● |
| 16 | Fuel Tank, Cap and Lines Inspection | Every 24 Months 30,000 Miles | | | | ● | | | | ● |
| 17 | Early Fuel Evaporation System Inspection | At 7,500 Miles and at 30,000 Miles than at 30,000 Mile intervals. | ● | | | ● | | | | ● |
| 18 | Evaporative Control System Inspection | Every 30,000 Miles | | | | ● | | | | ● |
| 19 | Fuel Filter Replacement | Every 30,000 Miles | | | | ● | | | | ● |
| 20 | Valve Lash Adjustment | Every 15,000 Miles | | ● | | ● | | ● | | ● |
| 21 | Thermostatically Controlled Air Cleaner Inspection | Every 30,000 Miles | | | | ● | | | | ● |

① Severe service  ② Normal service

Maintenance interval – schedule II

88261C06

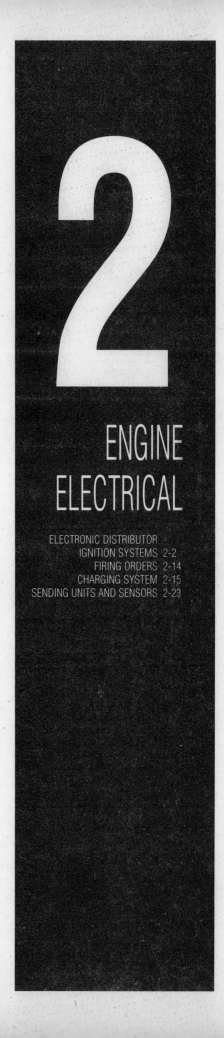

# 2

# ENGINE
# ELECTRICAL

## ELECTRONIC DISTRIBUTOR IGNITION SYSTEMS

➡For information on understanding electricity and troubleshooting electrical circuits, please refer to Section 6 of this manual.

### General Information

There are three general ignition systems used on these vehicles: High Energy Ignition (HEI), Electronic Spark Timing (EST) and High Voltage Switch (HVS). The HEI and EST systems are very similar to each other and differ more in nomenclature than anything else. These systems use distributors that contain pickups and electronic modules. The HVS system uses a distributor that contains nothing but a rotor and cap. All the HVS does is to distribute the spark to the appropriate cylinder; the engine control module (ECM) takes care of the rest of the timing parameters. The HVS distributor does contain a camshaft position sensor, but it is not used for timing determination.

### HIGH ENERGY IGNITION (HEI) AND ELECTRONIC SPARK TIMING (EST) SYSTEMS

#### ▶ See Figures 1 thru 15

The HEI/EST system operates in basically the same manner as the conventional points type ignition system, with the exception of the type of switching device used. A toothed iron timer core is mounted on the distributor shaft which rotates inside of an electronic pole piece. The pole piece has internal teeth (corresponding to those on the timer core) which contains a permanent magnet and pick-up coil (not to be confused with the ignition coil). The pole piece senses the magnetic field of the timer core teeth and sends a signal to the ignition module which electronically controls the primary coil voltage. The ignition coil operates in basically the same manner as a conventional ignition coil (though the ignition coils DO NOT interchange).

Some distributors use a Hall Effect device to act as the switching device. This type of distributor uses a slotted vane that passes between a magnet and the Hall Effect device to signal when to initiate a spark. The Hall Effect device is a solid state sensor that acts as a magnetic activated switch. The slots in the vane effectively change the magnetic field set up by the magnet, causing the Hall Effect device to switch on and off. This signal is sent to the ignition module and processed in the same way that the above mentioned pick-up coil type distributor does.

The 4.3L engines up to 1995 use a knock sensor to retard the timing when knock is sensed. The knock sensor is located on the block and it sends a signal to the Electronic Spark Control (ESC) module located on a bracket at the back of the engine. The ESC module in turn sends a signal to the ECM to retard the timing.

➡The HEI/EST systems uses a capacitor within the distributor which is primarily used for radio interference suppression purposes.

None of the electrical components used in the HEI systems are adjustable. If a component is found to be defective, it must be replaced.

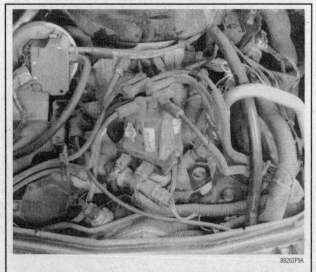

**Fig. 1 EST distributor at home nestled at the back of the 4.3L engine**

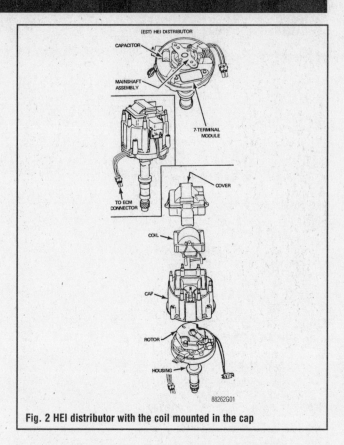

**Fig. 2 HEI distributor with the coil mounted in the cap**

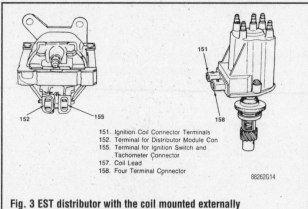

151. Ignition Coil Connector Terminals
152. Terminal for Distributor Module Con
155. Terminal for Ignition Switch and Tachometer Connector
157. Coil Lead
158. Four Terminal Connector

**Fig. 3 EST distributor with the coil mounted externally**

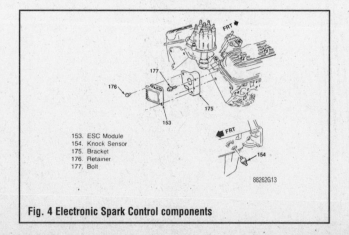

153. ESC Module
154. Knock Sensor
175. Bracket
176. Retainer
177. Bolt

**Fig. 4 Electronic Spark Control components**

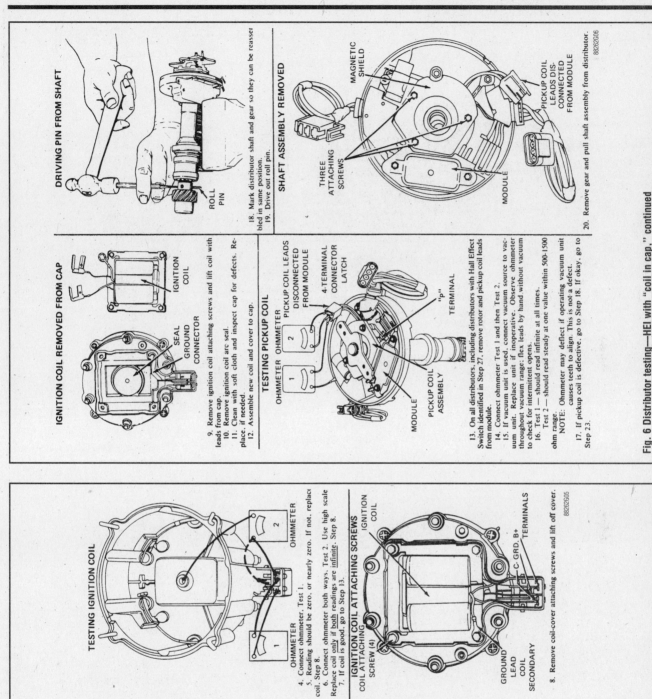

**DRIVING PIN FROM SHAFT**

ROLL PIN

18. Mark distributor shaft and gear so they can be reassembled in same position.
19. Drive out roll pin.

**SHAFT ASSEMBLY REMOVED**

MAGNETIC SHIELD

PICKUP COIL LEADS DISCONNECTED FROM MODULE

THREE ATTACHING SCREWS

MODULE

20. Remove gear and pull shaft assembly from distributor.

**IGNITION COIL REMOVED FROM CAP**

IGNITION COIL

SEAL

GROUND CONNECTOR

9. Remove ignition coil attaching screws and lift coil with leads from cap.
10. Remove ignition coil arc seal.
11. Clean with soft cloth and inspect cap for defects. Replace, if needed.
12. Assemble new coil and cover to cap.

**TESTING PICKUP COIL**

OHMMETER OHMMETER

PICKUP COIL LEADS DISCONNECTED FROM MODULE

4-TERMINAL CONNECTOR LATCH

"P" TERMINAL

MODULE

PICKUP COIL ASSEMBLY

13. On all distributors, including distributors with Hall Effect Switch identified in Step 27, remove rotor and pickup coil leads from module.
14. Connect ohmmeter Test 1 and then Test 2.
15. If vacuum unit is used, connect vacuum source to vacuum unit. Replace unit if inoperative. Observe ohmmeter throughout vacuum range; flex leads by hand without vacuum to check for intermittent opens.
16. Test 1 — should read infinite at all times.
    Test 2 — should read steady at one value within 500-1500 ohm range.
NOTE: Ohmmeter may deflect if operating vacuum unit causes teeth to align. This is not a defect.
17. If pickup coil is defective, go to Step 18. If okay, go to Step 23.

**Fig. 6 Distributor testing—HEI with "coil in cap," continued**

**TESTING IGNITION COIL**

OHMMETER

OHMMETER

4. Connect ohmmeter, Test 1.
5. Reading should be zero, or nearly zero. If not, replace coil. Step 8.
6. Connect ohmmeter both ways. Test 2. Use high scale. Replace coil only if both readings are infinite. Step 8.
7. If coil is good, go to Step 13.

**IGNITION COIL ATTACHING SCREWS**

COIL ATTACHING SCREW (4)

IGNITION COIL

C. GRD. B+ TERMINALS

GROUND LEAD COIL SECONDARY

8. Remove coil-cover attaching screws and lift off cover.

**"COIL IN CAP" DISTRIBUTOR**

TERMINALS C. B+

CONNECTOR (DISCONNECTED FROM CAP)

COIL AND CAP ASSEMBLY

LATCH (4)

4-TERMINAL CONNECTOR

1. A 6-cyl. EST distributor with coil-in-cap is illustrated.
2. Detach wiring connector from cap, as shown.
3. Turn four latches and remove cap and coil assembly from lower housing.

**Fig. 5 Distributor testing—HEI with "coil in cap"**

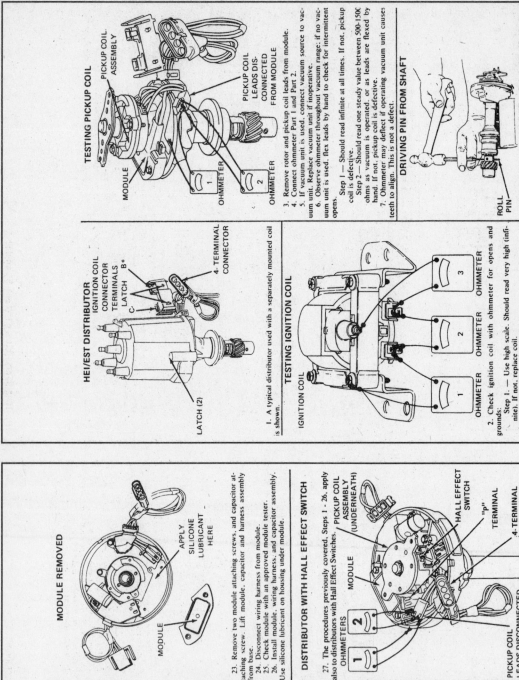

TESTING PICKUP COIL

PICKUP COIL ASSEMBLY

PICKUP COIL LEADS DISCONNECTED FROM MODULE

MODULE

OHMMETER 1

OHMMETER 2

3. Remove rotor and pickup coil leads from module.
4. Connect ohmmeter Part 1 and Part 2.
5. If vacuum unit is used, connect vacuum source to vacuum unit. Replace vacuum unit if inoperative.
6. Observe ohmmeter throughout vacuum range: if no vacuum unit is used, flex leads by hand to check for intermittent opens.

Step 1 — Should read infinite at all times. If not, pickup coil is defective.

Step 2 — Should read one steady value between 500-1500 ohms as vacuum is operated, or as leads are flexed by hand. If not, pickup coil is defective.

7. Ohmmeter may deflect if operating vacuum unit causes teeth to align. This is not a defect.

**DRIVING PIN FROM SHAFT**

ROLL PIN

8. If distributor has a Hall Effect Switch (identified in Step 12), remove this switch by detaching screws. Then drive roll pin from gear and remove shaft assembly. Mark gear and shaft for correct reassembly.

HEI/EST DISTRIBUTOR

IGNITION COIL CONNECTOR TERMINALS
LATCH B+
C

4 - TERMINAL CONNECTOR

LATCH (2)

1. A typical distributor used with a separately mounted coil is shown.

**TESTING IGNITION COIL**

IGNITION COIL

OHMMETER 1   OHMMETER 2   OHMMETER 3

2. Check ignition coil with ohmmeter for opens and grounds:

Step 1. — Use high scale. Should read very high (infinite). If not, replace coil.

Step 2. — Use low scale. Should read very low or zero. If not, replace coil.

Step 3. — Use high scale. Should not read infinite. If it does, replace coil.

**Fig. 8 Distributor testing—HEI with remote coil**

---

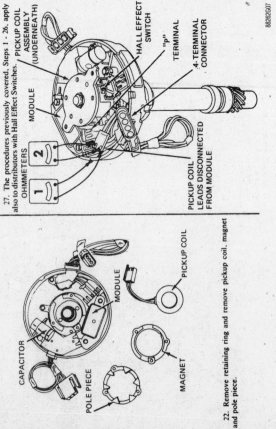

**MODULE REMOVED**

APPLY SILICONE LUBRICANT HERE

MODULE

23. Remove two module attaching screws, and capacitor attaching screw. Lift module, capacitor and harness assembly from base.
24. Disconnect wiring harness from module.
25. Check module with an approved module tester.
26. Install module, wiring harness, and capacitor assembly. Use silicone lubricant on housing under module.

**DISTRIBUTOR WITH HALL EFFECT SWITCH**

27. The procedures previously covered, Steps 1 - 26, apply also to distributors with Hall Effect Switches.

PICKUP COIL ASSEMBLY (UNDERNEATH)

HALL EFFECT SWITCH

"p"

TERMINAL

4-TERMINAL CONNECTOR

MODULE

OHMMETERS 1   2

PICKUP COIL LEADS DISCONNECTED FROM MODULE

**ALUMINUM NON-MAGNETIC SHIELD REMOVED**

PICKUP COIL ASSEMBLY

PICKUP COIL LEADS DISCONNECTED

MODULE

"C" WASHER

21. Remove three attaching screws and remove magnetic shield.

**PICKUP COIL REMOVED AND DISASSEMBLED**

CAPACITOR

POLE PIECE

MAGNET

MODULE

PICKUP COIL

22. Remove retaining ring and remove pickup coil, magnet and pole piece.

**Fig. 7 Distributor testing—HEI with "coil in cap," continued**

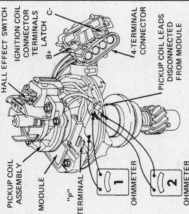

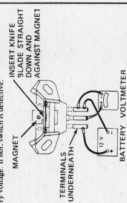

## IGNITION SYSTEM CHECK
### (REMOTE COIL) 2.5L TRUCK

**Test Description:** Numbers below refer to circled numbers on the diagnostic chart.

1. Two wires are checked, to ensure that an open is not present in a spark plug wire.

1A. If spark occurs with 4 terminal distributor connector disconnected, pick-up coil output is too low for EST operation.

2. A spark indicates the problem must be the distributor cap or rotor.

3. Normally, there should be battery voltage at the "C" and "+" terminals. Low voltage would indicate an open or a high resistance circuit from the distributor to the coil or ignition switch. If "C" terminal voltage was low, but "+" terminal voltage is 10 volts or more, circuit from "C" terminal to ignition coil or ignition coil primary winding is open.

4. Checks for a shorted module or grounded circuit from the ignition coil to the module. The dist. module should be turned "OFF," so normal voltage should be about 12 volts.
If the module is turned "ON," the voltage would be low, but above 1 volt. This could cause the ignition coil to fail from excessive heat.
With an open ignition coil primary winding, a small amount of voltage will leak through the module from the "Bat." to the "tach" terminal.

5. Applying a voltage (1.5 to 8 volts) to module terminal "P" should turn the module "ON" and the "Tach." terminal voltage should drop to about 7-9 volts. This test will determine whether the module or coil is faulty or if the pick-up coil is not generating the proper signal to turn the module "ON." This test can be performed by using a DC battery with a rating of 1.5 to 8 volts. The use of the test light is mainly to allow the "P" terminal to be probed more easily.
Some digital multi-meters can also be used to trigger the module by selecting ohms, usually the diode position. In this position, the meter may have a voltage across its terminals which can be used to trigger the module. The voltage in the ohm's position can be checked by using a second meter or by checking the manufacture's specification of the tool being used.

6. This should turn "OFF," the module and cause a spark. If no spark occurs, the fault is most likely in the ignition coil because most module problems would have been found before this point in the procedure. A module tester (J 24642) could determine which is at fault.

### Diagnostic Aids:

The "Scan" tool does not have any ability to help diagnose a ignition system check.

**Fig. 10 Ignition system check—2.5L engine**

88262C37

---

### DISTRIBUTOR WITH HALL EFFECT SWITCH

12. If distributor has a Hall Effect Switch, this switch was removed in Step 8.

13. The procedures previously covered, Steps 1-11, apply also to distributors with Hall Effect Switches.

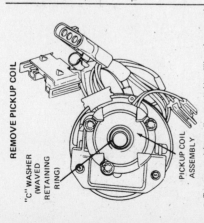

### REMOVE PICKUP COIL

9. To remove pickup coil, remove thin "C" washer (waved retaining ring).

### DISTRIBUTOR WITH PICKUP COIL REMOVED

10. Lift pickup coil assembly straight up to remove from distributor.

11. Disconnect wiring connectors from module. Remove two screws to remove module. Test module with an approved module tester.

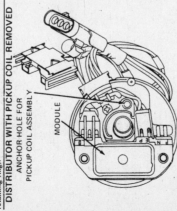

### TESTING HALL EFFECT SWITCH

14. Connect 12-volt battery and voltmeter to switch; carefully note polarity markings.

15. Without knife blade, voltmeter should read less than 0.5 volts. If not, switch is defective.

16. With knife blade, voltmeter should read within 0.5 volts of battery voltage. If not, switch is defective.

### REASSEMBLY

17. Wipe distributor base and module clean, apply silicone lubricant between module and base for heat dissipation.

18. Attach module to base. Attach wiring connectors to module.

19. Assemble pickup and thin "C" washer.

20. Assemble shaft, gear parts and roll pin.

21. If used, assemble Hall Effect Switch.

22. Spin shaft to insure that teeth do not touch.

23. Loosen, then re-tighten pickup coil teeth and Hall Effect Switch teeth, if used, to eliminate contact.

24. Install rotor and cap.

88262G09

**Fig. 9 Distributor testing—HEI with remote coil, continued**

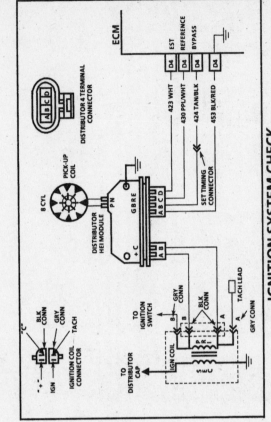

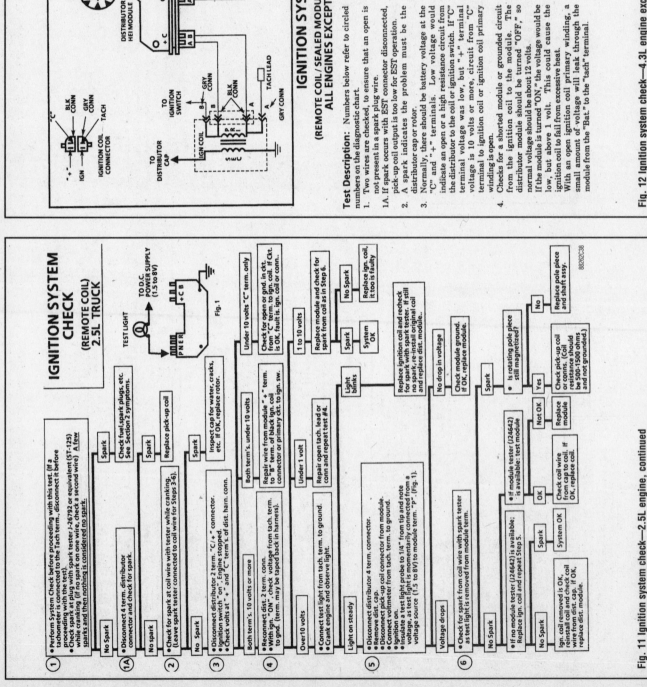

## IGNITION SYSTEM CHECK

### (REMOTE COIL / SEALED MODULE CONNECTOR DISTRIBUTOR) ALL ENGINES EXCEPT 2.5L TRUCK

**Test Description:** Numbers below refer to circled numbers on the diagnostic chart.

1. Two wires are checked, to ensure that an open is not present in a spark plug wire.

1A. If spark occurs with EST connector disconnected, pick-up coil output is too low for EST operation.

2. A spark indicates the problem must be the distributor cap or rotor.

3. Normally, there should be battery voltage at the "C" and "+" terminals. Low voltage would indicate an open or a high resistance circuit from the distributor to the coil or ignition switch. If "C" terminal voltage was low, but "+" terminal voltage is 10 volts or more, circuit from "C" terminal to ignition coil or ignition coil primary winding is open.

4. Checks for a shorted module or grounded circuit from the ignition coil to the module. The distributor module should be turned "OFF," so normal voltage should be about 12 volts. If the module is turned "ON," the voltage would be low, but above 1 volt. This could cause the ignition coil to fail from excessive heat. With an open ignition coil primary winding, a small amount of voltage will leak through the module from the "Bat." to the "tach" terminal.

5. Applying a voltage (1.5 to 8 volts) to module terminal "P" should turn the module "ON" and the "tach" terminal voltage should drop to about 7-9 volts. This test will determine whether the module or coil is faulty or if the pick-up coil is not generating the proper signal to turn the module "ON." This test can be performed by using a DC battery with a rating of 1.5 to 8 volts. The use of the test light is mainly to allow the "P" terminal to be probed more easily. Some digital multi-meters can also be used to trigger the module by selecting ohms, usually the diode position. In this position the meter may have a voltage across it's terminals which can be used to trigger the module. The voltage in the ohm's position can be checked by using a second meter or by checking the manufacturer's specification of the tool being used.

6. This should turn "OFF" the module and cause a spark. If no spark occurs, the fault is most likely in the ignition coil because most module problems would have been found before this point in the procedure. A module tester could determine which is at fault.

Fig. 12 Ignition system check—4.3L engine except with HVS

88262C39

Fig. 11 Ignition system check—2.5L engine, continued

88262C38

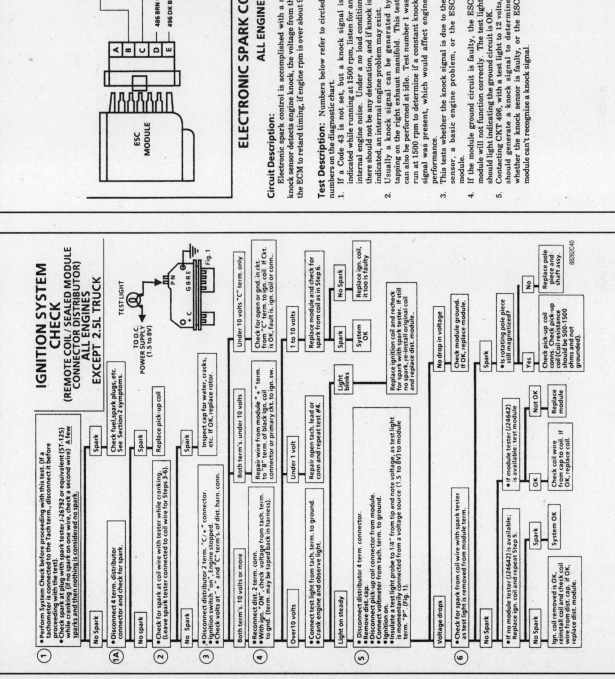

## ELECTRONIC SPARK CONTROL SYSTEM CHECK

### ALL ENGINES EXCEPT 2.5L

**Circuit Description:**

Electronic spark control is accomplished with a module that sends a voltage signal to the ECM. As the knock sensor detects engine knock, the voltage from the ESC module to the ECM is shut "OFF" and this signals the ECM to retard timing, if engine rpm is over about 900.

**Test Description:** Numbers below refer to circled numbers on the diagnostic chart.

1. If a Code 43 is not set, but a knock signal is indicated while running at 1500 rpm, listen for an internal engine noise. Under a no load condition there should not be any detonation, and if knock is indicated, an internal engine problem may exist.

2. Usually a knock signal can be generated by tapping on the right exhaust manifold. This test can also be performed at idle. Test number 1 was run at 1500 rpm to determine if a constant knock signal was present, which would affect engine performance.

3. This tests whether the knock signal is due to the sensor, a basic engine problem, or the ESC module.

4. If the module ground circuit is faulty, the ESC module will not function correctly. The test light should light indicating the ground circuit is OK.

5. Contacting CKT 496, with a test light to 12 volts, should generate a knock signal to determine whether the knock sensor is faulty, or the ESC module can't recognize a knock signal.

**Diagnostic Aids:**

"Scan" tools may be used to diagnose the ESC system. The knock signal can be monitored to see if the knock sensor is detecting a knock condition and if the ESC module is functioning, knock signal should display "YES," whenever detonation is present. For 2.5L engines, the knock retard position on the "Scan" displays the amount of spark retard the ECM is commanding. The ECM can retard the timing up to 20 degrees.

This check should be used after other causes of spark knock have been checked such as engine timing, EGR systems, engine temperature or excessive engine noise.

Fig. 14 Ignition system check—4.3L engine except with HVS, continued

---

## IGNITION SYSTEM CHECK

### (REMOTE COIL / SEALED MODULE CONNECTOR DISTRIBUTOR) ALL ENGINES EXCEPT 2.5L TRUCK

Fig. 13 Ignition system check—4.3L engine except with HVS, continued

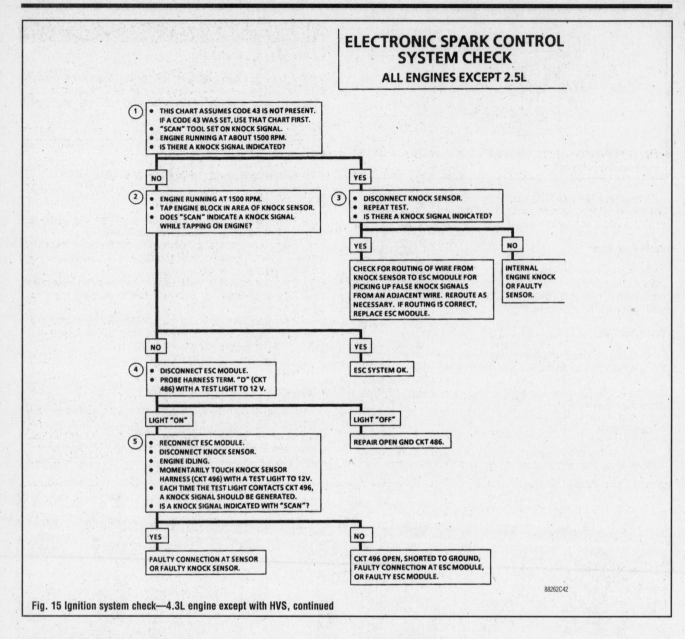

Fig. 15 Ignition system check—4.3L engine except with HVS, continued

## HIGH VOLTAGE SWITCH (HVS) SYSTEM

### ◆ See Figures 16 and 17

The High Voltage Switch (HVS) system is the highest evolution in distributor based ignition systems. The only purpose the distributor has in the systems is to distribute the spark to the cylinders. It contains no ignition pickup coils, no ignition high voltage coils, no weights or springs, nor does it contain any ignition modules. It does contain a camshaft position sensor, but that sensor does not effect the operation of the vehicle. The camshaft position sensor is utilized to determine which cylinder is misfiring, under misfire conditions. The Powertrain Control Module (PCM) controls the ignition coil based on inputs from the various engine sensors. It sends a signal to the Ignition Control Module which uses the low voltage control signal (approximately 4 volts) to ground the ignition coil, thus completing the circuit. When the ICM switches off, the ignition coil fires. The ICM module is attached to the same bracket as the ignition coil.

## PRECAUTIONS

Before troubleshooting the systems, it might be a good idea to take note of the following precautions:

### Timing Light Use

Inductive pick-up timing lights are the best kind to use. Timing lights which connect between the spark plug and the spark plug wire occasionally give false readings.

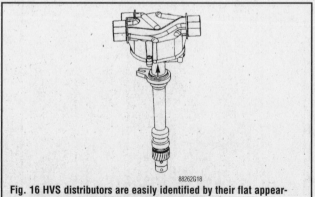

Fig. 16 HVS distributors are easily identified by their flat appearance and side mounted ignition wire towers

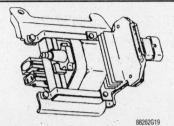

**Fig. 17 HVS ignition systems have the ICM module mounted to the same bracket as the coil**

Some engines incorporate a magnetic timing probe terminal (at the damper pulley) for use of special electronic timing equipment. Refer to the manufacturer's instructions when using this equipment.

### Spark Plug Wires

The plug wires are of a different construction than conventional wires. When replacing them, make sure to use the correct wires, since conventional wires won't carry the higher voltage. Also, handle them carefully to avoid cracking or splitting them and never pierce them.

### Tachometer Use

Not all tachometers will operate or indicate correctly. While some tachometers may give a reading, this does not necessarily mean the reading is correct. In addition, some tachometers connect differently than others. If you can't figure out whether or not your tachometer will work on your vehicle, check with the tachometer manufacturer.

### System Testers

Instruments designed specifically for testing the HEI system are available from several tool manufacturers. Some of these will even test the module.

## Ignition Coil

▶ **See Figures 18, 19 and 20**

The ignition coil on the 2.5L engine, is located on the right rear side of the engine; on the 4.3L (1985) engine, it is located in the top of the distributor cap; on the 1986 and later 4.3L engine, it is located on intake manifold to the right side of the engine.

### TESTING

▶ **See Figures 21 and 22**

➡ **The following procedures require the use of an ohmmeter.**

#### 2.5L Engine

For this procedure, the ignition coil may be removed from the engine or simply remove the electrical connectors and test it on the engine.

1. Using an ohmmeter (on the high scale), connect the probes between the primary (low-voltage) terminal and coil ground; the reading should be very high or infinity, if not, replace the coil.
2. Using an ohmmeter (on the low scale), connect the probes between both primary (low voltage) terminals; the reading should be very low or zero, if not, replace the coil.
3. Using an ohmmeter (on the high scale), connect the probes between a primary (low voltage) terminal and the secondary (high voltage) terminal; the reading should be high (not infinite), if not, replace the coil.

#### 4.3L Engine

*CARBURETED*

To test the ignition coil, the distributor cap must be removed from the distributor.

1. Remove the electrical connector from the distributor cap and the distributor cap from the distributor. Place the distributor cap on a workbench in the inverted position.

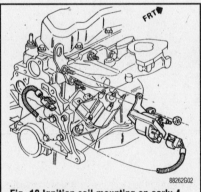

**Fig. 18 Ignition coil mounting on early 4-cylinder engines**

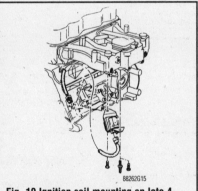

**Fig. 19 Ignition coil mounting on late 4-cylinder engines**

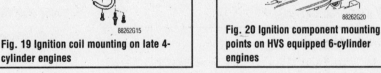

**Fig. 20 Ignition component mounting points on HVS equipped 6-cylinder engines**

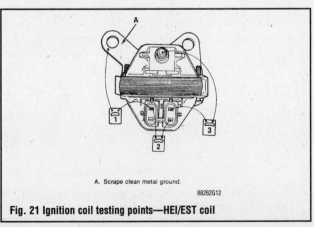

A. Scrape clean metal ground.

**Fig. 21 Ignition coil testing points—HEI/EST coil**

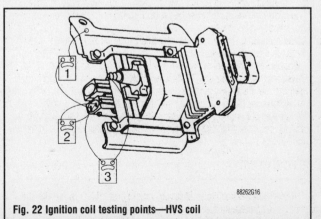

**Fig. 22 Ignition coil testing points—HVS coil**

2. Using an ohmmeter (on the low scale), connect the probes between the primary (low voltage) terminals; the reading should be low or nearly zero, if not, replace the coil.

3. Using an ohmmeter (on the high scale), connect the probes between a primary (low voltage) terminal and the secondary (center terminal or high voltage) terminal; the reading should be high (not infinite), if not, replace the coil.

### FUEL INJECTED

For this procedure, the ignition coil may be removed from the engine or simply remove the electrical connectors and test it on the engine.

1. Using an ohmmeter (on the high scale), connect the probes between the primary (low voltage) terminal and coil ground; the reading should be very high or infinity, if not, replace the coil.

2. Using an ohmmeter (on the low scale), connect the probes between both primary (low voltage) terminals; the reading should be very low or zero, if not, replace the coil.

3. Using an ohmmeter (on the high scale), connect the probes between a primary (low voltage) terminal and the secondary (high voltage) terminal; the reading should be high (not infinite), if not, replace the coil.

### REMOVAL & INSTALLATION

▶ **See Figures 23, 24, 25, 26 and 27**

#### 2.5L Engine

The ignition coil is located near the cylinder head at the right rear side of the engine. The coil is located under the intake manifold on the later model 2.5L engines.

1. Disconnect the negative battery terminal and remove the console cover.
2. At the ignition coil, disconnect the ignition switch-to-coil wire and the distributor-to-coil wires.
3. Remove the coil-to-engine nuts/bolts and the coil from the engine.
4. If necessary, test or replace the ignition coil.
5. To install, mount the coil onto the engine, torque the nuts to 20 ft. lbs. (27 Nm) and reconnect all coil and battery connectors.

#### 4.3L Engine

##### CARBURETED

The ignition coil is located in the top of the distributor which is positioned at the top rear of the engine.

1. Disconnect the negative battery terminal and remove the console cover from inside the vehicle.
2. At the ignition coil, on top of the distributor, disconnect the electrical connector and remove the spark plug wire retainer.
3. Remove the coil cover-to-distributor cap screws and the cover. Mark the coil terminals for installation purposes.
4. Remove the coil-to-distributor cap screws and the coil from the cap.
5. If necessary, test or replace the coil.
6. To install, position the high tension button and seal and coil into the cap.
7. Insert the terminals into the proper cap locations. Install the coil cover and spark plug retainer. Reconnect the coil and battery terminals.

##### FUEL INJECTED

The ignition coil is located, on top of the intake manifold, next to the distributor or midway along the valve cover.

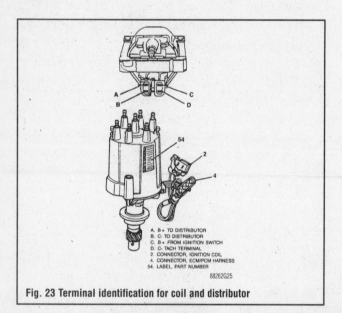

A. B+ TO DISTRIBUTOR
B. C- TO DISTRIBUTOR
C. B+ FROM IGNITION SWITCH
D. C- TACH TERMINAL
2. CONNECTOR, IGNITION COIL
4. CONNECTOR, ECM/PCM HARNESS
54. LABEL, PART NUMBER

88262G25

**Fig. 23 Terminal identification for coil and distributor**

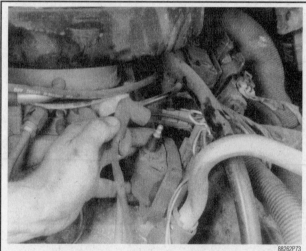

88262P73

**Fig. 24 Always pull on the boot to remove the ignition wires, never the wire itself**

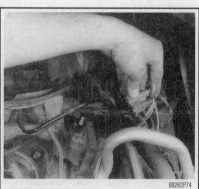

88262P74

**Fig. 25 Depress the tabs to release the connector from the coil**

88262P75

**Fig. 26 The coil will be mounted to the manifold directly or to a bracket which is bolted to the manifold**

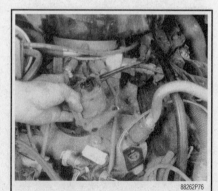

88262P76

**Fig. 27 Check the coil for cracks and other signs of damage before installation**

1. Disconnect the negative battery terminal and remove the console cover inside the vehicle.

2. Disconnect the engine control switch and tachometer terminals from the ignition coil.

3. Disconnect the ignition coil-to-distributor lead wire from the coil.

4. Remove the coil bracket/coil assembly-to-engine bracket nuts and the assembly from the engine.

5. If necessary, test or replace the coil.

6. If necessary to remove the coil from the bracket, perform the following procedures:
   a. Using a drill, drill out the coil-to-bracket rivets.
   b. Using a center punch, drive the rivets from the coil-to-bracket assembly.
   c. Remove the coil from the coil bracket.

7. **To install,** place the coil on the bracket with two screws, position the coil on the engine and torque the nuts to 20 ft. lbs. (27 Nm).

8. Connect the coil connectors and negative battery cable. Install the console cover.

## Ignition Module

The ignition module on the 2.5L and non-HVS 4.3L engine is located inside the distributor; it may be replaced without removing the distributor from the engine. The ignition control module (ICM) on 1995 and later VIN W 4.3L engines is just an electronic switch and does no controlling of the ignition system. It is attached to the ignition coil bracket.

### REMOVAL & INSTALLATION

#### 1985–94 (non-HVS) Engines

▶ See Figures 28, 29, 30 and 31

1. Disconnect the negative battery terminal and remove the console cover.
2. Remove the distributor cap and the rotor.
3. If the flange, of the distributor shaft is positioned above the module, place a socket on the crankshaft pulley bolt and rotate the crankshaft (turning the distributor shaft) to provide clearance to the ignition module.
4. Remove the ignition module-to-distributor bolts, lift the module and disconnect the electrical connectors from it.
5. If the module is suspected as being defective, take it to a module testing machine and have it tested.

➡When replacing the module, be sure to coat the module-to-distributor surface with silicone lubricant (dielectric compound) that will provide heat dissipation.

6. **To install,** apply silicone heat sink compound to the module mounting area of the distributor. Install the rotor, the distributor cap and connect the negative battery cable.

#### 1995–96 (HVS) Engines

1. Disconnect the negative battery terminal and remove the console cover inside the vehicle.

2. Disconnect the engine control switch and tachometer terminals from the ignition coil and module.

3. Disconnect the ignition coil-to-distributor lead wire from the coil.

4. Remove the coil bracket/module assembly-to-engine bracket nuts and lift the assembly from the engine.

5. If necessary to remove the module from the bracket, perform the following procedures:
   a. Using a drill, drill out the module-to-bracket rivets.
   b. Using a center punch, drive the rivets from the module-to-bracket assembly.
   c. Remove the module from the coil bracket.

6. **To install,** place the module on the bracket with two screws, position the coil on the engine and torque the nuts to 20 ft. lbs. (27 Nm).

7. Connect the coil connectors and negative battery cable. Install the console cover.

## Pickup Coil

▶ See Figure 32

### TESTING

1. With the ignition key **OFF**, remove the console cover, distributor cap, rotor and disconnect the pickup coil-to-module wire harness.

2. Connect an ohmmeter from the distributor housing to one pickup lead. The reading should be infinite at all times.

3. Connect an ohmmeter to both pickup coil wire terminals. The reading should be steady at one value within 500–1500 ohms. If not replace the pickup coil.

### REMOVAL & INSTALLATION

▶ See Figures 33, 34, 35 and 36

1. Disconnect the negative battery cable.

2. Remove the distributor cap and rotor. Do NOT remove the spark plug wires from the cap.

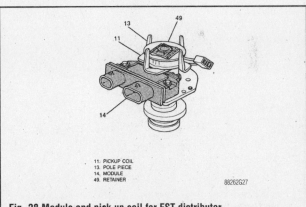

11. PICKUP COIL
13. POLE PIECE
14. MODULE
49. RETAINER

88262G27

**Fig. 28 Module and pick-up coil for EST distributor**

**Fig. 29 The module easily unbolts without disassembling the distributor on EST equipped engines**

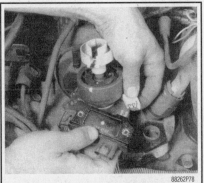

**Fig. 30 Unplug the internal connections before trying to remove the module**

**Fig. 31 Heat sink grease must be applied when installing the module or it may fail due to overheating**

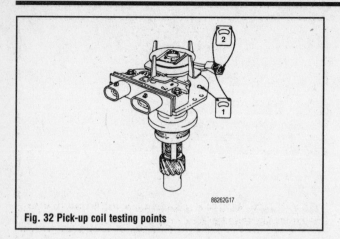

Fig. 32 Pick-up coil testing points

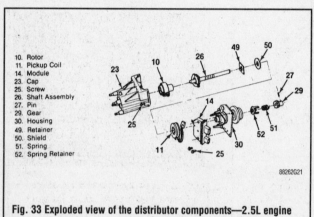

10. Rotor
11. Pickup Coil
14. Module
23. Cap
25. Screw
26. Shaft Assembly
27. Pin
29. Gear
30. Housing
49. Retainer
50. Shield
51. Spring
52. Spring Retainer

Fig. 33 Exploded view of the distributor components—2.5L engine

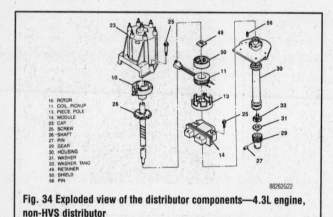

10. ROTOR
11. COIL, PICKUP
13. PIECE, POLE
14. MODULE
23. CAP
25. SCREW
26. SHAFT
27. PIN
29. GEAR
30. HOUSING
31. WASHER
33. WASHER, TANG
49. RETAINER
50. SHIELD
56. PIN

Fig. 34 Exploded view of the distributor components—4.3L engine, non-HVS distributor

3. Mark the distributor housing, position of rotor and relationship from the distributor housing-to-engine block for installation purposes.

4. Remove the distributor clamp and remove the distributor from the engine.

5. Place the distributor in a vise and mark the distributor shaft and gear so they can be reassembled in the same position.

6. Drive out the roll pin and remove the gear and shaft from the distributor. Remove the retainer clip by cutting it off.

7. Remove the attaching screws, magnetic shield, retaining ring, pickup coil and pole piece.

**To install:**

8. Install the pole piece, pickup coil, retaining ring, magnetic shield and retaining screws. Install a new retainer clip using a socket as a driver.

9. Install the gear and shaft to the distributor. Drive in the roll pin.

10. Install the distributor and clamp to the marked position.

11. Install the distributor cap and rotor.

12. Connect the negative battery cable, then adjust the timing.

## Distributor

### REMOVAL & INSTALLATION

◆ **See Figures 37 thru 48**

1. Disconnect the negative battery cable and remove the console cover.

2. Tag and disconnect the distributor electrical connector(s).

3. Remove the distributor cap (DO NOT remove the spark plug wires) from the distributor and move it aside.

4. Using a crayon or chalk, make locating marks (for installation purposes) on the rotor, the ignition module, the distributor housing and the engine block.

5. Loosen and remove the distributor clamp bolt and clamp, then lift the distributor from the engine.

➡**Noting the relative position of the rotor and the module alignment marks, make a second mark on the rotor to align it with the one mark on the module.**

6. Refer to the proper installation procedure for your vehicle, depending upon if the engine was rotated or not.

#### Engine Not Rotated

This procedure applies if the engine has not been rotated with the distributor removed.

1. Install a new O-ring on the distributor housing.

2. Align the second mark on the rotor with the mark on the module, then install the distributor, taking care to align the mark on the housing with the one on the engine.

➡**It may be necessary to lift the distributor and turn the rotor slightly to align the gears and the oil pump driveshaft. The crankshaft may have to moved very slightly to engage the oil pump driveshaft with the distributor. Do NOT force the distributor into the engine with the distributor clamp.**

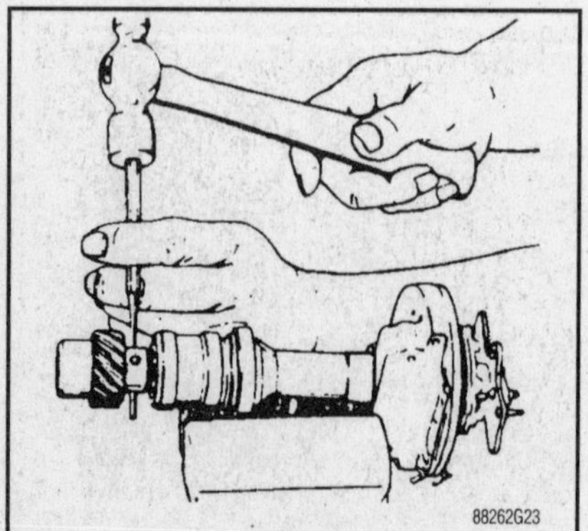

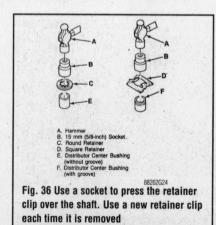

A. Hammer
B. 15 mm (5/8-inch) Socket
C. Round Retainer
D. Square Retainer
E. Distributor Center Bushing (without groove)
F. Distributor Center Bushing (with groove)

Fig. 36 Use a socket to press the retainer clip over the shaft. Use a new retainer clip each time it is removed

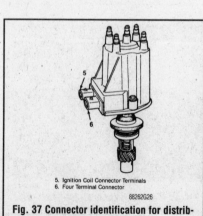

5. Ignition Coil Connector Terminals
6. Four Terminal Connector

Fig. 37 Connector identification for distributor—2.5L engine

Fig. 35 Support the distributor shaft while driving out the roll pin

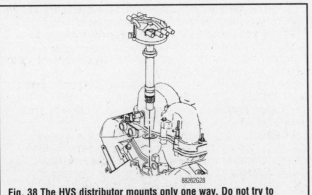

Fig. 38 The HVS distributor mounts only one way. Do not try to rotate the distributor to change the timing

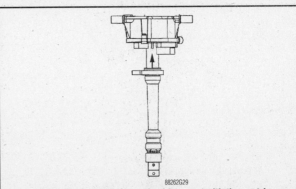

Fig. 39 Align the indent hole on the drive gear with the cast-in arrow before installation on the HVS distributor

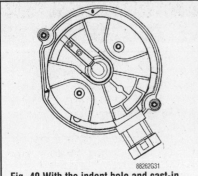

Fig. 40 With the indent hole and cast-in arrow aligned, the rotor should point in this direction

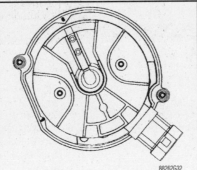

Fig. 41 With the HVS distributor properly aligned and installed, the rotor should point to the mark

Fig. 42 Tag all the ignition wires before removing them from the cap or the spark plugs

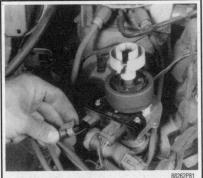

Fig. 43 Disconnect the harnesses from the module

Fig. 44 Mark the alignment of the rotor before removing the distributor

Fig. 45 Mark the distributor base-to-block alignment before removing the distributor

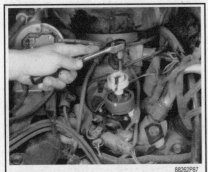

Fig. 46 The distributor hold-down bolt must be removed to be able to draw out the distributor

Fig. 47 Depending on the hold-down's shape, there may be a correct orientation, so note how it is mounted

Fig. 48 Draw the distributor body straight up and out

3. With the respective marks aligned, install the clamp and bolt finger tight.

4. Install and secure the distributor cap.

5. Connect the electrical connector(s) to the distributor.

6. Connect a timing light to the engine (following the manufacturer's instructions). Start the engine, then check and/or adjust the timing.

7. Turn the engine **OFF**, tighten the distributor clamp bolt and remove the timing light.

### Engine Rotated

This procedure applies when the engine has been rotated with the distributor removed.

1. Install a new O-ring on the distributor housing.

2. Rotate the crankshaft to position the No. 1 cylinder on the TDC of compression stroke. This may be determined by inserting a rag into the No. 1 spark plug hole and slowly turning the engine crankshaft. When the timing mark on the crankshaft pulley aligns with the **0** mark on the timing scale and the rag is blown out by the compression, the No. 1 piston is at top-dead-center (TDC).

3. Turn the rotor so that it will point to the No. 1 terminal of the distributor cap.

4. Install the distributor into the engine block. It may be necessary to turn the rotor, a little in either direction, in order to engage the gears.

5. Tap the starter a few times to ensure that the oil pump shaft is mated to the distributor shaft.

6. Bring the engine to No. 1 TDC again and check to see that the rotor is indeed pointing toward the No. 1 terminal of the cap.

7. With the respective marks aligned, install the clamp and bolt finger tight.

8. Install and secure the distributor cap.

9. Connect the distributor electrical connector(s).

10. Connect a timing light to the engine (following the manufacturer's instructions). Start the engine, then check and/or adjust the timing.

11. Turn the engine **OFF**, tighten the distributor clamp bolt and remove the timing light.

### Crankshaft and Camshaft Position Sensors

Refer to Section 5 for information on the crankshaft and camshaft sensors.

## FIRING ORDERS

◆ **See Figures 49 thru 56**

➡ **To avoid confusion, remove and tag the spark plug wires one at a time, for replacement.**

If a distributor is not keyed for installation with only one orientation, it could have been removed previously and rewired. The resultant wiring would hold the correct firing order, but could change the relative placement of the plug towers in relation to the engine. For this reason it is imperative that you label all wires before disconnecting any of them. Also, before removal, compare the current wiring with the accompanying illustrations. If the current wiring does not match, make notes in your book to reflect how your engine is wired.

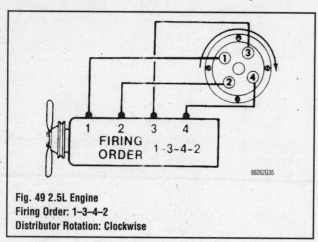

**Fig. 49 2.5L Engine**
**Firing Order: 1–3–4–2**
**Distributor Rotation: Clockwise**

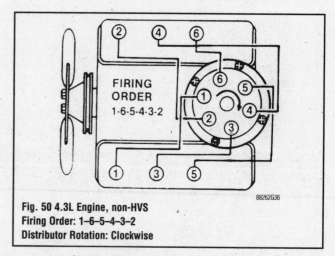

**Fig. 50 4.3L Engine, non-HVS**
**Firing Order: 1–6–5–4–3–2**
**Distributor Rotation: Clockwise**

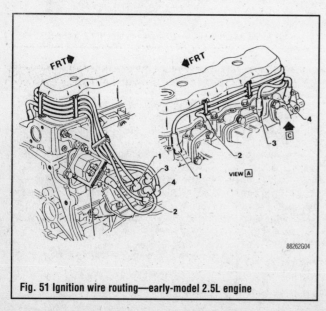

**Fig. 51 Ignition wire routing—early-model 2.5L engine**

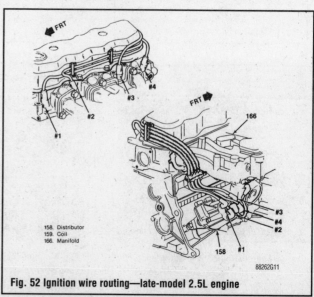

158. Distributor
159. Coil
166. Manifold

**Fig. 52 Ignition wire routing—late-model 2.5L engine**

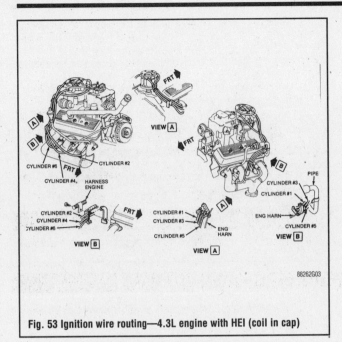

Fig. 53 Ignition wire routing—4.3L engine with HEI (coil in cap)

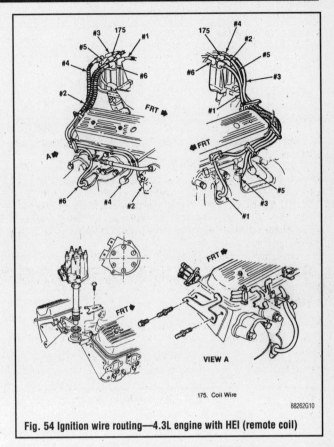

175. Coil Wire

Fig. 54 Ignition wire routing—4.3L engine with HEI (remote coil)

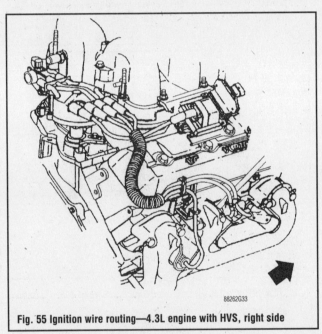

Fig. 55 Ignition wire routing—4.3L engine with HVS, right side

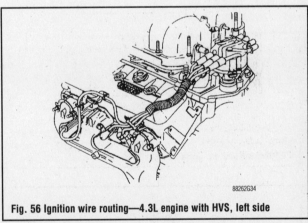

Fig. 56 Ignition wire routing—4.3L engine with HVS, left side

## CHARGING SYSTEM

## Alternator

▶ See Figures 57 and 58

The alternator charging system is a negative ground system which consists of an alternator, a regulator, a charge indicator, a storage battery and wiring connecting the components, and fuse link wire.

### ALTERNATOR PRECAUTIONS

Observing these precautions will ensure safe handling of the electrical system components and will avoid damage to the vehicle's electrical system:

1. Be absolutely sure of the polarity of a booster battery before making connections. Connect the cables positive-to-positive and negative-to-negative. If jump starting, connect the positive cables first and the last connection to a ground on the body of the booster vehicle, so that arcing cannot ignite the hydrogen gas that may have accumulated near the battery. Even a momentary connection of a booster battery with polarity reversed may damage the alternator diodes.

2. Disconnect both vehicle battery cables before attempting to charge the battery.

3. Never ground the alternator output or battery terminal. Be cautious when using metal tools around a battery to avoid creating a short circuit between the terminals.

4. Never run an alternator without a load unless the field circuit (1985) is disconnected.

5. Never attempt to polarize an alternator.

6. Never disconnect any electrical components with the ignition switch turned **ON**.

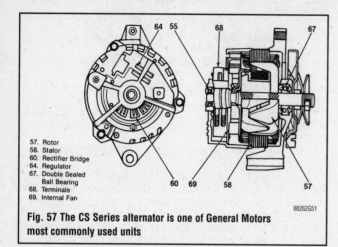

57. Rotor
58. Stator
60. Rectifier Bridge
64. Regulator
67. Double Sealed
    Ball Bearing
68. Terminals
69. Internal Fan

88262G51

**Fig. 57 The CS Series alternator is one of General Motors most commonly used units**

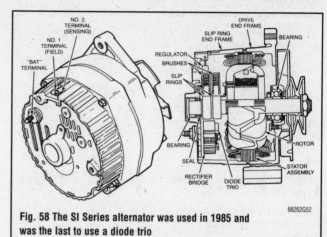

88262G52

**Fig. 58 The SI Series alternator was used in 1985 and was the last to use a diode trio**

## CHARGING SYSTEM TROUBLESHOOTING

♦ **See Figure 59**

There are many possible ways in which the charging system can malfunction. Often the source of a problem is difficult to diagnose, requiring special equipment and a good deal of experience. This is usually not the case, however, where the charging system fails completely and causes the dash board warning light to come on or the battery to become dead. To troubleshoot a complete system failure, only two pieces of equipment are needed: a test light, to determine that current is reaching a certain point; and a current indicator (ammeter), to determine the direction of the current flow and its measurement in amps.

This test works under three assumptions:

1. The battery is known to be good and fully charged.
2. The alternator belt is in good condition and adjusted to the proper tension.
3. All connections in the system are clean and tight.

➥**In order for the current indicator to give a valid reading, the truck must be equipped with battery cables which are of the same gauge size and quality as original equipment battery cables.**

4. Turn off all electrical components on the truck.
5. Make sure the doors of the truck are closed.
6. If the truck is equipped with a clock, disconnect the clock by removing the lead wire from the rear of the clock.
7. Disconnect the positive battery cable from the battery and connect the ground wire on a test light to the disconnected positive battery cable.
8. Touch the probe end of the test light to the positive battery post. The test light should not light. If the test light does light, there is a short or open circuit on the truck.

9. Disconnect the voltage regulator wiring harness connector at the voltage regulator.
10. Turn on the ignition key.
11. Connect the wire on a test light to a good ground (engine bolt).
12. Touch the probe end of a test light to the ignition wire connector into the voltage regulator wiring connector. This wire corresponds to the **I** terminal on the regulator. If the test light goes on, the charging system warning light circuit is complete. If the test light does not come on and the warning light on the instrument panel is on, either the resistor wire, which is parallel with the warning light, or the wiring to the voltage regulator, is defective. If the test light does not come on and the warning light is not on, either the bulb is defective or the power supply wire form the battery through the ignition switch to the bulb has an open circuit. Connect the wiring harness to the regulator.
13. Examine the fuse link wire in the wiring harness from the starter relay to the alternator. If the insulation on the wire is cracked or split, the fuse link may be melted.
14. Connect a test light to the fuse link by attaching the ground wire on the test light to an engine bolt and touching the probe end of the light to the bottom of the fuse link wire where it splices into the alternator output wire. If the bulb in the test light does not light, the fuse link is melted.
15. Start the engine and place a current indicator on the positive battery cable.
16. Turn off all electrical accessories and make sure the doors are closed. If the charging system is working properly, the gauge will show a draw of less than 5 amps. If the system is not working properly, the gauge will show a draw of more than 5 amps. A charge moves the needle toward the battery, a draw moves the needle away from the battery. Turn the engine off.
17. Disconnect the wiring harness from the voltage regulator at the regulator at the regulator connector.
18. Connect a male spade terminal (solderless connector) to each end of a jumper wire.
19. Insert one end of the wire into the wiring harness connector which corresponds to the **A** terminal on the regulator.
20. Insert the other end of the wire into the wiring harness connector which corresponds to the **F** terminal on the regulator.
21. Position the connector with the jumper wire installed so that it cannot contact any metal surface under the hood.
22. Position a current indicator gauge on the positive battery cable. Have an assistant start the engine. Observe the reading on the current indicator. Have your assistant slowly raise the speed of the engine to about 2,000 rpm or until the current indicator needle stops moving, whichever comes first. Do not run the engine for more than a short period of time in this condition. If the wiring harness connector or jumper wire becomes excessively hot during this test, turn off the engine and check for a grounded wire in the regulator wiring harness. If the current indicator shows a charge of about three amps less than the output of the alternator, the alternator is working properly. If the previous tests showed a draw, the voltage regulator is defective. If the gauge does not show the proper charging rate, the alternator is defective.

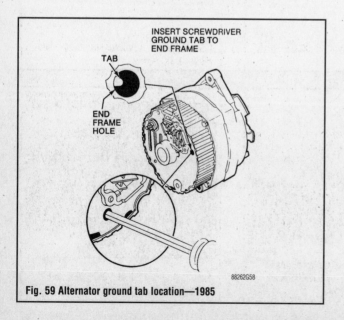

INSERT SCREWDRIVER
GROUND TAB TO
END FRAME

TAB

END
FRAME
HOLE

88262G58

**Fig. 59 Alternator ground tab location—1985**

## PRELIMINARY CHARGING SYSTEM TESTS

1. If you suspect a defect in your charging system, first perform these general checks before going on to more specific tests.
2. Check the condition of the alternator belt and tighten it if necessary.
3. Clean the battery cable connections at the battery. Make sure the connections between the battery wires and the battery clamps are good. Reconnect the negative terminal only and proceed to the next step.
4. With the key off, insert a test light between the positive terminal on the battery and the disconnected positive battery terminal clamp. If the test light comes on, there is a short in the electrical system of the truck. The short must be repaired before proceeding. If the light does not come on, proceed to the next step.

➡ **If the truck is equipped with an electric clock, the clock must be disconnected.**

5. Check the charging system wiring for any obvious breaks or shorts.
6. Check the battery to make sure it is fully charged and in good condition.

## CHARGING SYSTEM OPERATIONAL TEST

➡ **You will need a current indicator to perform this test. If the current indicator is to give an accurate reading, the battery cables must be the same gauge and length as the original equipment.**

1. With the engine running and all electrical systems turned off, place a current indicator over the positive battery cable.
2. If a charge of roughly 5 amps is recorded, the charging system is working. If a draw of about 5 amps is recorded, the system is not working. The needle moves toward the battery when a charge condition is indicated, and away from the battery when a draw condition is indicated.
3. If a draw is indicated, proceed with further testing. If an excessive charge (10–15 amps) is indicated, the regulator may be at fault.

## OUTPUT TEST

1. You will need an ammeter for this test.
2. Disconnect the battery ground cable.
3. Disconnect the wire from the battery terminal on the alternator.
4. Connect the ammeter negative lead to the battery terminal wire removed in step three, and connect the ammeter positive lead to the battery terminal on the alternator.
5. Reconnect the battery ground cable and turn on all electrical accessories. If the battery is fully charged, disconnect the coil wire and bump the starter a few times to partially discharge it.
6. Start the engine and run it until you obtain a maximum current reading on the ammeter.
7. If the current is not within 10 amps of the rated output of the alternator, the alternator is working properly. If the current is not within 10 amps, insert a screwdriver in the test hole in the end frame of the alternator and ground the tab in the test hole against the side of the hole.
8. If the current is now within 10 amps of the rated output, remove the alternator and have the voltage regulator replaced. If it is still below 10 amps of rated output, have the alternator repaired.

## REMOVAL & INSTALLATION

### 1985–90 Models

◆ **See Figures 60 thru 68**

➡ **The following procedures require the use of GM Belt Tension Gauge No. BT-33-95-ACBN for regular V-belts, or BT-33-97M for serpentine belts. The belt should deflect about 6mm (¼ in.) over a 178-254mm (7-10 in.) span, or 13mm (½ in.) over a 330-406mm (13-16 in.) span at this point.**

1. Disconnect the negative battery terminal from the battery.
2. Remove the top radiator hose bracket from the radiator.

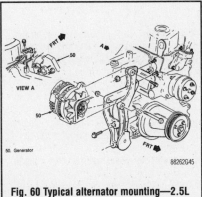

**Fig. 60 Typical alternator mounting—2.5L engine**

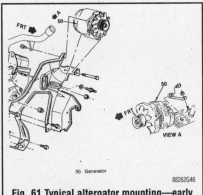

**Fig. 61 Typical alternator mounting—early model 4.3L engine**

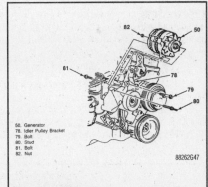

**Fig. 62 Typical alternator mounting—late model 4.3L engine**

**Fig. 63 Before removing the positive lead from the alternator, DISCONNECT the battery ground cable**

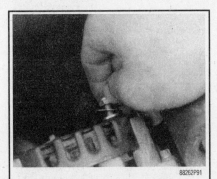

**Fig. 64 Be careful when removing the locknut as sometimes the terminal stud likes to rotate with the nut**

**Fig. 65 Remove the mounting bolts after removing the belt**

Fig. 66 This mounting stud holds a bracket in addition to mounting the alternator

Fig. 67 Once the bracket is removed, the mounting stud can be removed

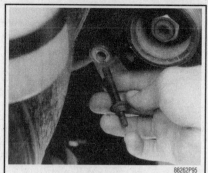

Fig. 68 If equipped, do not replace this stud with a regular bolt or the bracket will not have a mounting point

3. Remove the wiring harness that is clamped to the radiator core support.

4. Remove the upper fan support-to-radiator support bolts and the fan support.

5. Label and disconnect the alternator's electrical connectors.

6. Remove the alternator brace bolt and the drive belt.

7. Support the alternator, then remove the mounting bolts and the unit from the vehicle.

**To install:**

8. Install the alternator and adjust the drive belt tension. Tighten the top mounting bolt as follows:
- 2.5L to 20 ft. lbs. (27 Nm)
- 4.3L to 18.4 ft. lbs. (25 Nm)

9. Lower mounting bolt as follows:
- 2.5L to 37 ft. lbs. (50 Nm)
- 4.3L to 35 ft. lbs. (47 Nm)

10. The remainder of installation is the reverse of the removal procedure. Adjust the drive belt, as outlined in Section 1 of this manual.

**1991–96 Models**

▶ See Figures 60 thru 68

1. Disconnect the negative battery cable.
2. Disconnect the terminal plug and battery lead from the alternator.
3. Remove the drive belt.
4. Remove the alternator brace.
5. Remove the mounting bolts.
6. Remove the alternator from the alternator mounting bracket.
7. Installation is the reverse of the removal procedure. Tighten the following components to specifications:
- front mounting bolts: 36 ft. lbs. (50 Nm)
- alterator brace-to-bracket bolt: 36 ft. lbs. (50 Nm)
- brace-to-alternator bolt: 18 ft. lbs. (25 Nm)
8. Start the engine and check for proper charging system operation.

## Regulator

The voltage regulators are sealed units mounted within the alternator body and are nonadjustable.

### REMOVAL & INSTALLATION

#### 1985 Models

▶ See Figures 69, 70, 71 and 72

➡This procedure is to be performed with the alternator removed from the vehicle. The new alternators, 1986 and later models, are non-service-able.

1. Mark scribe lines on the end-frames to make the reassembly easier.
2. Remove the 4 through-bolts and separate the drive end-frame assembly from the rectifier end-frame assembly.

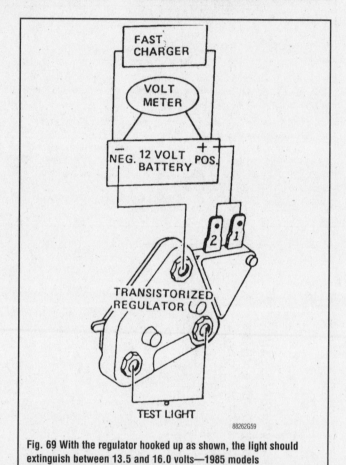

Fig. 69 With the regulator hooked up as shown, the light should extinguish between 13.5 and 16.0 volts—1985 models

3. Remove the 3 diode trio attaching nuts and the 3 regulator attaching screws.
4. Remove the diode trio and the regulator from the end frame.

➡Before installing the regulator, push the brushes into the brush holder and install a brush retainer or a tooth pick to hold the brushes in place.

5. To install the regulator, reverse the removal procedures. After the alternator is assembled, remove the brush retainer.

### VOLTAGE ADJUSTMENT

The voltage regulator is electronic and is housed within the alternator. Adjustment of the regulator is not possible. Should replacement of the regulator become necessary, the alternator must be disassembled.

BRUSHES RETAINED IN HOLDER
BRUSH RETAINER
BRUSHES

14. Clean brushes with soft, dry cloth.
15. Put brushes in holder and hold with brush retainer wire.

DRIVE END BEARING
END FRAME
SEALED BEARING
FAN
PULLEY
WASHER
NUT
SHAFT
COLLAR
COLLAR
SCREW
FLAT RETAINER
COLLAR

10SI, 12SI, AND LATE PRODUCTION 15SI AND 27SI

RETAINER
COLLAR OR SHAFT
BEARING
COLLAR
ROTOR SHAFT
END FRAME
SCREW

EARLY PRODUCTION 15SI AND 27SI

16. Observe stack-up of parts in both illustrations.
To remove rotor and drive end bearing, remove shaft nut, washer and pulley, fan and collar. Push rotor from housing.
17. Remove retainer plate inside drive end frame and push bearing out. Clean all parts with soft cloth.
18. Press against -outer race to push bearing in. Fill cavity between retainer plate and bearing with lubricant on early production 15SI and 27SI. Series 10SI, 12SI and late production 15SI and 27SI use sealed bearing – no lubricant is required. Assemble retainer plate.
19. Press rotor into end frame. Assemble collar, fan, pulley, washer and nut. Torque shaft nut to 40-60 lb.-ft. (54-82 N.M).

TESTING TRIO
SINGLE CONNECTOR
OHMMETER
THREE CONNECTORS

9. To check diode trio, connect ohmmeter as shown, then reverse lead connections. Should read high and low. If not, repeat diode trio.
10. Repeat same test between single connector and each of other connectors.

TESTING RECTIFIER BRIDGE
REGULATOR
INSULATING WASHER
OHMMETER
GROUNDED HEAT SINK
INSULATED HEAT SINK
BRUSH HOLDER

11. Check rectifier bridge with ohmmeter connected from grounded heat sink to flat metal on terminal. Reverse leads. If both readings are the same, replace rectifier bridge.
12. Repeat test between grounded heat sink and other two flat metal clips.
13. Repeat test between insulated heat sink and three flat metal clips.
To replace bridge, remove attaching screws.

Fig. 71 Alternator service—1985 models, continued

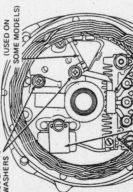

# DISASSEMBLY, TEST AND REASSEMBLY (GENERATOR REMOVED FROM ENGINE)

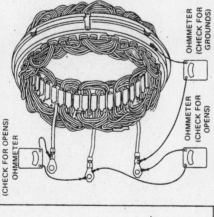

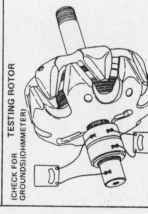

TESTING STATOR
(CHECK FOR OPENS)
OHMMETER
OHMMETER (CHECK FOR GROUNDS)
OHMMETER (CHECK FOR OPENS)

5. On 10SI only, check stator for opens with ohmmeter (two checks). If either reading is high (infinite), replace stator.
6. On all series, check stator for grounds. If reading is low, replace stator.

TESTING ROTOR
(CHECK FOR GROUNDS)(OHMMETER)
OHMMETER CHECK FOR OPENS

7. Check rotor for grounds with ohmmeter. Reading should be very high (infinite). If not, replace rotor.
8. Check rotor for opens. Should read 2.4-3.5 ohms. If not, replace rotor.

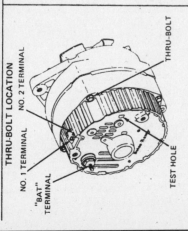

THRU-BOLT LOCATION
NO. 1 TERMINAL
NO. 2 TERMINAL
THRU-BOLT
"BAT" TERMINAL
TEST HOLE

1. Make scribe marks on end frames to facilitate reassembly.
2. Remove four thru-bolts and separate drive end frame assembly from rectifier end frame assembly.

END FRAME VIEW
RESISTOR (USED ON SOME MODELS)
DIODE TRIO
INSULATING WASHERS
RECTIFIER BRIDGE
CAPACITOR
ATTACHING NUTS

3. Remove three attaching nuts and regulator attaching screws.
4. Separate stator, diode trio and regulator from end frame. NOTE: The regulator cannot be tested on the work bench except with a regulator tester.

Fig. 70 Alternator service—1985 models

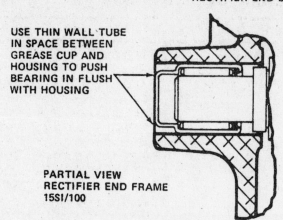

RECTIFIER END BEARING 15SI SERIES

USE THIN WALL TUBE IN SPACE BETWEEN GREASE CUP AND HOUSING TO PUSH BEARING IN FLUSH WITH HOUSING

PARTIAL VIEW RECTIFIER END FRAME 15SI/100

20. PUSH SLIP RING END BEARING OUT FROM OUTSIDE TOWARD INSIDE OF END FRAME.
21. ON 10SI AND 12SI, PLACE FLAT PLATE OVER NEW BEARING, PRESS FROM OUTSIDE TOWARD INSIDE UNTIL BEARING IS FLUSH WITH END FRAME.
22. ON 15SI, SEE ILLUSTRATION.
23. ASSEMBLE BRUSH HOLDER, REGULATOR, RESISTOR, DIODE TRIO, RECTIFIER BRIDGE AND STATOR TO SLIP RING END FRAME.
24. ASSEMBLE END FRAMES TOGETHER WITH THRU-BOLTS. REMOVE BRUSH RETAINER WIRE.

88262G56

**Fig. 72 Alternator service—1985 models, continued**

## Starter

▶ **See Figures 73 and 74**

The starter is located on the left side (2.5L) or right side (4.3L) of the engine. The 1985–87 2.5L is equipped with a 5MT starter. The 4.3L is equipped with a 10MT. In the model year 1988, the names of the 5MT changed to SD–200 and the 10MT changed to the SD–300. The starters are basically still the same.

### SHIMMING THE STARTER

▶ **See Figures 75 and 76**

Starter noise during cranking and after the engine fires is often a result of too much or too little distance between the starter pinion gear and the flywheel. A high pitched whine during cranking (before the engine fires) can be caused by the pinion and flywheel being too far apart. Likewise, a whine after the engine starts (as the key is released) is often a result of the pinion-flywheel relationship being too close. In both cases flywheel damage can occur. Shims are available in 0.015 in. sizes to properly adjust the starter on its mount. You will also need a flywheel turning tool, available at most auto parts stores or from any auto tool store or salesperson.

If your truck's starter emits the above noises, follow the shimming procedure below:

1. Disconnect the negative battery cable.
2. Remove the flywheel inspection cover on the bottom of the bellhousing.
3. Using the flywheel turning tool, turn the flywheel and examine the flywheel teeth. If damage is evident, the flywheel should be replaced.
4. Insert a screwdriver into the small hole in the bottom of the starter and move the starter pinion and clutch assembly so the pinion and flywheel teeth mesh. If necessary, rotate the flywheel so that a pinion tooth is directly in the center of the two flywheel teeth and on the centerline of the two gears, as shown in the accompanying illustration.
5. Check the pinion-to-flywheel clearance by using a 0.5mm (0.020 in.) wire gauge (a spark plug wire gauge may work here, or you can make your own). Make sure you center the pinion tooth between the flywheel teeth and the gauge not in the corners, as you may get a false reading. If the clearance is under this minimum, shim the starter away from the flywheel by adding shim(s) one at a time to the starter mount. Check clearance after adding each shim.
6. If the clearance is a good deal over 0.5mm (0.020 in.), in the vicinity of 1.3mm (0.050 in.) plus, shim the starter towards the flywheel. Broken or severely mangled flywheel teeth are also a good indicator that the clearance here is too great. Shimming the starter towards the flywheel is done by adding shims to the outboard starter mounting pad only. Check the clearance after each shim is added. A shim of 0.015 in. at this location will decrease the clearance about 0.010 in.

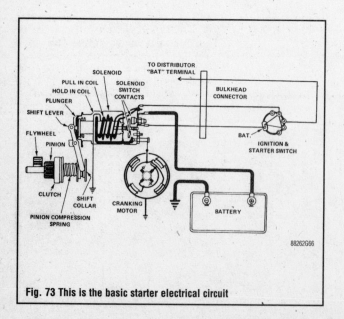

**Fig. 73 This is the basic starter electrical circuit**

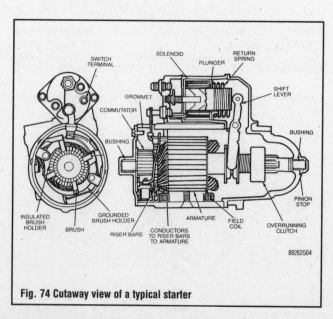

**Fig. 74 Cutaway view of a typical starter**

## Troubleshooting Basic Starting System Problems

| Problem | Cause | Solution |
|---|---|---|
| Starter motor rotates engine slowly | • Battery charge low or battery defective | • Charge or replace battery |
| | • Defective circuit between battery and starter motor | • Clean and tighten, or replace cables |
| | • Low load current | • Bench-test starter motor. Inspect for worn brushes and weak brush springs. |
| | • High load current | • Bench-test starter motor. Check engine for friction, drag or coolant in cylinders. Check ring gear-to-pinion gear clearance. |
| Starter motor will not rotate engine | • Battery charge low or battery defective | • Charge or replace battery |
| | • Faulty solenoid | • Check solenoid ground. Repair or replace as necessary. |
| | • Damaged drive pinion gear or ring gear | • Replace damaged gear(s) |
| | • Starter motor engagement weak | • Bench-test starter motor |
| | • Starter motor rotates slowly with high load current | • Inspect drive yoke pull-down and point gap, check for worn end bushings, check ring gear clearance |
| | • Engine seized | • Repair engine |
| Starter motor drive will not engage (solenoid known to be good) | • Defective contact point assembly | • Repair or replace contact point assembly |
| | • Inadequate contact point assembly ground | • Repair connection at ground screw |
| | • Defective hold-in coil | • Replace field winding assembly |
| Starter motor drive will not disengage | • Starter motor loose on flywheel housing | • Tighten mounting bolts |
| | • Worn drive end busing | • Replace bushing |
| | • Damaged ring gear teeth | • Replace ring gear or driveplate |
| | • Drive yoke return spring broken or missing | • Replace spring |
| Starter motor drive disengages prematurely | • Weak drive assembly thrust spring | • Replace drive mechanism |
| | • Hold-in coil defective | • Replace field winding assembly |
| Low load current | • Worn brushes | • Replace brushes |
| | • Weak brush springs | • Replace springs |

TCCS2C01

## REMOVAL & INSTALLATION

▶ **See Figures 77 thru 82**

1. Disconnect the negative battery cable.
2. Raise and support the front of the vehicle on jackstands.
3. If equipped, remove any starter braces or shields that may be in the way.
4. Disconnect the electrical connectors from the starter solenoid.
5. Remove the starter-to-engine bolts, nuts, washers and shims. Allow the starter to drop, then remove it from the engine.

➥**Be sure to keep the shims in order so that they may be reinstalled in the same order.**

6. Installation is the reverse of the removal procedure. Make sure to install any shims that were removed. Tighten the starter-to-engine bolts to 31 ft. lbs. (42 Nm) for the 2.5L and 28 ft. lbs. (38 Nm) for the 4.3L.

## SOLENOID REPLACEMENT

1. Remove the starter, then place it on a workbench.
2. Remove the screw and the washer from the motor connector strap terminal.
3. Remove the two solenoid retaining screws.
4. Twist the solenoid housing clockwise to remove the flange key from the keyway in the housing, then remove the housing.

**To install:**

5. Place the return spring on the plunger and place the solenoid body on the drive housing. Turn it counterclockwise to engage the flange key.
6. Place the two retaining screws in position, then install the screw and washer which secures the strap terminal. Install the unit on the starter.

465. Shim
469. Screwdriver

**Fig. 75 Insert a tool into the hole and push the pinion out until it engages the ring gear. This allows the pinion clearance to be measured**

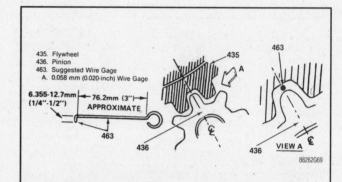

435. Flywheel
436. Pinion
463. Suggested Wire Gage
A. 0.058 mm (0.020-inch) Wire Gage

**Fig. 76 Make sure that you measure at the tip of the gear to get an accurate pinion clearance measurement**

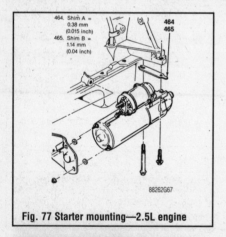

464. Shim A = 0.38 mm (0.015 inch)
465. Shim B = 1.14 mm (0.04 inch)

**Fig. 77 Starter mounting—2.5L engine**

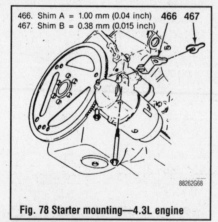

466. Shim A = 1.00 mm (0.04 inch)
467. Shim B = 0.38 mm (0.015 inch)

**Fig. 78 Starter mounting—4.3L engine**

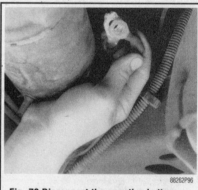

**Fig. 79 Disconnect the negative battery cable before removing the starter cables**

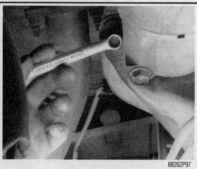

**Fig. 80 The torque converter cover may need to be removed on some versions to withdraw the starter**

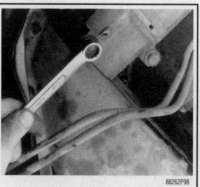

**Fig. 81 Support the starter when removing the mounting bolts**

**Fig. 82 The starter can be heavy, so be ready for its heft once the final mounting bolt is removed**

## SENDING UNITS AND SENSORS

The sensors covered in this section are not related to engine control. They are for gauges and warning lights only. For sensors related to engine control refer to Electronic Engine Controls in Section 4.

## Coolant Temperature Sensor

### OPERATION

The coolant temperature sensor changes resistance as the coolant temperature increases and decreases. The sensor is located on the left side of the engine on both the V6 and I4 engines. On the V6 it is screwed into the head between the rear two exhaust ports. On the I4 engine, it is screwed into the rear of the head just in front of the lifting eye.

### TESTING

1. Turn the ignition switch to **ON**, but do not start the engine.
2. Disconnect the sensor lead at the sensor. Connect a test lamp to the lead; The lamp should glow. If not, check the wiring, fuses and connections.
3. Disconnect the test lamp and ground the connector. The gauge should read at the **HOT** mark.
4. Remove the connector from ground. The gauge should read at the **COLD** mark.
5. At 104°F (40°C) the resistance of the sensor should be 1365 ohms.
6. At 257°F (125°C) the resistance of the sensor should be 55 ohms.

### REMOVAL & INSTALLATION

▶ **See Figure 83**

1. Disconnect the negative battery cable and drain the engine coolant. Remove the engine cover.
2. Disconnect the electrical lead and unscrew the sensor.
3. Installation is the reverse of the removal procedure. Tighten the sensor to 17 ft. lbs. (23 Nm). Make sure to fill the engine with the proper type and amount of coolant.

## Oil Pressure Sender

### OPERATION

The oil pressure sender relays to the dash gauge the oil pressure in the engine.

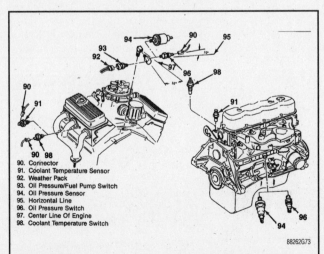

90. Connector
91. Coolant Temperature Sensor
92. Weather Pack
93. Oil Pressure/Fuel Pump Switch
94. Oil Pressure Sensor
95. Horizontal Line
96. Oil Pressure Switch
97. Center Line Of Engine
98. Coolant Temperature Switch

88262G73

**Fig. 83 Coolant temperature and oil pressure senders—2.5L and 4.3L engines**

### TESTING

1. Check the oil level and correct as necessary. Turn the ignition switch on, but do not start the engine.
2. Disconnect the sensor lead at the sensor. The gauge should read full scale.
3. Ground the connector. The gauge should read at the bottom of the scale.
4. At 0 psi (0 kPa) the resistance of the sensor should be 1 ohm.
5. At 40 psi (275 kPa) the resistance of the sensor should be 44 ohms.

### REMOVAL & INSTALLATION

▶ **See Figures 84, 85, 86 and 87**

1. Disconnect the negative battery cable. Remove the engine cover.
2. Disconnect the sensor electrical lead and unscrew the sensor. The sensor can be found on the top side of the engine, near the distributor.
**To install:**
3. Coat the first 2 or 3 threads with sealer. Install the sensor and tighten until snug. Engage the electrical lead.
4. Connect the battery cable and install the engine cover.

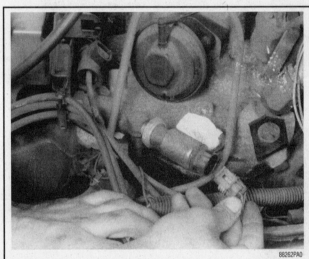

88262PA0

**Fig. 84 The oil pressure sender can be reached after removing the engine cover**

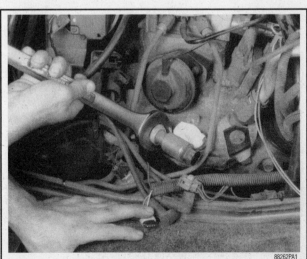

88262PA1

**Fig. 85 Do not put too much sideways force on the sender or you can damage the adapter**

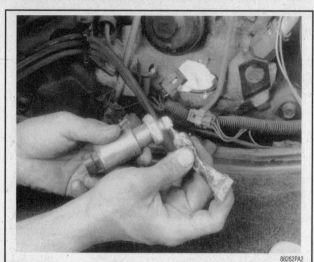

Fig. 86 You can use some pipe sealer to make sure oil doesn't leak past the sender threads

Fig. 87 Do not crossthread the sender into the adapter or you will definitely have a leak

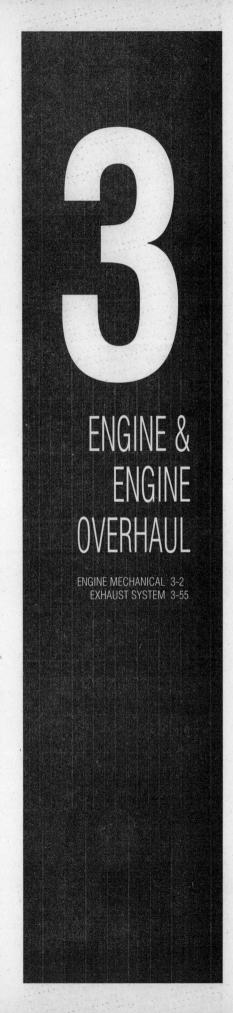

**3**

# ENGINE & ENGINE OVERHAUL

## ENGINE MECHANICAL

### Engine Overhaul Tips

Most engine overhaul procedures are fairly standard. In addition to specific parts replacement procedures and specifications for your individual engine, this section is also a guide to acceptable rebuilding procedures. Examples of standard rebuilding practice are given and should be used along with specific details concerning your particular engine.

Competent and accurate machine shop services will ensure maximum performance, reliability and engine life. In most instances it is more profitable for the do-it-yourself mechanic to remove, clean and inspect the component, buy the necessary parts and deliver these to a shop for actual machine work.

On the other hand, much of the rebuilding work (crankshaft, block, bearings, piston rods, and other components) is well within the scope of the do-it-yourself mechanic's tools and abilities. You will have to decide for yourself the depth of involvement you desire in an engine repair or rebuild.

### TOOLS

The tools required for an engine overhaul or parts replacement will depend on the depth of your involvement. With a few exceptions, they will be the tools found in a mechanic's tool kit (see Section 1 of this manual). More in-depth work will require some or all of the following:

- A dial indicator (reading in thousandths) mounted on a universal base
- Micrometers and telescope gauges
- Jaw and screw-type pullers
- Scraper
- Valve spring compressor
- Ring groove cleaner
- Piston ring expander and compressor
- Ridge reamer
- Cylinder hone or glaze breaker
- Plastigage®
- Engine stand

The use of most of these tools is illustrated in this chapter. Many can be rented for a one-time use from a local parts jobber or tool supply house specializing in automotive work.

Occasionally, the use of special tools is called for. See the information on Special Tools and the Safety Notice in the front of this book before substituting another tool.

### INSPECTION TECHNIQUES

Procedures and specifications are given in this chapter for inspecting, cleaning and assessing the wear limits of most major components. Other procedures such as Magnaflux® and Zyglo® can be used to locate material flaws and stress cracks. Magnaflux® is a magnetic process applicable only to ferrous materials. The Zyglo® process coats the material with a fluorescent dye penetrant and can be used on any material.

Checking for suspected surface cracks can be more readily made using spot check dye. The dye is sprayed onto the suspected area, wiped off and the area sprayed with a developer. Cracks will show up brightly.

### OVERHAUL TIPS

Aluminum has become extremely popular for use in engines, due to its low weight. Observe the following precautions when handling aluminum parts:

- Never hot tank aluminum parts (the caustic hot tank solution will eat the aluminum.
- Remove all aluminum parts (identification tag, etc.) from engine parts prior to the tanking.
- Always coat threads lightly with engine oil or anti-seize compounds before installation, to prevent seizure.
- Never overtorque bolts or spark plugs especially in aluminum threads.

Stripped threads in any component can be repaired using any of several commercial repair kits (Heli-Coil®, Microdot®, Keenserts®, etc.).

When assembling the engine, any parts that will be exposed to frictional contact must be prelubed to provide lubrication at initial start-up. Any product specifically formulated for this purpose can be used, but engine oil is not recommended as a prelube in most cases.

When semi-permanent (locked, but removable) installation of bolts or nuts is desired, threads should be cleaned and coated with Loctite® or another similar, commercial non-hardening sealant.

### REPAIRING DAMAGED THREADS

▶ See Figures 1, 2, 3, 4 and 5

Several methods of repairing damaged threads are available. Heli-Coil® (shown here), Keenserts® and Microdot® are among the most widely used. All involve basically the same principle—drilling out stripped threads, tapping the hole and installing a prewound insert—making welding, plugging and oversize fasteners unnecessary.

Two types of thread repair inserts are usually supplied: a standard type for most inch coarse, inch fine, metric course and metric fine thread sizes and a spark lug type to fit most spark plug port sizes. Consult the individual tool manufacturer's catalog to determine exact applications. Typical thread repair kits will contain a selection of prewound threaded inserts, a tap (corresponding to the outside diameter threads of the insert) and an installation tool. Spark plug inserts usually differ because they require a tap equipped with pilot threads and a combined reamer/tap section. Most manufacturers also supply blister-packed thread repair inserts separately in addition to a master kit containing a variety of taps and inserts plus installation tools.

Before attempting to repair a threaded hole, remove any snapped, broken or damaged bolts or studs. Penetrating oil can be used to free frozen threads. The offending item can usually be removed with locking pliers or using a screw/stud extractor. After the hole is clear, the thread can be repaired, as shown in the series of accompanying illustrations and in the kit manufacturer's instructions.

### Checking Engine Compression

▶ See Figure 6

A noticeable lack of engine power, excessive oil consumption and/or poor fuel mileage measured over an extended period are all indicators of internal engine wear. Worn piston rings, scored or worn cylinder bores, blown head gaskets, sticking or burnt valves and worn valve seats are all possible culprits here. A check of each cylinder's compression will help you locate the problems.

1. Make sure the battery is fully charged.
2. Warm up the engine to normal operating temperature, then shut the engine **OFF**.
3. Disable the ignition system by disconnecting the primary ignition wiring from the coil. On early models equipped with an external ignition coil it is also possible to disconnect the secondary wiring (coil-to-distributor lead).
4. Remove all spark plugs.
5. Block open the throttle linkage in the fully open position.
6. Screw the compression gauge into the No. 1 spark plug hole until the fitting is snug.

➡ Be careful not to crossthread the plug hole. Use extra care, as the spark plug threads are easily ruined.

7. Set the compression gauge to zero, then use the ignition switch to crank the engine through 4 compression strokes (four "puffs" on the compression gauge).
8. Record the highest reading, clear the compression gauge and repeat to be sure of your results. Record the highest obtained reading from both tests, then remove the compression gauge and repeat at each of the cylinders.
9. Compare the highest reading of each cylinder to the readings of the other cylinders. No cylinder should be less than 70 percent of the highest reading. For example, if the highest reading was 150 psi (1035 kPa), then the lowest cylinder should not be below 105 psi (725 kPa).

➡ A cylinder's compression pressure should not be below 100 psi (689 kPa) and the lowest cylinder should NOT be any lower than 70 percent of the highest cylinders reading.

10. If a cylinder is unusually low, pour a tablespoon of clean engine oil into the cylinder through the spark plug hole and repeat the compression test. If the compression rises after adding the oil, it is likely that the cylinder's piston rings

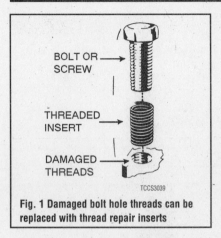

Fig. 1 Damaged bolt hole threads can be replaced with thread repair inserts

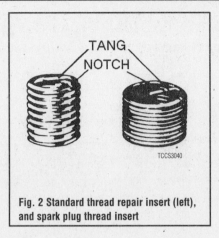

Fig. 2 Standard thread repair insert (left), and spark plug thread insert

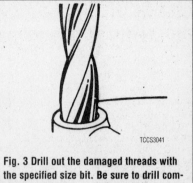

Fig. 3 Drill out the damaged threads with the specified size bit. Be sure to drill completely through the hole or to the bottom of a blind hole

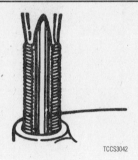

Fig. 4 Using the kit, tap the hole in order to receive the thread insert. Keep the tap well oiled and back it out frequently to avoid clogging the threads

Fig. 5 Screw the insert onto the installer tool until the tang engages the slot. Thread the insert into the hole until it is ¼–½ turn below the top surface, then remove the tool and break off the tang using a punch

or bore are damaged or worn. If the pressure remains low, the valves may not be seating properly (a valve job would be needed), or the head gasket may be blown near that cylinder. If compression in any two adjacent cylinders is low and if the addition of oil does not help the compression, there is probably leakage past the head gasket. Oil and coolant water in the combustion chamber can result from this problem. There may be evidence of water droplets on the engine dipstick when a head gasket has blown.

Different engine conditions should yield appropriate compression test results:

**NORMAL**—Compression builds up quickly and evenly to the specified compression on each cylinder.

**PISTON RINGS**—Compression low on the first stroke, then tends to build up on the following strokes, but does not reach normal. This reading should be tested with the addition of a few shots of engine oil into the cylinder. If the compression increases considerably, the rings are leaking compression.

**VALVES**—Low on the first stroke, does not tend to build up on following strokes. This reading will stay around the same with a few shots of engine oil in the cylinder.

**HEAD GASKET**—The compression reading is low between two adjacent cylinders. The head gasket between the two cylinders may be blown. If there is signs of white smoke coming from the exhaust while the engine is running may indicate water leaking into the cylinder and being converted into steam. Check around the cylinder head-to-cylinder block area for signs of coolant and oil leakage, indicating a leaking head gasket.

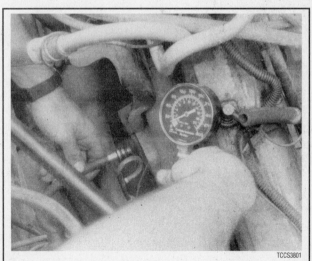

Fig. 6 A screw-in type compression gauge is more accurate and easier to use without an assistant

## GENERAL ENGINE SPECIFICATIONS

| Year | Engine ID/VIN | Engine Displacement Liters (cc) | Fuel System Type | Net Horsepower @ rpm | Net Torque @ rpm (ft. lbs.) | Bore x Stroke (in.) | Compression Ratio | Oil Pressure @ rpm |
|---|---|---|---|---|---|---|---|---|
| 1985 | E | 2.5 (2474) | TBI | 98@4400 | 134@3200 | 4.00x3.00 | 9.0:1 | 36-41@2000 |
| | N | 4.3 (4293) | 4BC | 150@4000 | 225@2400 | 4.00x3.48 | 9.3:1 | 30-35@2000 |
| 1986 | E | 2.5 (2474) | TBI | 98@4400 | 134@3200 | 4.00x3.00 | 9.0:1 | 36-41@2000 |
| | Z | 4.3 (4293) | TBI | 150@4000 | 230@2400 | 4.00x3.48 | 9.3:1 | 30-35@2000 |
| 1987 | E | 2.5 (2474) | TBI | 98@4400 | 134@3200 | 4.00x3.00 | 9.0:1 | 36-41@2000 |
| | Z | 4.3 (4293) | TBI | 150@4000 | 230@2400 | 4.00x3.48 | 9.3:1 | 30-35@2000 |
| 1988 | Z | 4.3 (4293) | TBI | 150@4000 | 230@2400 | 4.00x3.48 | 9.3:1 | 36-41@2000 |
| | E | 2.5 (2474) | TBI | 92@4400 | 134@3200 | 4.00x3.00 | 9.0:1 | 36-41@2000 |
| | Z | 4.3 (4293) | TBI | 145@4000 | 230@2400 | 4.00x3.48 | 9.3:1 | 30-35@2000 |
| 1989 | E | 2.5 (2474) | TBI | 92@4400 | 134@3200 | 4.00x3.00 | 9.0:1 | 36-41@2000 |
| | Z | 4.3 (4293) | TBI | 145@4000 | 230@2400 | 4.00x3.48 | 9.3:1 | 30-35@2000 |
| 1990 | E | 2.5 (2474) | TBI | 92@4400 | 134@3200 | 4.00x3.00 | 9.0:1 | 36-41@2000 |
| | B | 4.3 (4293) | TBI | 170@4000 | 235@2200 | 4.00x3.48 | 9.3:1 | 18@2000 |
| | Z | 4.3 (4293) | TBI | 150@4000 | 230@2400 | 4.00x3.48 | 9.3:1 | 30-35@2000 |
| 1991 | B | 4.3 (4293) | TBI | 170@4000 | 235@2400 | 4.00x3.48 | 9.3:1 | 18@2000 |
| | Z | 4.3 (4293) | TBI | 150@4000 | 230@2400 | 4.00x3.48 | 9.3:1 | 18@2000 |
| 1992 | W | 4.3 (4293) | CMFI | 200@4400 | 260@3600 | 4.00x3.48 | 9.05:1 | 18@2000 |
| | Z | 4.3 (4293) | TBI | 150@4000 | 230@2400 | 4.00x3.48 | 9.3:1 | 18@2000 |
| 1993 | W | 4.3 (4293) | CMFI | 200@4400 | 260@3600 | 4.00x3.48 | 9.05:1 | 18@2000 |
| | Z | 4.3 (4293) | TBI | 165@4000 | 235@2400 | 4.00x3.48 | 9.05:1 | 16@2000 |
| 1994 | W | 4.3 (4293) | CMFI | 200@4400 | 260@3600 | 4.00x3.48 | 9.05:1 | 18@2000 |
| | Z | 4.3 (4293) | TBI | 165@4000 | 235@2400 | 4.00x3.48 | 9.05:1 | 18@2000 |
| 1995 | W | 4.3 (4293) | CMFI | 190@4400 | 260@3400 | 4.00x3.48 | 9.1:1 | 18@2000 |
| 1996 | W | 4.3 (4293) | CSFI | 190@4400 | 250@2800 | 4.00x3.48 | 9.2:1 | 16@2000 |

BC - Barrel carburetor
CMFI - Central multi-port fuel injection
CSFI - Central sequential fuel injection
TBI - Throttle body fuel injection
1 Minimum oil pressure, engine HOT

88263C01

## VALVE SPECIFICATIONS

| Year | Engine ID/VIN | Engine Displacement Liters (cc) | Seat Angle (deg.) | Face Angle (deg.) | Spring Test Pressure (lbs. @ in.) | Spring Installed Height (in.) | Stem-to-Guide Clearance (in.) Intake | Stem-to-Guide Clearance (in.) Exhaust | Stem Diameter (in.) Intake | Stem Diameter (in.) Exhaust |
|---|---|---|---|---|---|---|---|---|---|---|
| 1985 | E | 2.5 (2474) | 46 | 45 | 78-86@1.66 | 1.69 | 0.0010-0.0027 | 0.0010-0.0027 | 0.3418-0.3425 | 0.3418-0.3425 |
| | N | 4.3 (4293) | 46 | 45 | 194-206@1.25 | 1.72 | 0.0010-0.0027 | 0.0010-0.0027 | 0.3410-0.3417 | 0.3410-0.3417 |
| 1986 | E | 2.5 (2474) | 46 | 45 | 78-86@1.66 | 1.69 | 0.0010-0.0027 | 0.0010-0.0027 | 0.3418-0.3425 | 0.3418-0.3425 |
| | Z | 4.3 (4293) | 46 | 45 | 194-206@1.25 | 1.72 | 0.0010-0.0027 | 0.0010-0.0027 | 0.3410-0.3417 | 0.3410-0.3417 |
| 1987 | E | 2.5 (2474) | 46 | 45 | 71-78@1.44 | 1.44 | 0.0010-0.0027 | 0.0013-0.0030 | 0.3133-0.3138 | 0.3128-0.3135 |
| | Z | 4.3 (4293) | 46 | 45 | 194-206@1.25 | 1.72 | 0.0010-0.0027 | 0.0010-0.0027 | 0.3410-0.3417 | 0.3410-0.3417 |
| 1988 | Z | 4.3 (4293) | 46 | 45 | 194-206@1.25 | 1.72 | 0.0010-0.0027 | 0.0010-0.0027 | 0.3410-0.3417 | 0.3410-0.3417 |
| | E | 2.5 (2474) | 46 | 45 | 71-78@1.44 | 1.44 | 0.0010-0.0025 | 0.0013-0.0030 | 0.3133-0.3138 | 0.3128-0.3136 |
| | Z | 4.3 (4293) | 46 | 45 | 194-206@1.25 | 1.72 | 0.0010-0.0027 | 0.0010-0.0027 | 0.3410-0.3417 | 0.3410-0.3417 |
| 1989 | E | 2.5 (2474) | 46 | 45 | 71-78@1.44 | 1.44 | 0.0010-0.0025 | 0.0013-0.0030 | 0.3133-0.3138 | 0.3128-0.3135 |
| | Z | 4.3 (4293) | 46 | 45 | 194-206@1.25 | 1.72 | 0.0010-0.0027 | 0.0010-0.0027 | 0.3410-0.3417 | 0.3410-0.3417 |
| 1990 | E | 2.5 (2474) | 46 | 45 | 71-78@1.44 | 1.44 | 0.0010-0.0025 | 0.0013-0.0030 | 0.3133-0.3138 | 0.3128-0.3135 |
| | B | 4.3 (4293) | 46 | 45 | 194-206@1.25 | 1.72 | 0.0010-0.0027 | 0.0010-0.0027 | 0.3410-0.3417 | 0.3410-0.3417 |
| | Z | 4.3 (4293) | 46 | 45 | 194-206@1.25 | 1.72 | 0.0010-0.0027 | 0.0010-0.0027 | 0.3410-0.3417 | 0.3410-0.3417 |
| 1991 | B | 4.3 (4293) | 46 | 45 | 194-206@1.25 | 1.72 | 0.0010-0.0027 | 0.0010-0.0027 | 0.3410-0.3417 | 0.3410-0.3417 |
| | Z | 4.3 (4293) | 46 | 45 | 194-206@1.25 | 1.72 | 0.0010-0.0027 | 0.0010-0.0027 | 0.3410-0.3417 | 0.3410-0.3417 |
| 1992 | W | 4.3 (4293) | 46 | 45 | 194-206@1.25 | 1.69-1.71 | 0.0010-0.0027 | 0.0010-0.0027 | 0.3410-0.3417 | NA |
| | Z | 4.3 (4293) | 46 | 45 | 194-206@1.25 | 1.69-1.71 | 0.0010-0.0027 | 0.0010-0.0027 | 0.3410-0.3417 | NA |
| 1993 | W | 4.3 (4293) | 46 | 45 | 194-206@1.25 | 1.69-1.71 | 0.0011-0.0027 | 0.0011-0.0027 | 0.3410-0.3417 | NA |
| | Z | 4.3 (4293) | 46 | 45 | 194-206@1.25 | 1.69-1.71 | 0.0010-0.0027 | 0.0010-0.0027 | 0.3410-0.3417 | NA |
| 1994 | W | 4.3 (4293) | 46 | 45 | 194-206@1.25 | 1.69-1.71 | 0.0011-0.0027 | 0.0011-0.0027 | 0.3410-0.3417 | NA |
| | Z | 4.3 (4293) | 46 | 45 | 194-206@1.25 | 1.69-1.71 | 0.0010-0.0027 | 0.0010-0.0027 | 0.3410-0.3417 | NA |
| 1995 | W | 4.3 (4293) | 46 | 45 | 194-206@1.25 | 1.69-1.71 | 0.0011-0.0027 | 0.0011-0.0027 | 0.3410-0.3417 | NA |
| 1996 | W | 4.3 (4293) | 46 | 45 | 187-203@1.27 | 1.69-1.71 | 0.0011-0.0027 | 0.0011-0.0027 | 0.3410-0.3417 | NA |

NA - Not Available
1 Maximum service limit is listed specification plus 0.001 (intake) or 0.002 (exhaust)

88263C02

## CRANKSHAFT AND CONNECTING ROD SPECIFICATIONS

All measurements are given in inches.

| Year | Engine ID/VIN | Engine Displacement Liters (cc) | Main Brg. Journal Dia. | Crankshaft Main Brg. Oil Clearance | Shaft End-play | Thrust on No. | Connecting Rod Journal Diameter | Connecting Rod Oil Clearance | Connecting Rod Side Clearance |
|---|---|---|---|---|---|---|---|---|---|
| 1985 | E | 2.5 (2474) | 2.3000 | 0.0005-0.0022 | 0.0035-0.0085 | 5 | 2.0000 | 0.0005-0.0026 | 0.0060-0.0220 |
|  | N | 4.3 (4293) | [1] | [1] | 0.0020-0.0060 | 4 | 2.2487-2.2497 | 0.0010-0.0032 | 0.0070-0.0150 |
| 1986 | E | 2.5 (2474) | 2.3000 | 0.0005-0.0022 | 0.0035-0.0085 | 5 | 2.0000 | 0.0005-0.0026 | 0.0060-0.0220 |
|  | Z | 4.3 (4293) | [1] | [3] | 0.0020-0.0060 | 4 | 2.2487-2.2497 | 0.0013-0.0035 | 0.0060-0.0140 |
| 1987 | E | 2.5 (2474) | 2.3000 | 0.0005-0.0022 | 0.0035-0.0085 | 5 | 2.0000 | 0.0005-0.0026 | 0.0060-0.0020 |
|  | Z | 4.3 (4293) | [1] | [3] | 0.0020-0.0060 | 4 | 2.2487-2.2497 | 0.0013-0.0035 | 0.0060-0.0140 |
| 1988 | E | 2.5 (2474) | 2.3000 | 0.0005-0.0022 | 0.0035-0.0085 | 5 | 2.0000 | 0.0005-0.0026 | 0.0060-0.0020 |
|  | Z | 4.3 (4293) | [1] | [3] | 0.0020-0.0060 | 4 | 2.2487-2.2497 | 0.0013-0.0035 | 0.0060-0.0140 |
| 1989 | E | 2.5 (2474) | 2.3000 | 0.0005-0.0022 | 0.0035-0.0085 | 5 | 2.0000 | 0.0005-0.0026 | 0.0060-0.0020 |
|  | Z | 4.3 (4293) | [1] | [3] | 0.0020-0.0060 | 4 | 2.2487-2.2497 | 0.0013-0.0035 | 0.0060-0.0140 |
| 1990 | E | 2.5 (2474) | 2.3000 | 0.0005-0.0022 | 0.0035-0.0085 | 5 | 2.0000 | 0.0005-0.0026 | 0.0060-0.0020 |
|  | B | 4.3 (4293) | [1] | [3] | 0.0020-0.0060 | 4 | 2.2487-2.2497 | 0.0013-0.0035 | 0.0060-0.0140 |
|  | Z | 4.3 (4293) | [1] | [3] | 0.0020-0.0060 | 4 | 2.2487-2.2497 | 0.0013-0.0035 | 0.0060-0.0140 |
| 1991 | B | 4.3 (4293) | [1] | [3] | 0.0020-0.0060 | 4 | 2.2487-2.2497 | 0.0013-0.0035 | 0.0060-0.0140 |
|  | Z | 4.3 (4293) | [1] | [3] | 0.0020-0.0060 | 4 | 2.2487-2.2497 | 0.0013-0.0035 | 0.0060-0.0140 |
| 1992 | W | 4.3 (4293) | [2] | [3] | 0.0020-0.0060 | 4 | 2.2487-2.2497 | 0.0013-0.0035 | 0.0060-0.0140 |
|  | Z | 4.3 (4293) | [1] | [3] | 0.0020-0.0060 | 4 | 2.2487-2.2497 | 0.0013-0.0035 | 0.0060-0.0140 |
| 1993 | W | 4.3 (4293) | [2] | [3] | 0.0020-0.0070 | 4 | 2.2487-2.2497 | 0.0013-0.0035 | 0.0060-0.0140 |
|  | Z | 4.3 (4293) | [1] | [3] | 0.0020-0.0060 | 4 | 2.2487-2.2497 | 0.0013-0.0035 | 0.0060-0.0140 |
| 1994 | W | 4.3 (4293) | [2] | [3] | 0.0020-0.0070 | 4 | 2.2487-2.2497 | 0.0013-0.0035 | 0.0060-0.0140 |
|  | Z | 4.3 (4293) | [1] | [3] | 0.0020-0.0060 | 4 | 2.2487-2.2497 | 0.0013-0.0035 | 0.0060-0.0140 |
| 1995 | W | 4.3 (4293) | [2] | [3] | 0.0050-0.0180 | 4 | 2.2487-2.2497 | 0.0013-0.0035 | 0.0150-0.0460 |
| 1996 | W | 4.3 (4293) | [2] | [4] | 0.0020-0.0080 | 4 | 2.2487-2.2497 | 0.0010-0.0030 | 0.0060-0.0170 |

NA - Not Available
[1] No.: 2.4484-2.4493; Nos. 2-3: 2.4481-2.4490; No. 4: 2.4479-2.4488
[2] No. 1: 2.4488-2.4495; Nos. 2-3: 2.4485-2.4494; No. 4: 2.4480-2.4489
[3] No. 1: 0.0008-0.0200; Nos. 2-3: 0.0011-0.0023; No. 4: 0.0017-0.0032
[4] No. 1: 0.0010-0.0015; Nos. 2-3: 0.0010-0.0025; No. 4: 0.0025-0.0035

88263C04

## CAMSHAFT SPECIFICATIONS

All measurements given in inches.

| Year | Engine ID/VIN | Engine Displacement Liters (cc) | Journal Diameter 1 | 2 | 3 | 4 | 5 | Elevation In. | Ex. | Bearing Clearance | Camshaft End Play |
|---|---|---|---|---|---|---|---|---|---|---|---|
| 1985 | E | 2.5 (2474) | 1.8690 | 1.8690 | 1.8690 | — | — | 0.3980 | 0.3980 | 0.0007-0.0027 | 0.0015-0.0050 |
|  | N | 4.3 (4293) | 1.8682-1.8692 | 1.8682-1.8692 | 1.8682-1.8692 | 1.8682-1.8692 | — | 0.3570 | 0.3900 | NA | 0.0040-0.0120 |
| 1986 | E | 2.5 (2474) | 1.8690 | 1.8690 | 1.8690 | — | — | 0.3980 | 0.3980 | 0.0007-0.0027 | 0.0015-0.0050 |
|  | Z | 4.3 (4293) | 1.8682-1.8692 | 1.8682-1.8692 | 1.8682-1.8692 | 1.8682-1.8692 | — | 0.3570 | 0.3900 | 0.0010-0.0030 | 0.0040-0.0120 |
| 1987 | E | 2.5 (2474) | 1.8690 | 1.8690 | 1.8690 | — | — | 0.3980 | 0.3980 | 0.0007-0.0027 | 0.0015-0.0050 |
|  | Z | 4.3 (4293) | 1.8682-1.8692 | 1.8682-1.8692 | 1.8682-1.8692 | 1.8682-1.8692 | — | 0.3570 | 0.3900 | 0.0010-0.0030 | 0.0040-0.0120 |
| 1988 | E | 2.5 (2474) | 1.8690 | 1.8690 | 1.8690 | — | — | 0.3980 | 0.3980 | 0.0007-0.0027 | 0.0015-0.0050 |
|  | Z | 4.3 (4293) | 1.8682-1.8692 | 1.8682-1.8692 | 1.8682-1.8692 | 1.8682-1.8692 | — | 0.3570 | 0.3900 | 0.0010-0.0030 | 0.0040-0.0120 |
| 1989 | E | 2.5 (2474) | 1.8690 | 1.8690 | 1.8690 | — | — | 0.3980 | 0.3980 | 0.0007-0.0027 | 0.0015-0.0050 |
|  | Z | 4.3 (4293) | 1.8682-1.8692 | 1.8682-1.8692 | 1.8682-1.8692 | 1.8682-1.8692 | — | 0.3570 | 0.3900 | 0.0010-0.0030 | 0.0040-0.0120 |
| 1990 | E | 2.5 (2474) | 1.8690 | 1.8690 | 1.8690 | — | — | 0.3980 | 0.3980 | 0.0007-0.0027 | 0.0015-0.0050 |
|  | B | 4.3 (4239) | 1.8682-1.8692 | 1.8682-1.8692 | 1.8682-1.8692 | 1.8682-1.8692 | — | 0.2570 | 0.2760 | NA | 0.0040-0.0120 |
|  | Z | 4.3 (4293) | 1.8682-1.8692 | 1.8682-1.8692 | 1.8682-1.8692 | 1.8682-1.8692 | — | 0.3570 | 0.3900 | 0.0010-0.0030 | 0.0040-0.0120 |
| 1991 | B | 4.3 (4239) | 1.8682-1.8692 | 1.8682-1.8692 | 1.8682-1.8692 | 1.8682-1.8692 | — | 0.2570 | 0.2760 | NA | 0.0040-0.0120 |
|  | Z | 4.3 (4293) | 1.8682-1.8692 | 1.8682-1.8692 | 1.8682-1.8692 | 1.8682-1.8692 | — | 0.3570 | 0.3900 | 0.0010-0.0030 | 0.0040-0.0120 |
| 1992 | W | 4.3 (4293) | 1.8682-1.8692 | 1.8682-1.8692 | 1.8682-1.8692 | 1.8682-1.8692 | — | 0.2340 | 0.2570 | NA | 0.0040-0.0120 |
|  | Z | 4.3 (4293) | 1.8682-1.8692 | 1.8682-1.8692 | 1.8682-1.8692 | 1.8682-1.8692 | — | 0.2880 | 0.2940 | NA | 0.0010-0.0090 |
| 1993 | W | 4.3 (4293) | 1.8682-1.8692 | 1.8682-1.8692 | 1.8682-1.8692 | 1.8682-1.8692 | — | 0.2340 | 0.2570 | NA | 0.0040-0.0120 |
|  | Z | 4.3 (4293) | 1.8682-1.8692 | 1.8682-1.8692 | 1.8682-1.8692 | 1.8682-1.8692 | — | 0.2880 | 0.2940 | NA | 0.0010-0.0090 |
| 1994 | W | 4.3 (4293) | 1.8682-1.8692 | 1.8682-1.8692 | 1.8682-1.8692 | 1.8682-1.8692 | — | 0.2340 | 0.2570 | NA | 0.0040-0.0120 |
|  | Z | 4.3 (4293) | 1.8682-1.8692 | 1.8682-1.8692 | 1.8682-1.8692 | 1.8682-1.8692 | — | 0.2880 | 0.294 | NA | 0.0010-0.0090 |
| 1995 | W | 4.3 (4293) | 1.8682-1.8692 | 1.8682-1.8692 | 1.8682-1.8692 | 1.8682-1.8692 | — | 0.288 | 0.257 | NA | 0.0040-0.0120 |
|  | Z | 4.3 (4293) | 1.8682-1.8692 | 1.8682-1.8692 | 1.8682-1.8692 | 1.8682-1.8692 | — | 0.234 | 0.294 | NA | 0.0010-0.0090 |
| 1996 | W | 4.3 (4293) | 1.8677-1.8697 | 1.8677-1.8697 | 1.8677-1.8697 | 1.8677-1.8697 | — | 0.2763 | 0.2855 | NA | 0.0010-0.0090 |

NA - Not Available

88263C03

## TORQUE SPECIFICATIONS

All readings in ft. lbs.

| Year | Engine ID/VIN | Engine Displacement Liters (cc) | Cylinder Head Bolts | Main Bearing Bolts | Rod Bearing Bolts | Crankshaft Damper Bolts | Flywheel Bolts | Manifold Intake | Manifold Exhaust | Spark Plugs | Lug Nut |
|---|---|---|---|---|---|---|---|---|---|---|---|
| 1985 | E | 2.5 (2474) | ④ | 70 | 32 | 160 | 44 | 25 ① | 2 | 7-15 | 90 |
| 1985 | N | 4.3 (4293) | 65 | 70 | 45 | 70 | 55-75 | 35 | 3 | 22 | 90 |
| 1986 | E | 2.5 (2474) | ④ | 70 | 32 | 160 | 5 | 25 ① | 2 | 7-15 | 90 |
| 1986 | Z | 4.3 (4293) | 65 | 75 | 45 | 70 | 75 | 35 | 3 | 22 | 90 |
| 1987 | E | 2.5 (2474) | ④ | 70 | 32 | 160 | 5 | 25 ① | 2 | 7-15 | 90 |
| 1987 | Z | 4.3 (4293) | 65 | 80 | 45 | 70 | 75 | 35 | 3 | 22 | 90 |
| 1988 | E | 2.5 (2474) | ④ | 70 | 32 | 160 | 5 | 25 ① | 2 | 7-15 | 90 |
| 1988 | Z | 4.3 (4293) | 65 | 80 | 45 | 70 | 75 | 35 | 3 | 22 | 90 |
| 1989 | E | 2.5 (2474) | ④ | 65 | 30 | 160 | 5 | 25 | 2 | 11 | 90 |
| 1989 | Z | 4.3 (4293) | 65 | 80 | 45 | 70 | 75 | 35 | 3 | 11 | 90 |
| 1990 | B | 2.5 (2474) | ④ | 65 | 30 | 160 | 5 | 25 | 2 | 11 | 90 |
| 1990 | B | 4.3 (4293) | 65 | 80 | 45 | 70 | 75 | 35 | 3 | 11 | 90 |
| 1991 | B | 4.3 (4293) | 65 | 75 | 6 | 70 | 75 | 35 ⑦ | 3 | 11 | 90 |
| 1992 | Z | 4.3 (4293) | 65 | 75 | 6 | 70 | 75 | 35 ⑦ | 3 | 11 | 90 |
| 1992 | W | 4.3 (4293) | 65 | 75 | 6 | 70 | 75 | 35 ⑧ | 3 | 11 | 100 |
| 1993 | Z | 4.3 (4293) | 65 | 75 | 6 | 70 | 75 | 35 ⑧ | 3 | 11 | 100 |
| 1993 | W | 4.3 (4293) | 65 | 75 | 6 | 70 | 75 | 35 ⑧ | 3 | 11 | 100 |
| 1994 | Z | 4.3 (4293) | 65 | 75 | 6 | 70 | 75 | 35 ⑦ | 3 | 11 | 100 |
| 1994 | W | 4.3 (4293) | 65 | 75 | 6 | 70 | 75 | 35 ⑧ | 3 | 11 | 100 |
| 1995 | Z | 4.3 (4293) | 65 | 75 | 6 | 70 | 75 | 35 ⑧ | 3 | 11 | 100 |
| 1995 | W | 4.3 (4293) | 65 | 75 | 6 | 70 | 75 | 35 ⑧ | 3 | 11 | 100 |
| 1996 | W | 4.3 (4293) | ⑨ | 77 | 6 | 74 | 75 | 35 ⑩ | 10 | 14 | 100 |

88263C06

① If equipped with bolts and studs refer to the illustration accompanying the repair procedure
② Center bolts: 36 ft. lbs.
   Outer bolts: 32 ft. lbs.
③ Center bolts: 26 ft. lbs.
   Other bolts: 20 ft. lbs.
④ Step 1: Tighten all head bolts to 18 ft. lbs.
   Step 2: Tighten all bolts to 26 ft. lbs. except No. 9
   Retighten No. 9 to 18 ft. lbs.
   Tighten all an additional 90 degrees (1/4 turn)
⑤ Automatic trans: 55 ft. lbs.
   Manual trans: 65 ft. lbs.
⑥ 20 ft. lbs. plus 60 degrees (1991-92) or plus 70 degrees (1993-96)
⑦ Last bolt, left side #9 in sequence: 41 ft. lbs.
   All others 35 ft. lbs.
⑧ Specification is for lower manifold. Upper: 124 inch lbs.
⑨ 1st pass 22 ft. lbs.
   2nd pass
   Short bolts: Plus 55 degrees
   Medium bolts: Plus 65 degrees
   Long bolts: Plus 75 degrees
⑩ Lower intake manifold:
   1st pass: 27 inch lbs.
   2nd pass: 106 inch lbs.
   Final pass: 11 ft. lbs.
   Upper manifold bolts:
   83 inch lbs.
⑪ Specification is for a used head; on new heads tighten to 20 ft. lbs.

## PISTON AND RING SPECIFICATIONS

All measurements are given in inches.

| Year | Engine ID/VIN | Engine Displacement Liters (cc) | Piston Clearance | Ring Gap Top Compression | Ring Gap Bottom Compression | Ring Gap Oil Control | Ring Side Clearance Top Compression | Ring Side Clearance Bottom Compression | Ring Side Clearance Oil Control |
|---|---|---|---|---|---|---|---|---|---|
| 1985 | E | 2.5 (2474) | 0.0014-0.0022 | 0.010-0.022 | 0.010-0.027 | 0.015-0.055 | 0.0015-0.0030 | 0.0015-0.0030 | NA |
| 1985 | N | 4.3 (4293) | 0.0007-0.0017 | 0.010-0.020 | 0.010-0.025 | 0.015-0.055 | 0.0012-0.0032 | 0.0012-0.0032 | 0.0020-0.0070 |
| 1986 | E | 2.5 (2474) | 0.0014-0.0022 | 0.010-0.020 | 0.010-0.020 | 0.020-0.060 | 0.0010-0.0030 | 0.0010-0.0030 | 0.0150-0.0550 |
| 1986 | Z | 4.3 (4293) | 0.0007-0.0017 | 0.010-0.020 | 0.010-0.025 | 0.015-0.055 | 0.0012-0.0032 | 0.0012-0.0032 | 0.0020-0.0070 |
| 1987 | E | 2.5 (2474) | 0.0014-0.0022 | 0.010-0.020 | 0.010-0.020 | 0.020-0.060 | 0.0010-0.0030 | 0.0010-0.0030 | 0.0150-0.0550 |
| 1987 | Z | 4.3 (4293) | 0.0007-0.0017 | 0.010-0.020 | 0.010-0.025 | 0.015-0.055 | 0.0012-0.0032 | 0.0012-0.0032 | 0.0020-0.0070 |
| 1988 | E | 2.5 (2474) | 0.0014-0.0022 | 0.010-0.020 | 0.010-0.020 | 0.020-0.060 | 0.0010-0.0030 | 0.0010-0.0030 | 0.0150-0.0550 |
| 1988 | Z | 4.3 (4293) | 0.0007-0.0017 | 0.010-0.020 | 0.010-0.025 | 0.015-0.055 | 0.0012-0.0032 | 0.0012-0.0032 | 0.0020-0.0070 |
| 1989 | E | 2.5 (2474) | 0.0096-0.0022 | 0.010-0.020 | 0.010-0.020 | 0.020-0.060 | 0.0020-0.0030 | 0.0012-0.0030 | 0.0150-0.0550 |
| 1989 | Z | 4.3 (4293) | 0.0007-0.0017 | 0.010-0.020 | 0.010-0.025 | 0.015-0.055 | 0.0012-0.0032 | 0.0012-0.0032 | 0.0020-0.0070 |
| 1990 | E | 2.5 (2474) | 0.0096-0.0022 | 0.010-0.020 | 0.010-0.020 | 0.015-0.060 | 0.0010-0.0020 | 0.0010-0.0030 | 0.0150-0.0020 |
| 1990 | B | 4.3 (4293) | 0.0007-0.0017 | 0.010-0.020 | 0.010-0.025 | 0.015-0.055 | 0.0012-0.0032 | 0.0012-0.0032 | 0.0020-0.0070 |
| 1991 | Z | 4.3 (4293) | 0.0007-0.0017 | 0.010-0.020 | 0.010-0.025 | 0.015-0.055 | 0.0012-0.0032 | 0.0012-0.0032 | 0.0020-0.0070 |
| 1991 | B | 4.3 (4293) | 0.0007-0.0017 | 0.010-0.020 | 0.010-0.025 | 0.015-0.055 | 0.0012-0.0032 | 0.0012-0.0032 | 0.0020-0.0070 |
| 1992 | Z | 4.3 (4293) | 0.0007-0.0017 | 0.010-0.020 | 0.010-0.025 | 0.015-0.055 | 0.0012-0.0032 | 0.0012-0.0032 | 0.0020-0.0070 |
| 1992 | W | 4.3 (4293) | 0.0007-0.0014 | 0.018-0.026 | 0.018-0.026 | 0.015-0.055 | 0.0014-0.0032 | 0.0014-0.0032 | 0.0014-0.0032 |
| 1993 | Z | 4.3 (4293) | 0.0007-0.0017 | 0.010-0.020 | 0.010-0.025 | 0.015-0.055 | 0.0012-0.0032 | 0.0012-0.0032 | 0.0020-0.0070 |
| 1993 | W | 4.3 (4293) | 0.0007-0.0014 | 0.018-0.026 | 0.018-0.026 | 0.015-0.055 | 0.0014-0.0032 | 0.0014-0.0032 | 0.0014-0.0032 |
| 1994 | W | 4.3 (4293) | 0.0007-0.0014 | 0.010-0.020 | 0.010-0.025 | 0.015-0.055 | 0.0014-0.0032 | 0.0012-0.0032 | 0.0014-0.0032 |
| 1994 | Z | 4.3 (4293) | 0.0007-0.0017 | 0.010-0.020 | 0.010-0.025 | 0.015-0.055 | 0.0012-0.0032 | 0.0012-0.0032 | 0.0020-0.0070 |
| 1995 | W | 4.3 (4293) | 0.0007-0.0024 ① | 0.010-0.020 | 0.018-0.026 | 0.015-0.055 | 0.0014-0.0032 | 0.0014-0.0032 | 0.0014-0.0032 |
| 1996 | W | 4.3 (4293) | 0.0024 ① | 0.035 | 0.035 | 0.065 | 0.0042 | 0.0042 | 0.0080 ① |

NA - Not Available
① MAX

88263C05

## Engine

### REMOVAL & INSTALLATION

> ※ **CAUTION**
>
> To reduce the risk of fire and personal injury, it is necessary to relieve the fuel system pressure before servicing any fuel system component. If this procedure is not performed, fuel may be sprayed out of the connection under pressure. Always keep a dry chemical (Class B) fire extinguisher near the work area. Relieve the pressure on the fuel system before disconnecting any fuel line connection.

➡All engine fasteners are important parts that may affect the performance of the components and systems. If replacement becomes necessary, they MUST BE replaced with the same part number or equivalent part. Use specific torque values when assembling the parts, to assure proper retention.

> ※ **CAUTION**
>
> When draining the coolant, keep in mind that cats and dogs are attracted by ethylene glycol antifreeze, and are quite likely to drink any that is left in an uncovered container or in puddles on the ground. This will prove fatal in sufficient quantity. Always drain the coolant into a sealable container. Coolant should be reused unless it is contaminated or several years old.

### 2.5L Engine

1. From inside the vehicle, remove the engine cover, as outlined in Section 1 of this manual.
2. Properly relieve the fuel system pressure, then disconnect the negative battery cable.
3. Drain the cooling system into a suitable container; be sure to save the cooling fluid for reuse.
4. Remove the headlight bezel and grille.
5. Remove the lower radiator close out panel and the radiator support brace.
6. Remove the lower tie bar, the cross braces and the hood latch assembly.
7. If equipped, remove the upper radiator core support.
8. Remove the radiator hoses, then disconnect and plug the transmission-to-radiator oil cooler lines (if equipped).
9. Remove the radiator filler panels, then the radiator and the fan shroud as an assembly.
10. At the bulkhead connector, disconnect the engine electrical harness. Disconnect the electrical harness from the ECM and pull it through the bulkhead.
11. Remove the heater hoses from the heater core.
12. Disconnect the accelerator, the cruise control and the detent (if equipped) cables. Disconnect the ground cable from the cylinder head.
13. Remove the oil filler neck and the thermostat housing from the engine.
14. Remove the purge hose from the charcoal canister, then the air cleaner and adapter from throttle body. Disconnect the fuel hoses from the throttle body.
15. Raise and support the front of the vehicle on jackstands.
16. Disconnect the exhaust pipe from the exhaust manifold. Remove the flywheel cover from the bellhousing.
17. Disconnect the electrical harness from the transmission and the frame, then the electrical connectors from the starter.
18. Remove the starter-to-engine bolts and the starter from the engine.
19. Remove the through-bolts from the engine mounts and install an engine lifting device to the engine.
20. Remove the bellhousing-to-engine bolts, then lower the vehicle. Using a floor jack, support the transmission.
21. Using an engine lifting device, lift the engine, separate it from the transmission and remove it from the vehicle.
   **To install:**
22. Using an engine lifting device, lift the engine, connect it to the transmission and install it in the vehicle.

23. Install the bellhousing-to-engine bolts, torque to 32 ft. lbs. (44 Nm) then lower the vehicle. Using a floor jack, support the transmission.
24. Install the through-bolts to the engine mounts and remove the engine lifting device from the engine.
25. The remainder of installation is the reverse of the removal procedure.
26. Refill the cooling system. Install the engine cover.
27. Connect the negative battery cable. Start the engine and check for fluid leaks and proper operation.

### 4.3L Engine

#### 1985–90 MODELS

1. If equipped, take the vehicle to a reputable repair facility to have the A/C system properly discharged and recovered.
2. Properly relieve the fuel system pressure and disconnect the negative battery cable.
3. Drain the engine coolant into a suitable container.
4. Raise and support the front of the vehicle on jackstands.
5. Disconnect the exhaust pipes from the exhaust manifolds.
6. At the flywheel cover, remove the strut rods, then the flywheel cover from the bellhousing. If equipped with an automatic transmission, mark the torque converter-to-flywheel position, then disconnect the torque converter from the flywheel.
7. Detach the connectors from the starter, then remove the starter from the engine. Disconnect the electrical harness and connectors from the transmission and the frame.
8. Remove the oil filter and the lower fan shroud bolts. Disconnect the fuel hoses from the frame.
9. From the radiator, disconnect the lower transmission oil cooler line (if used) and the lower engine oil cooler line (if used).
10. Remove the through-bolts of the engine-to-frame mounts, then remove the jackstands and lower the vehicle.
11. Remove the headlight bezels and the grille. At the radiator, remove the lower close-out panel, the support brace and the core support cross brace, then remove the lower tie-bar and the hood latch mechanism.
12. At the firewall, remove the master cylinder.
13. From the radiator, remove the upper fan shroud, the upper radiator core support, the filler panels and the radiator.

➡Before removing the radiator, be sure to discharge the air conditioning system (if equipped).

14. From inside the vehicle, remove the engine cover (for details, please refer to Section 1 of this manual) and the right side kick panel.
15. From the A/C system, remove the rear compressor brace, the hose from the accumulator, then the compressor (with the bracket) and the accumulator.
16. Remove the power steering pump (DO NOT disconnect the pressure hoses) and move it aside.
17. Disconnect the vacuum hoses from the intake manifold. Disconnect the electrical harness connector from the bulkhead and the Electronic Control Module (ECM); push the electrical harness connector through the bulkhead.
18. Remove the distributor cap, the fuel line(s) from the carburetor or throttle body and the diverter valve (if equipped).
19. Remove the transmission dipstick tube, the heater hose(s) from the heater core, the horn and the Air Injector Reactor (AIR) check valves.
20. Using and engine lifting device, attach it to the engine.
21. Using a floor jack, raise and support the transmission, then remove the bellhousing-to-engine bolts.
22. Raise the engine, disconnect it from the bellhousing and remove it from the vehicle.
   **To install:**
23. Place the engine on a lifting device and lower the engine into the vehicle. Connect it to the bellhousing.
24. Using a floor jack, raise and support the transmission, then install the bellhousing-to-engine bolts.
25. Remove the engine lifting device.
26. Installation of the remaining components is the reverse of the removal procedure.
27. Refill the engine with coolant and oil.
28. Connect the negative battery cable. Start the engine and check for leaks and proper operation.
29. If the A/C system was discharged, take the van to a reputable repair facility to have the system evacuated, recharged and leak tested. DO NOT WAIT

LONG to do this or moisture which entered the system while it was discharged will cause corrosion and internal system damage. ALSO, DO NOT run the compressor until the system has been properly recharged. Depending on how your model is equipped this may mean you CANNOT use the defogger (this automatically turns the compressor on in some vehicles).

### *1991–95 MODELS*

#### ♦ See Figures 7, 8 and 9

1. If equipped, take the vehicle to a reputable repair shop to have the A/C system properly discharged and recovered using the proper equipment.
2. Properly relieve the fuel system pressure and disconnect the negative battery cable.
3. Drain the cooling system.
4. Raise and safely support the vehicle. Disconnect the exhaust pipes at the manifolds.
5. If applicable, disconnect the strut rods at the flywheel housing.
6. Remove the torque converter cover, then remove the torque converter bolts.
7. Remove the starter assembly, then drain the oil and remove the and oil filter. Disconnect the wires at the transmission. Disconnect the fuel lines.
8. Tag and disengage the wires at the engine and frame. Disconnect the fuel lines at the frame.
9. Disconnect the transmission and engine oil cooler lines at the radiator.
10. Remove the lower fan shroud retainers, then remove the motor mount bolts.
11. Lower the vehicle. Remove the headlight bezels and/or grille, as necessary. On 1994–95 vehicles, remove the horns.
12. Remove the radiator close out panel and the radiator support brace.
13. Remove the hood latch mechanism. If necessary on vehicles through 1992, remove the master cylinder.
14. Remove the air cleaner assembly and ducts.
15. Remove the upper fan shroud.
16. For 1991–93 vehicles:
   a. Remove the upper radiator core support, then if equipped, remove the A/C condenser.
   b. Remove the radiator filler panels, then remove the radiator.
   c. Remove the lower radiator shroud, then remove the engine cover (for details, please refer to Section 1 of this manual).
   d. If equipped, disconnect the A/C hose at the accumulator.
   e. Remove the multi-ribbed accessory drive belt, then remove the fan.
17. For 1994–95 vehicles:
   a. If equipped, remove the A/C condenser.
   b. Remove the fan and clutch assembly, then remove the lower fan shroud.
   c. If not done already, disconnect the remaining oil cooler-to-radiator lines.
   d. Remove the radiator.
   e. Remove the engine cover (for details, please refer to Section 1 of this manual).
   f. If equipped, remove the A/C accumulator.
   g. If not done already, remove the multi-ribbed engine accessory drive belt.

18. Disconnect the power steering pump lines at the gearbox (1991–93) or from the hydro-boost, oil cooler and reservoir (1994–95).
19. If equipped, remove the A/C compressor pencil braces at the engine block.
20. Remove the power steering pump, bracket and A/C compressor as an assembly.
21. Disengage the alternator wiring, then remove the alternator and bracket assembly.
22. Disengage the wiring harness at the bulkhead. Except for 1995 vehicles, remove the right kick panel.
23. Disengage the wiring from the knock sensor module.
24. Disconnect the upper and lower radiator hoses, then disconnect the heater hose from the water pump.
25. Remove the oil filler tube, then remove the transmission filler tube (top bolt only).
26. Tag and disconnect the vacuum hoses at the intake manifold.
27. If equipped, remove the cruise control servo and bracket.
28. Matchmark and remove the distributor assembly or the High Voltage Switch (HVS) assembly, as applicable.
29. If equipped with the 4.3L (VIN W) engine, remove the upper intake manifold assembly, then disconnect the fuel lines and remove the lower intake manifold.
30. If equipped with the 4.3L (VIN B or Z) engine, disconnect the fuel lines from the TBI unit, tag and disengage all cables, wiring and hoses, then remove the TBI unit from the engine. Remove the MAP sensor bracket, then disconnect the heater hose from the engine block with bracket from the exhaust manifold.
31. Raise and support the vehicle safely, then If equipped, remove the transfer case brace.
32. For 1994–95 vehicles, remove the fuel line bracket and ground wire from the back of the left cylinder head.
33. Remove the transmission oil level indicator tube.
34. Disengage the necessary wiring from the transmission.
35. Remove the bellhousing bolts, then lower the vehicle.
36. For 1995 vehicles the tie bar must be cut from the vehicle in order to create sufficient clearance for engine removal:
   a. Remove the master cylinder retaining nuts, then reposition the cylinder assembly out of the way.
   b. Scribe marks for cutting the tie bar assembly. The marks should be made at the centerline between the indentations on the right and left side of the bar assembly.
   c. Using the replacement brackets from the service kit as a template over the indentations, center punch the holes for drilling.
   d. Drill out 8mm holes for the brace bolts.
   e. Carefully cut the tie bar cross section using a reciprocating power saw or hack saw.

➡**Extreme care must be taken when cutting out the tie bar cross section. The tie bar will be attached using brackets from the service kit. The cut out portion of the bar and the brackets must be treated with anti-corrosion materials and painted. Care taken during cutting will help save time on surface preparation and installation.**

37. Attach a suitable lifting device to the engine and support the transmission, then carefully remove the engine.

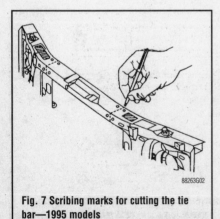

**Fig. 7 Scribing marks for cutting the tie bar—1995 models**

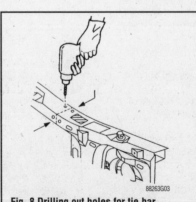

**Fig. 8 Drilling out holes for tie bar replacement brackets—1995 models**

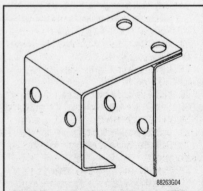

**Fig. 9 Tie bar bracket positioning—1995 models**

**To install:**

38. Carefully lower the engine into position and engage it to the transmission assembly. If possible, thread the bellhousing bolts to secure the engine to the transmission.

39. Remove the engine lifting device, then raise and support the vehicle safely. Install any remaining bellhousing bolts, then tighten the bolts and remove the transmission support.

40. Engage the wiring to the transmission assembly.

41. Install the transmission oil level indicator tube.

42. On 1994–95 vehicles install the fuel line bracket and ground wire to the back of the left cylinder head.

43. If equipped, install the transfer case brace.

44. Lower the vehicle.

45. If equipped with the 4.3L (VIN B or Z) engine, connect the heater hose to the engine block with the exhaust manifold bracket, then install the MAP sensor bracket. Install the TBI unit, connecting all wiring, cables and hoses. Connect the fuel lines.

46. If equipped with the 4.3L (VIN W) engine, install the lower intake manifold assembly, then connect the fuel lines and install the upper intake manifold assembly.

47. Align and install the distributor or the HVS assembly, as equipped.

48. If equipped, install the cruise control servo and bracket.

49. Connect the vacuum hoses to the intake manifold.

50. Install the transmission filler tube (upper bolt) and the oil filler tube.

51. If removed and applicable, install the ignition coil.

52. Except for 1995 vehicles, the air cleaner and ducts may be installed at this time.

53. Connect the heater and radiator hoses.

54. Connect the wiring harness to the knock sensor module, then for vehicles 1991–94 install the kick panel.

55. Engage the wiring harness at the bulkhead.

56. Install the alternator and bracket as an assembly, then engage the wiring.

57. Install the power steering pump, bracket and A/C compressor assembly. Connect the compressor pencil braces to the block and connect the hoses to the power steering pump, oil cooler and reservoir. Make sure all components are secure.

58. For 1991–93 vehicles, install the fan.

59. Position the multi-ribbed drive belt.

60. Install the accumulator and/or connect the refrigerant hoses to the accumulator assembly, as applicable.

61. Install the lower radiator shroud, then for 1994–95 vehicles, install the fan and clutch.

62. For 1995 vehicles install the tie bar assembly:

    a. File the rough edges of the tie bar and removed cross section.

    b. Clean the assembly, cross section and brackets using a wax and grease remover.

    c. Treat all bare metal surfaces with an anticorrosion primer.

    d. Apply primer surfaces to the tie bar assembly, cross section and brackets.

    e. Paint the components and allow to dry.

    f. Install the front brackets to the tie bar cross section and to the bar assembly using the 2 bolts and nuts facing the front of the vehicle.

    g. Install the U-nuts to the rear tie bar cross section and tie bar assembly.

    h. Install the rear bracket and remaining nuts and bolts, then tighten to 24 ft. lbs. (31 Nm)

    i. Reposition and secure the master cylinder assembly. If necessary, cut out indication hole in the air cleaner snorkel.

63. Install the radiator and connect the hoses.

64. If equipped, install the A/C condenser.

65. Install the upper fan shroud and, if applicable, the upper radiator core support.

66. Install the hood latch mechanism, then install the core support brace.

67. On vehicles 1991–94 install the radiator lower close out panel.

68. On 1994–95 vehicles, install the horns.

69. Install the remaining components in the reverse order of removal.

70. Refill the engine crankcase with engine oil, then connect the negative battery cable.

71. Properly refill the engine cooling system.

72. If the A/C system was discharged, take the van to a reputable repair facility to have the system evacuated, recharged and leak tested. DO NOT WAIT LONG to do this or moisture which entered the system while it was discharged will cause corrosion and internal system damage. ALSO, DO NOT run the compressor until the system has been properly recharged. Depending on how your model is equipped this may mean you CANNOT use the defogger (this automatically turns the compressor on in some vehicles).

### *1996 MODELS*

#### ◆ See Figures 10, 11, 12 and 13

For the 1996 model year, the manufacturer determined that lifting the engine from the van's engine compartment was no longer a viable option (especially if it involved cutting pieces of the radiator support in order to provide sufficient clearance). Although it still may be possible to remove the engine as outlined for similar late-model vehicles (under the 1991–95 procedures), IT IS NOT recommended.

→Because there is insufficient clearance to remove the engine from the van through the engine compartment, the body must be lifted off the frame assembly for access. This requires great care and patience to prevent unnecessary damage to the vehicle's body. ALSO, this procedure requires the use of a side lift or twin post hoist. If a suitable hoist is not available, it is recommended that you do NOT attempt this procedure, but instead have the work done by a reputable repair facility.

1. If equipped, take the vehicle to a reputable repair facility that has the proper equipment and have them recover the A/C system refrigerant.

2. Properly relieve the fuel system pressure.

3. Drain the engine cooling system.

4. Disconnect the negative battery, followed by the positive cable, then remove the battery from the engine compartment.

5. Remove the air cleaner assembly.

6. Disconnect the throttle cable, and cruise control cable (if equipped), from the throttle body bracket.

7. If equipped, disengage the cruise control stepper motor wiring.

8. If equipped, disconnect the A/C lines at the accumulator and condenser. Immediately plug all openings to prevent system contamination.

9. Remove the radiator assembly.

10. Remove the power steering reservoir and drain the fluid.

11. If equipped, disconnect the lines from the brake hydro-boost unit.

12. Remove the master cylinder from the hydro-boost unit, then tie it to the oil fill tube for support.

13. Matchmark, then disconnect the steering shaft from the gear. Make sure the steering wheel is locked in position and remains so to prevent possible damage to the Supplemental Inflatable Restraint (SIR or air bag) coil in the steering column).

14. Disconnect the heater hoses from the engine and the vacuum line from the vacuum tank.

15. Disengage the fuse box and wiring harness from the bulkhead connector and all related electrical connectors. Position the wiring harness over the engine.

16. Drain the engine crankcase.

17. Matchmark and remove the rear driveshaft.

18. Remove the starter and starter opening shield.

19. Matchmark the torque converter to the flywheel (flexplate), then remove the torque converter bolts through the starter opening.

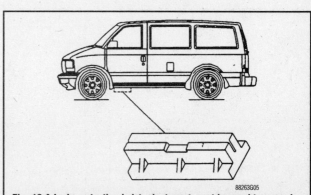

88263G05

**Fig. 10 A body protection hoist adapter set must be used to spread the weight evenly and prevent damage—1996 models**

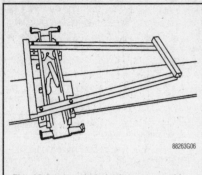

**Fig. 11 A twin post hoist frame assembly support bar is necessary unless you are using a side lift hoist**

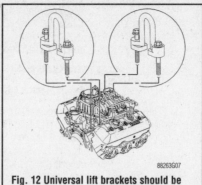

**Fig. 12 Universal lift brackets should be installed in place of the proper intake manifold bolts**

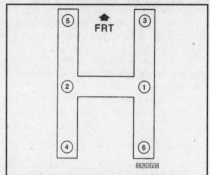

**Fig. 13 The proper frame bolt tightening sequence MUST BE OBSERVED to assure proper chassis-to-frame alignment**

20. Disconnect the shift linkage from the transmission.

21. Disconnect the exhaust system at the main flange behind the catalytic converter.

22. Disconnect the parking brake bracket from the frame.

23. Disconnect the brake line from the BMPV assembly.

24. Remove the front bumper.

25. Remove the power steering cooler from the front air deflector.

26. Disengage the SIR (air bag) sensor connector.

27. Remove the wheel housing splash shield's chassis-to-frame retainers.

28. If equipped, disconnect the rear air conditioning lines at the rear crossmember. Leave the A/C lines attached to the powertrain assembly.

29. Disconnect the fuel lines at the fuel filter. Carefully pull the lines through the crossmember (forward) and position them on the transmission.

30. Disengage the fuel tank electrical connector.

➡**Make sure that there are no connections between the chassis and frame.**

31. On All Wheel Drive (AWD) vehicles, remove the transfer case vent hose.

**✳✳ CAUTION**

**When working on a vehicle that is supported by a hoist, add extra support to the opposite end of the vehicle, from where the work is occurring to prevent the possibility of the vehicle falling from the lift. A sudden jarring motion that causes the vehicle to fall could also cause SEVERE personal injury or even death.**

32. If a side lift hoist is being used:

a. Install a body protection hoist adapter set such as J-41602, or equivalent, to the pinch weld area on both sides of the vehicle. A suitable replacement for this tool may be fabricated from blocks of wood, but be sure that they spread the weight across a sufficiently large area of the body around the weld point.

b. If raised, lower the vehicle.

c. Position the front hoist arms under the body protection adapter set, making sure the rear of the vehicle is slightly higher than the front.

d. Support the rear crossmember with jackstands.

e. Remove the 6 frame bolts.

f. Raise the hoist to separate the body from the frame assembly.

g. Install supports under the rear axle.

33. If a twin post hoist is being used:

a. Install a body protection hoist adapter set such as J-41602, or equivalent, to the pinch weld area on both sides of the vehicle. A suitable replacement for this tool may be fabricated from blocks of wood, but be sure that they spread the weight across a sufficiently large area of the body around the weld point.

b. Install jackstands under the body protection set and under the rear of the van to support the vehicle.

c. Lower the front post of the hoist, then install J-41617 or an equivalent twin post hoist frame assembly support bar to the hoist. Raise the front part of the hoist with the tool attached.

d. Remove the 6 frame bolts.

e. CAREFULLY lower the powertrain/frame assembly from the vehicle.

34. Install J-41427, or equivalent universal lift brackets, to the engine:

a. Tag and disconnect the spark plug wires, then remove the distributor cap from the top of the HVS assembly.

b. Remove the 2 rear right lower intake manifold bolts, then install the engine lift bracket marked RIGHT REAR. Tighten the bracket retaining bolts to 11 ft. lbs. (15 Nm).

c. Remove the air conditioning compressor and accessory drive bracket.

d. Disconnect the EGR tube from the intake manifold.

e. Remove the 2 left front lower intake manifold bolts, then install the engine lift bracket marked LEFT FRONT, with the arrow pointing to the front of the engine. Tighten the retaining bolts to 11 ft. lbs. (15 Nm).

35. Remove the engine mount through-bolts.

36. Disconnect the fuel line bracket from the rear of the left cylinder head.

37. Disconnect the fuel lines from the fuel rail.

38. Disengage the electrical harness at the transmission connectors and ALL of the emission sensors.

39. On All Wheel Drive (AWD) vehicles, remove the transfer case-to-engine support brace. Raise the engine slightly and support the transmission with jackstands and a block of wood. DO NOT support the transmission under the oil pan.

40. Disconnect the exhaust "Y" pipe from the manifolds.

41. Disconnect the engine from the transmission, then remove the engine from the frame.

**To install:**

➡**If you are installing a new motor, make sure that any remaining components, brackets or accessories are transferred from the old engine.**

42. Carefully position the engine to the frame, then install it to the transmission and tighten the retaining bolts. Remove the transmission jack, then lower the assembly onto the engine mountings.

43. Install and tighten the engine mount through-bolts.

44. Connect the exhaust pipe to the manifolds.

45. Install the fuel line bracket to the rear of the left cylinder head, then connect the fuel lines to the rail.

46. Engage the wiring harness to the transmission connectors and to the emission sensors.

47. If equipped, install the transfer case-to-engine block support brace.

48. Remove the universal lift brackets from the engine.

49. Install the intake manifold bolts where the lift hooks were installed.

50. Install the A/C compressor and accessory drive bracket.

51. Connect the EGR pipe to the intake manifold.

52. CAREFULLY lower the vehicle onto the frame (if using a side post hoist) OR raise the engine/frame assembly up and into the vehicle (if using a twin post hoist). As the body is assembled to the frame, use a prybar or dowel pin to properly align the components using the 2 alignment holes provided in each.

53. Loosely install the 6 frame mounting bolts, then tighten the bolts to specification using THE PROPER SEQUENCE:

a. First, tighten the right center bolt to 114 ft. lbs. (155 Nm).

b. Then, tighten the left center bolt to 114 ft. lbs. (155 Nm).

c. Next, tighten the right front bolt, followed by the left rear bolt each to 66 ft. lbs. (90 Nm).

d. Finally, tighten left front bolt, followed by the right rear bolt each to 66 ft. lbs. (90 Nm).

54. Remove the body protection hoist adapters and, if raised, lower the vehicle.

55. Install the remaining components in the reverse order of removal. Tighten all components securely.

56. Align the torque converter and flexplate matchmarks made earlier, then install and tighten the converter bolts. Tighten the bolts evenly to specification. For details, please refer to Section 7.

57. Refill the engine crankcase, then install and connect the battery (negative cable last).

58. Fill and bleed the hydraulic brake system.

59. Check and fill the transmission assembly, as necessary.

60. Refill the power steering system.

61. Fill and bleed the engine cooling system.

62. Properly refill the engine cooling system, then check for leaks.

63. Once the engine has cooled sufficiently, install the engine cover to the passenger compartment.

64. If the A/C system was discharged, take the van to a reputable repair facility to have the system evacuated, recharged and leak tested. DO NOT WAIT LONG to do this or moisture which entered the system while it was discharged will cause corrosion and internal system damage. ALSO DO NOT run the compressor until the system has been properly recharged, depending on how your model is equipped this may mean you CANNOT use the defogger (this automatically turns the compressor on in some vehicles).

## Pushrod Side Cover

### REMOVAL & INSTALLATION

#### 2.5L Engine

▶ See Figures 14 and 15

The pushrod side cover is located on the right side of the engine and must be removed to service the valve lifters:

1. Disconnect the negative battery cable for safety.

2. For access, remove the engine cover from the passenger compartment. For details, please refer to Section 1 of this manual.

3. If necessary, remove the alternator and the bracket from the engine.

4. Place a pan under the radiator, open the drain cock and drain the cooling system.

### ✳✳ CAUTION

**When draining the coolant, keep in mind that cats and dogs are attracted by ethylene glycol antifreeze, and are quite likely to drink any that is left in an uncovered container or in puddles on the ground. This will prove fatal in sufficient quantity. Always drain the coolant into a sealable container. Coolant should be reused unless it is contaminated or several years old.**

5. If necessary on early models, remove the intake manifold-to-engine brace, then remove the lower radiator and heater hoses.

6. Disengage the ignition coil wires, then remove the spark plug wires and bracket from the intake manifold.

7. Remove the fuel pipes and clips from the pushrod cover.

8. Remove the oil pressure gage sender or wiring (if equipped), then remove the wiring harness brackets from the pushrod cover.

9. Unscrew the nuts from the cover attaching studs, reverse 2 of the nuts so the washers face outward and screw them back onto the 2 inner studs.

10. Assemble the 2 remaining nuts to the same 2 inner studs with the washers facing inward, then using a small wrench on the inner nut (on each stud) jam the nuts slightly together.

11. Again using the wrench on the inner stud, unscrew the studs until the cover breaks loose, then remove the nuts from the studs and remove the cover from the engine. Remove the studs from the cover and reinstall them to the engine. Tighten the studs to 90 inch lbs. (10 Nm).

12. Using a plastic scraper, clean the gasket mounting surfaces.

➡Use a solvent to clean the oil and grease from the gasket mounting surfaces.

#### To install:

13. Apply a ³⁄₁₆ (5mm) bead of RTV sealant to the gasket mating surface of the pushrod cover.

14. Install the side cover to the engine and tighten the nuts to 90 inch lbs. (10 Nm).

15. Install the remaining components in the reverse order of removal.

16. Connect the negative battery cable, then properly refill and bleed the cooling system.

17. Start the engine and check for leaks.

18. Once the engine has cooled, install the engine cover.

## Rocker Arm (Valve) Cover

### REMOVAL & INSTALLATION

#### 2.5L Engine

▶ See Figures 15 and 16

1. Disconnect the negative battery cable for safety.

2. From inside the vehicle, remove the engine cover as outlined in Section 1 of this manual.

3. Remove the air cleaner.

4. Disconnect the Positive Crankcase Ventilation (PCV) valve hose, the ignition wires from the rocker arm cover.

5. Remove the Exhaust Gas Recirculation (EGR) valve.

6. From the intake stud, label and disconnect the vacuum hoses.

7. Remove the rocker arm cover-to-cylinder head bolts and the cover.

8. Using a plastic scraper, clean the gasket mounting surface.

➡Be sure to use solvent to remove any oil or grease that may remain on the sealing surfaces.

#### To install:

9. Apply a ³⁄₁₆ in. (5mm) continuous bead of RTV sealant to the cylinder head, inboard of the bolts holes. While the sealant is still wet (within about 10 minutes of applications), install the rocker arm cover, then tighten the retainers to 90 inch lbs. (10 Nm).

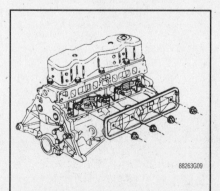

Fig. 14 Exploded view of the pushrod side cover mounting—2.5L engine

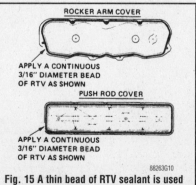

Fig. 15 A thin bead of RTV sealant is used on both the pushrod and rocker arm covers on the 2.5L engine

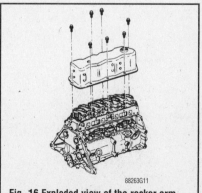

Fig. 16 Exploded view of the rocker arm cover mounting—2.5L engine

10. Connect the vacuum hoses to the intake stud as labeled.

11. Installation of the remaining components is the reverse of the removal procedure.

12. Connect the negative battery cable. Start the engine and check for leaks.

13. Once the engine has cooled, install the engine cover.

### 4.3L Engine

▶ See Figures 17, 18, 19, 20 and 21

### RIGHT SIDE (1985–92)

1. Disconnect the negative battery cable for safety.

2. From inside the vehicle, remove the engine cover. For details, please refer to Section 1 of this manual.

3. Remove the air cleaner. Disconnect the Air Injection Reaction (AIR) hoses from the diverter valve, then the diverter valve bracket from the intake manifold.

4. From the alternator bracket, remove the engine oil filler tube and the transmission (if equipped with an automatic transmission) oil filler tube.

5. From the valve cover, remove the Positive Crankcase Ventilation (PCV) valve.

6. From the back side of the right cylinder head, remove the AIR pipe-to-cylinder head bolts and move the pipe (hose) out of the way.

7. Remove the ignition wires from the valve cover and the distributor cap (with the wires attached), then move the cap out of the way.

8. Remove the rocker arm cover-to-cylinder head bolts and the cover.

9. Using a plastic scraper, clean the gasket mounting surfaces.

10. Using a new gasket, install the rocker cover and tighten the retainers to 90 inch lbs. (10 Nm).

11. The remainder of installation is the reverse of the removal procedure.

12. Connect the negative battery cable.

13. Start the engine and check for leaks.

14. Once the engine has cooled, install the engine cover.

### RIGHT SIDE (1993–95)

1. Disconnect the negative battery cable for safety.

2. From inside the vehicle, remove the engine cover. For details, please refer to Section 1 of this manual.

3. Remove the air cleaner, adapter and heat stove tube.

4. Disconnect the spark plug wire bracket at the side of the cylinder head, then remove the wires from the clip at the rear of the cylinder head.

5. Remove the Positive Crankcase Ventilation (PCV) valve and vacuum tube.

6. Disengage the wiring harness at the rocker arm cover including the connections for:

   a. Air conditioning compressor clutch (if equipped).

   b. Coolant temperature sensor.

   c. Manifold Absolute Pressure (MAP) sensor.

   d. Throttle Position (TP) sensor.

   e. Exhaust Gas Recirculation (EGR) solenoid.

   f. Fuel injector(s).

   g. Ignition coil.

   h. Knock sensor module.

   i. Wiring harness ground at the coolant outlet.

7. Tag and disconnect the vacuum tubes from the MAP sensor and EGR solenoid. Remove the sensor bracket.

8. Remove the rocker arm cover-to-cylinder head bolts, then remove the cover and gasket.

9. Using a plastic scraper, clean the gasket mounting surfaces.

10. Using a new gasket, install the rocker cover and tighten the retainers to 90 inch lbs. (10 Nm).

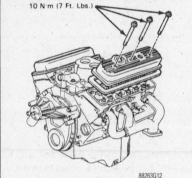

**Fig. 17 Exploded view of a typical 4.3L rocker arm cover mounting**

**Fig. 18 Loosen the rocker arm retaining bolts using a wrench or ratchet and suitable driver . . .**

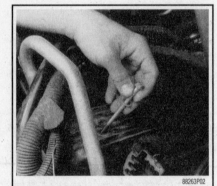

**Fig. 19 . . . then remove the bolts from the cylinder head and valve cover**

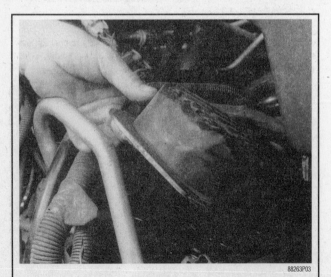

**Fig. 20 Lift and remove the valve cover from the cylinder head . . .**

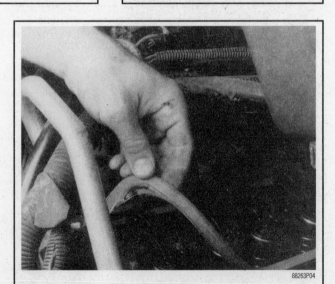

**Fig. 21 . . . then remove and discard the old gasket**

11. Install the remaining components in the reverse order of removal.
12. Connect the negative battery cable.
13. Start the engine and check for leaks.
14. Once the engine has cooled, install the engine cover.

### RIGHT SIDE (1996)

1. Disconnect the negative battery cable for safety.
2. From inside the vehicle, remove the engine cover. For details, please refer to Section 1 of this manual.
3. Disconnect the spark plug wires from the brackets. If any of the wires will interfere with cover removal, they should be TAGGED and disconnected from the spark plugs for additional clearance.
4. Disconnect the vent tube.
5. Remove the purge solenoid and bracket from the engine.
6. Disengage the wiring harness at the rocker arm cover, then remove the bracket.
7. Remove the rocker arm cover-to-cylinder head bolts, then remove the cover and gasket.
8. Using a plastic scraper, clean the gasket mounting surfaces.
9. Using a new gasket, install the rocker cover and tighten the retainers to 90 inch lbs. (10 Nm).
10. Installation of the remaining components is the reverse of the removal procedure.
11. Connect the negative battery cable.
12. Start the engine and check for leaks.
13. Once the engine has cooled, install the engine cover.

### LEFT SIDE (1985–92)

1. Disconnect the negative battery cable for safety.
2. From inside the vehicle, remove the engine cover. For details, please refer to Section 1 of this manual.
3. Remove the air cleaner.

➡**If equipped with a carburetor, remove the vacuum pipe from the carburetor.**

4. Disconnect the electrical harness from the rocker arm cover and any vacuum hoses (if necessary).
5. On late-model vehicles, remove the oil fill tube if necessary for clearance.
6. If necessary, disconnect the accelerator and the detent cables from the carburetor/throttle body, then remove the mounting brackets from the intake manifold.
7. Remove the rocker arm cover-to-cylinder head bolts and the cover.
8. Using a plastic scraper, clean the gasket mounting surfaces.
9. Install the cover using a new gasket, then tighten the rocker cover-to-cylinder head bolts to 90 inch lbs. (10 Nm).
10. Install the remaining components in the reverse order of removal.
11. Connect the negative battery cable. Start the engine and check for leaks.
12. Once the engine has sufficiently, install the engine cover.

### LEFT SIDE (1993–95)

1. Disconnect the negative battery cable for safety.
2. From inside the vehicle, remove the engine cover. For details, please refer to Section 1 of this manual.
3. Remove the air cleaner, adapter and heat stove tube.
4. Remove the multiple ribbed serpentine drive belt.
5. If equipped, remove the air conditioning compressor pencil braces at the rear of the compressor, then remove the compressor mounting bolts. Pull the compressor forward without disconnecting or damaging the refrigerant lines.
6. If equipped, disconnect the vacuum tube and disengage the wiring harness connector from the cruise control servo.
7. Remove the oil fill tube.
8. Disconnect the spark plug wire bracket from the side of the cylinder head.
9. Remove the rocker arm cover-to-cylinder head bolts, then remove the cover and gasket.
10. Using a plastic scraper, clean the gasket mounting surfaces.
11. Using a new gasket, install the rocker cover and tighten the retainers to 90 inch lbs. (10 Nm).
12. The remainder of installation is the reverse of the removal procedure.
13. Connect the negative battery cable. Start the engine and check for leaks.

14. Once the engine has cooled sufficiently, install the engine cover to the passenger compartment.

### LEFT SIDE (1996)

1. Disconnect the negative battery cable for safety.
2. From inside the vehicle, remove the engine cover. For details, please refer to Section 1 of this manual.
3. Remove the air cleaner box and intake duct.
4. Remove the PCV valve and oil fill tube.
5. Remove the serpentine drive belt.
6. If equipped, unbolt the air conditioning compressor and bracket, then slide the assembly forward without disconnecting or damaging the refrigerant lines.
7. Remove the EGR tube.
8. Disconnect the spark plug wires from the brackets. If any of the wires will interfere with cover removal, they should be TAGGED and disconnected from the spark plugs for additional clearance.
9. Remove the rocker arm cover-to-cylinder head bolts, then remove the cover and gasket.
10. Using a plastic scraper, clean the gasket mounting surfaces.
11. Using a new gasket, install the rocker cover and tighten the retainers to 90 inch lbs. (10 Nm).
12. The remainder of installation is the reverse of the removal procedure.
13. Connect the negative battery cable, then start the engine and check for leaks.
14. Once the engine has cooled, install the engine cover.

## Rocker Arms

The rocker arms open and close the valves through a very simple ball pivot type operation.

### REMOVAL & INSTALLATION

#### 2.5L Engine

♦ **See Figures 22 and 23**

1. Refer to the rocker arm (valve) cover, removal and installation procedures in this section and remove the valve cover.
2. Using a socket wrench, remove the rocker arm bolts, the ball washer and the rocker arm.

➡**If only the pushrod is to be removed, back off the rocker arm bolt, swing the rocker arm aside and remove the pushrod. When removing more than assembly, at the same time, be sure to keep them in order for reassembly purposes.**

3. Inspect the rocker arms and ball washers for scoring and/or other damage, replace them (if necessary).
**To install:**

➡**If replacing worn components with new ones, be sure to coat the new parts with Molykote® or an equivalent engine assembly pre-lube, before installation.**

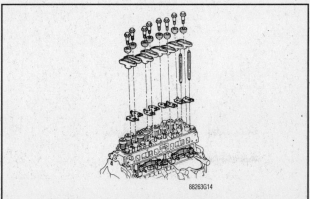

88263G14

**Fig. 22 Exploded view of the rocker arm assembly—2.5L engine**

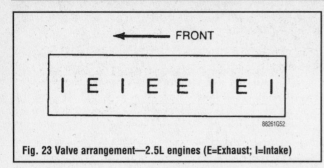

Fig. 23 Valve arrangement—2.5L engines (E=Exhaust; I=Intake)

4. Install the pushrod and pushrod guide, if removed.
5. Loosely install the ball washer, rocker arms and bolts.
6. Adjust the valves:
    a. Rotate the crankshaft until the mark on the damper pulley aligns with the **0** mark on the timing plate and the No. 1 cylinder is on the compression stroke.

➡**To determine if the No. 1 cylinder is on the compression stroke, shake the rocker arms of the No. 1 cylinder, if they move the cylinder is on the compression stroke, if they don't move the cylinder is on the exhaust stroke. If the cylinder is on the exhaust stroke, it will be necessary to rotate the crankshaft one more full revolution to bring No. 1 back to top on compression.**

    b. With the engine on the compression stroke, adjust the exhaust valves of cylinders No. 1 & 3 and the intake valves of cylinders No. 1 & 2.
    c. To adjust the valves, tighten the rocker arm studs to the specified torque:
    • 1985–86: 20 ft. lbs. (28 Nm).
    • 1987: 24 ft. lbs. (32 Nm).
    • 1988–90: 22 ft. lbs. (30 Nm).
    d. Rotate the crankshaft one complete revolution and align the mark on the damper pulley with the **0** mark on the timing plate.
    e. With the engine on the No. 4 compression stroke, tighten the retainers for the exhaust valves of cylinders No. 2 & 4 and the intake valves of cylinders No. 3 & 4.
7. Install the rocker arm cover. For details, please refer to the procedure found earlier in this section.

### 4.3L Engine

▶ **See Figures 24 thru 30**

1. Refer to the Valve Cover, Removal and Installation procedures in this section and remove the valve covers.
2. Using a socket wrench remove the rocker arm-to-cylinder head nuts, the ball washers, the rocker arms and the pushrods (if necessary).

➡**If you are removing more than one rocker arm, nut, washer and pushrod at a time, keep each assembly tagged, arranged and/or sorted to assure installation in their original locations.**

3. Inspect the parts for excessive wear and/or damage, then replace any parts (if necessary).

**To install:**

➡**If replacing any parts with new ones, coat the new parts with Molykote® or an equivalent engine assembly pre-lube.**

4. If removed, install the pushrod.
5. Loosely install the rocker arm, ball pivot and nut.
6. For the 4.3L (VIN W) engine and any 1993–94 4.3L (VIN Z) engines which are equipped with screw-in type rocker arm studs with positive stop shoulders, Tighten the rocker arm adjusting nuts against the stop shoulders to 20 ft. lbs. (27 Nm). No further adjustment is necessary, or possible.
7. For all 1985–92 and most later 4.3L (VIN B or Z) engines (which are not equipped with screw-in type rocker arm studs and positive stop shoulders), properly adjust the valve lash, as outlined in this following steps.
8. To prepare the engine for valve adjustment, rotate the crankshaft until the mark on the damper pulley aligns with the 0° mark on the timing plate and the No. 1 cylinder is on the compression stroke. You will know when the No. 1 piston is on it's compression stroke because both the intake and exhaust valves will remain closed as the crankshaft damper mark approaches the timing scale.

➡**Another method to tell when the piston is coming up on the compression stroke is by removing the spark plug and placing your thumb over the hole, you will feel the air being forced out of the spark plug hole. Stop turning the crankshaft when the TDC timing mark on the crankshaft pulley is directly aligned with the timing mark pointer or the zero mark on the scale.**

9. With the engine on the compression stroke, adjust the exhaust valves of cylinders No. 1, 5 and 6 and the intake valves of cylinders No. 1, 2 and 3 by performing the following procedures:
    a. Back out the adjusting nut until lash can be felt at the pushrod.
    b. While rotating the pushrod, turn the adjusting nut inward until all of the lash is removed.
    c. When the play has disappeared, turn the adjusting nut inward 1 additional turn for 1988–93 engines or 1¾ additional turns for 1994 engines.
10. Rotate the crankshaft 1 complete revolution and align the mark on the damper pulley with the 0° mark on the timing plate; the engine is now positioned on the No. 4 firing position. This time the No. 4 cylinder valves remain closed as the timing mark approaches the scale. Adjust the exhaust valves of cylinders No. 2, 3 and 4 and the intake valves of cylinders No. 4, 5 and 6, by performing the following procedures:
    a. Back out the adjusting nut until lash can be felt at the pushrod.
    b. While rotating the pushrod, turn the adjusting nut inward until all of the lash is removed.
    c. When the play has disappeared, turn the adjusting nut inward 1 additional turn for 1988–93 engines or 1¾ additional turns for 1994 engines.
11. Install the rocker arm cover(s) to the cylinder head.

## Thermostat

The thermostat is located inside a housing, which is attached to the front of the cylinder head (2.5L) or to the front of the intake manifold (4.3L).

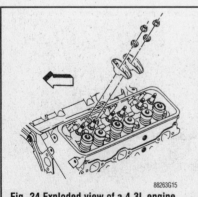

Fig. 24 Exploded view of a 4.3L engine rocker arm assembly

Fig. 25 To remove the rocker arm, loosen and remove the nut and ball washer (pivot) . . .

Fig. 26 . . . then lift the rocker arm from the stud

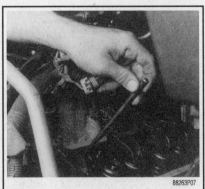

Fig. 27 If necessary, remove the pushrod for replacement or inspection

Fig. 28 Keep ALL PARTS sorted or tagged for installation in their original locations

Fig. 29 Most 4.3L engines (except VIN W and some 1993–94 VIN Z models) will require valve lash adjustment during installation

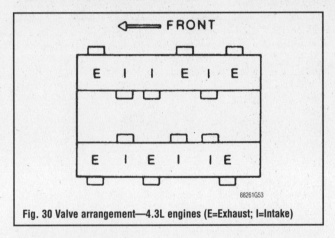

Fig. 30 Valve arrangement—4.3L engines (E=Exhaust; I=Intake)

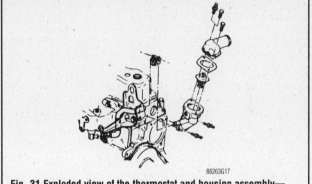

Fig. 31 Exploded view of the thermostat and housing assembly—2.5L engine

## REMOVAL & INSTALLATION

▶ See Figures 31 thru 39

1. Disconnect the negative battery cable for safety.
2. Place a catch pan under the radiator, open the drain cock and drain the cooling system to a level below the thermostat housing.

### ✳✳ CAUTION

**When draining the coolant, keep in mind that cats and dogs are attracted by ethylene glycol antifreeze, and are quite likely to drink any that is left in an uncovered container or in puddles on the ground. This will prove fatal in sufficient quantity. Always drain the coolant into a sealable container. Coolant should be reused unless it is contaminated or several years old.**

3. Remove the thermostat housing-to-engine bolts or bolt and stud, as applicable.
4. Separate the housing from the cylinder head (2.5L) or manifold (4.3L) and carefully remove the thermostat.
5. Using a plastic scraper, clean the gasket mounting surfaces.

**To install:**

6. Except for 1996 vehicles, place a ⅛ in. (3mm) bead of RTV sealant in the groove of the water outlet mating surface.
7. Place the thermostat in position, then install and secure the housing using a new gasket on all but 1996 vehicles.
8. Tighten the thermostat housing-to-engine bolts or bolt and nut to 21 ft. lbs. (28 Nm) for 1985–94 vehicles, 15 ft. lbs. (20 Nm) for 1995 vehicles or to 18 ft. lbs. (25 Nm) for 1996 vehicles.
9. Connect the battery cable, the properly refill and bleed the cooling system.
10. Run the engine and check for leaks.

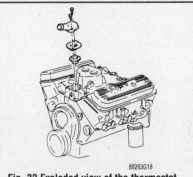

Fig. 32 Exploded view of the thermostat and housing assembly—carbureted and TBI 4.3L engines

Fig. 33 If access is difficult with the hose attached . . .

Fig. 34 . . . remove the hose, then loosen and remove the housing retainers

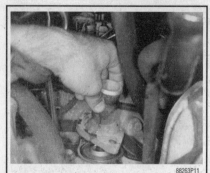

**Fig. 35 Once the housing is free, carefully lift it from the engine to expose the thermostat**

**Fig. 36 Sometimes, the thermostat will lift from the engine with the housing . . .**

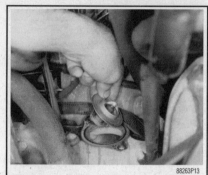

**Fig. 37 . . . but if not, note the direction it is installed, then lift if from the engine for replacement**

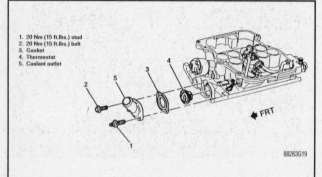

1. 20 Nm (15 ft.lbs.) stud
2. 20 Nm (15 ft.lbs.) bolt
3. Gasket
4. Thermostat
5. Coolant outlet

**Fig. 38 Exploded view of the thermostat and housing assembly—4.3L (1992–95 VIN W) CMFI engine**

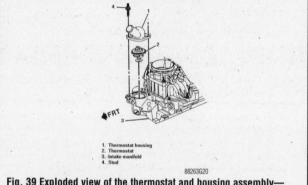

1. Thermostat housing
2. Thermostat
3. Intake manifold
4. Stud

**Fig. 39 Exploded view of the thermostat and housing assembly—4.3L (1996 VIN W) CSFI engine**

## Intake Manifold

### REMOVAL & INSTALLATION

#### 2.5L Engine

▶ See Figure 40

The intake manifold is located on the right side of the cylinder head.

### ✳✳ CAUTION

**Relieve the pressure on the fuel system before disconnecting any fuel line connection!**

1. From inside the vehicle, remove the engine cover. For details, please refer to Section 1 of this manual.
2. Properly relieve the fuel system pressure, then disconnect the negative battery cable.
3. Place a catch pan under the radiator, open the drain cock and drain the cooling system.

### ✳✳ CAUTION

**When draining the coolant, keep in mind that cats and dogs are attracted by ethylene glycol antifreeze, and are quite likely to drink any that is left in an uncovered container or in puddles on the ground. This will prove fatal in sufficient quantity. Always drain the coolant into a sealable container. Coolant should be reused unless it is contaminated or several years old.**

4. Remove the air cleaner assembly.
5. Label and disengage the wiring harnesses and connectors at the intake manifold.

6. Disconnect the accelerator, TVS, and cruise control cables (as equipped) with brackets.
7. If equipped, remove the cruise control transducer.
8. Disconnect the EGR vacuum line.
9. Remove the emission sensor bracket at the manifold.
10. Tag and disconnect the fuel lines, vacuum lines and wiring from the TBI unit.
11. Disconnect the water pump bypass hose and, if applicable, the heater hoses at the intake manifold.
12. Remove the alternator rear bracket.
13. Tag and disconnect the vacuum hoses and pipes from the intake manifold and the vacuum line clips at the thermostat and manifold.
14. If necessary, tag and disconnect the spark plug wires and the bracket at the manifold. Depending on how the wires are run it may be possible to leave them attached to the spark plugs, but if you disconnect them BE SURE TO LABEL THEM BEFORE REMOVAL.
15. Disconnect the coil wires.
16. Remove the intake manifold bolts, then remove the manifold from the engine.

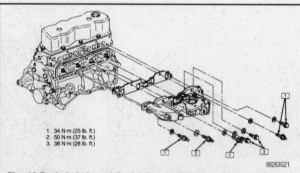

1. 34 N·m (25 lb. ft.)
2. 50 N·m (37 lb. ft.)
3. 38 N·m (28 lb. ft.)

**Fig. 40 Exploded view of the intake manifold mounting—early-model 2.5L engines (NOTE that torque values apply ONLY to models retained by bolts and STUDS)**

**To install:**

17. Using a plastic scraper, clean the gasket mounting surfaces.

18. Install the intake manifold to the engine using a new gasket and carefully thread the retainers.

19. Early-model 2.5L engines use a manifold retained by bolts and studs. For these engines (used through the mid-1980's) tighten the retainers slowly and evenly (starting at the middle and working outward) to 25–37 ft. lbs. (34–50 Nm) using the torque values for each specific fastener as shown in the accompanying illustration. For late-model engines which are retained only by bolts, slowly and evenly tighten all of the retainers to 25 ft. lbs. (34 Nm).

20. The remainder of installation is the reverse of the removal. Make sure to connect all wiring as tagged during removal.

21. Properly refill the engine cooling system, then check for leaks.

22. Once the engine has cooled, install the engine cover.

### 4.3L Engine

♦ **See Figures 41 thru 47**

*VIN B, N AND Z MODELS*

♦ **See Figures 48, 49 and 50**

The intake manifold is located between the cylinder heads.

### ✶✶ CAUTION

**If equipped with a TBI system, relieve the pressure on the fuel system before disconnecting any fuel line connection!**

1. From inside the vehicle, remove the engine cover. For details, please refer to Section 1 of this manual.

2. Properly relieve the fuel system pressure, then disconnect the negative battery cable.

3. Remove the air cleaner assembly and the heat stove tube.

4. Place a catch pan under the radiator, open the drain cock and drain the cooling system.

### ✶✶ CAUTION

**When draining the coolant, keep in mind that cats and dogs are attracted by ethylene glycol antifreeze, and are quite likely to drink any that is left in an uncovered container or in puddles on the ground. This will prove fatal in sufficient quantity. Always drain the coolant into a sealable container. Coolant should be reused unless it is contaminated or several years old.**

5. Matchmark and remove the distributor assembly.

6. If equipped, remove the cruise control transducer.

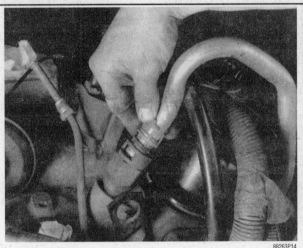

**Fig. 41 Disconnect all lines, hoses . . .**

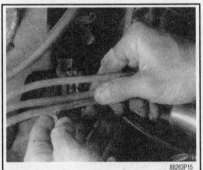

**Fig. 42 . . . and wiring from the intake manifold or from manifold mounted support brackets**

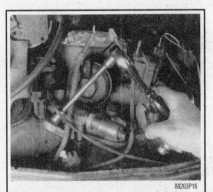

**Fig. 43 Loosen and remove the intake manifold retaining bolts . . .**

**Fig. 44 . . . a ratchet with various extensions will be very helpful for this, then carefully . . .**

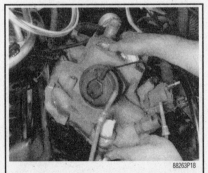

**Fig. 45 . . . remove the manifold—NOTE the TBI unit or carb need not be removed on VIN B, N or Z engines**

**Fig. 46 Once the manifold has been removed you have free access to the lifter valley**

**Fig. 47 To keep debris out of the engine, cover all openings before cleaning the gasket surfaces**

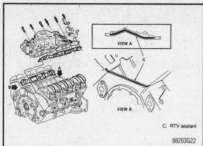

**Fig. 48 Exploded view of the 4.3L (VIN B, N and Z) engine intake manifold mounting and RTV sealant application—NOTE that bolt/stud locations will vary based on model year and emission packages**

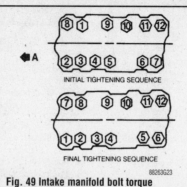

**Fig. 49 Intake manifold bolt torque sequence—1985–90 4.3L (VIN B, N and Z) engines**

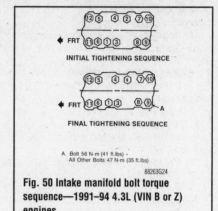

**Fig. 50 Intake manifold bolt torque sequence—1991–94 4.3L (VIN B or Z) engines**

7. Disconnect the throttle linkage (accelerator, cruise control and the transmission detent cables, as equipped).

8. Remove the A/C compressor from the engine and support aside, leaving the refrigerant lines connected. Be sure not to stretch, stress or otherwise damage the A/C lines.

9. Disconnect the engine oil filler tube (at the manifold bracket) and the transmission dipstick/oil filler tube (if equipped) at the manifold or alternator brackets (as applicable).

10. If applicable on early-model vehicles, remove the air conditioning compressor belt idler (if equipped) from the alternator bracket, then the alternator bracket.

11. Tag and disconnect the fuel hoses, the vacuum lines and the electrical connectors from the carburetor or the throttle body, as applicable.

12. On early-model vehicles so equipped, remove the Air Injection Reactor (AIR) hoses and brackets.

13. Disconnect the heater hose and the upper radiator hose.

14. If used, remove the power brake vacuum pipe.

15. If equipped with an external ignition coil, disengage the wiring, then remove the coil.

16. Disconnect the EGR vacuum line.

17. Remove the sensors and bracket from the right side of the engine.

➡When removing the intake manifold retainers, take careful note of the locations for all bolts and studs. The stud locations will vary based on production year and emission packages, but the studs must be installed in their original locations is all engine accessories and controls are to be properly reinstalled.

18. Remove the intake manifold-to-cylinder head bolts, then carefully lift and remove the intake manifold from the engine.

19. Using a plastic scraper, clean the gasket mounting surfaces, the carbon deposits from the exhaust/EGR passages and the scale/deposits from the coolant passages.

20. Inspect the intake manifold for cracks.

**To install:**

21. Use new gaskets and RTV sealant (apply a ¾₆ in. (5mm) bead to the front and rear manifold seals, extend the bead approximately ½ in. (13mm) up each cylinder head to seal and retain the gaskets). Tighten the intake manifold-to-cylinder head bolts/studs using 2 passes of the proper sequence to 35 ft. lbs. (48 Nm). On 1991–94 vehicles, then tighten bolt 9 to 41 ft. lbs. (56 Nm).

22. The remainder of installation is the reverse of the removal procedure.

23. Connect the negative battery cable.

24. Properly refill the engine cooling system, then check for leaks.

25. Once the engine has cooled, install the engine cover.

*CMFI VIN W MODELS—1992–95*

♦ **See Figures 51, 52 and 53**

➡The manufacturer warns that it may be necessary to disconnect the refrigerant lines from the back of the compressor in order to remove the upper intake manifold assembly. If your vehicle is equipped with A/C, before beginning this procedure you must determine if this is necessary. If so, take the vehicle to a reputable repair facility and have the A/C system discharged and recovered using a suitable recovery station. ALSO, remember that if you are wrong and later decide that the system must

be discharged, you may have to significantly reassemble the motor so the van may be driven to the repair facility.

Unlike previous versions of the 4.3L engine, the VIN W utilizes separate upper and lower intake manifold assemblies. It is possible to remove only the upper manifold assembly for access to fuel injection components. If this is all that is necessary on your vehicle, follow only the steps up to upper intake manifold removal, then skip to that portion of the installation procedure.

1. Open the hood, then from inside the vehicle, remove the engine cover. For details, please refer to Section 1 of this manual.

2. If your vehicle is equipped with A/C determine if the compressor can be unbolted and repositioned in order to allow upper manifold removal or if the A/C refrigerant lines will have to be removed from the compressor. If you determine they must be removed from the compressor, take the vehicle to a reputable repair facility to have the system discharged and recovered.

➡If only the upper intake manifold is being removed, the fuel system pressure does not need to be released. ALWAYS release the pressure before disconnecting any fuel lines.

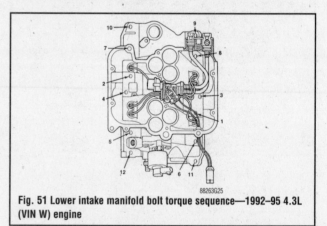

**Fig. 51 Lower intake manifold bolt torque sequence—1992–95 4.3L (VIN W) engine**

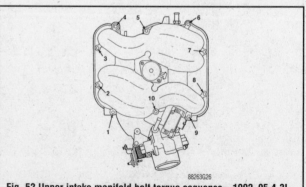

**Fig. 52 Upper intake manifold bolt torque sequence—1992–95 4.3L (VIN W) engine**

3.  Unless only the upper intake manifold is being removed, properly relieve the fuel system pressure.

4.  Disconnect the negative battery cable for safety.

5.  Unless only the upper intake manifold is being removed, drain the engine cooling system.

6.  Remove the air cleaner box and inlet duct.

7.  Disengage the wiring harness from the necessary upper intake components including:
- Throttle Position (TP) sensor
- Idle Air Control (IAC) motor
- Manifold Absolute Pressure (MAP) sensor
- Communicator valve

8.  Disengage the throttle linkage, and the TV linkage if applicable) from the upper intake manifold.

9.  Disengage the wiring, then remove the ignition coil.

10.  Disconnect the PCV hose at the rear of the upper intake manifold, then tag and disengage the vacuum hoses from both the front and rear of the upper intake.

11.  If equipped with A/C, either unbolt and reposition the compressor (you will have to remove the serpentine drive belt first) or disconnect the refrigerant lines from the rear of the compressor. Remember that the A/C refrigerant must be recovered using a suitable recycling/recovery station before the lines can be disconnected.

12.  Remove the upper intake manifold bolts and studs, making sure to note or mark the location of all studs to assure proper installation. Remove the upper intake manifold from the engine.

13.  Disengage the wiring from the distributor (or HVS as applicable, they both perform the job of "distributing" secondary ignition voltage to the plugs and are visually very similar) and matchmark the distributor or HVS, then remove the assembly from the engine.

14.  Disconnect the upper radiator hose at the thermostat housing and the heater hose at the lower intake manifold.

15.  Disconnect the fuel supply and return lines at the rear of the lower intake manifold.

16.  Disengage the wiring harness connectors from the necessary lower intake components including:
- Fuel injector
- Exhaust Gas Recirculation (EGR) valve
- Engine Coolant Temperature (ECT) sensor

17.  Remove the lower intake manifold retaining bolts, then remove the manifold from the engine.

18.  Using a plastic scraper, carefully clean the gasket mounting surfaces. Be sure to inspect the manifold for warpage and/or cracks; if necessary, replace the manifold.

**To install:**

19.  Position the gaskets to the cylinder heads with the port blocking plates to the rear and the "this side up" stamps facing upward, then apply a 3/16 in. (5mm) bead of RTV sealant to the front and rear of the engine block at the block-to-manifold mating surface. Extend the bead 1/2 in. (13mm) up each cylinder head to seal and retain the gaskets.

20.  Install the lower intake manifold taking care not to disturb the gaskets. Apply sealer such as GM 1052080 or equivalent to the lower manifold retaining bolts, then install and tighten the manifold retainers to 35 ft. lbs. (48 Nm) using the proper torque sequence.

21.  Engage the wiring harness to the lower manifold components, including the injector, EGR valve and ECT sensor.

22.  Connect the fuel supply and return lines to the rear of the lower intake. Temporarily reconnect the negative battery cable, then pressurize the fuel system (by cycling the ignition without starting the engine) and check for leaks. Disconnect the negative battery cable for safety and continue installation.

23.  The remainder of installation is the reverse of the removal procedure. Tighten the upper intake manifold retainers, making sure the studs are properly positioned, 124 inch lbs. (14 Nm).

24.  Properly refill the engine cooling system, then check for leaks.

25.  Once the engine has cooled, install the engine cover.

26.  If the A/C system was discharged, take the van to a reputable repair facility to have the system evacuated, recharged and leak tested. DO NOT WAIT LONG to do this or moisture which entered the system while it was discharged will cause corrosion and internal system damage. ALSO, DO NOT run the compressor until the system has been properly recharged. Depending on how your model is equipped this may mean you CANNOT use the defogger (this automatically turns the compressor on in some vehicles).

### CSFI VIN W MODELS—1996

▶ **See Figures 54, 55 and 56**

Unlike early versions of the 4.3L engine, the VIN W utilizes separate upper and lower intake manifold assemblies. It is possible to remove only the upper manifold assembly for access to fuel injection components. If this is all that is necessary on your vehicle, follow only the steps up to upper intake manifold removal, then skip to that portion of the installation procedure.

1.  From inside the vehicle, remove the engine cover. For details, please refer to Section 1 of this manual.

➡**If only the upper intake manifold is being removed, the fuel system pressure does not need to be released. ALWAYS release the pressure before disconnecting any fuel lines.**

2.  Unless only the upper intake manifold assembly is being removed, properly relieve the fuel system pressure.

3.  Disconnect the negative battery cable for safety.

4.  Unless only the upper intake manifold is being removed, drain the engine cooling system.

5.  Remove the air cleaner box and inlet duct.

6.  Disengage the wiring harness from the necessary upper intake components (including brackets), then position the harness aside.

7.  Disengage the throttle linkage and cruise control cable (if equipped), along with the bracket from the upper intake manifold.

8.  Disconnect the fuel line bracket from the rear of the lower intake manifold.

9.  Disconnect the PCV hose at the upper intake manifold.

10.  Disengage the wiring, then remove the ignition coil and bracket.

11.  Remove the purge solenoid and bracket.

12.  Remove the upper intake manifold bolts and studs, making sure to note or mark the location of all studs to assure proper installation. Remove the upper intake manifold from the engine.

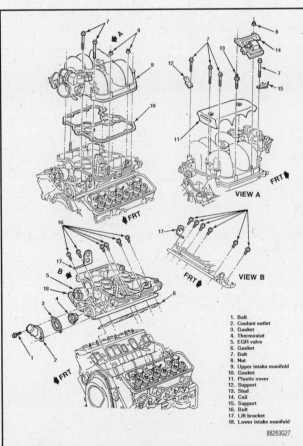

VIEW A

FRT

VIEW B

FRT

FRT

1.  Bolt
2.  Coolant outlet
3.  Gasket
4.  Thermostat
5.  EGR valve
6.  Gasket
7.  Bolt
8.  Nut
9.  Upper intake manifold
10.  Gasket
11.  Plastic cover
12.  Support
13.  Stud
14.  Coil
15.  Support
16.  Bolt
17.  Lift bracket
18.  Lower intake manifold

88263G27

**Fig. 53 Exploded view of the upper and lower intake manifold assembly—1992–95 4.3L (VIN W) engine**

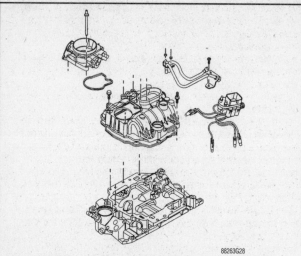

**Fig. 54 Exploded view of the upper intake manifold and Central Sequential Fuel Injection (CSFI) components**

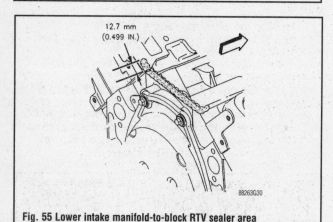

12.7 mm
(0.499 IN.)

**Fig. 55 Lower intake manifold-to-block RTV sealer area**

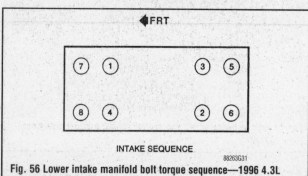

FRT

INTAKE SEQUENCE

**Fig. 56 Lower intake manifold bolt torque sequence—1996 4.3L (VIN W) CSFI engines**

13. Matchmark the relationship of the HVS housing and rotor for proper installation, then remove the HVS distributor assembly from the engine.

14. Disconnect the upper radiator hose at the thermostat housing and the heater hose at the lower intake manifold.

15. Remove the EGR valve.

16. Disconnect the coolant bypass hose.

17. Disconnect the fuel supply and return lines at the rear of the lower intake manifold.

18. Disengage the wiring harness connectors and brackets from the necessary lower intake components.

19. Remove the throttle linkage and cable(s) with bracket from the lower intake manifold.

20. Remove the transmission fluid level indicator tube.

21. Remove the EGR tube, clamp and bolt.

22. Remove the PCV valve and vacuum hoses.

23. Remove the air conditioning compressor, bracket and accessory drive bracket. Reposition and support the A/C compressor aside with the refrigerant lines intact.

24. If needed, remove the alternator bracket bolt next to the thermostat housing

25. Remove the lower intake manifold retaining bolts, then remove the manifold from the engine.

26. Using a plastic scraper, carefully clean the gasket mounting surfaces. Be sure to inspect the manifold for warpage and/or cracks; if necessary, replace the manifold.

**To install:**

27. Position the gaskets to the cylinder head with the port blocking plates to the rear and the "this side up" stamps facing upward, then apply a ³⁄₁₆ in. (5mm) bead of RTV sealant to the front and rear of the engine block at the block-to-manifold mating surface. Extend the bead ½ in. (13mm) up each cylinder head to seal and retain the gaskets.

28. Install the lower intake manifold taking care not to disturb the gaskets. Apply sealer such as GM 1052080 or equivalent to the lower manifold retaining bolts, then install and tighten the manifold retainers in 3 passes of the proper sequence.

    a. First, tighten lower manifold bolts to 26 inch lbs. (3 Nm).

    b. Then, tighten the bolts to 106 inch lbs. (12 Nm).

    c. Finally, tighten the bolts to 11 ft. lbs. (15 Nm).

29. Install the alternator bracket bolt, next to the thermostat housing.

30. Connect the coolant bypass hose, then install the EGR valve.

31. Connect the upper radiator hoses at the thermostat housing and the heater hose at the lower manifold.

32. Engage the wiring harness and brackets to the lower manifold components.

33. Connect the fuel supply and return lines at the rear of the lower intake. Temporarily reconnect the negative battery cable, then pressurize the fuel system (by cycling the ignition without starting the engine) and check for leaks. Disconnect the negative battery cable for safety and continue installation.

34. The remainder of installation is the reverse of the removal procedure.

35. Connect the negative battery cable.

36. Properly refill the engine cooling system and check for leaks.

37. Once the engine has cooled sufficiently, install the engine cover to the passenger compartment.

## Exhaust Manifold

### REMOVAL & INSTALLATION

Exhaust pipe and manifold fasteners suffer extreme corrosion due to the harsh operating conditions to which they are exposed. It is usually EASY to break or strip these fasteners if great care is not taken. It is usually a good idea to soak the fasteners with penetrating oil some time before the procedure is begun. Try letting the engine cool the night before and carefully spray the fasteners with a penetrating oil, then allow it to soak in and work while you sleep.

**2.5L Engine**

▶ See Figure 57

The exhaust manifold is located on the left side of the engine.

1. Disconnect the negative battery cable for safety.

2. From inside the vehicle, remove the engine cover. For details, please refer to Section 1 of this manual.

3. Disconnect the Thermac heat stove pipe from the exhaust manifold.

4. Disengage the wiring from the oxygen sensor. The sensor should be removed only if the manifold or sensor requires replacement.

5. Raise and support the front of the vehicle safely using jackstands.

6. Disconnect the exhaust pipe from the exhaust manifold.

7. If equipped, remove the rear air conditioning compressor bracket.

8. Remove the exhaust manifold-to-engine bolts and the manifold from the engine.

9. Using a plastic scraper, clean the gasket mounting surfaces.

**To install:**

10. Install the exhaust manifold to the cylinder head using a new gasket. Tighten the retaining bolts in sequence to 36 ft. lbs. (50 Nm) for the inner or center retainers and to 32 ft. lbs. (43 Nm) for the outer retainers.

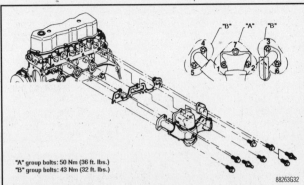

"A" group bolts: 50 Nm (36 ft. lbs.)
"B" group bolts: 43 Nm (32 ft. lbs.)

88263G32

**Fig. 57 Exploded view of the exhaust manifold mounting and retainer torque sequence—2.5L engine**

11. Install the remaining components in the reverse order of removal. Start the engine and check for leaks.

12. Once the engine has cooled, install the engine cover.

### 4.3L Engine

▶ See Figures 58, 59, 60, 61 and 62

#### RIGHT SIDE

1. Disconnect the negative battery cable for safety.

2. From inside the vehicle, remove the engine cover. For details, please refer to Section 1 of this manual.

3. Raise and support the front of the vehicle safely using jackstands.

4. Disconnect the right exhaust pipe from the exhaust manifold.

5. On models through 1990, disconnect the Air Injection Reactor (AIR) hose from the check valve (and, if necessary from the diverter valve). If applicable, remove the dipstick tube bracket at the manifold.

6. Except for 1996 models, disconnect the heat stove tube from the manifold.

7. Remove the exhaust manifold-to-engine bolts, washers and tab washers. Whenever tab washers are used, their edges should be straightened before you attempt to loosen the bolts.

8. If used, remove the heat shields (if removal is difficult, take them out with the manifold as an assembly).

9. Remove the manifold from the engine.

10. Using a plastic scraper, clean the gasket mounting surfaces.

**To install:**

11. Install the exhaust manifold assembly using a new gasket. Remember, that if heat shields were removed with the manifold as an assembly, it may be easier to position them at the same time you position the manifold. It also may help to be an octopus with 8 arms or to have an assistant nearby.

12. If used and not positioned already, install the heat shields.

13. Install the manifold retaining bolts, then tighten the inner (center tube) manifold bolts to 26 ft. lbs. (36 Nm), and the outer (front and rear tube) manifold bolts to 20 ft. lbs. (28 Nm). Once the bolts are tightened, bend the tab washers over the heads of the bolts in order to lock them in place and keep them from loosening in service.

14. Install the remaining components in the reverse order of removal.

15. Connect the negative battery cable. Start the engine and check for leaks.

16. Once the engine has cooled, install the engine cover.

#### LEFT SIDE

1. Disconnect the negative battery cable for safety.

2. From inside the vehicle, remove the engine cover. For details, please refer to Section 1 of this manual.

3. Raise and support the front of the vehicle safely using jackstands.

4. Disconnect the right exhaust pipe from the exhaust manifold.

5. On models through 1990, disconnect the Air Injection Reactor (AIR) hose from the check valve (and, if necessary from the diverter valve). If applicable, remove the power steering pump and alternator brackets from the manifold.

6. Except for 1996 models, disengage the oxygen sensor wiring. The sensor should only be removed if the manifold or sensor requires replacement.

7. On 1996 models, disconnect the EGR inlet pipe.

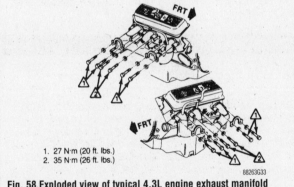

1. 27 N·m (20 ft. lbs.)
2. 35 N·m (26 ft. lbs.)

88263G33

**Fig. 58 Exploded view of typical 4.3L engine exhaust manifold mounting**

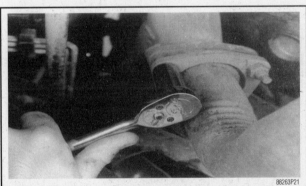

88263P21

**Fig. 59 Loosen the retainers and disconnect the exhaust pipe from the manifold**

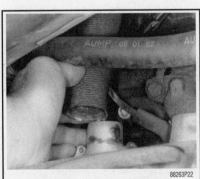

88263P22

**Fig. 60 Except for 1996 models, disconnect the heat stove tube from the exhaust manifold**

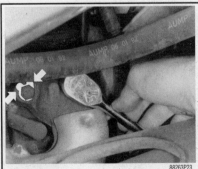

88263P23

**Fig. 61 Once the tab washers are flattened, loosen and remove the manifold retaining bolts . . .**

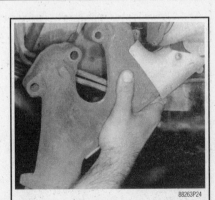

88263P24

**Fig. 62 . . . then carefully remove the manifold from the vehicle**

8. Remove the exhaust manifold-to-engine bolts, washers and tab washers. Whenever tab washers are used, their edges should be straightened before you attempt to loosen the bolts.

9. If used, remove the heat shields (if removal is difficult, take them out with the manifold as an assembly).

10. Remove the manifold from the engine.

11. Using a plastic scraper, clean the gasket mounting surfaces.

**To install:**

12. Install the exhaust manifold assembly using a new gasket. Remember, that if heat shields were removed with the manifold as an assembly, it may be easier to position them at the same time you position the manifold. It also may help to be an octopus with 8 arms or to have an assistant nearby.

13. If used and not positioned already, install the heat shields.

14. Install the manifold retaining bolts, then tighten the inner (center tube) manifold bolts to 26 ft. lbs. (36 Nm), and the outer (front and rear tube) manifold bolts to 20 ft. lbs. (28 Nm). Once the bolts are tightened, bend the tab washers over the heads of the bolts in order to lock them in place and keep them from loosening in service.

15. Install the remaining components in the reverse order of removal.

16. Connect the negative battery cable. Start the engine and check for leaks.

17. Once the engine has cooled, install the engine cover.

## Radiator

### REMOVAL & INSTALLATION

♦ **See Figures 63 thru 75**

### ✷✷ CAUTION

When draining the coolant, keep in mind that cats and dogs are attracted by ethylene glycol antifreeze, and are quite likely to drink any that is left in an uncovered container or in puddles on the ground. This will prove fatal in sufficient quantity. Always drain the coolant into a sealable container. Coolant should be reused unless it is contaminated or several years old.

### 1985–95 Models

➡For certain late-model vehicles (1993–94 AWD and all 1995 vehicles) you will need a special Quick-Connect fitting release tool, such as J-37088-2a or equivalent to release the transmission fluid cooler lines from the fittings at the radiator.

1. Disconnect the negative battery cable for safety.

2. Drain the cooling system into a suitable container.

3. For 1985–87 vehicles, remove the brake master cylinder from the firewall (non-power brakes) or the power booster (power brakes) and support it aside. Take care not to stress or damage the brake lines.

➡DO NOT disconnect the brake lines from the master cylinder, unless there is not enough room to move the master cylinder to provide enough room.

4. For 1992–95 vehicles, matchmark the position of the hood latch to the radiator support, then unbolt and position the latch aside for clearance. Also, if equipped, loosen the A/C accumulator brackets.

5. Separate the upper fan shroud from the bottom half of the shroud assembly, then remove the upper shroud from the vehicle. For many mid-to-late-model vehicles (late 80's to 1995) it will be necessary to unfasten upper radiator hose and power steering pressure switch harness from the shroud. It may also be necessary to remove the upper radiator hose from the radiator in order to provide sufficient clearance.

6. Disconnect the radiator hoses and the coolant overflow hose from the radiator.

### ✷✷ WARNING

When working on fluid lines BE VERY CAREFUL not to strip them. Although an open-end wrench must be used, the use of a special line wrench is HIGHLY recommended. Line wrenches are open-

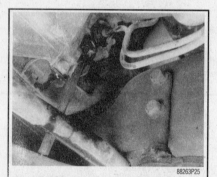

Fig. 63 Drain the cooling system using the radiator drain cock—a tube on the outlet may prevent a mess

Fig. 64 On some late-model vehicles you must remove the hood latch—start by matchmarking it . . .

Fig. 65 . . . then loosen the retaining bolts . . .

Fig. 66 . . . and remove the assembly from the radiator support

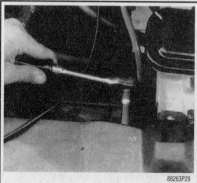

Fig. 67 Loosen the upper fan shroud retainers . . .

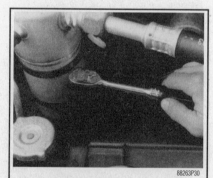

Fig. 68 . . . be careful not to miss any (a long extension is handy for the upper-to-lower shroud bolts)

Fig. 69 With the retainers removed, carefully lift the upper fan shroud from the engine compartment

Fig. 70 Loosen and disconnect any threaded transmission or engine oil cooler lines . . .

Fig. 71 . . . note the shape of this open-end wrench, it is a special line wrench just for this purpose

Fig. 72 Disengage the overflow hose from the radiator . . .

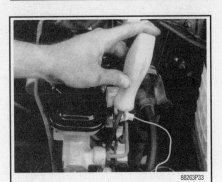

Fig. 73 . . . and finally, loosen the clamps and disconnect and remaining radiator hoses . . .

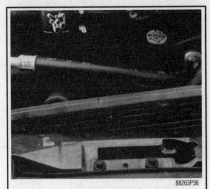

Fig. 74 . . . then CAREFULLY lift the radiator from the engine compartment

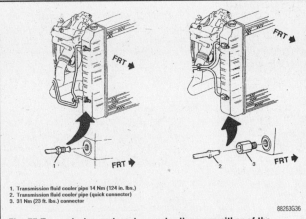

1. Transmission fluid cooler pipe 14 Nm (124 in. lbs.)
2. Transmission fluid cooler pipe (quick connector)
3. 31 Nm (23 ft. lbs.) connector

88263G36

Fig. 75 Transmission and engine cooler lines are either of the threaded type (left) or the Quick-Connect type (right)

ended wrenches with smaller openings (meaning a greater surface area to contact the line fitting) that are designed to be just large enough to fit over a line.

7. If equipped with an automatic transmission, disconnect the transmission fluid cooler lines from the radiator assembly. For most models, use the appropriate sized flare (line) wrench. For 1993–94 All Wheel Drive (AWD) models and all 1995 models, you must use J-37088-2a or an equivalent Quick-Connect Fitting tool to disengage the lines from the radiator.

➡Once transmission or engine oil cooler lines have been disconnected, immediately cap or plug the openings to prevent excessive fluid loss or system contamination. Golf tees or specially made plastic caps work well for this, but it is sometime difficult to really seal them. If neces-

sary, raise and support the front of the vehicle, this should keep fluid in the lines, but will help speed up the draining process of the oils in the radiator cooler tanks.

8. If equipped, loosen and disconnect the engine oil cooler lines from the radiator assembly.
9. Check the bottom of the radiator assembly for fasteners (some early-models are retained by mounting bolts which thread through the lower shroud and radiator), and remove if any are found.
10. Carefully lift the radiator from the vehicle, keeping in mind that the coolant tank and any oil cooler tanks (transmission and/or engine) are still filled with a pretty significant amount of fluid. Take care or get wet.
11. Inspect the radiator for leaks or physical damage, then repair (if necessary).

➡The radiator is constructed of aluminum. If repairs are necessary, it should be taken to a radiator repair shop.

12. Installation is the reverse of the removal procedure. Tighten the retainers to 18 ft. lbs. (25 Nm).

➡When reconnecting the Quick-Connect fittings on certain late-model transmission cooler lines, listen and feel for a distinct snap which should be heard when the line is fastened. The line must be fully inserted into the connector to assure proper seating. Check this by hand using a forceful pull on the fitting.

13. Connect the negative battery cable.
14. Properly refill and bleed the engine cooling system, then check for leaks.
15. If equipped with an engine oil cooler or with a transmission oil cooler, check and top-off those fluids, as necessary.

### 1996 Models

◆ See Figures 76 and 77

➡To assure a proper seal upon installation you will need NEW cooler line retaining clips for the transmission and engine oil cooler line fittings for this procedure.

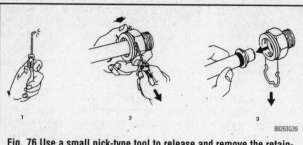

**Fig. 76 Use a small pick-type tool to release and remove the retaining clips from the cooler line fittings**

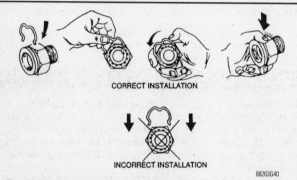

CORRECT INSTALLATION

INCORRECT INSTALLATION

**Fig. 77 When installing the replacement clips to the cooler line fittings, PROPER ALIGNMENT IS CRITICAL**

1. Disconnect the negative battery cable for safety.
2. Drain the cooling system into a suitable container.
3. Loosen the clamp, then remove the air cleaner assembly.
4. Remove the upper fan shroud retaining bolts, then remove the upper shroud from the vehicle.
5. Disconnect the radiator hoses and the coolant overflow hose from the radiator.

➡ **To disconnect the transmission or engine oil cooler lines, use a small pick-type tool or a small screwdriver to release one of retaining clip's open ends, then remove and discard the old clip.**

6. Disconnect the transmission oil cooler lines from the radiator, then discard the old retaining clips.
7. Disconnect the engine oil cooler lines from the radiator, then discard the old retaining clips.
8. Carefully lift the radiator from the vehicle, keeping in mind that the coolant tank and the engine/transmission oil cooler tanks are still filled with a pretty significant amount of fluid. Take care or get wet.
9. Inspect the radiator for leaks or physical damage, then repair (if necessary).

➡ **The radiator is constructed of aluminum. If repairs are necessary, it should be taken to a radiator repair shop.**

**To install:**
10. Carefully lower the radiator into the mounting insulators.

### ❈❈ WARNING

**DO NOT attempt to reuse the existing retaining clips that were removed from the cooler line connector fittings. ALSO, take care to assure that each clip engages all 3 slots in the connector fittings. Old, damaged or improperly installed clips could cause the cooler lines to loosen in service, allowing for fluid leaks which could damage the engine or transmission.**

11. Install the new retaining clips into the cooler line connector fittings. For each fitting, use your thumb and forefinger to insert a new clip into one of the 3 recesses in the connector fitting. With one end of the retaining clip engaged in the connector fitting slot, use your thumb to rotate the retaining clip around the connector fitting until it snaps into place.
12. Install the engine oil cooler lines to the radiator assembly. Make sure that your hear and/or feel a click as each line is snapped into place, then pull back sharply on the pipe to assure it is tightly fastened to the fitting.
13. Install the transmission cooler lines to the radiator assembly. Make sure that your hear and/or feel a click as each line is snapped into place, then pull back sharply on the pipe to assure it is tightly fastened to the fitting.
14. Connect the radiator and overflow hoses.
15. Install the upper shroud and secure using the retaining bolts.
16. Install the air cleaner assembly and tighten the clamp.
17. Connect the negative battery cable.
18. Properly refill and bleed the engine cooling system, then check for leaks.
19. Check the engine and transmission fluids and top-off, as necessary.

## Cooling Fan

### REMOVAL & INSTALLATION

### ❈❈ CAUTION

**DO NOT use or repair a damaged fan assembly. An unbalanced fan assembly could fly apart causing damage or severe personal injury. Always replace a damaged fan using a NEW assembly.**

**1985–95 Models**

◆ **See Figures 78 thru 83**

1. Disconnect the negative battery cable for safety.
2. For 1992–95 vehicles, matchmark the position of the hood latch to the radiator support, then unbolt and position the latch aside for clearance. Also, if equipped, loosen the A/C accumulator brackets.
3. Remove the upper fan shroud retainers, then separate the upper fan shroud from the bottom half of the shroud assembly. Remove the upper shroud from the vehicle. For many mid-to-late-model vehicles (late 80's to 1995) it will be necessary to unfasten upper radiator hose and power steering pressure

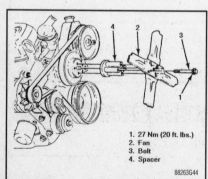

1. 27 Nm (20 ft. lbs.)
2. Fan
3. Bolt
4. Spacer

**Fig. 78 Exploded view of the cooling fan assembly for the 2.5L engine without a clutch**

**Fig. 79 Fan removal usually boils down to a simple matter of removing the retainers (without cutting your hand) . . .**

**Fig. 80 . . . then pulling the fan blade assembly from the water pump and pulley**

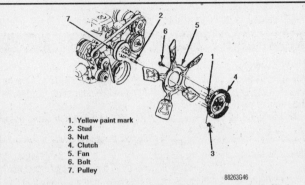

1. Yellow paint mark
2. Stud
3. Nut
4. Clutch
5. Fan
6. Bolt
7. Pulley

88263G46

**Fig. 81 Exploded view of the late-model 2.5L engine fan and clutch assembly**

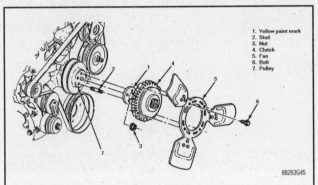

1. Yellow paint mark
2. Stud
3. Nut
4. Clutch
5. Fan
6. Bolt
7. Pulley

88263G45

**Fig. 82 Exploded view of an early-model 2.5L engine fan and clutch assembly**

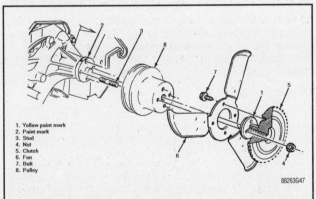

1. Yellow paint mark
2. Paint mark
3. Stud
4. Nut
5. Clutch
6. Fan
7. Bolt
8. Pulley

88263G47

**Fig. 83 Exploded view of a 4.3L engine fan and clutch assembly**

switch harness from the shroud. It may also be necessary to remove the upper radiator hose from the radiator in order to provide sufficient clearance. If the hose must be removed, first partially drain the cooling system (to a level below the upper radiator hose).

4. Remove the fan clutch-to-water pump nuts and bolts, then remove the fan and clutch assembly from the engine.

➡Some early-model 2.5L engines may not be equipped with a fan clutch assembly. For these models, the fan is bolted to directly to the water pump through a spacer. To remove the fan, simply unbolt and remove the blade with the spacer.

5. If necessary, remove the fan blade-to-clutch retainers, and separate the blade from the clutch assembly.

**To install:**

6. Installation is the reverse of the removal procedure.

7. If separated, install the fan blade to the clutch assembly and secure using the retainers. Tighten the fan-to-clutch retainers to 18 ft. lbs. (24 Nm) for

1985–92 4.3L engines or to 26 ft. lbs. (35 Nm) for 1993–95 4.3L engines. For 2.5L engines tighten the retainers to 89 inch lbs. (10 Nm) if they thread from the front of the fan, then back into the clutch, toward the engine or to 26 ft. lbs. (35 Nm) if they thread from the engine side, through the fan and THEN out toward the front of the vehicle and into the clutch.

8. Install the fan and clutch assembly (or fan and spacer on some early 2.5L engines) to the water pump pulley. Tighten the retainers to 18 ft. lbs. (24 Nm) for 2.5L engines with a clutch assembly, 20 ft. lbs. (27 Nm) for 2.5L engines with a spacer (and no clutch) or to 22 ft. lbs. (30 Nm) for 4.3L engines.

9. Connect the negative battery cable. Start the engine and check operation.

10. Remember that if the upper radiator hose was removed, you should bleed and top-off the cooling system.

**1996 Models**

▶ **See Figure 84**

1. Disconnect the negative battery cable for safety.

2. Place a catch pan under the radiator, open the drain cock and drain the cooling system.

> ☀ **CAUTION**

**When draining the coolant, keep in mind that cats and dogs are attracted by ethylene glycol antifreeze, and are quite likely to drink any that is left in an uncovered container or in puddles on the ground. This will prove fatal in sufficient quantity. Always drain the coolant into a sealable container. Coolant should be reused unless it is contaminated or several years old.**

3. Loosen the clamp, then remove the air cleaner assembly.

4. Remove the upper fan shroud retaining bolts, then remove the upper shroud from the vehicle.

5. Remove the fan and clutch assembly retainers using J-41240, or an equivalent fan clutch wrench.

6. If necessary, remove the 4 bolts holding the fan blade to the clutch, then separate the fan from the clutch assembly.

7. Installation is the reverse of the removal procedure. Tighten the components to the following specifications:

   a. If removed, tighten the fan-to-clutch bolts to 24 ft. lbs. (33 Nm).

   b. Install the fan blade and clutch assembly to the engine using J-41240 and tighten the retainers to 41 ft. lbs. (56 Nm).

8. Connect the negative battery cable. Start the engine and check operation.

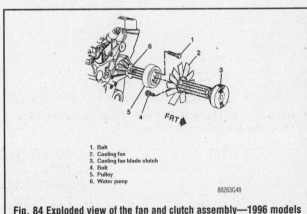

1. Bolt
2. Cooling fan
3. Cooling fan blade clutch
4. Bolt
5. Pulley
6. Water pump

88263G48

**Fig. 84 Exploded view of the fan and clutch assembly—1996 models**

## Water Pump

REMOVAL & INSTALLATION

▶ **See Figures 85 thru 91**

1. Disconnect the negative battery cable for safety.

2. Place a catch pan under the radiator, open the drain cock and drain the cooling system.

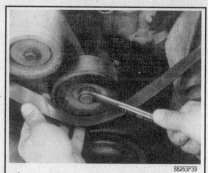
Fig. 85 Remove the accessory drive belt(s)—on most models that means the single serpentine belt

Fig. 86 Once the shroud, fan and clutch or spacer are out of the way, remove the water pump pulley

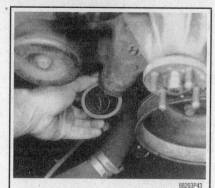
Fig. 87 Disconnect the hoses from the water pump . . .

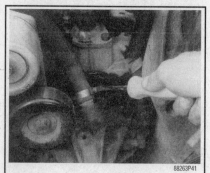
Fig. 88 . . . in most cases this means loosening the clamp and pulling off the hose . . .

Fig. 89 . . . but a stuck hose can be carefully cut away if you determine it should be replaced anyway

Fig. 90 Loosen and remove the retaining bolts, then remove the water pump from the engine

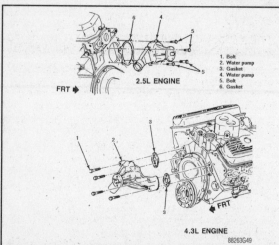

1. Bolt
2. Water pump
3. Gasket
4. Water pump
5. Bolt
6. Gasket

2.5L ENGINE

FRT ►

4.3L ENGINE

88263G49

Fig. 91 Exploded view of typical Astro and Safari water pump mountings—note that some early-models use studs at various locations to help mount engine accessories

**✳✳ CAUTION**

When draining the coolant, keep in mind that cats and dogs are attracted by ethylene glycol antifreeze, and are quite likely to drink any that is left in an uncovered container or in puddles on the ground. This will prove fatal in sufficient quantity. Always drain the coolant into a sealable container. Coolant should be reused unless it is contaminated or several years old.

3. Remove the accessory drive belt(s).

4. Remove the upper fan shroud and the engine cooling fan. For details, please refer to the procedure found earlier in this section.

5. Remove the water pump pulley.

6. Loosen the clamps, then disconnect the hoses from the water pump.

7. Remove the water pump-to-engine bolts. Because the bolt lengths and types may vary from location-to-location (some early-models may use studs in certain locations) on some models, tag or note all bolt locations as they are removed, this will help assure proper installation.

8. Carefully break the gasket seal and remove the water pump from the engine.

9. Using a plastic scraper, clean the gasket mounting surfaces.

**To install:**

10. For 2.5L engines, clean the water pump bolt threads, then apply a coating of GM 1052080 or an equivalent sealant.

11. Position the water pump to the engine using new gaskets, then install the retaining bolts. If any are of different lengths (or are bolts instead of studs) be sure they are installed in their original locations, as noted during removal.

12. Tighten the pump-to-engine bolts to 17 ft. lbs. (25 Nm) for the 2.5L, 22 ft. lbs. (29 Nm) 1985–92 4.3L engines, 30 ft. lbs. (41 Nm) 1993–95 4.3L engines, or 33 ft. lbs. (45 Nm) 1996 4.3L engines.

13. The remainder of installation is the reverse of the removal procedure.

14. If removed, install the water pump pulley and tighten to 18 ft. lbs. (25 Nm).

15. Connect the negative battery cable. Properly refill and bleed the engine cooling system, then check for leaks.

## Cylinder Head

REMOVAL & INSTALLATION

**✳✳ CAUTION**

When draining the coolant, keep in mind that cats and dogs are attracted by ethylene glycol antifreeze, and are quite likely to drink any that is left in an uncovered container or in puddles on the ground. This will prove fatal in sufficient quantity. Always drain the coolant into a sealable container. Coolant should be reused unless it is contaminated or several years old.

## 2.5L Engine

▶ See Figures 92 and 93

➡ Before disassembling the engine, make sure that it is overnight cold.

### ✳✳ CAUTION

**Relieve the pressure on the fuel system before disconnecting any fuel line connection!**

1. Remove the engine cover as outlined in Section 1 of this manual.
2. Properly relieve the fuel system pressure, then disconnect the negative battery cable for safety.
3. Place a catch pan under the radiator, open the drain cock and drain the cooling system.
4. Remove the rocker arm cover.
5. Disconnect the accelerator, cruise control and the TVS cables, as equipped.
6. From the intake manifold, remove the water pump bypass and heater hoses.
7. From the alternator, remove the front and rear braces, then move it aside.
8. Disconnect the air conditioning compressor brackets, then reposition and support the compressor aside. Be sure not to stress or damage the A/C refrigerant lines.
9. Remove the thermostat housing-to-cylinder head bolts and the housing from the engine.
10. Remove the ground cable and any necessary electrical connectors from the cylinder head. TAG and disconnect the ignition wires from the spark plugs and disengage the oxygen sensor lead. Disconnect and remove the ignition coil from the intake manifold and the cylinder head.
11. Tag and remove the vacuum lines and fuel hoses from the intake manifold and the TBI unit.

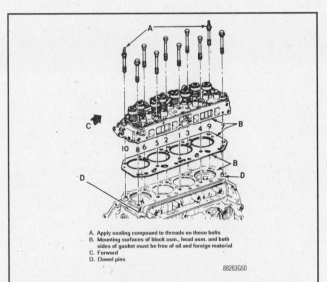

A. Apply sealing compound to threads on these bolts
B. Mounting surfaces of block asm., head asm. and both sides of gasket must be free of oil and foreign material
C. Forward
D. Dowel pins

88263G50

**Fig. 92 Exploded view of the cylinder head mounting—2.5L engine**

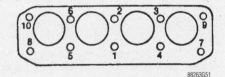

88263G51

**Fig. 93 Cylinder head bolt torque sequence—2.5L engine**

12. Disconnect the exhaust pipe from the exhaust manifold.
13. Remove the rocker arm nuts, the washers, the rocker arms and the pushrods from the cylinder head.

➡ If the rocker arm and pushrod assemblies are not being replaced BE SURE TO TAG or ARRANGE them. If they are reused, they MUST be installed in their original locations.

14. Remove the cylinder head-to-engine bolts, then remove the cylinder head from the engine (with the manifolds attached).
15. Place the assembly on a workbench. If necessary, remove the intake and the exhaust manifolds from the cylinder head.
16. Using a plastic scraper, clean the gasket mounting surfaces. Using a wire brush, clean the carbon deposits from the combustion chambers.
17. Inspect the cylinder head and block for cracks, nicks, heavy scratches or other damage.

**To install:**

18. If removed, install the intake and/or exhaust manifolds to the cylinder head using new gaskets.
19. Use new gaskets, sealant (where necessary, refer to the illustration and any instructions which came with the gasket kit) and install the cylinder head onto the block.
20. Tighten all of the cylinder head bolts (in sequence) to 18 ft. lbs. (25 Nm). Then tighten all bolts (except #9) to 26 ft. lbs. (35 Nm). Retighten the #9 bolt to 18 ft. lbs. (25 Nm). Then tighten all bolts an additional 90 degrees (¼ turn) in sequence.
21. Loosely install the pushrods, rocker arms and nuts. Adjust the valve lash and secure the rocker arm assemblies as detailed in Section 1 of this manual or earlier in this section under Rocker Arm removal and installation.
22. Connect the exhaust pipe to the exhaust manifold.
23. Install the remaining components in the reverse order of removal.
24. Connect the negative battery cable. Properly refill and bleed the engine cooling system, then check for leaks.
25. Once the engine has cooled, install the engine cover.

## 4.3L Engine

▶ See Figures 94 thru 101

### 1985–90 MODELS

### ✳✳ CAUTION

**If equipped with a TBI system, relieve the pressure on the fuel system before disconnecting any fuel line connection.**

1. Remove the engine cover as outlined in Section 1 of this manual.
2. Properly relieve the fuel system pressure, then disconnect the negative battery cable for safety.
3. Place a catch pan under the radiator, open the drain cock and drain the cooling system.
4. Remove the rocker arm cover.
5. Remove the intake manifold.
6. Remove the exhaust manifold.
7. Remove the AIR pipe at the rear of the head.
8. If removing the right cylinder head, remove or disconnect:
   - AIR pump mounting bolt and spacer at the head.
   - Engine accessory bracket bolts and studs at the head.
   - Wiring harness and clip at the rear of the head.
9. If removing the left cylinder head, remove or disconnect:
   - Engine accessory bracket bolts and studs at the head. It may be necessary to loosen the remaining bracket bolts to provide clearance for head removal.
   - Fuel pipes and bracket at the rear of the head.
   - Coolant sensor wire.
   - Cruise control transducer bracket, if equipped.
10. Tag and disconnect the wiring from the spark plugs. If necessary, remove the spark plugs from the cylinder head.
11. Loosen the rocker arms and remove the pushrods.

➡ If valve train components, such as the rocker arms or pushrods, are to be reused, they must be tagged or arranged to insure installation in their original locations.

12. Remove the cylinder head bolts by loosening them in the reverse of the torque sequence, then carefully remove the cylinder head.

Fig. 94 Prepare the cylinder head by removing the rocker arm cover, intake manifold, and exhaust manifold

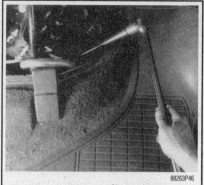

Fig. 95 Loosen the cylinder head bolts using the reverse of the torque sequence . . .

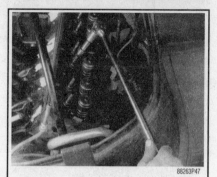

Fig. 96 . . . a breaker bar, socket and various length extensions are necessary to remove the bolts

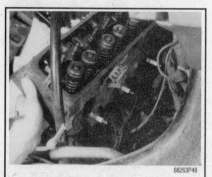

Fig. 97 Once all the bolts are removed, break the gasket seal and lift the cylinder head from the block

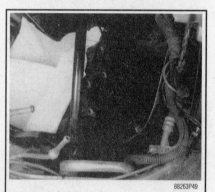

Fig. 98 Protect the lifter valley and pistons bores using rags or a plastic cover . . .

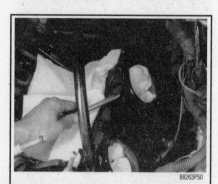

Fig. 99 . . . then carefully clean the gasket mating surfaces of all old gasket and debris

Fig. 100 Upon installation, tighten the cylinder head bolts using the proper torque sequence

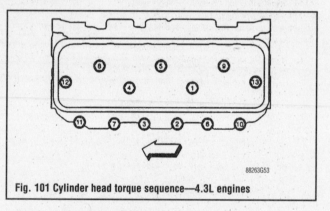

Fig. 101 Cylinder head torque sequence—4.3L engines

13. Using a plastic scraper, clean the gasket mounting surfaces.

14. Clean the carbon deposits from the combustion chambers.

15. Inspect the cylinder head and block for cracks, nicks, heavy scratches or other damage.

**To install:**

➡The gasket surfaces on both the head and block must be clean of any foreign matter and free of nicks or heavy scratches. The cylinder bolt threads in the block and threads on the bolts must be cleaned (dirt will affect the bolt torque).

➡DO NOT apply sealer to composition steel-asbestos gaskets.

16. If using a steel only gasket, apply a thin and even coat of sealer to both sides of the gaskets.

17. Place a new gasket over the dowel pins with the bead or the words "This Side Up" facing upwards (as applicable), then carefully lower the cylinder head into position over the gasket and dowels.

18. Apply a coating of GM 1052080 or an equivalent sealer to the threads of the cylinder head bolts, then thread the bolts into position until finger-tight. Using the proper torque sequence, tighten the bolts in 3 steps:

- First, tighten the bolts to 25 ft. lbs. (34 Nm).
- Next, tighten the bolts to 45 ft. lbs. (61 Nm).
- Finally, tighten the bolts to 65 ft. lbs. (90 Nm).

19. Install the pushrods, secure the rocker arms and adjust the valves.

20. If removed, install the spark plugs. Engage the spark plug wires and make sure they are positioned in the wire brackets.

21. Installation of the remaining components is the reverse of the removal procedure.

22. Properly refill the engine cooling system. Run the engine to check for leaks, then check and/or adjust the ignition timing.

23. Once the engine has cooled, install the engine cover.

*1991–95 MODELS*

### ❊❊ CAUTION

**Relieve the pressure on the fuel system before disconnecting any fuel line connection.**

1. From inside the vehicle, remove the engine cover. For details, please refer to Section 1 of this manual.
2. Properly relieve the fuel system pressure, then disconnect the negative battery cable for safety.
3. Place a catch pan under the radiator, open the drain cock and drain the cooling system.
4. Remove the rocker arm cover.
5. Remove the intake manifold.
6. Remove the exhaust manifold.
7. Remove the engine accessory bracket bolts and studs at the head.
8. Disconnect the wiring harness clip at the rear of the head.
9. Remove the fuel pipes and bracket from the rear of the head.
10. Disconnect the coolant sensor wire.
11. If equipped, remove the cruise control transducer bracket.
12. Tag and disconnect the wiring from the spark plugs. If necessary, remove the spark plugs from the cylinder head.
13. Loosen the rocker arms and remove the pushrods.

➡ **If valve train components, such as the rocker arms or pushrods, are to be reused, they must be tagged or arranged to insure installation in their original locations.**

14. Remove the cylinder head bolts by loosening them in the reverse of the torque sequence, then carefully remove the cylinder head.
15. Using a plastic scraper, clean the gasket mounting surfaces.
16. Clean the carbon deposits from the combustion chambers.
17. Inspect the cylinder head and block for cracks, nicks, heavy scratches or other damage.
   **To install:**

➡ **The gasket surfaces on both the head and block must be clean of any foreign matter and free of nicks or heavy scratches. The cylinder bolt threads in the block and threads on the bolts must be cleaned (dirt will affect the bolt torque).**

➡ **DO NOT apply sealer to composition steel-asbestos gaskets.**

18. If using a steel only gasket, apply a thin and even coat of sealer to both sides of the gaskets.
19. Place a new gasket over the dowel pins with the bead or the words "This Side Up" facing upwards (as applicable), then carefully lower the cylinder head into position over the gasket and dowels.
20. Apply a coating of GM 1052080 or an equivalent sealer to the threads of the cylinder head bolts, then thread the bolts into position until finger-tight. Using the proper torque sequence, tighten the bolts in 3 steps:
   • First, tighten the bolts to 25 ft. lbs. (34 Nm).
   • Next, tighten the bolts to 45 ft. lbs. (61 Nm).
   • Finally, tighten the bolts to 65 ft. lbs. (90 Nm).
21. Install the pushrods, secure the rocker arms and adjust the valves.
22. If removed, install the spark plugs. Engage the spark plug wires and make sure they are positioned in the wire brackets.
23. Install the remaining components in the reverse of the removal procedure.
24. Properly refill the engine cooling system. Run the engine to check for leaks, then check and/or adjust the ignition timing.
25. Once the engine has cooled, install the engine cover.

*1996 MODELS*

### ❊❊ CAUTION

**Relieve the pressure on the fuel system before disconnecting any fuel line connection.**

1. Remove the engine cover as outlined in Section 1 of this manual.
2. Properly relieve the fuel system pressure, then disconnect the negative battery cable for safety.
3. Place a catch pan under the radiator, open the drain cock and drain the cooling system.

4. Remove the rocker arm cover.
5. Remove the intake manifold.
6. Remove the exhaust manifold.
7. Remove the alternator and bracket.
8. Disconnect the wiring harness clip at the rear of the head.
9. Disconnect the coolant sensor wire.
10. Tag and disconnect the wiring from the spark plugs. If necessary, remove the spark plugs from the cylinder head.
11. Loosen the rocker arms and remove the pushrods.

➡ **If valve train components, such as the rocker arms or pushrods, are to be reused, they must be tagged or arranged to insure installation in their original locations.**

12. Remove the cylinder head bolts by loosening them in the reverse of the torque sequence, then carefully remove the cylinder head.
13. Using a plastic scraper, clean the gasket mounting surfaces.
14. Clean the carbon deposits from the combustion chambers.
15. Inspect the cylinder head and block for cracks, nicks, heavy scratches or other damage.
   **To install:**

➡ **The gasket surfaces on both the head and block must be clean of any foreign matter and free of nicks or heavy scratches. The cylinder bolt threads in the block and threads on the bolts must be cleaned (dirt will affect the bolt torque).**

➡ **DO NOT apply sealer to composition steel-asbestos gaskets.**

16. If using a steel only gasket, apply a thin and even coat of sealer to both sides of the gaskets.
17. Place a new gasket over the dowel pins with the bead or the words "This Side Up" facing upwards (as applicable), then carefully lower the cylinder head into position over the gasket and dowels.
18. Apply a coating of GM 1052080 or an equivalent sealer to the threads of the cylinder head bolts, then thread the bolts into position until finger-tight. Using the proper torque sequence, tighten the bolts to 22 ft. lbs. (30 Nm), then using a torque angle meter, tighten the bolts the additional specified amount based on bolt size and position in the torque sequence.
   • Short length bolts (11, 7, 3, 2, 6 and 10) should be tightened an additional 55 degrees.
   • Medium length bolts (12, and 13) should be tightened an additional 65 degrees.
   • Long length bolts (1, 4, 8, 5, and 9) should be tightened an additional 75 degrees.
19. Install the remaining components in the reverse order of removal.
20. Properly refill the engine cooling system. Run the engine to check for leaks, then check and/or adjust the ignition timing.
21. Once the engine has cooled, install the engine cover.

### CLEANING AND INSPECTION

▸ **See Figures 102, 103, 104 and 105**

1. With the valves installed to protect the valve seats, remove carbon deposits from the combustion chambers and valve heads using a drill-mounted wire brush. Be careful not to damage the cylinder head gasket surface. If the head is to be disassembled, proceed to Step 3. If the head is not to be disassembled, proceed to Step 2.
2. Remove all dirt, oil and old gasket material from the cylinder head with solvent. Clean the bolt holes and the oil passage. Be careful not to get solvent on the valve seals as the solvent may damage them. If available, dry the cylinder head with compressed air. Check the head for cracks or other damage, and check the gasket surface for burrs, nicks and flatness. If you are in doubt about the head's serviceability, consult a reputable automotive machine shop.
3. Remove the valves, springs and retainers, then clean the valve guide bores with a valve guide cleaning tool. Remove all dirt, oil and old gasket material from the cylinder head with solvent. Clean the bolt holes and the oil passage.

➡ **Excessive valve stem-to-bore clearance will cause excessive oil consumption and may cause valve breakage. Insufficient clearance will result in noisy and sticky functioning of the valve and disturb engine smoothness.**

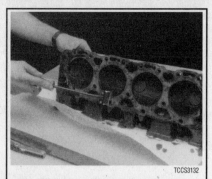

**Fig. 102 Use a gasket scraper to remove the bulk of the old head gasket material from the mating surface . . .**

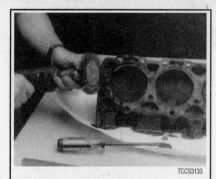

**Fig. 103 . . . but an electric drill equipped with a wire wheel will expedite complete gasket removal**

**Fig. 104 Clean the combustion chambers using a wire brush—if the valves are removed use care around the valve seats**

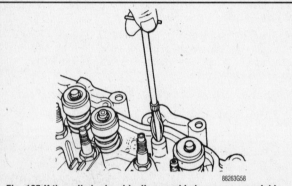

**Fig. 105 If the cylinder head is disassembled, use an expandable wire type tool to clean the valve guides**

4. Remove all deposits from the valves with a wire brush or buffing wheel. Inspect the valves as described later in this section.

5. Check the head for cracks using a dye penetrant in the valve seat area and ports, head surface and top. Check the gasket surface for burrs, nicks and flatness. If you are in doubt about the head's serviceability, consult a reputable automotive machine shop.

➡️If the cylinder head was removed due to an overheating condition and a crack is suspected, do not assume that the head is not cracked because a crack is not visually found. A crack can be so small that it cannot be seen by eye, but can pass coolant when the engine is at operating temperature. Consult an automotive machine shop that has pressure testing equipment to make sure the head is not cracked.

### RESURFACING

▶ **See Figures 106 and 107**

Whenever the cylinder head is removed, check the flatness of the cylinder head gasket surface as follows:

1. Make sure all dirt and old gasket material has been cleaned from the cylinder head. Any foreign material left on the head gasket surface can cause a false measurement.

2. Place a straightedge straight across and diagonally across the gasket surface of the cylinder head (in the positions shown in the figures). Using feeler gauges, determine the clearance at the center of the straightedge.

3. If warpage exceeds the 0.004 in. (0.10mm) then the cylinder head should likely be resurfaced or replaced. Contact a reputable machine shop for machining service and recommendations.

➡️When resurfacing the cylinder head(s), the intake manifold mounting position is altered and must be corrected by machining a proportionate amount from the intake manifold flange.

### CYLINDER BLOCK CLEANING

While the cylinder head is removed, the top of the cylinder block and pistons should also be cleaned. Before you begin, rotate the crankshaft until one or more pistons are flush with the top of the block. Carefully stuff clean rags into

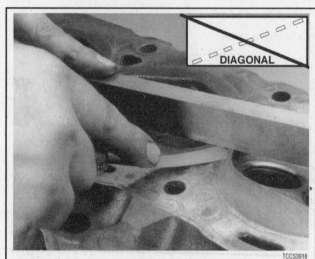

**Fig. 106 Check the cylinder head for flatness across the head surface**

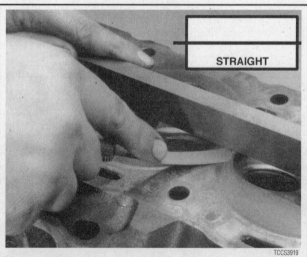

**Fig. 107 Checks should be made both straight across the head and a both diagonals**

the cylinders in which the pistons are down. This will help keep grit and carbon chips out during cleaning. Using care not to gouge or scratch the block-to-head mating surface and the piston top(s), clean away any old gasket material with a wire brush and/or scraper. On the piston tops, make sure you are actually removing the carbon and not merely burnishing it.

Remove the rags from the down cylinders after you have wiped the top of the block with a solvent soaked rag. Rotate the crankshaft until the other pistons come up flush with the top of the block, and clean those pistons.

➡**Because you have rotated the crankshaft, you may have to re-time the ignition during installation. It is probably easiest to set the engine to No. 1 TDC before installing the cylinder head. Also, make sure you wipe out each cylinder thoroughly with a solvent-soaked rag, to remove all traces of grit, before the head is reassembled to the block.**

## Valves

### REMOVAL & INSTALLATION

▶ **See Figures 108 thru 114**

➡**If the valve springs are suspect, you may wish to measure the installed height BEFORE removing them. For details, please refer to the valve spring inspection information, later in this section.**

New valve seals must be installed when the valve train is put back together. Certain seals slip over the valve stem and guide boss, while others require that

the boss be machined. In some applications Teflon guide seals are available. Check with a machinist and/or automotive parts store for a suggestion on the proper seals to use.

1. Remove the cylinder head(s), and place on a clean surface.
2. Using a suitable spring compressor (either a leverage or jawed type that is designed for pushrod overhead valve engines), compress the valve spring and remove the valve spring cap keys. Carefully release the spring compressor and remove the valve spring and cap (and valve rotator on some engines).

➡**Use care in removing the keys; they are easily lost.**

3. Remove the valve seals and the spring seat (if applicable) from the valve guides. Throw these old seals away, as you'll be installing new seals during reassembly.
4. Slide the valves out of the head from the combustion chamber side.
5. Make a holder for the valves out of a piece of wood with drilled holes or cardboard. Make sure you number each hole in the holder to keep the valves in proper order; they MUST be installed in their original locations. Another method of sorting the valve components is to use numbered containers, and make sure the components from each valve is stored in a separate container.
6. Use an electric drill and rotary wire brush to clean the intake and exhaust valve ports, combustion chamber and valve seats. In some cases, the carbon build-up will have to be chipped away. Use a blunt pointed drift for carbon chipping, being careful around valve seat areas.
7. Use a valve guide cleaning brush and suitable solvent to clean the valve guides.
8. Clean the valves with a revolving wire brush. Heavy carbon deposits may be removed with a blunt drift.

TCCS3809

Fig. 108 Compress the valve springs, then remove the valve keys in order to free the assembly . . .

TCCS3810

Fig. 109 . . . then remove the spring from the valve stem in order to access the seal

TCCS3811

Fig. 110 Remove the valve stem seal from the cylinder head

TCCS3141

Fig. 111 Invert the cylinder head and withdraw the valve from the cylinder head bore

88263G57

Fig. 112 A valve spring compressor is necessary to remove the valves—this C-clamp style model can only be used with the cylinder head removed from the engine. Jawed types, such as seen in the photos can also be used with the head installed

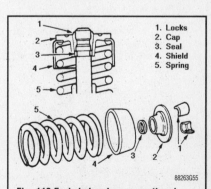

1. Locks
2. Cap
3. Seal
4. Shield
5. Spring

88263G55

Fig. 113 Exploded and cross-sectional view of a common valve component assembly—2.5L engine shown

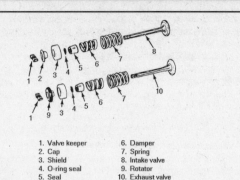

1. Valve keeper
2. Cap
3. Shield
4. O-ring seal
5. Seal
6. Damper
7. Spring
8. Intake valve
9. Rotator
10. Exhaust valve

88263G56

**Fig. 114 Exploded view of early-model 4.3L engine valves and components—late-model similar**

➡**When using a wire brush to remove carbon from the cylinder head or valves, make sure the deposits are actually removed and not just burnished.**

9. Wash and clean all valve springs, retainers etc., in safe solvent. Remember to keep parts from each valve separate.

10. Check the cylinder head for cracks. Cracks usually start around the exhaust valve seat because it is the hottest part of the combustion chamber. If a crack is suspected but cannot be detected visually, have the area checked by pressure testing, with a dye penetrant or other method by an automotive machine shop.

11. Inspect the valves, guides, springs and seats and machine or replace parts, as necessary.

**To install:**

12. Lubricate the valve stems with clean engine oil.

13. Install the valves in the cylinder head, one at a time, as numbered.

14. Lubricate and position the spring seats (if applicable), new seals and valve springs, again one valve at a time.

15. Install the spring caps, and compress the springs.

16. With the valve key groove exposed above the compressed valve spring, wipe some wheel bearing grease around the groove. This will retain the keys as you release the spring compressor.

17. Using needle-nose pliers (or your fingers), carefully place the keys in the key grooves. The grease should hold the keys in place. Slowly release the spring compressor; the valve cap or rotator will be raised as the compressor is released, retaining the key.

18. Install the cylinder head(s).

## INSPECTION

▶ **See Figures 115, 116, 117, 118 and 119**

➡**Excessive valve stem-to-bore clearance will cause excessive oil consumption and may cause valve breakage. Insufficient clearance will result in noisy and sticky functioning of the valve and disturb engine smoothness.**

Inspect the valve faces and seats (in the head) for pits, burned spots and other evidence of poor seating. Valves that are pitted must be refaced to the proper angle (45°). Valves that are warped excessively must be replaced. When a valve head that is warped excessively is refaced, a knife edge will be ground on part or all of the valve head due to the amount of material that must be removed to completely reface the valve. Knife edges lead to breakage, burning or preignition due to heat localizing on the knife edge. If the edge of the valve head is less than $\frac{1}{32}$ in. (0.8mm) after machining, replace the valve. We recommend that all machine work be performed by a reputable machine shop.

Make sure the valve stem is not bent. The valve may be rolled on a flat surface such as a mirror or glass. An even better indication of valve stem bending can be determined by carefully chocking the stem into an electric drill. Use the drill the spin the stem while you watch the valve head. A bent stem will be obvious by the wobbling of the head. Be very careful if this method is used. If the valve stem is not properly chocked in position it could come flying out of the drill and cause injury.

Some of the engines covered in this guide are equipped with valve rotators, which double as valve spring caps. In normal operation the rotators put a certain degree of wear on the tip of the valve stem; this wear appears as concentric rings on the stem tip. However, if the rotator is not working properly, the wear

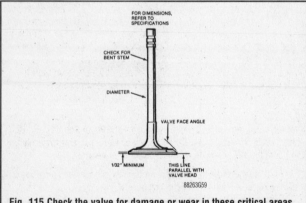

FOR DIMENSIONS, REFER TO SPECIFICATIONS

CHECK FOR BENT STEM

DIAMETER

VALVE FACE ANGLE

1/32" MINIMUM

THIS LINE PARALLEL WITH VALVE HEAD

88263G59

**Fig. 115 Check the valve for damage or wear in these critical areas**

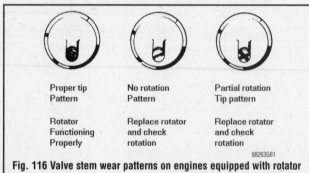

Proper tip Pattern

No rotation Pattern

Partial rotation Tip pattern

Rotator Functioning Properly

Replace rotator and check rotation

Replace rotator and check rotation

88263G61

**Fig. 116 Valve stem wear patterns on engines equipped with rotator cups**

TCCS3142

**Fig. 117 A dial gauge may be used to check valve stem-to-guide clearance**

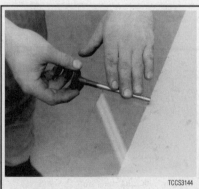

TCCS3144

**Fig. 118 Valve stems may be rolled on a flat surface to check for bends**

TCCS3910

**Fig. 119 Use a micrometer to check the valve stem diameter**

may appear as straight notches or **X** patterns across the valve stem tip. Whenever the valves are removed from the cylinder head, the tips should be inspected for improper pattern, which could indicate valve rotator problems. Valve stem tips will have to be ground flat if rotator patterns are severe.

Check the valve stem for scoring and burned spots. If not noticeably scored or damaged, clean the valve stem with solvent to remove all gum and varnish. Clean the valve guides using solvent and an expanding wire type valve guide cleaner. Check the valve stem-to-guide clearance in one or more of the following manners, but do not rely on the visual inspection alone:

1. A visual inspection can give you a fairly good idea if the guide, valve stem or both are worn. Insert the valve into the guide until the valve head is slightly away from the valve seat. Wiggle the valve sideways. A small amount of wobble is normal, excessive wobble means a worn guide and/or valve stem.

➡**If a dial indicator and micrometer are not available to you, take your cylinder head and valves to a reputable machine shop of inspection.**

2. If a dial indicator is on hand, mount the indicator so that gauge stem is 90° to the valve stem as close to the top of the valve guide as possible. Move the valve from the seat, and measure the valve guide-to-stem clearance by rocking the stem back and forth to actuate the dial indicator. Measure the valve stem using a micrometer and compare to specifications to determine whether stem or guide is causing excessive clearance.

3. If both a ball gauge and a micrometer are available, first, measure the inside diameter of the valve guide bushing at three locations using the ball gauge. Second, use the micrometer to measure the stem diameter. Finally, subtract the valve stem diameter from the corresponding valve guide inside diameter to arrive at the valve clearance. If clearance is greater than specification, the valve and guide bushing must be replaced.

The valve guide, if worn, must be repaired before the valve seats can be resurfaced. A new valve guide should be installed or, in some cases, knurled. Consult an automotive machine shop.

If the valve guide is okay, measure the valve seat concentricity using a runout gauge. Follow the manufacturers instructions. If runout is excessive, reface or replace the valve and machine or replace the valve seat.

➡**Valves and seats must always be machined together. Never use a refaced valve on a valve seat that has not been machined; never use a valve that has not been refaced on a machined valve seat.**

## REFACING

Valve refacing should only be handled by a reputable machine shop, as the experience and equipment needed to do the job are beyond that of the average owner/mechanic. Refacing may be necessary in order to correct seat and face wear. When the valves are reground (resurfaced), the valve seats must also be recut, again requiring special equipment and experience.

## VALVE LAPPING

▶ **See Figures 120 and 121**

After machine work has been performed on the valves, it may be necessary to lap the valves to assure proper contact. For this, you should first contact your machine shop to determine if lapping is necessary. Some machine shops will

perform this for you as part of the service. Keep in mind that the precision machining which is available today often makes lapping unnecessary. Additionally, the hardened valves/seats used in modern automobiles may make lapping difficult or impossible. If your machine shop recommends that you lap the valves, proceed as follows:

1. Set the cylinder head on the workbench, combustion chamber side up. Rest the head on wooden blocks on either end, so there are two or three inches between the tops of the valve guides and the bench.

2. Lightly lube the valve stem with clean engine oil. Coat the valve seat completely with valve grinding compound. Use just enough compound that the full width and circumference of the seat are covered.

3. Install the valve in its proper location in the head. Attach the suction cup end of the valve lapping tool to the valve head. It usually helps to put a small amount of saliva into the suction cup to aid its sticking to the valve.

4. Rotate the tool between your palms, changing position and lifting the tool often to prevent grooving. Lap the valve in until a smooth, evenly polished seat and valve face are evident.

5. Remove the valve from the head. Wipe away all traces of grinding compound from the valve face and seat. Wipe out the port with a solvent soaked rag, and swab out the valve guide with a piece of solvent soaked rag to make sure there are no traces of compound grit inside the guide. This cleaning is important.

6. Proceed through the remaining valves, one at a time. Make sure the valve faces, seats, cylinder ports and valve guides are clean before reassembling the valve train.

## Valve Springs and Stem Seals

### REMOVAL & INSTALLATION

▶ **See Figures 122 and 123**

➡**If the valve springs are suspect, you may wish to measure the installed height BEFORE removing them. For details, please refer to the valve spring inspection information, later in this section.**

Both the valve spring and stem seal must be removed if the valve is being removed from the cylinder head. If the cylinder head has been removed from the engine, then please refer to the Valve procedures found earlier in this section for details on spring or stem seal removal or installation. But unlike the valves which face into the combustion chamber (and therefore cannot be removed unless the cylinder head is off the engine) both the valve springs and the stem seals can be replaced with the cylinder head installed (if a special tool is used to keep the valves from falling into the combustion chambers).

➡**The following procedures requires the use of GM Air Adapter tool No. J–23590 or equivalent, and a jawed spring compressor or a lever style spring compressor tool such as No. J–5892 or equivalent.**

1. For access, remove the engine cover from the passenger compartment. For details, please refer to Section 1 of this manual.
2. Disconnect the negative battery cable.
3. Remove the rocker arm cover.

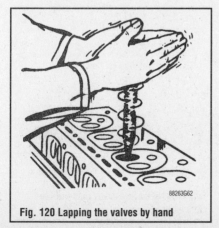

**Fig. 120 Lapping the valves by hand**

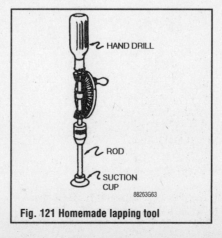

**Fig. 121 Homemade lapping tool**

**Fig. 122 With the proper tools, valve springs and stem seals can be replaced with the cylinder head installed**

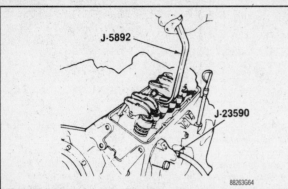

**Fig. 123 A lever type or jawed spring compressor can be used with the head installed**

➡The cylinder on whose valves you are working must have its piston at TDC of the compression stroke in order to follow this procedure. On the compression stroke, the cylinder's valves will be closed allowing the air pressure to hold the valve in position. The engine must therefore be turned slightly for each cylinder's valve springs or seals.

4. Remove the rocker arm and pushrod assemblies from the cylinders on which the valves are being serviced.

5. Remove the spark plug from the cylinder which is on its compression stroke and install a spark plug air fitting adapter with an in-line gauge set between the adapter and air compressor. Apply AT LEAST 100 psi (690 kPa) of compressed air to hold the valve in place.

### ✳✳ WARNING

**If air pressure is lost while the valve keepers are removed, the valve will drop into the cylinder. If this happens, the cylinder head must be removed in order to recover the valve.**

6. Compress the valve spring using a suitable compressor tool and remove the valve key. Carefully release the spring tension, then remove the valve cap and spring.

➡If the air pressure has forced the piston to the bottom of the cylinder, any removal of air pressure will allow the valves to fall into the cylinder. A rubber band, tape or string wrapped around the end of the valve stem will prevent this.

7. If the seals are being replaced, remove and discard the old seal from the valve stem.

**To install:**

8. If removed, install the new seal using a valve stem seal installer or other suitable driver.

9. Install the valve spring and cap, then compress the spring and install the valve keys.

10. When the valve springs are properly installed, release the air pressure from the cylinder using the gauge set, then remove the spark plug adapter.

11. Install the spark plug and turn the engine sufficiently to work on the next cylinder. Repeat the above steps until all seals are replaced.

12. Install the rocker arm and pushrod assemblies.

13. Install the rocker cover and connect the negative battery cable.

14. Install the engine cover to the passenger compartment.

### INSPECTION

▶ **See Figures 124, 125, 126, 127 and 128**

1. Before the springs are removed, check the installed height using a precision ruler. Compare the measurement to the specification found in the Valve chart at the beginning of this section.

2. Place the valve spring on a flat, clean surface next to a square.

3. Measure the height of the spring, and rotate it against the edge of the square to measure distortion (out-of-roundness). If spring height varies between springs by more than 1/16 in. (1.6mm) or if the distortion exceeds 1/16 in (1.6mm), replace the spring.

A valve spring tester is needed to test spring test pressure, so the valve springs must usually be taken to a professional machine shop for this test. Spring pressure at the installed and/or compressed heights is checked, depending on the specification.

### Valve Seats

▶ **See Figure 129**

The valve seats are cast into the cylinder head(s) and cannot be replaced; the seats can be machined during a valve job to provide optimum sealing between the valve and the seat. Valve seat concentricity should be checked by the machine shop, using special dial gauge.

The seating services should be performed by a professional machine shop which has the specialized knowledge and tools necessary to perform the service.

### Valve Guides

▶ **See Figures 130 and 131**

The engines covered in this guide use integral valves guides; that is, they are a part of the cylinder head and cannot be replaced. The guides can, however, be reamed oversize if they are found to be worn past an acceptable limit. Occasionally, a valve guide bore will be oversize as manufactured. These are marked on the inboard side of the cylinder heads on the machined surface just above the intake manifold.

If the guides must be reamed (this service is available at most machine shops), then valves with oversize stems must be fitted. Valves are usually available in 0.001 in. (0.0254mm), 0.003 in. (0.0762mm) and 0.005 in. (0.127mm) stem oversizes. Valve guides which are not excessively worn or distorted may, in some cases, be knurled rather than reamed. Knurling is a process in which the metal on the valve guide bore is displaced and raised, thereby reducing clearance. Knurling also provides excellent oil control. The option of knurling rather than reaming valve guides should be discussed with a reputable machinist or engine specialist.

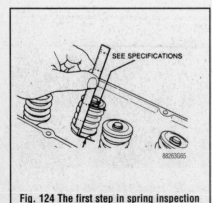

**Fig. 124 The first step in spring inspection is to measure the installed height**

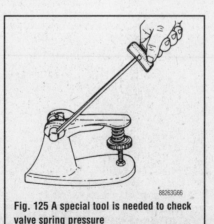

**Fig. 125 A special tool is needed to check valve spring pressure**

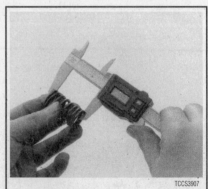

**Fig. 126 Use a caliper gauge to check the valve spring free-length**

**Fig. 127 Check the valve spring for squareness on a flat service; a carpenter's square can be used**

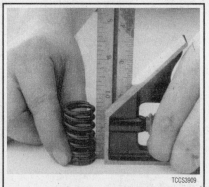

**Fig. 128 The valve spring should be straight up and down when placed like this**

**Fig. 129 Machine shops will check valve seat concentricity using a special dial gauge**

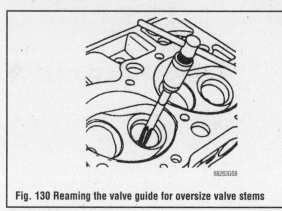

**Fig. 130 Reaming the valve guide for oversize valve stems**

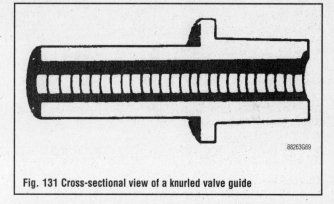

**Fig. 131 Cross-sectional view of a knurled valve guide**

## Oil Pan

### REMOVAL & INSTALLATION

▶ **See Figures 132 thru 137**

**1985–90 Models**

1. Disconnect the negative battery cable for safety.
2. Raise and support the front of the vehicle safely using jackstands.
3. Position a catch pan under the crankcase and drain the oil from the engine.

### ✴ CAUTION

The EPA warns that prolonged contact with used engine oil may cause a number of skin disorders, including cancer! You should make every effort to minimize your exposure to used engine oil. Protective gloves should be worn when changing the oil. Wash your hands and any other exposed skin areas as soon as possible after exposure to used engine oil. Soap and water, or waterless hand cleaner should be used.

4. Disconnect the strut rods at the flywheel/torque converter cover, then remove the cover from the bellhousing.
5. Disengage the electrical connectors from the starter, then remove the starter-to-engine bolts, the brace and the starter from the vehicle.
6. Disconnect the exhaust pipe(s) from the exhaust manifold(s) and, if necessary, at the exhaust pipe-to-catalytic converter hanger(s).
7. If necessary, remove the engine mount through-bolts, then using an engine lifting device, raise the engine (as needed) in order to make room for the oil pan removal.

### ✴ WARNING

If it is necessary to raise the engine, do so slowly, continually checking for possible interference with the firewall. DO NOT allow upper engine components to become damaged.

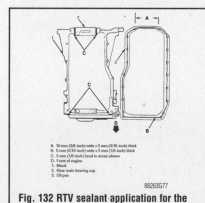

A. 10 mm (3/8-inch) wide x 5 mm (3/16-inch) thick
B. 5 mm (3/16-inch) wide x 3 mm (1/8-inch) thick
C. 3 mm (1/8-inch) bead in areas shown
D. Front of engine
1. Block
2. Rear main bearing cap
3. Oil pan

**Fig. 132 RTV sealant application for the 2.5L engine oil pan**

**Fig. 133 On most vehicles covered by this manual you will have to unbolt the exhaust pipe for clearance**

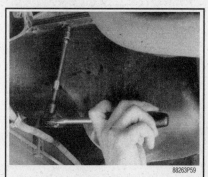

**Fig. 134 Loosen and remove the oil pan retaining bolts (a variety of ratchet extensions will be helpful)**

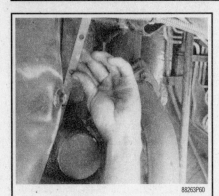

**Fig. 135 If equipped, remove the oil pan reinforcements . . .**

**Fig. 136 . . . then lower the pan from the engine**

**Fig. 137 CAREFULLY remove the old gasket (on 4.3L engines it can be reused if it is not damaged)**

8. Remove the oil pan-to-engine bolts and nuts (as applicable), then remove the oil pan from the engine.

9. Using a plastic scraper, clean the gasket mounting surfaces. Using solvent, clean the excess oil from the mounting surfaces.

**To install:**

10. On the 2.5L engine, apply a ⅙ in. (4.2mm) bead of RTV sealant to the oil pan flange (keep the bead inside the bolt holes), the rear main bearing, the timing gear cover and the engine block sealing surface. On the 4.3L engine, apply a small amount of RTV sealant to the front and rear corners of the oil pan; too much sealant may prevent sealing of the gasket.

➡**The 4.3L engine uses a one piece oil pan gasket.**

11. Use a new gasket (4.3L), RTV sealant and install the oil pan.

12. Tighten the oil pan-to-engine bolts to 100 inch lbs. (11 Nm) and the oil pan-to-engine nuts to 14 ft. lbs. (20 Nm) for the 4.3L.

13. If raised, lower the engine into position and install the mount through-bolts.

14. Install the remaining components in the reverse order of removal. Tighten all components securely and carefully lower the vehicle.

15. Immediately refill the crankcase with fresh oil. Don't risk someone accidentally trying to start a dry motor.

16. Connect the negative battery cable, then start the engine, establish normal operating temperatures and check for leaks.

**1991–95 Models**

1. Disconnect the negative battery cable for safety.
2. Raise and support the front of the vehicle safely using jackstands.
3. Position a catch pan under the crankcase and drain the oil from the engine.

**✻✻ CAUTION**

**The EPA warns that prolonged contact with used engine oil may cause a number of skin disorders, including cancer! You should make every effort to minimize your exposure to used engine oil. Protective gloves should be worn when changing the oil. Wash your hands and any other exposed skin areas as soon as possible after exposure to used engine oil. Soap and water, or waterless hand cleaner should be used.**

4. Disconnect the exhaust pipe from the manifolds.
5. Remove the torque converter cover from the bellhousing.
6. Remove the starter assembly from the vehicle.
7. Remove the oil pan-to-engine bolts, nuts and reinforcements, then carefully lower the oil pan from the engine.

➡**Remember that no matter how well you drained the crankcase, the oil pan will still be holding a decent amount of slimy residue.**

8. Carefully remove the rubber composite gasket from the mating surface. Take care because if the gasket is free of damage it can be reused.

9. Clean the gasket mounting surfaces of sealant, dirt or other residue. Using solvent, clean the excess oil from the mounting surfaces.

**To install:**

10. Inspect the oil pan gasket for damage and replace, if necessary. Position the gasket on the oil pan.

11. Apply sealant such as GM 12346141, or equivalent, to the front cover-to-block joint and to the rear crankshaft seal-to-block joint. Continue the sealant about 1 in. (25mm) in both directions from the 4 corners.

12. Carefully raise the oil pan into position with the reinforcements and thread the retainers.

13. Tighten the oil pan-to-engine bolts to 100 inch lbs. (11 Nm) and the oil pan-to-engine nuts to 17 ft. lbs. (23 Nm).

14. Install the remaining components in the reverse order of removal. Tighten all components securely and carefully lower the vehicle.

15. Immediately refill the crankcase with fresh oil. Don't risk someone accidentally trying to start a dry motor.

16. Connect the negative battery cable, then start the engine, establish normal operating temperatures and check for leaks.

**1996 Models**

◆ **See Figures 138, 139 and 140**

➡**Any time the transmission and oil pan are off the engine at the same time, the transmission MUST be installed before the oil pan. This will allow for proper measurement of the oil pan tolerance.**

1. Disconnect the negative battery cable for safety.
2. Raise and support the front of the vehicle safely using jackstands.
3. Position a catch pan under the crankcase and drain the oil from the engine.

**✻✻ CAUTION**

**The EPA warns that prolonged contact with used engine oil may cause a number of skin disorders, including cancer! You should make every effort to minimize your exposure to used engine oil. Protective gloves should be worn when changing the oil. Wash your hands and any other exposed skin areas as soon as possible after exposure to used engine oil. Soap and water, or waterless hand cleaner should be used.**

4. Remove the oil filter.
5. Disconnect the oil cooler lines from the oil pan and from the adapter. Immediately plug all openings to prevent system contamination or excessive fluid loss.

6. Remove the oil filter adapter.
7. Remove the starter assembly from the vehicle.
8. Remove the starter shield.
9. If necessary, remove the transmission oil cooler lines. Immediately plug all openings to prevent system contamination or excessive fluid loss.

10. On All Wheel Drive (AWD) vehicles, remove the front drive axle tube mount nuts and the left lower drive axle bushing bolt.

11. Remove the rubber bellhousing plugs.
12. Remove the oil pan-to-engine bolts and studs, then carefully lower the oil pan from the engine.

➡**Remember that no matter how well you drained the crankcase, the oil pan will still be holding a decent amount of slimy residue.**

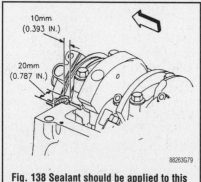

**Fig. 138 Sealant should be applied to this area during installation—1996 4.3L engines**

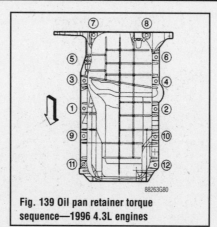

**Fig. 139 Oil pan retainer torque sequence—1996 4.3L engines**

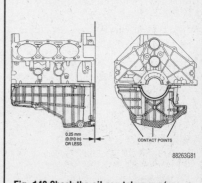

**Fig. 140 Check the oil pan tolerance (pan-to-transmission clearance) as these 3 points**

13. Carefully remove the rubber composite gasket from the mating surface. Take care because if the gasket is free of damage it can be reused.

14. Clean the gasket mounting surfaces of sealant, dirt or other residue. Using solvent, clean the excess oil from the mounting surfaces.

**To install:**

15. Inspect the oil pan gasket for damage and replace, if necessary. Position the gasket on the oil pan.

16. Apply sealant such as GM 12346141, or equivalent, to the front cover-to-block joint and to the rear crankshaft seal-to-block joint. Continue the sealant about 1 in. (25mm) in both directions from the 4 corners.

17. Carefully raise the oil pan into position and thread the retainers finger-tight.

18. Tighten the oil pan-to-engine retainers using the proper torque sequence to 18 ft. lbs. (25 Nm).

19. Use a feeler gauge to check for proper oil pan-to-transmission clearance at the points shown in the accompanying figure. If the clearance exceeds 0.010 in. (0.254) at ANY of the 3 contact points, loosen the retainers and reposition the pan until clearance is correct.

20. Install the remaining components in the reverse order of removal. Tighten all components securely and carefully lower the vehicle.

21. Immediately refill the crankcase with fresh oil. Don't risk someone accidentally trying to start a dry motor.

22. Connect the negative battery cable, then start the engine, establish normal operating temperatures and check for leaks.

## Oil Pump

### REMOVAL & INSTALLATION

#### ♦ See Figures 141, 142 and 143

1. Remove the oil pan, as outlined in this section.

2. Remove the oil pump-to-rear main bearing cap bolt(s), the pump and the extension shaft.

3. Remove the pump pickup screen only if replacement is necessary. Because the pickup tube has a press (interference) fit to the pump cover on most models it cannot be reinstalled.

**To install:**

4. Install the oil pump and extension shaft to the engine, while aligning the slot (on top of the extension shaft) with the drive tang (on the lower end of the distributor driveshaft). The oil pump should slide easily in place.

5. Tighten the oil pump-to-bearing cap bolt(s) to 22 ft. lbs. (30 Nm) for the 2.5L engine or 65 ft. lbs. (88 Nm) for the 4.3L engine.

6. Install the oil pan and refill the crankcase with fresh oil.

7. When starting the motor, MAKE SURE the oil pressure light goes out, or the gauge reads pressure almost immediately after starting. If it does not, shut the engine **OFF** and determine the cause of the problem.

## Crankshaft Pulley, Damper and Front Oil Seal

### REMOVAL & INSTALLATION

#### 2.5L Engine

➡The following procedure requires the use of the GM Seal Installer/Centering tool No. J–34995 or equivalent.

1. Disconnect the negative battery cable for safety.

2. If equipped, remove the power steering fluid reservoir from the radiator shroud.

3. Remove the upper fan shroud. Loosen and remove the accessory-to-damper pulley drive belts.

4. Remove the damper pulley/hub assembly-to-crankshaft bolt and washer, then the pulley/hub assembly from the crankshaft.

➡The damper pulley is connected to the damper pulley hub by 3 bolts; if necessary, remove the pulley-to-hub bolts and separate the pulley from the hub. When it becomes necessary to remove the damper pulley/hub assembly, ALWAYS replace the front oil seal with a new one.

**Fig. 141 Exploded view of a typical oil pump mounting—4.3L engine (late-model shown)**

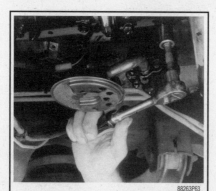

**Fig. 142 Loosen and remove the oil pump retaining bolt(s) . . .**

**Fig. 143 . . . then remove the pump and extension shaft from the engine**

5. Inspect the damper hub (oil seal surface) for rust or burrs; remove the roughness with fine emery cloth.

➡**When installing the damper pulley hub to the crankshaft, be careful not to damage the front oil seal.**

6. To replace the timing cover oil seal, perform the following procedures:

   a. Using a medium prybar, carefully pry the oil seal from the timing cover, making sure not to score the surface of the bore or the crankshaft.

   b. Using the GM Seal Installer/Centering tool No. J-34995 or equivalently sized driver, install the new oil seal into the timing cover, then remove the tool from the timing cover.

**To install:**

7. Lubricate (with clean engine oil) and install the damper hub. Align it onto the keyway and push onto crankshaft.

8. Install and tighten the damper pulley hub-to-crankshaft bolt to 160 ft. lbs. (217 Nm).

9. Install remaining components in the reverse order of removal.

10. Connect the negative battery cable. Start the engine, check for leaks and proper operation.

### 4.3L Engine

▸ **See Figures 144 thru 150**

➡**The following procedure requires the use of a torsional damper puller/installer tool such as GM tool no. J-23523-E (1985–92 models), J-39046 (1993–96 models) or an equivalent, and the GM seal installer tool No. J-35468 or equivalent.**

### ❊❊ WARNING

**DO NOT attempt to remove the damper using a jawed puller or the hub may be destroyed. The internal weight section of the balancer is assembled to the hub using a rubber-type material. The proper puller type tool is needed to prevent damage.**

1. Disconnect the negative battery cable for safety.

2. For 1985–90 vehicles, loosen and remove the accessory-to-damper pulley drive belt(s).

3. For 1991–96 vehicles, remove the engine cooling fan, along with the upper and lower shrouds. For details, please refer to the procedure found earlier in this section.

➡**Although fan and shroud removal is not required on many older vehicles covered by this manual, because of the tight working conditions, it is highly recommended.**

4. Remove the accessory drive belt pulley-to-damper bolts, then remove the pulley. On some models the center bolt (torsional damper bolt) is equipped with a LARGE flat washer which would prevent removal of the pulley. On these engines the pulley cannot be removed until the next step has been completed.

5. Remove the damper-to-crankshaft bolt. If removal is difficult, you have 2 options. The first is to hold the crankshaft from turning (on M/T vehicles this can be done by blocking the wheels, setting the parking brake and putting the van in gear. On A/T vehicles you must use a flywheel holding tool.). The second option is to cheat the bolt through impact (an air ratchet is best, though a sharp blow on the end of a wrench or breaker bar may also do the trick) or through using a penetrating oil. If the various special tools mentioned before are not available, apply penetrating oil to the bolt and allow it to sit overnight (this usually does the trick).

6. Using the a suitable torsional damper puller/installer tool (NOT AT JAWED TYPE) draw the damper from the end of the crankshaft.

➡**When performing this operation, ALWAYS replace the front oil seal with a new one.**

7. To replace the engine front oil seal in the timing cover, perform the following procedures (if the timing cover is being removed, this should be done after the cover is removed or during the beginning of the installation process):

   a. Using a medium prybar, carefully pry the oil seal from the timing cover. Take care not to score and damage the sealing surfaces and DO NOT distort the front cover.

   b. Coat the lips of the new seal with engine oil. The open end of the seal faces inside the engine.

Fig. 144 On some models you will have to remove the damper hub-to-crankshaft bolt before the pulley

Fig. 145 The hub bolt on this 4.3L engine has a LARGE flat washer which spreads the clamp load on the pulley

Fig. 146 Loosen and remove the retaining bolts around the perimeter of the pulley face . . .

Fig. 147 . . . then remove the pulley from the damper

Fig. 148 Use a suitable (NON-JAWED) puller to loosen the damper on the crankshaft

Fig. 149 Once loosened, the damper is easily removed

Fig. 150 If necessary, drive a new oil seal into place before reinstalling the damper

c. Using a suitable seal installer such as J-35468, or an equivalent sized driver, install the new oil seal into the timing cover.

8. Inspect the damper (oil seal surface) for rust or burrs; remove the roughness with fine emery cloth.

**To install:**

➡When installing the damper onto the crankshaft, be careful not to damage the front oil seal.

9. Lubricate the hub with engine oil, align it with the keyway and install it onto the crankshaft. Use the torsional damper puller/installer tool to slowly draw the damper into position.

➡If the tool is not available you MAY be able to align the damper and thread the retaining bolt a few turns, then use the hub retaining bolt to draw the damper into position. Be careful that sufficient threads are engaged first or you could strip the threads on the bolt or shaft. If the bolt cannot be started (because the distance is too great) obtain a second bolt of the same thread size, but of a longer length. You may also need some thick flat washers (in case the bolt is too long).

➡REMEMBER that the damper retaining bolt on some models MUST be installed AFTER the pulley (or stated another way, you may have to position the pulley before installing the damper bolt).

10. Tighten the damper hub-to-crankshaft bolt to 70 ft. lbs. (95 Nm) for 1985–95 vehicles or to 74 ft. lbs. (100 Nm) for 1996 vehicles.

11. If not done already, position the accessory drive belt pulley, then secure using the retaining bolts.

12. If removed, install the lower shroud, followed by the engine cooling fan and upper shroud.

13. Install the drive belt(s), then check and/or adjust the belt tension as applicable. For details, please refer to Section 1 of this manual.

14. Start the engine, then check for leaks or normal operation.

## Timing Cover and Front Oil Seal

### REMOVAL & INSTALLATION

#### 2.5L Engine

♦ See Figures 151, 152 and 153

➡This procedure requires the use of the GM Seal Installer/Centering tool No. J–34995 or equivalent.

1. Disconnect the negative battery cable for safety.

2. Refer to the Crankshaft Pulley, Damper and Oil Seal, Removal and Installation procedures in this section and remove the damper from the crankshaft.

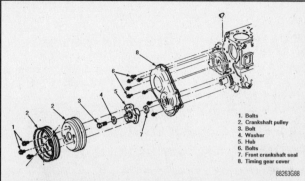

1. Bolts
2. Crankshaft pulley
3. Bolt
4. Washer
5. Hub
6. Bolts
7. Front crankshaft seal
8. Timing gear cover

Fig. 151 Exploded view of the crankshaft pulley, damper/hub and timing gear cover assembly—2.5L engine

Fig. 152 Apply RTV sealer to the timing gear cover as shown

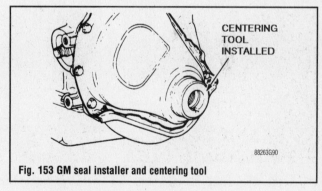

CENTERING TOOL INSTALLED

Fig. 153 GM seal installer and centering tool

3. If not done already, remove the fan and the pulley.

4. Remove the alternator and the brackets from the front of the engine.

5. Remove the lower radiator hose clamp at the water pump.

6. Remove the timing cover bolts and cover. Check for bolts threaded from the front of the oil pan to the bottom of the cover. If present, these must be removed before attempting to loosen the cover.

7. If the front seal is to be replaced, it can be pried out of the cover with a small prytool.

8. Using a plastic scraper, clean the gasket mounting surfaces. Then clean the surface with solvent to remove all traces of oil and grease.

➡The timing cover can become distorted very easily, so be careful when cleaning the gasket surface.

**To install:**

9. Apply engine oil to the lips of the new oil seal. Using the GM Seal Installer/Centering tool No. J–34995 or equivalent, install the new oil seal into the timing cover; leave the tool installed in the timing cover.

10. Using RTV sealant or equivalent, apply a ¼ in. (6mm) wide bead to the timing cover mounting surface and a ⅜ in. (9.5mm) wide bead to the oil pan at the timing cover sealing surface.

11. Using the GM Seal Installer/Centering Tool J-34995 or equivalent, align the front cover. Install the cover while the RTV sealant is still wet and finger-tighten the retainers.

12. Tighten the timing cover-to-engine bolts to 90 inch lbs. (10 Nm) first, then, tighten the timing cover-to-oil pan bolts to 90 inch lbs. (10 Nm). Remove the seal installer/centering tool from the timing cover.

13. Install the remaining components in the reverse order of removal. Tighten all components securely.

14. Connect the negative battery cable, start the engine and check for leaks.

### 4.3L Engine

♦ **See Figures 154, 155, 156 and 157**

#### 1985–95 MODELS

➡ The following procedure requires the use of a torsional damper puller/installer tool such as GM tool no. J-23523-E (1985–92 models), J-39046 (1993–95 models) or an equivalent, and the GM Seal Installer tool No. J-35468 or equivalent.

1. Disconnect the negative battery cable for safety.
2. Remove the water pump assembly from the engine. For details, please refer to the procedure found earlier in this section.
3. Remove the crankshaft pulley and damper. For details, please refer to the procedure found earlier in this section.
4. Either loosen or remove the oil pan, as necessary. For 1985–91 models the manufacturer recommends that the oil pan be removed. For 1992–95 models the manufacturer recommends that the pan just be loosened. It is possible that this can be done on earlier models as well, but caution must be taken to prevent front cover and oil pan seal damage.

**Fig. 154 Loosen and remove the timing cover retaining bolts . . .**

5. For 1995 vehicles, remove the crankshaft position sensor.
6. Remove the timing cover-to-engine bolts, then carefully remove the cover from the engine. If the oil pan was not removed, be careful not to damage the oil pan-to-front cover seal or sealing surfaces.
7. Using a plastic scraper, clean the gasket mounting surfaces. Using solvent and a rag, clean the oil and grease from the gasket mounting surfaces.
8. If the front cover seal is to be replaced, it may be pried front the front cover using a suitable prytool. Take care not to score and damage the seal bore, and take even greater care NOT TO distort the cover metal.
9. Inspect the timing cover for distortion and damage, if necessary, replace it.
**To install:**

➡ Beginning in 1992, the manufacturer began suggesting you wait until the front cover is mounted to the engine before you install the replacement crankshaft oil seal. This may be to assure the cover is properly supported. On earlier vehicles, the manufacturer allowed for installation with the cover removed or installed, so waiting would be acceptable for all years of the 4.3L engine.

10. If desired on early-model engines, install a new seal to the cover using a suitable installation driver, such as J-35468 or equivalent. Be sure to support the back of the seal cover area during installation to prevent the cover from becoming distorted or damaged. Lightly coat the lips of the new seal with clean engine oil.

➡ The oil seal is installed with the open end of the seal lips facing toward the inside of the engine.

11. Position a new front cover gasket to the engine or cover using a high-tack gasket cement to hold it in position. If the oil pan was not removed, lubricate the front of the oil pan seal with clean engine oil to aid in reassembly.

12. Install the front cover to the engine. If the oil pan is still in place, take care while engaging the front of the oil pan seal with the bottom of the cover.

13. Install front cover retaining bolts and tighten to 124 inch lbs. (14 Nm).

➡ Tighten the timing cover bolts alternately and evenly, while gently pressing on the cover.

14. If removed and not installed earlier, use the seal installation driver to install the new crankshaft seal at this time.

15. For 1995 vehicles, install the crankshaft position sensor.
16. Either secure or install the oil pan, depending on your decision earlier.
17. Install the crankshaft damper and pulley and the water pump.
18. Connect the negative battery cable, the properly refill and bleed the engine cooling system.
19. Run the engine and check for leaks.

#### 1996 MODELS

➡ The 1996 4.3L engine covered by this manual uses a composite engine front cover which must be discarded if it is removed from the engine. If a composite front cover is reused there is a good chance that it will leak.

1. Disconnect the negative battery cable for safety.
2. Remove the water pump assembly from the engine. For details, please refer to the procedure found earlier in this section.
3. Remove the crankshaft pulley and damper. For details, please refer to the procedure found earlier in this section.

**Fig. 155 . . . then carefully break the gasket seal and . . .**

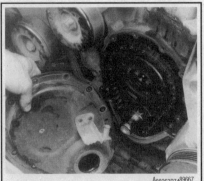

**Fig. 156 . . . remove the cover from the engine**

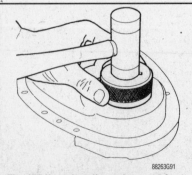

**Fig. 157 If you install a replacement front seal with the cover OFF the engine, BE SURE TO SUPPORT IT to prevent damage**

4. Loosen the oil pan to help provide clearance for front cover removal without damaging the front cover-to-oil pan seal.

5. Remove the crankshaft position sensor.

6. Remove the timing cover-to-engine bolts, then carefully remove the cover from the engine. Be careful not to damage the oil pan-to-front cover seal or sealing surfaces.

7. Discard the old timing cover.

8. Using a plastic scraper, solvent and a rag, clean the oil, grease and varnish from the mounting surfaces on the engine.

**To install:**

9. Lubricate the front of the oil pan seal with clean engine oil to aid in reassembly.

10. Install the new front cover to the engine, then tighten the front cover retaining bolts to 124 inch lbs. (14 Nm).

➡ **Tighten the timing cover bolts alternately and evenly, while gently pressing on the cover.**

11. Install the remaining components in the reverse order of removal.

12. Connect the negative battery cable, the properly refill and bleed the engine cooling system.

13. Run the engine and check for leaks.

## Timing Chain

### REMOVAL & INSTALLATION

#### 4.3L Engine

▶ **See Figures 158 thru 163**

The 4.3L engine is the only engine covered by this manual which uses a timing chain and gear (sprocket) assembly to turn the camshaft. The 2.5L engine uses a direct gear drive (without a chain).

➡ **The following procedure requires the use of the Crankshaft Sprocket Removal tool No. J-5825-A or equivalent, and the Crankshaft Sprocket Installation tool No. J-5590 or equivalent.**

1. Remove the timing cover from the engine.

2. Rotate the crankshaft until the No. 4 cylinder is on the TDC of its compression stroke and the camshaft sprocket mark aligns with the mark on the crankshaft sprocket (facing each other at a point closest together in their travel) and in line with the shaft centers.

3. For 1996 models, remove the crankshaft position sensor reluctor ring from the end of the crankshaft.

4. Remove the camshaft sprocket-to-camshaft nut and/or bolts, then remove the camshaft sprocket (and balance shaft drive gear on VIN W engines) along with the timing chain. If the sprocket is difficult to remove, use a plastic mallet to bump the sprocket from the camshaft.

➡ **The camshaft sprocket (located by a dowel) is lightly pressed onto the camshaft and should come off easily. The chain comes off with the camshaft sprocket.**

5. If necessary use J-5825-A or an equivalent crankshaft sprocket removal tool to free the timing sprocket from the crankshaft.

**To install:**

6. Inspect the timing chain and the timing sprockets for wear or damage, replace the damaged parts as necessary.

7. If removed, use J-5590, or an equivalent crankshaft sprocket installation tool and a hammer to drive the crankshaft sprocket onto the crankshaft, without disturbing the position of the crankshaft.

8. On VIN W engines, align and install the balance shaft drive gear. For details, please refer to the balance shaft procedure found later in this section.

➡ **During installation, coat the thrust surfaces lightly with Molykote® or an equivalent pre-lube.**

9. Position the timing chain over the camshaft sprocket. Arrange the camshaft sprocket in such a way that the timing marks will align between the shaft centers and the camshaft locating dowel will enter the dowel hole in the cam sprocket.

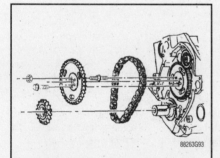

Fig. 158 Exploded view of a typical 4.3L engine timing chain and gear assembly—use of studs may vary

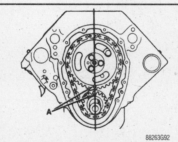

Fig. 159 Align the timing marks closest together (No. 4 TDC) before starting—NOTE that No. 1 TDC would be aligned, but with both timing marks at top of their travel

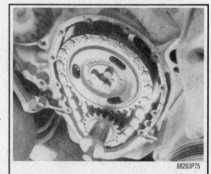

Fig. 160 Remove the timing cover, then turn the crankshaft as necessary to align the timing marks

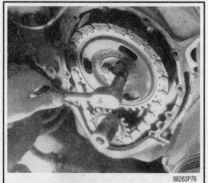

Fig. 161 Loosen and remove the camshaft sprocket retaining bolts . . .

Fig. 162 . . . then remove the camshaft sprocket along with the timing chain

Fig. 163 If necessary, use a suitable puller to remove the crankshaft sprocket

10. Position the chain under the crankshaft sprocket, then place the cam sprocket (on VIN W motors the balance shaft drive gear must still be in place), with the chain still mounted over it, in position on the front of the camshaft. Install and tighten the camshaft sprocket-to-camshaft retainers to 21 ft. lbs. (28 Nm).

11. With the timing chain installed, turn the crankshaft two complete revolutions, then check to make certain that the timing marks are in correct alignment between the shaft centers.

12. For 1996 models, install the crankshaft position reluctor ring to the end of the shaft.

13. Install the timing cover.

## Timing Gears

Unlike the rest of the engines covered by this manual, the 2.5L engine does not use a timing chain assembly. Instead the camshaft timing gear is directly driven by the crankshaft timing gear. The timing gear (camshaft sprocket) is pressed onto the camshaft and requires the use of an arbor press to remove.

### REMOVAL & INSTALLATION

#### 2.5L Engine

♦ **See Figures 164 and 165**

➡**The following procedure requires the use of an arbor press, a press plate, the GM gear removal tool No. J-971 or equivalent, and the GM gear installation tool No. J-21474-13, J-21795-1 or equivalent.**

1. Remove the camshaft. For details, please refer to the procedure later in this section.

2. Using an arbor press, a press plate and the GM Gear Removal tool No. J-971 or equivalent, press the timing gear from the camshaft.

➡**When pressing the timing gear from the camshaft, be certain that the position of the press plate does not contact the woodruff key.**

3. To assemble, position the press plate to support the camshaft at the back of the front journal. Place the gear spacer ring and the thrust plate over the end of the camshaft, then install the woodruff key. Press the timing gear onto the camshaft, until it bottoms against the gear spacer ring.

➡**The end clearance of the thrust plate should be 0.0015–0.005 in. (0.038–0.127mm). If less than 0.0015 in. (0.038mm), replace the spacer ring; if more than 0.005 in. (0.127mm), replace the thrust plate.**

4. To complete the installation, align the marks on the timing gears and install the camshaft. For details, please refer to the procedure later in this section.

## Camshaft

### REMOVAL & INSTALLATION

In 1987, the 4.3L TBI engine began using roller valve lifters instead of the standard flat bottom lifters. The roller lifter is still hydraulic requiring no valve adjustment. The roller lifter incorporates a roller that rides along the cam lobe reducing friction and component wear. A roller lifter restrictor and retainer is needed to keep the lifter from turning in the bore while the engine is running. All 2.5L TBI engines incorporate the roller lifter configuration.

➡**Valve lifters and pushrods MUST be kept in order so they can be reinstalled in their original positions.**

#### 2.5L Engine

♦ **See Figures 166, 167 and 168**

1. Disconnect the negative battery cable for safety.
2. Remove the rocker arm (valve) cover, then remove the rocker arms.
3. Refer to the Pushrod Cover Removal and Installation procedure in this section, then remove the cover and pushrods.

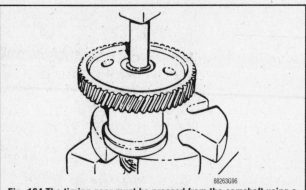

Fig. 164 The timing gear must be pressed from the camshaft using a suitable arbor press, driver and gear support

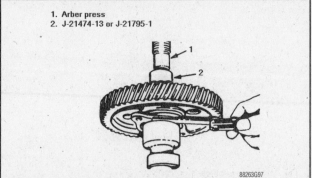

Fig. 165 Once the gear is pressed onto the camshaft, check the end clearance at the thrust plate using a feeler gauge

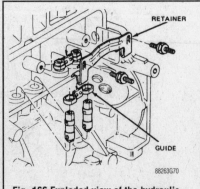

Fig. 166 Exploded view of the hydraulic lifter-to-engine mounting—2.5L engine

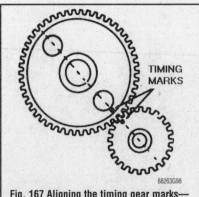

Fig. 167 Aligning the timing gear marks—2.5L engine

Fig. 168 Remove the camshaft-to-engine thrust plate bolts through the access hole in the gear—2.5L engine

➥When removing the pushrods and the valve lifters, be sure to keep them in order for reassembly purposes.

4. Remove the valve lifters, as follows:
This engine uses hydraulic lifters that are equipped with rollers to reduce engine friction.

   a. Remove the hydraulic lifter retainer studs, the retainer(s) and the guides. Lift the hydraulic lifter from the engine block.

   b. Inspect the hydraulic lifter for:
- Wear or scuffing.
- Wear or scuffing in the engine bore.
- Freedom of the roller movement.
- Flat spots or pitting on the roller surface.

➥If the hydraulic lifter is found to be defective, replace it. If installing a new lifter, be sure to remove all of the protective sealant from inside the body, then lubricate it and the roller with engine oil.

5. Place a catch pan under the radiator, open the drain cock and drain the cooling system.

### ✷✷ CAUTION

When draining the coolant, keep in mind that cats and dogs are attracted by ethylene glycol antifreeze, and are quite likely to drink any that is left in an uncovered container or in puddles on the ground. This will prove fatal in sufficient quantity. Always drain the coolant into a sealable container. Coolant should be reused unless it is contaminated or several years old.

6. Remove the power steering reservoir from the fan shroud, then remove the upper fan shroud and the radiator. Remove the grille, the headlight bezel and the bumper filler panel.

7. Remove the accessory drive belts, the cooling fan and the water pump pulley.

8. If equipped with air conditioning, disconnect the condenser baffles and the condenser attaching bolts, then raise the condenser and block it aside. Be careful not to stress or damage the A/C refrigerant lines.

9. Remove the crankshaft drive belt pulley and the damper hub. Remove the timing gear cover-to-engine bolts and the cover.

10. Label and disconnect the distributor electrical connectors, then remove the hold-down bolt and the distributor from the engine. Remove the oil pump driveshaft.

11. Label and disconnect the vacuum lines from the intake manifold and the thermostat housing, then remove the Exhaust Gas Recirculation (EGR) valve from the intake manifold.

12. Remove the camshaft thrust plate-to-engine bolts. While supporting the camshaft (to prevent damaging the bearing or lobe surfaces), remove it from the front of the engine.

13. Inspect the camshaft for scratches, pitting and/or wear on the bearing and lobe surfaces. Check the timing gear teeth for damage.

**To install:**

14. Lubricate all of the parts with engine oil and install the camshaft carefully so not to damage the cam bearings. Torque the camshaft thrust plate-to-engine bolts to 90 inch lbs. (10 Nm).

15. Connect the vacuum lines to the intake manifold and the thermostat housing, then install the Exhaust Gas Recirculation (EGR) valve to the intake manifold.

16. Install the oil pump driveshaft.

17. Install the distributor, adjust the timing and connect the distributor electrical connectors.

18. Install the timing gear cover-to-engine bolts and the cover. Install the crankshaft drive belt pulley and the damper hub.

19. If equipped with air conditioning, connect the condenser baffles and the condenser.

20. Install the accessory drive belts, the cooling fan and the water pump pulley.

21. Install the power steering reservoir to the fan shroud, then the upper fan shroud, the radiator. Install the grille, the headlight bezel and the bumper filler panel.

22. Connect the negative battery cable.

23. Install the lifters and retainers. If you are installing the old lifters, MAKE SURE they are being returned to their original positions.

24. Tighten the lifter retainer-to-engine studs to 96 inch lbs. (11 Nm).

25. Install the pushrods and reposition the rocker arms. Adjust the valve lash as detailed earlier in this section or in Section 1 of this manual.

26. Install the pushrod cover as outlined earlier in this section.

27. Install the rocker arm cover as outlined earlier in this section.

28. Refill the engine with coolant, connect the negative battery cable, start the engine and check for leaks.

### 4.3L Engine

▶ See Figures 169 thru 178

➥The following procedure requires the use of a torsional damper puller/installer tool such as GM tool no. J-23523-E (1985–92 models), J-39046 (1993–96 models) or an equivalent.

1. From inside the vehicle, remove the engine cover. For details, please refer to Section 1 of this manual.

2. Properly relieve the fuel system pressure, then disconnect the negative battery cable.

3. Place a catch pan under the radiator, open the drain cock and drain the cooling system.

### ✷✷ CAUTION

When draining the coolant, keep in mind that cats and dogs are attracted by ethylene glycol antifreeze, and are quite likely to drink any that is left in an uncovered container or in puddles on the ground. This will prove fatal in sufficient quantity. Always drain the coolant into a sealable container. Coolant should be reused unless it is contaminated or several years old.

4. Remove the engine cooling fan.

5. Remove the radiator assembly.

6. Remove the rocker arm covers.

7. Remove the intake manifold.

8. Remove the timing cover.

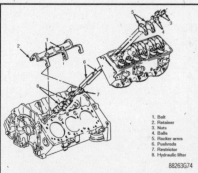

**Fig. 169 Exploded view of the hydraulic roller lifter, retainer and restrictor mounting—1987–93 4.3L engines**

1. Bolt
2. Retainer
3. Nuts
4. Balls
5. Rocker arms
6. Pushrods
7. Restrictor
8. Hydraulic lifter

88263G74

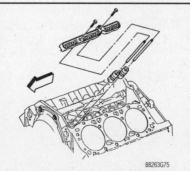

**Fig. 170 Exploded view of the hydraulic roller lifter and retainer mounting—1994–96 4.3L engines**

88263G75

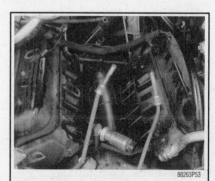

**Fig. 171 To remove the lifters, start by removing the intake manifold and the rocker arm cover**

88263P53

Fig. 172 Remove the bolts from the lifter retainer (this style was used from 1987–93) . . .

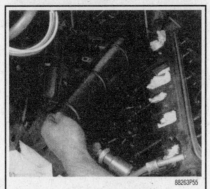

Fig. 173 . . . then remove the lifter retainer from the lifter valley

Fig. 174 Remove the restrictor for the lifter(s) you are removing . . .

Fig. 175 . . . then grasp and remove the lifter from the bore

Fig. 176 . . . a magnet is helpful to pull a well oiled lifter from the bore . . .

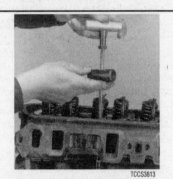

Fig. 177 . . . but a slide hammer type removal tool must be used if the lifter is stuck

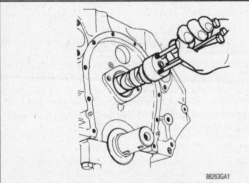

Fig. 178 Using bolts as a handle, pull STRAIGHT back and carefully remove the camshaft from the engine

9. Remove the valve lifters, as follows:

Some of the early 4.3L engines covered by this manual (1985–86 models), use a hydraulic lifter without a cam roller. All 1987 and later 4.3L engines use roller lifters. The removal procedures are basically the same except the roller lifters have retainers and guides (which are necessary to keep them from turning while the engine is running) that have to be removed to free the lifters.

a. Refer to the Rocker Arm, Removal and Installation procedures in this section, then loosen the rocker arm nuts, move the rocker arms aside and remove the pushrods.

➡Either work on only one lifter at a time, or label/arrange the pushrods to be assured that you can install them back to their original locations.

b. For 1987–93 models, remove the bolts from the lifter retainer, then remove the retainer from the lifter valley in order to access the lifter restrictors. Usually there will be 6 restrictors (one per cylinder or one per pair of lifters). Remove the restrictor for the lifter(s) you are servicing.

c. For 1994–96 models, remove the bolts from the retainer which is being removed. There is usually one on each side of the lifter valley.

d. Grasp the hydraulic lifter and remove it from the cylinder block, using a twisting action. If necessary use the GM Lifter Remover tool No. J–3049 (pliers type). In some cases, pliers can be used, but be careful not to score or damage the lifter.

e. If any lifters are stuck in the cylinder block, use the GM Lifter Removal tool No. J–9290–01 (or an equivalent slide hammer type tool) to pull the hydraulic lifter from the cylinder block.

➡When removing the hydraulic lifters, be sure to place them in an organizer rack so that they may be reinstalled in the same engine bore from which they were removed.

f. Inspect the lifters for:
• Wear or scuffing.
• Wear or scuffing in the engine bore.
• Lifter to bore clearance; if the clearance is excessive, replace the lifter.
• Worn spots, pitting or damage on the lifter surface; the lifter foot must be smooth and slightly convex.

➡If a new camshaft has been installed, install all new hydraulic lifters. If a new camshaft or new lifter(s) have been installed, add engine oil supplement to the crankcase. When removing the pushrods and the valve lifters, be sure to tag, arrange or otherwise keep them in order to assure installation in their original locations. Of course, if the camshaft is being replaced, this would not be necessary for the lifters, since they would have to be replaced as well.

10. Align the timing marks, then remove the timing chain and camshaft sprocket.

11. Thread two or three, ⁵⁄₁₆–18 in. bolts, which are 4–5 in. (100–125mm) long into the camshaft sprocket retaining holes. Using these camshaft bolts as handles, support the camshaft and pull it from the front of the engine block. Pull the shaft STRAIGHT back and from the bearings, while rotating it slightly; be careful not to damage the camshaft bearing or lobe surfaces.

12. Inspect the camshaft for scratches, pitting and/or wear on the bearing and lobe surfaces. Check the timing sprockets teeth and timing chain for damage and/or wear, replace the damaged parts (if necessary).

**To install:**

13. Before installing the camshaft, coat the lobes and bearings using either a high viscosity oil with zinc (such as GM 12345501) or with a suitable engine pre-lube.

➡**GM recommends that whenever a new camshaft and/or a set of new lifters has been installed, that you change the engine oil and filter, and then add GM engine oil supplement 1052367 to the engine oil upon refill.**

14. Using the bolts as handles, carefully slide the camshaft into the engine. Be certain to push the shaft straight inward to help prevent possible damage to the camshaft bearings.

15. Install the timing chain and camshaft sprocket, making sure to align the timing marks.

➡**REMEMBER that if the lifters and/or pushrods are not replaced, they must be reinstalled in their original positions.**

16. Install the valve lifters, as follows:

a. When new lifters are installed they should be coated using either a high viscosity oil with zinc (such as GM 12345501) or with a suitable engine pre-lube. It's also usually a good idea to prime any hydraulic lifter by submerging it in fresh engine oil and pumping the plunger gently a few times. This will provide lubrication to the internal components before assembly.

➡**GM recommends that whenever a new camshaft and/or a set of new lifters has been installed, that you change the engine oil and filter, and then add GM engine oil supplement 1052367 to the engine oil upon refill.**

b. Install the lifters. If you are reusing the old lifters MAKE SURE each is installed in the same bore from which it was removed.

c. Install the lifter retainer (and separate restrictors on 1987–93 models), then tighten the bolts to 12 ft. lbs. (16 Nm).

17. Install the pushrods and rotate the rocker arms back into position. Adjust the valve lash.

18. Install the remaining components in the reverse order of removal.

19. If the camshaft was replaced, change the engine oil and filter.

20. Connect the negative battery cable and properly refill the engine cooling system.

21. Run the engine and check for leaks. Check and/or adjust the engine timing, as necessary.

22. Once the engine has cooled sufficiently, install the engine cover to the passenger compartment.

### INSPECTION

▶ **See Figures 179, 180 and 181**

Using solvent, degrease the camshaft and clean out all of the oil holes. Visually inspect the cam lobes and bearing journals for excessive wear. If a lobe is questionable, check all of the lobes as indicated. If a journal or lobe is worn, the camshaft MUST BE reground or replaced.

➡**If a journal is worn, there is a good chance that the bushings are worn and need replacement.**

If the lobes and journals appear intact, place the front and rear journals in V-blocks and rest a dial indicator on the center journal. Rotate the camshaft to check the straightness. If deviation exceeds 0.001 in. (0.0254mm), replace the camshaft.

Check the camshaft lobes with a micrometer, by measuring the lobes from the nose to the base and again at 90° (see illustration). The lobe lift is determined by subtracting the second measurement from the first. If all of the exhaust and intake lobes are not identical, the camshaft must be reground or replaced.

➡**Camshaft lobe lift can also be measured with the shaft still installed.**

To determine camshaft lobe wear, with the shaft still installed.

1. Remove the rocker arm covers.

2. Loosen and reposition the rocker arms so the pushrods can be accessed.

3. Mount a dial gauge so the plunger rests on the end of the pushrod (so it will read pushrod movement).

4. Turn the crankshaft slowly in the normal direction of rotation until the lifter is on the base of the camshaft lobe (the pushrod will not be at its lowest point of travel), then zero the gauge.

5. Rotate the crankshaft slowly until the pushrod moves to the fully raised position.

6. Compare the readings for each camshaft lobe (as shown by the dial indicator) with the specifications.

➡**Keep in mind that hydraulic lifters can allow for some camshaft lobe height loss. If a camshaft is close, but out of specification, verify that plunger movement is not responsible for the difference before replacing the shaft.**

7. Reposition and install the rocker arms. For details, please refer to the procedure found earlier in this section.

8. Install the rocker arm covers.

### Pistons and Connecting Rods

REMOVAL

▶ **See Figures 182, 183 and 184**

➡**Although in some cases the pistons and connecting rods may be removed with the engine still in the vehicle, it is rarely worth the aggravation, especially when you are not working with a lift. On vehicles where this is possible (cylinder head and oil pan removal are both possible with the engine installed AND there is sufficient working clearance) take EXTREME care to assure no dirt or contamination is allowed into the cylinders during assembly and installation.**

Before removing the pistons, the top of the cylinder bore must be examined for a ridge. A ridge at the top of the bore is the result of normal cylinder wear, caused by the piston rings only traveling so far up the bore in the course of the piston stroke. The ridge can be felt by hand; it must be removed before the pistons are removed.

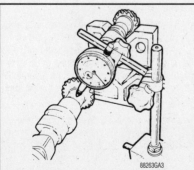

Fig. 179 Use a dial indicator to measure the camshaft for straightness (camshaft runout)

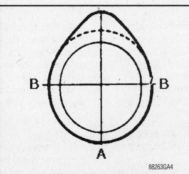

Fig. 180 Subtract measurement B from measurement A (width from height) in order to determine camshaft lobe lift

Fig. 181 A dial gauge can be used to measure lobe lift with the camshaft installed

Fig. 182 Normal cylinder wear and ridge formation

Fig. 183 Place hose over the connecting rod studs to protect the crankshaft and cylinders from damage

Fig. 184 Carefully tap the piston out of the bore using a wooden dowel

A ridge reamer is necessary for this operation. Place the piston at the bottom of its stroke, and cover it with a rag. Cut the ridge away with the ridge reamer, using extreme care to avoid cutting too deeply. Remove the rag, and remove the cuttings that remain on the piston with a magnet and a rag soaked in clean oil. Make sure the piston top and cylinder bore are absolutely clean before moving the piston. For more details, refer to the ridge removal and honing procedures later in this section.

➡️ If you plan on consulting a machine shop for hot tanking, honing, boring or other block service, you should do so BEFORE disassembling your engine. They may have specific preferences on whether or not you remove a cylinder ridge or how to you are to label parts.

1. Remove the engine assembly from the vehicle.
2. Remove the intake manifold and the cylinder head(s).
3. Remove the oil pan and the oil pump assembly.
4. Check the connecting rods and caps for identification marks. If none are present, stamp the cylinder number on the machined surfaces of the bolt bosses on the connecting rod and cap for identification when reinstalling. If the pistons are to be removed from the connecting rod, mark the cylinder number on the piston with a silver pencil or quick drying paint for proper cylinder identification and cap to rod location.

➡️ The 2.5L (4–cyl) engine is numbered 1–2–3–4 (front-to-rear); on the 4.3L (V6) engine, is numbered 1–3–5 (front-to-rear) on the left side and 2–4–6 (front-to-rear) on the right side.

5. Examine the cylinder bore above the ring travel. If a ridge exists, remove it with a ridge reamer before attempting to remove the piston and rod assembly.
6. Remove the rod bearing cap and bearing.
7. Install lengths of short rubber hose over the rod bolt threads; this will help prevent damage to the bearing journal and rod bolt threads.
8. Remove the rod and piston assembly through the top of the cylinder bore by gently tapping outward using a wooden dowel or wooden tool handle; remove the other rod and piston assemblies in the same manner.

➡️ BE SURE to note the direction in which the piston was facing. These engines usually use pistons which are notched to show proper orientation. Make sure you note where any notch (if present) is located, or mark the piston using paint for installation purposes. Also, if you had to mark the piston, be careful during cleaning either not to accidentally remove the mark (when you are not paying attention), or to place a new mark on the piston once it has been cleaned.

## CLEANING AND INSPECTION

Using a piston ring expanding tool, remove the piston rings from the pistons; any other method (screwdriver blades, pliers, etc.) usually results in the rings being bent, scratched or distorted and/or the piston itself being damaged.

### Pistons

◆ See Figures 185, 186, 187 and 188

Clean the varnish from the piston skirts and pins with a cleaning solvent. DO NOT WIRE BRUSH ANY PART OF THE PISTON. Clean the ring grooves with a groove cleaner and make sure that the oil ring holes and slots are clean.

### ❊❊ CAUTION

Do NOT use any solvent that will damage aluminum parts. Some hot tank solutions will dissolve aluminum.

Inspect the piston for cracked ring lands, scuffed or damaged skirts, eroded areas at the top of the piston. Replace the pistons that are damaged or show signs of excessive wear.

Inspect the grooves for nicks of burrs that might cause the rings to hang up.

Measure the piston skirt (across the center line of the piston pin) and check the piston clearance (the difference between the measurement you get at the piston skirt and the measurement of the cylinder bore). Compare the clearance to the specifications found in the charts at the beginning of this section. If clearance is excessive, consult a machine shop about boring the cylinders for over-size pistons.

Fig. 185 Use a ring expander tool to remove the piston rings

Fig. 186 Clean the piston grooves using a ring groove cleaner

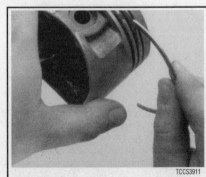

Fig. 187 You can use a piece of an old ring to clean the piston grooves, BUT be careful, the ring is sharp

Fig. 188 Measure the piston's outer diameter using a micrometer

Fig. 189 Cylinder bore measuring points

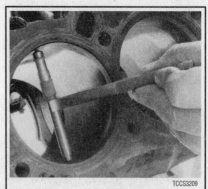

Fig. 190 A telescoping gauge may be used to measure the cylinder bore diameter

## Connecting Rods

Wash the connecting rods in cleaning solvent and dry with compressed air. Check for twisted or bent rods and inspect for nicks or cracks. Replace any connecting rods that are damaged.

## Cylinder Bores

### ▶ See Figures 189 and 190

Using a telescoping gauge or an inside micrometer, measure the diameter of the cylinder bore, perpendicular (90°) to the piston pin, at 2½ in. (63.5mm) below the surface of the cylinder block. The difference between the cylinder bore measurement and the piston skirt measurement is the piston clearance.

If the clearance is within specifications or slightly below (after the cylinders have been bored or honed), finish honing is all that is necessary, If the clearance is excessive, try to obtain a slightly larger piston to bring the clearance within specifications. If this is not possible obtain the first oversize piston and hone the cylinder or (if necessary) bore the cylinder to size. Generally, if the cylinder bore is tapered more than 0.005 in. (0.127mm) or is out-of-round more than 0.003 in. (0.0762mm), it is advisable to rebore for the smallest possible oversize piston and rings. After measuring, mark the pistons with a felt-tip pen for reference and for assembly.

➡Boring of the cylinder block should be performed by a reputable machine shop with the proper equipment. In some cases, clean-up honing can be done with the cylinder block in the vehicle, but most excessive honing and all cylinder boring MUST BE done with the block stripped and removed from the vehicle.

## RIDGE REMOVAL & HONING

### ▶ See Figures 191, 192, 193, 194 and 195

1. Before the piston is removed from the cylinder, check for a ridge at the top of the cylinder bore. This ridge occurs because the piston ring does not travel all the way to the top of the bore, thereby leaving an unworn portion of the bore.

2. Clean away any carbon buildup at the top of the cylinder with sand paper, in order to see the extent of the ridge more clearly. If the ridge is slight, it will be safe to remove the pistons without damaging the rings or piston ring lands. If the ridge is severe, and easily catches your fingernail, it will have to be removed using a ridge reamer.

➡A severe ridge is an indication of excessive bore wear. Before removing the piston, check the cylinder bore diameter with a bore gauge, as explained in the cleaning and inspection procedure. Compare your measurement with engine specification. If the bore is excessively worn, the cylinder will have to bored oversize and the piston and rings replaced.

3. Install the ridge removal tool in the top of the cylinder bore. Carefully follow the manufacturer's instructions for operation. Remove only the amount of material necessary to remove the ridge. Place the piston at the bottom of its stroke, and cover it with a rag. Cut the ridge away with the ridge reamer, using extreme care to avoid cutting too deeply. Remove the rag, and remove the cuttings that remain on the piston with a magnet and a rag soaked in clean oil. Make sure the piston top and cylinder bore are absolutely clean before moving the piston.

### ✳✳ WARNING

Be very careful if you are unfamiliar with operating a ridge reamer. It is very easy to remove more cylinder bore material than you want, possibly requiring a cylinder overbore and piston replacement that may not have been necessary.

4. After the piston and connecting rod assembly have been removed, check the clearances as explained earlier in this section under the cleaning and inspection procedure, to determine whether boring and honing or just light honing are required. If boring is necessary, consult an automotive machine shop. If light honing is all that is necessary, proceed with the next step.

5. Honing is best done with the crankshaft removed, to prevent damage to the crankshaft and to make post-honing cleaning easier, as the honing process will scatter metal particles. However, if you do not want to remove the crank-

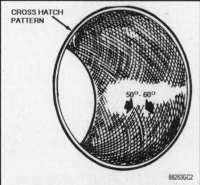

Fig. 191 Correct cylinder bore honing pattern

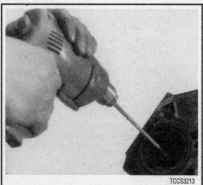

Fig. 192 Removing cylinder glazing using a flexible hone

Fig. 193 A solid hone can also be used to cross-hatch the cylinder bore

Fig. 194 As with a ball hone, work the hone carefully up and down the bore to achieve the desired results

Fig. 195 A properly cross-hatched cylinder bore

shaft, position the connecting rod journal for the cylinder being honed as far away from the bottom of the cylinder bore as possible, and wrap a shop cloth around the journal.

6. Honing can be done either with a flexible glaze breaker type hone or with a rigid hone that has honing stones and guide shoes. The flexible hone removes the least amount of metal, and is especially recommended if your piston-to-cylinder bore clearance is on the loose side. The flexible hone is useful to provide a finish on which the new piston rings will seat. A rigid hone will remove more material than the flexible hone and requires more operator skill.

7. Regardless of which type of hone you use, carefully follow the manufacturers instructions for operation.

8. The hone should be moved up and down the bore at sufficient speed to obtain a uniform finish. A rigid hone will provide a definite cross-hatch finish; operate the rigid hone at a speed to obtain a 45–65 degree included angle in the cross-hatch. The finish marks should be clean but not sharp, free from embedded particles and torn or folded metal.

9. Periodically during the honing procedure, thoroughly clean the cylinder bore and check the piston-to-bore clearance with the piston for that cylinder.

10. After honing is completed and BEFORE the piston is checked for fit, thoroughly wash the cylinder bores and the rest of the engine with hot water and detergent. Scrub the bores well with a stiff bristle brush and rinse thoroughly with hot water. Thorough cleaning is essential, for if any abrasive material is left

in the cylinder bore, it will rapidly wear the new rings and the cylinder bore. If any abrasive material is left in the rest of the engine, it will be picked up by the oil and carried throughout the engine, damaging bearings and other parts.

11. After the bores are cleaned, wipe them down with a clean cloth coated with light engine oil, to keep them from rusting.

### PISTON PIN REPLACEMENT

▶ **See Figures 196 and 197**

➡**The following procedure requires the use of the GM Fixture/Support Assembly tool No. J–24086–20 or equivalent, the GM Piston Pin Removal tool No. J–24086–8 or equivalent, and the GM Piston Pin Installation tool No. J–24086–9 or equivalent.**

Use care at all times when handling and servicing the connecting rods and pistons. To prevent possible damage to these units, DO NOT clamp the rod or piston in a vise since they may become distorted. DO NOT allow the pistons to strike one another, against hard objects or bench surfaces, since distortion of the piston contour or nicks in the soft aluminum material may result.

1. Using an arbor press, the GM Fixture/Support Assembly tool No. J–24086–20 or equivalent, and the GM Piston Pin Removal tool No. J–24086–8 or equivalent, place the piston assembly in the fixture/support tool and press the pin from the piston assembly.

➡**The piston and the piston pin are a matched set which are not serviced separately.**

2. Using solvent, wash the varnish and oil from the parts, then inspect the parts for scuffing or wear.

3. Using a micrometer, measure the diameter of the piston pin. Using a inside micrometer or a dial bore gauge, measure the diameter of the piston bore.

➡**If the piston pin-to-piston clearance is in excess of 0.001 in. (0.0254mm), replace the piston and piston pin assembly.**

4. Before installation, lubricate the piston pin and the piston bore with engine oil.

5. To install the piston pin into the piston assembly, use an arbor press, the GM Fixture/Support Assembly tool No. J–24086–20 or equivalent, and the GM Piston Pin Installation tool No. J–24086–9 or equivalent, then press the piston pin into the piston/connecting rod assembly.

➡**When installing the piston pin into the piston/connecting rod assembly and the installation tool bottoms onto the support assembly, DO NOT exceed 5000 psi (35,000 kPa) of pressure or structural damage may occur to the tool.**

6. After installing the piston pin, make sure that the piston has freedom of movement with the piston pin. The piston/connecting rod assembly is ready for installation into the engine block.

### PISTON RING REPLACEMENT AND SIDE CLEARANCE MEASUREMENT

▶ **See Figures 198, 199, 200 and 201**

Check the pistons to see that the ring grooves and oil return holes have been properly cleaned. Slide a piston ring into its groove and check the side clearance with a feeler gauge. Make sure the feeler gauge is inserted between the ring and its lower land (lower edge of the groove), because any wear that occurs forms a step at the inner portion of the lower land. If the piston grooves have been worn to the extent that relatively high steps exist on the lower land, the piston should be replaced, because these will interfere with the operation of the new rings and ring clearances will be excessive. Piston rings are not furnished in oversize widths to compensate for ring groove wear.

Once the ring end-gap has been checked and shown to be within specification, install the rings on the piston, bottom ring first, using a piston ring expander. There is a high risk of breaking or distorting the rings and/or scratching the piston, if the rings are installed by hand or other means.

Position the rings on the piston as illustrated; spacing of the various piston ring gaps is crucial to the proper oil retention and cylinder wear. When

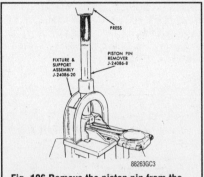

**Fig. 196 Remove the piston pin from the piston using an arbor press and suitable removal driver**

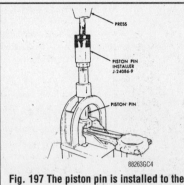

**Fig. 197 The piston pin is installed to the piston using the press and a suitable installer driver**

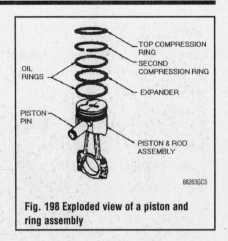

**Fig. 198 Exploded view of a piston and ring assembly**

**Fig. 199 Checking the ring-to-ring groove clearance (ring side clearance)**

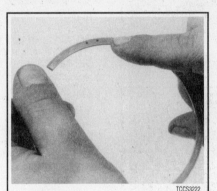

**Fig. 200 Most rings are marked to show which side should face upward**

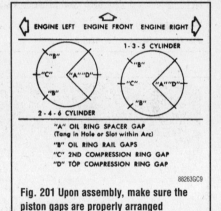

**Fig. 201 Upon assembly, make sure the piston gaps are properly arranged**

installing the new rings, refer to the installation diagram furnished with the new parts.

## CHECKING RING END-GAP

### ♦ See Figure 202

The piston ring end-gap should be checked while the rings are removed from the pistons. Incorrect end-gap indicates that the wrong size rings are being used; **ring breakage could result**.

1. Compress the new piston ring into a cylinder (one at a time).
2. Squirt some clean oil into the cylinder so that the ring and the top 2 in. (51mm) of the cylinder wall are coated.
3. Using an inverted piston, push the ring approximately 1 in. (25.4mm) below the top of the cylinder.
4. Using a feeler gauge, measure the ring gap and compare it to the Ring Gap chart in this section. Carefully remove the ring from the cylinder.

## ROD BEARING REPLACEMENT

### ♦ See Figures 203, 204, 205 and 206

Replacement bearings are available in standard size and undersize (for reground crankshafts). Connecting rod-to-crankshaft bearing clearance is checked using Plastigage® or an equivalent gauging material, at either the top or the bottom of each crank journal. The Plastigage® has a range of 0.001–0.003 in. (0.0254–0.0762mm).

1. Remove the rod cap with the bearing shell. Completely clean the bearing shell and the crank journal, blow any oil from the oil hole in the crankshaft; place the Plastigage® lengthwise along the bottom center of the lower bearing shell, then install the cap with the shell and torque the bolt or nuts to specification. DO NOT turn the crankshaft with the Plastigage® on the bearing.
2. Remove the bearing cap with the shell. The flattened Plastigage® will be found sticking to either the bearing shell or the crank journal. DO NOT remove it yet.

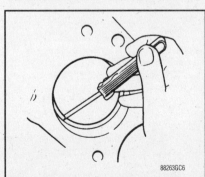

**Fig. 202 Ring end-gap is checked using a feeler gauge, after the ring is carefully inserted, square into the bore**

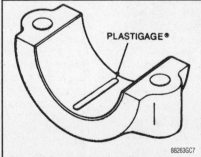

**Fig. 203 To check bearing clearance, apply a strip of gauging material to the bearing shell, then install and tighten the bearing cap . . .**

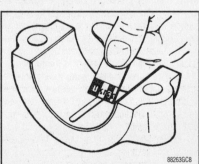

**Fig. 204 . . . after tightening to specification, remove the bearing cap and compare the thickness of the material to the scale provided**

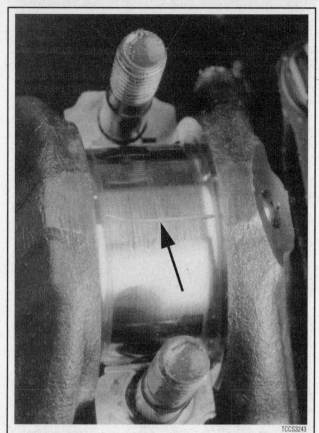

Fig. 205 You can apply the gauging material to bearing journal (shown) or to the bearing shell

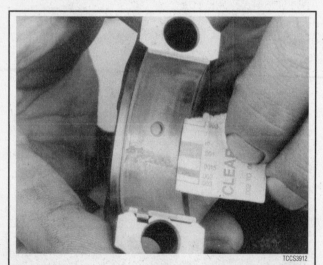

Fig. 206 Even if it was applied to the journal, it may wind up on the cap shell after it is tightened

3. Use the scale printed on the Plastigage® package to measure the flattened material at its widest point. The number within the scale which most closely corresponds to the width of the Plastigage® indicates the bearing clearance in thousandths of an inch.

4. Check the specifications chart in this section for the desired clearance. It is advisable to install a new bearing if the clearance exceeds 0.003 in. (0.0762mm); however, if the bearing is in good condition and is not being checked because of bearing noise, bearing replacement is not necessary.

5. If you are installing new bearings, try a standard size, then each undersize in order until one is found that is within the specified limits when checked for clearance with Plastigage®; each undersize shell has its size stamped on it.

6. When the proper size shell is found, clean off the Plastigage®, oil the bearing thoroughly, reinstall the cap with its shell and tighten the rod bolt nuts to specification.

➡ **With the proper bearing selected and the nuts torqued, it should be possible to move the connecting rod back and forth freely on the crank journal as allowed by the specified connecting rod end clearance. If the rod cannot be moved, either the rod bearing is too far undersize or the rod is misaligned.**

### INSTALLATION

▶ **See Figures 207, 208, 209 and 210**

Position the rings on the piston as illustrated; **spacing of the various piston ring gaps is crucial to proper oil retention and even cylinder wear.** When installing new rings, refer to the installation diagram furnished with the new parts.

Install the connecting rod to the piston, making sure that the piston installation notches and marks (if any) on the connecting rod are in proper relation to one another.

1. Make sure that the connecting rod big-end bearings (including the end cap) are of the correct size and properly installed.

2. Fit rubber hoses over the connecting rod bolts to protect the crankshaft journals, as in the Piston Removal procedure. Lubricate the connecting rod bearings with clean engine oil.

3. Using a suitable ring compressor positioned over the piston, compress the rings around the piston head. Insert the piston assembly into the cylinder, so that the notch (on top of the piston) faces the front of the engine.

4. From beneath the engine, coat each crank journal with clean oil. Using a hammer handle, gently drive the connecting rod/piston assembly into the cylinder bore. Align the connecting rod (with bearing shell) onto the crankshaft journal.

5. Remove the rubber hoses from the studs. Install the bearing cap (with bearing shell) onto the connecting rod and the cap nuts. Tighten the connecting rod cap nuts to specification.
- 2.5L engine (1985–88): 32 ft. lbs. (43 Nm)
- 2.5L engine (1989–90): 30 ft. lbs. (40 Nm)
- 4.3L engine (1985–90): 45 ft. lbs. (61 Nm)
- 4.3L engine (1991–92): 20 ft. lbs. (27 Nm) + a 60 ° turn
- 4.3L engine (1993–96): 20 ft. lbs. (27 Nm) + a 70 ° turn

➡ **When more than one connecting rod/piston assembly are being installed, the connecting rod cap nuts should only be tightened enough to keep each rod in position until all have been installed. This will ease the installation of the remaining piston assemblies.**

6. Check the clearance between the sides of the connecting rods and the crankshaft using a feeler gauge. Spread the rods slightly with a small prybar to insert the feeler gauge. If the clearance is below the minimum tolerance, the rod may be machined to provide adequate clearance. If the clearance is excessive,

Fig. 207 Install the pistons facing the proper direction (as noted during removal)—If present, a notch usually faces to the front of the engine

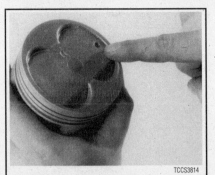

Fig. 208 Most pistons are marked to indicate in engine positioning (usually a mark means front)

TCCS3814

Fig. 209 Installing the piston into the block using a ring compressor and the handle of a hammer

TCCS3914

88263GD2

Fig. 210 After installation, check the connecting rod side clearance by CAREFULLY spreading the rods and inserting a feeler gauge

substitute an unworn rod and recheck. If clearance is still outside specifications, the crankshaft must be welded and reground or replaced.

7. Install the oil pump assembly and the oil pan.
8. Install the cylinder head(s) and the intake manifold.
9. Install the engine assembly to the vehicle.

## Rear Main Oil Seal

### REMOVAL & INSTALLATION

#### 2.5L Engine

▶ See Figure 211

The rear main oil seal is a one piece unit. It can be removed or installed without removing the oil pan or the crankshaft.

➡The following procedure requires the use of the GM Oil Seal Installation tool No. J-34924 or equivalent.

1. Disconnect the negative battery cable for safety.
2. Remove the transmission. For details, please refer to the Transmission, Removal and Installation procedures in Section 7.
3. If equipped with a manual transmission, remove the clutch assembly.
4. Matchmark and remove the flexplate or flywheel, as applicable.
5. Using a small prybar, carefully pry the oil seal from the rear of the crankshaft.

➡When removing the oil seal, be careful not to damage the crankshaft sealing surface.

6. To install the new oil seal into the rear retainer, perform the following procedures:

   a. Using fresh engine oil, lubricate the inner and outer diameter of the seal.

   b. Install the new seal onto the seal installation tool No. J-34924 or equivalent, then position the tool assembly against the crankshaft.

   c. Align the dowel with the alignment hole in the crankshaft and thread the attaching screws into the tapped holes in the crankshaft.

   d. Using a screwdriver, tighten the screws securely; this will ensure that the seal is installed squarely over the crankshaft.

   e. Turn the handle until it bottoms and remove the installation tool.

7. Align and install the flywheel or flexplate (as applicable).
8. If equipped with a manual transmission, install the clutch assembly.
9. Install the transmission.
10. Connect the negative battery cable.

#### 4.3L Engine

##### *1985 MODELS*

▶ See Figures 212, 213, 214 and 215

The 1985 4.3L engines covered by this manual were originally equipped with a 2-piece rear main seal.

1. Refer to the Oil Pan, Removal and Installation procedures in this section and remove the oil pan from the engine.
2. Remove the oil pump and the rear main bearing cap.
3. Pry the oil seal from the rear main bearing cap using a small suitable prytool.
4. Using a small hammer and a brass pin punch, CAREFULLY drive the top half of the oil seal from the rear main bearing. Drive it out far enough, so it may be removed with a pair of pliers.
5. Using a non-abrasive cleaner, clean the rear main bearing cap and the crankshaft.

**To install:**

6. Fabricate an oil seal installation tool from 0.004 in. (0.01mm) shim stock, shape the end to ½ in. (12.7mm) long by 11/64 in. (4.4mm) wide.
7. Coat the new oil seal with engine oil; DO NOT coat the mating ends of the seal.
8. Position the fabricated tool between the crankshaft and seal seat in the cylinder case.
9. Position the new half seal between the crankshaft and the tip of the tool, so that the seal bead contacts the tip of the tool.

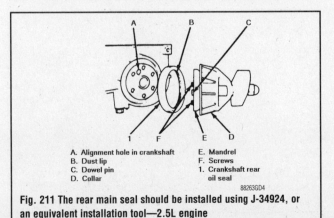

A. Alignment hole in crankshaft
B. Dust lip
C. Dowel pin
D. Collar
E. Mandrel
F. Screws
1. Crankshaft rear oil seal

88263GD4

Fig. 211 The rear main seal should be installed using J-34924, or an equivalent installation tool—2.5L engine

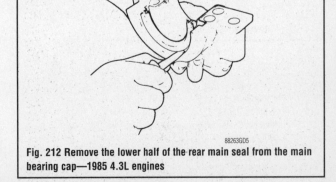

88263GD5

Fig. 212 Remove the lower half of the rear main seal from the main bearing cap—1985 4.3L engines

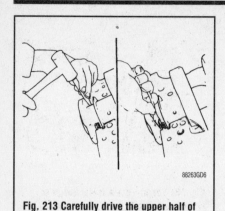

**Fig. 213 Carefully drive the upper half of the seal from the engine block**

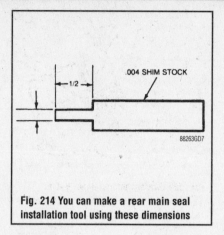

**Fig. 214 You can make a rear main seal installation tool using these dimensions**

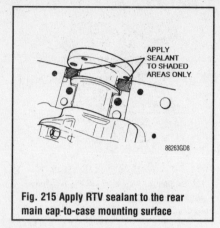

**Fig. 215 Apply RTV sealant to the rear main cap-to-case mounting surface**

➡ **Make sure that the seal lip is positioned toward the front of the engine.**

10. Using the fabricated tool as a shoe horn, to protect the seal's bead from the sharp edge of the seal seat surface in the cylinder case, roll the seal around the crankshaft. When the seal's ends are flush with the engine block, remove the installation tool.

11. Using the same manner of installation, install the lower seal half onto the lower half of the rear main bearing cap.

12. Apply sealant to the cap-to-case mating surfaces and install the lower rear main bearing half to the engine; keep the sealant off of the seal's mating line.

13. Install the rear main bearing cap bolts and tighten to specification. Using a lead hammer, tap the crankshaft forward and rearward, to align the thrust bearing surfaces.

14. Install the oil pan.

15. Refill the crankcase with clean engine oil and connect the negative battery cable.

16. Start the engine, allow it to reach normal operating temperatures and check for leaks.

### 1986–96 MODELS

▶ **See Figures 216 and 217**

Unlike the 1985 4.3L engines covered by this manual (which were equipped with a 2-piece rear main seal), the 1986–96 4.3L engines utilize a 1-piece seal which is installed to a rear seal retainer that bolts to the back of the block.

➡ **The following procedure requires the use of the GM Oil Seal Installation tool No. J-35621 or equivalent.**

1. Disconnect the negative battery cable for safety.

2. Remove the transmission. For details, please refer to the Transmission, Removal and Installation procedures in Section 7.

3. If equipped with a manual transmission, remove the clutch assembly.

4. Matchmark and remove the flexplate or flywheel, as applicable.

5. Insert a small prytool into the notches provided in the oil seal retainer and carefully pry the oil seal from the retainer.

➡ **When removing the oil seal from the retainer, be careful not to nick the crankshaft sealing surface.**

### To install:

6. Install the new oil seal into the rear retainer:

a. Using engine oil, lubricate the inner and outer diameter of the seal.

b. Install a new oil seal onto the GM Oil Seal Installation tool No. J-35621 (or equivalent), then position the tool and seal assembly against the crankshaft and thread the attaching screws into the tapped holes in the crankshaft.

c. Using a screwdriver, tighten the screws securely; this will ensure that the seal is installed squarely over the crankshaft.

d. Turn the handle until it bottoms and remove the installation tool.

7. Align and install the flywheel or flexplate (as applicable).

8. If equipped with a manual transmission, install the clutch assembly.

9. Install the transmission.

10. Connect the negative battery cable.

## Crankshaft and Main Bearings

### REMOVAL & INSTALLATION

▶ **See Figures 218, 219, 220, 221 and 222**

1. Drain the crankcase oil and remove the engine from the van.

2. Remove the flywheel/flexplate and mount the engine on a work stand in a suitable working area. Invert the engine, so the oil pan is facing up.

➡ **If the cylinder heads are not being removed, the spark plugs should be removed in order to release engine compression and allow for easier rotation of the crankshaft when necessary.**

3. Remove the engine front (timing) cover.

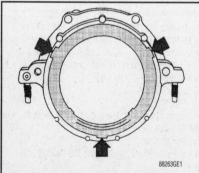

**Fig. 216 Carefully pry the seal from the retainer using a small prytool at the notches provided in the retainer**

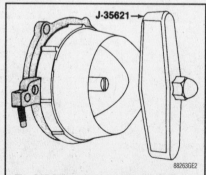

**Fig. 217 A threaded seal installation tool such as J-35621 is necessary to properly seat the new seal**

**Fig. 218 Place hose over the connecting rod studs to protect the crankshaft and cylinders from damage**

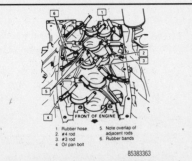

Fig. 219 Support the connecting rods with rubber bands and install rubber rod bolt caps to protect the crankshaft during removal and installation

1. Rubber hose
2. #4 rod
3. #3 rod
4. Oil pan bolt
5. Note overlap of adjacent rods
6. Rubber bands

FRONT OF ENGINE

85383363

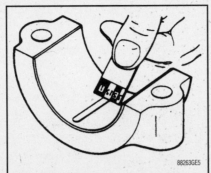

Fig. 220 Plastigage® or an equivalent gauging material should be used to check main bearing clearances

88263GE5

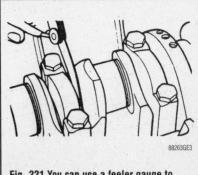

Fig. 221 You can use a feeler gauge to check the crankshaft end-play during installation

88263GE3

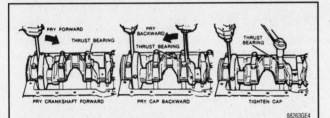

PRY FORWARD
THRUST BEARING
PRY CRANKSHAFT FORWARD

PRY BACKWARD
THRUST BEARING
PRY CAP BACKWARD

THRUST BEARING
TIGHTEN CAP

88263GE4

Fig. 222 Align the thrust bearing (as illustrated), then tighten the main bearing caps to specification

4. Align the timing marks, then remove the timing chain (on the 4.3L engine) and gears.

➡️After removing the timing gear or sprocket from the crankshaft, be sure to remove the woodruff key from the crankshaft.

5. Remove the oil pan.

### ✳✳ CAUTION

**The EPA warns that prolonged contact with used engine oil may cause a number of skin disorders, including cancer! You should make every effort to minimize your exposure to used engine oil. Protective gloves should be worn when changing the oil. Wash your hands and any other exposed skin areas as soon as possible after exposure to used engine oil. Soap and water, or waterless hand cleaner should be used.**

6. If necessary, remove the oil pump assembly.

7. Inspect the connecting rods and bearing caps for identification marks (numbers). If there are none, stamp the cylinder number on the machined surfaces of the bolt bosses of the connecting rods and caps for identification when reinstalling. If the pistons are to be removed eventually from the connecting rod, mark the cylinder number on the pistons with silver paint or felt-tip pen for proper cylinder identification and cap-to-rod location.

8. Remove the connecting rod nuts and caps, then store them in the order of removal. Place short pieces of rubber hose on the connecting rod studs to prevent damaging the crankshaft bearing surfaces.

9. Check the main bearing caps for identification marks (if not identified, mark them). Remove the main bearing caps and store them in order, for reassembly purposes; the caps must be reinstalled in their original position.

10. If equipped, remove the 1-piece rear main seal retainer from the engine.

11. Install rubber bands between a bolt on each connecting rod and oil pan bolts that have been reinstalled in the block (see illustration). This will keep the rods from banging on the block when the crank is removed.

12. Carefully lift the crankshaft out of the block. The rods will pivot to the center of the engine when the crank is removed.

➡️When removing the bearing shells, it is recommended to replace them with new ones.

13. Using solvent, clean all of the parts for inspection purposes. If necessary, replace any part that may be questionable.

**To install:**

14. Install new bearing shell inserts and check the bearing clearances. For details, please refer to the crankshaft cleaning and inspection information found later in this section.

➡️**If necessary, deliver the crankshaft to an automotive machine shop, have the crankshaft journals ground and new bearing shells matched.**

15. Lubricate all of the parts and oil seals with clean engine oil.

16. Using a feeler gauge and a medium prybar, move the crankshaft forward-and-rearward. Check the crankshaft end-play by inserting a feeler gauge between the crankshaft and the thrust bearing shell. An alternate method is to use a dial indicator at the crankshaft snout. Install the indicator, move the crankshaft rearward, zero the indicator and then move the crankshaft forward. The dial indicator will read the end-play.

17. Tighten main bearing caps (in three steps) to specification:
- 2.5L engine (1985–88): 70 ft. lbs. (95 Nm)
- 2.5L engine (1989–90): 65 ft. lbs. (88 Nm)
- 4.3L engine (1985): 70 ft. lbs. (95 Nm)
- 4.3L engine (1986): 75 ft. lbs. (100 Nm)
- 4.3L engine (1987–90): 80 ft. lbs. (108 Nm)
- 4.3L engine (1991–95): 75 ft. lbs. (95 Nm)
- 4.3L engine (1996): 77 ft. lbs. (105 Nm)

18. Remove the rubber hoses from the studs. Install the bearing cap (with bearing shell) onto the connecting rod and the cap nuts. Tighten the connecting rod cap nuts to specification.
- 2.5L engine (1985–88): 32 ft. lbs. (43 Nm)
- 2.5L engine (1989–90): 30 ft. lbs. (40 Nm)
- 4.3L engine (1985–90): 45 ft. lbs. (61 Nm)
- 4.3L engine (1991–92): 20 ft. lbs. (27 Nm) + a 60° turn
- 4.3L engine (1993–96): 20 ft. lbs. (27 Nm) + a 70° turn

➡️**When there is more than one connecting rod/piston assembly being installed, the connecting rod cap nuts should only be tightened enough to keep each rod in position until all have been installed. This will ease the installation of the remaining piston assemblies.**

19. Check the clearance between the sides of the connecting rods and the crankshaft using a feeler gauge. Spread the rods slightly with a small prybar to insert the feeler gauge. If the clearance is below the minimum tolerance, the rod may be machined to provide adequate clearance. If clearance is excessive, substitute an unworn rod and recheck. If clearance is still outside specifications, the crankshaft must be welded and reground or replaced.

20. If necessary, install the pump assembly.

21. Install the oil pan.

22. Make sure the woodruff key is installed in the end of the crankshaft, then install the timing chain (4.3L only) and gears.

23. Install the engine front (timing) cover.

24. Remove the engine from the work stand, then install the flywheel/flexplate.

25. Refill the crankcase and install the engine to the van.

## CLEANING & INSPECTION

### ♦ See Figures 220, 223 thru 227

1. Clean the crankshaft with solvent and a brush. Clean the oil passages with a suitable brush, then blow them out with compressed air.

2. Inspect the crankshaft for obvious damage or wear. Check the main and connecting rod journals for cracks, scratches, grooves or scores. Inspect the crankshaft oil seal surface for nicks, sharp edges or burrs that could damage the oil seal or cause premature seal wear.

3. If the crankshaft passes a visual inspection, check journal runout using a dial indicator. Support the crankshaft in V-blocks (or in the bearings on the engine block as shown if V-blocks are not available) and check the shaft runout. If crankshaft runout exceeds 0.001 in. (0.025mm) the shaft should be replaced. Consult a machine shop for advice.

4. Measure the main and connecting rod journals for wear, out-of-roundness or taper, using a micrometer. Measure in at least 4 places around each journal and compare your findings with the journal diameter specifications.

5. If the crankshaft fails any inspection for wear or damage, it must be reground or replaced.

➡The crankshaft used on the 2.5L engine is of the rolled fillet type and cannot be reground. If the measurements do not meet specification, replace the shaft.

6. Once the crankshaft has been cleared for a return to service, check the bearings using Plastigage® or an equivalent gauging material. The bearings must be checked regardless of whether they are new or used. To check the bearings:

   a. Temporarily install the upper and lower bearing halves to the block and main bearing cap (respectively).

   b. Wipe all oil from the crankshaft journal and outer/inner surfaces of the bearing shell.

   c. Temporarily position the crankshaft to the block and upper bearing journals.

   d. Place a piece of Plastigage® material in the center of the bearing.

   e. Install the bearing cap and bearing. Lubricate the main bearing bolts with engine oil, install the bolts and tighten them to specifications.

   f. Remove the bearing cap and determine the bearing clearance by comparing the width of the flattened Plastigage® material at its widest point with the graduations on the gauging material container. The number within the graduation on the envelope indicates the clearance in millimeters or thousandths of an inch. If the clearance is greater than allowed, REPLACE BOTH BEARING SHELLS AS A SET. Recheck the clearance after replacing the shells.

## MAIN BEARING REPLACEMENT

### ♦ See Figures 220 and 228

Main bearing clearances must be corrected by the use of selective upper and lower shells. under NO circumstances should the use of shims behind the shells to compensate for wear be attempted. The bearings are easily replaced if the crankshaft is removed from the engine, but provided that no refinishing or replacement of the crankshaft is necessary, the bearings can also be replaced with the engine and crankshaft still installed in the van. To replace the main bearing shells, proceed as follows:

1. Refer to the Oil Pan, Removal and Installation procedures in this section and remove the oil pan.

2. If necessary, remove the oil pump assembly.

3. Loosen all of the main bearing cap bolts.

4. Remove the bearing cap bolts, the caps and the lower bearing shell.

5. Insert a flattened cotter pin or a roll out pin in the oil passage hole in the crankshaft, then rotate the crankshaft in the direction opposite to the cranking rotation. The pin will contact the outside edge of the upper shell and roll it out.

6. The main bearing journals should be checked for roughness and wear. Slight roughness may be removed with a fine grit polishing cloth, saturated with engine oil. Burrs may be removed with a fine oil stone. If the journals are scored or ridged, the crankshaft must be replaced.

➡The journals can be measured for out-of-round with the crankshaft installed by using a crankshaft caliper and inside micrometer or a main

Fig. 223 A dial gauge may be used to check crankshaft end-play

Fig. 224 Carefully pry the shaft back and forth while reading the dial gauge for play

Fig. 225 A dial gauge may also be used to check crankshaft run-out

Fig. 226 Mounting a dial gauge to read crankshaft run-out

Fig. 227 Turn the crankshaft slowly by hand while checking the gauge

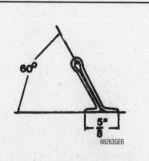
Fig. 228 A roll-out pin can be fabricated from a cotter pin and used to replace bearings with the crankshaft installed

**bearing micrometer. The upper bearing shell must be removed when measuring the crankshaft journals. Maximum out-of-round of the crankshaft journal must not exceed 0.0010 in. (0.025mm).**

7. Clean the crankshaft journals and bearing caps thoroughly before installing the new main bearings.
8. Place the new upper shell on the crankshaft journal with the locating tang in the correct position and rotate the shaft to turn it into place using a cotter pin or a roll out pin as during removal.
9. Place a new bearing shell in the bearing cap.
10. Check the main bearing clearances using a gauging material. In order to do this you will have to support the crankshaft (at the flywheel and damper) to be certain that all clearance is taken-up between the upper bearing half and the shaft journal. Then apply a strip of gauging material to each of the bearings, install and tighten all of the main bearing caps, then remove the caps again and check the gauging material. For more details, please refer to the crankshaft cleaning and inspection information, found earlier in this section.
11. Lubricate the new bearings and the main bearing cap bolts with engine oil, then install the main bearing caps and tighten to specification.
12. Using a feeler gauge, pry the crankshaft forward and rearward, then check for the crankshaft (thrust bearing) end-play.

**➡In order to prevent the possibility of cylinder block and/or main bearing cap damage, the main bearing caps are to be tapped into their cylinder block cavity, using a brass or leather mallet before the bolts are installed. Do not use the bolts to pull the main bearing caps into their seats. Failure to observe this procedure may damage the cylinder block or bearing cap.**

13. Install the oil pump assembly.
14. Install the oil pan.

## Flywheel/Flexplate

The flywheel and the ring gear are machined from one piece of metal and cannot be separated.

**➡The flywheel on automatic transmission vehicles is usually referred to as a flexplate. Though the job they do is quite different, the two terms are often interchanged.**

### REMOVAL & INSTALLATION

**See Figure 229**

1. Remove the transmission assembly from the vehicle.
2. If equipped with a manual transmission, remove the clutch and pressure plate assembly.
3. Remove the flywheel-to-crankshaft bolts, then remove the flywheel from the engine.

**To install:**

4. Inspect the flywheel for cracks, and inspect the ring gear for burrs or worn teeth. Replace the flywheel if any damage is apparent. Remove burrs with a mill file. On manual transmission vehicles, check the wheel for scoring, wear or other damage. If the scoring or wear is minimal, it may be possible to have the flywheel machined (turned) in order to keep it in service.
5. Install the flywheel. Most flywheels will attach to the crankshaft in only one position, as the bolt holes are unevenly spaced and/or the crankshaft is fitted with a dowel pin. Install the bolts and tighten to specification using a criss-cross pattern.
6. If equipped, install the clutch and pressure plate assembly.
7. Install the transmission assembly.

FLYWHEEL
PRESSURE PLATE AND COVER ASSEMBLY
J-33169
DRIVEN PLATE ASSEMBLY
88263GE7

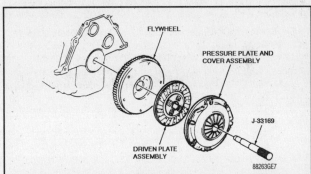

**Fig. 229 Exploded view of a typical Astro and Safari flywheel mounting—flexplate mounting similar, but without a clutch and pressure plate assembly**

## EXHAUST SYSTEM

**See Figures 230 and 231**

### Safety

For a number of different reasons, exhaust system work can be the most dangerous type of work you can do on your van. Always observe the following precautions:

- Support the van extra securely. Not only will you often be working directly under it, but you'll frequently be using a lot of force, such as heavy hammer blows to dislodge rusted parts. This can cause an improperly supported van to shift and possibly fall.
- Wear goggles. Exhaust system parts are always rusty. Metal chips can be dislodged, even when you're only turning rusted bolts. Attempting to pry pipes apart with a chisel makes chips fly even more frequently. Gloves are also recommended to protect against rusty chips and sharp, jagged edges.
- If you're using a cutting torch, keep it at a great distance from either the fuel tank or lines. Stop frequently and check the temperature of fuel and brake lines or the tank. Even slight heat can expand or vaporize the fuel, resulting in accumulated vapor or a liquid leak near your torch.
- Watch where your hammer blows fall. You could easily tap a brake or fuel line when you hit an exhaust system part with a glancing blow. Inspect all lines and hoses in the work area before driving the van.

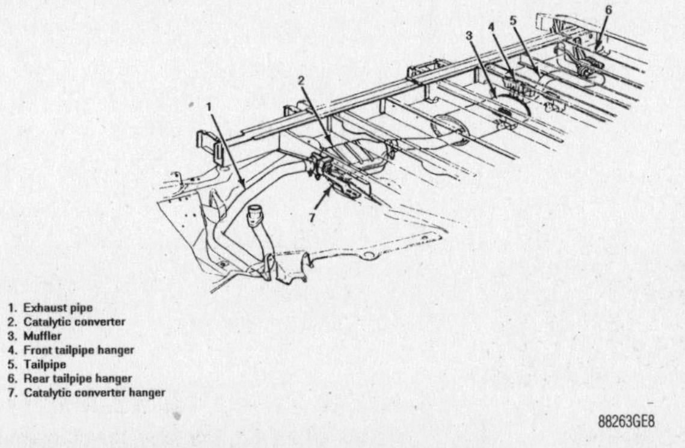

1
2
3
4
5
6
7
1. Exhaust pipe
2. Catalytic converter
3. Muffler
4. Front tailpipe hanger
5. Tailpipe
6. Rear tailpipe hanger
7. Catalytic converter hanger
88263GE8

**Fig. 230 Exhaust system components—2.5L engine**

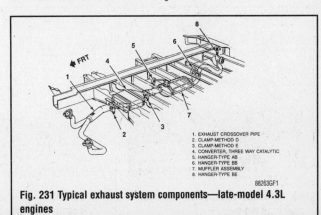

FRT
1
2
3
4
5
6
7
8
1. EXHAUST CROSSOVER PIPE
2. CLAMP-METHOD D
3. CLAMP-METHOD E
4. CONVERTER, THREE WAY CATALYTIC
5. HANGER-TYPE AB
6. HANGER-TYPE BB
7. MUFFLER ASSEMBLY
8. HANGER-TYPE BE
88263GF1

**Fig. 231 Typical exhaust system components—late-model 4.3L engines**

## ✳✳ CAUTION

**Be very careful when working on or near the catalytic converter. External temperatures can reach 1500°F (815°C) and more, causing severe burns. Removal or installation should be performed only on a cold exhaust system.**

A number of special exhaust system tools can be rented from auto supply houses or local stores that rent special equipment. A common one is a tail pipe expander, designed to enable you to join pipes of identical diameter.

It may also be quite helpful to use solvents designed to loosen rusted bolts or flanges. Soaking rusted hardware the night before you do the job can speed the work of freeing rusted parts considerably. Remember that some solvents are flammable. Apply them only after the parts are cool.

Two types of pipe connections are used on the exhaust system, they are: the ball joint (to allow angular movement for alignment purposes) and the slip joint. No gaskets are used in the entire system.

The system is supported by free hanging rubber mountings which permit some movement of the exhaust system but do not allow the transfer of noise and vibration into the passenger compartment. Any noise vibrations or rattles in the exhaust system are usually caused by misalignment of the parts.

## ✳✳ CAUTION

**Before performing any operation on the exhaust system, be sure to allow it to cool down.**

## Component Replacement

♦ See Figures 230 and 231

### REMOVAL & INSTALLATION

### Front Pipe

♦ See Figure 232

Most of the early models covered by this manual and some of the late-model or Canada emission vehicles utilize a front exhaust pipe to convey gases from the manifolds to the converter or muffler (again, depending on the emission package). Certain California emission and late-model vehicles utilize a close-mount catalytic converter where the front pipe is part of the converter assembly.

1. Raise and support the front of the vehicle safely using jackstands.
2. Remove the front pipe(s)-to-manifold(s) nuts and separate (pry, if necessary) the front pipe (ball joint) from the exhaust manifold(s).
3. At the catalytic converter, loosen the front pipe-to-converter clamp nuts, slide the clamp away from converter and separate the front pipe from the converter.

➡**Use a twisting motion to separate the front pipe-to-converter slip joint connection. If the front pipe cannot be removed from the catalytic converter, use a hammer (to loosen the connection) or wedge tool separate the connection.**

4. Inspect the pipe for holes, damage or deterioration; if necessary, replace the front pipe.
5. **To install,** lubricate the front pipe-to-manifold(s) studs/nuts and the front pipe-to-converter clamp threads, then tighten the clamps to 20 ft. lbs. (27 Nm).
6. Start the engine and check for exhaust leaks.

### Catalytic Converter

The catalytic converter is an emission control device added to the exhaust system to reduce the emission of hydrocarbon and carbon monoxide pollutants.

Most of the early models covered by this manual and some of the late-model or Canada emission vehicles utilize a front exhaust pipe to convey gases from the manifolds to the converter or muffler (again, depending on the emission package). Certain California emission and late-model vehicles utilize a close-mount catalytic converter where the front pipe is part of the converter assembly.

#### WITHOUT INTEGRAL FRONT PIPE

1. Raise and support the front of the vehicle on jackstands.
2. Remove the catalytic converter-to-muffler stud nuts and separate the muffler from the converter.

➡**The connection between the converter and the muffler is a ball joint type, which can be easily separated.**

3. Remove the catalytic converter-to-front pipe clamp nuts and move the clamp forward.
4. Remove the converter-to-mounting bracket bolts (if equipped), then twist the converter to separate it from the front pipe.
5. Inspect the condition of the catalytic converter for physical damage, replace it, if necessary.

➡**When installing the catalytic converter, be sure that it is installed with adequate clearance from the floor pan, to prevent overheating of the vehicle floor.**

6. **To install,** align the components and reverse the removal procedures; be careful not to damage the pipe sealing surfaces when tightening the retaining clamps. Tighten the clamps to 20 ft. lbs. (27 Nm).
7. Start the engine and check for exhaust leaks.

#### WITH INTEGRAL FRONT PIPE

♦ See Figures 233 and 234

1. Raise and support the front of the vehicle safely using jackstands.
2. Support the catalytic converter assembly to keep it from falling and becoming damaged when it is detached.
3. Disengage the oxygen sensor electrical connection. For 1996 vehicles, you have 4 oxygen sensors, so make sure the wiring to all of them has been disengaged. Remove the wiring from any necessary clips and reposition it out of the way.
4. If equipped with a slip-joint at the rear of the converter, remove the clamp and separate the pipe from the converter.
5. If equipped with a bolted flange-joint at the rear of the converter, remove the converter-to-muffler retaining nuts.

**Fig. 232 A deep socket is usually VERY helpful when trying to loosen exhaust pipe studs**

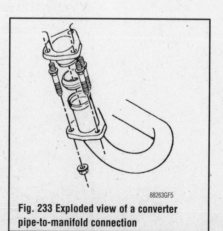

**Fig. 233 Exploded view of a converter pipe-to-manifold connection**

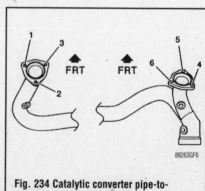

**Fig. 234 Catalytic converter pipe-to-exhaust manifold tightening sequence—1996 models**

6. Remove the nuts from the exhaust manifold studs. If equipped, remove the collars from the exhaust manifold studs.

7. Separate the converter pipe from the muffler and the exhaust manifolds, then carefully lower the front of the converter pipe down and remove the assembly from the hanger. Rotate the assembly over the rear of the transmission crossmember and remove it from the vehicle.

## ✳✳ CAUTION

**Be very careful not to damage the converter or the oxygen sensor(s).**

8. **To install,** align the components and reverse the removal procedures; be careful not to damage the pipe sealing surfaces when tightening the retainers. Tighten the exhaust manifold stud nuts to 15 ft. lbs. (20 Nm), except for on 1996 vehicles where the manifold stud nuts must be tightened to 18 ft. lbs. (24 Nm), using the proper sequence.

9. Either tighten the converter-to-muffler nuts to 30 ft. lbs. (40 Nm) or the converter rear slip-joint clamp to 27 ft. lbs. (37 Nm) for all except 1995 models which should be tightened to 44 ft. lbs. (60 Nm).

10. Start the engine and check for exhaust leaks.

### Muffler

➡The following procedure requires the use of GM Sealing Compound No. 1051249 or equivalent. When replacing the muffler, always replace the tail pipe.

1. Refer to the Tail Pipe, Removal and Installation procedures in this section and remove the tail pipe from the vehicle.

2. Loosen and move the catalytic converter-to-muffler clamp or remove the catalytic converter-to-muffler flange bolts and separate the items.

3. Remove the muffler-to-mounting bracket bolts and lower the muffler from the vehicle.

4. **To install,** coat the slip joints with GM Sealing Compound No. 1051249 or equivalent and loosely install the components onto the vehicle.

5. After aligning the components, tighten the connecting bolts and clamps to 20 ft. lbs. (27 Nm).

➡When torquing the exhaust system connectors, be careful not to tighten the pipe clamps too tightly, or deformation of the pipes may occur.

6. Start the engine and check for exhaust leaks.

### Tail Pipe

➡The following procedure requires the use of GM Sealing Compound No. 1051249 or equivalent.

➡Normally, when the tail pipe requires replacement, the muffler should be replaced also.

1. Raise and support the rear of the vehicle on jackstands.
2. Remove the tail pipe-to-muffler clamp, then slide the clamp rearward.
3. Remove the tail pipe-to-mounting bracket clamp.
4. Using a twisting motion, remove the tail pipe from the muffler.

➡If removal of the tail pipe difficult, use a hammer to free the pipe from the muffler.

5. Inspect the tail pipe for holes of physical damage.
6. **To install,** use a new tail pipe (if necessary), a new muffler (if necessary), apply GM Sealing Compound No. 1051249 or equivalent to the slip joint(s), lubricate the pipe clamp threads with engine oil, loosely assemble the exhaust system, then tighten the components to 20 ft. lbs. (27 Nm).
7. Start the engine and check for exhaust leaks.

## TORQUE SPECIFICATIONS—2.5L ENGINE

| Component | U.S. | Metric |
|---|---|---|
| Bellhousing-to-Engine Bolts: | 32 ft. lbs. | 43 Nm |
| Camshaft Thrust Plate-to-Engine Bolts: | 90 inch lbs. | 10 Nm |
| Connecting Rods | | |
| 1985-88: | 32 ft. lbs. | 43 Nm |
| 1989-90: | 30 ft. lbs. | 40 Nm |
| Cylinder Head (in sequence) | | |
| Step 1: | 18 ft. lbs. | 25 Nm |
| Step 2 (all bolts except #9 in sequence): | 26 ft. lbs. | 35 Nm |
| Step 3 (retighten #9 ONLY): | 18 ft. lbs. | 25 Nm |
| Step 4 (tighten all bolts with a torque angle meter): | 90 degrees (1/4 turn) | 90 degrees (1/4 turn) |
| Damper Pulley Hub-to-Crankshaft Bolt: | 160 ft. lbs. | 217 Nm |
| Exhaust Manifold (in sequence) | | |
| Inner or center retainers: | 36 ft. lbs. | 50 Nm |
| Outer retainers: | 32 ft. lbs. | 43 Nm |
| Exhaust Pipe Slip-Joint Clamps: | 15 ft. lbs. | 20 Nm |
| Exhaust Pipe-to-Manifold Nuts: | 20 ft. lbs. | 27 Nm |
| Fan Assembly-to-Water Pump | | |
| With clutch assembly: | 18 ft. lbs. | 24 Nm |
| With a spacer (no clutch): | 20 ft. lbs. | 27 Nm |
| Fan Blade-to-Clutch Assembly | | |
| Threaded from front, through clutch, toward the engine: | 89 inch lbs. | 10 Nm |
| Threaded from engine, through fan and then clutch: | 26 ft. lbs. | 35 Nm |
| Intake Manifold (in sequence) | | |
| Early-Model (retained by bolts and studs): | refer to illustration accompanying procedure | |
| Late-Model (retained only by bolts): | 25 ft. lbs. | 34 Nm |
| Lifter Retainer-to-Engine: | 96 inch lbs. | 11 Nm |
| Main Bearing Caps (in 3 steps) | | |
| 1985-88: | 70 ft. lbs. | 95 Nm |
| 1989-90: | 65 ft. lbs. | 88 Nm |
| Oil Pan-to-Engine Bolts: | 100 inch lbs. | 11 Nm |
| Rocker Arm Cover Retainers: | 90 inch lbs. | 10 Nm |
| Rocker Arm Retainers | | |
| 1985-86: | 20 ft. lbs. | 28 Nm |
| 1987: | 24 ft. lbs. | 32 Nm |
| 1988-90: | 22 ft. lbs. | 30 Nm |
| Thermostat Housing-to-Engine (bolts or bolt and nut): | 21 ft. lbs. | 28 Nm |
| Timing Cover-to-Engine Bolts: | 90 inch lbs. | 10 Nm |
| Timing Cover-to-Oil Pan Bolts: | 90 inch lbs. | 10 Nm |
| Water Pump-to-Engine Bolts: | 17 ft. lbs. | 25 Nm |

88263C08

## TORQUE SPECIFICATIONS—4.3L ENGINE

| Component | U.S. | Metric |
|---|---|---|
| Balance Shaft (VIN W only) | | |
| Shaft drive gear retaining stud: | 12 ft. lbs. | 16 Nm |
| Shaft driven gear | | |
| Step 1: | 15 ft. lbs. | 20 Nm |
| Step 2: | 35 degree turn | 35 degree turn |
| Shaft retainer bolts: | 120 inch lbs. | 14 Nm |
| Camshaft Sprocket-to-Camshaft Retainers: | 21 ft. lbs. | 28 Nm |
| Connecting Rods | | |
| 1985-90: | 45 ft. lbs. | 61 Nm |
| 1991-92 | | |
| Step 1: | 20 ft. lbs. | 27 Nm |
| Step 2: | 60 degree turn | 60 degree turn |
| 1993-96 | | |
| Step 1: | 20 ft. lbs. | 27 Nm |
| Step 2: | 70 degree turn | 70 degree turn |
| Cylinder Head (in sequence) | | |
| 1985-95 | | |
| Step 1: | 25 ft. lbs. | 34 Nm |
| Step 2: | 45 ft. lbs. | 61 Nm |
| Step 3: | 65 ft. lbs. | 90 Nm |
| 1996 | | |
| Step 1: | 22 ft. lbs. | 30 Nm |
| Step 2 plus (according to bolt size) | | |
| Short bolts (#'s 11, 7, 3, 2, 6 & 10): | 55 degree turn | 55 degree turn |
| Medium bolts (#'s 12 & 13): | 65 degree turn | 65 degree turn |
| Long bolts (#'s 1, 4, 8, 5 & 9): | 75 degree turn | 75 degree turn |
| Damper Hub-to-Crankshaft Bolt | | |
| 1985-95: | 70 ft. lbs. | 95 Nm |
| 1996: | 74 ft. lbs. | 100 Nm |
| Exhaust Close-Mount Converter nuts: | 30 ft. lbs. | 40 Nm |
| Exhaust Manifold (in sequence) | | |
| Inner (center tube) retainers: | 26 ft. lbs. | 36 Nm |
| Outer (front and rear tube) retainers: | 20 ft. lbs. | 28 Nm |
| Exhaust Pipe-to-Manifold Nuts: | | |
| 1985-95: | 15 ft. lbs. | 20 Nm |
| 1996 (in sequence): | 18 ft. lbs. | 24 Nm |
| Exhaust Pipe Slip-Joint Clamps | | |
| Except Converter: | 20 ft. lbs. | 27 Nm |
| Converter | | |
| Except 1995: | 27 ft. lbs. | 37 Nm |
| 1995: | 44 ft. lbs. | 60 Nm |
| Fan Assembly-to-Water Pump | | |
| 1985-95: | 22 ft. lbs. | 30 Nm |
| 1996: | 41 ft. lbs. | 56 Nm |
| Fan Blade-to-Clutch Assembly | | |
| 1985-92: | 18 ft. lbs. | 24 Nm |
| 1993-95: | 26 ft. lbs. | 35 Nm |
| 1996: | 24 ft. lbs. | 33 Nm |

88263C09

### TORQUE SPECIFICATIONS—4.3L ENGINE

| Component | U.S. | Metric |
|---|---|---|
| **Intake Manifold (in sequence)** | | |
| VIN B, N & Z engines | | |
| 1985-90: | 35 ft. lbs. | 48 Nm |
| 1991-94 | | |
| Step 1: | 35 ft. lbs. | 48 Nm |
| Step 2 (tighten bolt 9): | 41 ft. lbs. | 56 Nm |
| VIN W | | |
| 1992-95 | | |
| Lower Manifold: | 35 ft. lbs. | 48 Nm |
| Upper Manifold: | 124 inch lbs. | 14 Nm |
| 1996 | | |
| Lower Manifold | | |
| Step 1: | 26 inch lbs. | 3 Nm |
| Step 2: | 106 inch lbs. | 12 Nm |
| Step 3: | 11 ft. lbs. | 15 Nm |
| Upper Manifold: | 83 inch lbs. | 10 Nm |
| **Lifter Retainer Bolts:** | 12 ft. lbs. | 16 Nm |
| **Main Bearing Caps (in 3 steps)** | | |
| 1985: | 70 ft. lbs. | 95 Nm |
| 1986: | 75 ft. lbs. | 100 Nm |
| 1987-90: | 80 ft. lbs. | 108 Nm |
| 1991-95: | 75 ft. lbs. | 100 Nm |
| 1996: | 77 ft. lbs. | 105 Nm |
| **Oil Pan-to-Engine** | | |
| 1985-90 | | |
| Bolts: | 100 inch lbs. | 11 Nm |
| Nuts: | 14 ft. lbs. | 20 Nm |
| 1991-95 | | |
| Bolts: | 100 inch lbs. | 11 Nm |
| Nuts: | 17 ft. lbs. | 23 Nm |
| 1996 (in sequence): | 18 ft. lbs. | 25 Nm |
| **Rocker Arm Cover Retainers:** | 90 inch lbs. | 10 Nm |
| **Rocker Arm Stud Nuts** | | |
| VIN B, N & Z engines | | |
| Except 1993-94 with positive stop studs: | Adjust valve lash using proper procedure | |
| 1993-94 equipped with positive stop studs: | 20 ft. lbs. | 27 Nm |
| VIN W: | 20 ft. lbs. | 27 Nm |
| **Thermostat Housing-to-Engine Retainers** | | |
| 1985-94: | 21 ft. lbs. | 28 Nm |
| 1995: | 15 ft. lbs. | 20 Nm |
| 1996: | 18 ft. lbs. | 25 Nm |
| **Timing Cover-to-Engine Bolts:** | | |
| 1985-95: | 124 inch lbs. | 14 Nm |
| 1996 (use a NEW front cover): | 124 inch lbs. | 14 Nm |
| **Water Pump-to-Engine Bolts** | | |
| 1985-92: | 22 ft. lbs. | 29 Nm |
| 1993-95: | 30 ft. lbs. | 41 Nm |
| 1996: | 33 ft. lbs. | 45 Nm |

88263C10

## USING A VACUUM GAUGE

*White needle = steady needle*     *Dark needle = drifting needle*

The vacuum gauge is one of the most useful and easy-to-use diagnostic tools. It is inexpensive, easy to hook up, and provides valuable information about the condition of your engine.

**Indication: Normal engine in good condition**

Gauge reading: Steady, from 17–22 in./Hg.

**Indication: Sticking valve or ignition miss**

Gauge reading: Needle fluctuates from 15–20 in./Hg. at idle

**Indication: Late ignition or valve timing, low compression, stuck throttle valve, leaking carburetor or manifold gasket.**

Gauge reading: Low (15–20 in./Hg.) but steady

**Indication: Improper carburetor adjustment, or minor intake leak at carburetor or manifold**

*NOTE: Bad fuel injector O-rings may also cause this reading.*

Gauge reading: Drifting needle

**Indication: Weak valve springs, worn valve stem guides, or leaky cylinder head gasket (vibrating excessively at all speeds).**

*NOTE: A plugged catalytic converter may also cause this reading.*

Gauge reading: Needle fluctuates as engine speed increases

**Indication: Burnt valve or improper valve clearance. The needle will drop when the defective valve operates.**

Gauge reading: Steady needle, but drops regularly

**Indication: Choked muffler or obstruction in system. Speed up the engine. Choked muffler will exhibit a slow drop of vacuum to zero.**

Gauge reading: Gradual drop in reading at idle

**Indication: Worn valve guides**

Gauge reading: Needle vibrates excessively at idle, but steadies as engine speed increases

TCCS3C01

# Troubleshooting the Serpentine Drive Belt

| Problem | Cause | Solution |
| --- | --- | --- |
| Tension sheeting fabric failure (woven fabric on outside circumference of belt has cracked or separated from body of belt) | • Grooved or backside idler pulley diameters are less than minimum recommended<br>• Tension sheeting contacting (rubbing) stationary object<br>• Excessive heat causing woven fabric to age<br>• Tension sheeting splice has fractured | • Replace pulley(s) not conforming to specification<br>• Correct rubbing condition<br>• Replace belt<br>• Replace belt |
| Noise (objectional squeal, squeak, or rumble is heard or felt while drive belt is in operation) | • Belt slippage<br>• Bearing noise<br>• Belt misalignment<br>• Belt-to-pulley mismatch<br>• Driven component inducing vibration<br>• System resonant frequency inducing vibration | • Adjust belt<br>• Locate and repair<br>• Align belt/pulley(s)<br>• Install correct belt<br>• Locate defective driven component and repair<br>• Vary belt tension within specifications. Replace belt. |
| Rib chunking (one or more ribs has separated from belt body) | • Foreign objects imbedded in pulley grooves<br>• Installation damage<br>• Drive loads in excess of design specifications<br>• Insufficient internal belt adhesion | • Remove foreign objects from pulley grooves<br>• Replace belt<br>• Adjust belt tension<br>• Replace belt |
| Rib or belt wear (belt ribs contact bottom of pulley grooves) | • Pulley(s) misaligned<br>• Mismatch of belt and pulley groove widths<br>• Abrasive environment<br>• Rusted pulley(s)<br>• Sharp or jagged pulley groove tips<br>• Rubber deteriorated | • Align pulley(s)<br>• Replace belt<br>• Replace belt<br>• Clean rust from pulley(s)<br>• Replace pulley<br>• Replace belt |
| Longitudinal belt cracking (cracks between two ribs) | • Belt has mistracked from pulley groove<br>• Pulley groove tip has worn away rubber-to-tensile member | • Replace belt<br>• Replace belt |
| Belt slips | • Belt slipping because of insufficient tension<br>• Belt or pulley subjected to substance (belt dressing, oil, ethylene glycol) that has reduced friction<br>• Driven component bearing failure<br>• Belt glazed and hardened from heat and excessive slippage | • Adjust tension<br>• Replace belt and clean pulleys<br>• Replace faulty component bearing<br>• Replace belt |
| "Groove jumping" (belt does not maintain correct position on pulley, or turns over and/or runs off pulleys) | • Insufficient belt tension<br>• Pulley(s) not within design tolerance<br>• Foreign object(s) in grooves | • Adjust belt tension<br>• Replace pulley(s)<br>• Remove foreign objects from grooves |

TCCS3C09

## Troubleshooting the Serpentine Drive Belt

| Problem | Cause | Solution |
|---|---|---|
| "Groove jumping" (belt does not maintain correct position on pulley, or turns over and/or runs off pulleys) | • Excessive belt speed<br><br>• Pulley misalignment<br>• Belt-to-pulley profile mismatched<br>• Belt cordline is distorted | • Avoid excessive engine acceleration<br>• Align pulley(s)<br>• Install correct belt<br>• Replace belt |
| Belt broken (Note: identify and correct problem before replacement belt is installed) | • Excessive tension<br><br>• Tensile members damaged during belt installation<br>• Belt turnover<br>• Severe pulley misalignment<br>• Bracket, pulley, or bearing failure | • Replace belt and adjust tension to specification<br>• Replace belt<br><br>• Replace belt<br>• Align pulley(s)<br>• Replace defective component and belt |
| Cord edge failure (tensile member exposed at edges of belt or separated from belt body) | • Excessive tension<br>• Drive pulley misalignment<br>• Belt contacting stationary object<br>• Pulley irregularities<br>• Improper pulley construction<br>• Insufficient adhesion between tensile member and rubber matrix | • Adjust belt tension<br>• Align pulley<br>• Correct as necessary<br>• Replace pulley<br>• Replace pulley<br>• Replace belt and adjust tension to specifications |
| Sporadic rib cracking (multiple cracks in belt ribs at random intervals) | • Ribbed pulley(s) diameter less than minimum specification<br>• Backside bend flat pulley(s) diameter less than minimum<br>• Excessive heat condition causing rubber to harden<br>• Excessive belt thickness<br>• Belt overcured<br>• Excessive tension | • Replace pulley(s)<br><br>• Replace pulley(s)<br><br>• Correct heat condition as necessary<br>• Replace belt<br>• Replace belt<br>• Adjust belt tension |

TCCS3C10

## Troubleshooting the Cooling System

| Problem | Cause | Solution |
|---|---|---|
| High temperature gauge indication—overheating | · Coolant level low<br>· Improper fan operation<br>· Radiator hose(s) collapsed<br>· Radiator airflow blocked<br><br>· Faulty pressure cap<br>· Ignition timing incorrect<br>· Air trapped in cooling system<br>· Heavy traffic driving<br><br><br>· Incorrect cooling system component(s) installed<br>· Faulty thermostat<br>· Water pump shaft broken or impeller loose<br>· Radiator tubes clogged<br>· Cooling system clogged<br>· Casting flash in cooling passages<br><br><br><br>· Brakes dragging<br>· Excessive engine friction<br>· Antifreeze concentration over 68%<br><br>· Missing air seals<br>· Faulty gauge or sending unit<br><br>· Loss of coolant flow caused by leakage or foaming<br>· Viscous fan drive failed | · Replenish coolant<br>· Repair or replace as necessary<br>· Replace hose(s)<br>· Remove restriction (bug screen, fog lamps, etc.)<br>· Replace pressure cap<br>· Adjust ignition timing<br>· Purge air<br>· Operate at fast idle in neutral intermittently to cool engine<br>· Install proper component(s)<br><br><br>· Replace thermostat<br>· Replace water pump<br><br>· Flush radiator<br>· Flush system<br>· Repair or replace as necessary. Flash may be visible by removing cooling system components or removing core plugs.<br>· Repair brakes<br>· Repair engine<br>· Lower antifreeze concentration percentage<br>· Replace air seals<br>· Repair or replace faulty component<br>· Repair or replace leaking component, replace coolant<br>· Replace unit |
| Low temperature indication—undercooling | · Thermostat stuck open<br>· Faulty gauge or sending unit | · Replace thermostat<br>· Repair or replace faulty component |
| Coolant loss—boilover | · Overfilled cooling system<br><br>· Quick shutdown after hard (hot) run<br>· Air in system resulting in occasional "burping" of coolant<br>· Insufficient antifreeze allowing coolant boiling point to be too low<br>· Antifreeze deteriorated because of age or contamination<br>· Leaks due to loose hose clamps, loose nuts, bolts, drain plugs, faulty hoses, or defective radiator | · Reduce coolant level to proper specification<br>· Allow engine to run at fast idle prior to shutdown<br>· Purge system<br><br>· Add antifreeze to raise boiling point<br><br>· Replace coolant<br><br>· Pressure test system to locate source of leak(s) then repair as necessary |

TCCS3C11

## Troubleshooting the Cooling System

| Problem | Cause | Solution |
|---|---|---|
| Coolant loss—boilover | • Faulty head gasket<br>• Cracked head, manifold, or block<br>• Faulty radiator cap | • Replace head gasket<br>• Replace as necessary<br>• Replace cap |
| Coolant entry into crankcase or cylinder(s) | • Faulty head gasket<br>• Crack in head, manifold or block | • Replace head gasket<br>• Replace as necessary |
| Coolant recovery system inoperative | • Coolant level low<br>• Leak in system<br><br>• Pressure cap not tight or seal missing, or leaking<br>• Pressure cap defective<br>• Overflow tube clogged or leaking<br>• Recovery bottle vent restricted | • Replenish coolant to FULL mark<br>• Pressure test to isolate leak and repair as necessary<br>• Repair as necessary<br><br>• Replace cap<br>• Repair as necessary<br>• Remove restriction |
| Noise | • Fan contacting shroud<br><br>• Loose water pump impeller<br>• Glazed fan belt<br>• Loose fan belt<br>• Rough surface on drive pulley<br>• Water pump bearing worn<br><br>• Belt alignment | • Reposition shroud and inspect engine mounts (on electric fans inspect assembly)<br>• Replace pump<br>• Apply silicone or replace belt<br>• Adjust fan belt tension<br>• Replace pulley<br>• Remove belt to isolate. Replace pump.<br>• Check pulley alignment. Repair as necessary. |
| No coolant flow through heater core | • Restricted return inlet in water pump<br>• Heater hose collapsed or restricted<br>• Restricted heater core<br>• Restricted outlet in thermostat housing<br>• Intake manifold bypass hole in cylinder head restricted<br>• Faulty heater control valve<br>• Intake manifold coolant passage restricted | • Remove restriction<br><br>• Remove restriction or replace hose<br>• Remove restriction or replace core<br>• Remove flash or restriction<br><br>• Remove restriction<br><br>• Replace valve<br>• Remove restriction or replace intake manifold |

**NOTE:** *Immediately after shutdown, the engine enters a condition known as heat soak. This is caused by the cooling system being inoperative while engine temperature is still high. If coolant temperature rises above boiling point, expansion and pressure may push some coolant out of the radiator overflow tube. If this does not occur frequently it is considered normal.*

TCCS3C12

# 4

# DRIVEABILITY AND EMISSION CONTROLS

## GASOLINE ENGINE EMISSION CONTROLS

### Crankcase Ventilation System

OPERATION

▶ **See Figures 1 and 2**

The Positive Crankcase Ventilation (PCV) system is used to evacuate the crankcase vapors. Outside vehicle air is routed through the air cleaner to the crankcase where it mixes with the blow-by gases and is passed through the PCV valve. It is then routed into the intake manifold. The PCV valve meters the air flow rate which varies under engine operation depending on manifold vacuum. In order to maintain idle quality, the PCV valve limits the air flow when intake manifold vacuum is high. If abnormal operating conditions occur, the system will allow excessive blow-by gases to back flow through the crankcase vent tube into the air cleaner. These blow-by gases will then be burned by normal combustion.

A plugged PCV valve or hose may cause rough idle, stalling or slow idle speed, oil leaks, oil in the air cleaner or sludge in the engine. A leaking PCV valve or hose could cause rough idle, stalling or high idle speed.

Other than checking and replacing the PCV valve and associated hoses, there is not service required. Engine operating conditions that would direct suspicion to the PCV system are rough idle, oil present in the air cleaner, oil leaks and excessive oil sludging or dilution. If any of the above conditions exist, remove the PCV valve and shake it. A clicking sound indicates that the valve is free. If no clicking sound is heard, replace the valve. Inspect the PCV breather in the air

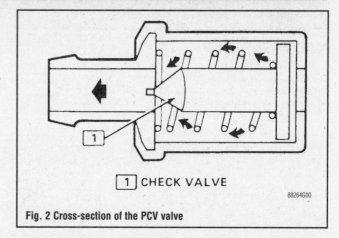

**1** CHECK VALVE

88264G00

**Fig. 2 Cross-section of the PCV valve**

cleaner. Replace the breather if it is so dirty that it will not allow gases to pass through. Check all the PCV hoses for condition and tight connections. Replace any hoses that have deteriorated.

TESTING

With the engine running, remove the PCV from the valve cover and place your thumb over the end of the valve. Check if vacuum is present at the valve. If vacuum is not present, check for plugged hoses, blockage of the manifold port at the throttle body/carburetor unit or a faulty PCV valve. Replace as necessary. With the engine not running, remove the PCV valve from the vehicle. Shake the valve and listen for the rattle of the check valve needle. If no rattle is heard the valve is defective and must be replaced.

REMOVAL & INSTALLATION

▶ **See Figure 3**

1. To replace the valve, gently pull the hose from the top of the valve, then pull the valve out of the cover grommet.
2. Installation is the reverse of removal.

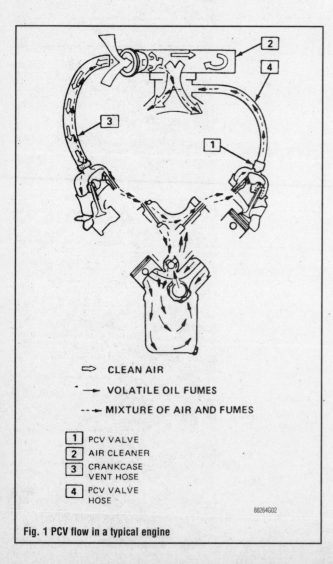

⇨ CLEAN AIR

→ VOLATILE OIL FUMES

--→ MIXTURE OF AIR AND FUMES

**1** PCV VALVE
**2** AIR CLEANER
**3** CRANKCASE VENT HOSE
**4** PCV VALVE HOSE

88264G02

**Fig. 1 PCV flow in a typical engine**

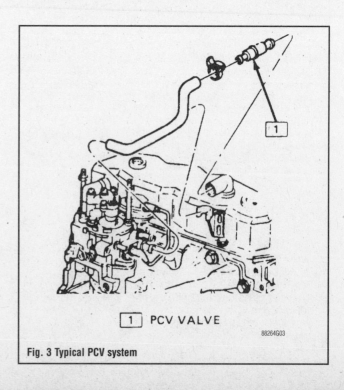

**1** PCV VALVE

88264G03

**Fig. 3 Typical PCV system**

## Evaporative Emission Control System

### OPERATION

#### ▶ See Figures 4 thru 9

The Evaporative Emission Control System (EECS) is designed to prevent fuel tank vapors from being emitted into the atmosphere. Gasoline vapors are absorbed and stored by a fuel vapor charcoal canister. The charcoal canister absorbs the gasoline vapors and stores them until certain engine conditions are met and the vapors can be purged and burned by the engine.

- A disconnected, misrouted, kinked or damaged vapor pipe or canister hoses
- A damaged air cleaner or improperly seated air cleaner gasket

### TESTING

#### Vapor Canister

1. Apply a length of hose to the lower tube of the purge valve assembly and attempt to blow air through it. There should be little or no air should passing into the canister.

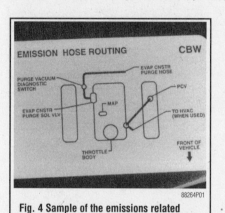

Fig. 4 Sample of the emissions related hose routing sticker found on most vehicles

Fig. 5 The emissions label under the hood has all of the information pertinent to that vehicle on it

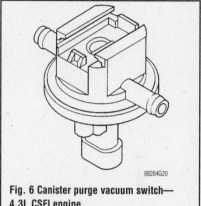

Fig. 6 Canister purge vacuum switch—4.3L CSFI engine

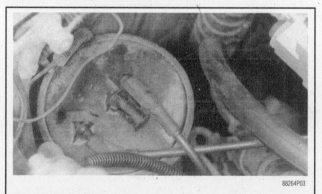

Fig. 7 Typical canister mounting—it has two hoses attached with a third nipple blocked-off

The charcoal canister purge cycle is controlled by a thermostatic vacuum switch, a timed vacuum source or by a solenoid valve the receives its instruction from the engine management system. The thermostatic switch is installed in the coolant passage and prevents canister purge when engine operating temperature is below 115°F (46°C). The timed vacuum source uses a manifold vacuum-controlled diaphragm to control canister purge. When the engine is running, full manifold vacuum is applied to the top tube of the purge valve which lifts the valve diaphragm and opens the valve. The solenoid valve is usually mounted on or near the intake manifold. In general, none of the systems, regardless of type, allow canister purge below 115°F (46°C).

A vent located in the fuel tank, allows fuel vapors to flow to the charcoal canister. A tank pressure control valve, used on high altitude applications, prevents canister purge when the engine is not running. The fuel tank cap does not normally vent to the atmosphere but is designed to provide both vacuum and pressure relief.

Poor engine idle, stalling and poor driveability can be caused by a damaged canister or split, damaged or improperly connected hoses.

Evidence of fuel loss or fuel vapor odor can be caused by a liquid fuel leak:
- A cracked or damaged vapor canister

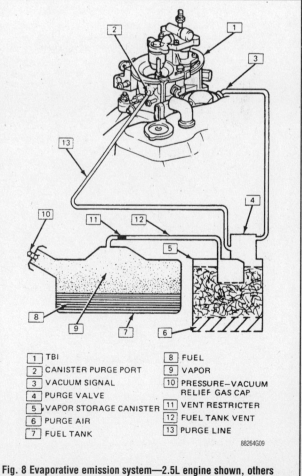

| 1 | TBI | 8 | FUEL |
| 2 | CANISTER PURGE PORT | 9 | VAPOR |
| 3 | VACUUM SIGNAL | 10 | PRESSURE-VACUUM RELIEF GAS CAP |
| 4 | PURGE VALVE | 11 | VENT RESTRICTER |
| 5 | VAPOR STORAGE CANISTER | 12 | FUEL TANK VENT |
| 6 | PURGE AIR | 13 | PURGE LINE |
| 7 | FUEL TANK | | |

Fig. 8 Evaporative emission system—2.5L engine shown, others similar

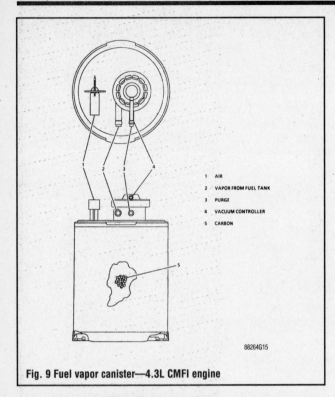

Fig. 9 Fuel vapor canister—4.3L CMFI engine

**Thermostatic Vacuum Switch**

1. With engine temperature below 100°F (38°C), apply vacuum to the manifold side of the switch. The switch should hold vacuum.
2. Start and continue to run the engine until the engine temperature increases above 122°F (50°C). The vacuum should drop off.
3. Replace the switch if it fails either test.

### REMOVAL & INSTALLATION

#### *VAPOR CANISTER*
▶ See Figures 11 and 12

1. Tag and disconnect the hoses from the canister.
2. Remove the vapor canister retaining nut.
3. Remove the canister from the vehicle.
4. To install, reverse the removal procedure, If necessary, refer to the vehicle emission control label, located in the engine compartment for proper routing of the vacuum hoses.

#### Thermostatic Vacuum Switch

1. Drain the cooling system to below the switch level.
2. Tag and disconnect the vacuum hoses from the switch.
3. Remove the thermostatic vacuum switch.
4. **To install,** apply sealer to the switch threads and reverse the removal procedure.

➡If the canister is equipped with a constant purge hole, a small amount of air will pass into the canister.

2. Using a hand-held vacuum pump, apply a vacuum of 15 in. Hg (51 kPa) to the control vacuum (upper) tube. If the vacuum does not hold for at least 20 seconds, the diaphragm is leaking. Replace the canister.
3. If the diaphragm holds vacuum, attempt to blow air through the hose connected to the PCV tube while vacuum is still being applied. An increase of air should be observed. If no increase is noted, the canister must be replaced.

#### Fuel Tank Pressure Control Valve
▶ See Figure 10

1. Attach a length of hose to the tank side of the valve assembly and try to blow air through it. Little or no air should pass into the canister.
2. Using a hand-held vacuum pump, apply vacuum equivalent to 15 in. Hg (51 kPa) to the control vacuum tube. If the diaphragm does not hold vacuum, the diaphragm is leaking. Replace the valve.
3. If the diaphragm holds vacuum, attempt to blow air through the hose connected to the valve while vacuum is still being applied. Air should pass. If no air is noted, the valve must be replaced.

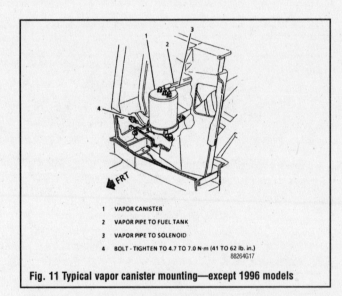

Fig. 11 Typical vapor canister mounting—except 1996 models

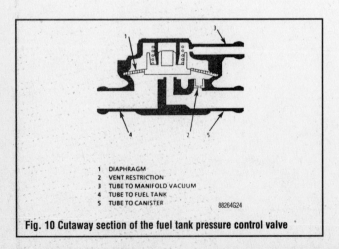

Fig. 10 Cutaway section of the fuel tank pressure control valve

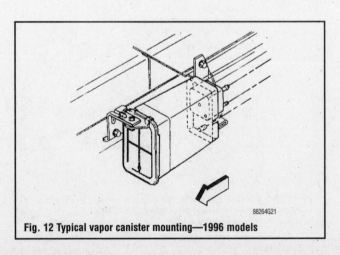

Fig. 12 Typical vapor canister mounting—1996 models

**Canister Purge Solenoid**

▶ **See Figures 13, 14 and 15**

1. Disconnect the negative battery cable.
2. Disconnect the electrical connectors and hoses from the solenoid.
3. Pull the solenoid away from the bracket and remove the assembly.
4. **To install,** slide the solenoid into place on the bracket, attach the connectors, hoses and connect the negative battery cable.

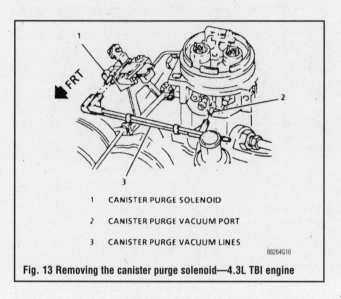

| | |
|---|---|
| 1 | CANISTER PURGE SOLENOID |
| 2 | CANISTER PURGE VACUUM PORT |
| 3 | CANISTER PURGE VACUUM LINES |

88264G16

**Fig. 13 Removing the canister purge solenoid—4.3L TBI engine**

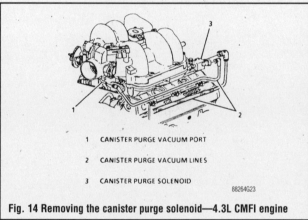

| | |
|---|---|
| 1 | CANISTER PURGE VACUUM PORT |
| 2 | CANISTER PURGE VACUUM LINES |
| 3 | CANISTER PURGE SOLENOID |

88264G23

**Fig. 14 Removing the canister purge solenoid—4.3L CMFI engine**

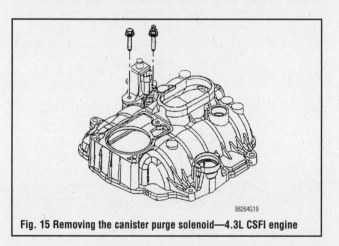

88264G19

**Fig. 15 Removing the canister purge solenoid—4.3L CSFI engine**

## Early Fuel Evaporation System

OPERATION

▶ **See Figures 16, 17 and 18**

The Early Fuel Evaporation (EFE) system, used on carbureted models, consists of an EFE valve at the flange of the exhaust manifold, an actuator, and a thermal vacuum switch. The TVS is located in the coolant outlet housing and directly controls vacuum.

In both systems, manifold vacuum is applied to the actuator, which in turn,

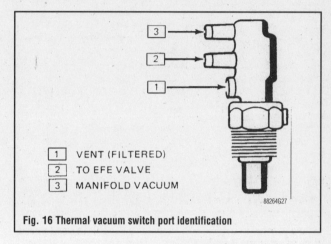

| | |
|---|---|
| 1 | VENT (FILTERED) |
| 2 | TO EFE VALVE |
| 3 | MANIFOLD VACUUM |

88264G27

**Fig. 16 Thermal vacuum switch port identification**

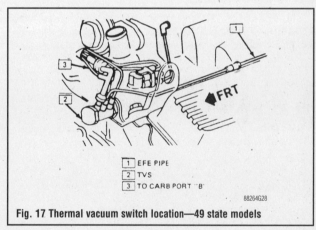

| | |
|---|---|
| 1 | EFE PIPE |
| 2 | TVS |
| 3 | TO CARB PORT "B" |

88264G28

**Fig. 17 Thermal vacuum switch location—49 state models**

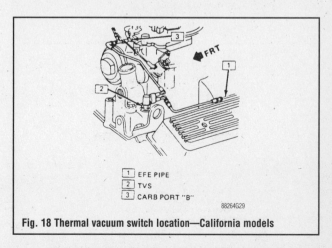

| | |
|---|---|
| 1 | EFE PIPE |
| 2 | TVS |
| 3 | CARB PORT "B" |

88264G29

**Fig. 18 Thermal vacuum switch location—California models**

closes the EFE valve. This routes hot exhaust gases to the base of the carburetor. When coolant temperatures reach a set limit, vacuum is denied to the actuator allowing an internal spring to return the actuator to its normal position, opening the EFE valve.

## TESTING

1. Locate the EFE valve on the exhaust manifold and note the position of the actuator arm. On some vehicles, the valve and arm are covered by a two-piece cover which must be removed for access. Make sure the engine is overnight cold.

2. Watch the actuator arm when the engine is started. The valve should close when the engine is started cold; the actuator link will be pulled into the diaphragm housing.

3. If the valve does not close, stop the engine. Remove the hose from the EFE valve and apply 10 in. Hg (33.8 kPa) of vacuum by hand pump. The valve should close and stay closed for at least 20 seconds (you will hear it close). If the valve opens in less than 20 seconds, replace it. The valve could also be seized if it does not close; lubricate it with spray type manifold heat valve lube. If the valve does not close when vacuum is applied and when it is lubricated, replace the valve.

4. If the valve closes, the problem is not with the valve. Check for loose, cracked, pinched or plugged hoses, and replace as necessary. Test the EFE solenoid (located on the valve cover bracket); if it is working, the solenoid plunger will emit a noise when the current is applied.

5. Warm up the engine to operating temperature.

6. Watch the EFE valve to see if it has opened. It should now be open. If the valve is still closed, replace the solenoid if faulty, and/or check the engine thermostat; the engine coolant may not be reaching normal operating temperature.

## REMOVAL & INSTALLATION

▶ See Figure 19

➡ If the vehicle is equipped with an oxygen sensor, it is located near the EFE valve. Use care when removing the EFE valve as not to damage the oxygen sensor.

1. Disconnect the negative (-) battery cable and vacuum hose at the EFE valve.

2. Remove the exhaust pipe-to-manifold nuts, and the washers and tension springs if used.

3. Lower the exhaust cross-over pipe. On some models, complete removal of the pipe is not necessary.

4. Remove the EFE valve.

**To install:** Always install new seals and gaskets. Tighten the exhaust nuts to 15 ft. lbs. (20 Nm). Connect the negative battery cable and vacuum hose to the valve.

## Exhaust Gas Recirculation (EGR)

### OPERATION

▶ See Figures 20, 21 and 22

The EGR system's purpose is to control oxides of nitrogen which are formed during the peak combustion temperatures. The end products of combustion are relatively inert gases derived from the exhaust gases which are directed into the EGR valve to help lower peak combustion temperatures.

The port EGR valve is controlled by a flexible diaphragm which is spring loaded to hold the valve closed. Vacuum applied to the top side of the diaphragm overcomes the spring pressure and opens the valve which allows exhaust gas to be pulled into the intake manifold and enter the engine cylinders.

The negative backpressure EGR valve has a bleed valve spring below the diaphragm, and the valve is normally closed. The valve varies the amount of exhaust flow into the manifold depending on manifold vacuum and variations in exhaust backpressure.

The diaphragm on this valve has an internal air bleed hole which is held closed by a small spring when there is no exhaust backpressure. Engine vacuum opens the EGR valve against the pressure of a large. When manifold vacuum combines with negative exhaust backpressure, the vacuum bleed hole opens and the EGR valve closes. This valve will open if vacuum is applied with the engine not running.

The linear EGR valve is operated exclusively by the control module command. The control module monitors various engine parameters:
- Throttle Position Sensor (TPS)

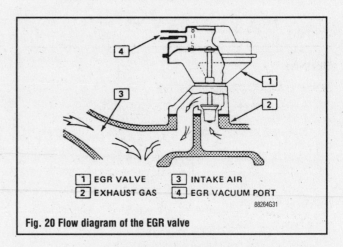

| 1 | EGR VALVE | 3 | INTAKE AIR |
| 2 | EXHAUST GAS | 4 | EGR VACUUM PORT |

88264G31

**Fig. 20 Flow diagram of the EGR valve**

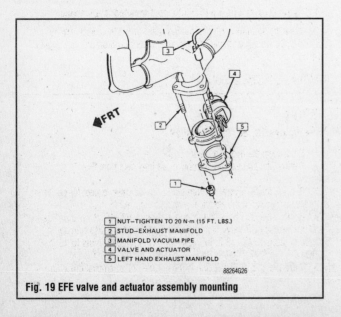

| 1 | NUT—TIGHTEN TO 20 N·m (15 FT. LBS.) |
| 2 | STUD—EXHAUST MANIFOLD |
| 3 | MANIFOLD VACUUM PIPE |
| 4 | VALVE AND ACTUATOR |
| 5 | LEFT HAND EXHAUST MANIFOLD |

88264G26

**Fig. 19 EFE valve and actuator assembly mounting**

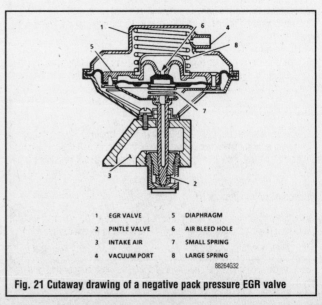

| 1 | EGR VALVE | 5 | DIAPHRAGM |
| 2 | PINTLE VALVE | 6 | AIR BLEED HOLE |
| 3 | INTAKE AIR | 7 | SMALL SPRING |
| 4 | VACUUM PORT | 8 | LARGE SPRING |

88264G32

**Fig. 21 Cutaway drawing of a negative pack pressure EGR valve**

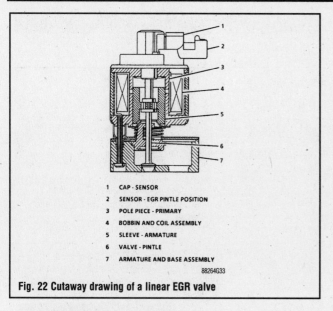

1  CAP - SENSOR
2  SENSOR - EGR PINTLE POSITION
3  POLE PIECE - PRIMARY
4  BOBBIN AND COIL ASSEMBLY
5  SLEEVE - ARMATURE
6  VALVE - PINTLE
7  ARMATURE AND BASE ASSEMBLY

88264G33

**Fig. 22 Cutaway drawing of a linear EGR valve**

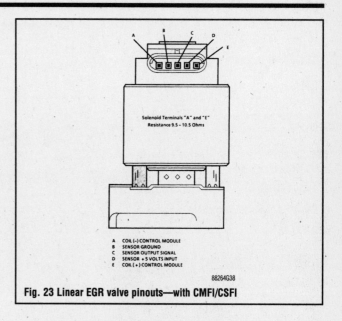

Solenoid Terminals "A" and "E"
Resistance 9.5 - 10.5 Ohms

A  COIL (−) CONTROL MODULE
B  SENSOR GROUND
C  SENSOR OUTPUT SIGNAL
D  SENSOR + 5 VOLTS INPUT
E  COIL (+) CONTROL MODULE

88264G38

**Fig. 23 Linear EGR valve pinouts—with CMFI/CSFI**

- Manifold Absolute Pressure (MAP)
- Engine Coolant Temperature (ECT) sensor
- Pintle position sensor

Output messages are then sent to the EGR system indicating the proper amount of exhaust gas recirculation necessary to lower combustion temperatures.

## TESTING

### EGR Valve

#### NEGATIVE BACKPRESSURE EGR VALVE

1. Remove the vacuum hose from the EGR valve.
2. Using a vacuum source, connect it to the EGR valve hose fitting and apply 10 in. Hg (33.8 kPa); the valve should lift off of its seat. If not, replace the EGR valve.
3. Clean the carbon deposits from the valve and intake manifold. With the valve removed, run the engine for 3–5 seconds to blow the carbon out of the intake manifold.

#### LINEAR EGR VALVE

▶ See Figures 23 and 24

1. Remove the electrical connector from the EGR valve.
2. Measure the resistance between terminals A and E.
3. The resistance should be 9.5–10.5 ohms. Replace the valve if that is not correct
4. Remove the EGR valve from the engine.
5. Measure the resistance between terminals B and C while moving the pintle in and out. The resistance should change in a smooth fashion without skips or jumps. Replace if necessary.

### EGR Control Solenoid

1. Disconnect the electrical connector from the solenoid.
2. Using an ohmmeter, measure the solenoid's resistance, it should be more than 20 ohms. If less than 20 ohms, replace the solenoid and/or possibly the ECM.

### Thermostatic Vacuum Switch

If the thermostatic vacuum switch is not working, a Code 32 will store in the ECM memory and a Service Engine Soon" lamp will light on the instrument panel.
1. Remove the TVS from the engine.
2. Using a vacuum gauge, connect it to one of the hose connections and apply 10 in. Hg (33.8 kPa).

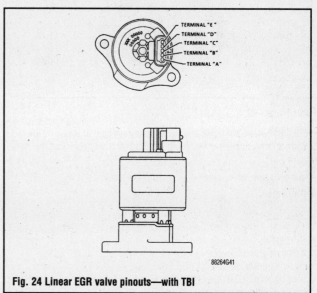

TERMINAL "E"
TERMINAL "D"
TERMINAL "C"
TERMINAL "B"
TERMINAL "A"

88264G41

**Fig. 24 Linear EGR valve pinouts—with TBI**

➡A vacuum drop of 2 in. Hg (6.7 kPa) in 2 minutes is allowable.

3. Place the tip of the switch in boiling water. When the switch reaches 195°F (91°C), the valve should open and the vacuum will drop; if not, replace the switch.

## REMOVAL & INSTALLATION

### EGR Valve

▶ See Figures 25, 26, 27, 28 and 29

1. Disconnect the negative battery cable.
2. Remove the air cleaner assembly or air inlet duct from the engine.
3. Remove the EGR valve vacuum tube from the valve, except for the linear EGR valves from which the electrical plug is disconnected.
4. Remove the EGR bolts and/or nuts and remove the EGR valve and gasket.
5. Install the EGR valve, using a new gasket to the EGR valve and tighten the bolts to 17–18 ft. lbs. (24–25 Nm) and/or the nuts to 15 ft. lbs. (20 Nm).
6. The remainder of installation is the reverse of the removal procedure.

1  EGR VALVE
2  GASKET
3  STUDS OR BOLTS
4  NUT - TIGHTEN TO 20 N·m (15 lb. ft.)

88264G44

**Fig. 25 Typical EGR mounting—4.3L TBI engine**

88264P04

**Fig. 26 Disconnect the vacuum hose and tag it for identification**

88264P05

**Fig. 27 A distributor wrench makes accessing the mounting hardware much easier**

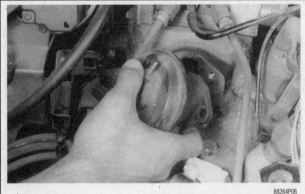

88264P06

**Fig. 28 Pull the EGR valve away along with the old gasket**

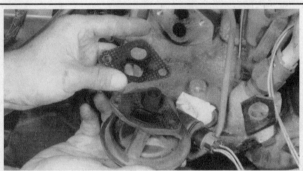

88264P07

**Fig. 29 Always use a new gasket when installing. Notice that this one is burned in the center**

## Air Injector Reactor (AIR) System

▶ See Figure 30

The AIR system injects compressed air into the exhaust system, near enough to the exhaust valves to continue the burning of the normally unburned segment of the exhaust gases. To do this, it employs an air injection pump and a system of hoses, valves, tubes, etc., necessary to carry the compressed air from the pump to the exhaust manifolds.

A diverter valve is used to prevent backfiring. The valve senses sudden increases in manifold vacuum and ceases the injection of air during rich periods. During coasting, this valve diverts the entire air flow through a muffler and during high engine speeds, expels it through a relief valve. Check valves in the system prevent exhaust gases from entering the pump.

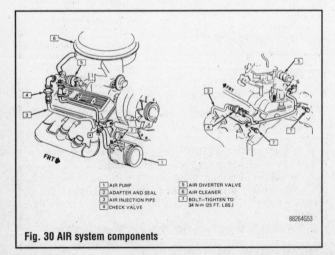

| 1 AIR PUMP | 5 AIR DIVERTER VALVE |
| 2 ADAPTER AND SEAL | 6 AIR CLEANER |
| 3 AIR INJECTION PIPE | 7 BOLT–TIGHTEN TO |
| 4 CHECK VALVE | 34 N·m (25 FT. LBS.) |

88264G53

**Fig. 30 AIR system components**

### TESTING

➡The AIR system is not completely silent under normal conditions. Noises will rise in pitch as engine speed increases. If the noise is excessive, eliminate the air pump itself by disconnecting the drive belt. If the noise disappears, the air pump is at fault.

#### Check Valve

To test the check valve, disconnect the hose at the diverter valve. Place your hand over the check valve and check for exhaust pulses. If exhaust pulses are present, the check valve must be replaced.

#### Diverter Valve

Pull off the vacuum line to the top of the valve with the engine running. There should be vacuum in the line, if not replace the line. No air should be escaping with the engine running at a steady idle. Open and quickly close the throttle. A blast of air should come out of the valve muffler for at least one second.

#### Air Pump

Disconnect the hose from the diverter valve. Start the engine and accelerate it to about 1500 rpm. The air flow should increase as the engine is accelerated. If no air flow is noted or it remains constant, check the following:

1. Drive belt tension.
2. Listen for a leaking pressure relief valve. If it is defective, replace the whole relief/diverter valve.
3. Foreign matter in pump filter openings. If the pump is defective or excessively noisy, it must be replaced.

## REMOVAL & INSTALLATION

### ♦ See Figures 31 and 32

All hoses and fittings should be inspected for condition and tightness of connections. Check the drive belt for wear and tension periodically.

### Air Pump

1. Disconnect the output hose.
2. Hold the pump from turning by squeezing the drive belt.
3. Loosen, but do not remove, the pulley bolts.
4. Loosen the alternator so the belt can be removed.
5. Remove the pulley.
6. Remove the pump mounting bolts and the pump.
7. Installation is the reverse of the removal procedure. Tighten the pump mounting bolts to 25 ft. lbs. (33 Nm) and the pulley bolts to 90 inch lbs. (10 Nm).
8. Check and adjust the belt tension.
9. Connect the hose. If any hose leaks are suspected, pour soapy water over the suspected area with the engine running. Bubbles will form wherever air is escaping.

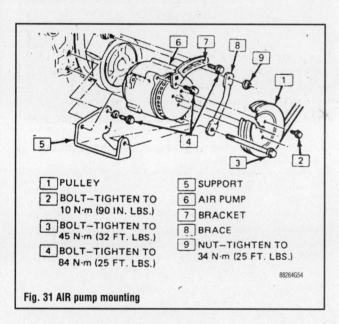

| 1 | PULLEY | 5 | SUPPORT |
|---|--------|---|---------|
| 2 | BOLT—TIGHTEN TO 10 N·m (90 IN. LBS.) | 6 | AIR PUMP |
| 3 | BOLT—TIGHTEN TO 45 N·m (32 FT. LBS.) | 7 | BRACKET |
| | | 8 | BRACE |
| 4 | BOLT—TIGHTEN TO 84 N·m (25 FT. LBS.) | 9 | NUT—TIGHTEN TO 34 N·m (25 FT. LBS.) |

88264G54

**Fig. 31 AIR pump mounting**

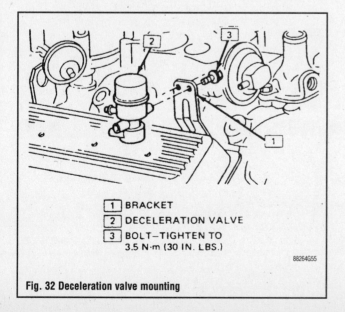

| 1 | BRACKET |
|---|---------|
| 2 | DECELERATION VALVE |
| 3 | BOLT—TIGHTEN TO 3.5 N·m (30 IN. LBS.) |

88264G55

**Fig. 32 Deceleration valve mounting**

## Filter

### ♦ See Figure 33

1. Remove the pump and the diverter valve as an assembly.

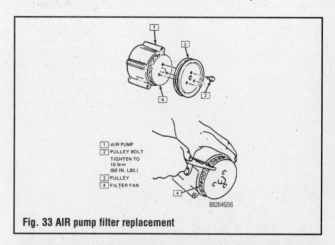

| 1 | AIR PUMP |
| 2 | PULLEY BOLT TIGHTEN TO 10 N·m (90 IN. LBS.) |
| 3 | PULLEY |
| 4 | FILTER FAN |

88264G56

**Fig. 33 AIR pump filter replacement**

### ✳✳ WARNING

**Do not clamp the pump in a vise or use a hammer or pry bar on the pump housing! Damage to the housing may result.**

2. To change the filter, break the plastic fan from the hub. It is seldom possible to remove the fan without breaking it. Wear safety glasses.
3. Remove the remaining portion of the fan filter from the pump hub. Be careful that filter fragments do not enter the air intake hole.
4. Installation is the reverse of the removal procedure. Tighten the screws alternately to 95 inch lbs. (10 Nm). Install the pump on the engine and adjust the drive belt.

## Thermostatic Air Cleaner

### OPERATION

### ♦ See Figure 34

This system is designed to warm the air entering the carburetor/TBI unit when underhood temperatures are low. This allows more precise calibration of the fuel system.

The thermostatically controlled air cleaner is composed of the air cleaner

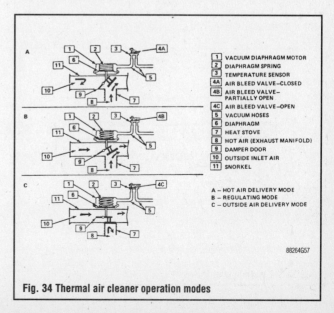

| 1 | VACUUM DIAPHRAGM MOTOR |
| 2 | DIAPHRAGM SPRING |
| 3 | TEMPERATURE SENSOR |
| 4A | AIR BLEED VALVE—CLOSED |
| 4B | AIR BLEED VALVE— PARTIALLY OPEN |
| 4C | AIR BLEED VALVE—OPEN |
| 5 | VACUUM HOSES |
| 6 | DIAPHRAGM |
| 7 | HEAT STOVE |
| 8 | HOT AIR (EXHAUST MANIFOLD) |
| 9 | DAMPER DOOR |
| 10 | OUTSIDE INLET AIR |
| 11 | SNORKEL |

A – HOT AIR DELIVERY MODE
B – REGULATING MODE
C – OUTSIDE AIR DELIVERY MODE

88264G57

**Fig. 34 Thermal air cleaner operation modes**

body, a filter, sensor unit, vacuum diaphragm, damper door and associated hoses and connections. Heat radiating from the exhaust manifold is trapped by a heat stove and is ducted to the air cleaner to supply heated air to the fuel system. A movable door in the air cleaner snorkel allows air to be drawn in from the heat stove (cold operation) or from the underhood air (warm operation). Periods of extended idling, climbing a grade or high speed operation are followed by a considerable increase in engine compartment temperature. Excessive fuel vapors enter the intake manifold causing an over-rich mixture, resulting in a rough idle. To overcome this, some engines may be equipped with a hot idle compensator.

## TESTING

1. Remove the air cleaner assembly and cool to below 40°F (4°C). The damper door should be closed to outside air.
2. Check for the presence and condition of the air cleaner gasket.
3. Reinstall the air cleaner assembly and check to make sure the heat stove tube is connected at the air cleaner snorkel and exhaust manifold.
4. Start the engine and watch the damper in the air cleaner snorkel. As the air cleaner warms up, the damper door should open slowly to the outside air.
5. If the damper fails to operate, check for vacuum at the port on the carburetor/TBI unit. If vacuum is not present, the port must be unclogged.
6. If vacuum was OK at the port, check for vacuum at the damper. If vacuum is present and the damper fails to operate, the vacuum diaphragm must be replaced. If vacuum is not present, the sensor unit in the air cleaner is probably faulty.

## REMOVAL & INSTALLATION

▶ **See Figure 35**

**Vacuum Diaphragm**

1. Remove the air cleaner.
2. If the truck uses a plastic heat tube elbow, use a ⅛ in. bit to drill out the two rivets that secure it to the heat tube and remove the elbow.

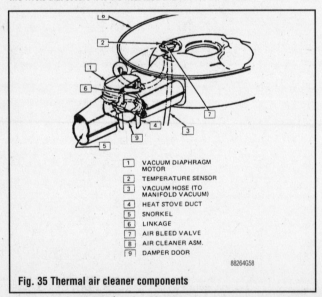

| 1 | VACUUM DIAPHRAGM MOTOR |
| 2 | TEMPERATURE SENSOR |
| 3 | VACUUM HOSE (TO MANIFOLD VACUUM) |
| 4 | HEAT STOVE DUCT |
| 5 | SNORKEL |
| 6 | LINKAGE |
| 7 | AIR BLEED VALVE |
| 8 | AIR CLEANER ASM. |
| 9 | DAMPER DOOR |

88264G58

**Fig. 35 Thermal air cleaner components**

3. Using a ⅛ in. drill bit again, drill out the two rivets that secure the vacuum diaphragm assembly.
4. Remove the blow down spring and the carrier assembly.
5. Examine the spring clip on the hot air damper. Replace if necessary.
**To install:**
6. Install a new assembly with two pop rivets. Install a new blow down spring.
7. Install the heat elbow with two rivets, if equipped. Install the air cleaner.

**Sensor Unit**

1. Remove the air cleaner.
2. Label and disconnect the vacuum hoses leading to the sensor.
3. Remove the two clips securing the sensor to the air cleaner.
**To install:**
4. Position the sensor on the air cleaner, then install the retaining clips.
5. Connect the vacuum hoses and install the air cleaner.

## Catalytic Converter

### OPERATION

The catalytic converter is a muffler-like container built into the exhaust system to aid in the reduction of exhaust emissions. The catalyst element is coated with a noble metal such as platinum, palladium, rhodium or a combination of them. When the exhaust gases come into contact with the catalyst, a chemical reaction occurs which reduces the pollutants into harmless substances such as water and carbon dioxide.

There are two types of catalytic converters: an oxidizing type and a three-way type. The oxidizing catalyst requires the addition of oxygen to spur the catalyst into reducing the engine's HC and CO emissions into $H_2O$ and $CO_2$.

### PRECAUTIONS

1. Use only unleaded fuel.
2. Avoid prolonged idling; the engine should run no longer than 20 min. at curb idle and no longer than 10 min. at fast idle.
3. Don't disconnect any of the spark plug leads while the engine is running. If any engine testing procedure requires disconnecting or bypassing a control component, perform the procedure as quickly as possible. A misfiring engine can overheat the catalyst and damage the oxygen sensor.
4. Make engine compression checks as quickly as possible.
5. Whenever under the vehicle or around the catalytic converter, remember that it has a very high outside or skin temperature. During operation, the catalyst must reach very high temperatures to work efficiently. Be very wary of burns, even after the engine has been shut off for a while. Additionally, because of the heat, never park the vehicle on or over flammable materials, particularly dry grass or leaves. Inspect the heat shields frequently and correct any bends or damage.
6. In the unlikely event that the catalyst must be replaced, DO NOT dispose of the old one where anything containing grease, gas or oil can come in contact with it. The catalytic action with these substances will result in heat which may start a fire.

## CARBURETED ELECTRONIC ENGINE CONTROLS

### Electronic Control Module (ECM)

▶ **See Figures 36 and 37**

### OPERATION

➥ **When the term Electronic Control Module (ECM) is used in this manual it will refer to the engine control computer regardless that it may be a Vehicle Control Module (VCM), Powertrain Control Module (PCM) or Engine Control Module (ECM).**

The ECM is a reliable solid state computer, protected in a metal box. It is used to monitor and control all the functions of the Computer Command Control (CCC) system and is located in the passenger side footwell at the kick panel. The ECM can perform several on-car functions at the same time and has the ability to diagnose itself as well as other CCC system circuits.

### REMOVAL & INSTALLATION

1. Disconnect the negative battery cable.
2. Disengage the connectors from the ECM.
3. Remove the ECM mounting hardware.

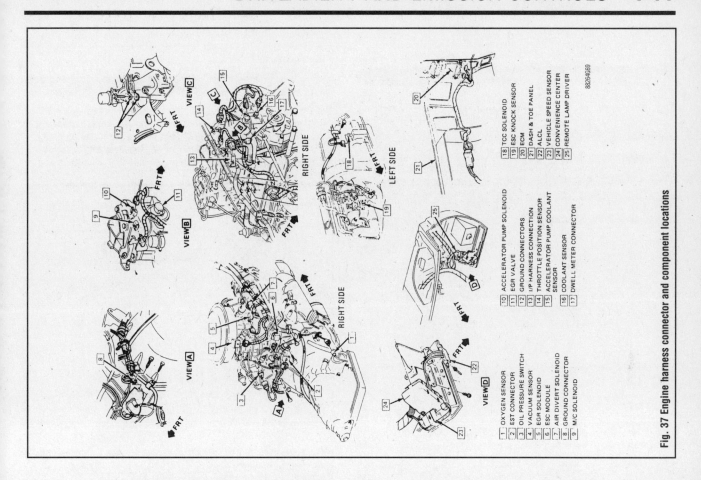

| | |
|---|---|
| 1 — OXYGEN SENSOR | 10 — ACCELERATOR PUMP SOLENOID | 18 — TCC SOLENOID |
| 2 — EST CONNECTOR | 11 — EGR VALVE | 19 — ESC KNOCK SENSOR |
| 3 — OIL PRESSURE SWITCH | 12 — GROUND CONNECTORS | 20 — ECM |
| 4 — VACUUM SENSOR | 13 — I/P HARNESS CONNECTION | 21 — DASH & TOE PANEL |
| 5 — EGR SOLENOID | 14 — THROTTLE POSITION SENSOR | 22 — ALCL |
| 6 — ESC MODULE | 15 — ACCELERATOR PUMP COOLANT SENSOR | 23 — VEHICLE SPEED SENSOR |
| 7 — AIR DIVERT SOLENOID | 16 — COOLANT SENSOR | 24 — CONVENIENCE CENTER |
| 8 — GROUND CONNECTOR | 17 — DWELL METER CONNECTOR | 25 — REMOTE LAMP DRIVER |
| 9 — M/C SOLENOID | | |

**Fig. 37 Engine harness connector and component locations**

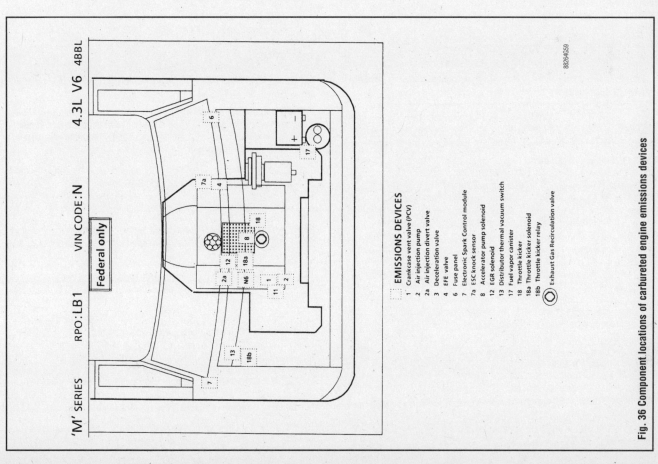

'M' SERIES   RPO: LB1   VIN CODE: N   4.3L V6   4BBL

Federal only

### EMISSIONS DEVICES

1  Crankcase vent valve (PCV)
2  Air injection pump
2a Air injection divert valve
3  Deceleration valve
4  EFE valve
6  Fuse panel
7  Electronic Spark Control module
7a ESC knock sensor
8  Accelerator pump solenoid
12 EGR solenoid
13 Distributor thermal vacuum switch
17 Fuel vapor canister
18 Throttle kicker
18a Throttle kicker solenoid
18b Throttle kicker relay
Exhaust Gas Recirculation valve

**Fig. 36 Component locations of carbureted engine emissions devices**

4. Remove the ECM from the passenger compartment.
5. Installation is the reverse of removal.

## Oxygen Sensor

### OPERATION

▶ **See Figure 38**

The oxygen sensor is a spark plug shaped device that is screwed into the exhaust pipe. It monitors the oxygen content of the exhaust gases and sends a voltage signal to the ECM. The ECM monitors this voltage and, depending on the value of the received signal, issues a command to the mixture control solenoid on the carburetor to adjust for rich or lean conditions.

The proper operation of the oxygen sensor depends upon four basic conditions:

1. Good electrical connections. Since the sensor generates low currents, good clean electrical connections at the sensor are a must.
2. Outside air supply. Air must circulate to the internal portion of the sensor. When servicing the sensor, do not restrict the air passages.
3. Proper operating temperatures. The ECM will not recognize the sensor's signals until the sensor reaches approximately 600°F (316°C).
4. Non-leaded fuel. The use of leaded gasoline will damage the sensor very quickly.

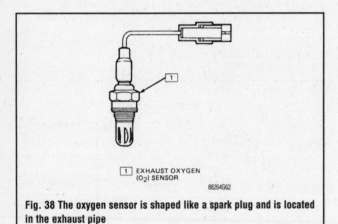

| 1 | EXHAUST OXYGEN (O₂) SENSOR |

88264G62

**Fig. 38 The oxygen sensor is shaped like a spark plug and is located in the exhaust pipe**

### TESTING

1. Start the engine and bring it to normal operating temperature, then run the engine above 1200 rpm for two minutes.
2. Backprobe with a high impedance averaging voltmeter (set to the DC voltage scale) between the oxygen sensor (O₂S) and battery ground.
3. Verify that the O₂S voltage fluctuates rapidly between 0.40–0.60 volts.
4. If the O₂S voltage is stabilized at the middle of the specified range (approximately 0.45–0.55 volts) or if the O₂S voltage fluctuates very slowly between the specified range (O₂S signal crosses 0.5 volts less than 5 times in ten seconds), the O₂S may be faulty.
5. If the O₂S voltage stabilizes at either end of the specified range, the ECM is probably not able to compensate for a mechanical problem such as a vacuum leak or a high float level. These types of mechanical problems will cause the O₂S to sense a constant lean or constant rich mixture. The mechanical problem will first have to be repaired and then the O₂S test repeated.
6. Pull a vacuum hose located after the throttle plate. Voltage should drop to approximately 0.12 volts (while still fluctuating rapidly). This tests the ability of the O₂S to detect a lean mixture condition. Reattach the vacuum hose.
7. Richen the mixture using a propane enrichment tool. Voltage should rise to approximately 0.90 volts (while still fluctuating rapidly). This tests the ability of the O₂S to detect a rich mixture condition.
8. If the O₂S voltage is above or below the specified range, the O₂S and/or the O₂S wiring may be faulty. Check the wiring for any breaks, repair as necessary and repeat the test.

### REMOVAL & INSTALLATION

▶ **See Figure 39**

#### ❋❋ WARNING

**The sensor uses a permanently attached pigtail and connector. This pigtail should not be removed from the sensor. Damage or removal of the pigtail or connector could affect the proper operation of the sensor. Keep the electrical connector and louvered end of the sensor clean and free of grease. NEVER use cleaning solvents of any type on the sensor!**

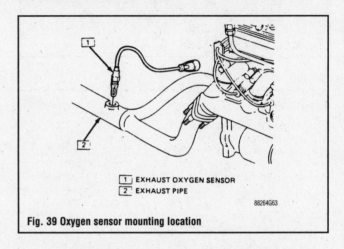

| 1 | EXHAUST OXYGEN SENSOR |
| 2 | EXHAUST PIPE |

88264G63

**Fig. 39 Oxygen sensor mounting location**

➡ **The oxygen sensor may be difficult to remove when the temperature of the engine is below 120°F (49°C). Excessive force may damage the threads in the exhaust manifold or exhaust pipe.**

1. Unplug the electrical connector and any attaching hardware.
2. Remove the sensor using an appropriate sized wrench or special socket.

**To install:**
3. Coat the threads of the sensor with a GM anti-seize compound, part number 5613695, or its equivalent, before installation. New sensors are usually precoated with this compound.

➡ **The GM anti-seize compound is NOT a conventional anti-seize paste. The use of a regular paste may electrically insulate the sensor, rendering it useless. The threads MUST be coated with the proper electrically conductive anti-seize compound.**

4. Install the sensor and tighten to 30 ft. lbs. (40 Nm). Use care in making sure the silicone boot is in the correct position to avoid melting it during operation.
5. Engage the electrical connector and attaching hardware if used.

## Coolant Temperature Sensor (CTS)

### OPERATION

▶ **See Figure 40**

The coolant temperature sensor is a thermistor (a resistor which changes value based on temperature). Low coolant temperatures produce high resistance (100,000 ohms at -40°F/-40°C) while low temperatures causes low resistance (70 ohms at 266°F/130°C). The sensor is mounted in the coolant stream and the ECM supplies a 5 volt signal to the sensor through a resistor in the ECM and measures the voltage. The voltage will be high when the engine is cold, and low when the engine is hot. By measuring the voltage, the ECM knows the engine coolant temperature effects most systems the ECM controls.

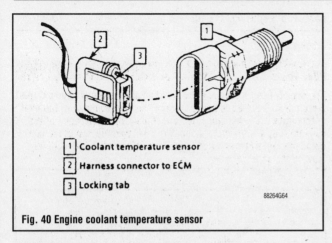

1 Coolant temperature sensor

2 Harness connector to ECM

3 Locking tab

88264G64

**Fig. 40 Engine coolant temperature sensor**

## TESTING

▶ **See Figure 41**

1. Remove the sensor from the vehicle.
2. Immerse the tip of the sensor in container of water.
3. Connect a digital ohmmeter to the two terminals of the sensor.
4. Using a calibrated thermometer, compare the resistance of the sensor to the temperature of the water. Refer to the engine coolant sensor temperature vs. resistance chart.
5. Repeat the test at two other temperature points, heating or cooling the water as necessary.
6. If the sensor does not meet specification, it must be replaced.

## REMOVAL & INSTALLATION

1. Disconnect the negative battery cable.
2. Drain the cooling system below the level of the sensor and disengage the sensor electrical connection.
3. Remove the coolant sensor.
4. Installation is the reverse of removal.

| TEMPERATURE TO RESISTANCE VALUES (APPROXIMATE) | | |
|---|---|---|
| °F | °C | OHMS |
| 210 | 100 | 185 |
| 160 | 70 | 450 |
| 100 | 38 | 1,600 |
| 70 | -20 | 3,400 |
| 40 | -4 | 7,500 |
| 20 | -7 | 13,500 |
| 0 | -18 | 25,000 |
| -40 | -40 | 100,700 |

88264G65

**Fig. 41 Coolant temperature sensor resistance chart**

## Differential Pressure (Vacuum) Sensor

### OPERATION

The differential pressure sensor measures the changes in intake manifold pressure, which result from the engine load and speed changes, and converts this to a voltage output. The differential pressure sensor operates opposite of a MAP sensor

A closed throttle on engine coastdown will produce a high output, while a wide-open throttle will produce a low output. This low output is produced because the pressure inside the manifold is the same as outside the manifold, so 100 percent of the outside air pressure is measured.

The ECM sends a 5 volt reference signal to the sensor. As the manifold pressure changes, the electrical resistance of the sensor also changes. By monitoring the sensor output voltage, the ECM knows the manifold pressure. A higher pressure, low vacuum (high voltage) requires more fuel, while a lower pressure, higher vacuum (low voltage) requires less fuel.

The ECM uses the sensor to control fuel delivery and ignition timing.

### TESTING

▶ **See Figure 42**

1. Backprobe with a high impedance voltmeter at sensor terminals A and C.
2. With the key **ON** and engine off, the voltmeter reading should be approximately 5.0 volts.
3. If the voltage is not as specified, either the wiring to the sensor or the ECM may be faulty. Correct any wiring or ECM faults before continuing test.
4. Backprobe with a high impedance voltmeter at MAP sensor terminals B and A.
5. Verify that the sensor voltage is less then 1.0 volts with the engine not running.
6. Start the vehicle.
7. Verify that the sensor voltage is greater than 3.0 volts at idle.
8. Verify that the sensor voltage drops at Wide Open Throttle (WOT).
9. If the sensor voltage is as specified, the sensor is functioning properly.
10. If the sensor voltage is not as specified, check the sensor and the sensor vacuum source for a leak or a restriction. If no leaks or restrictions are found, the sensor may be defective and should be replaced.

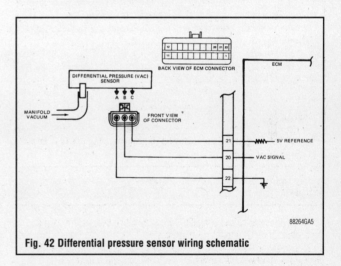

**Fig. 42 Differential pressure sensor wiring schematic**

### REMOVAL & INSTALLATION

▶ **See Figure 43**

1. Disconnect the negative battery cable.
2. Tag and disconnect the vacuum harness assembly.
3. Disengage the electrical connector.
4. Release the locktabs, unfasten the bolts and remove the sensor.
5. Installation is the reverse of removal.

## Throttle Position Sensor (TPS)

### OPERATION

The Throttle Position Sensor (TPS) is located inside the carburetor. It is a potentiometer with one wire connected to 5 volts from the ECM and the other to ground. A third wire is connected to the ECM to measure the voltage from the TPS.

As the accelerator pedal is moved, the output of the TPS also changes. At a

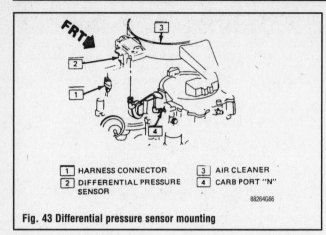

**1** HARNESS CONNECTOR
**2** DIFFERENTIAL PRESSURE
SENSOR
**3** AIR CLEANER
**4** CARB PORT "N"

88264G66

**Fig. 43 Differential pressure sensor mounting**

closed throttle position, the output of the TPS is low (approximately 0.5 volts). As the throttle valve opens, the output increases so that, at wide-open throttle, the output voltage should be approximately 4.5 volts.

By monitoring the output voltage from the TPS, the ECM can determine fuel delivery based on throttle valve angle (driver demand).

### TESTING

1. Backprobe with a high impedance voltmeter at TPS terminals A and B.
2. With the key **ON** and engine off, the voltmeter reading should be approximately 5.0 volts.
3. If the voltage is not as specified, either the wiring to the TPS or the ECM may be faulty. Correct any wiring or ECM faults before continuing test.
4. Backprobe with a high impedance voltmeter at terminals C and B.
5. With the key **ON** and engine off and the throttle closed, the TPS voltage should be approximately 0.5–1.2 volts.
6. Verify that the TPS voltage increases or decreases smoothly as the throttle is opened or closed. Make sure to open and close the throttle very slowly in order to detect any abnormalities in the TPS voltage reading.
7. If the sensor voltage is not as specified, replace the sensor.

### REMOVAL & INSTALLATION

The throttle position sensor is located in the carburetor. Please refer to Section 5 for the procedures to remove the TPS.

## Vehicle Speed Sensor (VSS)

### OPERATION

The vehicle speed sensor is sometimes located behind the speedometer or more commonly on the transmission. It sends a pulsing voltage signal to the ECM, which the ECM converts to vehicle speed. This sensor mainly controls the operation of the Torque Converter Clutch (TCC) system, shift light and cruise control.

### TESTING

1. Backprobe the VSS terminals with a high impedance voltmeter (set at the AC voltage scale).
2. Safely raise and support the entire vehicle using jackstands. Make absolutely sure the vehicle is secure.
3. Start the vehicle and place it in gear.
4. Verify that the VSS voltage increases as the speed increases.
5. If the VSS voltage is not as specified the VSS may be faulty.

### REMOVAL & INSTALLATION

1. Raise and safely support the vehicle.
2. Unplug the electrical connector.
3. Remove the sensor from the transmission or transfer case.
4. Installation is the reverse of removal.

## Knock Sensor

### OPERATION

▶ **See Figure 44**

Located in the engine block, the Knock Sensor (KS) retards ignition timing during a spark knock condition to allow the ECM to maintain maximum timing advance under most conditions.

### TESTING

1. Connect a timing light to the vehicle and start the engine.
2. Check that the timing is correct before testing knock sensor operation.
3. If timing is correct, tap on the front of the engine block with a metal object while observing the timing to see if the timing retards.
4. If the timing does not retard, the knock sensor may be defective.

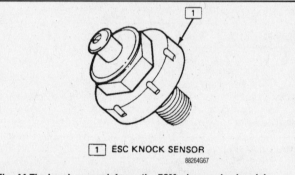

**1** ESC KNOCK SENSOR

88264G67

**Fig. 44 The knock sensor informs the ECM when engine knock is occurring by producing a voltage via a piezoelectric crystal inside the housing**

### REMOVAL & INSTALLATION

▶ **See Figure 45**

1. Disconnect the negative battery cable.
2. Disengage the wiring harness connector from the knock sensor.
3. Remove the knock sensor from the engine block.

**To install:**

4. Apply a water base caulk to the knock sensor threads and install the sensor in the engine block.

### ✳✳ WARNING

**Do not use silicon tape to coat the knock sensor threads as this will insulate the sensor from the engine block.**

5. Engage the wiring harness connector.
6. Connect the negative battery cable.

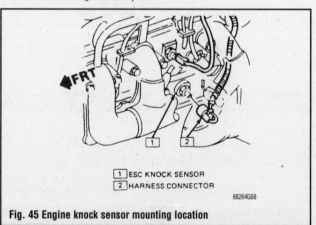

**1** ESC KNOCK SENSOR
**2** HARNESS CONNECTOR

88264G68

**Fig. 45 Engine knock sensor mounting location**

## FUEL INJECTED ELECTRONIC ENGINE CONTROLS

### Electronic Control Module (ECM)

#### OPERATION

➡When the term Electronic Control Module (ECM) is used in this manual it will refer to the engine control computer regardless that it may be a Vehicle Control Module (VCM), Powertrain Control Module (PCM) or Engine Control Module (ECM).

The Electronic Control Module (ECM) is required to maintain the exhaust emissions at acceptable levels. The module is a small, solid state computer which receives signals from many sources and sensors; it uses these data to make judgments about operating conditions and then control output signals to the fuel and emission systems to match the current requirements.

Engines coupled to electronically controlled transmissions employ a Powertrain Control Module (PCM) or Vehicle Control Module (VCM) to oversee both engine and transmission operation. The integrated functions of engine and transmission control allow accurate gear selection and improved fuel economy.

In the event of an ECM failure, the system will default to a pre-programmed set of values. These are compromise values which allow the engine to operate, although at a reduced efficiency. This is variously known as the default, limp-in or back-up mode. Driveability is almost always affected when the ECM enters this mode.

#### REMOVAL & INSTALLATION

▶ **See Figures 46 and 47**

The ECM is located in the passenger side footwell in the kick panel up to 1996. In 1996, the ECM is located in the engine compartment next to the battery.
1. Disconnect the negative battery cable.
2. Disengage the connectors from the ECM.
3. Remove the spring retainer off and over the rail of the ECM on vehicles except 1996.
4. Slide the ECM out of the bracket at an angle.
5. Remove the ECM.
6. Installation is the reverse of removal.

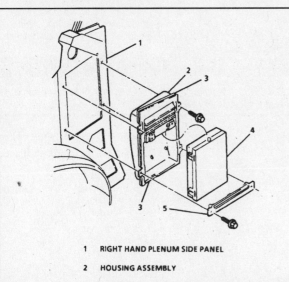

| | |
|---|---|
| 1 | RIGHT HAND PLENUM SIDE PANEL |
| 2 | HOUSING ASSEMBLY |
| 3 | SEAL |
| 4 | ELECTRONIC CONTROL MODULE |
| 5 | RETAINER |

88264G71

**Fig. 46 ECM mounting scheme—except 1996 models**

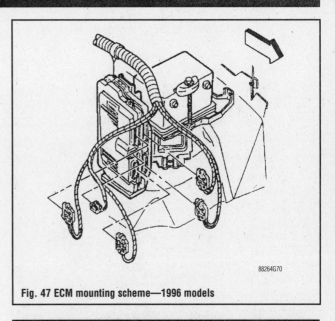

88264G70

**Fig. 47 ECM mounting scheme—1996 models**

### Oxygen Sensor

#### OPERATION

▶ **See Figure 48**

There are two types of oxygen sensors used in these vehicles. They are the single wire oxygen sensor ($O_2S$) and the heated oxygen sensor ($HO_2S$). The oxygen sensor is a spark plug shaped device that is screwed into the exhaust manifold. It monitors the oxygen content of the exhaust gases and sends a voltage signal to the Electronic Control Module (ECM). The ECM monitors this voltage and, depending on the value of the received signal, changes the injection parameters to maintain a proper air/fuel ratio. The 1996 models use 4 oxygen sensors. Two are used as inputs to adjust the mixture while the other two are used to monitor the condition of the catalytic converter.

The heated oxygen sensor has a heating element incorporated into the sensor to aid in the warm up to the proper operating temperature and to maintain that temperature.

The proper operation of the oxygen sensor depends upon four basic conditions:
1. Good electrical connections. Since the sensor generates low currents, good clean electrical connections at the sensor are a must.
2. Outside air supply. Air must circulate to the internal portion of the sensor. When servicing the sensor, do not restrict the air passages.
3. Proper operating temperatures. The ECM will not recognize the sensor's signals until the sensor reaches approximately 600°F (316°C).
4. Non-leaded fuel. The use of leaded gasoline will damage the sensor very quickly.

#### TESTING

**Single Wire Sensor**

1. Start the engine and bring it to normal operating temperature, then run the engine above 1200 rpm for two minutes.
2. Backprobe with a high impedance averaging voltmeter (set to the DC voltage scale) between the oxygen sensor ($O_2S$) and battery ground.
3. Verify that the $O_2S$ voltage fluctuates rapidly between 0.40–0.60 volts.
4. If the $O_2S$ voltage is stabilized at the middle of the specified range (approximately 0.45–0.55 volts) or if the $O_2S$ voltage fluctuates very slowly between the specified range ($O_2S$ signal crosses 0.5 volts less than 5 times in ten seconds), the $O_2S$ may be faulty.
5. If the $O_2S$ voltage stabilizes at either end of the specified range, the ECM is probably not able to compensate for a mechanical problem such as a vacuum

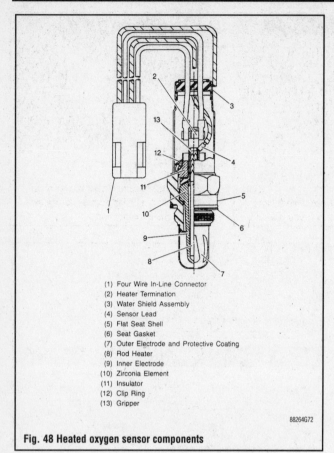

(1) Four Wire In-Line Connector
(2) Heater Termination
(3) Water Shield Assembly
(4) Sensor Lead
(5) Flat Seat Shell
(6) Seat Gasket
(7) Outer Electrode and Protective Coating
(8) Rod Heater
(9) Inner Electrode
(10) Zirconia Element
(11) Insulator
(12) Clip Ring
(13) Gripper

88264G72

**Fig. 48 Heated oxygen sensor components**

leak or a faulty pressure regulator. These types of mechanical problems will cause the $O_2S$ to sense a constant lean or constant rich mixture. The mechanical problem will first have to be repaired and then the $O_2S$ test repeated.

6. Pull a vacuum hose located after the throttle plate. Voltage should drop to approximately 0.12 volts (while still fluctuating rapidly). This tests the ability of the $O_2S$ to detect a lean mixture condition. Reattach the vacuum hose.

7. Richen the mixture using a propane enrichment tool. Voltage should rise to approximately 0.90 volts (while still fluctuating rapidly). This tests the ability of the $O_2S$ to detect a rich mixture condition.

8. If the $O_2S$ voltage is above or below the specified range, the $O_2S$ and/or the $O_2S$ wiring may be faulty. Check the wiring for any breaks, repair as necessary and repeat the test.

### Heated Oxygen Sensor

1. Start the engine and bring it to normal operating temperature, then run the engine above 1200 rpm for two minutes.

2. Turn the ignition **OFF** disengage the $HO_2S$ harness connector.

3. Connect a test light between harness terminals A and B on three wire sensors or C and D on four wire sensors. With the ignition switch **ON** and the engine off, verify that the test light is lit. If the test light is not lit, either the supply voltage to the $HO_2S$ heater or the ground circuit of the $HO_2S$ heater is faulty. Check the $HO_2S$ wiring and the fuse.

4. Next, connect a high impedance ohmmeter between the $HO_2S$ terminals B and A on 3 wire sensors or C and D on four wire sensors. Verify that the resistance is 3.5–14.0 ohms.

5. If the $HO_2S$ heater resistance is not as specified, the $HO_2S$ may be faulty.

6. Start the engine and bring it to normal operating temperature, then run the engine above 1200 rpm for two minutes.

7. Backprobe with a high impedance averaging voltmeter (set to the DC voltage scale) between the oxygen sensor ($O_2S$) and battery ground.

8. Verify that the $O_2S$ voltage fluctuates rapidly between 0.40–0.60 volts.

9. If the $O_2S$ voltage is stabilized at the middle of the specified range

(approximately 0.45–0.55 volts) or if the $O_2S$ voltage fluctuates very slowly between the specified range ($O_2S$ signal crosses 0.5 volts less than 5 times in ten seconds), the $O_2S$ may be faulty.

10. If the $O_2S$ voltage stabilizes at either end of the specified range, the ECM is probably not able to compensate for a mechanical problem such as a vacuum leak or a faulty fuel pressure regulator. These types of mechanical problems will cause the $O_2S$ to sense a constant lean or constant rich mixture. The mechanical problem will first have to be repaired and then the $O_2S$ test repeated.

11. Pull a vacuum hose located after the throttle plate. Voltage should drop to approximately 0.12 volts (while still fluctuating rapidly). This tests the ability of the $O_2S$ to detect a lean mixture condition. Reattach the vacuum hose.

12. Richen the mixture using a propane enrichment tool. Voltage should rise to approximately 0.90 volts (while still fluctuating rapidly). This tests the ability of the $O_2S$ to detect a rich mixture condition.

13. If the $O_2S$ voltage is above or below the specified range, the $O_2S$ and/or the $O_2S$ wiring may be faulty. Check the wiring for any breaks, repair as necessary and repeat the test.

### REMOVAL & INSTALLATION

▶ **See Figures 49, 50, 51 and 52**

**✳✳ WARNING**

**The sensor uses a permanently attached pigtail and connector. This pigtail should not be removed from the sensor. Damage or removal of the pigtail or connector could affect the proper operation of the sensor. Keep the electrical connector and louvered end of the sensor clean and free of grease. NEVER use cleaning solvents of any type on the sensor!**

➡**The oxygen sensor may be difficult to remove when the temperature of the engine is below 120°F (49°C). Excessive force may damage the threads in the exhaust manifold or exhaust pipe.**

1. Disconnect the negative battery cable.
2. Unplug the electrical connector and any attaching hardware.
3. Remove the sensor.
**To install:**
4. Coat the threads of the sensor with a GM anti-seize compound, part number 5613695, or its equivalent, before installation. New sensors are precoated with this compound.

➡**The GM anti-seize compound is NOT a conventional anti-seize paste. The use of a regular paste may electrically insulate the sensor, rendering it useless. The threads MUST be coated with the proper electrically conductive anti-seize compound.**

5. Install the sensor and tighten to 30 ft. lbs. (40 Nm). Use care in making sure the silicone boot is in the correct position to avoid melting it during operation.

6. Engage the electrical connector and connect the negative battery cable.

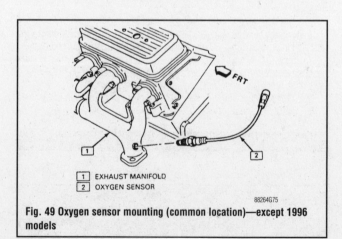

1 EXHAUST MANIFOLD
2 OXYGEN SENSOR

88264G75

**Fig. 49 Oxygen sensor mounting (common location)—except 1996 models**

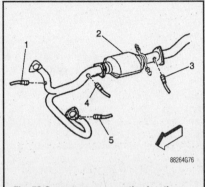

Fig. 50 Oxygen sensor mounting locations—1996 4.3L engine

Fig. 51 This oxygen sensor wrench has a cut out to allow the wires to pass through

Fig. 52 Do not contaminate the tip of the oxygen sensor or the accuracy of the sensor will be affected

## Crankshaft Position (CKP) Sensor

### OPERATION

The Crankshaft Position (CKP) Sensor provides a signal through the ignition module which the ECM uses as a reference to calculate rpm and crankshaft position.

### TESTING

1. Disconnect the CKP sensor harness. Connect an LED test light between battery ground and CKP harness terminal A.
2. With the ignition **ON** and the engine off, verify that the test light illuminates.
3. If not as specified, repair or replace the fuse and/or wiring.
4. Carefully connect the test light between CKP harness terminal A and B. Verify that the test light illuminates.
5. If not as specified, repair the CKP harness ground circuit (terminal B).
6. Turn the ignition **OFF** and disconnect the test light.
7. Next, connect suitable jumper wires between the CKP sensor and CKP sensor harness. Connect a duty cycle meter to the jumper wire corresponding to CKP terminal C and battery ground.
8. Crank the engine and verify that the duty cycle signal is between 40–60%.
9. If it is not as specified, the CKP sensor may be faulty.
10. Next, connect a AC volt meter to the jumper wire corresponding to CKP terminal C and battery ground.
11. Crank the engine and verify that the AC voltage signal is at least 10.0 volts.
12. If not as specified the CKP sensor may be faulty.

### REMOVAL & INSTALLATION

▶ See Figure 53

1. Disconnect the negative battery cable.
2. Detach the sensor harness connector at the sensor.
3. Unfasten the retaining bolt, then remove the sensor from the front cover. Inspect the sensor O-ring for wear, cracks or leakage and replace if necessary.
   **To install:**
4. Lubricate the O-ring with clean engine oil, then place on the sensor. Install the sensor into the front cover.
5. Tighten the retaining bolt and attach the sensor harness connector.
6. Connect the negative battery cable.

## Mass Air Flow (MAF) Sensor

### OPERATION

▶ See Figure 54

The Mass Air Flow (MAF) Sensor measures the amount of air entering the engine during a given time. The ECM uses the mass airflow information for fuel delivery calculations. A large quantity of air entering the engine indicates an

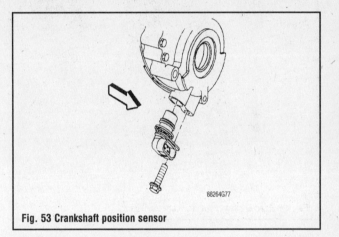

Fig. 53 Crankshaft position sensor

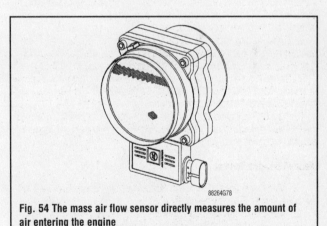

Fig. 54 The mass air flow sensor directly measures the amount of air entering the engine

acceleration or high load situation, while a small quantity of air indicates deceleration or idle.

### TESTING

1. Backprobe with a high impedance voltmeter between MAF sensor terminals C and B.
2. With the ignition **ON** engine off, verify that battery voltage is present.
3. If the voltage is not as specified, either the wiring to the MAF sensor, fuse or the ECM may be faulty. Correct any wiring or ECM faults before continuing test.
4. Disconnect the voltmeter and backprobe with a frequency meter between MAF sensor terminals A and B.
5. Start the engine and wait until it reaches normal idle speed and verify that the MAF sensor output is approximately 2000 Hz.

6. Slowly raise engine speed up to maximum recommended rpm and verify that the MAF sensor output rises smoothly to approximately 8000 Hz.

7. If MAF sensor output is not as specified the sensor may be faulty.

## REMOVAL & INSTALLATION

▶ See Figures 55 and 56

1. Disconnect the negative battery cable.
2. Unplug the electrical connector.
3. Remove the air intake hoses from the sensor, then remove its attaching bolts, if equipped on some versions.
4. Installation is the reverse of removal.

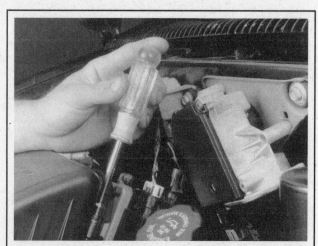

Fig. 55 This style MAF sensor is mounted directly behind the air cleaner assembly

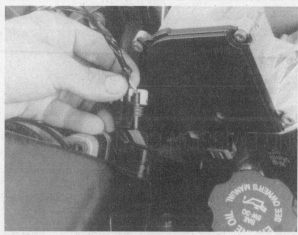

Fig. 56 Dirty contacts can cause the MAF to send bad signals to the ECM, so check it before installation

## Engine Coolant Temperature (ECT) Sensor

### OPERATION

▶ See Figure 57

The Engine Coolant Temperature (ECT) sensor is mounted near the thermostat housing and sends engine temperature information to the ECM. The ECM

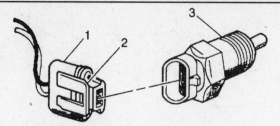

(1) ECT Electrical Connector
(2) Connector Tab
(3) Engine Coolant Temperature (ECT) Sensor

Fig. 57 Engine coolant temperature sensors are always mounted in a coolant passage, usually near the thermostat

supplies 5 volts to the coolant temperature sensor circuit. The sensor is a thermistor which changes internal resistance as temperature changes. When the sensor is cold (internal resistance high), the ECM monitors a high signal voltage which it interprets as a cold engine. As the sensor warms (internal resistance low), the ECM monitors a low signal voltage which it interprets as warm engine.

### TESTING

▶ See Figure 58

1. Remove the ECT sensor from the vehicle.
2. Immerse the tip of the sensor in container of water.
3. Connect a digital ohmmeter to the two terminals of the sensor.
4. Using a calibrated thermometer, compare the resistance of the sensor to the temperature of the water. Refer to the engine coolant sensor temperature vs. resistance illustration.
5. Repeat the test at two other temperature points, heating or cooling the water as necessary.
6. If the sensor does not met specification, it must be replaced.

| TEMPERATURE TO RESISTANCE VALUES (APPROXIMATE) | | |
|---|---|---|
| °F | °C | OHMS |
| 210 | 100 | 185 |
| 160 | 70 | 450 |
| 100 | 38 | 1,600 |
| 70 | -20 | 3,400 |
| 40 | -4 | 7,500 |
| 20 | -7 | 13,500 |
| 0 | -18 | 25,000 |
| -40 | -40 | 100,700 |

Fig. 58 Engine coolant temperature and Intake air temperature sensor resistance chart

### REMOVAL & INSTALLATION

▶ See Figures 59 and 60

1. Disconnect the negative battery cable.
2. Drain the cooling system below the level of the sensor and disengage the sensor electrical connection.
3. Remove the coolant sensor.
4. Installation is the reverse of removal.

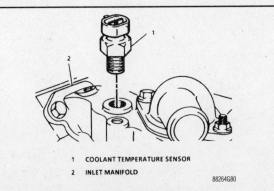

1  COOLANT TEMPERATURE SENSOR
2  INLET MANIFOLD

88264G80

**Fig. 59 The ECT is mounted in the intake manifold next to the thermostat housing on the V6 TBI engines**

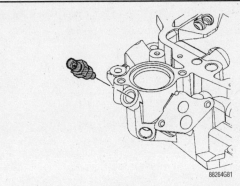

88264G81

**Fig. 60 The ECT is mounted in the lower intake manifold in the thermostat housing on the V6 engines**

## Intake Air Temperature (IAT) Sensor

### OPERATION

▶ **See Figure 61**

The Intake Air Temperature (IAT) Sensor is a thermistor which changes value based on the temperature of the air entering the engine. Low temperature produces a high resistance, while a high temperature causes a low resistance. The ECM supplies a 5 volt signal to the sensor through a resistor in the ECM and measures the voltage. The voltage will be high when the incoming air is cold, and low when the air is hot. By measuring the voltage, the ECM calculates the incoming air temperature.

The IAT sensor signal is used to adjust spark timing according to incoming air density.

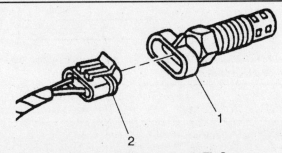

(1)  Intake Air Temperature (IAT) Sensor
(2)  Electrical Harness Connector

88264G82

**Fig. 61 Typical intake air temperature sensor**

### TESTING

▶ **See Figure 58**

1. Remove the Intake Air Temperature (IAT) sensor.
2. Connect a digital ohmmeter to the two terminals of the sensor.
3. Using a calibrated thermometer, compare the resistance of the sensor to the temperature of the ambient air. Refer to the temperature vs. resistance illustration.
4. Repeat the test at two other temperature points, heating or cooling the air as necessary with a hair dryer or other suitable tool.
5. If the sensor does not meet specification, it must be replaced.

### REMOVAL & INSTALLATION

▶ **See Figures 62, 63 and 64**

1. Disconnect the negative battery cable.
2. Disengage the sensor electrical connection.
3. Loosen and remove the IAT sensor.
4. Installation is the reverse of removal.

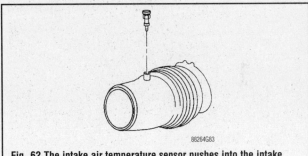

88264G83

**Fig. 62 The intake air temperature sensor pushes into the intake duct on the CMFI engines**

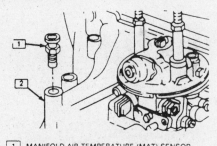

1  MANIFOLD AIR TEMPERATURE (MAT) SENSOR
   (APPLY SEALER TO THREADS ONLY)
2  ENGINE INTAKE MANIFOLD

88264G84

**Fig. 63 The intake air temperature sensor screws into the intake manifold on the 4–cylinder engine**

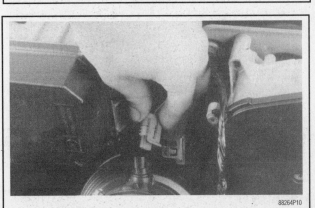

88264P10

**Fig. 64 Intake air temperature sensor location on 1996 CSFI engine**

## Throttle Position Sensor (TPS)

### OPERATION

The Throttle Position Sensor (TPS) is connected to the throttle shaft on the throttle body. It is a potentiometer with one end connected to 5 volts from the ECM and the other to ground.

A third wire is connected to the ECM to measure the voltage from the TPS. As the throttle valve angle is changed (accelerator pedal moved), the output of the TPS also changes. At a closed throttle position, the output of the TPS is low (approximately .5 volts). As the throttle valve opens, the output increases so that, at wide-open throttle, the output voltage should be approximately 4.5 volts.

By monitoring the output voltage from the TPS, the ECM can determine fuel delivery based on throttle valve angle (driver demand).

### TESTING

▶ **See Figure 65**

1. Backprobe with a high impedance voltmeter at TPS terminals A and B.
2. With the key **ON** and engine off, the voltmeter reading should be approximately 5.0 volts.
3. If the voltage is not as specified, either the wiring to the TPS or the ECM may be faulty. Correct any wiring or ECM faults before continuing test.
4. Backprobe with a high impedance voltmeter at terminals C and B.
5. With the key **ON** and engine off and the throttle closed, the TPS voltage should be approximately 0.5–1.2 volts.
6. Verify that the TPS voltage increases or decreases smoothly as the throttle is opened or closed. Make sure to open and close the throttle very slowly in order to detect any abnormalities in the TPS voltage reading.
7. If the sensor voltage is not as specified, replace the sensor.

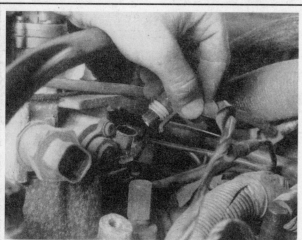

Fig. 65 Most testing of the TPS can be done while it is still mounted on the throttle body

### REMOVAL & INSTALLATION

▶ **See Figures 66 and 67**

1. Disconnect the negative battery cable and remove the air cleaner and gasket.
2. Disengage the electrical connector.
3. Unfasten the one or two TPS attaching screw assemblies.
4. Remove the TPS from the throttle body assembly.
5. Remove the TPS seal.

**To install:**
6. Install the TPS seal over the throttle shaft.
7. With the throttle valve closed, install the TPS on the throttle shaft. Rotate it counterclockwise, to align the mounting holes.

Fig. 66 Even though the TPS is not adjustable, marking its location before removal is a good idea

Fig. 67 Use the correct size bit in the mounting screws. This one just might strip out the screw

8. Install the 2 TPS attaching screw assemblies.
9. Engage the electrical connector.
10. Install the air cleaner and gasket and connect the negative battery cable.

## Manifold Absolute Pressure (MAP) Sensor

### OPERATION

The Manifold Absolute Pressure (MAP) sensor measures the changes in intake manifold pressure, which result from the engine load and speed changes, and converts this to a voltage output.

A closed throttle on engine coast-down will produce a low MAP output, while a wide-open throttle will produce a high output. This high output is produced because the pressure inside the manifold is the same as outside the manifold, so 100 percent of the outside air pressure is measured.

The MAP sensor reading is the opposite of what you would measure on a vacuum gauge. When manifold pressure is high, vacuum is low. The MAP sensor is also used to measure barometric pressure under certain conditions, which allows the ECM to automatically adjust for different altitudes.

The ECM sends a 5 volt reference signal to the MAP sensor. As the manifold pressure changes, the electrical resistance of the sensor also changes. By monitoring the sensor output voltage, the ECM knows the manifold pressure. A higher pressure, low vacuum (high voltage) requires more fuel, while a lower pressure, higher vacuum (low voltage) requires less fuel.

The ECM uses the MAP sensor to control fuel delivery and ignition timing.

## TESTING

1. Backprobe with a high impedance voltmeter at MAP sensor terminals A and C.
2. With the key **ON** and engine off, the voltmeter reading should be approximately 5.0 volts.
3. If the voltage is not as specified, either the wiring to the MAP sensor or the ECM may be faulty. Correct any wiring or ECM faults before continuing test.
4. Backprobe with the high impedance voltmeter at MAP sensor terminals B and A.
5. Verify that the sensor voltage is approximately 0.5 volts with the engine not running (at sea level).
6. Record MAP sensor voltage with the key **ON** and engine off.
7. Start the vehicle.
8. Verify that the sensor voltage is greater than 1.5 volts (above the recorded reading) at idle.
9. Verify that the sensor voltage increases to approximately 4.5. volts (above the recorded reading) at Wide Open Throttle (WOT).
10. If the sensor voltage is as specified, the sensor is functioning properly.
11. If the sensor voltage is not as specified, check the sensor and the sensor vacuum source for a leak or a restriction. If no leaks or restrictions are found, the sensor may be defective and should be replaced.

## REMOVAL & INSTALLATION

▶ **See Figures 68, 69 and 70**

1. Disconnect the negative battery cable.
2. Tag and disconnect the vacuum harness assembly, except 1996.
3. Disengage the electrical connector.
4. Release the locktabs, unfasten the bolts and remove the sensor.
5. Installation is the reverse of removal.

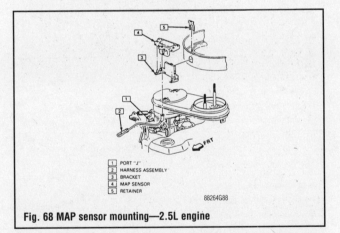

| 1 | PORT "J" |
| 2 | HARNESS ASSEMBLY |
| 3 | BRACKET |
| 4 | MAP SENSOR |
| 5 | RETAINER |

88264G88

**Fig. 68 MAP sensor mounting—2.5L engine**

## Vehicle Speed Sensor (VSS)

## OPERATION

▶ **See Figure 71**

The vehicle speed sensor is made up of a coil mounted on the transmission and a tooth rotor mounted to the output shaft of the transmission. As each tooth nears the coil, the coil produces an AC voltage pulse. As the vehicle speed increases the number of voltage pulses per second increases.

## TESTING

1. To test the VSS, backprobe the VSS terminals with a high impedance voltmeter (set at the AC voltage scale).

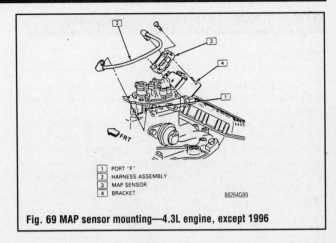

| 1 | PORT "F" |
| 2 | HARNESS ASSEMBLY |
| 3 | MAP SENSOR |
| 4 | BRACKET |

88264G89

**Fig. 69 MAP sensor mounting—4.3L engine, except 1996**

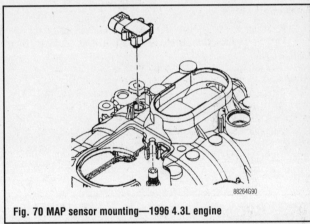

88264G90

**Fig. 70 MAP sensor mounting—1996 4.3L engine**

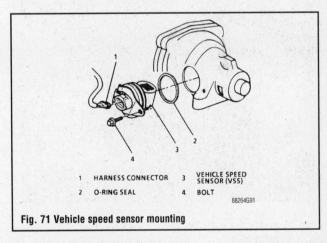

| 1 | HARNESS CONNECTOR | 3 | VEHICLE SPEED SENSOR (VSS) |
| 2 | O-RING SEAL | 4 | BOLT |

88264G91

**Fig. 71 Vehicle speed sensor mounting**

2. Safely raise and support the entire vehicle using jackstands. Make absolutely sure the vehicle is stable.
3. Start the vehicle and place it in gear.
4. Verify that the VSS voltage increases as the driveshaft speed increases.
5. If the VSS voltage is not as specified the VSS may be faulty.

## REMOVAL & INSTALLATION

1. Disconnect the negative battery cable.
2. Disengage the electrical connection.
3. Unfasten the sensor retainers.
4. Remove the sensor and gasket or O-ring.
5. Installation is the reverse of removal. Install the sensor with a new gasket or O-ring.

## Knock Sensor

### OPERATION

Located in the engine block, the knock sensor retards ignition timing during a spark knock condition to allow the ECM to maintain maximum timing advance under most conditions.

### TESTING

1. Connect a timing light to the vehicle and start the engine.
2. Check that the timing is correct before testing knock sensor operation.
3. If timing is correct, tap on the front of the engine block with a metal object while observing the timing to see if the timing retards.
4. If the timing does not retard, the knock sensor may be defective.

### REMOVAL & INSTALLATION

♦ **See Figure 72**

1. Disconnect the negative battery cable.
2. Disengage the wiring harness connector from the knock sensor.
3. Remove the knock sensor from the engine block.
**To install:**
4. Apply a water base caulk to the knock sensor threads and install the sensor in the engine block.

### ❋❋ WARNING

**Do not use silicon tape to coat the knock sensor threads as this will insulate the sensor from the engine block.**

5. Engage the wiring harness connector.
6. Connect the negative battery cable.

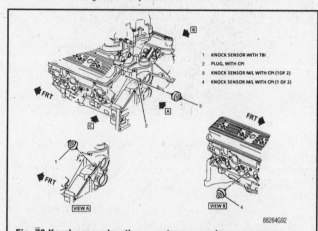

1 KNOCK SENSOR WITH TBI
2 PLUG, WITH CPI
3 KNOCK SENSOR M/L WITH CPI (1 OF 2)
4 KNOCK SENSOR M/L WITH CPI (1 OF 2)

88264G92

**Fig. 72 Knock sensor locations—note your engine may use one or more**

## TROUBLE CODES

### General Information

Since the control module is programmed to recognize the presence and value of electrical inputs, it will also note the lack of a signal or a radical change in values. It will, for example, react to the loss of signal from the vehicle speed sensor or note that engine coolant temperature has risen beyond acceptable (programmed) limits. Once a fault is recognized, a numeric code is assigned and held in memory. The dashboard warning lamp: CHECK ENGINE or SERVICE ENGINE SOON (SES), will illuminate to advise the operator that the system has detected a fault. This lamp is also known as the Malfunction Indicator Lamp (MIL).

More than one code may be stored. Keep in mind not every engine uses every code. Additionally, the same code may carry different meanings relative to each engine or engine family.

In the event of an computer control module failure, the system will default to a pre-programmed set of values. These are compromise values which allow the engine to operate, although possibly at reduced efficiency. This is variously known as the default, limp-in or back-up mode. Driveability is almost always affected when the ECM enters this mode.

### SCAN TOOLS

♦ **See Figures 73, 74 and 75**

On most models, the stored codes may be read with only the use of a small jumper wire, however the use of a hand-held scan tool such as GM's TECH-1® or equivalent is recommended. On 1996 models, an OBD-II compliant scan tool must be used. There are many manufacturers of these tools; a purchaser must be certain that the tool is proper for the intended use. If you own a scan type tool, it probably came with comprehensive instructions on proper use. Be sure to follow the instructions that came with your unit if they differ from what is given here; this is a general guide with useful information included.

The scan tool allows any stored codes to be read from the ECM or PCM memory. The tool also allows the operator to view the data being sent to the computer control module while the engine is running. This ability has obvious diagnostic advantages; the use of the scan tool is frequently required for component testing. The scan tool makes collecting information easier; the data must be correctly interpreted by an operator familiar with the system.

An example of the usefulness of the scan tool may be seen in the case of a temperature sensor which has changed its electrical characteristics. The ECM is reacting to an apparently warmer engine (causing a driveability problem), but the sensor's voltage has not changed enough to set a fault code. Connecting the scan tool, the voltage signal being sent to the ECM may be viewed; comparison to normal values or a known good vehicle reveals the problem quickly.

### ELECTRICAL TOOLS

The most commonly required electrical diagnostic tool is the digital multimeter, allowing voltage, ohmage (resistance) and amperage to be read by one

| "SCAN" Position | Units Displayed | Typical Data Value |
|---|---|---|
| Engine Speed | Rpm | ± 50 RPM from desired rpm in drive (A/T) ± 100 RPM from desired rpm in neutral (M/T) |
| Desired Idle | Rpm | ECM idle command (varies with temp.) |
| Coolant Temperature | Degrees Celsius | 85° - 105° |
| IAT/MAT | Degrees Celsius | 10° - 90° (varies with underhood temp. and sensor location) |
| MAP | kPa/Volts | 29-48 kPa/1 - 2 volts (varies with manifold and barometric pressures) |
| Open/Closed Loop | Open/Closed | "Closed Loop" (may enter "Open Loop" with extended idle) |
| Throt Position | Volts | .30 - 1.33 |
| Throttle Angle | 0 - 100% | 0 |
| Oxygen Sensor | Millivolts | 100 - 999 (varies continuously) |
| Inj. Pulse Width | Milliseconds | .8 - 3.0 |
| Spark Advance | Degrees | Varies |
| Engine Speed | Rpm | ± 50 RPM from desired rpm in drive (A/T) ± 100 RPM from desired rpm in neutral (M/T) |
| Fuel Integrator | Counts | 110-145 |
| Block Learn | Counts | 118-138 |
| Idle Air Control | Counts (steps) | 1 - 50 |
| P/N Switch | P-N and R-D-L | Park/Neutral (P/N) |
| MPH/KPH | 0-255 | 0 |
| TCC | "ON"/"OFF" | "OFF" |
| Crank Rpm | Rpm | 〉796 |
| Ign/Batt Voltage | Volts | 13.5 - 14.5 |
| Cooling Fan Relay | "ON"/"OFF" | "OFF" (coolant temperature below 102°C) |
| A/C Request | "YES"/"NO" | No |
| A/C Clutch | "ON"/"OFF" | "OFF" |
| Power Steering | Normal/High Pressure | Normal |
| Shift Light (M/T) | "ON"/"OFF" | "OFF" |

84904059

**Fig. 73 Example of scan tool data and typical or baseline values**

**Fig. 74 Different types of computerized test equipment are available from aftermarket tool manufacturers**

**Fig. 75 Inexpensive scan tools, such as this Auto X-ray®, can interface with your General Motors vehicle**

instrument. The multimeter must be a high-impedance unit, with 10 megohms of impedance in the voltmeter. This type of meter will not place an additional load on the circuit it is testing; this is extremely important in low voltage circuits. The multimeter must be of high quality in all respects. It should be handled carefully and protected from impact or damage. Replace batteries frequently in the unit.

Other necessary tools include an unpowered test light, a quality tachometer with an inductive (clip-on) pick up, and the proper tools for releasing GM's Metri-Pack, Weather Pack and Micro-Pack terminals as necessary. The Micro-Pack connectors are used at the ECM electrical connector. A vacuum pump/gauge may also be required for checking sensors, solenoids and valves.

## Diagnosis and Testing

Diagnosis of a driveability and/or emissions problem requires attention to detail and following the diagnostic procedures in the correct order. Resist the temptation to perform any repairs before performing the preliminary diagnostic steps. In many cases this will shorten diagnostic time and often cure the problem without electronic testing.

The proper troubleshooting procedure for these vehicles is as follows:

### VISUAL/PHYSICAL INSPECTION

This is possibly the most critical step of diagnosis and should be performed immediately after retrieving any codes. A detailed examination of connectors, wiring and vacuum hoses can often lead to a repair without further diagnosis. Performance of this step relies on the skill of the technician performing it; a careful inspector will check the undersides of hoses as well as the integrity of hard-to-reach hoses blocked by the air cleaner or other component. Wiring

should be checked carefully for any sign of strain, burning, crimping, or terminal pull-out from a connector. Checking connectors at components or in harnesses is required; usually, pushing them together will reveal a loose fit.

### INTERMITTENTS

If a fault occurs intermittently, such as a loose connector pin breaking contact as the vehicle hits a bump, the ECM will note the fault as it occurs and energize the dash warning lamp. If the problem self-corrects, as with the terminal pin again making contact, the dash lamp will extinguish after 10 seconds but a code will remain stored in the computer control module's memory.

When an unexpected code appears during diagnostics, it may have been set during an intermittent failure that self-corrected; the codes are still useful in diagnosis and should not be discounted.

### CIRCUIT/COMPONENT REPAIR

The fault codes and the scan tool data will lead to diagnosis and checking of a particular circuit. It is important to note that the fault code indicates a fault or loss of signal in an ECM-controlled system, not necessarily in the specific component.

Refer to the appropriate Diagnostic Code chart to determine the codes meaning. The component may then be tested following the appropriate component test procedures found in this section. If the component is OK, check the wiring for shorts or opens. Further diagnoses should be left to an experienced driveability technician.

If a code indicates the ECM to be faulty and the ECM is replaced, but does not correct the problem, one of the following may be the reason:

• There is a problem with the ECM terminal connections: The terminals may have to be removed from the connector in order to check them properly.

• The ECM or PROM is not correct for the application: The incorrect ECM or PROM may cause a malfunction and may or may not set a code.

• The problem is intermittent: This means that the problem is not present at the time the system is being checked. In this case, make a careful physical inspection of all portions of the system involved.

• Shorted solenoid, relay coil or harness: Solenoids and relays are turned on and off by the ECM using internal electronic switches called drivers. Each driver is part of a group of four called Quad-Drivers. A shorted solenoid, relay coil or harness may cause an ECM to fail, and a replacement ECM to fail when it is installed. Use a short tester, J34696, BT 8405, or equivalent, as a fast, accurate means of checking for a short circuit.

• The Programmable Read Only Memory (PROM) may be faulty: Although the PROM rarely fails, it operates as part of the ECM. Therefore, it could be the cause of the problem. Substitute a known good PROM.

• The replacement ECM may be faulty: After the ECM is replaced, the system should be rechecked for proper operation. If the diagnostic code again indicates the ECM is the problem, substitute a known good ECM. Although this is a very rare condition, it could happen.

## Reading Codes

### 1988–95 MODELS

▶ See Figures 76, 77, 78, 79 and 80

Listings of the trouble for the various engine control system covered in this manual are located in this section. Remember that a code only points to the

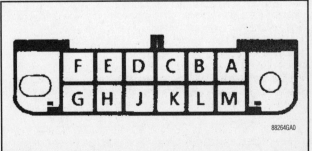

**Fig. 76 The ALDL connector is also known as the DLC**

## DIAGNOSTIC CODE IDENTIFICATION

The "Service Engine Soon" light will only be "ON" if the malfunction exists under the conditions listed below. If the malfunction clears, the light will go out and the code will be stored in the ECM/PCM. Any codes stored will be erased if no problem reoccurs within 50 engine starts.

| CODE AND CIRCUIT | PROBABLE CAUSE | CODE AND CIRCUIT | PROBABLE CAUSE |
|---|---|---|---|
| Code 13 - Oxygen $O_2$ Sensor Circuit (Open Circuit) | Indicates that the oxygen sensor circuit or sensor was open for one minute while off idle. | Code 33 - Manifold Absolute Pressure (MAP) Sensor Circuit (Signal Voltage High- Low Vacuum) | MAP sensor output to high for 5 seconds or an open signal circuit. |
| Code 14 - Coolant Temperature Sensor (CTS) Circuit (High Temperature Indicated) | Sets if the sensor or signal line becomes grounded for 3 seconds. | Code 34 - Manifold Absolute Pressure (MAP) Sensor Circuit (Signal Voltage Low- High Vacuum) | Low or no output from sensor with engine running. |
| Code 15 - Coolant Temperature Sensor (CTS) Circuit (Low Temperature Indicated) | Sets if the sensor, connections, or wires open for 3 seconds. | Code 35 - Idle Air Control (IAC) System | IAC error |
| Code 21 - Throttle Position Sensor (TPS) Circuit (Signal Voltage High) | TPS voltage greater than 2.5 volts for 3 seconds with less than 1200 RPM. | Code 42 - Electronic Spark Timing (EST) | ECM/PCM has seen an open or grounded EST or bypass circuit. |
| Code 22 - Throttle Position Sensor (TPS) Circuit (Signal Voltage Low) | A shorted to ground or open signal circuit will set code in 3 seconds. | Code 43 - Electronic Spark Control (ESC) Circuit | Signal to the ECM/PCM has remained low for too long or the system has failed a functional check. |
| Code 23 - Intake Air Temperature (IAT) Sensor Circuit (Low Temperature Indicated) | Sets if the sensor, connections, or wires open for 3 seconds | Code 44 - Oxygen ($O_2$) Sensor Circuit (Lean Exhaust Indicated) | Sets if oxygen sensor voltage remains below .2 volt for about 20 seconds. |
| Code 24 - Vehicle Speed Sensor (VSS) | No vehicle speed present during a road load deceleration. | Code 45 - Oxygen ($O_2$) Sensor Circuit (Rich Exhaust Indicated) | Sets if oxygen sensor voltage remains above .7 volt for about 1 minute. |
| Code 25 - Intake Air Temperature (IAT) Sensor Circuit (High Temperature Indicated) | Sets if the sensor or signal line becomes grounded for 3 seconds. | Code 51 - Faulty MEM-CAL, PROM, or ECM/PCM | Fuel CAL-PAK missing or faulty. |
| Code 32 - Exhaust Gas Recirculation (EGR) System | Vacuum switch shorted to ground on start up OR Switch not closed after the ECM/PCM has commanded EGR for a specified period of time. OR EGR solenoid circuit open for a specified period of time. | Code 52 - Fuel CALPAK Missing | System overvoltage. Indicates a basic generator problem. |
| | | Code 53 - System Over Voltage | Sets when the fuel pump voltage is less than 2 volts when reference pulses are being received. |
| | | Code 54 - Fuel Pump Circuit (Low Voltage) | Faulty ECM/PCM |
| | | Code 55 - Faulty ECM/PCM | |

88264G95

**Fig. 78 Fuel injected engine trouble codes through 1995, except with 4L60E and 4L80E transmissions**

## CODE IDENTIFICATION

The "Service Engine Soon" light will only be "ON" if the malfunction exists under the conditions listed below. If the malfunction clears, the light will go out and the code will be stored in the ECM. Any Codes stored will be erased if no problem reoccurs within 50 engine starts.

| CODE AND CIRCUIT | PROBABLE CAUSE | CODE AND CIRCUIT | PROBABLE CAUSE |
|---|---|---|---|
| Code 12 - No engine speed reference pulse. | No engine speed sensor reference pulses to the ECM. This code is not stored in memory and will only flash while the fault is present. Normal code with ignition "ON", engine not running. | Code 31 - MAP Sensor Too Low | Absolute Pressure (MAP) circuit signal voltage too low. Engine must run at curb idle for 10 seconds before this code will set. |
| Code 14 - Coolant Sensor High Temperature Indication | Sets if the sensor or signal line becomes grounded for 10 seconds. | Code 32 - EGR Loop Error | Exhaust Gas Recirculation (EGR) vacuum circuit has seen improper EGR vacuum. Vehicle must be running at road speed approximately 30 mph (48 Km/h) for 10 seconds before this code will set. |
| Code 15 - Coolant Sensor Low Temperature Indication | Sets if the sensor, connections, or wires open for 10 seconds. | Code 33 - MAP Sensor Too High | Absolute Pressure (MAP) circuit signal voltage too high. Engine must run at curb idle for 10 seconds before this code will set. |
| Code 21 - TPS Signal Voltage High | Throttle Position Sensor (TPS) circuit voltage high (open circuit or misadjusted TPS). Engine must run 30 seconds, at curb idle speed, before this code will set | Code 51 - PROM | Faulty or improperly installed PROM. It takes approximately 10 seconds before this code will set. |
| Code 22 - TPS Signal Voltage Low | Throttle Position Sensor (TPS) circuit voltage low (grounded circuit). Engine must run 2 minutes at 1250 rpm or above before this code will set. | Code 52 - ECM | Fault in ECM circuit. It takes 10 seconds before this code will set. |
| Code 23 - TPS Not Calibrated | Throttle Position Sensor (TPS) circuit. Voltage not between 25 and 1.3 volts at curb idle and Engine must run for 30 seconds, at curb idle, before this code will set. | Code 53 - Five volt Reference Overload | 5 volt reference (Vref) circuit overloaded (grounded circuit). It takes 10 seconds before this Code will set. |
| Code 24 - VSS No Vehicle Speed Indication | Vehicle speed sensor (VSS) circuit (open or grounded circuit). Vehicle must operate at road speed for 10 seconds before this code will set. | | |

88264G94

**Fig. 77 Carbureted engine trouble codes**

## DIAGNOSTIC TROUBLE CODE (DTC) IDENTIFICATION

The MIL (Service Engine Soon) will only be "ON" if the malfunction exists with the conditions listed below. If the malfunction clears, the lamp will go out and the DTC will be stored in the PCM. Any DTCs stored will be erased if no problem reoccurs within 50 engine starts

| DTC AND CIRCUIT | PROBABLE CAUSE | DTC AND CIRCUIT | PROBABLE CAUSE |
|---|---|---|---|
| DTC 51 - Faulty PROM (MEM-CAL) Problem | Faulty PROM (MEM-CAL) or PCM. | DTC 69 - TCC Stuck "ON" | Slip > -20 and slip 20 TCC is not locked gear ≠ 2, 3 or 4 TPS > 25%, not in P/R/N for 4 seconds. |
| DTC 53 - System Voltage High | System overvoltage of 19.5 volts for 2 seconds | DTC 72 - Vehicle Speed Sensor Loss | Not in P/N - Output speed changes greater than 1000 RPM • P/N - Output speed changes greater than 2050 RPM • For 2 seconds |
| DTC 54 - Fuel Pump Circuit (Low Voltage) | Sets when the fuel pump voltage is less than 2 volts when reference pulses are being received. | DTC 73 - Pressure Control Solenoid | If return amperage varies more than 0.16 amps from commanded amperage |
| DTC 55 - Faulty PCM | Faulty PCM. | DTC 75 - System Voltage Low | System voltage < 7.3 at low temperature or < 11.7 at high temperature for 4 seconds. |
| DTC 58 - Transmission Fluid Temperature High | Transmission fluid temperature greater than 154°C (309°F) for one second. | DTC 79 - Transmission Fluid Over Temperature | Transmission fluid Temperature > 150°C and < 154°C for 15 minutes. |
| DTC 59 - Transmission Fluid Temperature Low | Transmission fluid temperature greater than -33°C (-27°F) for one second. | DTC 81 - 2-3 Shift Solenoid Circuit Fault | 2-3 shift solenoid is command "ON", and circuit voltage is high for two seconds OR 2-3 shift solenoid is command "OFF", and circuit voltage is low for two seconds |
| DTC 66 - 3-2 Control Solenoid Circuit Fault | At High Duty Cycle the circuit voltage is high OR at Low Duty Cycle the Circuit Voltage is low for four seconds. | DTC 82 - 1-2 Shift Solenoid Circuit Fault | 1-2 shift solenoid is command "ON," and circuit voltage is high for two seconds OR 1-2 shift solenoid is command "OFF" and circuit voltage is low for two seconds |
| DTC 67 Torque Converter Clutch Circuit | TCC is commanded "ON" and circuit voltage remains high for two seconds OR TCC is commanded "OFF" and circuit voltage remains low for two seconds. | | |

Fig. 80 Fuel injected engine trouble codes through 1995 with 4L60E transmissions (continued)

## DIAGNOSTIC TROUBLE CODE (DTC) IDENTIFICATION

The MIL (Service Engine Soon) will only be "ON" if the malfunction exists with the conditions listed below. If the malfunction clears, the lamp will go out and the DTC will be stored in the PCM. Any DTCs stored will be erased if no problem reoccurs within 50 engine starts.

| DTC AND CIRCUIT | PROBABLE CAUSE | DTC AND CIRCUIT | PROBABLE CAUSE |
|---|---|---|---|
| DTC 13 - Oxygen O2S Sensor Circuit (Open Circuit) | Indicates that the oxygen sensor circuit or sensor was open for one minute while off idle. | DTC 33 - Manifold Absolute Pressure (MAP) Sensor Circuit (Signal Voltage High - Low Vacuum) | MAP sensor output high for 5 seconds or an open signal circuit. |
| DTC 14 - Engine Coolant Temperature (ECT) Sensor Circuit (High Temperature Indicated) | Sets if the sensor or signal line becomes grounded or greater than 145°C (294°F) for 0.5 seconds. | DTC 34 - Manifold Absolute Pressure (MAP) Sensor Circuit (Signal Voltage Low- High Vacuum) | Low or no output from MAP sensor with engine operating. |
| DTC 15 - Engine Coolant Temperature (ECT) Sensor Circuit (Low Temperature Indicated) | Sets if the sensor, connections, or wires open or less than -33°C (-27°F) for 0.5 seconds. | DTC 35 - IAC | IAC error |
| DTC 16 - Transmission Output Speed Low | Open in CKT 1697/1716 or power loss to VSS buffer | DTC 37 - Brake Switch Stuck On | With no voltage and vehicle speed is less than 5 mph for 6 seconds, then vehicle speed is 5 - 20 MPH for 6 seconds, then vehicle speed is greater than 20 MPH for 6 seconds, this must occur for 7 times. |
| DTC 21 - Throttle Position (TP) Sensor Circuit (Signal Voltage High) | TP voltage greater than 4.88 volts 4 seconds with less than 1200 RPM. | DTC 38 - Brake Switch Stuck Off | With voltage and vehicle speed is greater than 20 MPH for 6 seconds, then vehicle speed is 5 - 20 MPH for 6 seconds. This must occur 7 times. |
| DTC 22 - Throttle Position (TP) Sensor Circuit (Signal Voltage Low) | A short to ground,open signal circuit, or TP voltage less than 0.16 volts for 4 seconds. | DTC 42 - Ignition Control (IC) | PCM detects an open or grounded IC or bypass circuit. |
| DTC 24 - Vehicle Speed Sensor (VSS) Signal Low | No vehicle speed sensor signal present during a road load decel. | DTC 43 - Knock Sensor (KS) Circuit | Signal to the PCM has remained low for too long, or the system has failed a functional system check. |
| DTC 28 - Fluid Pressure Switch Assembly | PCM detects 1 of 2 invalid combinations of the fluid pressure switch range signals | DTC 44 - Oxygen Sensor (O2S) Circuit (Lean Exhaust Indicated) | Sets if oxygen sensor voltage remains less than 0.2 volt for 20 seconds. |
| DTC 32 - Exhaust Gas Recirculation (EGR) System | Vacuum switch shorted to ground on start up OR Switch not closed after the PCM has commanded EGR for a specified period of time. OR EGR solenoid circuit open for a specified period of time. | DTC 45 - Oxygen Sensor (O2S) Circuit (Rich Exhaust Indicated) | Sets if oxygen sensor voltage remains greater than 0.7 volt for about 1 minute. |

Fig. 79 Fuel injected engine trouble codes through 1995 with 4L60E transmissions

faulty circuit NOT necessarily to a faulty component. Loose, damaged or corroded connections may contribute to a fault code on a circuit when the sensor or component is operating properly. Be sure that the components are faulty before replacing them, especially the expensive ones.

The Assembly Line Diagnostic Link (ALDL) connector or Data Link Connector (DLC) may be located under the dash and sometimes covered with a plastic cover labeled DIAGNOSTIC CONNECTOR.

1. The diagnostic trouble codes can be read by grounding test terminal B. The terminal is most easily grounded by connecting it to terminal A (internal ECM ground). This is the terminal to the right of terminal B on the top row of the ALDL connector.

2. Once the terminals have been connected, the ignition switch must be moved to the **ON** position with the engine not running.

3. The Service Engine Soon or Check Engine light should be flashing. If it isn't, turn the ignition **OFF** and remove the jumper wire. Turn the ignition **ON** and confirm that light is now on. If it is not, replace the bulb and try again. If the bulb still will not light, or if it does not flash with the test terminal grounded, the system should be diagnosed by an experienced driveability technician. If the light is OK, proceed as follows.

4. The code(s) stored in memory may be read through counting the flashes of the dashboard warning lamp. The dash warning lamp should begin to flash Code 12. The code will display as one flash, a pause and two flashes. Code 12 is not a fault code. It is used as a system acknowledgment or handshake code; its presence indicates that the ECM can communicate as requested. Code 12 is used to begin every diagnostic sequence. Some vehicles also use Code 12 after all diagnostic codes have been sent.

5. After Code 12 has been transmitted 3 times, the fault codes, if any, will each be transmitted 3 times. The codes are stored and transmitted in numeric order from lowest to highest.

➡**The order of codes in the memory does not indicate the order of occurrence.**

6. If there are no codes stored, but a driveability or emissions problem is evident, the system should be diagnosed by an experienced driveability technician.

7. If one or more codes are stored, record them. Refer to the applicable Diagnostic Code chart in this section.

8. Switch the ignition **OFF** when finished with code retrieval or scan tool readings.

➡**After making repairs, clear the trouble codes and operate the vehicle to see if it will reset, indicating further problems.**

## 1996 MODELS

▶ **See Figures 81 and 82**

On 1996 models, an OBD-II compliant scan tool must be used to retrieve the trouble codes. Follow the scan tool manufacturer's instructions on how to connect the scan tool to the vehicle and how to retrieve the codes.

## Clearing Codes

Stored fault codes may be erased from memory at any time by removing power from the ECM for at least 30 seconds. It may be necessary to clear stored codes during diagnosis to check for any recurrence during a test drive, but the stored codes must be written down when retrieved. The codes may still be required for subsequent troubleshooting. Whenever a repair is complete, the stored codes must be erased and the vehicle test driven to confirm correct operation and repair.

## ✳✳ WARNING

**The ignition switch must be OFF any time power is disconnected or restored to the ECM. Severe damage may result if this precaution is not observed.**

Depending on the electrical distribution of the particular vehicle, power to the ECM may be disconnected by removing the ECM fuse in the fusebox, disconnecting the in-line fuse holder near the positive battery terminal or disconnecting the ECM power lead at the battery terminal. Disconnecting the negative battery cable to clear codes is not recommended as this will also clear other memory data in the vehicle such as radio presets.

DTC P0101 - Mass Air Flow (MAF) System Performance

DTC P0102 - Mass Air Flow (MAF) Sensor Circuit Low Frequency

DTC P0103 - Mass Air Flow (MAF) Sensor Circuit High Frequency

DTC P0106 - Manifold Absolute Pressure (MAP) System Performance

DTC P0107 - Manifold Absolute Pressure (MAP) Sensor Circuit Low Voltage

DTC P0108 - Manifold Absolute Pressure (MAP) Sensor Circuit High Voltage

P0112 - Intake Air Temperature (IAT) Sensor Circuit Low Voltage

P0113 - Intake Air Temperature (IAT) Sensor Circuit High Voltage

P0117 - Engine Coolant Temperature (ECT) Sensor Circuit Low Voltage

P0118 - Engine Coolant Temperature (ECT) Sensor Circuit High Voltage

P0121 - Throttle Position (TP) System Performance

P0122 - Throttle Position (TP) Sensor Circuit Low Voltage

P0123 - Throttle Position (TP) Sensor Circuit High Voltage

P0125 - Engine Coolant Temperature (ECT) Excessive Time to Closed Loop Fuel Control

P0131 - Heated Oxygen Sensor (HO2S) Circuit Low Voltage Bank 1, Sensor 1

P0132 - Heated Oxygen Sensor (HO2S) Circuit High Voltage Bank 1, Sensor 1

P0133 - Heated Oxygen Sensor (HO2S) Slow Response Bank 1, Sensor 1

P0134 - Heated Oxygen Sensor (HO2S) Circuit Insufficient Activity Bank 1, Sensor 1

P0135 - Heated Oxygen Sensor (HO2S) Heater Circuit Bank 1, Sensor 1

P0137 - Heated Oxygen Sensor (HO2S) Circuit Low Voltage Bank 1, Sensor 2

P0138 - Heated Oxygen Sensor (HO2S) Circuit High Voltage Bank 1, Sensor 2

P0140 - Heated Oxygen Sensor (HO2S) Circuit Insufficient Activity Bank 1, Sensor 2

P0141 - Heated Oxygen Sensor (HO2S) Heater Circuit Bank 1, Sensor 2

P0143 - Heated Oxygen Sensor (HO2S) Circuit Low Voltage Bank 1, Sensor 3

P0144 - Heated Oxygen Sensor (HO2S) Circuit High Voltage Bank 1, Sensor 3

P0146 - Heated Oxygen Sensor (HO2S) Circuit Insufficient Activity Bank 1, Sensor 3

P0147 - Heated Oxygen Sensor (HO2S) Heater Circuit Bank 1, Sensor 3

P0151 - Heated Oxygen Sensor (HO2S) Circuit Low Voltage Bank 2, Sensor 1

P0152 - Heated Oxygen Sensor (HO2S) Circuit High Voltage Bank 2, Sensor 1

P0153 - Heated Oxygen Sensor (HO2S) Slow Response Bank 2, Sensor 1

P0154 - Heated Oxygen Sensor (HO2S) Circuit Insufficient Activity Bank 2, Sensor 1

P0155 - Heated Oxygen Sensor (HO2S) Heater Circuit Bank 2, Sensor 1

P0157 - Heated Oxygen Sensor (HO2S) Circuit Low Voltage Bank 2, Sensor 2

P0158 - Heated Oxygen Sensor (HO2S) Circuit High Voltage Bank 2, Sensor 2

P0160 - Heated Oxygen Sensor (HO2S) Circuit Insufficient Activity Bank 2, Sensor 2

P0161 - Heated Oxygen Sensor (HO2S) Heater Circuit Bank 2, Sensor 2

P0171 - Fuel Trim System Lean Bank 1

P0172 - Fuel Trim System Rich Bank 1

P0174 - Fuel Trim System Lean Bank 2

P0175 - Fuel Trim System Rich Bank 2

P0300 - Engine Misfire Detected

P0301 - Cylinder 1 Misfire Detected

P0302 - Cylinder 2 Misfire Detected

P0303 - Cylinder 3 Misfire Detected

P0304 - Cylinder 4 Misfire Detected

P0305 - Cylinder 5 Misfire Detected

P0306 - Cylinder 6 Misfire Detected

P0307 - Cylinder 7 Misfire Detected

P0308 - Cylinder 8 Misfire Detected

P0325 - Knock Sensor (KS) Module Circuit

P0327 - Knock Sensor (KS) Circuit Low Voltage

P0336 - Crankshaft Position (CKP) Sensor Circuit Performance

P0337 - Crankshaft Position (CKP) Sensor Circuit Low Frequency

P0338 - Crankshaft Position (CKP) Sensor Circuit High Frequency

P0339 - Crankshaft Position (CKP) Sensor Circuit Intermittent

P0340 - Camshaft Position (CMP) Sensor Circuit

P0341 - Camshaft Position (CMP) Sensor Circuit Performance

P0401 - Exhaust Gas Recirculation (EGR) System

P0410 - AIR System

P0420 - Three Way Catalytic Converter (TWC) System Low-Efficiency Bank 1

P0430 - Three Way Catalytic Converter (TWC) System Low Efficiency Bank 2

P0441 - Evaporative Emission (EVAP) System No Flow During Purge

88264G98

**Fig. 81 Trouble code list for 1996 gasoline engines**

P0500 - Vehicle Speed Sensor (VSS)
Circuit

P0506 - Idle System Low - Idle Air Control (IAC)
Responding

P0507 - Idle System High - Idle Air Control (IAC)
Responding

P1106 - Manifold Absolute Pressure (MAP) Sensor
Circuit Intermittent High Voltage

P1107 - Manifold Absolute Pressure (MAP) Sensor
Circuit Intermittent Low Voltage

P1111 - Intake Air Temperature (IAT) Sensor
Circuit Intermittent High Voltage

P1112 - Intake Air Temperature (IAT) Sensor
Circuit Intermittent Low Voltage

P1114 - Engine Coolant Temperature (ECT)
Sensor Circuit Intermittent
Low Voltage

P1115 - Engine Coolant Temperature (ECT)
Sensor Circuit Intermittent
High Voltage

P1121 - Throttle Position (TP) Sensor Circuit
Intermittent High Voltage

P1122 - Throttle Position (TP) Sensor Circuit
Intermittent Low Voltage

P1133 - Heated Oxygen Sensor (HO2S)
Insufficient Switching Bank 1, Sensor 1

P1134 - Heated Oxygen Sensor (HO2S) Transition
Time Ratio Bank 1, Sensor 1

P1153 - Heated Oxygen Sensor (HO2S)
Insufficient Switching Bank 2, Sensor 1

P1154 - Heated Oxygen Sensor (HO2S) Transition
Time Ratio Bank 2, Sensor 1

P1345 - Crankshaft Position/Camshaft Position
(CKP/CMP) Correlation

P1351 - Ignition Control (IC) Circuit High
Voltage

P1361 - Ignition Control (IC) Circuit Low
Voltage

P1380 - Electronic Brake Control Module (EBCM)
DTC Detected - Rough Road Data
Unusable

P1381 - Misfire Detected - No Electronic Brake
Control Module (EBCM) VCM Serial
Data

P1406 - Exhaust Gas Recirculation (EGR) Valve
Pintle Position Circuit

P1415 - AIR System Bank 1

P1416 - AIR System Bank 2

P1441 - Evaporative Emission (EVAP) System
Flow During Non-Purge

P1508 - Idle Air Control (IAC) System Low
RPM

P1509 - Idle Air Control (IAC) System High
RPM

88264G99

**Fig. 82 Trouble code list for 1996 gasoline engines (continued)**

## VACUUM DIAGRAMS

Following is a listing of vacuum diagrams for many of the engine and emissions package combinations covered by this manual. Because vacuum circuits will vary based on various engine and vehicle options, always refer first to the vehicle emission control information label. Should the label be missing, or should the vehicle be equipped with a different engine from the original equipment, refer to the diagrams below for the same or similar configuration. New labels specific to your vehicle are available from the manufacturer.

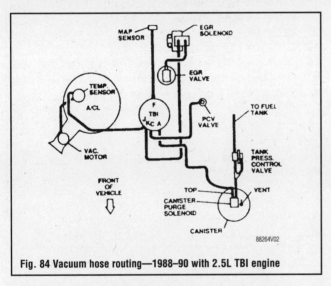

Fig. 83 Vacuum hose routing—1985–87 with 2.5L TBI engine

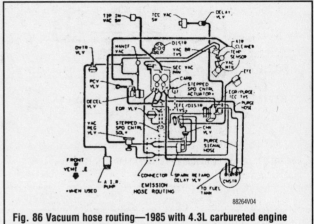

Fig. 86 Vacuum hose routing—1985 with 4.3L carbureted engine (Federal and low altitude)

Fig. 84 Vacuum hose routing—1988–90 with 2.5L TBI engine

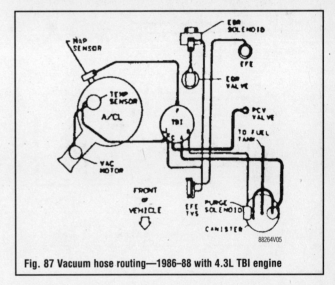

Fig. 87 Vacuum hose routing—1986–88 with 4.3L TBI engine

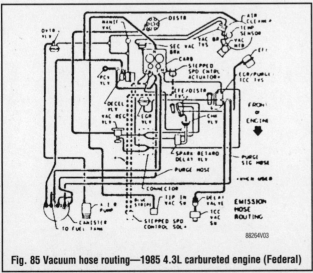

Fig. 85 Vacuum hose routing—1985 4.3L carbureted engine (Federal)

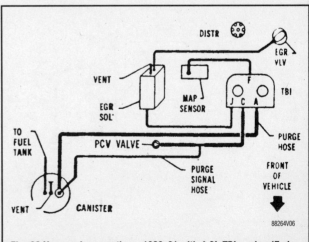

Fig. 88 Vacuum hose routing—1988–91 with 4.3L TBI engine (Federal without air pump)

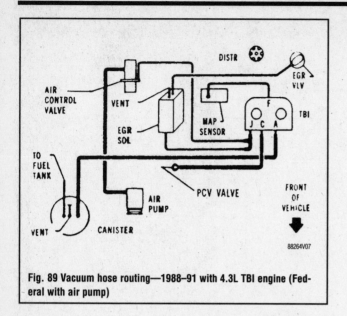

Fig. 89 Vacuum hose routing—1988–91 with 4.3L TBI engine (Federal with air pump)

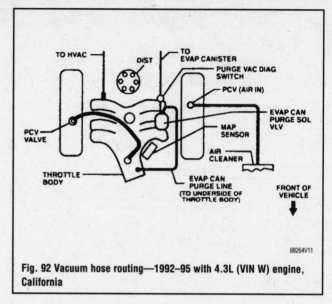

Fig. 92 Vacuum hose routing—1992–95 with 4.3L (VIN W) engine, California

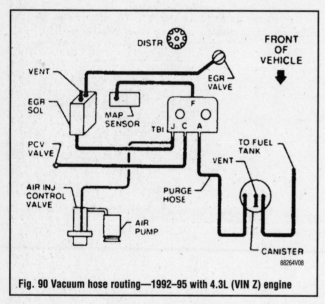

Fig. 90 Vacuum hose routing—1992–95 with 4.3L (VIN Z) engine

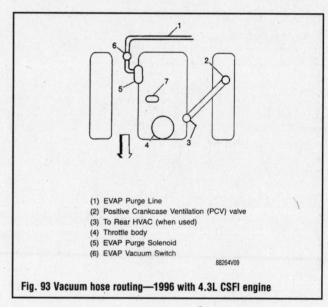

(1) EVAP Purge Line
(2) Positive Crankcase Ventilation (PCV) valve
(3) To Rear HVAC (when used)
(4) Throttle body
(5) EVAP Purge Solenoid
(6) EVAP Vacuum Switch

Fig. 93 Vacuum hose routing—1996 with 4.3L CSFI engine

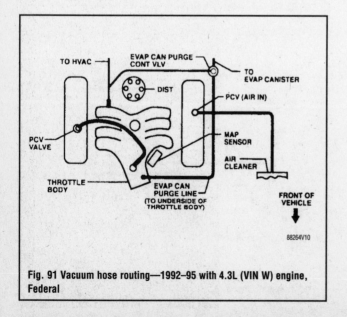

Fig. 91 Vacuum hose routing—1992–95 with 4.3L (VIN W) engine, Federal

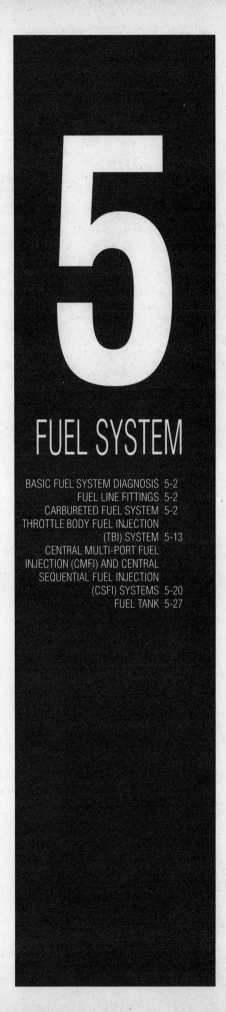

# 5

## FUEL SYSTEM

## BASIC FUEL SYSTEM DIAGNOSIS

When there is a problem starting or driving a vehicle, two of the most important checks involve the ignition and the fuel systems. The questions most mechanics attempt to answer first, "is there spark?" and "is there fuel?" will often lead to solving most basic problems. For ignition system diagnosis and testing, please refer to the information on engine electrical components and ignition systems found earlier in this manual. If the ignition system checks out (there is spark), then you must determine if the fuel system is operating properly (is there fuel?).

## FUEL LINE FITTINGS

### Quick-Connect Fittings

REMOVAL & INSTALLATION

▶ See Figure 1

➡This procedure requires Tool Set J37088–A or an equivalent aftermarket fuel line quick-connect separator.

1. Grasp both sides of the fitting. Twist the female connector ¼ turn in each direction to loosen any dirt within the fittings. Using compressed air, blow out the dirt from the quick-connect fittings at the end of the fittings.

### ✳✳ CAUTION

**Safety glasses MUST be worn when using compressed air to avoid eye injury due to flying dirt particles!**

2. For plastic (hand releasable) fittings, squeeze the plastic retainer release tabs, then pull the connection apart.
3. For metal fittings, choose the correct tool from kit J37088–A or its equivalent for the size of the fitting to be disconnected. Insert the proper tool into the female connector, then push inward to release the locking tabs. Pull the connection apart.
4. If it is necessary to remove rust or burrs from the male tube end of a quick-connect fitting, use emery cloth in a radial motion with the tube end to prevent damage to the O-ring sealing surfaces. Using a clean shop towel, wipe off the male tube ends. Inspect all connectors for dirt and burrs. Clean and/or replace if required.

**To install:**

5. Apply a few drops of clean engine oil to the male tube end of the fitting.
6. Push the connectors together to cause the retaining tabs/fingers to snap into place.
7. Once installed, pull on both ends of each connection to make sure they are secure and check for leaks.

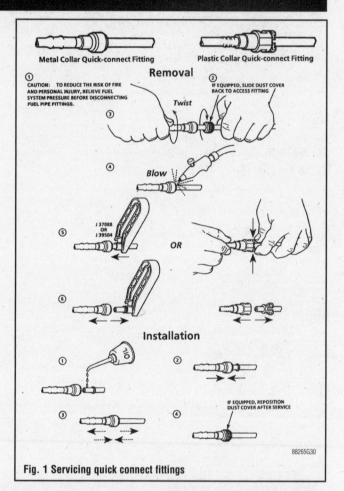

**Fig. 1 Servicing quick connect fittings**

## CARBURETED FUEL SYSTEM

Only the 1985 4.3L engine uses a carburetor.

### Mechanical Fuel Pump

The mechanical fuel pump is located on the right front of the engine.

REMOVAL & INSTALLATION

### ✳✳ CAUTION

**Before removing any component of the fuel system, be sure to reduce the fuel pressure in the system. Keep a fire extinguisher close by when servicing the fuel system. Place a rag under the fuel line and slowly remove the line from the fitting.**

1. Disconnect the negative battery cable, the fuel inlet hose from the fuel pump and the vapor return hose (if equipped).
2. Disconnect the fuel outlet hose from the fuel pump.
3. Remove the fuel pump-to-engine bolts, the fuel pump, the pushrod, the gasket and the mounting plate.
4. Using a putty knife, clean the gasket mounting surfaces.

**To install:**

5. Use a new gasket with silicone sealer.
6. Installation is the reverse of the removal procedure. Tighten the mounting bolts to 27 ft. lbs. (37 Nm).
7. Connect the negative battery cable, start the engine and check for fuel leaks.

TESTING

#### Flow Test

1. Remove the fuel pump-to-carburetor line from the carburetor.
2. Place the fuel line into a clean container.
3. Crank the engine; approximately ½ pint of the fuel should be delivered in 15 seconds.
4. If the fuel flow is below minimum, inspect the fuel system for restrictions; if no restrictions are found, replace the fuel pump.

#### Pressure Test

➡The following procedure requires the use of a GM Fuel Pressure Gauge tool No. J–29658–A or equivalent.

1.  Remove the air cleaner, then disconnect and plug the THERMAC vacuum port on the carburetor.

2.  Place a rag (to catch excess fuel) under the fuel line-to-carburetor connection. Disconnect the fuel line from the carburetor.

➡**When disconnecting the fuel line, use a back-up wrench to hold the fuel nut on the carburetor.**

3.  Using a GM Fuel Pressure Gauge tool No. J–29658–A or equivalent, install it into the fuel line.

4.  Start the engine and observe the fuel pressure. The pressure should be 4–6.5 psi (27.5–44.9 kPa).

➡**If the fuel pressure does not meet specifications, inspect the fuel system for restrictions or replace the fuel pump.**

5.  Stop the engine, relieve the fuel pressure and remove the GM Fuel Pressure Gauge tool No. J–29658–A or equivalent.

6.  Install a new fuel line-to-carburetor O-ring or washer. Unplug the THERMAC vacuum port. Start the engine and check for fuel leaks.

## Carburetor

### ADJUSTMENTS

#### Idle Speed and Mixture Adjustments

➡**The following procedure requires the use of a dwell meter, GM tool No. J–29030–B, BT–7610–B or equivalent, a center punch, a hammer, a hacksaw, GM tool No. J–33815, BT–8253–B or equivalent.**

The idle air bleed valve and the idle mixture needles are sealed with hardened plugs, to protect the factory settings. These settings are not to be tampered with, except for, cleaning, part replacement or if the carburetor is the cause of trouble.

1.  If necessary to remove the idle air bleed cover, perform the following procedures:

   a.  Remove the air cleaner and the gasket.

   b.  Using masking tape or equivalent, cover the internal bowl vents and the air inlets to the idle air bleed valve.

   c.  Carefully drill out the idle air bleed cover pop rivet heads.

   d.  Using a drift and a small hammer, drive out the remaining portions of the rivet shanks.

   e.  Remove/discard the idle air bleed cover and the masking tape used to cover the vents and the air passages.

2.  To set the idle air bleed valve, perform the following procedures:

   a.  Using the GM tool No. J–33815, BT–8253–B or equivalent, position it in the throttle side D-shaped hole in the air horn casting. The tool's upper end should be positioned over the open cavity next to the idle air bleed valve.

   b.  Holding the gauging tool down slightly, so that the solenoid plunger is against the solenoid stop, adjust the idle air bleed valve so that the gauging tool will pivot over and just contact the top of the valve.

3.  Using a new idle air bleed cover and pop rivets, install the cover to the air horn casting.

4.  If necessary to adjust the idle mixture needle screws, perform the following procedures to remove the hardened steel plugs:

   a.  Remove the carburetor from the engine.

   b.  Invert the carburetor and drain the fuel from the float bowl.

   c.  Position the carburetor, in the inverted position, in a holding fixture to gain access to the idle mixture needle plugs.

➡**When positioning the carburetor, be careful not to damage the linkage, the tubes and other parts protruding from the air horn.**

   d.  Using a hacksaw, make two parallel cuts into the throttle body; cut on each side of the locator points beneath the idle mixture needle plugs.

   e.  Using a punch and a hammer, drive the casting segment toward the hardened plug, be sure to drive out the plug.

   f.  Repeat this process for the other plug.

5.  Using the GM tool No. J–29030–B, BT–7610–B or equivalent, turn the idle mixture needle screws clockwise until they are lightly seated, then turn them counterclockwise 3 turns.

6.  Using a new carburetor-to-intake manifold gasket, install the carburetor onto the engine, DO NOT install the air cleaner or gasket.

7.  Disconnect the vacuum hose-to-canister purge valve and plug it. At the carburetor, disconnect the electrical connector from the Mixture Control (M/C) solenoid.

8.  Using a dwell meter, connect it to the M/C solenoid electrical connector and set it on the 6-cyl. scale.

9.  Start the engine and allow it to reach normal operating temperatures.

10.  Place the transmission in Drive (AT) or Neutral (MT), then adjust the idle mixture needle screws, in ⅛ turn increments, until the dwell reading varies within the 25–35° range (be as close to 30° as possible). If the reading is too low, turn the idle mixture needle screws counterclockwise. If the reading is too high, turn the idle mixture needle screws clockwise.

➡**Be sure to allow the engine to stabilize between adjustments.**

11.  After the adjustment is complete, seal the idle mixture screw openings with silicone sealant, this will prevent any further adjustment of the idle mixture screws and prevent any fuel vapor loss.

12.  Adjust the curb idle speed, if necessary.

13.  Check and/or adjust the fast idle speed by referring information on the Vehicle Emission Control Information Label in the engine compartment.

**Float and Fuel Level Adjustment**

◆ **See Figure 2**

➡**The following procedure requires the use of the GM Float Gauge tool No. J–34935, BT–8420–A or equivalent.**

1.  Remove the air cleaner from the carburetor.

2.  With the engine idling and the choke plate in the wide-open position, insert the GM Float Gauge tool No. J–34935, BT–8420–A or equivalent, into the vent hole (slot) of the air horn; allow the gauge to float freely.

➡**DO NOT press down on the gauge, for flooding or float damage may occur.**

3.  Observe the mark (on the gauge) that aligns with the top of the air horn; the float setting should be within 0.0625 in. (1.5mm) of the specifications.

➡**Incorrect fuel pressure will adversely affect the fuel level.**

4.  If the float level is not correct, perform the following procedures:

   a.  Turn the ignition switch **OFF**.

   b.  Disconnect the fuel line, the throttle linkage and/or any electrical connectors from the top of the carburetor (air horn).

   c.  Remove the air horn-to-fuel bowl screws. Lift the air horn from the fuel bowl and discard the gasket.

   d.  Bend the float tang (at the needle valve) to the correct specifications.

   e.  To install the air horn, use a new fuel bowl gasket, install the air horn and the air horn-to-fuel bowl screws.

   f.  Install the throttle linkage and the fuel line.

5.  To complete the installation, install the air cleaner. Start the engine and check for fuel leaks.

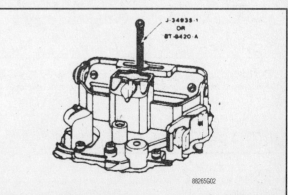

**Fig. 2 Using the GM float gauge tool No. J–34935–1, BT–8420–A or equivalent, to check the float level**

## Air Valve Spring Adjustment

▶ See Figure 3

1. Using a ³⁄₃₂ in. Allen wrench, loosen the air valve spring lock screw.
2. Turning the tension adjusting screw counterclockwise, open the air valve part way.
3. Turning the tension adjusting screw clockwise, close the air valve, then turn it an additional number of specified turns.
4. Tighten the lock screw, then apply Lithium grease to the spring-to-lever contact area.

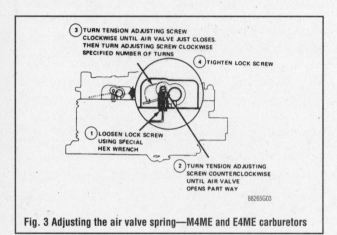

Fig. 3 Adjusting the air valve spring—M4ME and E4ME carburetors

## Choke Coil Lever Adjustment

▶ See Figure 4

1. Drill out and remove the choke coil housing cover rivets. Retain the choke housing cover, then remove the thermostatic cover and coil assembly from the choke housing.
2. Place the fast idle cam follower on the high step of the fast idle cam.
3. Close the choke valve by pushing up on the thermostatic coil tang (counterclockwise).
4. Insert a drill or gauge, of the specified size, into the hole in the choke housing. The lower edge of the choke lever should be just touching the side of the gauge.
5. If the choke lever is not touching the side of the gauge, bend the choke rod until you see that it does.

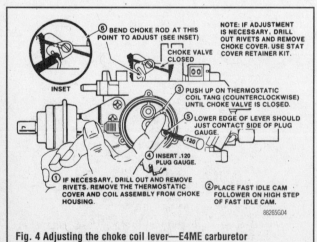

Fig. 4 Adjusting the choke coil lever—E4ME carburetor

## Fast Idle Cam (Choke Rod) Adjustment

▶ See Figures 5 and 6

➡ The following procedure requires the use of the GM Valve Angle Gauge tool No. J–26701, BT–7704 or equivalent.

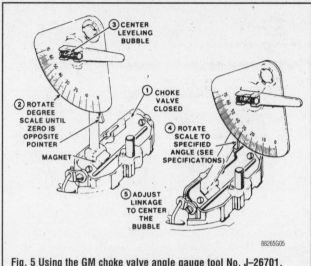

Fig. 5 Using the GM choke valve angle gauge tool No. J–26701, BT–7740 or equivalent, to check the choke valve

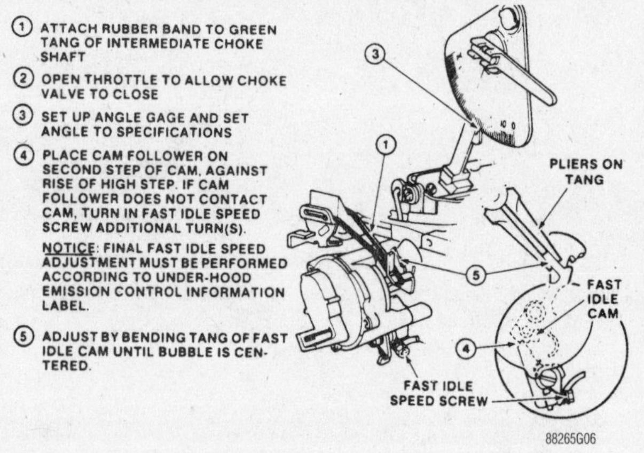

① ATTACH RUBBER BAND TO GREEN TANG OF INTERMEDIATE CHOKE SHAFT
② OPEN THROTTLE TO ALLOW CHOKE VALVE TO CLOSE
③ SET UP ANGLE GAGE AND SET ANGLE TO SPECIFICATIONS
④ PLACE CAM FOLLOWER ON SECOND STEP OF CAM, AGAINST RISE OF HIGH STEP. IF CAM FOLLOWER DOES NOT CONTACT CAM, TURN IN FAST IDLE SPEED SCREW ADDITIONAL TURN(S). NOTICE: FINAL FAST IDLE SPEED ADJUSTMENT MUST BE PERFORMED ACCORDING TO UNDER-HOOD EMISSION CONTROL INFORMATION LABEL.
⑤ ADJUST BY BENDING TANG OF FAST IDLE CAM UNTIL BUBBLE IS CENTERED.

Fig. 6 Fast idle cam (choke rod) adjustment—E4ME carburetor

1. Using a rubber band, attach it between the green tang of the intermediate choke shaft and the air horn housing.
2. Open the throttle and allow the choke valve to close.
3. Using the GM Valve Angle Gauge tool No. J–26701, BT–7704 or equivalent, attach it to the choke plate, then perform the following procedures:
   a. Rotate the degree scale until the zero is opposite the pointer.
   b. Center the leveling bubble.
   c. Rotate the scale to the specified angle degrees.
4. Position the cam follower on the 2nd step (against the rise of the high step) of the fast idle cam.

➡ If the cam follower does not contact the cam, adjust the fast idle speed screw. Final fast idle speed adjustment MUST BE performed according to the underhood emission control information label.

5. Center the bubble of the Valve Angle Gauge, by bending the fast idle cam tang.

## Front (Primary Side) Vacuum Break Adjustment

▶ See Figure 7

➡ The following procedure requires the use of the GM Valve Angle Gauge tool No. J–26701, BT–7704 or equivalent.

1. Using a rubber band, attach it between the green tang of the intermediate choke shaft and the air horn housing.
2. Open the throttle and allow the choke valve to close.

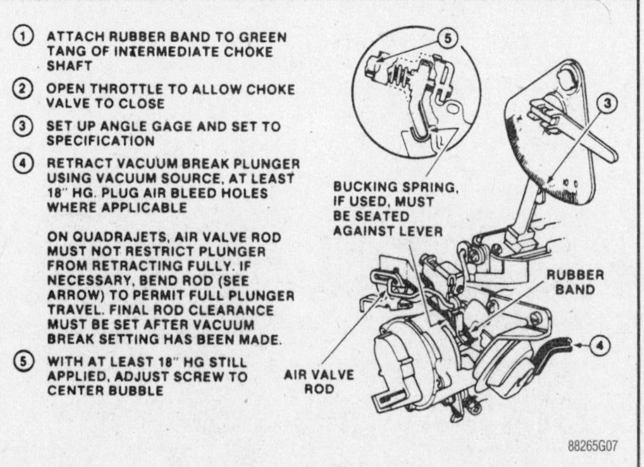

① ATTACH RUBBER BAND TO GREEN TANG OF INTERMEDIATE CHOKE SHAFT

② OPEN THROTTLE TO ALLOW CHOKE VALVE TO CLOSE

③ SET UP ANGLE GAGE AND SET TO SPECIFICATION

④ RETRACT VACUUM BREAK PLUNGER USING VACUUM SOURCE, AT LEAST 18" HG. PLUG AIR BLEED HOLES WHERE APPLICABLE

ON QUADRAJETS, AIR VALVE ROD MUST NOT RESTRICT PLUNGER FROM RETRACTING FULLY. IF NECESSARY, BEND ROD (SEE ARROW) TO PERMIT FULL PLUNGER TRAVEL. FINAL ROD CLEARANCE MUST BE SET AFTER VACUUM BREAK SETTING HAS BEEN MADE.

⑤ WITH AT LEAST 18" HG STILL APPLIED, ADJUST SCREW TO CENTER BUBBLE

BUCKING SPRING, IF USED, MUST BE SEATED AGAINST LEVER

RUBBER BAND

AIR VALVE ROD

88265G07

**Fig. 7 Front (primary side) vacuum break adjustment—E4ME carburetor**

3. Using the GM Valve Angle Gauge tool No. J–26701, BT–7704 or equivalent, attach it to the choke plate, then perform the following procedures:
    a. Rotate the degree scale until the zero is opposite the pointer.
    b. Center the leveling bubble.
    c. Rotate the scale to the specified angle degrees.
4. Apply a vacuum source (18 in. Hg) to retract the vacuum break and plug the air bleed holes.
5. Center the bubble of the Valve Angle Gauge, by turning the adjusting screw.

### Rear (Secondary Side) Vacuum Break Adjustment

♦ See Figures 8 and 9

➡The following procedure requires the use of the GM Valve Angle Gauge tool No. J–26701, BT–7704 or equivalent.

1. Using a rubber band, attach it between the green tang of the intermediate choke shaft and the air horn housing.
2. Open the throttle and allow the choke valve to close.
3. Using the GM Valve Angle Gauge tool No. J–26701, BT–7704 or equivalent, attach it to the choke plate, then perform the following procedures:
    a. Rotate the degree scale until the zero is opposite the pointer.
    b. Center the leveling bubble.
    c. Rotate the scale to the specified angle degrees.
4. Apply an 18 in. Hg (60 kPa) vacuum source to retract the vacuum break and plug the air bleed holes.
5. Center the bubble of the Valve Angle Gauge by performing one of the following procedures:
    a. Using a ⅛ in. Allen wrench, turn the vacuum break adjusting screw.

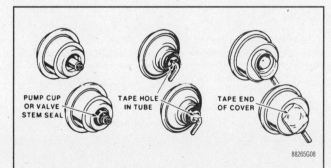

**Fig. 8 Plugging the air bleed holes of the vacuum break—E4ME carburetor**

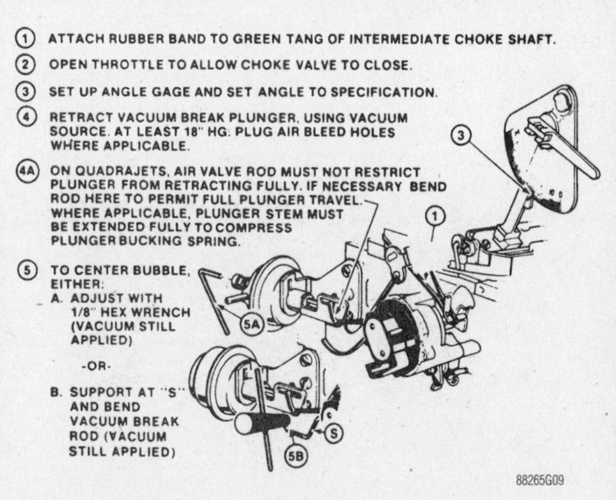

PUMP CUP OR VALVE STEM SEAL

TAPE HOLE IN TUBE

TAPE END OF COVER

88265G08

① ATTACH RUBBER BAND TO GREEN TANG OF INTERMEDIATE CHOKE SHAFT.

② OPEN THROTTLE TO ALLOW CHOKE VALVE TO CLOSE.

③ SET UP ANGLE GAGE AND SET ANGLE TO SPECIFICATION.

④ RETRACT VACUUM BREAK PLUNGER, USING VACUUM SOURCE. AT LEAST 18" HG. PLUG AIR BLEED HOLES WHERE APPLICABLE.

④A ON QUADRAJETS, AIR VALVE ROD MUST NOT RESTRICT PLUNGER FROM RETRACTING FULLY. IF NECESSARY BEND ROD HERE TO PERMIT FULL PLUNGER TRAVEL. WHERE APPLICABLE, PLUNGER STEM MUST BE EXTENDED FULLY TO COMPRESS PLUNGER BUCKING SPRING.

⑤ TO CENTER BUBBLE, EITHER:
  A. ADJUST WITH 1/8" HEX WRENCH (VACUUM STILL APPLIED)
    -OR-
  B. SUPPORT AT "S" AND BEND VACUUM BREAK ROD (VACUUM STILL APPLIED)

88265G09

**Fig. 9 Rear (secondary side) vacuum break adjustment—E4ME carburetor**

    b. Using a rod bending tool, support the S-rod and bend the vacuum break rod.

### Air Valve Rod Adjustment

♦ See Figure 10

➡The following procedure requires the use of an 18 in. Hg (60 kPa) vacuum source and a 0.025 in. plug gauge.

1. Apply an 18 in. Hg (60 kPa) vacuum source to retract the vacuum break and plug the air bleed holes.
2. Open the throttle and allow the choke valve to close.
3. Using a 0.025 in. plug gauge, position it between the control rod and the slot in the choke valve cam.
4. To adjust, bend (using a bending tool) the air valve rod.

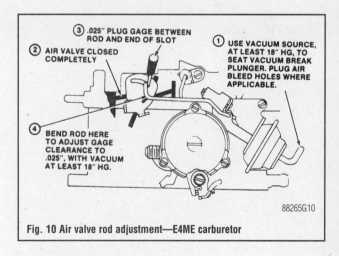

③ .025" PLUG GAGE BETWEEN ROD AND END OF SLOT

② AIR VALVE CLOSED COMPLETELY

① USE VACUUM SOURCE, AT LEAST 18" HG, TO SEAT VACUUM BREAK PLUNGER. PLUG AIR BLEED HOLES WHERE APPLICABLE.

④ BEND ROD HERE TO ADJUST GAGE CLEARANCE TO .025", WITH VACUUM AT LEAST 18" HG.

88265G10

**Fig. 10 Air valve rod adjustment—E4ME carburetor**

### Secondary Lockout Adjustment

♦ See Figure 11

➡The following procedure requires the use of a 0.015 in. plug gauge and a rod bending tool.

1. Pull the choke wide open by pushing out on the choke lever.
2. Open the throttle until the end of the secondary actuating lever is opposite the toe of the lockout lever.
3. Measure the clearance between the lockout lever and the secondary lever.
4. Bend the lockout pin until the clearance is 0.015 in.

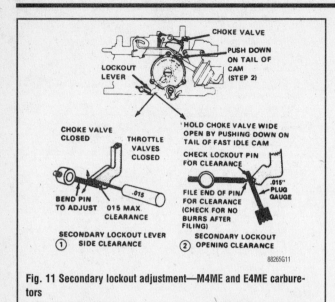

Fig. 11 Secondary lockout adjustment—M4ME and E4ME carburetors

### Unloader Adjustment

▶ See Figure 12

➡The following procedure requires the use of the GM Valve Angle Gauge tool No. J–26701, BT–7704 or equivalent, a rubber band and a bending tool.

1. Using a rubber band, attach it between the green tang of the intermediate choke shaft and the air horn housing.
2. Open the throttle and allow the choke valve to close.
3. Using the GM Valve Angle Gauge tool No. J–26701, BT–7704 or equivalent, attach it to the choke plate, then perform the following procedures:
   a. Rotate the degree scale until the zero is opposite the pointer.
   b. Center the leveling bubble.
   c. Rotate the scale to the specified angle degrees.

➡On a Quadrajet, hold the secondary lockout lever away from the pin.

4. Adjust and hold the throttle lever in the wide-open position.
5. Center the bubble of the Valve Angle Gauge, by bending the fast idle lever tang.

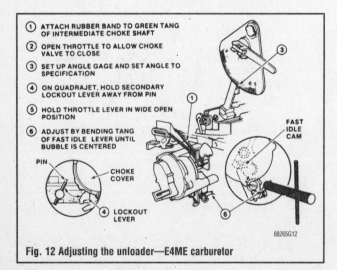

Fig. 12 Adjusting the unloader—E4ME carburetor

### Throttle Position Sensor (TPS)

▶ See Figures 13 and 14

The throttle position sensor is a position meter, mounted on the carburetor; one end is connected to the ECM and the other to a ground. As the throttle plate

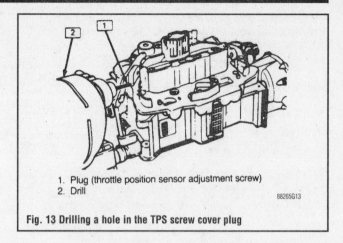

1. Plug (throttle position sensor adjustment screw)
2. Drill

Fig. 13 Drilling a hole in the TPS screw cover plug

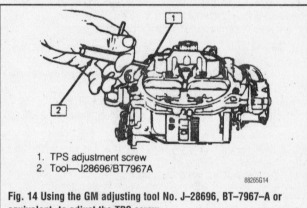

1. TPS adjustment screw
2. Tool—J28696/BT7967A

Fig. 14 Using the GM adjusting tool No. J–28696, BT–7967–A or equivalent, to adjust the TPS screw

opens, the output voltage increases; at wide-open throttle the output voltage is approximately 5V.

➡The following procedure requires the use of GM Adjustment tool No. J–28696 or equivalent, a digital voltmeter tool No. J–29125–A, a drill, a $\frac{5}{64}$ in. drill bit.

1. Disconnect the negative battery cable from the battery.
2. Remove the air cleaner and stuff a clean rag into the intake bore to keep the carburetor clean.
3. To remove the throttle position plug cover, perform the following procedures:
   a. Using a $\frac{5}{64}$ in. drill bit, drill a hole in the aluminum plug covering the throttle position solenoid adjusting screw.

➡When drilling the hole in the aluminum plug, be careful not to damage the adjusting screw head.

   b. Using a No. 8, $\frac{1}{2}$ in. self-tapping screw, install it into the drilled hole.
   c. Using a wide blade screwdriver, pry against the screw head to remove the plug, then discard the plug.
4. Using the GM adjusting tool No. J–28696, BT–7967–A or equivalent, remove the throttle position solenoid adjusting screw.
5. Using the digital voltmeter tool No. J–29125–A or equivalent, connect one probe to the center terminal and the other to the bottom terminal of the throttle position solenoid connector.
6. Turn the ignition switch **ON** with the engine stopped. Install the throttle position solenoid adjustment screw.
7. Using the GM adjusting tool No. J–28696, BT–7967–A or equivalent, install the throttle position solenoid adjusting screw and turn it to obtain a voltage of 0.255V (air conditioning off and at curb idle).
8. After the adjustment is complete, install a new throttle position solenoid plug cover; drive the plug in until it flush with the raised pump lever boss on the casting.

➡If a throttle position solenoid plug is not available, apply Delco Threadlock Adhesive X-10® or equivalent, to the screw threads and repeat the adjustment.

9. After adjustment, clear the trouble code memory.

**Mixture Control Solenoid (Plunger Travel)**

If the dwell is off at 3000 rpm, perform this check and/or adjustment procedure.

### CHECKING

▶ **See Figure 15**

➡The following procedure requires the use of the GM Float Gauge tool No. J–34935, BT–8420–A or equivalent.

1. With the engine not running, remove the air cleaner from the carburetor.
2. Insert the GM Float Gauge tool No. J–34935–1, BT–8420–A or equivalent, into the vertical D-shaped vent hole of the air horn; allow the gauge to touch the solenoid plunger.

➡If difficulty is experienced in inserting the gauge into the hole, it may be necessary to grind some of the material from it.

3. With the gauge released (plunger in the Up position), observe and record the mark (on the gauge) that aligns with the top of the air horn.
4. Press down (lightly) on the gauge until it bottoms, then read and record the mark that aligns with the top of the air horn.
5. Subtract the Up position from the Down position; the difference is the total plunger travel:

   a. If the plunger travel is 1/16–3/16 in. (1.5–4.8mm) and the dwell reading was OK at 3,000 rpm (10°–50°).

   b. If the plunger travel is less than 1/16 in. (1.5mm) or greater than 3/16 in. (4.8mm) or the dwell reading was off at 3,000 rpm, adjust the mixture control solenoid plunger travel.

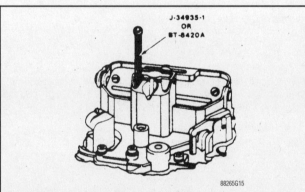

**Fig. 15 Checking the mixture control solenoid plunger travel—E4ME carburetor**

### ADJUSTMENT

▶ **See Figures 16, 17 and 18**

➡The following procedure requires the use of the GM Mixture Solenoid Gauge tool No. J–33815–1, BT–8253–A or equivalent, and the GM Adjustment tool No. J–28696–10, BT–7928 or equivalent.

1. Disconnect the negative battery terminal from the battery, then the mixture control solenoid, the throttle position sensor and the idle speed solenoid connectors from the carburetor.
2. To remove the air horn, perform the following procedures:

   a. Remove the idle speed solenoid-to-air horn screws and the solenoid.

   b. Remove the choke lever-to-choke shaft screw, rotate the upper choke lever and remove the choke rod from the slot in the lever.

   c. To remove the choke rod from the lower lever (inside the float bowl casting), use a small screwdriver to hold the lower lever outward and twist the rod counterclockwise.

   d. Remove the fuel pump link from the pump lever; DO NOT remove the pump link from the air horn.

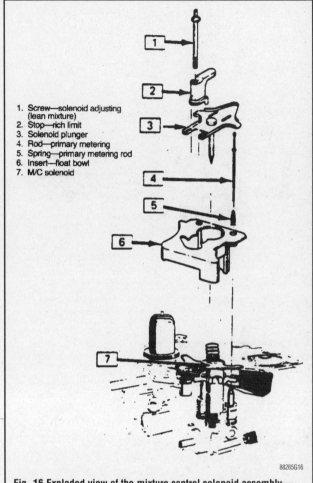

1. Screw—solenoid adjusting (lean mixture)
2. Stop—rich limit
3. Solenoid plunger
4. Rod—primary metering
5. Spring—primary metering rod
6. Insert—float bowl
7. M/C solenoid

**Fig. 16 Exploded view of the mixture control solenoid assembly— E4ME carburetor**

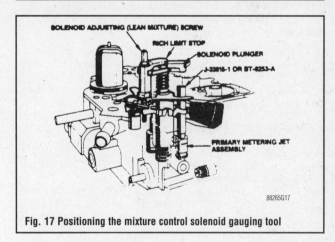

**Fig. 17 Positioning the mixture control solenoid gauging tool**

   e. From the front of the float bowl, remove the front vacuum break hose from the tube.

   f. Remove the air horn-to-fuel bowl screws and lift the air horn straight up from the float bowl; discard the gasket.

➡When removing the air horn-to-float bowl screws, be sure to remove the 2 countersunk screws located next to the venturi.

3. Remove the solenoid adjustment screw, the rich limit stop, the mixture control solenoid plunger, the primary metering rods with the springs, the plastic filler block and the mixture control solenoid.
4. Inspect the carburetor for the cause of an incorrect mixture:

   a. Inspect for a worn mixture control solenoid bore or sticking plunger.

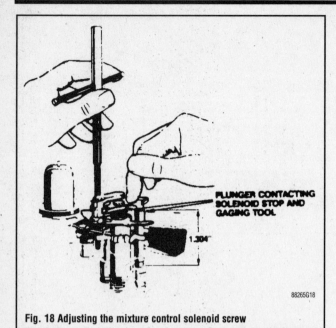

**Fig. 18 Adjusting the mixture control solenoid screw**

b. Inspect the metering rods for an incorrect part number, sticking condition and improperly installed rods or springs.

c. Inspect for dirt in the jets.

5. Using the GM Mixture Solenoid Gauging tool No. J–33815–1, BT–8253–A or equivalent, install it over the throttle side metering jet rod guide and temporarily reinstall the solenoid adjusting screw spring, the mixture control solenoid, the plunger, the rich limit stop and the solenoid adjusting screw.

6. To adjust the solenoid plunger, perform the following procedures:

a. Using light finger pressure, as close to the plunger shaft as possible, hold the solenoid plunger in the Down position.

b. Using the GM Adjustment tool No. J–28696–10, BT–7928 or equivalent, turn the solenoid adjusting screw clockwise until the plunger contacts the gauging tool.

c. Turn the tool counterclockwise until the plunger breaks contact with the gauging tool.

➡**When the solenoid plunger contacts both the solenoid stop and the gauge tool, the adjustment is correct.**

7. Noting the position of the tool's tee handle, turn the solenoid's adjusting screw clockwise (counting and recording the number of turns) until the solenoid bottoms against the float bowl.

8. Remove the solenoid adjusting screw, the rich limit stop, the mixture control solenoid, the plunger, the solenoid adjusting screw spring and the gauging tool.

9. Install the solenoid adjusting screw spring, the mixture control solenoid, the plastic filler block, the primary metering rods/springs, the mixture control solenoid plunger, the rich limit stop and the solenoid adjusting screw.

10. Using the GM Adjustment tool No. J–28696–10, BT–7928 or equivalent, turn the adjusting screw clockwise (counting the exact number of turns from Step 7) until the solenoid bottoms against the float bowl.

11. To install the air horn, use a new gasket and reverse the removal procedures. Start the engine and check the dwell at 3000 rpm.

12. To set the engine for dwell inspection, perform the following procedures:

a. Disconnect and plug the vacuum line-to-canister purge valve.

b. Ground the diagnostic test terminal.

c. Attach a dwell meter to the engine.

d. Operate the engine until normal operating temperature is established; the upper radiator hose is Hot.

13. To inspect the dwell, operate the engine at 3000 rpm and check for the following conditions:

a. If the dwell is 10–50° the mixture control solenoid adjustment is complete.

b. If the dwell is greater than 50°, check the carburetor for a rich condition.

c. If the dwell is less than 10°, check for vacuum leaks or a lean operating carburetor.

## REMOVAL & INSTALLATION

### Carburetor

▶ **See Figures 19, 20, 21 and 22**

1. Raise the hood. From inside the vehicle, remove the engine cover.
2. Disconnect the negative battery cable from the battery.
3. Remove the air cleaner and the accelerator linkage.
4. If equipped with an AT, remove the detent cable from the carburetor.
5. Disconnect the cruise control, if equipped.
6. Label and disconnect all of the necessary vacuum lines.
7. Place a shop cloth under the fuel line-to-carburetor connection and disconnect the fuel line from the carburetor; the cloth will catch the excess fuel.
8. Label and disconnect all of the necessary electrical connections.
9. Remove the carburetor-to-intake manifold bolts, the carburetor and the gasket (discard it).

**To install:**

10. Use a new carburetor-to-intake manifold gasket and install the carburetor onto the manifold. Torque the carburetor-to-intake manifold bolts to 84 inch lbs. (9.5 Nm) or 132 inch lbs. (14 Nm).

11. Connect all of the necessary electrical connections. Place a shop cloth under the fuel line-to-carburetor connection and connect the fuel line to the carburetor; the cloth will catch the excess fuel.

12. Installation of the remaining components is the reverse of the removal procedure.

13. Connect the negative battery cable, install the engine cover and lower the hood.

14. Start the engine and check for leaks and proper operation.

## Throttle Position Sensor (TPS)

### REMOVAL & INSTALLATION

▶ **See Figures 23 and 24**

1. Disconnect the negative battery cable from the battery, then the mixture control solenoid, the throttle position sensor and the idle speed solenoid connectors from the carburetor.

2. At the air horn, remove the following items by performing the following procedures:

a. Remove the idle speed solenoid-to-air horn screws and the solenoid.

b. Remove the choke lever-to-choke shaft screw, rotate the upper choke lever and remove the choke rod from the slot in the lever.

c. To remove the choke rod from the lower lever (inside the float bowl casting), use a small screwdriver to hold the lower lever outward and twist the rod counterclockwise.

d. Remove the fuel pump link from the pump lever; DO NOT remove the pump link from the air horn.

e. From the front of the float bowl, remove the front vacuum break hose from the tube.

f. Remove the air horn-to-fuel bowl screws and lift the air horn straight up from the float bowl; discard the gasket.

➡**When removing the air horn-to-float bowl screws, be sure to remove the 2 countersunk screws located next to the venturi.**

3. To remove the throttle position solenoid from the float bowl, perform the following procedures:

a. Using a flat tool or a piece of metal, lay it across the float bowl to protect the gasket sealing surface.

b. Using a small prybar, lightly depress the throttle position solenoid sensor and hold against the spring tension.

c. Using a small chisel, pry upward (against the bowl staking) to remove the staking.

➡**When removing the bowl staking, be sure to apply prying force against the metal piece and not the bowl casting.**

d. Pushing up on the bottom of the throttle position solenoid electrical connector, remove it and the connector assembly from the fuel bowl.

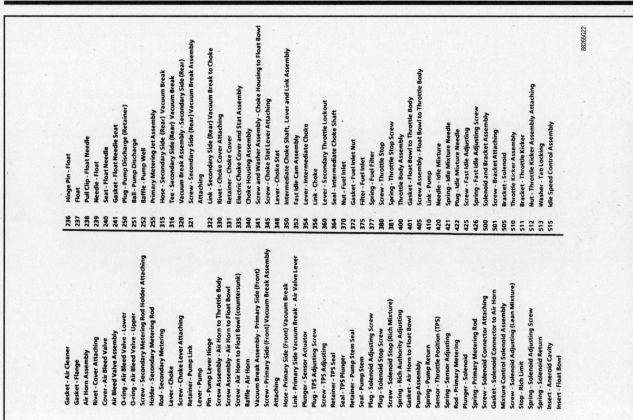

| | |
|---|---|
| 236 | Hinge Pin - Float |
| 237 | Float |
| 238 | Pull Clip - Float Needle |
| 239 | Needle - Float |
| 240 | Seat - Float Needle |
| 241 | Gasket - Float Needle Seat |
| 250 | Plug - Pump Discharge (Retainer) |
| 251 | Ball - Pump Discharge |
| 252 | Baffle - Pump Well |
| 255 | Primary Metering Jet Assembly |
| 315 | Hose - Secondary Side (Rear) Vacuum Break |
| 316 | Tee - Secondary Side (Rear) Vacuum Break |
| 320 | Vacuum Break Assembly - Secondary Side (Rear) |
| 321 | Screw - Secondary Side (Rear) Vacuum Break Assembly Attaching |
| 322 | Link - Secondary Side (Rear) Vacuum Break to Choke |
| 330 | Rivet - Choke Cover Attaching |
| 331 | Retainer - Choke Cover |
| 335 | Electric Choke Cover and Stat Assembly |
| 340 | Choke Housing Assembly |
| 341 | Screw and Washer Assembly - Choke Housing to Float Bowl |
| 345 | Screw - Choke Stat Lever Attaching |
| 348 | Lever - Choke Stat |
| 350 | Intermediate Choke Shaft, Lever and Link Assembly |
| 352 | Fast Idle Cam Assembly |
| 354 | Lever - Intermediate Choke |
| 356 | Link - Choke |
| 360 | Lever - Secondary Throttle Lockout |
| 364 | Seal - Intermediate Choke Shaft |
| 370 | Nut - Fuel Inlet |
| 372 | Gasket - Fuel Inlet Nut |
| 375 | Filter - Fuel Filter |
| 377 | Spring - Fuel Filter |
| 380 | Screw - Throttle Stop |
| 381 | Spring - Throttle Stop Screw |
| 400 | Throttle Body Assembly |
| 401 | Gasket - Float Bowl to Throttle Body |
| 405 | Screw and Washer Assembly - Float Bowl to Throttle Body |
| 410 | Link - Pump |
| 420 | Needle - Idle Mixture |
| 421 | Spring - Idle Mixture Needle |
| 422 | Plug - Idle Mixture Needle |
| 425 | Screw - Fast Idle Adjusting |
| 426 | Spring - Fast Idle Adjusting Screw |
| 500 | Solenoid and Bracket Assembly |
| 501 | Screw - Bracket Attaching |
| 505 | Bracket - Solenoid |
| 510 | Throttle Kicker Assembly |
| 511 | Bracket - Throttle Kicker |
| 512 | Nut - Throttle Kicker Assembly Attaching |
| 513 | Washer - Tab Locking |
| 515 | Idle Speed Control Assembly |

| | |
|---|---|
| 1 | Gasket - Air Cleaner |
| 5 | Gasket - Flange |
| 10 | Air Horn Assembly |
| 11 | Rivet - Cover Attaching |
| 12 | Cover - Air Bleed Valve |
| 15 | Air Bleed Valve Assembly |
| 16 | O-ring - Air Bleed Valve - Lower |
| 17 | O-ring - Air Bleed Valve - Upper |
| 30 | Screw - Secondary Metering Rod Holder Attaching |
| 31 | Holder - Secondary Metering Rod |
| 32 | Rod - Secondary Metering |
| 35 | Lever - Choke |
| 36 | Screw - Choke Lever Attaching |
| 40 | Retainer - Pump Link |
| 41 | Lever - Pump |
| 42 | Pin - Pump Lever Hinge |
| 45 | Screw Assembly - Air Horn to Throttle Body |
| 46 | Screw Assembly - Air Horn to Float Bowl |
| 47 | Screw - Air Horn to Float Bowl (countersunk) |
| 50 | Baffle - Air Horn |
| 55 | Vacuum Break Assembly - Primary Side (Front) |
| 56 | Screw - Primary Side (Front) Vacuum Break Assembly Attaching |
| 57 | Hose - Primary Side (Front) Vacuum Break |
| 58 | Link - Primary Side Vacuum Break - Air Valve Lever |
| 60 | Plunger - Sensor Actuator |
| 61 | Plug - TPS Adjusting Screw |
| 62 | Screw - TPS Adjusting |
| 65 | Retainer - TPS Seal |
| 66 | Seal - TPS Plunger |
| 67 | Retainer - Pump Stem Seal |
| 68 | Seal - Pump Stem |
| 70 | Plug - Solenoid Adjusting Screw |
| 71 | Plug - Solenoid Stop Screw |
| 72 | Screw - Solenoid Stop (Rich Mixture) |
| 73 | Spring - Rich Authority Adjusting |
| 201 | Gasket - Air Horn to Float Bowl |
| 205 | Pump - Pump |
| 206 | Spring - Pump Return |
| 210 | Sensor - Throttle Position (TPS) |
| 211 | Spring - Sensor Adjusting |
| 213 | Rod - Primary Metering |
| 215 | Plunger - Solenoid |
| 217 | Spring - Primary Metering Rod |
| 221 | Screw - Solenoid Connector Attaching |
| 222 | Gasket - Air Horn to Float Bowl |
| 225 | Gasket - Solenoid Connector to Air Horn |
| 226 | Mixture Control Solenoid Assembly |
| 227 | Screw - Solenoid Adjusting (Lean Mixture) |
| 228 | Stop - Rich Limit |
| 229 | Spring - Solenoid Adjusting Screw |
| 234 | Spring - Solenoid Return |
| 235 | Insert - Aneroid Cavity |
| 235 | Insert - Float Bowl |

**Fig. 20 Exploded view of the carburetor assembly—E4ME carburetor, continued**

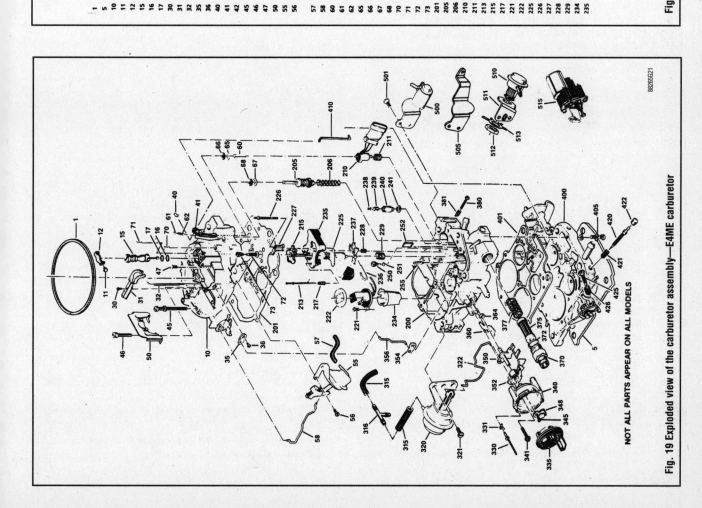

NOT ALL PARTS APPEAR ON ALL MODELS

**Fig. 19 Exploded view of the carburetor assembly—E4ME carburetor**

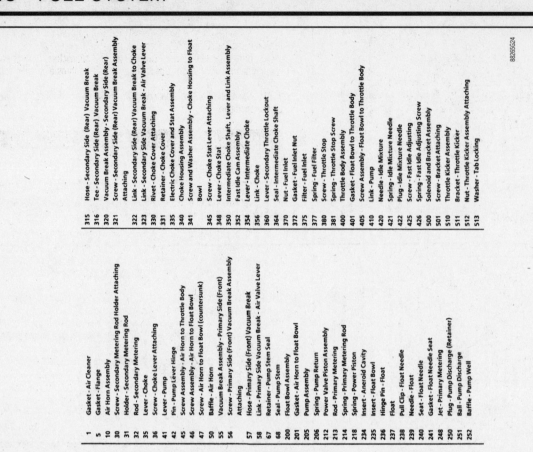

| | |
|---|---|
| 315 | Hose - Secondary Side (Rear) Vacuum Break |
| 316 | Tee - Secondary Side (Rear) Vacuum Break |
| 320 | Vacuum Break Assembly - Secondary Side (Rear) |
| 321 | Screw - Secondary Side (Rear) Vacuum Break Assembly Attaching |
| 322 | Link - Secondary Side (Rear) Vacuum Break to Choke |
| 323 | Link - Secondary Side Vacuum Break - Air Valve Lever |
| 330 | Rivet - Choke Cover Attaching |
| 331 | Retainer - Choke Cover |
| 335 | Electric Choke Cover and Stat Assembly |
| 340 | Choke Housing Assembly |
| 341 | Screw and Washer Assembly - Choke Housing to Float Bowl |
| 345 | Screw - Choke Stat Lever Attaching |
| 348 | Lever - Choke Stat |
| 350 | Intermediate Choke Shaft, Lever and Link Assembly |
| 352 | Fast Idle Cam Assembly |
| 354 | Lever - Intermediate Choke |
| 356 | Link - Choke |
| 360 | Lever - Secondary Throttle Lockout |
| 364 | Seal - Intermediate Choke Shaft |
| 370 | Nut - Fuel Inlet |
| 372 | Gasket - Fuel Inlet Nut |
| 375 | Filter - Fuel Inlet |
| 377 | Spring - Fuel Filter |
| 380 | Screw - Throttle Stop |
| 381 | Spring - Throttle Stop Screw |
| 400 | Throttle Body Assembly |
| 401 | Gasket - Float Bowl to Throttle Body |
| 405 | Screw Assembly - Float Bowl to Throttle Body |
| 410 | Link - Pump |
| 420 | Needle - Idle Mixture |
| 421 | Spring - Idle Mixture Needle |
| 422 | Plug - Idle Mixture Needle |
| 425 | Screw - Fast Idle Adjusting |
| 426 | Spring - Fast Idle Adjusting Screw |
| 500 | Solenoid and Bracket Assembly |
| 501 | Screw - Bracket Attaching |
| 510 | Throttle Kicker Assembly |
| 511 | Bracket - Throttle Kicker |
| 512 | Nut - Throttle Kicker Assembly Attaching |
| 513 | Washer - Tab Locking |

| | |
|---|---|
| 1 | Gasket - Air Cleaner |
| 5 | Gasket - Flange |
| 10 | Air Horn Assembly |
| 30 | Screw - Secondary Metering Rod Holder Attaching |
| 31 | Holder - Secondary Metering Rod |
| 32 | Rod - Secondary Metering |
| 35 | Lever - Choke |
| 36 | Screw - Choke Lever Attaching |
| 41 | Lever - Pump |
| 42 | Pin - Pump Lever Hinge |
| 45 | Screw Assembly - Air Horn to Throttle Body |
| 46 | Screw Assembly - Air Horn to Float Bowl |
| 47 | Screw - Air Horn to Float Bowl (countersunk) |
| 50 | Baffle - Air Horn |
| 55 | Vacuum Break Assembly - Primary Side (Front) |
| 56 | Screw - Primary Side (Front) Vacuum Break Assembly Attaching |
| 57 | Hose - Primary Side (Front) Vacuum Break |
| 58 | Link - Primary Side Vacuum Break - Air Valve Lever |
| 67 | Retainer - Pump Stem Seal |
| 68 | Seal - Pump Stem |
| 200 | Float Bowl Assembly |
| 201 | Gasket - Air Horn to Float Bowl |
| 205 | Spring - Pump Return |
| 206 | Power Valve Piston Assembly |
| 212 | Rod - Primary Metering |
| 213 | Spring - Primary Metering Rod |
| 214 | Spring - Power Piston |
| 218 | Insert - Aneroid Cavity |
| 234 | Insert - Float Bowl |
| 235 | Hinge Pin - Float |
| 236 | Float |
| 237 | Pull Clip - Float Needle |
| 238 | Needle - Float |
| 239 | Seat - Float Needle |
| 240 | Gasket - Float Needle Seat |
| 241 | Jet - Primary Metering |
| 248 | Plug - Pump Discharge (Retainer) |
| 250 | Ball - Pump Discharge |
| 251 | Baffle - Pump Well |
| 252 | |

Fig. 22 Exploded view of the carburetor assembly—M4ME carburetor, continued

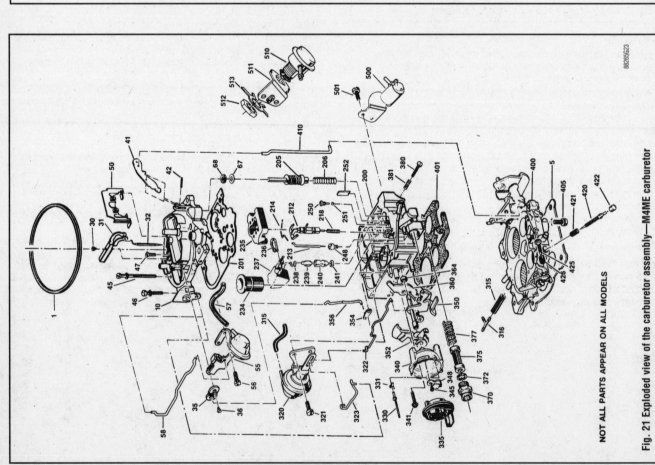

NOT ALL PARTS APPEAR ON ALL MODELS

Fig. 21 Exploded view of the carburetor assembly—M4ME carburetor

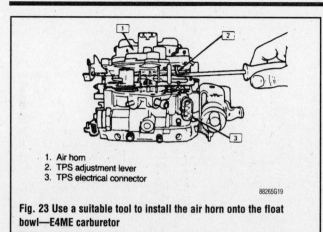

1. Air horn
2. TPS adjustment lever
3. TPS electrical connector

88265G19

**Fig. 23 Use a suitable tool to install the air horn onto the float bowl—E4ME carburetor**

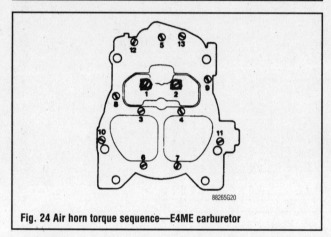

88265G20

**Fig. 24 Air horn torque sequence—E4ME carburetor**

### To install:

4. Install the throttle position solenoid/connector assembly, align the groove in the electrical connector with the slot in the float bowl casting. Push down on the assembly so that the connector and wires are located below the bowl casting surface; be sure the green throttle position solenoid actuator plunger is aligned in the air horn.

5. Install the air horn, hold the pump plunger assembly down against the return spring tension. Align the pump plunger stem with the hole in the gasket and the gasket over the throttle position solenoid plunger, the solenoid plunger return spring, the metering rods, the solenoid mounting screws and the electrical connector. Use the two dowel locating pins (on the float bowl) to align the gasket.

6. While holding the solenoid metering rod plunger, the air horn gasket and the pump plunger assembly, align the slot in the end of the plunger with the solenoid mounting screw.

7. While lowering the air horn assembly (carefully) onto the float bowl, position the throttle position solenoid adjustment lever of the throttle position solenoid sensor and guide the pump plunger stem through the air horn casting seal.

➡**To ease the installation of the air horn onto the float bowl, insert a thin screwdriver between the air horn gasket and the float bowl to raise the throttle position solenoid adjustment lever while positioning it over the throttle position solenoid sensor.**

8. Install the air horn-to-float bowl screws and tighten all of the screws evenly, using the torquing sequence.

9. Reconnect all of the vacuum and electrical connectors. Clear the trouble code from the ECM memory. Check and/or adjust the throttle position solenoid voltage.

10. Connect the negative battery cable, start the engine, check for leaks and proper operation.

## Mixture Control Solenoid

### REMOVAL & INSTALLATION

➡**The following procedure requires the use of GM Solenoid Adjusting tool No. J–28696–1 or equivalent.**

1. Disconnect the negative battery cable from the battery, then the mixture control solenoid and the Throttle Position Sensor (TPS) electrical connectors from the carburetor.

2. Remove the air horn, by performing the following procedures:

a. Remove the choke lever-to-choke shaft screw, rotate the upper choke lever and remove the choke rod from the slot in the lever.

b. To remove the choke rod from the lower lever (inside the float bowl casting), use a small screwdriver to hold the lower lever outward and twist the rod counterclockwise.

c. Remove the fuel pump link from the pump lever; DO NOT remove the pump link from the air horn.

d. From the front of the float bowl, remove the front vacuum break hose from the tube.

e. Remove the air horn-to-fuel bowl screws and lift the air horn straight up from the float bowl; discard the gasket.

➡**When removing the air horn-to-float bowl screws, be sure to remove the 2 countersunk screws located next to the venturi.**

f. Lift the air horn straight up from the float bowl.

3. Using the GM Solenoid Adjusting tool No. J–28696–1 or equivalent, remove the mixture control solenoid adjusting screw.

4. Lift the air horn-to-float bowl gasket from the dowel locating pins and discard it.

5. Remove the plastic filler block from over the float bowl.

6. Lift (carefully) each metering rod from the guided metering jet; be sure to remove the return spring with each rod.

7. Remove the mixture control solenoid-to-float bowl screw, then lift the solenoid and the connector assembly from the float bowl.

➡**If a new mixture control solenoid package is being installed, the solenoid and the plunger MUST BE installed as a matched set.**

8. When installing the mixture control solenoid, perform the following procedures:

a. Align the solenoid's pin with the hole in the raised boss at the bottom of the float bowl.

b. Align the wires of the solenoid's connector in the bowl slot or the plastic insert (if used).

c. Install the solenoid-to-fuel bowl mounting screw and engage the first 6 screw threads (to assure proper thread engagement).

9. To complete the installation, use a new gasket and reverse the removal procedures. Calibrate the mixture control solenoid plunger.

**M4ME CARBURETOR ADJUSTMENT SPECIFICATIONS**

| CARBURETOR PART NO. | FLOAT LEVEL mm (Inches) + 1/16" | PUMP ROD SETTING mm (Inches) | PUMP ROD LOCATION | AIR VALVE SPRING (Turns) | CHOKE COIL LEVER | FAST IDLE CAM (CHOKE ROD) ± 2.5° | VACUUM BREAK FRONT ± 2.5° | VACUUM BREAK REAR ± 3.5° | AIR VALVE ROD mm (Inches) | UNLOADER ± 4° | PROPANE ENRICHMENT SPEED |
|---|---|---|---|---|---|---|---|---|---|---|---|
| 17080212 | 9.5 (12/32) | 7.0 (9/32) | INNER | 3/4 | .120 | 46° | 24° | 30° | .025 | 40° | |
| 17080213 | 9.5 (12/32) | 7.0 (9/32) | INNER | 1 | .120 | 37° | 23° | 30° | .025 | 40° | |
| 17080298 | 9.5 (12/32) | 7.0 (9/32) | INNER | 1 | .120 | 37° | 23° | 30° | .025 | 40° | |
| 17082213 | 9.5 (12/32) | 7.0 (9/32) | INNER | 1 | .120 | 37° | 23° | 30° | .025 | 40° | |
| 17083298 | 9.5 (12/32) | 7.0 (9/32) | INNER | 1 | .120 | 37° | 23° | 30° | .025 | 40° | |
| 17084500 | 9.5 (12/32) | 7.0 (9/32) | INNER | 1 | .120 | 37° | 23° | 30° | .025 | 40° | |
| 17084501 | 9.5 (12/32) | 7.0 (9/32) | INNER | 1 | .120 | 37° | 23° | 30° | .025 | 40° | |
| 17084502 | 9.5 (12/32) | 7.0 (9/32) | INNER | 7/8 | .120 | 46° | 24° | 30° | .025 | 40° | |
| 17085000 | 9.5 (12/32) | 7.0 (9/32) | INNER | 7/8 | .120 | 46° | 24° | 30° | 0.6 (.025) | 40° | |
| 17085001 | 9.5 (12/32) | 7.0 (9/32) | INNER | 1 | .120 | 46° | 23° | 30° | 0.6 (.025) | 40° | |
| 17085003 | 10.0 (13/32) | 7.0 (9/32) | INNER | 7/8 | .120 | 46° | 23° | — | 0.6 (.025) | 35° | |
| 17085004 | 10.0 (13/32) | 7.0 (9/32) | INNER | 7/8 | .120 | 46° | 23° | — | 0.6 (.025) | 35° | |
| 17085205 | 10.0 (13/32) | 7.0 (9/32) | INNER | 7/8 | .120 | 20° | 26° | 38° | 0.6 (.025) | 39° | |
| 17085206 | 10.0 (13/32) | 7.0 (9/32) | INNER | 7/8 | .120 | 46° | — | 26° | 0.6 (.025) | 39° | 20 |
| 17085208 | 10.0 (13/32) | 7.0 (9/32) | INNER | 7/8 | .120 | 20° | 26° | 38° | 0.6 (.025) | 39° | 10 |
| 17085209 | 10.0 (13/32) | 9.5 (3/8) | OUTER | 7/8 | .120 | 20° | 26° | 36° | 0.6 (.025) | 39° | 50 |
| 17085210 | 10.0 (13/32) | 7.0 (9/32) | INNER | 7/8 | .120 | 20° | 26° | 38° | 0.6 (.025) | 39° | 10 |
| 17085211 | 10.0 (13/32) | 9.5 (3/8) | OUTER | 7/8 | .120 | 20° | 26° | 36° | 0.6 (0.25) | 39° | 50 |
| 17085212 | 10.0 (13/32) | 7.0 (9/32) | INNER | 7/8 | .120 | 46° | 23° | — | 0.6 (.025) | 35° | |
| 17085213 | 10.0 (13/32) | 7.0 (9/32) | INNER | 7/8 | .120 | 46° | 23° | — | 0.6 (.025) | 35° | |
| 17085215 | 10.0 (13/32) | 7.0 (9/32) | INNER | 7/8 | .120 | 46° | — | 26° | 0.6 (.025) | 32° | |
| 17085216 | 10.0 (13/32) | 7.0 (9/32) | INNER | 7/8 | .120 | 20° | 26° | 38° | 0.6 (.025) | 39° | |
| 17085217 | 10.0 (13/32) | 7.0 (9/32) | INNER | 1/2 | .120 | 20° | 26° | 36° | 0.6 (.025) | 39° | |
| 17085219 | 10.0 (13/32) | 7.0 (9/32) | INNER | 1/2 | .120 | 20° | 26° | 36° | 0.6 (.025) | 39° | |
| 17085220 | 10.0 (13/32) | 9.5 (3/8) | OUTER | 7/8 | .120 | 20° | — | 26° | 0.6 (.025) | 32° | 75 |
| 17085221 | 10.0 (13/32) | 9.5 (3/8) | OUTER | 7/8 | .120 | 20° | — | 26° | 0.6 (.025) | 32° | 75 |
| 17085222 | 10.0 (13/32) | 7.0 (9/32) | INNER | 1/2 | .120 | 20° | 26° | 36° | 0.6 (.025) | 39° | 20 |

88265C25

**M4ME CARBURETOR ADJUSTMENT SPECIFICATIONS**

| CARBURETOR PART NO. | FLOAT LEVEL mm (Inches) + 1/16" | PUMP ROD SETTING mm (Inches) | PUMP ROD LOCATION | AIR VALVE SPRING (Turns) | CHOKE COIL LEVER | FAST IDLE CAM (CHOKE ROD) + 2.5° | VACUUM BREAK FRONT + 2.5° | VACUUM BREAK REAR + 3.5° | AIR VALVE ROD mm (Inches) | UNLOADER + 4° | PROPANE ENRICHMENT SPEED |
|---|---|---|---|---|---|---|---|---|---|---|---|
| 17085223 | 10.0 (13/32) | 9.5 (3/8) | OUTER | 1/2 | .120 | 20° | 26° | 36° | 0.6 (.025) | 39° | 50 |
| 17085224 | 10.0 (13/32) | 7.0 (9/32) | INNER | 1/2 | .120 | 20° | 26° | 36° | 0.6 (.025) | 39° | 20 |
| 17085225 | 10.0 (13/32) | 9.5 (3/8) | OUTER | 1/2 | .120 | 20° | 26° | 36° | 0.6 (.025) | 39° | 50 |
| 17085226 | 10.0 (13/32) | 7.0 (9/32) | INNER | 7/8 | .120 | 20° | — | 24° | 0.6 (.025) | 32° | 20 |
| 17085227 | 10.0 (13/32) | 7.0 (9/32) | INNER | 7/8 | .120 | 20° | — | 24° | 0.6 (.025) | 32° | 20 |
| 17085228 | 10.0 (13/32) | 7.0 (9/32) | INNER | 7/8 | .120 | 46° | — | 24° | 0.6 (.025) | 39° | 30 |
| 17085229 | 10.0 (13/32) | 7.0 (9/32) | INNER | 7/8 | .120 | 46° | — | 24° | 0.6 (.025) | 39° | 30 |
| 17085230 | 10.0 (13/32) | 7.0 (9/32) | INNER | 7/8 | .120 | 20° | — | 26° | 0.6 (.025) | 32° | 20 |
| 17085231 | 10.0 (13/32) | 7.0 (9/32) | INNER | 7/8 | .120 | 20° | — | 26° | 0.6 (.025) | 32° | 40 |
| 17085235 | 10.0 (13/32) | 7.0 (9/32) | INNER | 7/8 | .120 | 46° | — | 26° | 0.6 (.025) | 39° | 80 |
| 17085238 | 10.0 (13/32) | 9.5 (3/8) | OUTER | 7/8 | .120 | 20° | — | 26° | 0.6 (.025) | 32° | 75 |
| 17085239 | 10.0 (13/32) | 9.5 (3/8) | OUTER | 7/8 | .120 | 20° | — | 26° | 0.6 (.025) | 32° | 75 |
| 17085290 | 10.0 (13/32) | 7.0 (9/32) | INNER | 7/8 | .120 | 46° | — | 24° | 0.6 (.025) | 39° | 30 |
| 17085291 | 10.0 (13/32) | 9.5 (3/8) | OUTER | 7/8 | .120 | 46° | — | 26° | 0.6 (.025) | 39° | 100 |
| 17085292 | 10.0 (13/32) | 7.0 (9/32) | INNER | 7/8 | .120 | 46° | — | 24° | 0.6 (.025) | 39° | 30 |
| 17085293 | 10.0 (13/32) | 9.5 (3/8) | OUTER | 7/8 | .120 | 46° | — | 26° | 0.6 (.025) | 39° | 100 |
| 17085294 | 10.0 (13/32) | 7.0 (9/32) | INNER | 7/8 | .120 | 46° | — | 26° | 0.6 (.025) | 39° | |
| 17085298 | 10.0 (13/32) | 7.0 (9/32) | INNER | 7/8 | .120 | 46° | — | 26° | 0.6 (.025) | 39° | |

88265C26

| CARBU-RETOR NUMBER | FLOAT LEVEL + 1/16" | LEAN MIXTURE SCREW | RICH MIXTURE SCREW + 2/32" | IDLE MIXTURE NEEDLE (NO. OF TURNS) | IDLE AIR BLEED VALVE | AIR VALVE SPRING (NO. OF TURNS) | CHOKE STAT LEVER | CHOKE ROD CAM + 2.5° | VACUUM BREAK FRONT + 2.5° | VACUUM BREAK REAR + 3.5° | AIR VALVE ROD | UNLOADER +4° |
|---|---|---|---|---|---|---|---|---|---|---|---|---|
| 17085202 | 11/32 (8I7 mm) | 1.304 Gage | 4/32 | 3-3/8 | NOTE 1 | 7/8 | .120 Gage | 20° | 27° | – | .025 | 38° |
| 17085203 | 11/32 (8.7 mm) | 1.304 Gage | 4/32 | 3-3/8 | NOTE 1 | 7/8 | .120 Gage | 20° | 27° | – | .025 | 38° |
| 17085204 | 11/32 (8.7 mm) | 1.304 Gage | 4/32 | 3-3/8 | NOTE 1 | 7/8 | .120 Gage | 20° | 27° | – | .025 | 38° |
| 17085207 | 11/32 (8.7 mm) | 1.304 Gage | 4/32 | 3-3/8 | NOTE 1 | 7/8 | .120 Gage | 38° | 27° | – | .025 | 38° |
| 17085218 | 11/32 (8.7 mm) | 1.304 Gage | 4/32 | 3-3/8 | NOTE 1 | 7/8 | .120 Gage | 20° | 27° | – | .025 | 38° |
| 17085502 | 7/16 11.0 mm | 1.304 Gage | – | NOTE 2 | 1.756 Gage | 7/8 | .120 Gage | 20° | 26° | 36° | .025 | 39° |
| 17085503 | 7/16 11.0 mm | 1.304 Gage | – | NOTE 2 | 1.756 Gage | 7/8 | .120 Gage | 20° | 26° | 36° | .025 | 39° |
| 17085506 | 7/16 11.0 mm | 1.304 Gage | – | NOTE 2 | 1.756 Gage | 1 | .120 Gage | 20° | 27° | 36° | .025 | 36° |
| 17085508 | 7/16 11.0 mm | 1.304 Gage | – | NOTE 2 | 1.756 Gage | 1 | .120 Gage | 20° | 27° | 36° | .025 | 36° |
| 17085524 | 7/16 11.0 mm | 1.304 Gage | – | NOTE 2 | 1.756 Gage | 1 | .120 Gage | 20° | 25° | 36° | .025 | 36° |
| 17085526 | 7/16 11.0 mm | 1.304 Gage | – | NOTE 2 | 1.756 Gage | 1 | .120 Gage | 20° | 25° | 36° | .025 | 36° |

MODEL E4ME CARBURETOR ADJUSTMENT SPECIFICATIONS

1  PRESET WITH 1.756 GAGE, FINAL ADJUSTMENT ON VEHICLE
2  PRESET 3 TURNS, FINAL ADJUSTMENT ON VEHICLE

88265C27

# THROTTLE BODY FUEL INJECTION (TBI) SYSTEM

## Relieving Fuel System Pressure

### 2.5L ENGINE

1. Loosen the fuel filler cap.
2. Unplug the fuel pump wiring at the fuel tank or from the fuse block, located in the passenger compartment, remove the fuse labeled, **Fuel Pump**.
3. Start the engine.

➡ **The engine will start and run, for a short period of time, until the remaining fuel is used up.**

4. Engage the starter, a few more times, to relieve any remaining pressure.
5. Turn the ignition switch to **OFF** and install the fuel pump fuse into the fuse block or plug in the fuel pump wiring connector.
6. Tighten the fuel filler cap.

### 4.3L ENGINE

Loosen the fuel filler cap and allow the engine to sit for 5–10 minutes; this will allow the orifice (in the fuel system) to bleed off the pressure.

## Electric Fuel Pump

The electric fuel pump is attached to the fuel sending unit, located in the fuel tank.

### REMOVAL & INSTALLATION

Because removal and installation of the fuel pump requires the removal of the fuel tank, refer to the procedures in the fuel tank portion of this section.

### TESTING

#### Flow Test

1. Relieve the fuel system pressure.
2. Remove the fuel pump feed line from the fuel inlet on the throttle body.

3. Place the fuel line in a clean container.
4. Turn the ignition switch **ON**; approximately ½ pint of the fuel should be delivered in 15 seconds.
5. If the fuel flow is below minimum, inspect the fuel system for restrictions; if no restrictions are found, replace the fuel pump.

#### Pressure Test

▶ **See Figure 25**

➡ **The following procedure requires the use of a GM Fuel Pressure Gauge tool No. J–29658–A or equivalent.**

1. Properly relieve the fuel system pressure.
2. If necessary for access, remove the air cleaner assembly and plug the vacuum port(s).

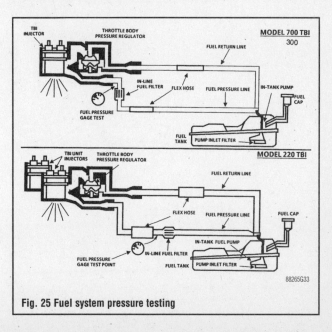

**Fig. 25 Fuel system pressure testing**

3. Disconnect the flexible fuel supply line, located in the engine compartment between the fuel filter and throttle body.

4. Install a fuel pressure gauge, such as J-29658 or equivalent, in-line between the fuel filter and throttle body unit (between the steel line and flexible hose). If necessary use an adapter or Tee fitting in order to connect the gauge and complete the fuel circuit.

➡**A Tee fitting may be fabricated for this purpose. Depending on the fuel pressure gauge, short lengths of steel tubing, appropriately sized flare nuts and a flare nut adapter may be used.**

5. If the engine will run, start the engine and allow it to run at normal idle speed. The fuel pressure should be 9–13 psi (62–90 kPa).

6. If the engine does not run, turn the ignition **ON**, but do not attempt to start the engine. Listen for the fuel pump to run. Within 2 seconds of turning the ignition **ON**, pressure should be 9–13 psi (62–90 kPa). If necessary, cycle the ignition **OFF**, then **ON** again, in order to build up system pressure.

7. If the fuel pump did not run or system pressure did not reach specification, locate the fuel pump test connector. The test connector is usually found on the driver's side of the engine compartment (on or near the fender), with a single wire (usually red) leading from the relay to the connector. Using a jumper wire, apply battery voltage to the test connector in order to energize and run the fuel pump. The pump should run and produce fuel pressure of 9–13 psi (62–90 kPa). If the pump does not run, check the relay and fuel pump wiring.

8. If the pump pressure was lower than specification, first check for a restricted fuel line or filter and replace, as necessary. If no restrictions can be found, restrict the fuel supply line between the pressure gauge and the TBI unit (a flexible hose may be temporarily clamped to produce the restriction), then apply voltage to the test connector again. If pressure is now above 13 psi (90 kPa), replace the faulty pressure regulator. If pressure remains below 9 psi (62 kPa), then the problem is located in the fuel tank (the fuel pump, coupling hose or inlet filter).

9. If during Step 7, the pressure was higher than specification, disengage the injector connector, then disconnect the fuel return line flexible hose which connects the line from the throttle body to the tank line. Attach a 5/16 ID flex hose to the fuel line from the throttle body and place the other end into an approved gasoline container. Cycle the ignition in order to energize the fuel pump and watch system pressure. If pressure is still higher, check for restrictions in the throttle body return line. Repair or replace the line if restrictions are found or replace the faulty pressure regulator if no other causes of high pressure are identified. If fuel pressure is normal only with the flexible hose-to-fuel tank line out of the circuit, check that line for restrictions and repair or replace, as necessary.

10. Once the test is completed, depressurize the fuel system and remove the gauge.

11. Secure the fuel lines and check for leaks.

12. If removed, install the air cleaner assembly.

## Fuel Pump Relay

▶ **See Figure 26**

The fuel pump relay is mounted on the right-side of the engine compartment. Check for loose electrical connections; no other service is possible, except replacement.

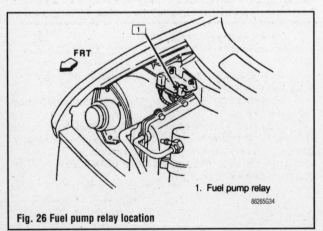

1. Fuel pump relay

88265G34

**Fig. 26 Fuel pump relay location**

## REMOVAL & INSTALLATION

1. Disconnect the negative battery cable from the battery.
2. Disconnect the relay/electrical connector assembly from the bracket.
3. Pull the fuel pump relay from the electrical connector.
4. Installation is the reverse of the removal procedure.

## Throttle Body

▶ **See Figures 27, 28 and 29**

The Model 300 throttle body, used on the 2.5L engine (1985–87), is a single barrel, single injector type. The 1988–90 2.5L engine is equipped with a model 700 single barrel, single injector type. The Model 220 throttle body, used on the 4.3L engine (1986–on), is a dual barrel, twin injector type. The operation of all three types are basically the same. This system is not to be confused with the direct port injection Central Multiport Fuel Injection (CMFI) or Central Sequential Multiport Fuel Injection (CSFI) systems.

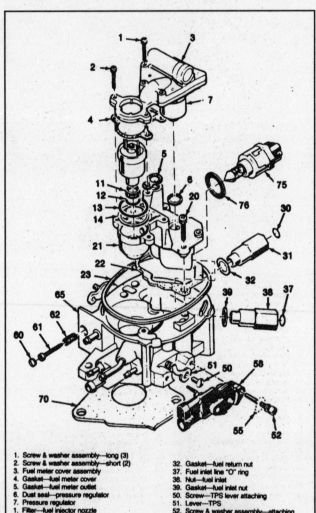

1. Screw & washer assembly—long (3)
2. Screw & washer assembly—short (2)
3. Fuel meter cover assembly
4. Gasket—fuel meter cover
5. Gasket—fuel meter outlet
6. Dust seal—pressure regulator
7. Pressure regulator
1. Filter—fuel injector nozzle
2. Lower "O" ring
3. Upper "O" ring
4. Back-up washer—fuel injector
0. Screw & washer assembly—attaching (3)
1. Fuel meter body assembly
2. Gasket—fuel meter body
3. Gasket—air filter
0. Fuel return line "O" ring
1. Nut—fuel return

32. Gasket—fuel return nut
37. Fuel inlet line "O" ring
38. Nut—fuel inlet
39. Gasket—fuel inlet nut
50. Screw—TPS lever attaching
51. Lever—TPS
52. Screw & washer assembly—attaching
55. Retainer—TPS attaching screw
58. Sensor—throttle position
60. Plug—idle stop screw
61. Screw—throttle stop
62. Spring—throttle stop screw
65. Throttle body assembly
70. Gasket—flange mounting
75. Idle air control assembly
76. Gasket—IAC to throttle body

88265G37

**Fig. 27 Exploded view of the Model 300 throttle body—2.5L engine**

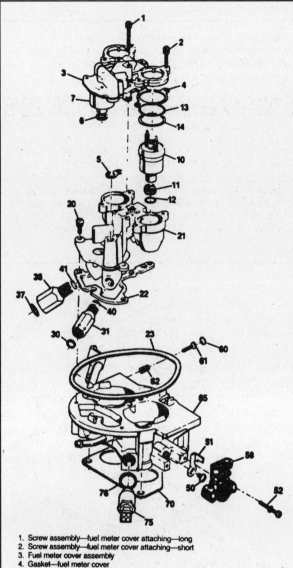

1. Screw assembly—fuel meter cover attaching—long
2. Screw assembly—fuel meter cover attaching—short
3. Fuel meter cover assembly
4. Gasket—fuel meter cover
5. Gasket—fuel meter outlet
6. Seal—pressure regulator
7. Pressure regulator
10. Injector—fuel
11. Filter—fuel injector inlet
12. O-ring—fuel injector—lower
13. O-ring—fuel injector—upper
14. Washer—fuel injector
20. Screw assembly—fuel meter body—throttle body attaching
21. Fuel meter body assembly
22. Gasket—throttle body to fuel meter body
23. Gasket—air filter
30. O-ring—fuel return line
31. Nut—fuel outlet
37. O-ring—fuel inlet line
38. Nut—fuel inlet
40. Gasket—fuel outlet nut
41. Gasket—fuel inlet nut
50. Screw—TPS lever attaching
51. Lever—TPS
52. Screw assembly—TPS attaching
58. Sensor—throttle position (TPS)
60. Plug—idle stop screw
61. Screw assembly—idle stop
62. Spring—idle stop screw
65. Throttle body assembly
70. Gasket—flange
75. Valve assembly—idle air control (IAC)
76. Gasket—idle air control valve assembly

88265G38

**Fig. 28 Exploded view of the Model 220 throttle body—4.3L engine**

Both throttle bodies are constantly monitored by the ECM to produce a 14.7:1 air/fuel ratio, which is vital to the catalytic converter operation.

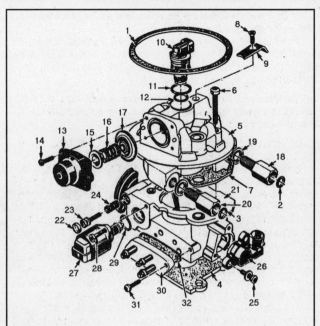

| 1. Gasket | 17. Pressure regulator diaphragm |
|---|---|
| 2. Fuel inlet O-ring | 18. Fuel inlet nut |
| 3. Fuel outlet O-ring | 19. Fuel nut seal |
| 4. Flange gasket | 20. Fuel outlet nut |
| 5. Fuel meter assembly | 21. Throttle body assembly |
| 6. Fuel meter screws | 22. Idle stop screw plug |
| 7. Fuel meter-to-throttle body gasket | 23. Idle stop screw and washer |
| 8. Injector retainer screw | 24. Idle stop screw spring |
| 9. Injector retainer | 25. Throttle position sensor |
| 10. Fuel injector | 26. TPS attaching screw |
| 11. Upper injector O-ring | 27. Idle air control valve |
| 12. Lower injector O-ring | 28. IAC valve screw |
| 13. Pressure regulator cover | 29. IAC O-ring |
| 14. Pressure regulator screw | 30. Tube module |
| 15. Spring seat | 31. Tube module attaching screw |
| 16. Pressure regulator spring | 32. Tube module gasket |

88265G40

**Fig. 29 Exploded view of the Model 700 throttle body—2.5L engine**

## REMOVAL & INSTALLATION

▶ **See Figures 30 thru 38**

### ✷✷ CAUTION

**Before removing any component of the fuel system, be sure to reduce the fuel pressure in the system. The pressure regulator contains an orifice in the fuel system; when the engine is turned Off, the pressure in the system will bleed down within a few minutes.**

1. Relieve the pressure in the fuel system.
2. Remove the air cleaner. Disconnect the negative battery cable from the battery.
3. Disconnect the electrical connectors from the idle air control valve, the throttle position sensor and the fuel injector(s).
4. Remove the throttle return spring(s), the cruise control (if equipped) and the throttle linkage.
5. Label and disconnect the vacuum hoses from the throttle body.
6. Place a rag (to catch the excess fuel) under the fuel line-to-throttle body connection, then disconnect the fuel line from the throttle body.
7. Remove the attaching hardware, the throttle body-to-intake manifold bolts, the throttle body and the gasket.

➡Be sure to place a cloth in the intake manifold to prevent dirt from entering the engine.

8. Using a gasket remover (if necessary), clean the gasket mounting surfaces.

**To install:**

9. Install a new gasket, throttle body and mounting bolts. Tighten the nuts/bolts to 13 ft. lbs. (17 Nm).

10. The remainder of installation is the reverse of the removal procedure.

11. Depress the accelerator pedal to the floor and release it, to see if the pedal returns freely.

12. Start the engine, check for leaks and proper operation.

## ADJUSTMENTS

### Idle Speed and Mixture

#### 1985–87 2.5L ENGINE

➡The following procedures require the use a tachometer, GM tool No. J–33047 or equivalent, GM Torx® Bit No. 20, silicone sealant, a 5/32 in. drill bit, a prick punch and a 1/16 in. pin punch.

The throttle stop screw, used in regulating the minimum idle speed, is adjusted at the factory and is not necessary to perform. This adjustment should be performed ONLY when the throttle body has been replaced.

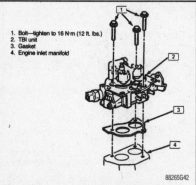

1. Bolt—tighten to 16 N·m (12 ft. lbs.)
2. TBI unit
3. Gasket
4. Engine inlet manifold

Fig. 30 Exploded view of a typical throttle body mounting—4.3L engine shown

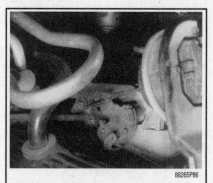

Fig. 31 Both the throttle cable and the cruise control linkage need to removed

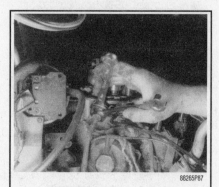

Fig. 32 Use a backup wrench and a flare wrench when disconnection the fuel lines

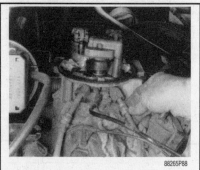

Fig. 33 Some fuel may spill out of the line connections, so place a rag under the fittings to catch it

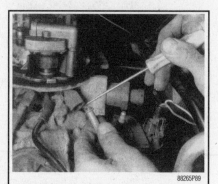

Fig. 34 Always replace the fuel line O-rings

Fig. 35 Remove the 3 bolts holding the throttle body

Fig. 36 Lift the throttle body straight up and be careful not to drop anything into the manifold

Fig. 37 Slide the electrical connection from the groove

Fig. 38 Always replace the throttle body base gasket, otherwise a vacuum leak may occur

➡ **The factory supplied replacement throttle body assembly will have the minimum idle adjusted at the factory.**

1. Remove the air cleaner and the gasket. Be sure to plug the THERMAC vacuum port (air cleaner vacuum line-to-throttle body) on the throttle body.
2. Remove the throttle valve cable from the throttle control bracket to provide access to the minimum air adjustment screw.
3. Using the manufacturer's instructions, connect a tachometer to the engine.
4. Remove the electrical connector from the Idle Air Control (IAC) valve, located on the throttle body.
5. To remove the throttle stop screw cover, perform the following procedures:
   a. Using a prick punch, mark the housing at the top over the center line of the throttle stop screw.
   b. Using a 5/32 in. drill bit, drill (on an angle) a hole through the casting to the hardened cover.
   c. Using a 1/16 in. pin punch, place it through the hole and drive out the cover to expose the throttle stop screw.
6. Place the transmission in Park (AT) or Neutral (MT), start the engine and allow the idle speed to stabilize.
7. Using the GM tool No. J–33047 or equivalent, install it into the idle air passage of the throttle body; be sure that the tool is fully seated in the opening and no air leaks exist.
8. Using the GM Torx® Bit No. 20, turn the throttle stop screw until the engine speed is 475–525 rpm (AT in Park or Neutral) or 750–800 rpm (MT in Neutral).
9. With the idle speed adjusted, stop the engine, remove the tool No. J–33047 from the throttle body.
10. Reconnect the Idle Air Control (IAC) electrical connector.
11. Using silicone sealant or equivalent, cover the throttle stop screw.
12. Reinstall the gasket and the air cleaner assembly.

### 1985–87 4.3L ENGINE

➡ **The following procedure requires the use of a tachometer, a prick punch, a 5/32 in. drill bit, a 1/16 in. pin punch, a grounding wire and silicone sealant.**

1. Remove the air cleaner and the gasket.
2. Remove the throttle stop screw cover by performing the following procedures:
   a. Using a prick punch, mark the housing at the top over the center line of the throttle stop screw.
   b. Using a 5/32 in. drill bit, drill (on an angle) a hole through the casting to the hardened cover.
   c. Using a 1/16 in. pin punch, place it through the hole and drive out the cover to expose the throttle stop screw.

➡ **The following adjustment should be performed ONLY when the throttle body assembly has been replaced; the engine should be at normal operating temperatures before making this adjustment.**

3. With the Idle Air Control (IAC) connected, ground the diagnostic terminal of the Assembly Line Communications Link (ALCL) connector.

➡ **The Assembly Line Communications Link (ALCL) connector is located in the engine compartment on the left side firewall.**

4. Turn the ignition switch ON but DO NOT start the engine. Wait 30 seconds, this will allow the IAC valve pintle to extend and seat in the throttle body.
5. With the ignition switch turned On, disconnect the Idle Air Control (IAC) valve electrical connector.
6. Remove the ground from the Diagnostic Terminal ALCL connector and start the engine.
7. Adjust the idle stop screw to obtain 400–450 rpm (AT in Drive).
8. Turn the ignition OFF and reconnect the IAC valve electrical connector.
9. Using silicone sealant or equivalent, cover the throttle stop screw.
10. Reinstall the gasket and the air cleaner assembly.

### 1988–90 2.5L AND 1988–ON 4.3L ENGINES

▶ **See Figure 39**

Before performing this check, there should be no codes displayed, idle air control system has been checked and ignition timing is correct.

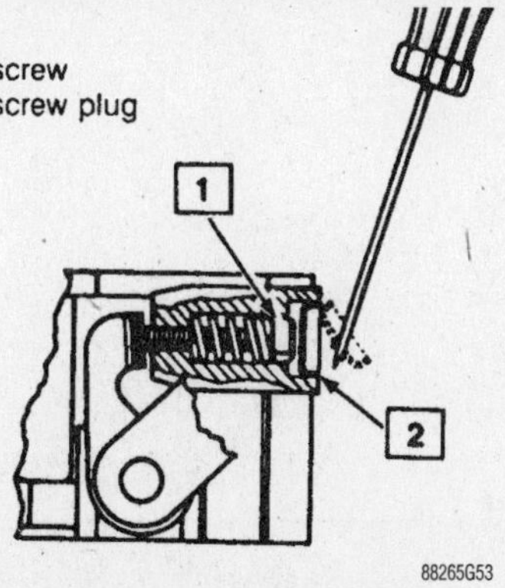

1. Idle stop screw
2. Idle stop screw plug

88265G53

**Fig. 39 Removing the idle stop screw plug—Model 700**

1. CONTROLLED IDLE SPEED CHECK: set the parking brake and block the wheels.
2. Connect a SCAN tool to the ALDL connector with the tool in the OPEN MODE.
3. Start the engine and bring it to normal operating temperature.
4. Check for correct state of Park/Neutral switch on the SCAN tool.
5. If the idle and IAC counts are not within specifications:
   • 2.5L MT in NEUTRAL 800 rpm, 5–20 IAC valve counts and in the closed loop.
   • 2.5L AT in DRIVE 750 rpm, 5–20 IAC valve counts and in the closed loop.
   • 4.3L MT in NEUTRAL 500–550 rpm, 2–12 IAC valve counts and in the closed loop.
   • 4.3L AT in DRIVE 500–550 rpm, 10–25 IAC valve counts and in the closed loop.
6. MINIMUM IDLE AIR RATE CHECK: check the controlled idle speed and perform the idle air control system check first.
7. With the IAC valve connected, ground the diagnostic A and B terminals of the ALDL connector.
8. Turn ON the ignition with engine NOT running, wait for ten seconds to allow the IAC valve to stabilize. Remove the ground from the ALDL and disconnect the IAC valve.
9. Connect the SCAN tool to the ALDL connector and place in the open mode. If a SCAN tool is not available, connect a tachometer to the engine.
10. Start the engine and allow to stabilize.
11. Check the rpm using the specifications.
12. If the minimum idle rate is not within specifications perform the following:
   a. Remove the idle stop screw plug by piercing it with an awl, then apply leverage to remove the plug.
   b. Adjust the screw to the specified rpm.
   c. Turn the engine OFF, disconnect the SCAN tool, reconnect the IAC valve and cover the idle stop screw with silicone sealer.
13. Install the air cleaner, adapter and gasket.

### Fuel Injectors

REMOVAL & INSTALLATION

▶ **See Figures 40, 41 and 42**

**✳✳ CAUTION**

**When removing the injector(s), be careful not to damage the electrical connector pins (on top of the injector), the injector fuel filter and the nozzle. The fuel injector is serviced as a complete assembly ONLY. It is an electrical component and should not be immersed in any kind of cleaner.**

1. Remove the air cleaner. Disconnect the negative battery cable from the battery.
2. Refer to the Fuel Pressure Relief procedures in this section and relieve the fuel pressure.

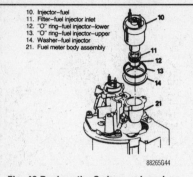

Fig. 40 Replace the O-rings and washers whenever the injector is removed—Model 220 (Model 300 is similar)

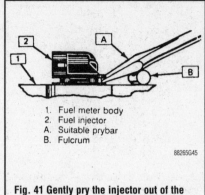

1. Fuel meter body
2. Fuel injector
A. Suitable prybar
B. Fulcrum

Fig. 41 Gently pry the injector out of the bore

Fig. 42 Replace the O-rings on the injector body when removed—Model 220, 4.3L engine shown

3. At the injector connector, squeeze the 2 tabs together and pull it straight up.

4. Remove the fuel meter cover and leave the cover gasket in place.

5. Using a small pry bar or tool No. J–26868, carefully lift the injector until it is free from the fuel meter body.

6. Remove the small O-ring from the nozzle end of the injector. Carefully rotate the injector's fuel filter back-and-forth to remove it from the base of the injector.

7. Discard the fuel meter cover gasket.

8. Remove the large O-ring and back-up washer from the top of the counterbore of the fuel meter body injector cavity.

**To install:**

9. Lubricate the O-rings with automatic transmission fluid and push the fuel injector into the cavity.

10. Install a new fuel meter cover gasket and install the cover (Model 300 and 220). Install the retainer and screw (Model 700).

11. Attach the injector electrical connector.

12. Install the air cleaner and connect the negative battery cable.

13. Start the engine, check for leaks and proper operation.

### Fuel Meter Cover

REMOVAL & INSTALLATION

▶ **See Figures 43 thru 54**

➡The fuel meter cover does not have to be removed to replace the single fuel injector for the Model 700 throttle body (1987–90 2.5L engine). For the Model 220 and 300, the fuel meter cover does have to be removed to replace the injector.

1. Remove the air cleaner. Disconnect the negative battery cable from the battery.

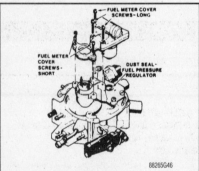

Fig. 43 Removing the fuel meter cover from the throttle body—Model 300 (Model 220 is similar)

Fig. 44 The throttle body can be accessed once the engine cover and air cleaner have been removed

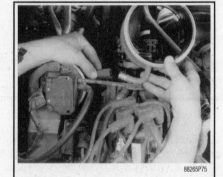

Fig. 45 Remove the adapter ring and disconnect from the breather hose

Fig. 46 Unplug the injector electrical connectors

Fig. 47 Use clean rags to block the throttle openings and prevent debris from dropping in the engine

Fig. 48 Remove the mounting screws from the meter body

Fig. 49 Lift the meter body up and off the injectors. The injectors can be removed at this point

Fig. 50 Check the condition of the gaskets. This one is torn and would leak fuel if reused

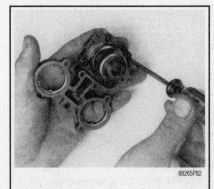

Fig. 51 The fuel pressure regulator can be removed from the meter cover

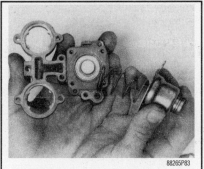

Fig. 52 The fuel pressure regulator diaphragm must be intact for proper operation

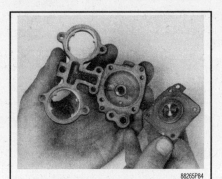

Fig. 53 Check the condition of the diaphragm and seating area before reassembly

Fig. 54 Exploded view of the fuel metering cover

2. At the injector electrical connector, squeeze the 2 tabs together and pull it straight up.

3. Remove the fuel meter-to-fuel meter body screws and lockwashers.

➡**When removing the fuel meter cover screws, note the location of the two short screws.**

4. Remove the fuel meter cover and discard the gasket.

5. Installation is the reverse of the removal procedure. Make sure to use a new gasket and install the injector if removed. Tighten the cover screws to 30 inch lbs. (4.0 Nm).

6. Connect the negative battery cable, then start the engine, check for leaks and proper operation.

## Idle Air Control (IAC) Valve

### TESTING

▶ See Figure 55

1. Disconnect the negative battery cable.
2. Test resistance between terminals A and B, then test between C and D.
3. If the resistance is nor 40–80 ohms, replace the IAC.
4. Connect the negative battery cable.

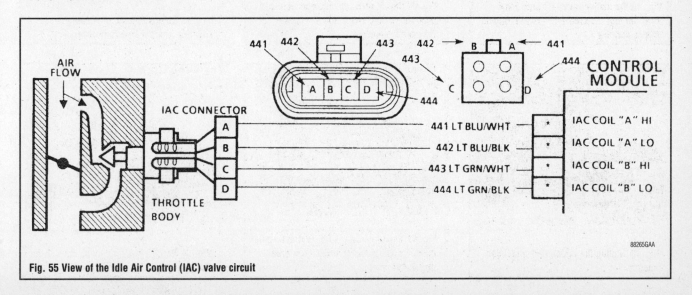

Fig. 55 View of the Idle Air Control (IAC) valve circuit

### REMOVAL & INSTALLATION

◢ **See Figures 56 and 57**

➡ The following procedure requires the use of the GM Removal tool No. J–33031 or equivalent.

1. From inside the vehicle, remove the engine cover.
2. Remove the air cleaner. Disconnect the negative battery cable.
3. Disconnect the electrical connector from the idle air control valve.
4. Using a 1¼ in. (approx. 32mm) wrench or the GM Removal tool No. J–33031, remove the idle air control valve (Model 220 and 300). Remove the two retaining screws and valve (Model 700).

### ☀ CAUTION

Before installing a new idle air control valve, measure the distance that the valve extends (from the motor housing to the end of the cone); the distance should be no greater than 1⅛ in. (28mm). If it extends to far, damage will occur to the valve when it is installed. Push the valve pintle in slowly with finger pressure until the correct measurement is obtained.

**To install:**

5. Use a new gasket and the correct IAC replacement valve.
6. Install the valve and torque the thread mounted valve to 13 ft. lbs. (18 Nm) and the screw mounted valve to 28 inch lbs. (3.3 Nm). Use thread locking compound on the retaining screws before assembly.
7. Connect the valve and negative battery cable.
8. Start the engine and allow it to reach normal operating temperatures. Check for fuel leaks.
9. Turn the ignition **ON** for 5 seconds and **OFF** for 10 seconds to allow the IAC valve to reset.
10. The vehicle may have to driven a few miles before the IAC valve will return to normal.

➡ The ECM will reset the idle speed when the vehicle is driven at 30 mph (48 kph).

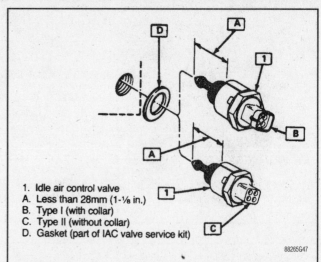

1. Idle air control valve
A. Less than 28mm (1-⅛ in.)
B. Type I (with collar)
C. Type II (without collar)
D. Gasket (part of IAC valve service kit)

88265G47

**Fig. 56 Exploded view of the Idle Air Control (IAC) valves—Model 220 and 300**

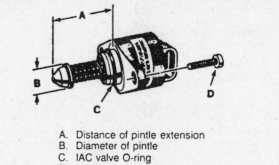

A. Distance of pintle extension
B. Diameter of pintle
C. IAC valve O-ring
D. Valve attaching screw

88265G48

**Fig. 57 Idle Air Control (IAC) valve—Model 700**

## CENTRAL MULTI-PORT FUEL INJECTION (CMFI) AND CENTRAL SEQUENTIAL FUEL INJECTION (CSFI) SYSTEMS

### General Information

◢ **See Figures 58, 59 and 60**

The 4.3L (VIN W) engine is equipped with a Central Multi-port Fuel Injection (CMFI) and Central Sequential Fuel Injection (CSFI) systems. The system functions similarly to the TBI system in that an injection assembly (CMFI/CSFI unit) is centrally mounted on the engine intake manifold. The major differences come in the incorporation of a split (upper and lower) intake manifold assembly with a variable tuned plenum (using an intake manifold tuning valve) and the CMFI unit's single fuel injector which feeds 6 poppet valves (1 for each individual cylinder). On the Central Sequential Fuel Injection (CSFI) there are 6 injectors for 6 poppet valves. This allows sequential fuel injection to occur. Unless otherwise broken out, CMFI and CSFI will be dealt with as a single system.

The non-repairable CMFI/CSFI assembly or injection unit consists of a fuel meter body, gasket seal, fuel pressure regulator, fuel injector(s) and 6 poppet nozzles with fuel tubes. The assembly is housed in the lower intake manifold. Should a failure occur in the CMFI/CSFI assembly, the entire component must be replaced as a unit.

As with other fuel injection systems, all injection and ignition functions are controlled by the computer control module. The module accepts inputs from various sensors and switches, calculates the optimum air/fuel mixture and operates the various output devices to provide peak performance within specific emissions limits. If a system failure occurs that is not serious enough to stop

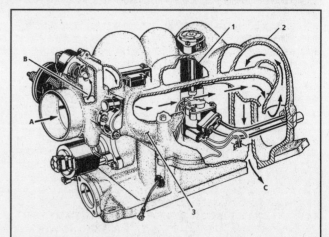

| 1 | INTAKE MANIFOLD TUNING VALVE ASSEMBLY | A | AIR INLET |
| 2 | TRI-LOBULAR RUNNER | B | IAC VALVE BYPASS AIR |
| 3 | ZIP TUBE | C | TO HEAD INTAKE PORT |

88265G54

**Fig. 58 CMFI air flow schematic**

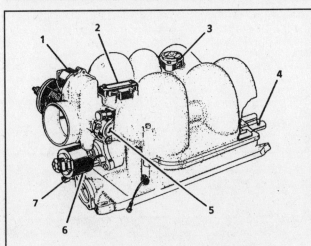

1   VALVE ASSEMBLY - IDLE AIR CONTROL (IAC)

2   SENSOR - MANIFOLD ABSOLUTE PRESSURE (MAP)

3   VALVE ASSEMBLY - INTAKE MANIFOLD TUNING

4   CONNECTION - FUEL PRESSURE

5   SENSOR - THROTTLE POSITION (TP)

6   VALVE ASSEMBLY - EXHAUST GAS RECIRCULATION (EGR)

7   SENSOR - ENGINE COOLANT TEMPERATURE

88265G55

**Fig. 59 Various CMFI engine components are mounted to the intake manifolds (the CMFI unit is located under the upper intake)**

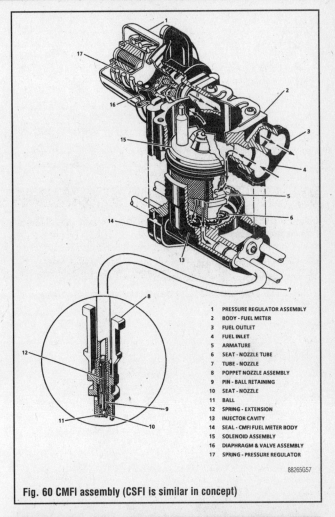

| | |
|---|---|
| 1 | PRESSURE REGULATOR ASSEMBLY |
| 2 | BODY - FUEL METER |
| 3 | FUEL OUTLET |
| 4 | FUEL INLET |
| 5 | ARMATURE |
| 6 | SEAT - NOZZLE TUBE |
| 7 | TUBE - NOZZLE |
| 8 | POPPET NOZZLE ASSEMBLY |
| 9 | PIN - BALL RETAINING |
| 10 | SEAT - NOZZLE |
| 11 | BALL |
| 12 | SPRING - EXTENSION |
| 13 | INJECTOR CAVITY |
| 14 | SEAL - CMFI FUEL METER BODY |
| 15 | SOLENOID ASSEMBLY |
| 16 | DIAPHRAGM & VALVE ASSEMBLY |
| 17 | SPRING - PRESSURE REGULATOR |

88265G57

**Fig. 60 CMFI assembly (CSFI is similar in concept)**

the engine, the module will illuminate the SERVICE ENGINE SOON light and will continue to operate the engine, although it may need to operate in a backup or fail-safe mode.

Fuel is supplied to the injector through an electric fuel pump assembly which is mounted in the vehicle's fuel tank. The module provides a signal to operate the fuel pump though the fuel pump relay and oil pressure switch. The CMFI/CSFI unit internal pressure regulator maintains a system pressure of approximately 55–61 psi (380–420 kPa). When the injector is energized by the control module, an armature lifts allowing pressurized fuel to travel down the fuel tubes to the poppet valves. In the poppet valves, fuel pressure (working against the extension spring force) will cause the nozzle ball to open from its seat and fuel will flow from the nozzle. It takes approximately 51 psi (350 kPa) to force fuel from the poppet nozzle. Once the module de-energizes the injector, the armature will close, allowing fuel pressure in the tubes to drop and the spring force will close off fuel flow.

Other system components include a pressure regulator, an Idle Air Control (IAC) valve, a Throttle Position (TP) sensor, Intake Air Temperature (IAT) sensor, Engine Coolant Temperature (ECT) sensor, a Manifold Absolute Pressure (MAP) sensor and an oxygen sensor.

The idle air control valve is a stepper motor that controls the amount of air allowed to bypass the throttle plate. With this valve the computer control module can closely control idle speed even when the engine is cold or when there is a high engine load at idle.

The computer module used on CMFI/CSFI vehicles has a learning capability which is used to provide corrections for a particular engine's condition. If the battery is disconnected to clear diagnostic codes, or for safety during a repair, the learning process must start all over again. A change may be noted in vehicle performance. In order to "teach" the vehicle, make sure the vehicle is at normal operating temperature, then drive at part throttle, under moderate acceleration and idle conditions, until normal performance returns.

## Fuel Pressure Relief

▶ See Figure 61

Prior to servicing any component of the fuel injection system, the fuel pressure must relieved. If fuel pressure is not relieved, serious injury could result.

A Schrader valve is provided on this fuel system in order to conveniently test or release the fuel system pressure. A fuel pressure gauge and adapter will be necessary to connect the gauge to the fitting. The CMFI system covered here uses a valve located on the inlet pipe fitting, immediately before it enters the CMFI assembly (towards the rear of the engine).

1. Disconnect the negative battery cable to assure the prevention of fuel spillage if the ignition switch is accidentally turned **ON** while a fitting is still disconnected.

2. Loosen the fuel filter cap to release the fuel tank pressure.

3. Make sure the release valve on the fuel gauge is closed, then connect the fuel gauge to the pressure fitting located on the inlet fuel pipe fitting.

➡**When connecting the gauge to the fitting, be sure to wrap a rag around the fitting to avoid spillage. After repairs, place the rag in an approved container.**

4. Install the bleed hose portion of the fuel gauge assembly into an approved container, then open the gauge release valve and bleed the fuel pressure from the system.

5. When the gauge is removed, be sure to open the bleed valve and drain all fuel from the gauge assembly.

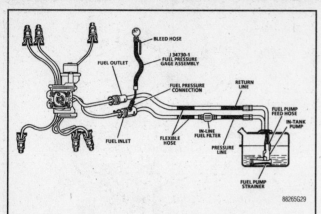

**Fig. 61 Use a fuel pressure gauge with a bleed hose to relieve the fuel system pressure**

## Electric Fuel Pump

The electric pump is attached to the fuel sending unit, located in the fuel tank.

### TESTING

▶ **See Figure 61**

1. Properly relieve the fuel system pressure.
2. Leave the gauge attached to the pressure fitting on the fuel inlet pipe.
3. If disconnected during the fuel pressure relief procedure, reconnect the negative battery cable.
4. If the engine will run, start the engine and allow it to run at normal idle speed. The fuel pressure should be 55–61 psi (380–420 kPa). Once the engine is at normal operating temperature, open the throttle quickly while noting fuel pressure; it should quickly approach 61 psi (420 kPa) if all components are operating properly (there is no need to proceed further). If the pressure was in specification before, but does not approach 61 psi (420 kPa) on acceleration, the pressure regulator in the CMFI/CSFI unit is faulty and the assembly should be replaced.
5. If the engine does not run, turn the ignition **ON**, but do not attempt to start the engine. Listen for the fuel pump to run. Within 2 seconds of turning the ignition **ON** pressure should be 55–61 psi (380–420 kPa) while the pump is running. Once the pump stops, pressure may vary by several pounds, then it should hold steady. If the pressure does not hold steady, wait 10 seconds and repeat this step, but pinch the fuel pressure line flexible hose and watch if the pressure holds. If it still does not hold, the CMFI/CSFI unit should be replaced. If the pressure holds with the pressure line pinched, check for a partially disconnected fuel dampener (pulsator) or faulty in-tank fuel pump.
6. If the fuel pump did not run or system pressure did not reach specification, locate the fuel pump test connector. The test connector is usually found on the driver's side of the engine compartment (on or near the fender), with a single wire (usually red) leading from the relay to the connector. Using a 10 amp fused jumper wire, apply battery voltage to the test connector in order to energize and run the fuel pump. The pump should run and produce fuel pressure of 55–61 psi (380–420 kPa). If the pump does not run, check the relay and fuel pump wiring.
7. If the pump pressure was lower than specification, first check for a restricted fuel line, filter or a disconnected fuel pulse dampener (pulsator) and repair/replace, as necessary. If no restrictions can be found, restrict the flexible fuel return line (by gradually pinching it) until the pressure rises above 61 psi (420 kPa), but DO NOT allow pressure to exceed 75 psi (517 kPa). If the fuel pressure rises above specification with the return line restricted, then the pressure regulator is faulty and the CMFI assembly should be replaced. If pressure still does not reach specification, check for a faulty fuel pump, partially disconnected fuel pulse dampener (pulsator), partially restricted pump strainer or an incorrect pump.
8. If during the previous steps, the fuel pressure was higher than specification, relieve the system pressure, then disconnect the engine compartment fuel return line. Attach a 5⁄16 ID flex hose to the fuel line from the throttle body and place the other end into an approved gasoline container. Cycle the ignition in

order to energize the fuel pump and watch system pressure. If pressure is still higher, check for restrictions in the line between the pressure regulator and the point where it was disconnected. Repair or replace the line if restrictions are found or replace the CMFI/CSFI assembly with the faulty internal pressure regulator if no other causes of high pressure are identified. If fuel pressure is normal only with the rest of the return line out of the circuit, check that remaining line for restrictions and repair or replace, as necessary.
9. Once the test is completed, depressurize the fuel system and remove the gauge.

### REMOVAL & INSTALLATION

Removal and installation of the fuel pump and sending unit assembly requires the removal of the fuel tank. Please refer to the procedures later in this section.

## Fuel Pump Relay

For CMFI/CSFI vehicles, the fuel pump relay is normally found in the convenience center, located under the center of the dashboard. If a problem is suspected, first check for loose electrical connections; no other service is possible, except replacement.

### REMOVAL & INSTALLATION

▶ **See Figure 62**

1. Disconnect the negative battery cable.
2. Remove the retainer, if equipped.
3. Disengage the relay electrical connector.
4. Remove the relay by depressing the bracket clip at the rear of the relay, or removing the bolts from the retaining bracket, as applicable.
5. If necessary, use a new relay, then reverse the removal procedures.

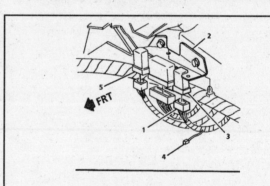

| 1 | ELECTRICAL CONNECTOR |
| 2 | BRACKET |
| 3 | FUEL PUMP RELAY |
| 4 | FUEL PUMP PRIME TERMINAL |
| 5 | INTAKE MANIFOLD TUNING VALVE RELAY |

**Fig. 62 Common fuel pump relay mounting—CMFI/CSFI vehicles**

## CMFI Assembly

### REMOVAL & INSTALLATION

#### Except 1996

▶ **See Figures 63 and 64**

The CMFI assembly is mounted to the lower intake manifold. The upper intake manifold assembly must be removed for access. The CMFI assembly includes a fuel meter body, gasket seal, fuel pressure regulator, fuel injector and 6 poppet nozzles with fuel tubes. Should a failure occur in any components of the CMFI unit, the entire assembly must be replaced.

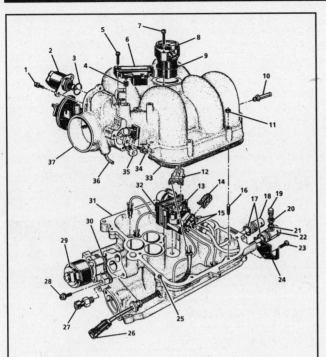

**Fig. 63 Exploded view of the upper and lower intake manifolds and the CMFI system components**

| # | | # | |
|---|---|---|---|
| 1 | BOLT/SCREW - IDLE AIR CONTROL VALVE | 20 | FUEL PRESSURE CONNECTION ASSEMBLY |
| 2 | VALVE ASSEMBLY - IDLE AIR CONTROL (IAC) | 21 | SEAL - FUEL PRESSURE CONNECTION |
| 3 | SEAL - IDLE AIR CONTROL VALVE (O-RING) | 22 | PIPE ASSEMBLY - FUEL INJECTION FUEL FEED |
| 4 | SEAL - MAP SENSOR | 23 | BOLT/SCREW - FUEL INJECTION FUEL FEED AND RETURN PIPE RETAINER |
| 5 | BOLT/SCREW - MAP SENSOR | 24 | RETAINER - FUEL INJECTION FUEL FEED AND RETURN PIPE |
| 6 | SENSOR ASSEMBLY - MANIFOLD ABSOLUTE PRESSURE (MAP) | 25 | PIN - UPPER INTAKE MANIFOLD LOCATING |
| 7 | BOLT/SCREW - INTAKE MANIFOLD TUNING VALVE | 26 | HARNESS ASSEMBLY - CENTRAL MULTIPORT FUEL INJECTOR WIRING |
| 8 | VALVE ASSEMBLY - INTAKE MANIFOLD TUNING | 27 | SENSOR ASSEMBLY - ENGINE COOLANT TEMPERATURE (ECT) |
| 9 | SEAL - INTAKE MANIFOLD VALVE (O-RING) | 28 | BOLT/SCREW - EGR VALVE |
| 10 | FITTING - POWER BRAKE BOOSTER VACUUM | 29 | VALVE ASSEMBLY - EGR |
| 11 | NUT - UPPER INTAKE MANIFOLD | 30 | GASKET - EGR VALVE |
| 12 | CONNECTOR ASSEMBLY - CENTRAL MULTIPORT FUEL INJECTOR WIRING HARNESS | 31 | MANIFOLD ASSEMBLY - LOWER INTAKE |
| 13 | INJECTOR ASSEMBLY - CENTRAL MULTIPORT FUEL INJECTOR (CMFI) | 32 | SEAL - CENTRAL MULTIPORT FUEL INJECTOR (CMFI) |
| 14 | CLIP - FUEL INJECTION FUEL FEED AND RETURN PIPE | 33 | GASKET - UPPER INTAKE MANIFOLD |
| 15 | SEAL - FUEL INJECTION FUEL FEED AND RETURN PIPE (O-RING) | 34 | BOLT/SCREW - THROTTLE POSITION SENSOR |
| 16 | STUD - UPPER INTAKE MANIFOLD | 35 | SENSOR ASSEMBLY - THROTTLE POSITION (TP) SENSOR |
| 17 | SEAL - LOWER INTAKE MANIFOLD FUEL FEED AND RETURN PIPE (O-RING) | 36 | TUBE - FUEL VAPOR CANISTER PURGE |
| 18 | PIPE ASSEMBLY - FUEL INJECTION FUEL RETURN | 37 | MANIFOLD ASSEMBLY - UPPER INTAKE (WITH THROTTLE BODY) |
| 19 | CAP - FUEL PRESSURE CONNECTION | | |

88265G59

1. Remove the plastic cover and properly relieve the fuel system pressure.

2. Disconnect the negative battery cable, then remove the air cleaner and air inlet duct.

3. Disengage the wiring harness from the necessary upper intake components including:

 • Throttle Position (TP) sensor
 • Idle Air Control (IAC) motor

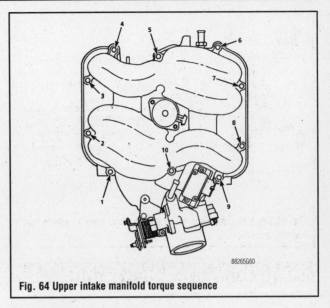

**Fig. 64 Upper intake manifold torque sequence**

88265G60

 • Manifold Absolute Pressure (MAP) sensor
 • Intake Manifold Tuning Valve (IMTV)

4. Disengage the throttle linkage from the upper intake manifold, then remove the ignition coil.

5. Disconnect the PCV hose at the rear of the upper intake manifold, then tag and disengage the vacuum hoses from both the front and rear of the upper intake manifold.

6. Remove the upper intake manifold bolts and studs, making sure to note or mark the location of all studs to assure proper installation. Remove the upper intake manifold from the engine.

7. Disengage the injector wiring harness connector at the CMFI assembly.

8. Remove and discard the fuel fitting clip.

9. Disconnect the fuel inlet and return tube and fitting assembly. Discard the old O-rings.

10. Squeeze the poppet nozzle locktabs together while lifting each nozzle out of the casting socket. Once all 6 nozzles are released, carefully lift the CMFI assembly out of the casting.

**To install:**

11. Align the CMFI assembly grommet with the casting grommet slots and push downward until it is seated in the bottom guide hole.

### ✳✳ CAUTION

**To reduce the risk of fire and personal injury, be ABSOLUTELY SURE that the poppet nozzles are firmly seated and locked into their casting sockets. An unlocked poppet nozzle could work loose from its socket resulting in a dangerous fuel leak.**

12. Carefully insert the poppet nozzles into the casting sockets. Make sure they are FIRMLY SEATED and locked into the casting sockets.

13. Position new O-ring seals (lightly coated with clean engine oil), then connect the fuel inlet and return tube and fitting assembly.

14. Install a new fuel fitting clip.

15. Temporarily connect the negative battery cable, then pressurize the fuel system by cycling the ignition switch **ON** for 2 seconds, then **OFF** for 10 seconds and repeating, as necessary. Once the fuel system is pressurized, check for leaks.

16. Disconnect the negative battery cable.

17. Position a new upper intake manifold gasket on the engine, making sure the green sealing lines are facing upward.

18. Install the upper intake manifold being careful not to pinch the fuel injector wires between the manifolds. Install the manifold retainers, making sure the studs are properly positioned, then tighten them using the proper sequence to 124 inch lbs. (14 Nm).

19. Install the remaining components in the reverse order of removal.

20. Connect the negative battery cable.

**1996 CSFI**

◆ **See Figures 65 and 66**

The 1996 4.3L engine is equipped with a sequential version of CMFI. It is very similar to the standard non-sequential CMFI except that there is a separate injector for each cylinder. This allows each cylinder to receive a timed pulse of fuel exactly when needed.

1. Clean the upper manifold area and fuel meter body area before disassembly to help prevent dirt from entering the air intake tract when the manifold is removed.

2. Disconnect the negative battery cable. Relieve the fuel system pressure.

3. Disconnect the wiring from the fuel meter body.

4. Remove the fuel inlet and return pipes from the fuel meter body and upper manifold. Keep dirt from falling into the now open fuel ports on the meter body.

5. Remove the upper manifold from the lower section. The air inlet tract is now open to contamination, so stuff some rags into the openings to prevent dirt from falling in.

6. Mark the poppet valves relative to their cylinders. This will prevent mixing them up during installation.

7. Release the poppet valves from the lower manifold by squeezing the tabs together and pulling out.

8. Release the fuel meter body from the lower manifold by unlocking the tabs from the bracket and removing the bolts.

9. Pull up on the fuel meter body to remove it from the manifold.

**To install:**

10. Install the fuel meter body and tighten the bolts to 88 inch lbs. (10.0 Nm). Make sure the body has locked all the tabs in place.

11. Install the poppet valves into the bores in the same locations as they were removed. Be sure the tabs lock into place or fuel leakage will occur.

12. Install the upper intake manifold electrical connector.

13. Install new O-rings on the fuel lines. Install the fuel lines on the manifold and tighten the connections to 22 ft. lbs. (30.0 Nm).

14. Connect the negative battery cable. Turn the ignition switch **ON** for 2 seconds, **OFF** for 10 seconds, **ON** for 2 seconds and then **OFF** again. Check for leaks from the fuel connections. Fix as necessary.

15. Disconnect the negative battery cable and the fuel lines.

16. Install the upper intake manifold.

17. Connect the fuel lines and check the fuel meter body electrical connection.

18. Connect the negative battery cable.

## Throttle Body

This procedure is for the CSFI system. The CMFI system uses a throttle plate integral with the upper manifold.

### REMOVAL & INSTALLATION

◆ **See Figures 67 and 68**

1. Disconnect the negative battery cable.

2. Remove the air inlet fastener and duct.

3. Disengage the Idle Air Control (IAC) valve and the Throttle Position Sensor (TPS) electrical connectors.

4. Disconnect the throttle and cruise control cables.

5. Disconnect the accelerator cable bracket bolts and nuts.

6. Disengage the wiring harness fastener nut.

7. Unfasten the throttle body retaining nuts and remove the throttle body.

8. Remove and discard the flange gasket.

9. Clean both gasket mating surfaces.

➡**When cleaning the old gasket from the machined aluminum surfaces be careful as sharp tools may damage the sealing surfaces**

10. Installation is the reverse of the removal procedure. Make sure all components and connectors are secured. Position a new flange gasket and the throttle body, then tighten the attaching nuts to 18 ft. lbs. (25 Nm).

11. Tighten the accelerator cable bracket bolts and nuts 18 ft. lbs. (25 Nm).

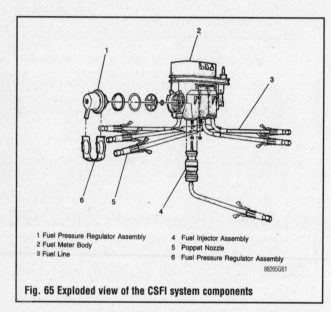

1 Fuel Pressure Regulator Assembly
2 Fuel Meter Body
3 Fuel Line
4 Fuel Injector Assembly
5 Poppet Nozzle
6 Fuel Pressure Regulator Assembly

88265G61

**Fig. 65 Exploded view of the CSFI system components**

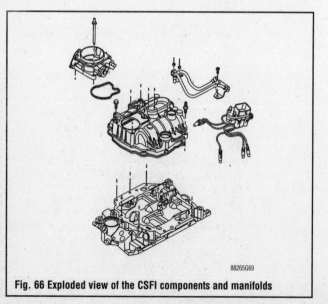

88265G69

**Fig. 66 Exploded view of the CSFI components and manifolds**

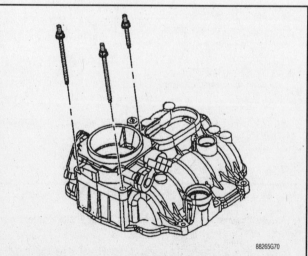

88265G70

**Fig. 67 These 3 long bolts or studs hold the throttle body to the upper manifold**

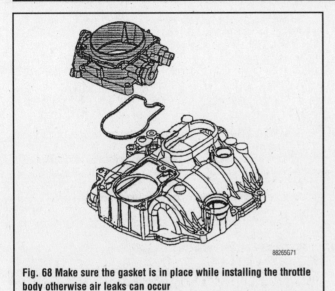

**Fig. 68 Make sure the gasket is in place while installing the throttle body otherwise air leaks can occur**

## CSFI Fuel Injectors

### REMOVAL & INSTALLATION

1. Disconnect the negative battery cable.
2. Relieve the fuel system pressure.
3. Disengage the fuel meter body electrical connection and the fuel feed and return hoses from the engine fuel pipes.
4. Remove the upper manifold assembly.
5. Tag and remove the poppet nozzle out of the casting socket.
6. Remove the fuel meter body by releasing the locktabs.

➠**Each injector is calibrated. When replacing the fuel injectors, be sure to replace it with the correct injector.**

7. Disassemble the lower hold-down plate and nuts.
8. While pulling the poppet nozzle tube downward, push with a small screwdriver down between the injector terminals and remove the injectors.
   **To install:**
9. Install the fuel meter body assembly into the intake manifold and tighten the fuel meter bracket retainer bolts to 88 inch. lbs. (10 Nm).

### ✳✳ CAUTION

**To reduce the risk of fire or injury ensure that the poppet nozzles are properly seated and locked in their casting sockets**

10. Install the fuel meter body into the bracket and lock all the tabs in place.
11. Install the poppet nozzles into the casting sockets.
12. Engage the electrical connections and install new O-ring seals on the fuel return and feed hoses.
13. Install the fuel feed and return hoses and tighten the fuel pipe nuts to 22 ft. lbs. (30 Nm).
14. Connect the negative battery cable.
15. Turn the ignition **ON** for 2 seconds and then turn it **OFF** for 10 seconds. Again turn the ignition **ON** and check for leaks.
16. Install the manifold plenum.

### TESTING

▶ **See Figure 69**

➠**This test requires the use of Fuel Injector Tester J 39021 or its equivalent.**

1. Disconnect the fuel injector harness and attach a noid light in order to test for injector pulse.
2. With the engine cool and the ignition turned **OFF**, install the fuel pres-

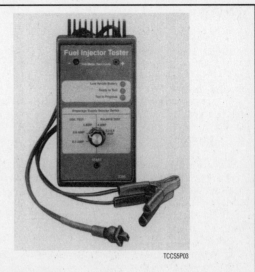

**Fig. 69 Fuel injector testers can be purchased or sometimes rented**

sure gauge to the fuel pressure connection. Wrap a shop towel around the fitting while connecting the gauge to prevent spillage.
3. Turn **ON** the ignition and record the fuel gauge pressure with the pump running.
4. Turn **OFF** the ignition. Pressure should drop and hold steady at this point.
5. To perform this test, set the selector switch to the balance test 2.5 amp position.
6. Turn the injector **ON** by depressing the button on the injector tester. Note this pressure reading the instant the gauge needle stops.
7. Repeat the balance test on the remaining injectors and record the pressure drop on each.
8. Start the engine to clear fuel from the intake. Retest the injectors that appear faulty. Any injector that has a plus or minus 1.5 psi (10 kPa) difference from the other injectors is suspect.

## Fuel Pressure Regulator

This procedure is for the CSFI system as the CMFI system uses an integral fuel pressure regulator. The CSFI uses a replaceable unit mounted on the CSFI assembly.

### REMOVAL & INSTALLATION

▶ **See Figures 70 and 71**

1. Disconnect the negative battery cable.
2. Relieve the fuel system pressure. Refer to the fuel system relief procedure in this section.

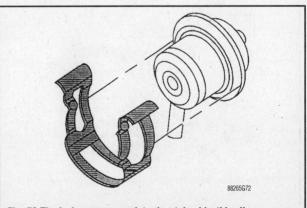

**Fig. 70 The fuel pressure regulator is retained by this clip**

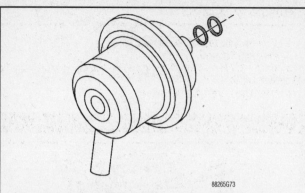

**Fig. 71 Replace the O-rings whenever the fuel pressure regulator is removed**

3. Remove the upper manifold assembly.
4. Remove the fuel pressure regulator vacuum tube.
5. Disassemble the fuel pressure regulator snapring retainer.
6. Remove the fuel pressure regulator assembly and the O-rings. Discard the O-rings, filter and back-up O-rings.

**To install:**
7. Lubricate the O-rings with clean engine oil and install as an assembly.
8. Install the fuel pressure regulator, attach the vacuum tube.
9. Install the snapring retainer.
10. Install the upper manifold assembly.
11. Connect the negative battery cable.

## Idle Air Control Valve

### REMOVAL & INSTALLATION

▶ **See Figure 72**

1. Disconnect the negative battery cable.
2. Disengage the electrical connector from the idle air control valve.
3. Loosen and remove the IAC valve retaining bolts, then remove the valve from the engine.

**To install:**

### ✳✳ WARNING

Before installing a new idle air control valve, measure the distance that the valve extends (from the motor housing to the end of the cone); the distance should be no greater than 1⅛ in. (28mm). If it is extended too far, damage may occur to the valve when it is installed.

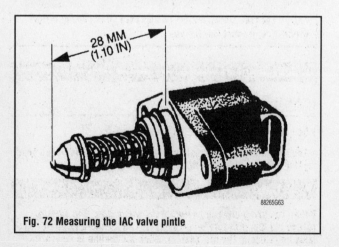

**Fig. 72 Measuring the IAC valve pintle**

4. Measure the valve pintle extension. To retract the pintle on a NEW valve, use firm thumb pressure and, if necessary, rock the pintle with a slight side-to-side motion. BUT, if reinstalling a used valve on which the pintle is extended further than specification, an IAC tester MUST be used to electrically retract the pintle.

➡ **Do not attempt to physically retract a pintle on an IAC valve that has been in service, the force may damage the pintle threads. The force required to retract the pintle is only safe on NEW IAC valves.**

5. Lightly coat the IAC valve O-ring with clean engine oil.
6. Inspect the retaining screw threads for threadlocking material. If there is no longer sufficient material on the threads, clean the threads and apply Loctite®262 or equivalent. DO NOT use a stronger compound or future bolt removal may be difficult.
7. Install the IAC valve and tighten the retaining bolts to 27 inch lbs. (3.0 Nm).
8. Engage the valve electrical connector.
9. Connect the negative battery cable.
10. Reset the IAC valve pintle: turn the ignition **ON** (engine NOT running) for 5 seconds, then turn the ignition **OFF** for 10 seconds. Start the engine and check for proper idle operation.

## Intake Manifold Tuning Valve

▶ **See Figure 73**

The upper intake manifold on the CMFI engine is of a variable tuned split plenum design. The manifold uses a centrally mounted tuning valve to equalize pressure in the side by side inlet plenums. The valve is electronically operated by the computer control module. The CSFI system does not utilize this component.

### REMOVAL & INSTALLATION

1. Disconnect the negative battery cable.
2. Remove the tuning valve attaching screws.
3. Remove the tuning valve from the top of the upper intake manifold assembly.
4. Remove and discard the old O-ring seal.

**To install:**
5. Lubricate the new O-ring seal with clean engine oil.
6. Make sure the threads of the retaining screws are coated with Loctite®262, or an equivalent threadlocking compound.
7. Position the tuning valve to the upper intake manifold, then carefully thread the retaining screws.

➡ **To avoid breaking the valve mounting ears, alternately tighten the attaching screws until they engage the mounting ear surface, then carefully tighten the screws to specification.**

8. Tighten the retaining screws to 18 inch lbs. (2 Nm).

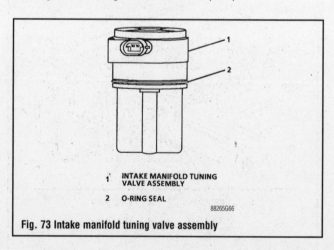

1   **INTAKE MANIFOLD TUNING VALVE ASSEMBLY**
2   **O-RING SEAL**

**Fig. 73 Intake manifold tuning valve assembly**

9. Engage the valve electrical connector, then connect the negative battery cable.

## Oil Pressure Switch

The oil pressure switch is mounted to a fitting in the left rear of the engine block.

## FUEL TANK

The fuel tank is located under the left side, center of the vehicle and is held in place by two metal straps.

### Fuel Tank Assembly

REMOVAL & INSTALLATION

▶ **See Figures 74 and 75**

1. Disconnect the negative battery cable from the battery.

➡ **Be sure to keep a Class B (dry chemical) fire extinguisher nearby.**

### ❊ CAUTION

**Due to the possibility of fire or explosion, never drain or store gasoline in an open container.**

2. Using a hand pump or a siphon hose, drain the gasoline into an approved container.
3. Raise and support the vehicle on jackstands.
4. Support the fuel tank and remove the fuel tank-to-vehicle straps.
5. Lower the tank slightly, then remove the sender unit wires, the hoses and the ground strap.
6. Remove the fuel tank from the vehicle.

**To install:**

➡ **Be sure to connect the sender unit wires and the hoses before final installation of the fuel tank.**

7. Align the insulator strips and position the tank into the vehicle. Torque the inner fuel tank bolts to 26 ft. lbs. (35 Nm) and the outer strap bolts to 30 ft. lbs. (40 Nm) in alternating sequence. Torque the nuts to 26 ft. lbs. (35 Nm). This must be done to prevent the bottom of the tank from bowing up and effecting the fuel level sender.
8. Make sure all hoses and electrical connectors are secure and properly routed to prevent damage.
9. Lower the vehicle, connect the negative battery cable, start the engine and check for leaks and proper operation.

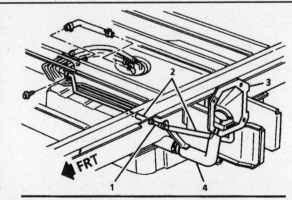

| | | | |
|---|---|---|---|
| 1 | VENT PIPE | 3 | HOUSING |
| 2 | INSULATOR | 4 | FILLER PIPE |

88265G67

**Fig. 74 Fuel filler neck assembly**

REMOVAL & INSTALLATION

1. Disconnect the negative battery cable.
2. Disengage the switch connector.
3. Using J-35748 or an equivalent wrench, carefully loosen and remove the oil pressure switch.
4. Installation is the reverse of removal.

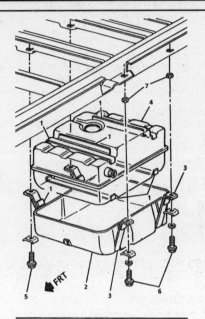

COMPLETELY INSTALL ONE STRAP PRIOR TO INSTALLATION OF THE SECOND STRAP, HOWEVER, THE TANK MUST REMAIN SUPPORTED UNTIL ALL FOUR BOLTS ARE TORQUED TO SPECIFICATIONS.

| | |
|---|---|
| 1 | INSULATOR |
| 2 | LOWER SHIELD |
| 3 | STRAP |
| 4 | FUEL TANK |
| | INSTALLATION SEQUENCE |
| 5 | BOLT - TIGHTEN TO 35 N·m (26 lb. ft.) |
| 6 | BOLT - TIGHTEN TO 3.4 N·m (30 lb. in.) |
| 7 | NUT - TIGHTEN TO 35 N·m (26 lb. ft.) |

88265G68

**Fig. 75 The fuel tank bolts must be tightened alternately to prevent distortion of the fuel tank bottom**

## Electric Fuel Pump

REMOVAL & INSTALLATION

▶ **See Figures 76, 77, 78 and 79**

➡ **The following procedure requires the use of the GM Fuel Gauge Sending Unit Retaining Cam tool No. J–24187 or equivalent.**

### ❊ CAUTION

**Before removing any component of the fuel system, be sure to reduce the fuel pressure in the system. The pressure regulator contains an orifice in the fuel system; when the engine is turned Off, the pressure in the system will bleed down within a few minutes.**

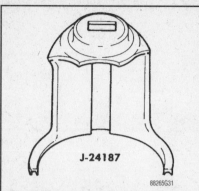

Fig. 76 The fuel pump locking ring can be removed using this tool

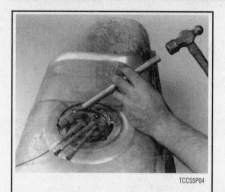

Fig. 77 The fuel pump locking ring can also be removed using a brass drift

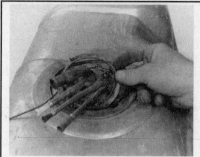

Fig. 78 With the locking ring removed, the fuel pump (and/or gauge sender) can be lifted from the tank

1. If the fuel system has been in use, turn the ignition switch to **OFF** and allow the system time to reduce the fuel pressure.
2. Disconnect the negative battery terminal from the battery.

➡Be sure to keep a Class B (dry chemical) fire extinguisher nearby.

### ✳✳ CAUTION

**Due to the possibility of fire or explosion, never drain or store gasoline in an open container.**

3. Using a hand pump or a siphon hose, drain the gasoline into an approved container.
4. Raise and support the vehicle on jackstands.
5. Support the fuel tank and remove the fuel tank-to-vehicle straps.
6. Lower the tank slightly, then remove the sender unit wires, the hoses and the ground strap.
7. Remove the fuel tank from the vehicle.
8. Using the GM Fuel Gauge Sending Unit Retaining Cam tool No. J–24187 (or equivalent) or a brass drift and a hammer, remove the cam locking ring (fuel sending unit) counterclockwise, then lift the sending unit from the fuel tank.
9. Remove the fuel pump from the fuel sending unit, by performing the following procedures:
   a. Pull the fuel pump up into the mounting tube, while pulling outward (away) from the bottom support.

➡When removing the fuel pump from the sending unit, be careful not to damage the rubber insulator and the strainer.

   b. When the pump assembly is clear of the bottom support, pull it out of the rubber connector.
**To install:**
10. Inspect the fuel pump hose and bottom sound insulator for signs of deterioration, then replace it, if necessary.
11. Push the fuel pump onto the sending tube.
12. Using a new sending unit-to-fuel tank O-ring, install the sending unit into the fuel tank.

➡When installing the sending unit, be careful not to fold or twist the fuel strainer, for it will restrict the fuel flow.

13. Using the GM Fuel Gauge Sending Unit Retaining Cam tool No. J–24187 (or equivalent) or a brass drift and a hammer, turn the sending unit-to-fuel tank locking ring clockwise.
14. Install the fuel tank, align the insulator strips and install the strap bolts.

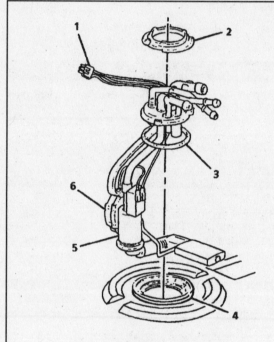

| 1 | ELECTRICAL CONNECTOR |
| 2 | CAM |
| 3 | SEAL |
| 4 | FUEL TANK |
| 5 | FUEL PUMP |
| 6 | SENDER |

Fig. 79 The fuel pump and fuel gauge sender assembly

Torque the inner fuel tank strap-to-vehicle bolts to 26 ft. lbs. (35 Nm) and the outer fuel tank strap-to-vehicle nuts/bolts to 26 ft. lbs. (35 Nm).
15. Attach the fuel lines, then connect the negative battery cable, start the engine and check for leaks.
16. Lower the vehicle.

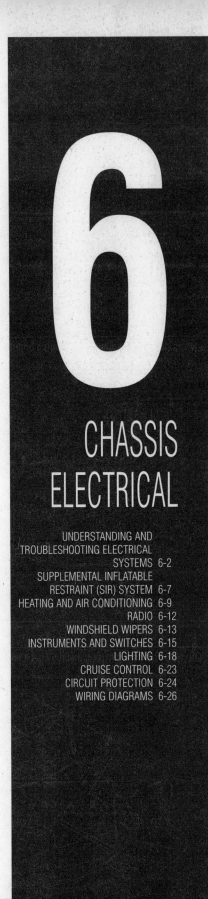

**6**

**CHASSIS ELECTRICAL**

## UNDERSTANDING AND TROUBLESHOOTING ELECTRICAL SYSTEMS

### Basic Electrical Theory

▶ See Figure 1

For any 12 volt, negative ground, electrical system to operate, the electricity must travel in a complete circuit. This simply means that current (power) from the positive (+) terminal of the battery must eventually return to the negative (-) terminal of the battery. Along the way, this current will travel through wires, fuses, switches and components. If, for any reason, the flow of current through the circuit is interrupted, the component fed by that circuit will cease to function properly.

Perhaps the easiest way to visualize a circuit is to think of connecting a light bulb (with two wires attached to it) to the battery—one wire attached to the negative (-) terminal of the battery and the other wire to the positive (+) terminal. With the two wires touching the battery terminals, the circuit would be complete and the light bulb would illuminate. Electricity would follow a path from the battery to the bulb and back to the battery. It's easy to see that with longer wires on our light bulb, it could be mounted anywhere. Further, one wire could be fitted with a switch so that the light could be turned on and off.

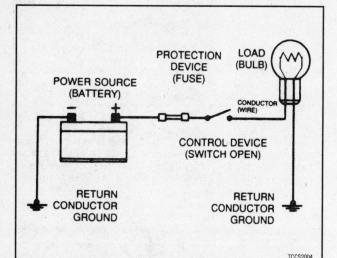

TCCS2004

**Fig. 1 This example illustrates a simple circuit. When the switch is closed, power from the positive (+) battery terminal flows through the fuse and the switch, and then to the light bulb. The light illuminates and the circuit is completed through the ground wire back to the negative (-) battery terminal. In reality, the two ground points shown in the illustration are attached to the metal frame of the vehicle, which completes the circuit back to the battery**

The normal automotive circuit differs from this simple example in two ways. First, instead of having a return wire from the bulb to the battery, the current travels through the frame of the vehicle. Since the negative (-) battery cable is attached to the frame (made of electrically conductive metal), the frame of the vehicle can serve as a ground wire to complete the circuit. Secondly, most automotive circuits contain multiple components which receive power from a single circuit. This lessens the amount of wire needed to power components on the vehicle.

### HOW DOES ELECTRICITY WORK: THE WATER ANALOGY

Electricity is the flow of electrons—the subatomic particles that constitute the outer shell of an atom. Electrons spin in an orbit around the center core of an atom. The center core is comprised of protons (positive charge) and neutrons (neutral charge). Electrons have a negative charge and balance out the positive charge of the protons. When an outside force causes the number of electrons to unbalance the charge of the protons, the electrons will split off the atom and look for another atom to balance out. If this imbalance is kept up, electrons will continue to move and an electrical flow will exist.

Many people have been taught electrical theory using an analogy with water. In a comparison with water flowing through a pipe, the electrons would be the water and the wire is the pipe.

The flow of electricity can be measured much like the flow of water through a pipe. The unit of measurement used is amperes, frequently abbreviated as amps (a). You can compare amperage to the volume of water flowing through a pipe. When connected to a circuit, an ammeter will measure the actual amount of current flowing through the circuit. When relatively few electrons flow through a circuit, the amperage is low. When many electrons flow, the amperage is high.

Water pressure is measured in units such as pounds per square inch (psi); The electrical pressure is measured in units called volts (v). When a voltmeter is connected to a circuit, it is measuring the electrical pressure.

The actual flow of electricity depends not only on voltage and amperage, but also on the resistance of the circuit. The higher the resistance, the higher the force necessary to push the current through the circuit. The standard unit for measuring resistance is an ohm. Resistance in a circuit varies depending on the amount and type of components used in the circuit. The main factors which determine resistance are:

• Material—some materials have more resistance than others. Those with high resistance are said to be insulators. Rubber materials (or rubber-like plastics) are some of the most common insulators used in vehicles as they have a very high resistance to electricity. Very low resistance materials are said to be conductors. Copper wire is among the best conductors. Silver is actually a superior conductor to copper and is used in some relay contacts, but its high cost prohibits its use as common wiring. Most automotive wiring is made of copper.

• Size—the larger the wire size being used, the less resistance the wire will have. This is why components which use large amounts of electricity usually have large wires supplying current to them.

• Length—for a given thickness of wire, the longer the wire, the greater the resistance. The shorter the wire, the less the resistance. When determining the proper wire for a circuit, both size and length must be considered to design a circuit that can handle the current needs of the component.

• Temperature—with many materials, the higher the temperature, the greater the resistance (positive temperature coefficient). Some materials exhibit the opposite trait of lower resistance with higher temperatures (negative temperature coefficient). These principles are used in many of the sensors on the engine.

### OHM'S LAW

There is a direct relationship between current, voltage and resistance. The relationship between current, voltage and resistance can be summed up by a statement known as Ohm's law.

Voltage (E) is equal to amperage (I) times resistance (R): $E = I \times R$

Other forms of the formula are $R = E/I$ and $I = E/R$

In each of these formulas, E is the voltage in volts, I is the current in amps and R is the resistance in ohms. The basic point to remember is that as the resistance of a circuit goes up, the amount of current that flows in the circuit will go down, if voltage remains the same.

The amount of work that the electricity can perform is expressed as power. The unit of power is the watt (w). The relationship between power, voltage and current is expressed as:

Power (w) is equal to amperage (I) times voltage (E): $W = I \times E$

This is only true for direct current (DC) circuits; The alternating current formula is a tad different, but since the electrical circuits in most vehicles are DC type, we need not get into AC circuit theory.

### Electrical Components

### POWER SOURCE

Power is supplied to the vehicle by two devices: The battery and the alternator. The battery supplies electrical power during starting or during periods when the current demand of the vehicle's electrical system exceeds the output capacity of the alternator. The alternator supplies electrical current when the engine is running. Just not does the alternator supply the current needs of the vehicle, but it recharges the battery.

### The Battery

In most modern vehicles, the battery is a lead/acid electrochemical device consisting of six 2 volt subsections (cells) connected in series, so that the unit is capable of producing approximately 12 volts of electrical pressure. Each subsection consists of a series of positive and negative plates held a short distance apart in a solution of sulfuric acid and water.

The two types of plates are of dissimilar metals. This sets up a chemical reaction, and it is this reaction which produces current flow from the battery when its positive and negative terminals are connected to an electrical load . The power removed from the battery is replaced by the alternator, restoring the battery to its original chemical state.

### The Alternator

On some vehicles there isn't an alternator, but a generator. The difference is that an alternator supplies alternating current which is then changed to direct current for use on the vehicle, while a generator produces direct current. Alternators tend to be more efficient and that is why they are used.

Alternators and generators are devices that consist of coils of wires wound together making big electromagnets. One group of coils spins within another set and the interaction of the magnetic fields causes a current to flow. This current is then drawn off the coils and fed into the vehicles electrical system.

## GROUND

Two types of grounds are used in automotive electric circuits. Direct ground components are grounded to the frame through their mounting points. All other components use some sort of ground wire which is attached to the frame or chassis of the vehicle. The electrical current runs through the chassis of the vehicle and returns to the battery through the ground (-) cable; if you look, you'll see that the battery ground cable connects between the battery and the frame or chassis of the vehicle.

➡ **It should be noted that a good percentage of electrical problems can be traced to bad grounds.**

## PROTECTIVE DEVICES

▶ **See Figure 2**

It is possible for large surges of current to pass through the electrical system of your vehicle. If this surge of current were to reach the load in the circuit, the surge could burn it out or severely damage it. It can also overload the wiring, causing the harness to get hot and melt the insulation. To prevent this, fuses, circuit breakers and/or fusible links are connected into the supply wires of the electrical system. These items are nothing more than a built-in weak spot in the system. When an abnormal amount of current flows through the system, these protective devices work as follows to protect the circuit:

• Fuse—when an excessive electrical current passes through a fuse, the fuse "blows" (the conductor melts) and opens the circuit, preventing the passage of current.

• Circuit Breaker—a circuit breaker is basically a self-repairing fuse. It will open the circuit in the same fashion as a fuse, but when the surge subsides, the circuit breaker can be reset and does not need replacement.

• Fusible Link—a fusible link (fuse link or main link) is a short length of special, high temperature insulated wire that acts as a fuse. When an excessive electrical current passes through a fusible link, the thin gauge wire inside the link melts, creating an intentional open to protect the circuit. To repair the circuit, the link must be replaced. Some newer type fusible links are housed in plug-in modules, which are simply replaced like a fuse, while older type fusible links must be cut and spliced if they melt. Since this link is very early in the electrical path, it's the first place to look if nothing on the vehicle works, yet the battery seems to be charged and is properly connected.

---
**✷✷ CAUTION**
---

**Always replace fuses, circuit breakers and fusible links with identically rated components. Under no circumstances should a component of higher or lower amperage rating be substituted.**

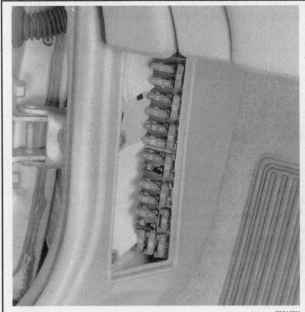

**Fig. 2 Most vehicles use one or more fuse panels. This one is located on the driver's side kick panel**

## SWITCHES & RELAYS

▶ **See Figures 3 and 4**

Switches are used in electrical circuits to control the passage of current. The most common use is to open and close circuits between the battery and the various electric devices in the system. Switches are rated according to the amount of amperage they can handle. If a sufficient amperage rated switch is not used in a circuit, the switch could overload and cause damage.

Some electrical components which require a large amount of current to operate use a special switch called a relay. Since these circuits carry a large amount of current, the thickness of the wire in the circuit is also greater. If this large wire were connected from the load to the control switch, the switch would have to carry the high amperage load and the fairing or dash would be twice as large to accommodate the increased size of the wiring harness. To prevent these problems, a relay is used.

Relays are composed of a coil and a set of contacts. When the coil has a current passed though it, a magnetic field is formed and this field causes the con-

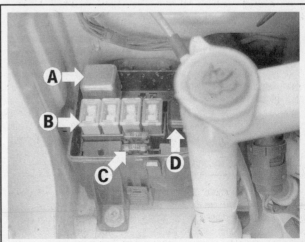

**Fig. 3 The underhood fuse and relay panel usually contains fuses, relays, flashers and fusible links**

tacts to move together, completing the circuit. Most relays are normally open, preventing current from passing through the circuit, but they can take any electrical form depending on the job they are intended to do. Relays can be considered "remote control switches." They allow a smaller current to operate devices that require higher amperages. When a small current operates the coil, a larger current is allowed to pass by the contacts. Some common circuits which may use relays are the horn, headlights, starter, electric fuel pump and other high draw circuits.

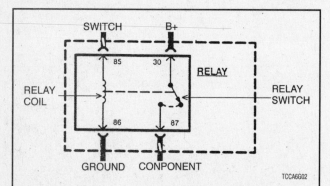

**Fig. 4 Relays are composed of a coil and a switch. These two components are linked together so that when one operates, the other operates at the same time. The large wires in the circuit are connected from the battery to one side of the relay switch (B+) and from the opposite side of the relay switch to the load (component). Smaller wires are connected from the relay coil to the control switch for the circuit and from the opposite side of the relay coil to ground**

## LOAD

Every electrical circuit must include a "load" (something to use the electricity coming from the source). Without this load, the battery would attempt to deliver its entire power supply from one pole to another. This is called a "short circuit." All this electricity would take a short cut to ground and cause a great amount of damage to other components in the circuit by developing a tremendous amount of heat. This condition could develop sufficient heat to melt the insulation on all the surrounding wires and reduce a multiple wire cable to a lump of plastic and copper.

## WIRING & HARNESSES

The average vehicle contains meters and meters of wiring, with hundreds of individual connections. To protect the many wires from damage and to keep them from becoming a confusing tangle, they are organized into bundles, enclosed in plastic or taped together and called wiring harnesses. Different harnesses serve different parts of the vehicle. Individual wires are color coded to help trace them through a harness where sections are hidden from view.

Automotive wiring or circuit conductors can be either single strand wire, multi-strand wire or printed circuitry. Single strand wire has a solid metal core and is usually used inside such components as alternators, motors, relays and other devices. Multi-strand wire has a core made of many small strands of wire twisted together into a single conductor. Most of the wiring in an automotive electrical system is made up of multi-strand wire, either as a single conductor or grouped together in a harness. All wiring is color coded on the insulator, either as a solid color or as a colored wire with an identification stripe. A printed circuit is a thin film of copper or other conductor that is printed on an insulator backing. Occasionally, a printed circuit is sandwiched between two sheets of plastic for more protection and flexibility. A complete printed circuit, consisting of conductors, insulating material and connectors for lamps or other components is called a printed circuit board. Printed circuitry is used in place of individual wires or harnesses in places where space is limited, such as behind instrument panels.

Since automotive electrical systems are very sensitive to changes in resistance, the selection of properly sized wires is critical when systems are repaired. A loose or corroded connection or a replacement wire that is too small for the circuit will add extra resistance and an additional voltage drop to the circuit.

The wire gauge number is an expression of the cross-section area of the conductor. Vehicles from countries that use the metric system will typically describe the wire size as its cross-sectional area in square millimeters. In this method, the larger the wire, the greater the number. Another common system for expressing wire size is the American Wire Gauge (AWG) system. As gauge number increases, area decreases and the wire becomes smaller. An 18 gauge wire is smaller than a 4 gauge wire. A wire with a higher gauge number will carry less current than a wire with a lower gauge number. Gauge wire size refers to the size of the strands of the conductor, not the size of the complete wire with insulator. It is possible, therefore, to have two wires of the same gauge with different diameters because one may have thicker insulation than the other.

It is essential to understand how a circuit works before trying to figure out why it doesn't. An electrical schematic shows the electrical current paths when a circuit is operating properly. Schematics break the entire electrical system down into individual circuits. In a schematic, usually no attempt is made to represent wiring and components as they physically appear on the vehicle; switches and other components are shown as simply as possible. Face views of harness connectors show the cavity or terminal locations in all multi-pin connectors to help locate test points.

## CONNECTORS

### ▶ See Figures 5 and 6

Three types of connectors are commonly used in automotive applications—weatherproof, molded and hard shell.

• Weatherproof—these connectors are most commonly used where the connector is exposed to the elements. Terminals are protected against moisture and dirt by sealing rings which provide a weathertight seal. All repairs require the use of a special terminal and the tool required to service it. Unlike standard blade type terminals, these weatherproof terminals cannot be straightened once they are bent. Make certain that the connectors are properly seated and all of the sealing rings are in place when connecting leads.

• Molded—these connectors require complete replacement of the connector if found to be defective. This means splicing a new connector assembly into the harness. All splices should be soldered to insure proper contact. Use care when probing the connections or replacing terminals in them, as it is possible to create a short circuit between opposite terminals. If this happens to the wrong terminal pair, it is possible to damage certain components. Always use jumper wires between connectors for circuit checking and NEVER probe through weatherproof seals.

• Hard Shell—unlike molded connectors, the terminal contacts in hard-shell connectors can be replaced. Replacement usually involves the use of a special terminal removal tool that depresses the locking tangs (barbs) on the connector terminal and allows the connector to be removed from the rear of the shell. The connector shell should be replaced if it shows any evidence of burning, melting, cracks, or breaks. Replace individual terminals that are burnt, corroded, distorted or loose.

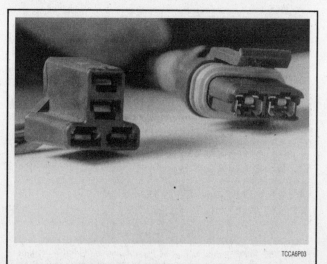

**Fig. 5 Hard shell (left) and weatherproof (right) connectors have replaceable terminals**

**Fig. 6 Weatherproof connectors are most commonly used in the engine compartment or where the connector is exposed to the elements**

## Test Equipment

Pinpointing the exact cause of trouble in an electrical circuit is most times accomplished by the use of special test equipment. The following describes different types of commonly used test equipment and briefly explains how to use them in diagnosis. In addition to the information covered below, the tool manufacturer's instructions booklet (provided with the tester) should be read and clearly understood before attempting any test procedures.

### JUMPER WIRES

### ✻✻ CAUTION

**Never use jumper wires made from a thinner gauge wire than the circuit being tested. If the jumper wire is of too small a gauge, it may overheat and possibly melt. Never use jumpers to bypass high resistance loads in a circuit. Bypassing resistances, in effect, creates a short circuit. This may, in turn, cause damage and fire. Jumper wires should only be used to bypass lengths of wire or to simulate switches.**

Jumper wires are simple, yet extremely valuable, pieces of test equipment. They are basically test wires which are used to bypass sections of a circuit. Although jumper wires can be purchased, they are usually fabricated from lengths of standard automotive wire and whatever type of connector (alligator clip, spade connector or pin connector) that is required for the particular application being tested. In cramped, hard-to-reach areas, it is advisable to have insulated boots over the jumper wire terminals in order to prevent accidental grounding. It is also advisable to include a standard automotive fuse in any jumper wire. This is commonly referred to as a "fused jumper". By inserting an in-line fuse holder between a set of test leads, a fused jumper wire can be used for bypassing open circuits. Use a 5 amp fuse to provide protection against voltage spikes.

Jumper wires are used primarily to locate open electrical circuits, on either the ground (-) side of the circuit or on the power (+) side. If an electrical component fails to operate, connect the jumper wire between the component and a good ground. If the component operates only with the jumper installed, the ground circuit is open. If the ground circuit is good, but the component does not operate, the circuit between the power feed and component may be open. By moving the jumper wire successively back from the component toward the power source, you can isolate the area of the circuit where the open is located. When the component stops functioning, or the power is cut off, the open is in the segment of wire between the jumper and the point previously tested.

You can sometimes connect the jumper wire directly from the battery to the "hot" terminal of the component, but first make sure the component uses 12 volts in operation. Some electrical components, such as fuel injectors or sensors, are designed to operate on about 4 to 5 volts, and running 12 volts directly to these components will cause damage.

### TEST LIGHTS

#### ▶ See Figure 7

The test light is used to check circuits and components while electrical current is flowing through them. It is used for voltage and ground tests. To use a 12 volt test light, connect the ground clip to a good ground and probe wherever necessary with the pick. The test light will illuminate when voltage is detected. This does not necessarily mean that 12 volts (or any particular amount of voltage) is present; it only means that some voltage is present. It is advisable before using the test light to touch its ground clip and probe across the battery posts or terminals to make sure the light is operating properly.

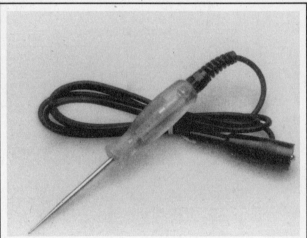

**Fig. 7 A 12 volt test light is used to detect the presence of voltage in a circuit**

### ✻✻ WARNING

**Do not use a test light to probe electronic ignition, spark plug or coil wires. Never use a pick-type test light to probe wiring on computer controlled systems unless specifically instructed to do so. Any wire insulation that is pierced by the test light probe should be taped and sealed with silicone after testing.**

Like the jumper wire, the 12 volt test light is used to isolate opens in circuits. But, whereas the jumper wire is used to bypass the open to operate the load, the 12 volt test light is used to locate the presence of voltage in a circuit. If the test light illuminates, there is power up to that point in the circuit; if the test light does not illuminate, there is an open circuit (no power). Move the test light in successive steps back toward the power source until the light in the handle illuminates. The open is between the probe and a point which was previously probed.

The self-powered test light is similar in design to the 12 volt test light, but contains a 1.5 volt penlight battery in the handle. It is most often used in place of a multimeter to check for open or short circuits when power is isolated from the circuit (continuity test).

The battery in a self-powered test light does not provide much current. A weak battery may not provide enough power to illuminate the test light even when a complete circuit is made (especially if there is high resistance in the circuit). Always make sure that the test battery is strong. To check the battery, briefly touch the ground clip to the probe; if the light glows brightly, the battery is strong enough for testing.

➡A self-powered test light should not be used on any computer controlled system or component. The small amount of electricity transmitted by the test light is enough to damage many electronic automotive components.

### MULTIMETERS

Multimeters are an extremely useful tool for troubleshooting electrical problems. They can be purchased in either analog or digital form and have a price range to suit any budget. A multimeter is a voltmeter, ammeter and ohmmeter (along with other features) combined into one instrument. It is often used when testing solid state circuits because of its high input impedance (usually 10 megaohms or more). A brief description of the multimeter main test functions follows:

• Voltmeter—the voltmeter is used to measure voltage at any point in a circuit, or to measure the voltage drop across any part of a circuit. Voltmeters usually have various scales and a selector switch to allow the reading of different voltage ranges. The voltmeter has a positive and a negative lead. To avoid damage to the meter, always connect the negative lead to the negative (-) side of the circuit (to ground or nearest the ground side of the circuit) and connect the positive lead to the positive (+) side of the circuit (to the power source or the nearest power source). Note that the negative voltmeter lead will always be black and that the positive voltmeter will always be some color other than black (usually red).

• Ohmmeter—the ohmmeter is designed to read resistance (measured in ohms) in a circuit or component. Most ohmmeters will have a selector switch which permits the measurement of different ranges of resistance (usually the selector switch allows the multiplication of the meter reading by 10, 100, 1,000 and 10,000). Some ohmmeters are "auto-ranging" which means the meter itself will determine which scale to use. Since the meters are powered by an internal battery, the ohmmeter can be used like a self-powered test light. When the ohmmeter is connected, current from the ohmmeter flows through the circuit or component being tested. Since the ohmmeter's internal resistance and voltage are known values, the amount of current flow through the meter depends on the resistance of the circuit or component being tested. The ohmmeter can also be used to perform a continuity test for suspected open circuits. In using the meter for making continuity checks, do not be concerned with the actual resistance readings. Zero resistance, or any ohm reading, indicates continuity in the circuit. Infinite resistance indicates an opening in the circuit. A high resistance reading where there should be none indicates a problem in the circuit. Checks for short circuits are made in the same manner as checks for open circuits, except that the circuit must be isolated from both power and normal ground. Infinite resistance indicates no continuity, while zero resistance indicates a dead short.

### ✳✳ WARNING

**Never use an ohmmeter to check the resistance of a component or wire while there is voltage applied to the circuit.**

• Ammeter—an ammeter measures the amount of current flowing through a circuit in units called amperes or amps. At normal operating voltage, most circuits have a characteristic amount of amperes, called "current draw" which can be measured using an ammeter. By referring to a specified current draw rating, then measuring the amperes and comparing the two values, one can determine what is happening within the circuit to aid in diagnosis. An open circuit, for example, will not allow any current to flow, so the ammeter reading will be zero. A damaged component or circuit will have an increased current draw, so the reading will be high. The ammeter is always connected in series with the circuit being tested. All of the current that normally flows through the circuit must also flow through the ammeter; if there is any other path for the current to follow, the ammeter reading will not be accurate. The ammeter itself has very little resistance to current flow and, therefore, will not affect the circuit, but it will measure current draw only when the circuit is closed and electricity is flowing. Excessive current draw can blow fuses and drain the battery, while a reduced current draw can cause motors to run slowly, lights to dim and other components to not operate properly.

### Troubleshooting Electrical Systems

When diagnosing a specific problem, organized troubleshooting is a must. The complexity of a modern automotive vehicle demands that you approach any problem in a logical, organized manner. There are certain troubleshooting techniques, however, which are standard:

• Establish when the problem occurs. Does the problem appear only under certain conditions? Were there any noises, odors or other unusual symptoms?

Isolate the problem area. To do this, make some simple tests and observations, then eliminate the systems that are working properly. Check for obvious problems, such as broken wires and loose or dirty connections. Always check the obvious before assuming something complicated is the cause.

• Test for problems systematically to determine the cause once the problem area is isolated. Are all the components functioning properly? Is there power going to electrical switches and motors. Performing careful, systematic checks will often turn up most causes on the first inspection, without wasting time checking components that have little or no relationship to the problem.

• Test all repairs after the work is done to make sure that the problem is fixed. Some causes can be traced to more than one component, so a careful verification of repair work is important in order to pick up additional malfunctions that may cause a problem to reappear or a different problem to arise. A blown fuse, for example, is a simple problem that may require more than another fuse to repair. If you don't look for a problem that caused a fuse to blow, a shorted wire (for example) may go undetected.

Experience has shown that most problems tend to be the result of a fairly simple and obvious cause, such as loose or corroded connectors, bad grounds or damaged wire insulation which causes a short. This makes careful visual inspection of components during testing essential to quick and accurate troubleshooting.

### Testing

### OPEN CIRCUITS

#### ▶ See Figure 8

This test already assumes the existence of an open in the circuit and it is used to help locate the open portion.

1. Isolate the circuit from power and ground.
2. Connect the self-powered test light or ohmmeter ground clip to the ground side of the circuit and probe sections of the circuit sequentially.
3. If the light is out or there is infinite resistance, the open is between the probe and the circuit ground.
4. If the light is on or the meter shows continuity, the open is between the probe and the end of the circuit toward the power source.

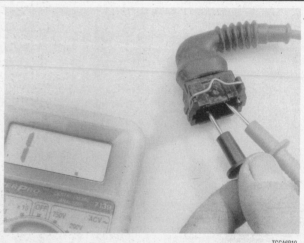

TCCA6P10

**Fig. 8 The infinite reading on this multimeter indicates that the circuit is open**

### SHORT CIRCUITS

➡**Never use a self-powered test light to perform checks for opens or shorts when power is applied to the circuit under test. The test light can be damaged by outside power.**

1. Isolate the circuit from power and ground.
2. Connect the self-powered test light or ohmmeter ground clip to a good ground and probe any easy-to-reach point in the circuit.

3. If the light comes on or there is continuity, there is a short somewhere in the circuit.

4. To isolate the short, probe a test point at either end of the isolated circuit (the light should be on or the meter should indicate continuity).

5. Leave the test light probe engaged and sequentially open connectors or switches, remove parts, etc. until the light goes out or continuity is broken.

6. When the light goes out, the short is between the last two circuit components which were opened.

## VOLTAGE

This test determines voltage available from the battery and should be the first step in any electrical troubleshooting procedure after visual inspection. Many electrical problems, especially on computer controlled systems, can be caused by a low state of charge in the battery. Excessive corrosion at the battery cable terminals can cause poor contact that will prevent proper charging and full battery current flow.

1. Set the voltmeter selector switch to the 20V position.

2. Connect the multimeter negative lead to the battery's negative (-) post or terminal and the positive lead to the battery's positive (+) post or terminal.

3. Turn the ignition switch **ON** to provide a load.

4. A well charged battery should register over 12 volts. If the meter reads below 11.5 volts, the battery power may be insufficient to operate the electrical system properly.

## VOLTAGE DROP

▶ **See Figure 9**

When current flows through a load, the voltage beyond the load drops. This voltage drop is due to the resistance created by the load and also by small resistances created by corrosion at the connectors and damaged insulation on the wires. The maximum allowable voltage drop under load is critical, especially if there is more than one load in the circuit, since all voltage drops are cumulative.

1. Set the voltmeter selector switch to the 20 volt position.

2. Connect the multimeter negative lead to a good ground.

3. Operate the circuit and check the voltage prior to the first component (load).

4. There should be little or no voltage drop in the circuit prior to the first component. If a voltage drop exists, the wire or connectors in the circuit are suspect.

5. While operating the first component in the circuit, probe the ground side of the component with the positive meter lead and observe the voltage readings. A small voltage drop should be noticed. This voltage drop is caused by the resistance of the component.

6. Repeat the test for each component (load) down the circuit.

7. If a large voltage drop is noticed, the preceding component, wire or connector is suspect.

## RESISTANCE

▶ **See Figures 10 and 11**

### ✳✳ WARNING

**Never use an ohmmeter with power applied to the circuit. The ohmmeter is designed to operate on its own power supply. The normal 12 volt electrical system voltage could damage the meter!**

1. Isolate the circuit from the vehicle's power source.

2. Ensure that the ignition key is **OFF** when disconnecting any components or the battery.

3. Where necessary, also isolate at least one side of the circuit to be checked, in order to avoid reading parallel resistances. Parallel circuit resistances will always give a lower reading than the actual resistance of either of the branches.

4. Connect the meter leads to both sides of the circuit (wire or component) and read the actual measured ohms on the meter scale. Make sure the selector switch is set to the proper ohm scale for the circuit being tested, to avoid misreading the ohmmeter test value.

## Wire and Connector Repair

Almost anyone can replace damaged wires, as long as the proper tools and parts are available. Wire and terminals are available to fit almost any need. Even the specialized weatherproof, molded and hard shell connectors are now available from aftermarket suppliers.

Be sure the ends of all the wires are fitted with the proper terminal hardware and connectors. Wrapping a wire around a stud is never a permanent solution and will only cause trouble later. Replace wires one at a time to avoid confusion. Always route wires exactly the same as the factory.

➡ **If connector repair is necessary, only attempt it if you have the proper tools. Weatherproof and hard shell connectors require special tools to release the pins inside the connector. Attempting to repair these connectors with conventional hand tools will damage them.**

Fig. 9 This voltage drop test revealed high resistance (low voltage) in the circuit

TCCA6P07

Fig. 10 Checking the resistance of a coolant temperature sensor with an ohmmeter. Reading is 1.04 kilohms

TCCA6P08

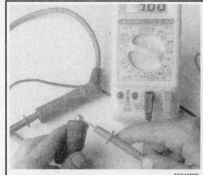

Fig. 11 Spark plug wires can be checked for excessive resistance using an ohmmeter

TCCA6P09

## SUPPLEMENTAL INFLATABLE RESTRAINT (SIR) SYSTEM

### General Information

▶ **See Figure 12**

The Supplemental Inflatable Restraint (SIR) system offers protection in addition to that provided by the seat belt by deploying an air bag from the center of the steering wheel and dash panel (passenger side air bag, if equipped). The air bag deploys when the vehicle is involved in a frontal crash of sufficient force up to 30° off the centerline of the vehicle. To further absorb the crash energy, there is also a knee bolster located beneath the instrument panel in the driver's area and the steering column is collapsible.

The system has an energy reserve, which can store a large enough electrical

88266P01

**Fig. 12 This sticker warns of air bag components. Be careful when working around the SIR wiring harness**

charge to deploy the air bag(s) for up to ten minutes after the battery has been disconnected or damaged. The system **MUST** be disabled before any service is performed on or around SIR components or SIR wiring.

## SYSTEM OPERATION

The SIR system contains a deployment loop for each air bag and a Diagnostic Energy Reserve Module (DERM). The deployment loop supplies current through the inflator module which will cause air bag deployment in the event of a frontal collision of sufficient force. The DERM supplies the necessary power, even if the battery has been damaged.

The deployment loop is made up of the arming sensors, coil assembly, inflator module and the discriminating sensors. The inflator module is only supplied sufficient current when the arming sensor and at least one of the two discriminating sensors close simultaneously. The function of the DERM is to supply the deployment loop a 36 Volt Loop Reserve (36VLR) to assure sufficient voltage to deploy the air bag if ignition voltage is lost in a frontal crash.

The DERM, in conjunction with the sensor resistors, makes it possible to detect circuit and component malfunctions within the deployment loop. If the voltages monitored by the DERM fall outside expected limits, the DERM will indicate a malfunction by storing a diagnostic trouble code and illuminating the AIR BAG lamp.

## SYSTEM COMPONENTS

### Diagnostic Energy Reserve Module (DERM)/Sensing and Diagnostic Module (SDM)

This component is known as the DERM on 1993—95 vehicles and the SDM on 1996 vehicles. The term DERM will be used in this section. The DERM is designed to perform five main functions: energy reserve, malfunction detection, malfunction recording, driver notification and frontal crash recording.

The DERM maintains a reserve voltage supply to provide deployment energy for a few seconds when the vehicle voltage is low or lost in a frontal crash. The DERM performs diagnostic monitoring of the SIR system and records malfunctions in the form of diagnostic trouble codes, which can be obtained from a hand scan tool and/or on-board diagnostics. The DERM warns the driver of SIR system malfunctions by controlling the AIR BAG warning lamp and records SIR system status during a frontal crash.

### Air Bag Warning Lamp

The AIR BAG warning/indicator lamp is used to verify lamp and DERM operation by flashing 7 times when the ignition is first turned **ON**. It is also used to warn the driver of an SIR system malfunction.

### Discriminating Sensors

There are two discriminating sensors in the SIR system, the LH forward and RH forward discriminating sensors. These sensors are located on the right frame rail for the RH sensor and the left front frame rail for the LH sensor.

The discriminating sensor consists of a sensing element, diagnostic resistor and normally open switch contacts. The sensing element closes the switch contact when vehicle velocity changes are severe enough to warrant air bag deployment.

### Arming Sensor

The arming sensor is located on the left hand frame rail. The arming sensor is a switch located in the power side of the deployment loop. It is calibrated to close at low level velocity changes (lower than the discriminating sensors), assuring that the inflator module is connected directly to the 36VLR output of the DERM or Ignition 1 voltage when any discriminating sensor closes.

### SIR Coil Assembly

The SIR coil assembly consists of two current carrying coils. They are attached to the steering column and allow rotation of the steering wheel while maintaining continuous deployment loop contact through the inflator module.

There is a shorting bar on the lower steering column connector that connects the SIR coil to the SIR wiring harness. The shorting bar shorts the circuit when the connector is disengaged. The circuit to the inflator module is shorted in this way to prevent unwanted air bag deployment when servicing the steering column or other SIR components.

### Inflator Module

The inflator module is located on the steering wheel hub. The inflator module consists of an inflatable bag and an inflator (a canister of gas-generating material and an initiating device). When the vehicle is in a frontal crash of sufficient force to close the arming sensor and at least one discriminating sensor simultaneously, current flows through the deployment loop. Current passing through the initiator ignites the material in the inflator module, causing a reaction which produces a gas that rapidly inflates the air bag.

## SERVICE PRECAUTIONS

- When performing service around the SIR system components or wiring, the SIR system **MUST** be disabled. Failure to do so could result in possible air bag deployment, personal injury or unneeded SIR system repairs.
- When carrying a live inflator module, make sure that the bag and trim cover are pointed away from you. Never carry the inflator module by the wires or connector on the underside of the module. In case of accidental deployment, the bag will then deploy with minimal chance of injury.
- When placing a live inflator module on a bench or other surface, always face the bag and trim cover up, away from the surface.

## DISABLING THE SYSTEM

▶ See Figures 13, 14 and 15

➡ With the AIR BAG fuse removed and the ignition switch ON, the AIR BAG warning lamp will be on. This is normal and does not indicate any system malfunction.

1. Turn the steering wheel so that the vehicle's wheels are pointing straight ahead.
2. Turn the ignition switch to **LOCK**, remove the key, then disconnect the negative battery cable.
3. Remove the AIR BAG fuse from the fuse block.
4. Remove the steering column filler panel.
5. Disengage the Connector Position Assurance (CPA) and the yellow two way connector located at the base of the steering column.
6. Connect the negative battery cable.

## ENABLING THE SYSTEM

1. Disconnect the negative battery cable.
2. Turn the ignition switch to **LOCK**, then remove the key.

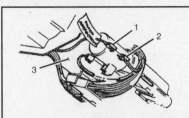

1. YELLOW 2 – WAY (SIR) CONNECTOR (STEERING COLUMN)
2. YELLOW 2 – WAY (SIR) CONNECTOR (SIR WIRING HARNESS)
3. STEERING COLUMN

88266G93

Fig. 13 Driver's side 2-way SIR connector—1993–95 models

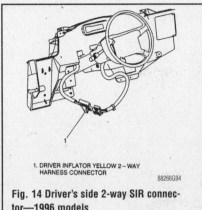

1. DRIVER INFLATOR YELLOW 2 – WAY HARNESS CONNECTOR

88266G94

Fig. 14 Driver's side 2-way SIR connector—1996 models

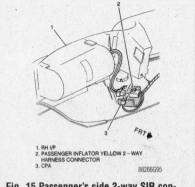

1. RH I/P
2. PASSENGER INFLATOR YELLOW 2 – WAY HARNESS CONNECTOR
3. CPA

88266G95

Fig. 15 Passenger's side 2-way SIR connector—1996 models

3. Engage the yellow SIR connector and CPA located at the base of the steering column.
4. Install the steering column filler panel.
5. Install the AIR BAG fuse to the fuse block.
6. Connect the negative battery cable.

7. Turn the ignition switch to **RUN** and make sure that the AIR BAG warning lamp flashes seven times and then shuts off. If the warning lamp does not shut off, make sure that the wiring is properly connected. If the light remains on, take the vehicle to a reputable repair facility for service.

## HEATING AND AIR CONDITIONING

→Refer to Section 1 for discharging, evacuating and recharging the air conditioning system. The system should be discharged by a qualified technician with proper recovery equipment. It is illegal to discharge refrigerant into the atmosphere and you may need a permit to purchase new refrigerant. If you do not possess the proper equipment, training and permits to perform refrigerant recovery, allow a repair shop to do that step for you.

## Heater Blower Motor

### REMOVAL & INSTALLATION

#### Front (Main) Motor

▶ **See Figures 16, 17, 18 and 19**

The blower motor is located in the engine compartment on the right side of the firewall.
1. Disconnect the negative battery cable from the battery.
2. Disconnect the electrical connectors from the blower motor.
3. Remove the radiator coolant collecting bottle from the right side of the engine compartment.
4. Remove the windshield washer fluid bottle from the right side of the engine compartment.
5. If equipped with an acoustic cover over the motor, cut the cover between the clip lands and save the cover for reassembly.
6. Remove the blower motor-to-duct housing screws and the blower motor from the vehicle.
7. If necessary, replace the blower motor-to-duct housing gasket.
8. Installation is the reverse of the removal procedure. Tighten the retaining screws to 18 inch lbs. (1.6 Nm).

#### Rear (Overhead) Motor

▶ **See Figure 20**

A rear overhead heater provides heating to the rear of the vehicle. It is located on the left side of the vehicle, in front of the wheel fender and is concealed behind a cover.
1. Disconnect the negative battery cable from the battery.
2. Remove the cover-to-heater unit and the cover.
3. Disconnect the electrical connector from the blower motor.
4. Remove the blower motor-to-heater housing screws and the blower motor.

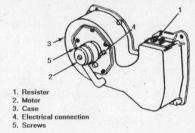

1. Resistor
2. Motor
3. Case
4. Electrical connection
5. Screws

88266G01

Fig. 16 The heater blower motor is mounted on the heater case assembly. This is shown without AC, but it is similar with AC

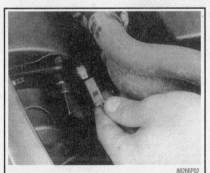

88266P02

Fig. 17 Both the ground connector and the power connector need to be removed from the push on tabs

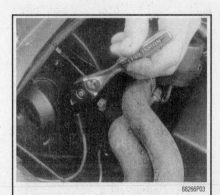

88266P03

Fig. 18 The blower motor is held on its circumference by screws

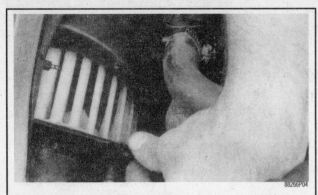

Fig. 19 Pulling the housing back will expose the fan blade connected to the motor shaft

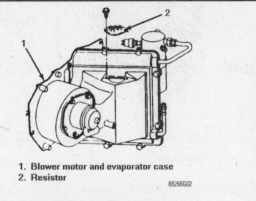

1. Blower motor and evaporator case
2. Resistor

Fig. 21 Blower motor resistor mounting location

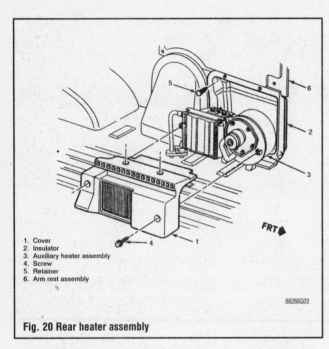

1. Cover
2. Insulator
3. Auxiliary heater assembly
4. Screw
5. Retainer
6. Arm rest assembly

Fig. 20 Rear heater assembly

5. If necessary, replace the blower motor-to-heater housing gasket.
6. Installation is the reverse of the removal procedure. Tighten the retaining screws to 18 inch lbs. (1.6 Nm).

## Blower Motor Resistor

♦ See Figure 21

A blower motor resistor is mounted on top of each blower/heater or blower/evaporator case.

### REMOVAL & INSTALLATION

1. Disconnect the negative battery cable from the battery.
2. Disconnect the electrical connector from the resistor.
3. Remove the resistor-to-case screws and lift the resistor from the case.
4. Install the resistor and retaining screws. Connect the electrical connector and negative battery cable.

## Heater Core

### REMOVAL & INSTALLATION

### ✳ CAUTION

**When draining the coolant, keep in mind that cats and dogs are attracted by the ethylene glycol antifreeze, and are quite likely to drink any that is left in an uncovered container or in puddles on the ground. This will prove fatal in sufficient quantity. Always drain the coolant into a sealable container. Coolant should be reused unless it is contaminated or several years old.**

### Front Core

♦ See Figures 22 thru 31

The front heater core is located on the right side of the passenger compartment, under the dash.
1. Disconnect the negative battery cable.
2. Place a catch pan under the radiator, open the drain cock and drain the coolant to a level below the heater core.
3. Remove the radiator overflow coolant bottle and the windshield washer fluid bottle.
4. In the engine compartment, remove the inlet/outlet hose clamps from the heater core. Remove and plug the heater hoses to prevent coolant spillage.
5. From inside the vehicle, remove the engine cover to provide extra room.
6. From under the dash, remove the lower right filler panel.
7. Remove the distributor duct, for extra room.
8. Remove the heater-to-cowl bolts and the heater assembly from the vehicle. In some instances this may not be necessary.
9. Separate the cover plate and the heater core from the heater assembly.
10. To install, reverse the removal procedure.
11. Refill the coolant to the proper level and check for leaks. Start the engine and recheck for leaks after it has reached operating temperature.

### Rear Core

A rear heater core provides heating to the rear of the vehicle. It is located on the left side of the vehicle, in front of the wheel fender and is concealed behind a cover.
1. Disconnect the negative battery terminal from the battery.
2. Place a catch pan under the radiator, open the drain cock and drain the cooling system.
3. From under the vehicle (at the rear heating unit), remove the inlet/outlet hose clamps from the heater core. Remove and plug the heater hoses to prevent coolant excess spillage.

Fig. 22 The heater core has its water connections in the engine compartment

Fig. 23 With the engine cover off, the trim panel bolts are accessible

Fig. 24 Remove the trim panel to access the heater box

Fig. 25 The air distribution duct is mounted in front of the heater box

Fig. 26 Note the seal at the top of the duct. Make sure it is in place when assembling the duct

Fig. 27 The side cover is held by 2 bolts

Fig. 28 The side cover is also gasketed. Check its condition once removed

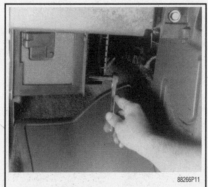
Fig. 29 The heater core is held by small bolts and molded-in brackets

Fig. 30 In most cases, the core can be separated from the heater box without removing the entire assembly

4. From inside the vehicle, remove the heating unit cover.
5. Remove the heater core from the blower assembly.
6. Inspect the heater hoses for deterioration, then replace (if necessary).
7. Installation is the reverse of the removal procedure. Refill the radiator to the proper level.
8. Start the engine and check for leaks.

## Evaporator Blower Motor

### REMOVAL & INSTALLATION

#### Front System

The blower motor is located in the engine compartment on the right side of the firewall. It is shared by the heater core.

1. Disconnect the negative battery cable from the battery.
2. Disconnect the electrical connector from the blower motor.
3. Remove the radiator coolant collecting bottle from the right side of the engine compartment.
4. Remove the windshield washer fluid bottle from the right side of the engine compartment.
5. Remove the relay bracket and move it aside.
6. Remove the blower motor-to-duct housing screws and the blower motor from the vehicle.
7. If necessary, replace the blower motor-to-duct housing gasket.
8. Installation is the reverse of the removal procedure. Tighten all components securely.
9. Connect the negative battery cable and check for proper operation.

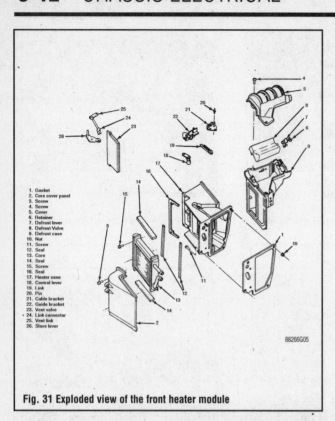

1. Gasket
2. Core cover panel
3. Screw
4. Screw
5. Cover
6. Retainer
7. Defrost lever
8. Defrost Valve
9. Defrost case
10. Nut
11. Screw
12. Seal
13. Core
14. Seal
15. Screw
16. Seal
17. Heater case
18. Control lever
19. Link
20. Pin
21. Cable bracket
22. Guide bracket
23. Vent valve
24. Link connector
25. Vent link
26. Slave lever

88266G05

**Fig. 31 Exploded view of the front heater module**

### Rear Overhead System

The rear overhead blower motor is located at the rear door on the left side.
1. Disconnect the negative battery cable from the battery.
2. Remove the rear blower motor-to-vehicle cover.
3. Disconnect the electrical connectors from the rear blower motor.
4. Remove the blower motor-to-blower case screws and the blower motor from the vehicle.
5. Installation is the reverse of the removal procedure. Tighten all components securely.
6. Connect the negative battery cable and check for normal operation.

## Air Conditioning

### REMOVAL & INSTALLATION

Repair or service of air conditioning components is not covered by this manual, because of the risk of personal injury or death, and because of the legal ramifications of servicing these components without the proper EPA certification and experience. Cost, personal injury or death, environmental damage, and legal considerations (such as the fact that it is a federal crime to vent refrigerant into the atmosphere), dictate that the A/C components on your vehicle should be serviced only by a Motor Vehicle Air Conditioning (MVAC) trained, and EPA certified automotive technician.

➡ **If your vehicle's A/C system uses R-12 refrigerant and is in need of recharging, the A/C system can be converted over to R-134a refrigerant (less environmentally harmful and expensive). Refer to Section 1 for additional information on R-12 to R-134a conversions, and for additional considerations dealing with your vehicle's A/C system.**

## RADIO

### Radio Assembly

### REMOVAL & INSTALLATION

◆ **See Figures 32 thru 39**

1. Disconnect the negative battery cable.
2. On some models you will need to remove the instrument panel-to-engine cover assembly.

3. Remove the radio-to-instrument panel bezel.
4. Remove the radio-to-instrument panel fasteners, except on 1996 models. On 1996 models, squeeze the clips to release the radio or remote cassette deck
5. Pull the radio (slightly) from the instrument, then disconnect the antenna and electrical connectors.
6. Remove the radio from the instrument panel.
7. Install the radio into the instrument panel after connecting the antenna and electrical connectors.
8. Install remaining components in the reverse order of removal.
9. Connect the negative battery cable to the battery and check operation.

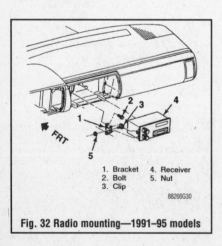

1. Bracket   4. Receiver
2. Bolt      5. Nut
3. Clip

88266G30

**Fig. 32 Radio mounting—1991–95 models**

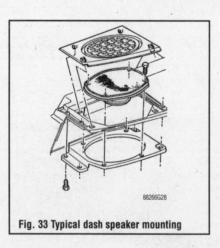

88266G28

**Fig. 33 Typical dash speaker mounting**

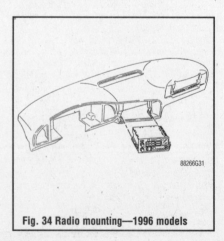

88266G31

**Fig. 34 Radio mounting—1996 models**

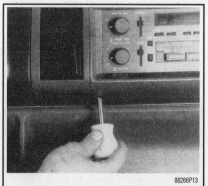

Fig. 35 The trim piece around the radio is held by 2 screws at the bottom

Fig. 36 Pull the trim piece off and disconnect the wiring to switches

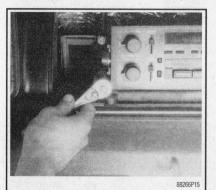

Fig. 37 Unbolt the 4 fasteners at the mounting bracket to free the radio

Fig. 38 The radio slides straight in and out

Fig. 39 Don't forget to unplug the connections at the back of the radio!

## WINDSHIELD WIPERS

▶ See Figures 40, 41 and 42

The windshield wiper units are of the 2-speed, non-depressed park type, a washer pump mounted under the washer bottle and turn signal type wiper/washer switch. A single wiper motor operates both wiper blades. Rotating the switch to either **LO** or **HI** speed position completes the circuit and the wiper motor runs at that speed.

The pulse/demand wash functions are controlled by a plug-in printed circuit board enclosed in the wiper housing cover.

### Blade and Arm

REMOVAL & INSTALLATION

▶ See Figures 43, 44, 45, 46 and 47

➡The following procedure is easier if you use GM Windshield Wiper Blade/Arm Removal tool No. J8966 or equivalent.

Fig. 40 The washer bottle has the washer pump built into the side of it. Removing the bottle allows access

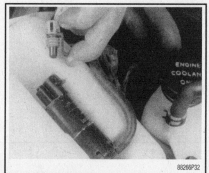

Fig. 41 The electrical connector is the watertight and has a catch to keep it secure

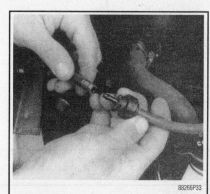

Fig. 42 The check valve keeps fluid in the line at all time

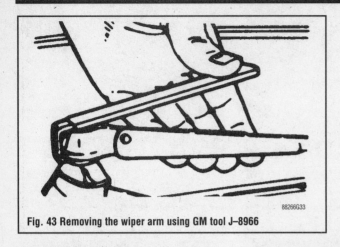

Fig. 43 Removing the wiper arm using GM tool J–8966

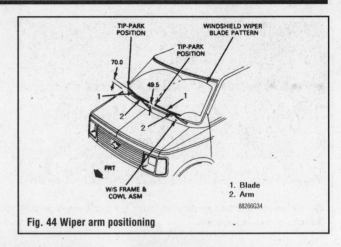

Fig. 44 Wiper arm positioning

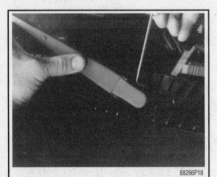

Fig. 45 If you don't have the special wiper arm tool, just pull back on the arm's side latch

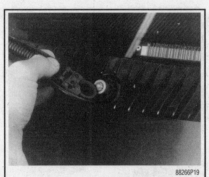

Fig. 46 The arm is splined to meet the linkage. Note the latch at the bottom of the wiper arm

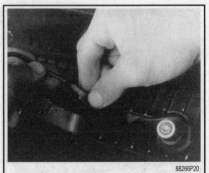

Fig. 47 On wiper arms with the washer nozzle built into it, you will need to disconnect the fluid hose

If the wiper assembly has a press type release tab at the center, simply depress the tab and remove the blade. If the blade has no release tab, use a screwdriver to depress the spring at the center; this will release the assembly. To install the assembly, position the blade over the pin (at the tip of the arm) and press until the spring retainer engages the groove in the pin.

To remove the element, either depress the release button or squeeze the spring type retainer clip (at the outer end) together and slide the blade element out. To install, slide the new element in until it latches.

1. Insert the tool under the wiper arm and lever the arm off the shaft. If you do not have the tool, use a pick to release the latch at the bottom of the arm.

2. Disconnect the washer hose from the arm (if equipped), then remove the arm.

**To install:**

3. Operate the wiper motor (momentarily) to position the pivot shafts into the park position. The proper park position for the arms is with the blades approximately 50mm on the driver's side, or 70mm on the passenger's side, above the lower windshield molding.

4. Connect the water hose and check operation.

## Windshield Wiper Motor

The windshield wiper motor is located in the engine compartment on the left side of the cowl.

### REMOVAL & INSTALLATION

#### Front Wipers

▶ See Figures 48, 49 and 50

1. Disconnect the negative battery cable and the electrical connector from the windshield wiper motor.

2. Remove the transmission link from the wiper motor crank arm by pulling or prying it toward the rear of the vehicle.

3. Remove the wiper motor-to-cowl bolts and the wiper motor from the vehicle.

4. Installation is the reverse of the removal procedure.

5. Connect the negative battery cable and check for proper operation.

#### Rear Wipers

▶ See Figure 51

1. Disconnect the negative battery cable. Remove the electrical connector from the windshield wiper motor.

2. Remove the trim from over the motor assembly.

Fig. 48 The connector has a positive lock on it that will need to be pressed in to unplug it

**Fig. 49 The bolts go through rubber isolators. Check the condition of the rubber when dismounting**

**Fig. 50 Once the linkage has been disconnected from the motor, the unit will pull right out**

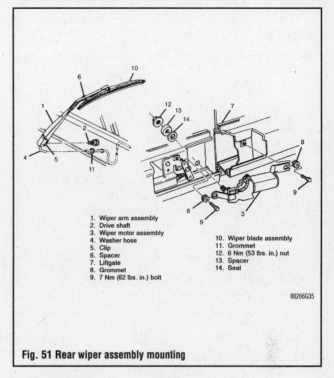

1. Wiper arm assembly
2. Drive shaft
3. Wiper motor assembly
4. Washer hose
5. Clip
6. Spacer
7. Liftgate
8. Grommet
9. 7 Nm (62 lbs. in.) bolt
10. Wiper blade assembly
11. Grommet
12. 6 Nm (53 lbs. in.) nut
13. Spacer
14. Seal

**Fig. 51 Rear wiper assembly mounting**

3. Disconnect the wiper motor electrical plug.
4. Remove the wiper arm from the wiper motor shaft.
5. Remove the nut, spacer, seal and the 2 bolts from the motor. Lift the motor out of the tailgate.
6. Installation is the reverse of the removal procedure. Tighten the bolts to 62 inch lbs. (7 Nm).
7. Connect the negative battery cable and check for proper operation.

## INSTRUMENTS AND SWITCHES

### Instrument Cluster

REMOVAL & INSTALLATION

**Except 1996 Models**

▶ See Figures 52 and 53

1. Disconnect the negative battery cable from the battery.
2. Remove the lower steering column cover-to-instrument panel screws and the cover.
3. Remove the instrument cluster trim plate-to-instrument cluster screws and the panel, then allow the panel to hang to the left side by the wiring.
4. Remove the air conditioning control-to-instrument panel screws and move the control assembly aside.
5. For access, remove the seat alarm assembly from the bracket, on the left side of the instrument panel.
6. Remove the instrument panel cluster-to-instrument panel fasteners and the cluster assembly.
7. Disconnect the speedometer cable (of applicable), the speed sensor and any other necessary electrical connectors.
8. Installation is the reverse of the removal procedure.
9. Connect the negative battery cable to the battery and check operation.

**1996 Models**

▶ See Figures 54 and 55

1. Disconnect the negative battery cable.
2. Apply the parking brake and turn the key to the **ON** position. Place the gear selector in 1st gear.

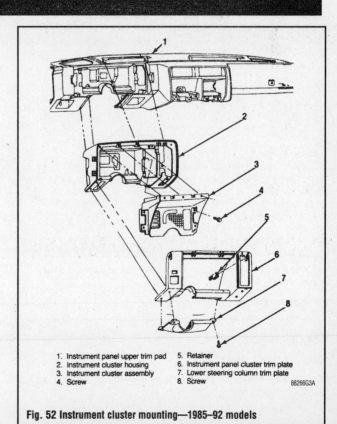

1. Instrument panel upper trim pad
2. Instrument cluster housing
3. Instrument cluster assembly
4. Screw
5. Retainer
6. Instrument panel cluster trim plate
7. Lower steering column trim plate
8. Screw

**Fig. 52 Instrument cluster mounting—1985–92 models**

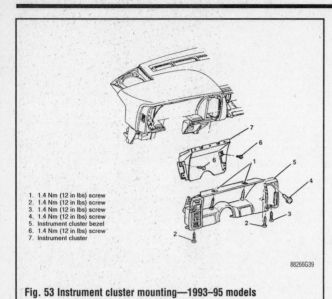

1. 1.4 Nm (12 in lbs) screw
2. 1.4 Nm (12 in lbs) screw
3. 1.4 Nm (12 in lbs) screw
4. 1.4 Nm (12 in lbs) screw
5. Instrument cluster bezel
6. 1.4 Nm (12 in lbs) screw
7. Instrument cluster

88266G39

Fig. 53 Instrument cluster mounting—1993–95 models

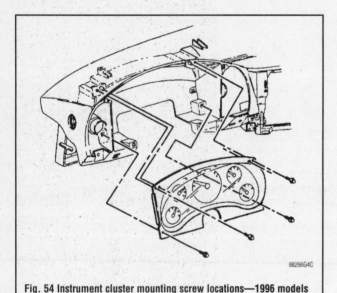

88266G4C

Fig. 54 Instrument cluster mounting screw locations—1996 models

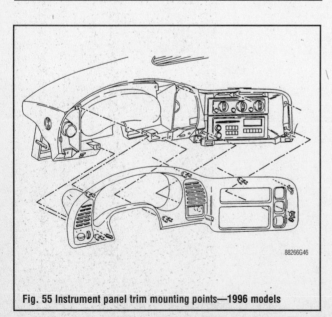

88266G46

Fig. 55 Instrument panel trim mounting points—1996 models

3. Pull the trim plate away from the dash until all the connectors are released. Unplug any electrical connections.

4. Remove the 4 screws holding the instrument cluster to the dash. Pull the cluster out from the electrical connectors.

**To install:**

5. Align the instrument cluster with the electrical connectors and push into place. Secure with the 4 retaining screws.

6. Place the trim plate in place and connect the electrical plugs. Press the trim plate into the connectors until they are all firmly attached.

7. Return the gear selector to **PARK** and turn the ignition switch to **OFF**. Connect the negative battery cable.

## Gauges

### REMOVAL & INSTALLATION

1. Disconnect the negative battery cable.
2. Remove the instrument cluster from the instrument panel.
3. Remove the gauge retaining screws and gauge.
4. Installation is the reverse of the removal procedure. Tighten all components securely.
5. Check for proper operation.

## Windshield Wiper Switch

The windshield wiper switch is located within the steering column and is actuated by the external lever, except on 1996 vehicles. In 1996 a new steering column was introduced. The switch is now located up at the top of the column, just underneath the steering wheel.

### REMOVAL & INSTALLATION

➡ Refer to the Combination Switch, Removal and Installation procedures in Section 8 to replace the combination switch.

## Headlight Switch

◗ See Figures 56 and 57

The headlight switch, a push button (rotary dial on 1996) switch to turn the lights on and off, is located on the left side of the instrument panel. A rheostat dial, located with the headlight/parking light switch, is used to control the illumination of the instrument panel.

A dimmer switch (part of the combination switch), to control the **Hi** and **Lo** beam operation, is located in the steering column; the lights are changed by pulling the lever toward the driver.

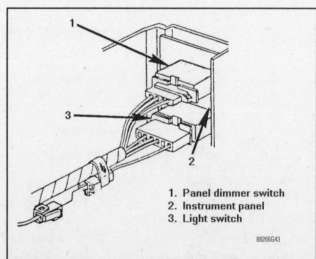

1. Panel dimmer switch
2. Instrument panel
3. Light switch

88266G43

Fig. 56 Headlight switch electrical connections—1985–95 shown, 1996 similar

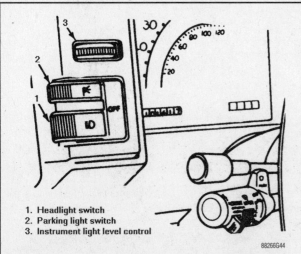

1. Headlight switch
2. Parking light switch
3. Instrument light level control

88266G44

**Fig. 57 This style headlight switch was used up to 1995. In 1996 a rotary switch was used**

## REMOVAL & INSTALLATION

1. Disconnect the negative battery cable from the battery.
2. Remove the lower steering column cover-to-instrument panel screws and the cover.
3. Remove the instrument cluster trim plate-to-instrument cluster screws and the panel, then allow the panel to hang to the left side by the wiring.
4. Disconnect the electrical connector from the rear of the headlight switch.
5. Disengage and remove the headlight switch from the instrument cluster trim plate.

**To install:**

6. Connect the electrical connector to the rear of the headlight switch.
7. Engage and install the headlight switch in the instrument cluster trim plate.
8. Install the remaining components in the reverse order of removal.
9. Connect the negative battery cable and check operation.

## Back-Up Light Switch

### REMOVAL & INSTALLATION

#### Automatic Transmission

▶ **See Figure 58**

Vehicles up to and including 1995 model year have the back-up light switch mounted on the steering column. On the 1996 model year vehicles, the back-up light switch is part of the neutral safety switch mounted on the side of the trans-

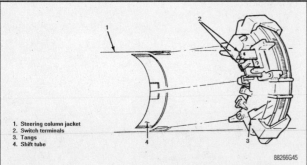

1. Steering column jacket
2. Switch terminals
3. Tangs
4. Shift tube

88266G45

**Fig. 58 The back up light switch also contains the neutral safety switch on automatic transmission equipped vehicles—1985-95 models**

mission. Refer to the procedure for replacement of the neutral safety switch is Section 7.

1. Disconnect the negative battery cable from the battery.
2. From the steering column, disconnect the electrical harness connector from the back-up light switch.
3. Using a small pry bar, expand the back-up switch-to-steering column retainers and remove the switch from the steering column.

**To install:**

4. Place the gear selector in **NEUTRAL** and align the actuator on the switch with the hole in the shift tube. Align the mounting tangs with the mounting holes and press down to lock in place.
5. Connect the electrical harness connector to the back-up light switch.
6. Connect the negative battery cable to the battery.
7. Move the gear selector through all the positions including **PARK** and **LOW**. This should ratchet the switch and self adjust it.
8. Place the gear shift lever in the **REVERSE** position and check that the back-up lights turn on.

#### Manual Transmission

To replace the back-up light switch, refer to the Back-Up Light Switch, Removal and Installation procedures in Section 7.

## Speedometer Cable

### REMOVAL & INSTALLATION

#### Mechanical Speedometer

▶ **See Figure 59**

1. Refer to the Instrument Cluster, Removal and Installation procedures in this section and remove the instrument cluster.
2. From the rear of the instrument cluster, remove the speedometer cable-to-head fitting.
3. If replacing ONLY the speedometer cable core, perform the following procedures:
   a. Disconnect the speedometer casing from the speedometer head.
   b. Pull the speedometer cable core from the speedometer casing.
   c. Using lubricant P/N 6478535 or equivalent, lubricate a new speedometer cable core and install the cable into the casing.
4. If replacing the speedometer cable core and the speedometer cable casing, perform the following procedures:
   a. Disconnect the speedometer cable casing from the speedometer head.
   b. Disconnect the speedometer cable casing from the transmission.
   c. Remove the various speedometer cable/casing retaining clips.
   d. Remove the speedometer cable/casing assembly from the vehicle.

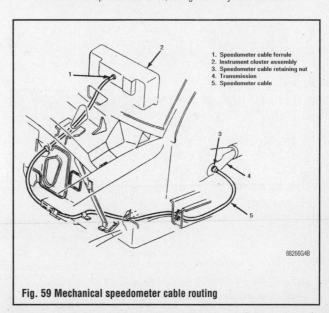

1. Speedometer cable ferrule
2. Instrument cluster assembly
3. Speedometer cable retaining nut
4. Transmission
5. Speedometer cable

88266G4B

**Fig. 59 Mechanical speedometer cable routing**

**Electronic Speedometer**

▶ **See Figure 60**

1. Disconnect the negative battery cable.
2. Raise and safely support the vehicle with jackstands.
3. Disconnect the harness connector at the transmission.
4. Remove the retaining bolt and sensor.
5. Drain the excess fluid into a drain pan.
6. Replace the O-ring seal if damaged.

**To install:**

7. Install the sensor with a new O-ring. Coat the seal with a film of transmission fluid.
8. Install the bolt and tighten to 96 inch lbs. (11 Nm).
9. Connect the harness connector and negative battery cable.
10. Start the engine and allow it to reach normal operating temperature.
11. Refill the transmission with fluid to the proper level and check operation.

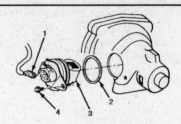

1. Harness connector
2. O-ring seal
3. Vehicle speed sensor (VSS)
4. Bolt

88266G47

**Fig. 60 Typical electronic speedometer speed sensor mounted in the transmission or the transfer case**

## LIGHTING

### Headlights

REMOVAL & INSTALLATION

➡ **The following procedures may require the use of the GM Safety Aimer tool No. J687801 or equivalent.**

**Sealed Beam**

▶ **See Figures 61, 62, 63, 64 and 65**

1. Disconnect the negative battery cable from the battery.
2. Remove the headlight bezel-to-fender screws and the bezel; allow the bezel to hang by the parking/side marker light wires.
3. Remove the headlight retaining-to-fender spring.
4. Remove the headlight retaining ring-to-fender screws and the retaining ring.
5. Disconnect the electrical connector from the headlight and remove the headlight from the vehicle.
6. Installation is the reverse of the removal procedure.
7. Connect the negative battery cable and check the headlight operation. Although, adjustment procedures may not be necessary, DO check the aim of the headlight.

➡ **If necessary to adjust the headlight aim, use the GM Safety Aimer tool No. J687801 or equivalent.**

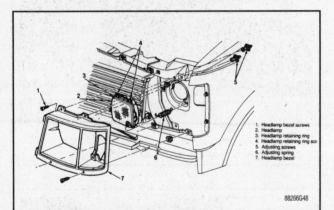

1. Headlamp bezel screws
2. Headlamp
3. Headlamp retaining ring
4. Headlamp retaining ring scr
5. Adjusting screws
6. Adjusting spring
7. Headlamp bezel

88266G48

**Fig. 61 Sealed beam headlight mounting**

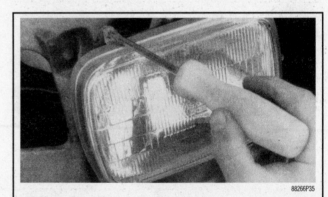

88266P35

**Fig. 63 Be careful with the headlight retaining ring screws. They can strip out easily**

88266P34

**Fig. 62 The headlight bezel needs to be removed to access the mounting screws for the bulb itself**

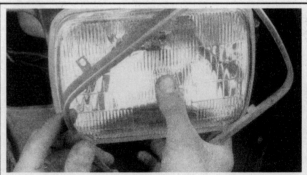

88266P36

**Fig. 64 If the ring becomes damaged, it can be replaced with parts from most auto supply stores**

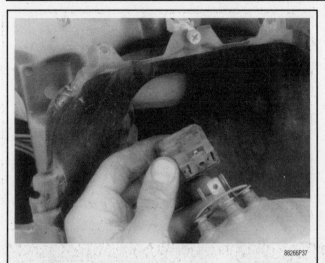

**Fig. 65 Check the terminals for signs of burning. A bad connection here can cause all sorts of light problems**

### Composite Headlamp

▶ See Figures 66 thru 75

1. Open the hood. Disconnect the negative battery cable from the battery.
2. Remove the composite headlamp side lens.
3. Remove the 3 bolts holding the composite headlight assembly to the body.
4. Unplug the bulb connector and remove the assembly from the vehicle.
5. Installation is the reverse of removal.

### HEADLIGHT AIMING

▶ See Figures 76, 77 and 78

Horizontal and vertical aiming of each headlight is done by 2 adjusting screws which move the mounting ring against the tension of the coil spring.

Some state and local authorities have specific requirements for aiming headlights and these requirements should be followed.

## Signal and Marker Lights

### REMOVAL & INSTALLATION

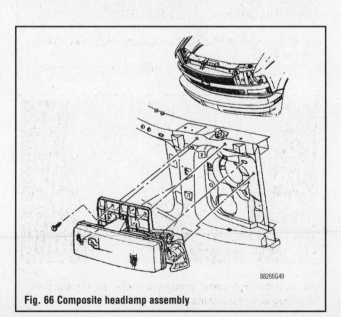

**Fig. 66 Composite headlamp assembly**

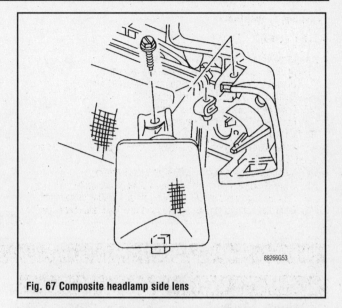

**Fig. 67 Composite headlamp side lens**

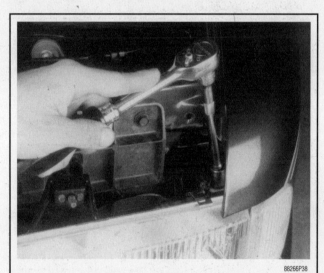

**Fig. 68 Remove this screw to release the side lens**

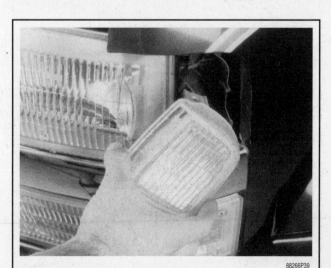

**Fig. 69 Pull the side lens out to expose the main headlight mounting points**

Fig. 70 Headlight side mounting bolt

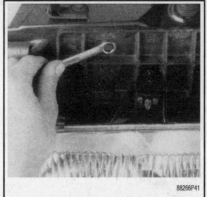

Fig. 71 Headlight bracket mounting bolt

Fig. 72 Pull the entire headlight unit out from the body

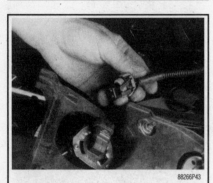

Fig. 73 The composite headlights use separate bulbs that mount to the headlight assembly

Fig. 74 Do not touch the surface of the bulb or it will burn out prematurely

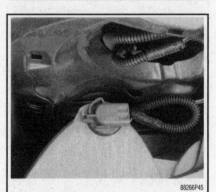

Fig. 75 With the headlight removed, you can get to the parking light bulbs

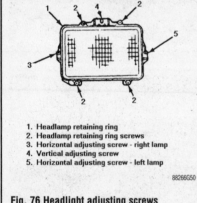

1. Headlamp retaining ring
2. Headlamp retaining ring screws
3. Horizontal adjusting screw - right lamp
4. Vertical adjusting screw
5. Horizontal adjusting screw - left lamp

Fig. 76 Headlight adjusting screws

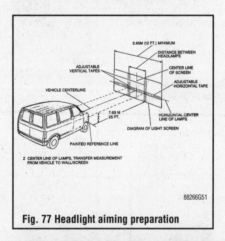

Fig. 77 Headlight aiming preparation

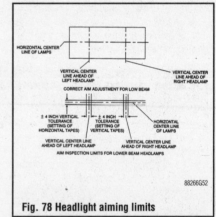

Fig. 78 Headlight aiming limits

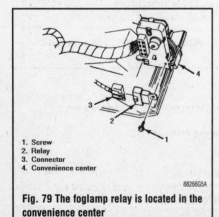

1. Screw
2. Relay
3. Connector
4. Convenience center

Fig. 79 The foglamp relay is located in the convenience center

Fig. 80 The bulb is mounted in the fog light by a bayonet mount

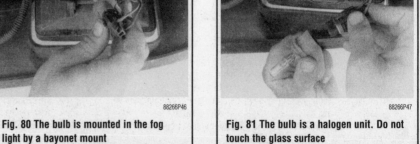

Fig. 81 The bulb is a halogen unit. Do not touch the glass surface

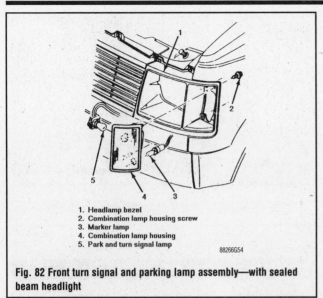

1. Headlamp bezel
2. Combination lamp housing screw
3. Marker lamp
4. Combination lamp housing
5. Park and turn signal lamp

88266G54

Fig. 82 Front turn signal and parking lamp assembly—with sealed beam headlight

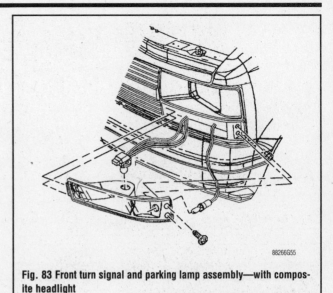

88266G55

Fig. 83 Front turn signal and parking lamp assembly—with composite headlight

88266P48

Fig. 84 The headlight bezel contains the turn signal and parking lamps

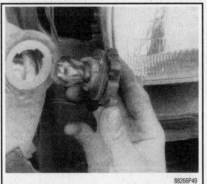

88266P49

Fig. 85 Note the seal around the socket. Check its condition before installation

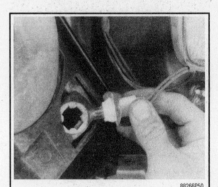

88266P50

Fig. 86 This socket is a twist to lock design

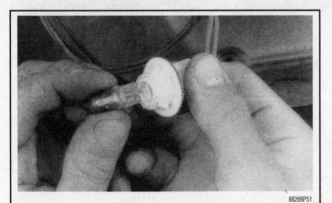

88266P51

Fig. 87 The replacement bulb just pushes into the socket

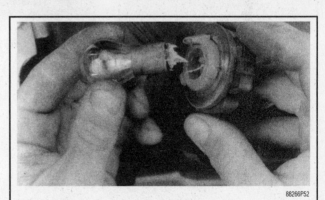

88266P52

Fig. 88 The grease at the bottom of the bulb is to help prevent corrosion

### Front Turn Signal and Parking Lights

▶ See Figures 79 thru 88

1. Disconnect the negative battery cable from the battery.
2. Remove the headlight bezel-to-fender screws and the bezel; allow the bezel to hang by the turn signal/parking/marker light wires.
3. From the rear headlight bezel, remove the turn signal/parking/marker lamp-to-bezel screws and the turn signal/parking/marker lamp.
4. Disconnect the turn signal bulb and the parking/marker bulb from the lamp housing and the housing from the vehicle.

5. To install, use new bulbs (if necessary) and reverse the removal procedures. Check the turn signal and the parking/marker light operations

### Rear Turn Signal, Brake and Parking Lights

▶ See Figures 89 and 90

1. Disconnect the negative battery cable from the battery.
2. Remove the rear turn signal/brake/parking lamp-to-vehicle screw and the lamp housing from the vehicle.
3. Replace the defective bulb(s).
4. To install, reverse the removal procedures.

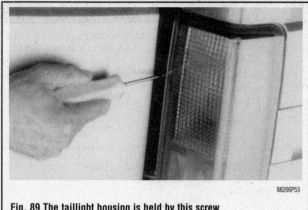

Fig. 89 The taillight housing is held by this screw

Fig. 90 The bulbs mount in sockets that twist into the taillight housing

## License Plate Lamp

### REMOVAL & INSTALLATION

▶ **See Figures 91, 92, 93 and 94**

Remove the mounting screws, lamp assembly and light bulb.

## Center High Mounted Stop Lamp

### REMOVAL & INSTALLATION

▶ **See Figure 95**

Remove the mounting screws, unplug the wires and remove the lamp assembly.

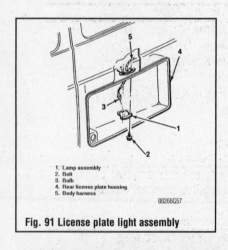

1. Lamp assembly
2. Bolt
3. Bulb
4. Rear license plate housing
5. Body harness

Fig. 91 License plate light assembly

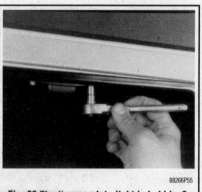

Fig. 92 The license plate light is held by 2 bolts

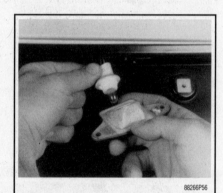

Fig. 93 The socket twists into the light housing

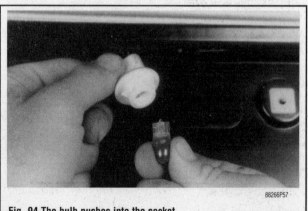
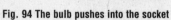

Fig. 94 The bulb pushes into the socket

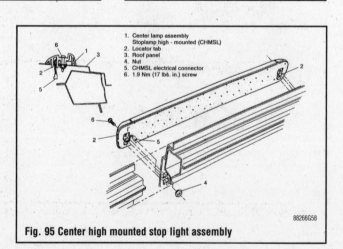

1. Center lamp assembly
   Stoplamp high - mounted (CHMSL)
2. Locator tab
3. Roof panel
4. Nut
5. CHMSL electrical connector
6. 1.9 Nm (17 lbs. in.) screw

Fig. 95 Center high mounted stop light assembly

## CRUISE CONTROL

The cruise control system is a speed control system which maintains a desired vehicle speed under normal driving conditions. However, steep grades up or down may cause variations in the selected speed.

The main components of the cruise control system are the mode control switches, controller (module), servo unit, speed sensor, vacuum supply, electrical and vacuum release switches.

To release the system, 2 release switches are provided. An electrical release switch is mounted on the brake pedal bracket and clutch pedal bracket on the vehicles equipped with manual transmissions. A vacuum release valve is mounted on the brake pedal bracket. The valve vents the trapped vacuum in the servo when the brake pedal is depressed, allowing the servo to return the throttle to idle position.

➡The 1995–96 models use an all electric system. There are no vacuum systems used.

## Operation

The controller interprets the position of the servo, position of the mode control switches and the output of the speed sensor. The servo consists of a vacuum tank and an open solenoid valve to vent the diaphragm chamber to atmosphere, except for the electric systems which use an electric stepper motor. The digital ratio adapter is a solid state device that is used to change the signal from the vehicle speed sensor to a digital signal. The adapter is matched to the final drive of each vehicle and most be replaced with the proper adapter to match the final drive. This unit is located inside the vehicle speed sensor at the transmission.

DIAGNOSIS

A problem can be mechanical, electrical and/or vacuum.

**Initial Inspection**

1. Check for bare, broken or disconnected wires and vacuum hoses.
2. Make sure the servo and throttle linkages operate freely and smoothly.
3. Check the "Ignition/Gauges" 20 amp fuse.
4. Verify that the check valve functions properly.

# CRUISE CONTROL TROUBLESHOOTING

| Problem | Possible Cause |
|---|---|
| Will not hold proper speed | Incorrect cable adjustment |
| | Binding throttle linkage |
| | Leaking vacuum servo diaphragm |
| | Leaking vacuum tank |
| | Faulty vacuum or vent valve |
| | Faulty stepper motor |
| | Faulty transducer |
| | Faulty speed sensor |
| | Faulty cruise control module |
| Cruise intermittently cuts out | Clutch or brake switch adjustment too tight |
| | Short or open in the cruise control circuit |
| | Faulty transducer |
| | Faulty cruise control module |
| Vehicle surges | Kinked speedometer cable or casing |
| | Binding throttle linkage |
| | Faulty speed sensor |
| | Faulty cruise control module |
| Cruise control inoperative | Blown fuse |
| | Short or open in the cruise control circuit |
| | Faulty brake or clutch switch |
| | Leaking vacuum circuit |
| | Faulty cruise control switch |
| | Faulty stepper motor |
| | Faulty transducer |
| | Faulty speed sensor |
| | Faulty cruise control module |

Note: Use this chart as a guide. Not all systems will use the components listed.

TCCA6C01

## CIRCUIT PROTECTION

### Fuses

▶ **See Figures 96 thru 103**

The fuses are of the miniaturized (compact) size and are located on a fuse block, they provide increased circuit protection and reliability. Access to the fuse block is gained either through a swing-down unit (located on the underside of the instrument panel, near the steering column) or through the glove box opening. On 1996 models, there is a fuse/relay panel mounted underhood. Each fuse receptacle is marked as to the circuit it protects and the correct amperage of the fuse.

#### REPLACEMENT

1. Pull the fuse from the fuse block.
2. Inspect the fuse element (through the clear plastic body) to the blade terminal for defects.

➡ **When replacing the fuse, DO NOT use one of a higher amperage.**

3. To install, reverse the removal procedures.

### Convenience Center

▶ **See Figures 104 and 105**

The Convenience Center is a swing-down unit located on the underside of the instrument panel, near the steering column. The swing-down feature provides central location and easy access to buzzers, relays and flasher units. All units are serviced by plug-in replacement.

### Fusible Links

In addition to fuses, the wiring harness incorporates fusible links (in the battery feed circuits) to protect the wiring. Fusible links are 4 in. (102mm) sections of copper wire, 4 gauges smaller than the circuit(s) they are protecting, designed to melt under electrical overload. There are 4 different gauge sizes used. The fusible links are color coded so that they may be installed in their original positions.

Here are some common fusible links and their locations. Refer to the wiring diagrams for specific fusible link information.
• Fusible link A — Rust/silver, to ECM, located at starter solenoid.
• Fusible link B — Gray/silver, to air conditioning blower, located at battery connection block.
• Fusible link C — Black/silver, to fuel pump circuit, located at battery connection block.
• Fusible link D — Black/silver, to ignition switch, located at battery connection block.
• Fusible link E — Rust/silver, to alternator, located at starter solenoid.
• Fusible link F — Rust/silver, to alternator (2.5L), located at starter solenoid.

### Circuit Breakers

A circuit breaker is an electrical switch which breaks the circuit in case of an overload. The circuit breaker is located on the lower center of the fuse block. The circuit breaker will remain open until the short or overload condition in the circuit is corrected.

Fig. 96 Remove the cover to expose the fuse panel

Fig. 97 Without a tester, it is impossible to check the fuses unless they are removed

Fig. 98 The underhood fuse panel has the fuse identification in the lid of the panel

Fig. 99 This puller will help remove the mini fuses

Fig. 100 These maxi fuses take the place of many of the fusible links

Fig. 101 The relays just plug into the panel

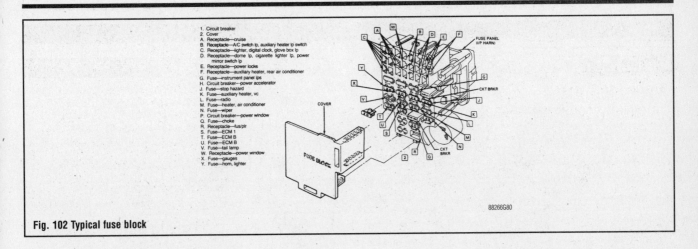

1. Circuit breaker
2. Cover
A. Receptacle—cruise
B. Receptacle—A/C switch lp, auxiliary heater lp switch
C. Receptacle—lighter, digital clock, glove box lp
D. Receptacle—dome lp, cigarette lighter lp, power mirror switch lp
E. Receptacle—power locks
F. Receptacle—auxiliary heater, rear air conditioner
G. Fuse—instrument panel lps
H. Circuit breaker—power accelerator
J. Fuse—stop hazard
K. Fuse—auxiliary heater, vc
L. Fuse—radio
M. Fuse—heater, air conditioner
N. Fuse—wiper
P. Circuit breaker—power window
Q. Fuse—choke
R. Receptacle—lus/plr
S. Fuse—ECM 1
T. Fuse—ECM B
U. Fuse—ECM B
V. Fuse—tail lamp
W. Receptacle—power window
X. Fuse—gauges
Y. Fuse—horn, lighter

**Fig. 102 Typical fuse block**

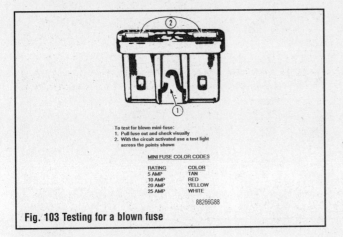

To test for blown mini-fuse:
1. Pull fuse out and check visually
2. With the circuit activated use a test light across the points shown

MINI FUSE COLOR CODES

| RATING | COLOR |
|--------|-------|
| 5 AMP | TAN |
| 10 AMP | RED |
| 20 AMP | YELLOW |
| 25 AMP | WHITE |

**Fig. 103 Testing for a blown fuse**

## RESETTING

Locate the circuit breaker on the fuse block, then push the circuit breaker in until it locks. If the circuit breaker kicks itself Off again, locate and correct the problem in the electrical circuit. The windshield wiper motor has a self setting circuit breaker built into the motor assembly. This breaker is non-serviceable and requires replacement of the wiper motor unit if defective.

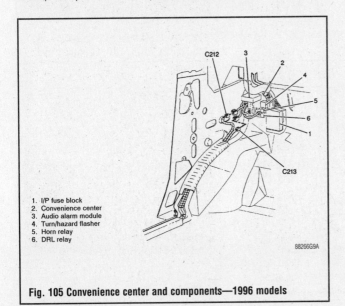

1. I/P fuse block
2. Convenience center
3. Audio alarm module
4. Turn/hazard flasher
5. Horn relay
6. DRL relay

**Fig. 105 Convenience center and components—1996 models**

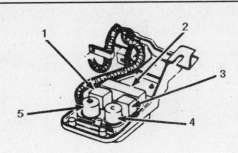

1. Horn relay
2. Seat belt - ignition key - headlight buzzer
3. Choke relay (vacant w/EFI)
4. Hazard flasher
5. Signal flasher

**Fig. 104 Convenience center and components—1985–95 models**

## Flashers

The turn signal flasher is mounted under the instrument panel to the right of the steering column.

The hazard flasher is mounted in the convenience center. The convenience center is located to the left of the steering column and at the lower edge of the instrument panel.

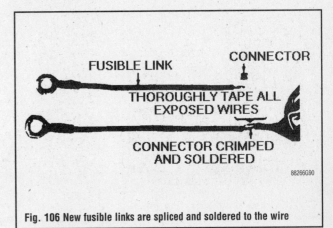

FUSIBLE LINK    CONNECTOR

THOROUGHLY TAPE ALL
EXPOSED WIRES

CONNECTOR CRIMPED
AND SOLDERED

**Fig. 106 New fusible links are spliced and soldered to the wire**

## WIRING DIAGRAMS

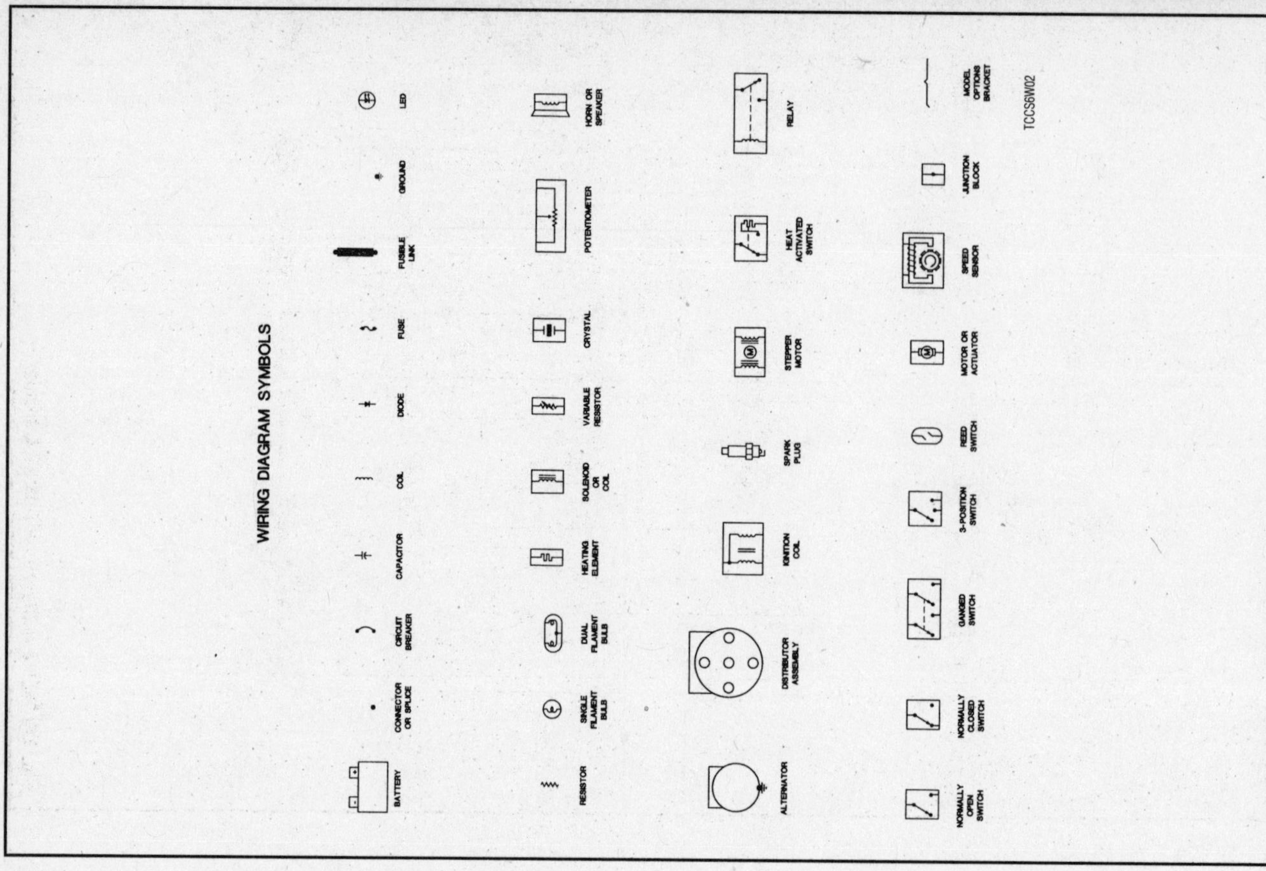

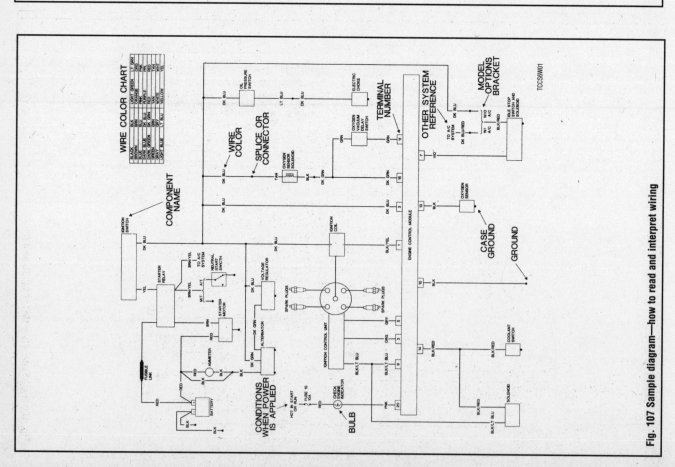

Fig. 108 Common wiring diagram symbols

Fig. 107 Sample diagram—how to read and interpret wiring

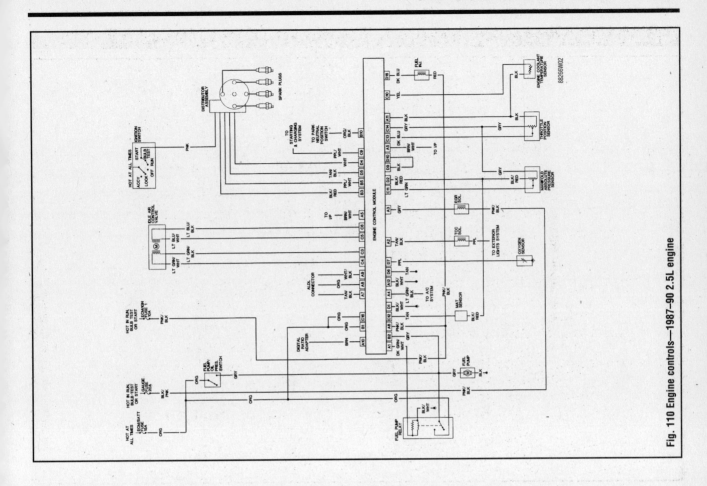

Fig. 110 Engine controls—1987-90 2.5L engine

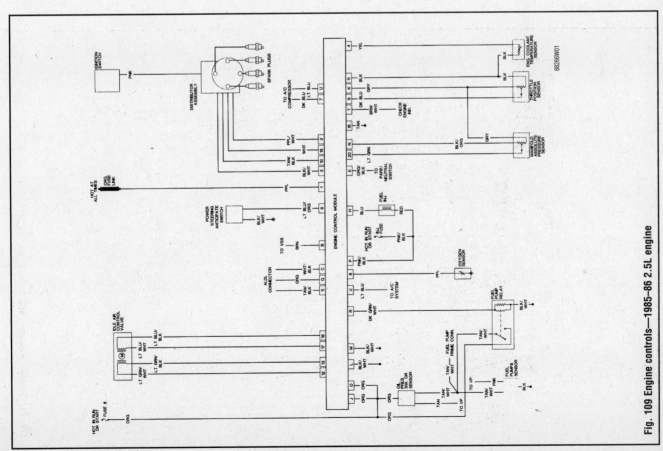

Fig. 109 Engine controls—1985-86 2.5L engine

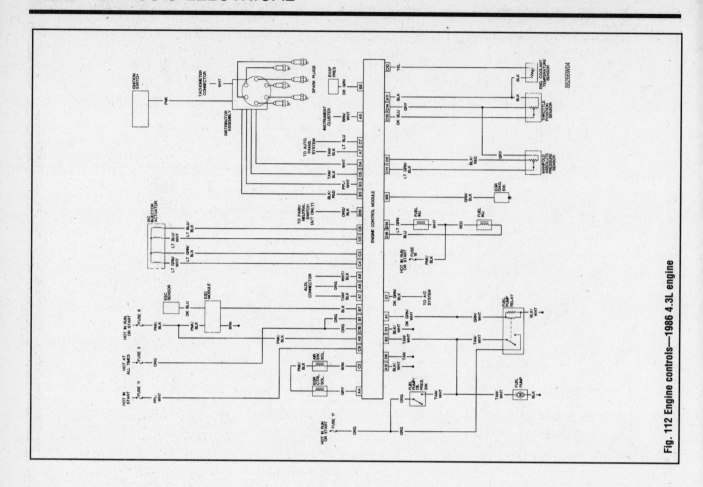

Fig. 112 Engine controls—1986 4.3L engine

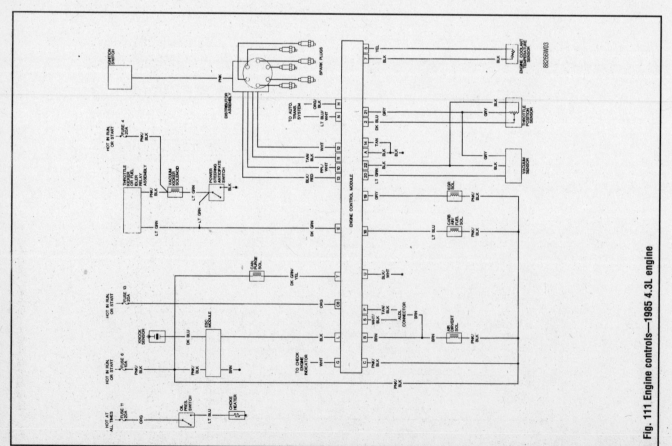

Fig. 111 Engine controls—1985 4.3L engine

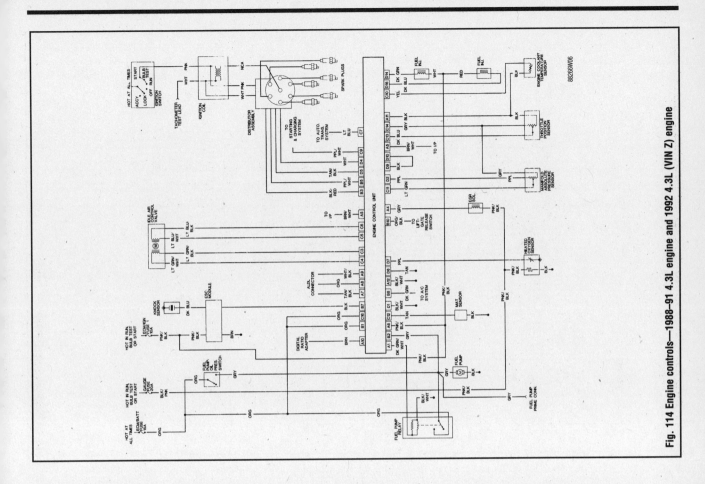

Fig. 114 Engine controls—1988-91 4.3L engine and 1992 4.3L (VIN Z) engine

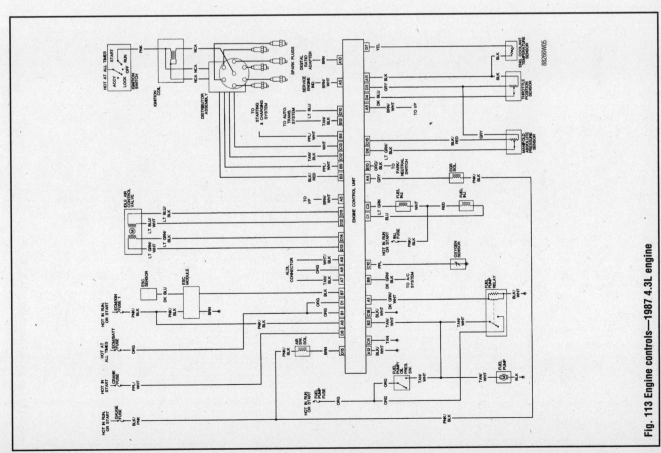

Fig. 113 Engine controls—1987 4.3L engine

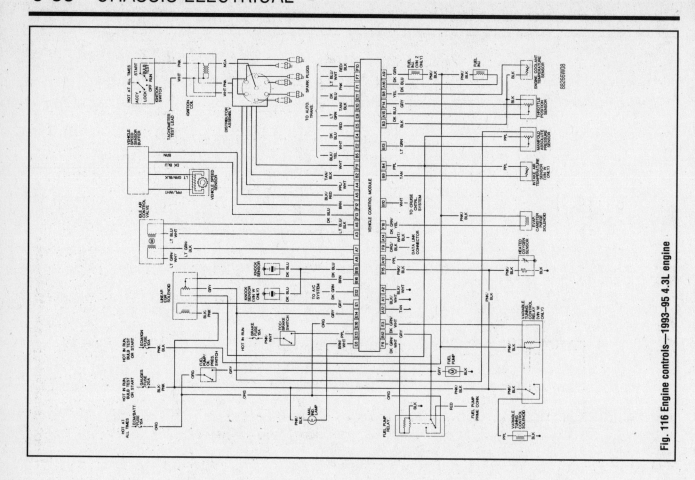

Fig. 116 Engine controls—1993–95 4.3L engine

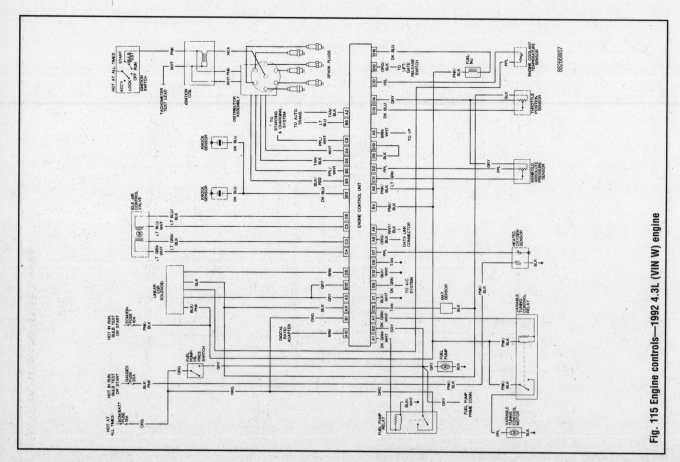

Fig. 115 Engine controls—1992 4.3L (VIN W) engine

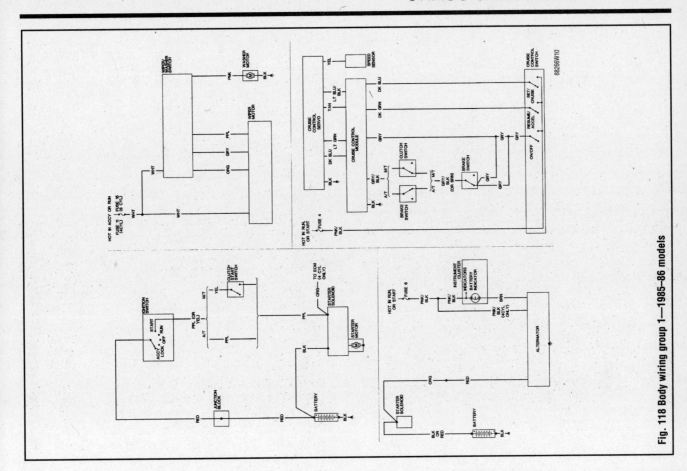

Fig. 118 Body wiring group 1—1985–86 models

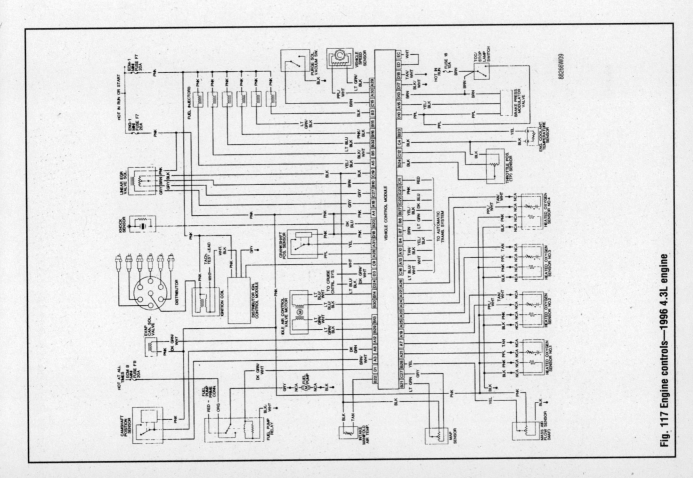

Fig. 117 Engine controls—1996 4.3L engine

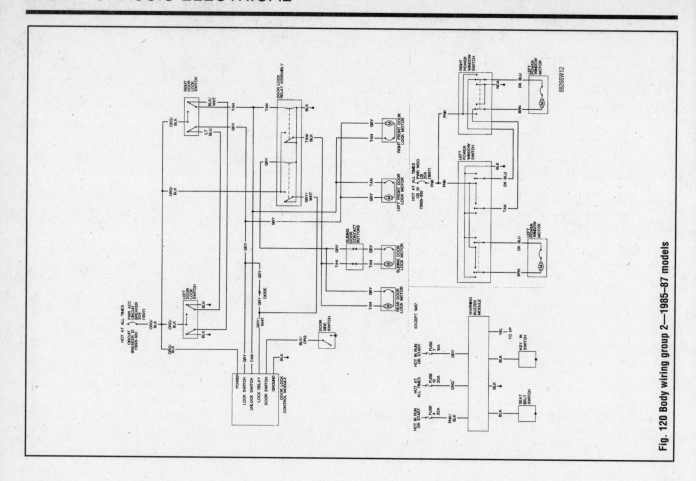

Fig. 120 Body wiring group 2—1985-87 models

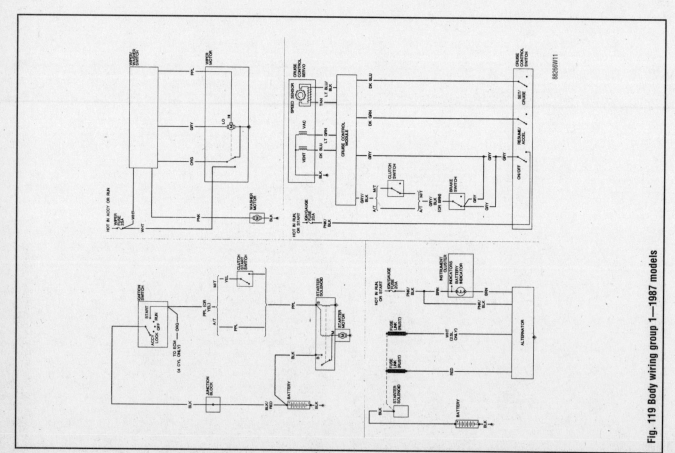

Fig. 119 Body wiring group 1—1987 models

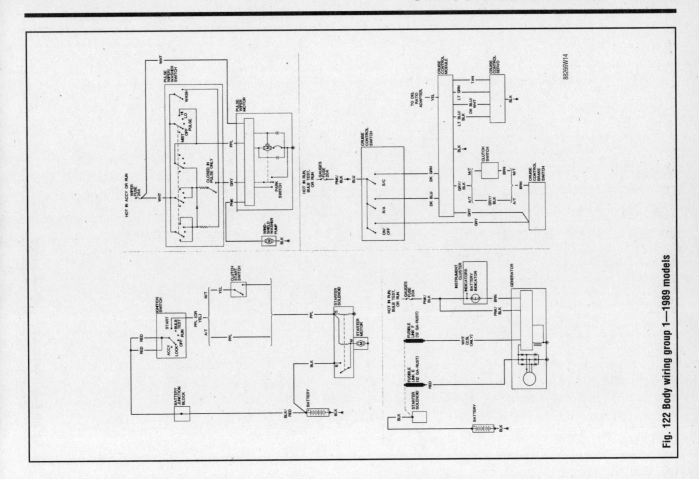

**Fig. 122 Body wiring group 1—1989 models**

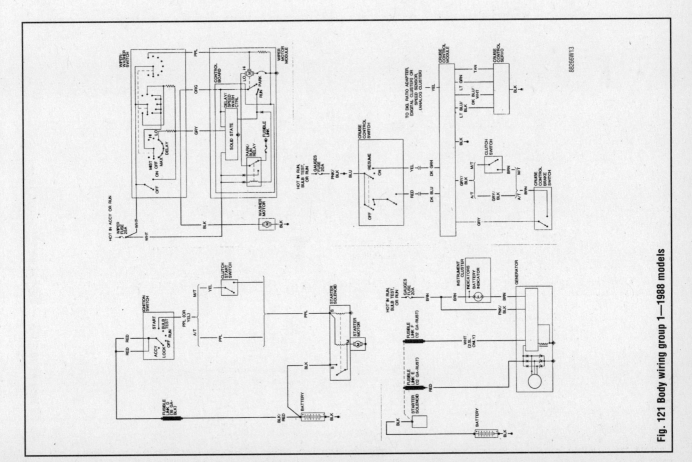

**Fig. 121 Body wiring group 1—1988 models**

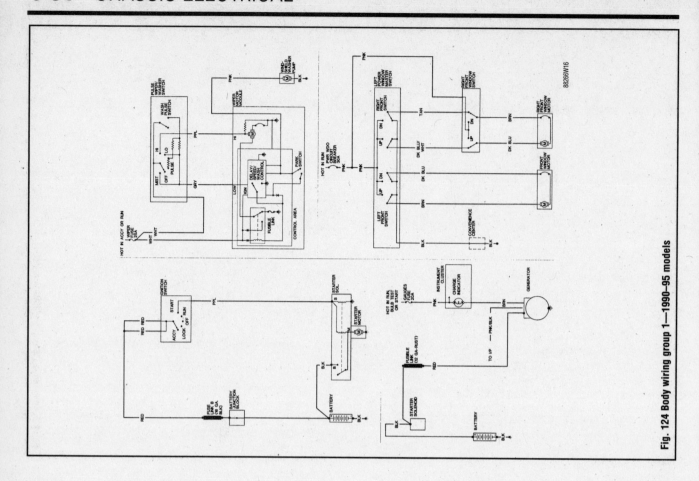

**Fig. 124 Body wiring group 1—1990–95 models**

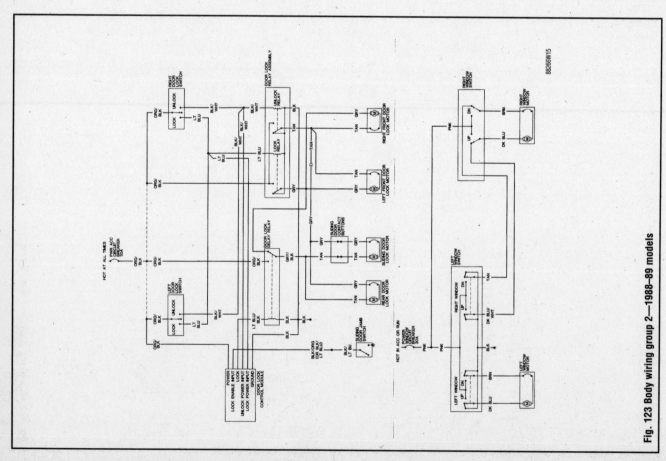

**Fig. 123 Body wiring group 2—1988–89 models**

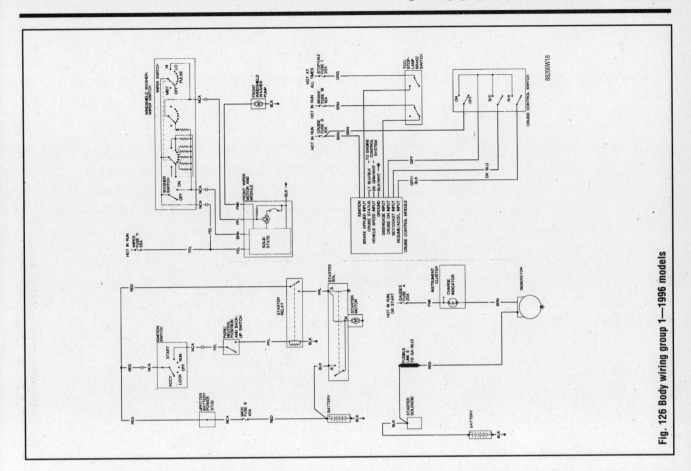

**Fig. 126 Body wiring group 1—1996 models**

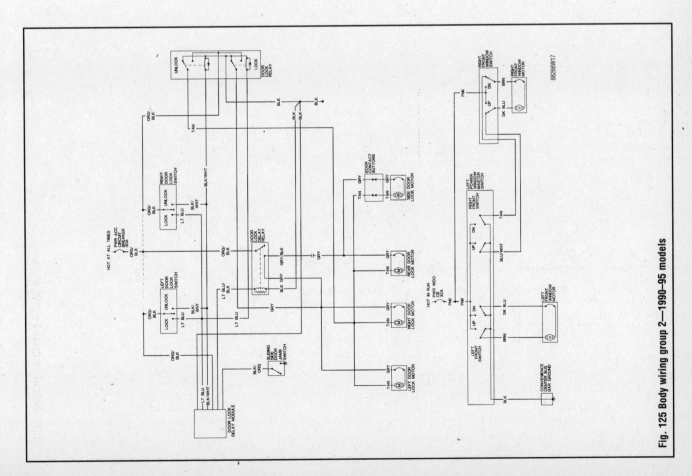

**Fig. 125 Body wiring group 2—1990-95 models**

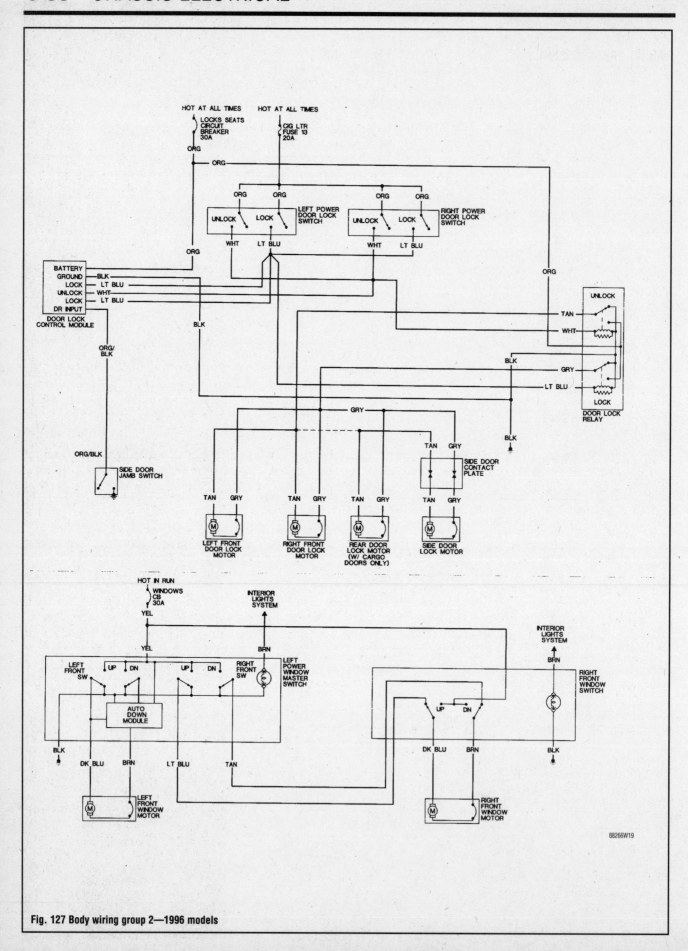

**Fig. 127 Body wiring group 2—1996 models**

88266W19

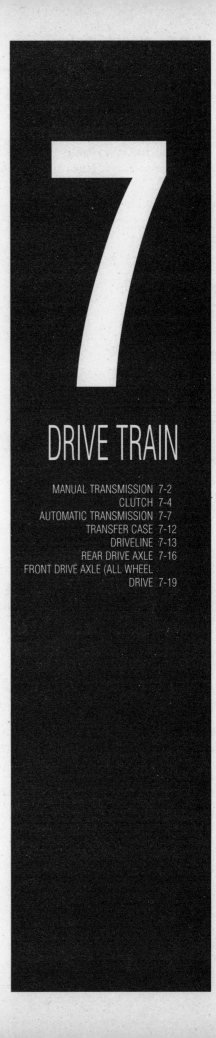

# 7

## DRIVE TRAIN

## MANUAL TRANSMISSION

▶ See Figure 1

### Adjustment

➡The shifter mechanism, of the 5-speed transmission, does not require adjustment and can be serviced independently.

#### SHIFTER RODS

#### 4-Speed (MR2)

▶ See Figures 2 and 3

➡The following procedure requires the use of ¼ in. pin gauge.

1. Raise and support the front of the vehicle safely using jackstands. This is necessary for access to the transmission housing and shifter rods.

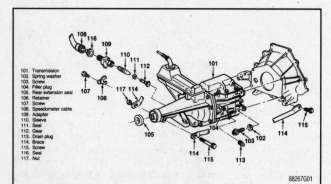

101. Transmission
102. Spring washer
103. Screw
104. Filler plug
105. Rear extension seal
106. Retainer
107. Screw
108. Speedometer cable
109. Adapter
110. Sleeve
111. Seal
112. Gear
113. Drain plug
114. Brace
115. Screw
116. Seal
117. Nut

88267G01

**Fig. 1 Exploded view of the MH3/ML3 5-speed transmission housing external components—MR2, 4-speed similar**

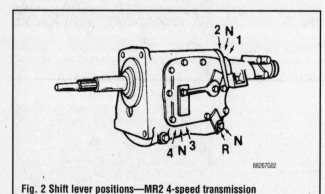

88267G02

**Fig. 2 Shift lever positions—MR2 4-speed transmission**

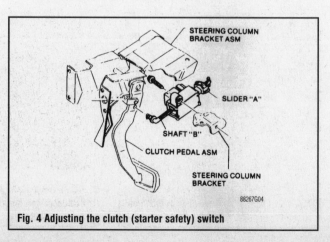

120. Shift lever
121. Shift control
122. Retainer
123. Washer
124. Control lever
125. Shift rod, 1st/2nd
126. Shift rod, 3rd/4th
127. Shift rod, rev.
128. Nut
129. Swivel
130. Nut
131. Shift lever
132. Washer
133. Retainer
A. Gage pin hole

88267G03

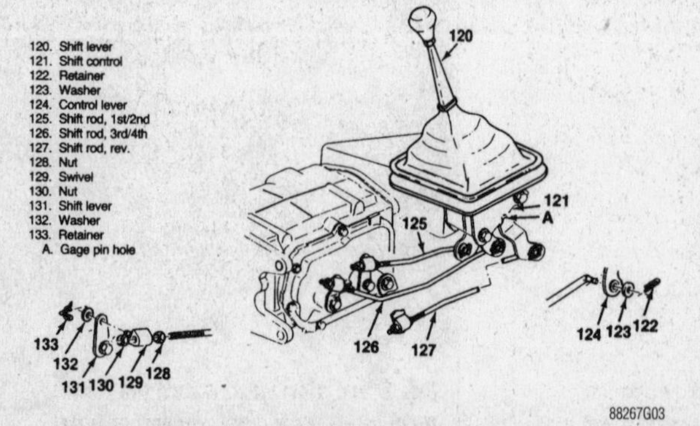

**Fig. 3 Adjusting the shifter rod linkage—MR2 4-speed transmission**

2. At each shifting swivel (located on the shifter side cover), loosen the jam nuts on the shifter rods.

3. From inside the vehicle, place the floor mounted, gear shift lever in the Neutral position.

4. From under the vehicle, place the shifter rods in the Neutral position. Refer to the accompanying illustration for help locating Neutral on the transmission housing.

5. Using a ¼ in. pin gauge, position it in the holes of the gear shift control levers.

6. While applying forward pressure (separately) on each shifter rod, tighten the shifter rod jam nuts, located on each side of the shifting swivel.

7. Remove the pin gauge and check the shifting operation. Lubricate the shifting levers.

8. Remove the jackstands and carefully lower the vehicle.

#### CLUTCH SWITCH

▶ See Figure 4

A clutch switch is located under the instrument panel and attached to the top of the clutch pedal. The switch is provided for safety to keep the vehicle from starting unless the pedal is depressed (disengaging the clutch).

1. Disconnect the negative battery cable for safety.
2. Remove the lower steering column-to-instrument panel cover.
3. Disengage the electrical connector from the clutch switch.

➡Be sure to leave any carpets and floor mats (being used in the vehicle) in place, when making the adjustment.

4. At the clutch switch, move the slider (adjuster) to the rear of the clutch switch shaft.
5. Push the clutch pedal to the floor.
6. While holding the clutch pedal to the floor, move the slider down the clutch switch shaft until it stops.

➡When moving the slider down the clutch switch shaft, a clicking noise can be heard.

7. Release the clutch pedal; the adjustment is complete.
8. Engage the electrical connector and connect the negative battery cable.
9. Verify proper switch operation.
10. Install the lower steering column cover.

### Back-up Light Switch

#### REMOVAL & INSTALLATION

▶ See Figure 5

1. Disconnect the negative battery cable for safety.
2. Raise and support the rear of the vehicle safely using jackstands. Support the rear, not the front of the vehicle, so the back of the switch is facing upward.

STEERING COLUMN BRACKET ASM

SLIDER "A"

SHAFT "B"

CLUTCH PEDAL ASM

STEERING COLUMN BRACKET

88267G04

**Fig. 4 Adjusting the clutch (starter safety) switch**

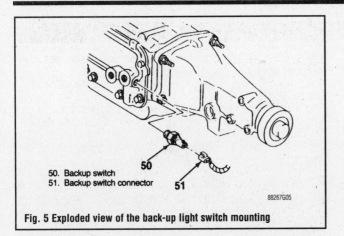

**Fig. 5 Exploded view of the back-up light switch mounting**

50. Backup switch
51. Backup switch connector

88267G05

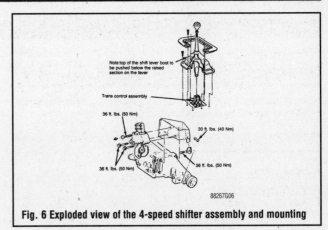

**Fig. 6 Exploded view of the 4-speed shifter assembly and mounting**

88267G06

This should help minimize the amount of the transmission fluid which might weep from the bore once the switch is removed.

3. Position a small drain pan or rag under the switch, just in case the vehicle is not supported at an angle which would prevent transmission fluid leakage when the switch is removed.

4. From the left rear of the transmission, disengage the electrical connector from the back-up light switch.

➡**If you are simply replacing the switch, prepare the replacement now (refer to the first installation step) and keep it handy. You can also minimize fluid loss by removing the old switch and immediately threading the new one.**

5. Loosen the back-up light switch using a suitably sized box wrench or deep socket made for switch removal, then remove the switch from the transmission assembly.

6. Installation is the reverse of the removal procedure. Apply thread sealing compound, install the switch and tighten to 17 ft. lbs. (23 Nm) using a deep socket and torque wrench.

7. Place the gear shift lever in the Reverse position and check the back-up lights are turned On.

➡**On some vehicles the ignition must be in the ON position in order for the reverse lights to work.**

## Shift Linkage

### REMOVAL & INSTALLATION

#### 4-Speed

♦ **See Figure 6**

1. Disconnect the negative battery cable for safety.
2. Raise the vehicle and support with jackstands.
3. Disconnect the shift rods from the control lever.

4. Remove the control mounting bolts and shifter.
5. If necessary for access inside the van, remove the jackstands and carefully lower the vehicle.
6. Remove the shifter knob, boot retaining screws and boot.
7. Pull the shifter assembly from the floor.
8. Installation is the reverse of the removal procedure.

#### 5-Speed

♦ **See Figure 7**

1. Disconnect the negative battery cable for safety.
2. Remove the transmission from the vehicle as detailed later in this section.
3. Remove the four dust cover clips, rubber boot and dust cover.
4. Remove the four control base-to-extension housing mounting bolts.
5. Remove the control assembly from the transmission.
6. Installation is the reverse of removal. Tighten the side bolts to 35 ft. lbs. (47 Nm) and the top bolts to 13 ft. lbs. (17 Nm). Apply a bead of RTV sealer to the groove around the base of the dust cover before installing the cover and retaining clips.

## Rear Extension Seal

### REMOVAL & INSTALLATION

♦ **See Figures 8 and 9**

1. Disconnect the negative battery cable for safety.
2. Raise and support the rear of the vehicle safely using jackstands. The rear of the vehicle should be raised high enough to prevent fluid loss from the rear of the transmission housing once the seal is removed.
3. Matchmark and remove the driveshaft as outlined in this section.
4. Using a suitable prybar or better yet, a seal removal tool (these are usually inexpensive and make the job much easier), pry the rear seal out of the extension housing.

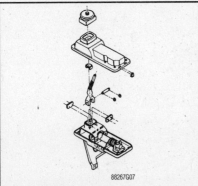

**Fig. 7 Exploded view of the 5-speed shifter assembly mounting**

88267G07

**Fig. 8 Use a seal puller to remove the extension housing seal (be careful not to damage the bore)**

88267P01

**Fig. 9 Use a driver to install the replacement seal—Automatic shown, manual similar**

88267P02

## ✷✷ WARNING

**The use of an improper tool to pry the seal from the housing could allow the bore to be damaged, preventing the seal's replacement from fully "sealing" the transmission. Fluid leaks could result.**

5. Installation is the reverse of the removal procedure. Coat the outside of the seal with silicone sealer and the lip of the seal with chassis grease.

## Transmission

### REMOVAL & INSTALLATION

▶ **See Figures 6 and 10**

1. Disconnect the negative battery cable for safety.
2. Raise and support the vehicle safely using jackstands.
3. Matchmark and remove the driveshaft from the vehicle.
4. Drain the transmission fluid into a suitable container, then install the drain plug to keep any remaining fluid from dripping throughout the procedure.
5. Loosen the shifter control knob-to-shifter control lever nut, then remove the shifter control knob. Remove the shifter control boot-to-chassis plate and the shifter control boot.
6. If removing an MH3/ML3, 5-speed transmission, unscrew the shift lever from the control lever.
7. If removing an MR2, 4-speed transmission, remove the shifter rods, then the shifter control assembly from the extension housing.
8. Disconnect the speedometer cable and seal, and the electrical connector from the transmission.
9. If necessary for clearance, disconnect and lower the exhaust pipe(s).
10. Place a transmission jack under the transmission housing, then secure it to the transmission. Raise the jack slightly so that it supports the weight of the transmission.
11. Remove the transmission-to-crossmember nuts/bolts and the transmission-to-chassis braces nuts/bolts, then remove the braces and the crossmember.

➡**If any spacers are used, make a note of them so that they may be installed in their original positions.**

12. While supporting the transmission, remove the transmission-to-bellhousing bolts; DO NOT allow it to hang on the input shaft.
13. Move the transmission and jack assembly rearward, then carefully lower and remove the transmission from the vehicle.

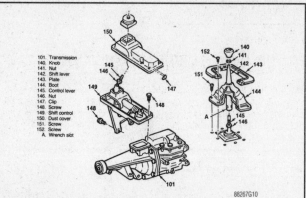

Fig. 10 Exploded view of the shift lever mounting—MH3/ML3 5-speed transmission

**To install:**

14. Place a thin coat of high temperature grease on the main drive gear splines.
15. Align the transmission's input shaft with the bellhousing and clutch assembly, then slide the transmission into the clutch.

➡**When installing the transmission, shift the transmission into High gear, then turn the output shaft to align the input shaft splines with the clutch plate.**

16. The balance of installation is the reverse of the removal procedure. Be sure to tighten all fasteners properly including:
- transmission-to-bellhousing bolts: 50 ft. lbs. (68 Nm).
- transmission-to-mount bolts: 40 ft. lbs. (54 Nm) for the MR2 or 33 ft. lbs. (45 Nm) for the for the MH3/ML3
- crossmember-to-mount bolts: 26 ft. lbs. (35 Nm) for the MR2 or 18 ft. lbs. for the MH3/ML3
- crossmember-to-chassis bolts: 37 ft. lbs. (50 Nm).
- transmission-to-brace bolts: 26 ft. lbs. (35 Nm).
- shifter control assembly-to-extension housing bolts: 23 ft. lbs. (31 Nm).
- shifter rod swivel nut: 18 ft. lbs. (24 Nm).
- shifter lever nut: 35 ft. lbs. (47 Nm).
17. Align and install the driveshaft, using the marks made during removal.
18. Remove the jackstands and carefully lower the vehicle.
19. Connect the negative battery cable.

## CLUTCH

▶ **See Figure 11**

### Adjustments

Since the hydraulic system provides automatic clutch adjustment, no adjustment of the clutch linkage or pedal height is required. For more details on how the hydraulic clutch actuation system operates, please refer to the general clutch information provided in this section.

## Clutch Disc and Pressure Plate

▶ **See Figures 12 and 13**

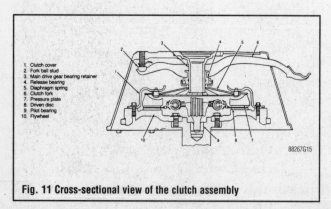

Fig. 11 Cross-sectional view of the clutch assembly

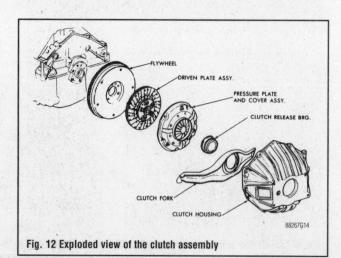

Fig. 12 Exploded view of the clutch assembly

REMOVAL & INSTALLATION

♦ **See Figures 14 thru 20**

1. Remove the transmission assembly from the vehicle. For details, please refer to the manual transmission procedure found earlier in this section.
2. Remove the slave cylinder attaching bolts, then position the cylinder aside.
3. Remove the clutch inspection cover.
4. Remove the retaining bolts, then remove the bellhousing.
5. Slide the clutch fork from the ball stud and remove the fork from the dust boot.

➡The ball stud is threaded into the clutch housing and can be easily replaced.

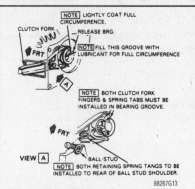

Fig. 13 Typical clutch release bearing lubrication points

Fig. 14 A clutch alignment arbor is used for removal or installation of the clutch and pressure plate assembly

Fig. 15 Remove the transmission and bellhousing for access to the pressure plate

Fig. 16 Loosen the pressure plate (clutch cover) bolts gradually and evenly in a cross-wise pattern

Fig. 17 Removing the clutch and pressure plate

Fig. 18 Be sure that the flywheel surface is clean of grease or contaminants, before installing the clutch

Fig. 19 Use a clutch alignment arbor, to align the clutch assembly during installation

Fig. 20 Clutch plate and pressure plate installed with the alignment arbor in place

6. Install the Clutch Pilot tool No. J–33169 into the clutch plate to support it during removal.

7. The flywheel and clutch cover (pressure plate assembly) are marked with **X**'s for correct assembly or white painted letters, if these are not visible, scribe new matchmarks.

8. Gradually loosen the clutch pressure plate-to-flywheel bolts (one turn at a time) until all of the spring pressure is released.

9. Remove the bolts and the clutch assembly.

➡The clutch pilot bearing is an oil impregnated type bearing pressed into the crankshaft. This bearing requires attention when the clutch is removed from the vehicle, at which time it should be cleaned and inspected for excessive wear or damage and should be replaced (if necessary).

10. Inspect the flywheel for wear, scoring or damage and machine or replace, if necessary.

**To install:**

11. Crank the engine over by hand until the X-mark on the flywheel is on the bottom.

12. Position the clutch disc and pressure plate in the same relative location as removed and support with a clutch pilot tool.

➡The clutch disc is installed with the damper springs and slinger toward the transmission.

13. Rotate the clutch assembly until the X-marks on the flywheel and clutch cover align. Make sure the cover bolt holes are aligned with those in the flywheel.

14. Install the bolts, then tighten them evenly and gradually using a cross-wise pattern. Tighten the bolts evenly to 15–22 ft. lbs. (20–29 Nm). Do NOT overtighten.

15. Remove the clutch pilot tool.

16. Lubricate the ball socket on the clutch fork (using a high temperature grease) and reinstall on the ball stud.

17. Pack the recess on the inside of the throw out bearing collar and the throw out groove with graphite grease.

18. Install the bellhousing and the slave cylinder.

19. Install the throw out bearing on the fork. Lubricate the bearing groove (using a high temperature grease).

20. The balance of the installation procedure is the reverse of the removal steps. Be sure to properly tighten all fasteners including:
- Pressure plate-to-flywheel bolts: 15–22 ft. lbs. (20–30 Nm) for the 4-speed or 25–35 ft. lbs. (34–47 Nm) for the 5-speed
- Flywheel-to-crankshaft bolts: 60–75 ft. lbs. (81–102 Nm) for the 4-speed or 55–75 ft. lbs. (75–102 Nm) for the 5-speed
- Slave cylinder-to-bellhousing bolts: 10–15 ft. lbs. (14–20 Nm).

21. Install the transmission assembly.

➡If installing an MR2, 4-speed transmission, lubricate and adjust the transmission shift linkages (using a high temperature grease).

## Pilot Bearing

### REMOVAL & INSTALLATION

♦ **See Figure 21**

1. Disconnect the negative battery cable for safety.
2. Remove the transmission assembly. For details, please refer to the manual transmission procedure found earlier in this section.

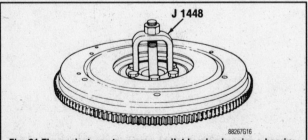

**Fig. 21 The easiest way to remove a pilot bearing is using a bearing puller tool**

3. Remove the clutch disc and pressure plate assembly. For details, please refer to the procedure found earlier in this section.

### ✳✳ WARNING

**The release bearing is permanently packed with lubricant and should NOT be soaked in a cleaning solvent as this would dissolve the lubricant.**

4. Using a pilot bearing removing tool J–1448, remove the pilot bearing from the crankshaft.

➡If a bearing puller is not available, thoroughly pack the bearing cavity with fresh grease, then position a drift (whose outer diameter is close to, but not the same size as the bearing's inner diameter) in the center of the bearing. Drive the drift inward using a mallet, this should force the grease against the bearing cage, freeing it from the flywheel. Just be careful that enough grease is used to keep the drift from damaging the flywheel or other engine components.

**To install:**

5. Apply a few drops of machine oil to the bearing.
6. Using a pilot bearing installing tool J–1522, or an equivalent driver, install the new pilot bearing.
7. Install the clutch and pressure plate assembly.
8. Install the transmission assembly to the vehicle.
9. Connect the negative battery cable and check operation.

## Master Cylinder

The clutch master cylinder is located in the engine compartment, on the left side of the firewall, above the steering column.

### REMOVAL & INSTALLATION

♦ **See Figures 22 and 23**

1. Disconnect negative battery cable.
2. Remove hush panel from under the dash.
3. Disconnect pushrod from clutch pedal.
4. Disconnect hydraulic line from the clutch master cylinder using a flare nut wrench.
5. Remove the master cylinder-to-cowl brace nuts. Remove master cylinder and overhaul (if necessary).
6. Using a putty knife, clean the master cylinder and cowl mounting surfaces.
7. Installation is the reverse of the removal procedure. Tighten the master cylinder-to-cowl brace nuts to 10–15 ft. lbs. (14–20 Nm). Fill master cylinder with clean, fresh hydraulic fluid conforming to DOT 3 specifications.
8. Bleed the hydraulic clutch system and check for leaks.

## Slave (Secondary) Cylinder

The slave cylinder is located on the left side of the bellhousing and controls the clutch release fork operation.

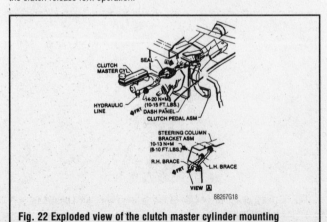

**Fig. 22 Exploded view of the clutch master cylinder mounting**

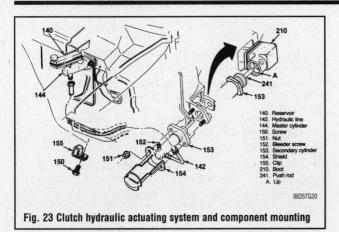

**Fig. 23 Clutch hydraulic actuating system and component mounting**

140. Reservoir
142. Hydraulic line
144. Master cylinder
150. Screw
151. Nut
152. Bleeder screw
153. Secondary cylinder
154. Shield
155. Clip
210. Boot
241. Push rod
A. Lip

## REMOVAL & INSTALLATION

▶ See Figure 23

1. Disconnect the negative battery cable.
2. Raise and support the front of the vehicle on jackstands.
3. Disconnect the hydraulic line from clutch master cylinder. Remove the hydraulic line-to-chassis screw and the clip from the chassis.

➡ Be sure to plug the line opening to keep dirt and moisture out of the system.

4. Remove the slave cylinder-to-bellhousing nuts.
5. Remove the pushrod and the slave cylinder from the vehicle, then overhaul it (if necessary).

**To install:**

6. Lubricate the leading end of the slave cylinder with Girling® Rubber Lube or equivalent.
7. Install the pushrod and the slave cylinder into the vehicle.

8. Install the slave cylinder-to-bellhousing nuts.
9. Connect the hydraulic line to the clutch master cylinder.
10. Fill the master cylinder with new brake fluid conforming to DOT 3 specifications. Bleed the hydraulic system. If the front of the vehicle is still raised, keep in mind that the clutch master cylinder cannot be properly filled. Check the fluid level often, then recheck and top off once the vehicle is lowered.
11. Tighten the slave cylinder-to-bellhousing nuts to 10–15 ft. lbs. (14–20 Nm).
12. Lower the front of the vehicle, then top off the clutch master cylinder reservoir.
13. Connect the negative battery cable.

## BLEEDING THE HYDRAULIC CLUTCH

Bleeding air from the hydraulic clutch system is necessary whenever any part of the system has been disconnected or the fluid level (in the reservoir) has been allowed to fall so low, that air has been drawn into the master cylinder.

1. Fill master cylinder reservoir with clean, fresh brake fluid conforming to DOT 3 specifications.

### ✳ WARNING

**Never, under any circumstances, use fluid which has been bled from a system to fill the reservoir as it may be aerated, have too much moisture content and possibly be contaminated.**

2. Raise and support the front of the vehicle on jackstands.
3. Remove the slave cylinder attaching bolts.
4. Hold the slave cylinder at approximately 45° with the bleeder at its highest point. Fully depress the clutch pedal and open the bleeder screw.
5. Close the bleeder screw and release the clutch pedal.
6. Repeat the procedure until all of the air is evacuated from the system. Check and refill the master cylinder reservoir as required to prevent air from being drawn through the master cylinder.

➡ Never release a depressed clutch pedal with the bleeder screw open or air will be drawn into the system.

## AUTOMATIC TRANSMISSION

### Adjustments

#### SHIFT LINKAGE

▶ See Figures 24, 25 and 26

The 1985–95 vehicles covered by this manual that are equipped with automatic transmissions utilize a mechanical shift lever and linkage assembly. Starting in 1996, the shift linkage was replaced by a shift cable. For 1996 vehicles, please refer to the cable replacement and adjustment procedure found later in this section.

1. Firmly apply the parking brake and block the rear wheels.

2. Raise and support the front of the vehicle on jackstands.
3. At the left side of the transmission, loosen the shift rod swivel-to-equalizer lever nut on 1985–89 vehicles or the bracket-to-frame screw on 1990–95 vehicles.
4. At the steering column, place the gear selector lever into the Neutral position.

➡ When positioning the gear selector lever, DO NOT use the steering column indicator to find the Neutral position, instead count gate positions from Park, through Reverse to the Neutral gate.

5. Rotate the transmission shift lever counterclockwise (toward the front of the transmission) to the first (Park) position, then turn it clockwise (rearward) to the 2nd detent (Neutral) position. Remember that the first position and the first

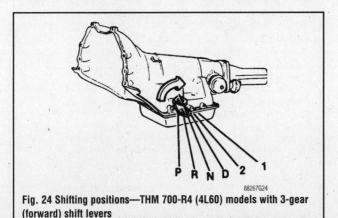

**Fig. 24 Shifting positions—THM 700-R4 (4L60) models with 3-gear (forward) shift levers**

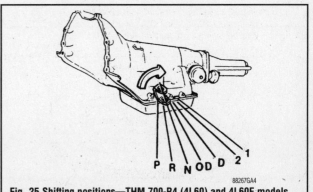

**Fig. 25 Shifting positions—THM 700-R4 (4L60) and 4L60E models with 4-gear (forward) shift levers**

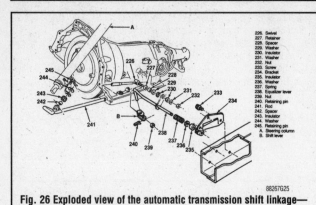

**Fig. 26 Exploded view of the automatic transmission shift linkage—1985–94 models (1995 similar)**

detent are not the same. The first position, or fully counterclockwise is Park, when you turn the lever clockwise 1 detent, the transmission will be in Reverse, then turn it to the second detent and it will be in Neutral.

6. Holding the rod tightly in the swivel, tighten the retainer which was loosened to allow the adjustment. For 1985–89 vehicles, you should have loosened the equalizer lever nut and it should be tightened to 11 ft. lbs. (14 Nm). For 1990–95 vehicles, the bracket-to-frame screw should be tightened to 21 ft. lbs. (28 Nm).

7. Place the gear selector lever (on the steering column) in the **P** position and check the adjustment. Move the gear selector lever into the various positions; the engine must start ONLY in the **P** and the **N** positions.

8. If the engine will not start in the **N** and/or **P** positions, refer to the Back-Up Light Switch adjustment information in Section 6 and adjust the switch.

### ❄❄ CAUTION

**With the gear selector lever in the PARK position, the parking pawl should engage the rear internal gear lugs or output ring gear lugs to prevent the vehicle from rolling and causing personal injury.**

9. Align the gear selector lever indicator, if necessary.
10. Remove the jackstands and carefully lower the vehicle

## THROTTLE VALVE (TV) CABLE

▶ **See Figure 27**

Only the THM 700-R4 (4L60) transmission (1985–92) utilizes a Throttle Valve (TV) and cable. Shift control on the 4L60-E is electronically controlled.

If the TV cable is broken, sticky, misadjusted or is the incorrect part for the model, the vehicle may exhibit various malfunctions, such as delayed or full throttle shifts.

### Preliminary Checks

1. Inspect and, if necessary, correct the transmission fluid level.
2. Make sure that the brakes are not dragging and that the engine is operating correctly.

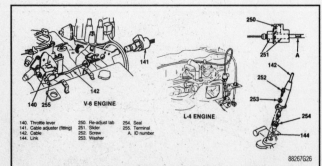

**Fig. 27 Adjusting the TV cable—V-6 on left, L-4 at middle and close-up of the adjuster assembly at right**

3. Make sure that the cable is connected at both ends.
4. Make sure that the correct cable is installed.

### Adjustment

1. Remove the engine cover in the passenger compartment for access to the throttle lever. For details on cover removal, please refer to Section 1 of this manual.
2. If necessary, remove the air cleaner.
3. If the cable has been removed and installed, check to see that the cable slider is in the zero or the fully adjusted position; if not, perform the following procedures:
   a. Depress and hold the readjust tab (located at the engine end of the TV cable).
   b. Move the slider back through the fitting (away from the throttle lever) until it stops against the fitting.
   c. Release the readjust tab.
4. Rotate the throttle lever to the Full Throttle Stop position. Be sure to manually operate the throttle lever, DO NOT use the accelerator pedal. The slider will ratchet toward the lever as it is rotated, so listen for at least 1 click.
5. Release the throttle lever.
6. Verify that the cable moves freely. The cable may appear to function properly with a stopped and cold engine. Recheck after normal operating temperature has been reached.
7. If removed for access, install the air cleaner assembly.
8. Road test the vehicle and confirm proper operation.
9. Install the engine cover to the passenger compartment.

## Shift Cable

▶ **See Figures 28, 29 and 30**

### REPLACEMENT & ADJUSTMENT

The 1985–95 vehicles covered by this manual that are equipped with automatic transmissions utilize a mechanical shift lever and linkage assembly. Starting in 1996, the shift linkage was replaced by a shift cable. For 1985–95 vehicles, please refer to the shift linkage adjustment procedure found earlier in this section.

Before attempting to remove the shift cable from the van, make sure that the transmission is in the mechanical Neutral position. You can verify this at the control lever on the transmission assembly by rotating it clockwise until it reaches the FULL STOP position, then rotating it back counterclockwise 2 detents.

1. Raise and support the front of the vehicle safely using jackstands.
2. Climb under the vehicle and verify that the transmission is in mechanical Neutral.
3. Remove the clip from the bracket securing the shift cable to the transmission.
4. Disconnect the shift cable end from the transmission shift lever stud ball.
5. Remove the 3 shift cable clips from the body.
6. Remove the grommet from the hole in the floor panel.
7. On All Wheel Drive (AWD) vehicles, remove the bolt and washer securing the clip and shift cable to the transfer case assembly.
8. Move to the passenger compartment, then disconnect the clip securing the shift cable to the steering column bracket.
9. Disconnect the shift cable end from the steering column shift controller stud ball.

**To install:**
10. Make sure the transmission is still in mechanical Neutral (double-check if it might have accidentally been changed during cable removal).
11. Feed the steering column end of the shift cable through the grommet hole in the floor panel of the vehicle.
12. Install the shift cable end to the steering column shift controller stud ball, then fasten using the retaining clip.
13. Route the cable to the transmission bracket. DO NOT depress the locking tab that secures the shift cable to the transmission bracket. Make sure that the tab remains in the OUT position. Also, DO NOT install the shift cable end to the transmission shift lever stud ball.

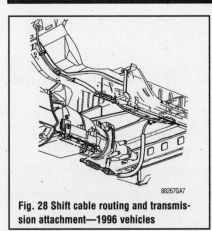

**Fig. 28 Shift cable routing and transmission attachment—1996 vehicles**

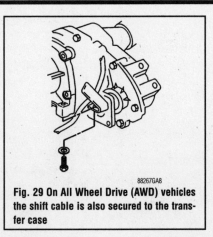

**Fig. 29 On All Wheel Drive (AWD) vehicles the shift cable is also secured to the transfer case**

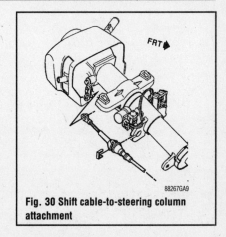

**Fig. 30 Shift cable-to-steering column attachment**

**To adjust:**

14. Place the steering column shift lever into the Neutral position.

15. Make sure that the shift cable is properly routed and that it is not restricted. The shift cable must assume a natural routing. It must be free to move 0.80 in. (20mm) axially during the adjustment under adjustment spring loads.

16. Pull the cable completely forward and release it. When the cable is pulled COMPLETELY forward and released, the adjustment spring will position the cable at its most rearward position.

17. Connect the end of the shift cable to the transmission shift lever ball stud.

➡DO NOT pull the shift cable end forward of the ball stud prior to connecting the two. A poor adjustment could result.

18. Press the locking tab IN to secure the shift cable to the transmission bracket.

19. Complete the cable installation:
   a. On AWD vehicles, install the bolt and washer securing the clip and shift cable to the transfer case.
   b. Position the grommet in the floor panel hole.
   c. Install the 3 shift cable clips to the body.

20. Remove the jackstands and carefully lower the vehicle, then road test to confirm proper operation.

## Neutral Safety Switch

On 1985–95 vehicles covered by this manual, the Neutral Safety Switch is a part of the Back-Up Light Switch and is mounted to the steering column. For replacement or adjustment, please refer to the Back-Up Light Switch, Removal and Installation procedures in Section 6 of this manual.

In 1996, the neutral safety switch was relocated to the side of the transmission assembly. This change corresponds to the change made that year from shift linkage to a shift cable.

### REPLACEMENT & ADJUSTMENT

♦ See Figures 31 and 32

➡Any removal of the switch will require that the switch is adjusted before installation. Switch adjustment should only be accomplished using J-41364-A or an equivalent switch adjustment and alignment tool. If the tool is not available, you may be able to successfully adjust the switch using a hit and miss method, moving the switch slightly each time and rechecking to verify that the switch works properly (the vehicle starts ONLY when the transmission is in Park or Neutral). But, this could take some time and be quite frustrating, so an attempt to buy or borrow the adjustment tool first may be well worth it.

1. Firmly apply the parking brake and block the rear wheels.
2. Disconnect the negative battery cable for safety.
3. Shift the transmission into Neutral.
4. Raise and support the front of the vehicle safely using jackstands.
5. Before attempting to remove or adjust the switch, make sure that the transmission is in the mechanical Neutral position. You can verify this at the control lever on the transmission assembly by rotating it clockwise until it reaches the FULL STOP position, then rotating it back counterclockwise 2 detents.

6. Disconnect the shift cable end from the transmission shift control lever by pulling the cable end from the lever ball stud.

7. Remove the nut securing the control lever to the manual shaft.

8. Disengage the wiring connectors from the neutral safety/back-up light switch.

9. Remove the 2 bolts which secure the switch to the transmission assembly.

10. Slide the switch from the manual shaft. If there is difficulty removing the switch, file the outer edge of the manual shaft lightly to remove any burrs from the shaft.

**To adjust:**

11. Position J-41364-A, or an equivalent adjustment tool, onto the neutral safety switch, making sure that the 2 slots on the switch (located where the manual shaft is inserted) are aligned with the 2 lower tabs on the tool. Then, rotate the tool until the tool's upper locator pin is aligned with the slot on the top of the switch.

➡During installation, leave the adjustment tool mounted to the switch until the switch is secured and the position cannot change.

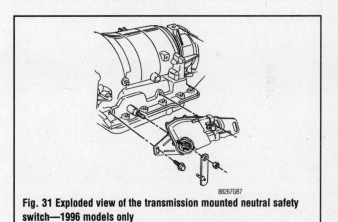

**Fig. 31 Exploded view of the transmission mounted neutral safety switch—1996 models only**

**Fig. 32 Use the adjustment tool to greatly ease your job during neutral safety switch adjustment or installation**

**To install:**

12. Check the outer edge of the manual shaft to make sure there are no burrs which could prevent switch installation. If necessary, file the edge lightly to remove any remaining burrs.

13. Align the switch hub flats with the flats on the manual shaft.

14. Slide the switch onto the transmission manual shaft until the switch mounting bracket contacts the mounting bosses on the transmission.

15. Secure the switch to the transmission using the 2 retaining bolts. Tighten the bolts to 21 ft. lbs. (28 Nm).

16. Remove the switch adjustment tool from the switch assembly.

17. Engage the wiring harness connectors to the switch.

18. Install the transmission control lever to the manual shaft, then secure using the retaining nut. Tighten the nut to 21 ft. lbs. (28 Nm).

19. Connect the negative battery cable, then verify proper switch operation. The engine MUST start ONLY with the transmission in Park or Neutral. If further adjustment is required, loosen the switch retaining bolts and rotate the switch slightly, then tighten the bolts and check for proper operation.

20. Remove the jackstands and carefully lower the vehicle.

## Back-up Light Switch

On 1985–95 vehicles covered by this manual, the Back-Up Light Switch and is mounted to the steering column. For replacement or adjustment, please refer to the Back-Up Light Switch, Removal and Installation procedures in Section 6 of this manual.

In 1996, the back-up light and neutral safety switch assembly was relocated to the side of the transmission assembly. This change corresponds to the change made that year from shift linkage to a shift cable. For replacement and adjustment procedures, please refer to the neutral safety switch information found earlier in this section.

## Extension Housing Seal

### REMOVAL & INSTALLATION

▶ **See Figures 33, 34 and 35**

1. Disconnect the negative battery cable for safety.
2. Block the front wheels.
3. Raise and support the rear of the vehicle safely using jackstands. Raise the rear of the vehicle sufficiently to keep all of the fluid in the transmission, away from the rear extension housing. If this cannot be done, the transmission pan will have to be removed in order to drain the fluid.
4. Matchmark and remove the driveshaft as outlined in this section.
5. Using a suitable prybar or better yet, a seal removal tool (these are usually inexpensive and make the job much easier), pry the rear seal out of the extension housing.

### ✷✷ WARNING

**The use of an improper tool to pry the seal from the housing could allow the bore to be damaged, preventing the seal's replacement from fully "sealing" the transmission. Fluid leaks could result.**

6. Coat the outside of the seal with a suitable non-hardening sealer and install with a suitable driver or seal installer.

7. The remainder of installation is the reverse of the removal procedure.

## Transmission

### REMOVAL & INSTALLATION

➡**The following procedures require the use of the Torque Converter Holding tool No. J–21366 or equivalent.**

The manufacturer recommends that you drain the transmission fluid before attempting to remove the transmission assembly from the vehicle. The major reason for this is that depending on the condition of the transmission's seals and how the transmission is manipulated during removal, there is a good chance that the fluid will spill causing quite a mess. Keep in mind that in almost all instances, the transmission dipstick tube must be removed from the housing before the transmission can be removed from the vehicle. This provides a great escape route for fluid unless it can be thoroughly and safely plugged for the duration of the procedure. The bottom line is that you will have to make up your own mind.

➡**If you decide to drain the fluid from a transmission that you are also planning on returning to service, it may be a good idea to drive the vehicle and thoroughly warm the fluid before draining. This will assure you the best fluid change possible.**

#### THM 700 R-4 (4L60) Transmission

▶ **See Figure 36**

1. Disconnect the negative battery cable for safety.
2. Remove the engine cover from the passenger compartment for access. For details, please refer to Section 1 of this manual.
3. Remove the air cleaner for access, then disconnect the Throttle Valve (TV) cable from the throttle lever.
4. Raise and support the front of the vehicle safely using jackstands.
5. Drain the transmission fluid by removing the pan.
6. Disconnect the shift linkage from the transmission assembly.
7. Matchmark and remove the driveshaft from the vehicle. On All Wheel Drive (AWD) vehicles, the front driveshaft should be removed as well.
8. Disconnect the support bracket at the catalytic converter along with any other components which must be removed for clearance.
9. Support the transmission or transmission and transfer case (as applicable) using a suitable floor jack.
10. Remove the transmission crossmember.

### ✷✷ WARNING

**DO NOT stretch or otherwise damage any cables, wires or other components when lowering the transmission in the next step.**

11. Carefully lower the transmission in order to provide the necessary clearance to reach other components.

12. Remove the dipstick tube and seal from the transmission assembly, then cover or plug the opening to prevent dirt or contamination from entering the

Fig. 33 Remove the driveshaft for access to the rear transmission (extension housing) seal

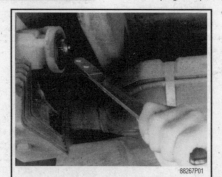

Fig. 34 Use a seal puller to remove the extension housing seal (BE CAREFUL not to damage the bore)

Fig. 35 Use a suitable driver to install the replacement seal into the housing

transmission and to minimize fluid leakage. Remember that even if you drained the transmission there is still a decent amount of the slimly fluid in the assembly and it will seep out of any opening you make during the procedure.

13. Disconnect the speedometer cable, on early-models or disengage speedometer harness (speed sensor) connector on late-models.

14. If used, disconnect the vacuum modulator line.

15. Disengage the electrical connectors and any electrical connector retaining clips from the transmission.

16. Disconnect the oil cooler lines. Immediately cap all openings in the transmission assembly and the lines to prevent excessive fluid loss or system contamination.

17. If equipped, remove the dampener and support.

18. On AWD vehicles, check the transfer case for any wires, hoses, cables or other connections, then disengage them and position aside.

➡️**Before removal, note the position of the transmission support braces as they must be reinstalled in their original positions.**

19. Remove the transmission support braces (at the torque converter cover).

20. Remove the torque converter cover, then matchmark the flexplate to the torque converter; re-aligning the marks during installation will maintain the original balance.

21. Remove the torque converter-to-flywheel bolts and slide the converter back into the transmission.

22. Place a block of wood and a jackstand under the rear of the engine and support it.

23. Remove the transmission-to-engine mounting bolts. Note the location of any clips or brackets for installation purposes, then position them aside.

24. With the transmission still supported by the first floor jack, carefully slide the transmission back off the locating pins. Once there is sufficient clearance, install a torque converter holding tool such as No. J–21366 or equivalent.

25. Carefully lower the transmission assembly from the vehicle.

**To install:**

26. Make sure the torque converter is properly seated in the transmission assembly and install the converter holding tool.

220. Harness
221. Dipstick Tube
222. Support Brace
223. Cooler Lines
224. Seal
225. Transmission
226. Screws, Transmission to Engine
228. Converter Housing Cover
229. Flywheel
230. Screw, Flywheel To Torque Converter
231. Dampener
232. Insulator
233. Support
A. Locating Pins

88267GD1

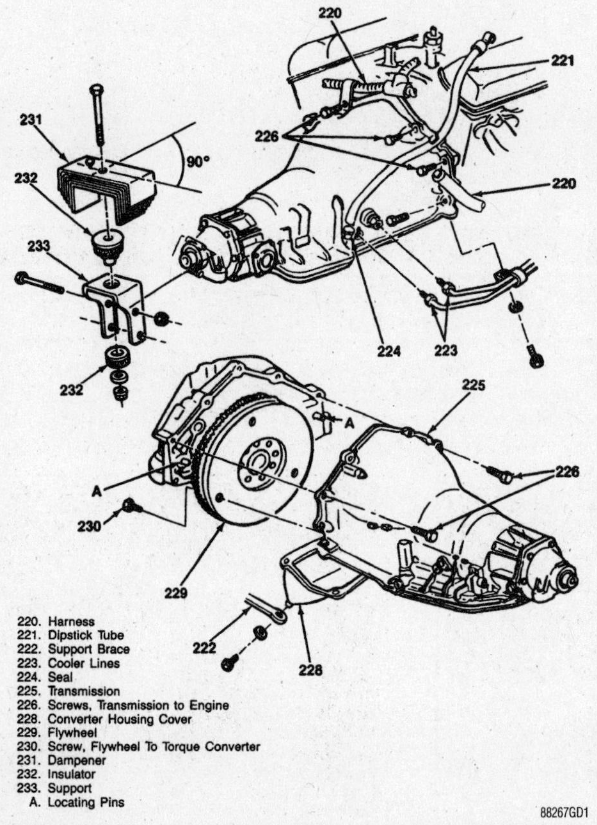

**Fig. 36 Exploded view of the automatic transmission mounting— 1985–93 vehicles shown (1994–96 similar)**

27. Support the transmission assembly (and transfer case on AWD vehicles) on a floor jack, then position it under the vehicle.

28. Carefully raise the transmission into position and remove the torque converter holding tool.

29. Slide the transmission straight onto the locating pins while aligning the flexplate and torque converter matchmarks which were made during removal.

➡️**Once in position, the torque converter must be flush onto the flexplate and must be able to rotate freely by hand.**

30. Install the transmission assembly-to-engine retaining bolts along with any brackets or clips which were positioned aside during removal. Tighten the transmission retaining bolts to 55 ft. lbs. (75 Nm) for 2.5L engines or to 35 ft. lbs. (47 Nm) for 1985–90 4.3L engines or to 23 ft. lbs. (32 Nm) for 1991–92 4.3L engines.

31. Thread the torque converter-to-flexplate screws by hand until they are finger-tight to assure proper converter seating.

32. Tighten the torque converter bolts to 46 ft. lbs. (63 Nm) slowly and evenly.

33. Install the converter cover, carefully hooking the cover under the lip of the engine oil pan.

34. If equipped, install the support and dampener. Make sure the dampener is positioned 90° from the transmission's centerline.

35. Install the remaining components in the reverse order of removal.

➡️**When raising the transmission into place, be sure NOT to pinch or damage any cables, wires or other components.**

36. If drained earlier, IMMEDIATELY refill the transmission using fresh fluid.

### 4L60-E Transmission

♦ **See Figure 36**

1. Disconnect the negative battery cable for safety.

2. Raise and support the front of the vehicle safely using jackstands.

3. Drain the transmission fluid by removing the pan.

4. Disconnect the shift linkage (1993–95 vehicles) or the shift cable (1996 vehicles) from the transmission assembly, as applicable.

5. Matchmark and remove the driveshaft from the vehicle. On All Wheel Drive (AWD) vehicles, the front driveshaft should be removed as well.

6. On 1996 vehicles, remove the transfer case and adapter from the transmission assembly. For details, please refer to the transfer case removal procedure found later in this section.

7. On 1993–95 vehicles, disconnect the support bracket at the catalytic converter along with any other components which must be removed for clearance.

8. Support the transmission or transmission and transfer case (as applicable) using a suitable floor jack.

9. On 1996 vehicles, remove the 2 front torsion bars. For details, please refer to Section 8 of this manual.

10. On 1994–95 vehicles, unload the torsion bars. For details, please refer to Section 8 of this manual.

11. On 1994–96 vehicles, remove the rear transmission mount.

12. On 1993–95 vehicles, remove the transmission crossmember.

**✳️✳️ WARNING**

**DO NOT stretch or otherwise damage any cables, wires or other components when lowering the transmission in the next step.**

13. Carefully lower the transmission in order to provide the necessary clearance to reach other components.

14. Remove the dipstick tube and seal from the transmission assembly, then cover or plug the opening to prevent dirt or contamination from entering the transmission and to minimize fluid leakage. Remember that even if you drained the transmission there is still a decent amount of the slimly fluid in the assembly and it will seep out of any opening you make during the procedure.

15. Disengage speedometer harness (speed sensor) connector.

16. Disengage the electrical connectors and any electrical connector retaining clips from the transmission.

17. Disconnect the oil cooler lines. Immediately cap all openings in the transmission assembly and the lines to prevent excessive fluid loss or system contamination.

18. On 1993 AWD vehicles, check the transfer case for any wires, hoses, cables or other connections, then disengage them and position aside.

➡ **On vehicles so equipped, before removal of the transmission support braces, note the brace positioning as they must be reinstalled in their original positions.**

19. On 1993–95 vehicles, remove the transmission support braces (at the torque converter cover).
20. On 1996 vehicles, remove the starter motor assembly from the engine.
21. Remove the torque converter cover, then matchmark the flexplate to the torque converter; re-aligning the marks during installation will maintain the original balance.
22. Remove the torque converter-to-flywheel bolts and slide the converter back into the transmission.
23. Place a block of wood and a jackstand under the rear of the engine and support it.
24. Remove the transmission-to-engine mounting bolts. Note the location of any clips or brackets for installation purposes, then position them aside.
25. With the transmission still supported by the first floor jack, carefully slide the transmission back off the locating pins., Once there is sufficient clearance, install a torque converter holding tool such as No. J–21366 or equivalent.
26. Carefully lower the transmission assembly from the vehicle.

**To install:**

27. Make sure the torque converter is properly seated in the transmission assembly and install the converter holding tool.

28. Support the transmission assembly (and the transfer case if it was removed with the transmission earlier AWD vehicles) on a floor jack, then position it under the vehicle.
29. Carefully raise the transmission into position and remove the torque converter holding tool.
30. Slide the transmission straight onto the locating pins while aligning the flexplate and torque converter matchmarks which were made during removal.

➡ **Once in position, the torque converter must be flush onto the flexplate and must be able to rotate freely by hand.**

31. Install the transmission assembly-to-engine retaining bolts along with any brackets or clips which were positioned aside during removal. Tighten the transmission retaining bolts to 23 ft. lbs. (32 Nm).
32. Thread the torque converter-to-flexplate screws by hand until they are finger-tight to assure proper converter seating.
33. Tighten the torque converter bolts to 46 ft. lbs. (63 Nm) slowly and evenly.
34. Remove the jackstand which was positioned to support the engine.
35. Install the remaining components in the reverse order of removal.

➡ **When raising the transmission into place, be sure NOT to pinch or damage any cables, wires or other components.**

36. If drained earlier, IMMEDIATELY refill the transmission using fresh fluid.

## TRANSFER CASE

### Identification

▶ **See Figure 37**

### Transfer Case Assembly

#### REMOVAL & INSTALLATION

▶ **See Figure 38**

The manufacturer recommends that you drain the transmission fluid before attempting to remove the transfer case assembly from the vehicle. The major reason for this is that depending on the condition of the case's seals and how the case assembly is manipulated during removal, there is a chance that the fluid will spill causing quite a mess. Even if the seals are in good condition, with the driveshafts removed, fluid will be able leak past them readily. The vent hose is another possible escape route. The bottom line is that you will have to make up your own mind.

➡ **If you decide to drain the fluid from a transfer case that you are also planning on returning to service, it may be a good idea to drive the vehicle and thoroughly warm the fluid before draining. This will assure you the best fluid change possible.**

1. Disconnect the negative battery cable for safety.
2. Raise and support the vehicle safely using jackstands.

3. Drain the oil from the transfer case into a suitable container.
4. Matchmark and remove the driveshafts.
5. If necessary, disconnect the breather hose.
6. Disengage all electrical connectors.
7. Support the transfer case with a suitable jack.
8. Remove the transfer case support bracket and adapter-to-case bolts.
9. Remove the transfer case mount nuts and washers, then carefully lower the transfer case from the vehicle.
10. Remove and discard the old adapter gasket.
11. Install a new transfer case-to-adapter gasket with sealer.
12. Carefully raise the transfer case assembly into position and Install the transfer case-to-adapter bolts. Tighten the bolts to 38 ft. lbs. (52 Nm).
13. Remove the jack from the transfer case assembly.
14. Install the remaining components in the reverse order of removal. Tighten the following to specifications:
   - case mount-to-crossmember nuts: 26 ft. lbs. (35 Nm)
   - bracket-to-engine bolts: 94 ft. lbs. (128 Nm)

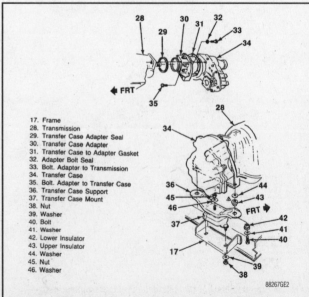

```
17. Frame
28. Transmission
29. Transfer Case Adapter Seal
30. Transfer Case Adapter
31. Transfer Case to Adapter Gasket
32. Adapter Bolt Seal
33. Bolt, Adapter to Transmission
34. Transfer Case
35. Bolt, Adapter to Transfer Case
36. Transfer Case Support
37. Transfer Case Mount
38. Nut
39. Washer
40. Bolt
41. Washer
42. Lower Insulator
43. Upper Insulator
44. Washer
45. Nut
46. Washer
```

88267GE2

**Fig. 38 Exploded view of the transfer case assembly mounting**

```
1. Front output flange nut
2. Front output flange
3. Front cover bolts
4. Input shaft
5. Input shaft oil seal
6. Identification tag
```

88267G32

**Fig. 37 The BW-4472 transfer case assembly**

• bracket-to-transfer case bolts: 66 ft. lbs. (90 Nm)

15. Check the transfer case lubricant as outlined in Section 1. Remember the vehicle MUST be level so you may have to raise and support the other end as well, unless there is sufficient clearance with the vehicle completely lowered.

If fluid does not spill out of the hole, add the proper type of fluid to the fill hole until lubricant reaches the top of the hole.

16. Remove the jackstands and carefully lower the vehicle.
17. Connect the negative battery cable and check operation.

## DRIVELINE

▶ **See Figures 39, 40 and 41**

The Astro and Safari van's rear driveshaft is of the conventional, open type. Located at either end of the driveshaft is a universal joint (U-joint), which allows the driveshaft to move up and down to match the motion of the front and rear axle. The main problem with the simple U-joint is that as the angle of the shaft increases past three to four degrees, the driven yoke rotates slower or faster than the drive yoke. This problem can be reduced by adding an additional U-joint or incorporating a constant velocity joint.

For most of the All Wheel Drive (AWD) vehicles covered by this manual, the front driveshaft uses two Constant Velocity (CV) joints to transfer the power from the transfer case to the front drive axle. The constant velocity joint is used because it allows the driveline angle to be adjusted according to the up and down movement of the vehicle without disturbing the power flow. For 1995–96 AWD vehicles the rear CV-joint (driveshaft-to-transfer case connection) was replaced with a double cardan joint, which serves a similar purpose, through the use of 2 spider and yoke assemblies.

As for the rear driveshaft, both ends are attached using U-joints, but the design is slightly different between the front and rear of the shaft itself. The rear driveshaft's front U-joint (injected nylon or internal snaprings) connects the driveshaft to a slip-jointed yoke. This yoke is internally splined and allows the driveshaft to move in and out on the transmission splines. On the production U-joints, nylon is injected through a small hole in the yoke during manufacture and flows along a circular groove between the U-joint and the yoke, creating a non-metallic snapring.

The rear driveshaft's rear U-joint is clamped to the rear axle pinion. The rear U-joint is secured in the yoke, using external snaprings (inside the yoke ears). It is attached to the rear axle pinion by use of bolted straps.

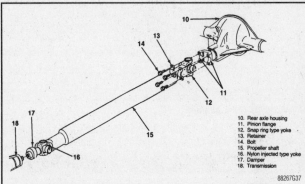

Fig. 41 Exploded view of the rear driveshaft mounting—1985–94 vehicles (1995–96 similar)

10. Rear axle housing
11. Pinion flange
12. Snap ring type yoke
13. Retainer
14. Bolt
15. Propeller shaft
16. Nylon injected type yoke
17. Damper
18. Transmission

Bad U-joints, requiring replacement, will produce a clunking sound when the vehicle is put into gear and when the transmission shifts from gear-to-gear. This is due to worn needle bearings or scored trunnion end possibly caused by improper lubrication during assembly. U-joints require no periodic maintenance and therefore have no lubrication fittings.

A vibration damper is employed as part of the slip joint. This damper cannot be serviced separately from the slip joint; if either component goes bad, the two must be replaced as a unit.

## Driveshaft and U-Joints

### ✱✱ WARNING

**If the vehicle is to be undercoated, the driveshaft and U-joints must be removed or completely covered to protect them from the undercoating. Failure to do this will most likely result in a loss of balance to the driveshaft leading to vibration and possible early U-joint failure.**

### REMOVAL & INSTALLATION

▶ **See Figures 39, 40 and 41**

➡**The driveshaft and its companion flanges are balanced at the factory. They must maintain this original alignment in order to maintain proper balance. Before removing any driveshaft ALWAYS matchmark the shaft to the flanges.**

**Front**

1. Disconnect the negative battery cable for safety.
2. Raise and support the front of the vehicle safely using jackstands.
3. Matchmark the positions of the driveshaft components relative to the driveshaft and flanges. The components must be reassembled in the same position to maintain proper balance.
4. Remove the transfer case flange and front axle flange-to-driveshaft bolts.
5. Pull the driveshaft forward and down to remove.

**To install:**

6. Inspect the plastic shrouds (CV-joints) for cracking or deterioration, replace if necessary.
7. Install the shaft, while aligning the reference marks made during removal. The importance of this step cannot be over-emphasized.
8. Install the flange-to-driveshaft bolts at both ends of the shaft.
9. Tighten the transfer case flange bolts to 92 ft. lbs. (125 Nm) for 1990–95 vehicles or to 55 ft. lbs. (75 Nm) for 1996 vehicles.

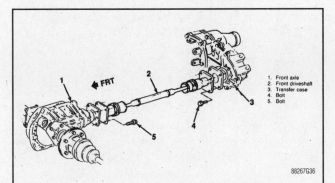

Fig. 39 Exploded view of the front driveshaft mounting—1990–94 AWD vehicles

1. Front axle
2. Front driveshaft
3. Transfer case
4. Bolt
5. Bolt

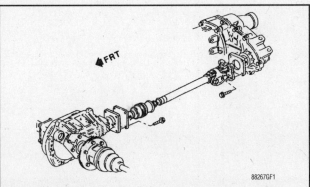

Fig. 40 Exploded view of the front driveshaft mounting—1995–96 AWD vehicles

10. Tighten the front axle flange bolts to 53 ft. lbs. (72 Nm) for 1990–95 vehicles or to 55 ft. lbs. (75 Nm) for 1996 vehicles.

11. Remove the jackstands and carefully lower the vehicle.

12. Connect the negative battery cable and check for proper operation.

### Rear

♦ **See Figures 42, 43, 44 and 45**

1. Disconnect the negative battery cable for safety.

2. Raise and support the rear of the vehicle safely using jackstands.

3. Using paint, matchmark the relationship of the driveshaft-to-pinion flange. The components must be reassembled in the same position to maintain proper balance.

4. Remove the universal joint-to-rear axle retainers.

➡ **If the bearing cups are loose, tape them together to prevent dropping or loosing the roller bearings.**

5. Remove the driveshaft by sliding it forward, to disengage it from the axle flange, and then rearward, passing it under the axle housing.

### ✳ WARNING

**When removing the driveshaft, DO NOT drop it or allow the universal joints to bend at extreme angles, for this may fracture the plastic injected joints.**

6. Inspect the driveshaft splines and surfaces for burrs, damage or wear.

**To install:**

7. Position the driveshaft into the transmission, then raise the rear and align it with the matchmarks on the axle flange. The importance of properly aligning the matchmarks made earlier cannot be over-emphasized.

8. Install the universal joint-to-pinion flange bolts and tighten to 27 ft. lbs. (37 Nm).

9. Remove the jackstands and carefully lower the vehicle.

10. Connect the negative battery cable and check for proper operation.

## U-JOINT OVERHAUL

♦ **See Figure 46**

Two types of universal joints are used: The front of the rear driveshaft uses an internal snapring (production is plastic injected), while the rear driveshaft's rear joint and the double cardan joint used on the rear of the 1995–96 front driveshafts use an external snapring.

➡ **KEEP IN MIND that if the U-joints have been replaced, it is possible that one type was substituted for another, since they are often available in the same sizes. To be sure with which type your driveshaft is equipped, visually inspect the trunnion bore on the outside of the flange. A snapring should be readily visible if you are using the external snapring type joint. If no snapring is visible, check for a retaining ring at the inner ear of the yoke to make sure there is no internal snapring.**

➡ **The following procedure requires the use of an Arbor Press, the GM Cross Press tool No. J–9522–3 or equivalent, the GM Spacer tool No. J–9522–5 or equivalent, and a 1⅛ in. socket.**

**Internal Snapring (Nylon Injected) Type**

♦ **See Figures 47 thru 52**

1. While supporting the driveshaft, in the horizontal position, place it so that the lower ear of the front universal joint's shaft yoke is supported on a 1⅛ in. (30mm) socket.

➡ **DO NOT clamp the driveshaft tube in a vise, for the tube may become damaged.**

2. Using the GM Cross Press tool No. J–9522–3 or equivalent, place it on the horizontal bearing cups and press the lower bearing cup out of the yoke ear; the pressing action will shear the plastic retaining ring from the lower bearing cup. If the bearing cup was not completely removed, insert the GM Spacer tool No. J–9522–5 or equivalent, onto the universal joint, then complete the pressing procedure to remove the joint.

**Fig. 42 ALWAYS matchmark the driveshaft yoke to the companion flange to assure proper installation**

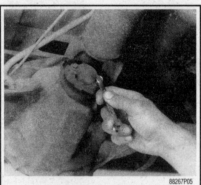

**Fig. 43 Remove the U-joint-to-companion flange retainers, then . . .**

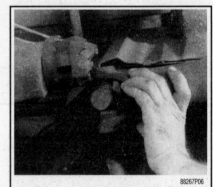

**Fig. 44 . . . push the driveshaft forward slightly and lower the rear from the flange**

**Fig. 45 Be sure to tape the U-joint caps to prevent bearing loss or damage should they come loose**

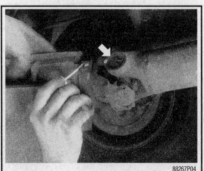

**Fig. 46 An external snapring type U-joint is easily identified by the visible snapring in the yoke bore**

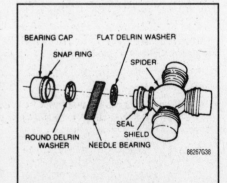

**Fig. 47 Exploded view of an internal snapring U-joint assembly**

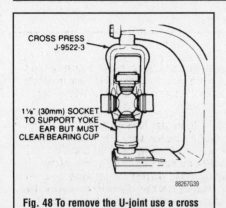

Fig. 48 To remove the U-joint use a cross press and a 1⅛ in. (30mm) socket

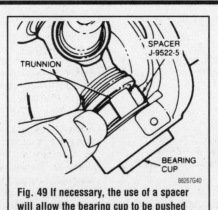

Fig. 49 If necessary, the use of a spacer will allow the bearing cup to be pushed further from the yoke

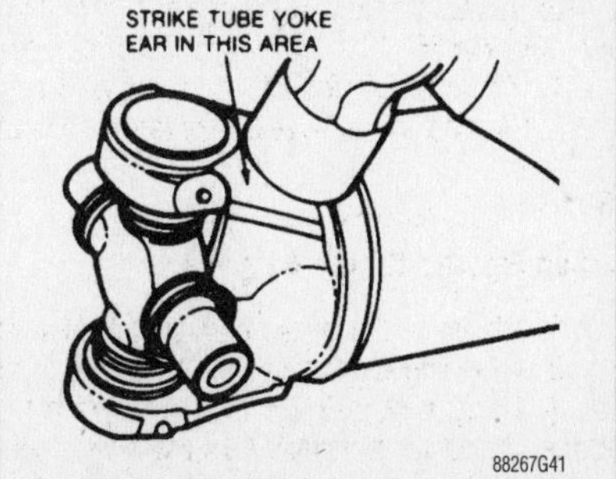

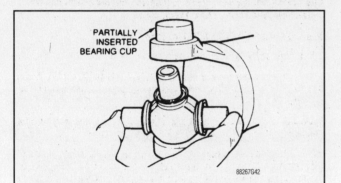

Fig. 50 A hammer may be used to relieve preload from a snapring (during removal) or to help seat the snapring (during installation)

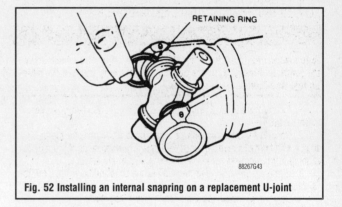

Fig. 51 Installing the U-joint bearing cross (spider) to the yoke

Fig. 52 Installing an internal snapring on a replacement U-joint

3. Rotate the driveshaft and shear the plastic retainer from the opposite side of the yoke.

4. Disengage the slip yoke from the driveshaft.

5. To remove the universal joint from the slip yoke, perform the procedures used in Steps 1–4.

➡When the front universal joint has been disassembled, it must usually be discarded and replaced with a service kit joint, as the production joint is not usually equipped with bearing retainer grooves on the bearing cups.

6. Clean (remove any remaining plastic particles), then inspect the slip yoke and driveshaft for damage, wear or burrs.

➡The universal joint service kit includes: A pregreased cross assembly, four bearing cups with seals, needle rollers, washers, four bearing retainers and grease. Make sure that the bearing cup seals are installed to hold the needle bearings in place for handling.

**To install:**

7. Position one bearing cup assembly part way into the yoke ear (turn the ear to the bottom), insert the bearing cross (into the yoke) so that the trunnion seats freely into the bearing cup. Turn the yoke 180° and install the other bearing cup assembly.

➡When installing the bearing cup assemblies, make sure the trunnions are started straight and true into the bearing cups.

8. Using the arbor press, press the bearing cups onto the cross trunnion, until they seat.

➡While installing the bearing cups, twist the cross trunnion to work it into the bearings. If there seems to be a hangup, stop the pressing and recheck the needle roller alignment.

9. Once the bearing cup retainer grooves have cleared the inside of the yoke, stop the pressing and install the snaprings.

10. If the other bearing cup retainer groove has not cleared the inside of the yoke, use a hammer to aid in the seating procedure.

11. To install the yoke/universal assembly to the driveshaft, perform the Steps 7–10 of this procedure.

**External Snapring Type**

➧ See Figures 48, 49, 50, 51, 53 and 54

1. Remove the snaprings from inside the yoke ears. This is done by carefully pinching the ends together using a pair of pliers (snapring or needlenose pliers work best).

➡If the ring does not readily snap from the yoke groove, tap the end of the bearing cup lightly to relieve the preload from the snapring.

2. While supporting the driveshaft, in the horizontal position, position it so that the lower ear of the front universal joint's shaft yoke is supported on a 1⅛ in. (30mm) socket.

➡DO NOT clamp the driveshaft tube in a vise, for the tube may become damaged.

3. Using the GM Cross Press tool No. J–9522–3 or equivalent, place it on the horizontal bearing cups and press the lower bearing cup out of the yoke ear. If the bearing cup was not completely removed, insert the GM Spacer tool No. J–9522–5 or equivalent, onto the universal joint, then complete the pressing procedure.

4. Rotate the driveshaft (or double cardan joint on late-model front shafts) and press the bearing cup from the opposite side of the yoke.

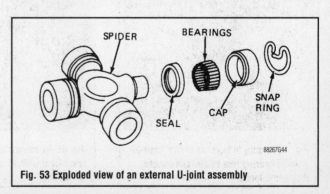

Fig. 53 Exploded view of an external U-joint assembly

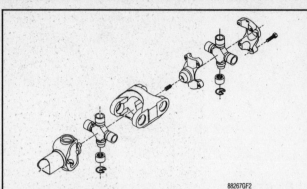

**Fig. 54 Exploded view of the double cardan U-joint—1995-96 front driveshaft (AWD vehicles)**

5. Disengage the slip yoke from the driveshaft (or the cardan joint from the front driveshaft, as applicable).

6. To remove the universal joint from the slip yoke (or to further disassemble the double cardan joint), perform Steps 1–4 which were used to remove the joint from the driveshaft.

## REAR DRIVE AXLE

♦ See Figure 55

### Axle Shaft, Bearing and Seal

REMOVAL & INSTALLATION

♦ See Figures 56 thru 69

A new pinion shaft lock bolt should be installed whenever either of the axle shafts are removed. You should probably purchase this and 2 new seals if you are planning on removing or replacing any components covered by this procedure.

➡ Axle shaft seal removal and installation uses the following special tools: the GM Axle Shaft Seal Installer tool No. J–33782 or equivalent and the Axle Shaft Bearing Installer tool No. J–34974 or equivalent.

The axle shaft and seal may be removed and replaced without disturbing the bearing or seal, BUT is highly recommended that you replace the seals as-long-as you've gone through the trouble to remove the axle shaft. Seal replacement is simple and it is cheap insurance against an oil leak which could ruin your brake shoes.

➡ If the bearing requires replacement, you will also need the following tools: GM Slide Hammer tool No. J–2619 or equivalent, the GM Adapter tool No. J–2619–4 or equivalent, the GM Axle Bearing Puller tool No. J–22813–01 or equivalent.

1. Raise and support the rear of the vehicle safely using jackstands.
2. Remove the rear wheel assemblies, then remove the brake drums.

7. Clean and inspect the yoke and the driveshaft for damage, wear or burrs.
   **To install:**
8. Position one bearing cup assembly part way into the yoke ear (turn the ear to the bottom), insert the bearing cross (into the yoke) so that the trunnion seats freely into the bearing cup. Turn the yoke 180° and install the other bearing cup assembly.

➡ When installing the bearing cup assemblies, make sure the trunnions are started straight and true into the bearing cups.

9. Using the arbor press, press the bearing cups onto the cross trunnion, until they seat.

➡ While installing the bearing cups, twist the cross trunnion to work it into the bearings. If there seems to be a hangup, stop the pressing and recheck the needle roller alignment.

10. Once the bearing cup clears the retainer grooves (inside of the yoke ear), stop the pressing and install the snaprings.
11. If the other bearing cup has not cleared the retainer groove (inside the yoke ear), use a hammer and a brass drift punch to aid in the seating procedure.
12. To install the yoke (joint)/universal assembly to the driveshaft, perform the Steps 8–11 of this procedure.

## ❊❊ CAUTION

Brake shoes may contain asbestos, which has been determined to be a cancer causing agent. Never clean the brake surfaces with compressed air! Avoid inhaling any dust from any brake surface! When cleaning brake surfaces, use a commercially available brake cleaning fluid.

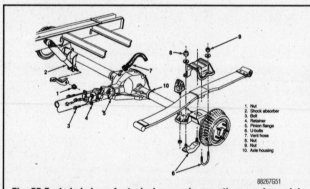

**Fig. 55 Exploded view of a typical rear axle mounting—early-model vehicles shown**

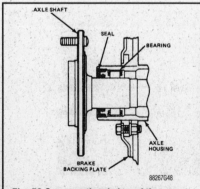

**Fig. 56 Cross-sectional view of the rear axle, bearing and seal assembly**

**Fig. 57 Remove the tire and wheel assembly, along with the brake drum for access to the shaft**

**Fig. 58 Loosen the pinion shaft lock bolt using a ratchet or a box-end wrench (shown) . . .**

Fig. 59 . . . then remove and discard the old lock bolt

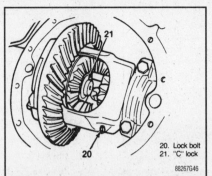

Fig. 60 Pinion shaft lock bolt and rear axle C-lock locations (note a separate C-lock is used for each axle shaft)

20. Lock bolt
21. "C" lock

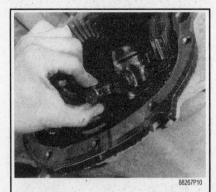

Fig. 61 Grasp the end of the pinion shaft and pull

Fig. 62 Once the pinion shaft is fully removed . . .

Fig. 63 . . . the axle shaft can be pushed inward and the C-lock can be withdrawn

Fig. 64 Pull the shaft STRAIGHT back from the axle tube (be careful not to damage any components)

Fig. 65 On late-model vehicles with ABS carefully clean the ABS reluctor ring with a soft-bristled brush

Fig. 66 Keep the seal puller away from the ABS speed sensor, as pictured it could damage the sensor

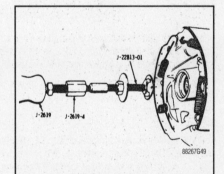

Fig. 67 If removal is necessary use a slide hammer and bearing puller assembly to remove the rear axle wheel bearings

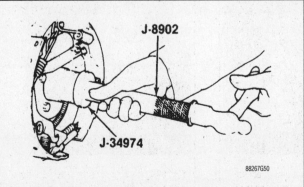

Fig. 68 The rear axle wheel bearings are installed using a driver

Fig. 69 During seal installation, KEEP THE DRIVER away from the speed sensor

Using a wire brush, clean the dirt/rust from around the rear axle cover.

4. Place a catch pan under the differential, then remove the drain plug (if equipped) or rear axle cover and drain the fluid (discard the old fluid).

5. At the differential, remove the rear pinion shaft lock bolt and the pinion shaft.

6. Push the axle shaft inward and remove the C-lock from the button end of the axle shaft.

7. Remove the axle shaft from the axle housing. Be careful not to damage the oil seal.

### ✳✳ WARNING

**On late-model vehicles equipped with an Anti-Lock Brake System (ABS) be careful not to damage the reluctor ring on the axle shaft or the speed sensor bolted to the backing plate, immediately adjacent to the shaft.**

8. Using a putty knife, clean the gasket mounting surfaces.

➡ It is recommended, when the axle shaft is removed, to replace the oil seal.

9. To replace the oil seal use a medium prybar or, better yet, an inexpensive seal removal tool, to pry the oil seal from the end of the rear axle housing. DO NOT damage the housing oil seal surface. And again, on late-model ABS equipped vehicles, STAY CLEAR OF THE SPEED SENSOR.

10. If replacing the wheel bearing, perform the following procedures:

a. Using the GM Slide Hammer tool No. J–2619 or equivalent, the GM Adapter tool No. J–2619–4 or equivalent and the GM Axle Bearing Puller tool No. J–22813–01 or equivalent, install the tool assembly so that the tangs engage the outer race of the bearing.

b. Using the action of the slide hammer, pull the wheel bearing from the axle housing.

**To install:**

11. If the wheel bearing was removed:

a. Using solvent, thoroughly clean the wheel bearing, then blow dry with compressed air. Inspect the wheel bearing for excessive wear or damage, then replace it (if necessary).

b. With a new or the reused bearing, thoroughly coat the bearing with gear lubricant.

c. Using the Axle Shaft Bearing Installer tool No. J–34974 or equivalent, drive the bearing into the axle housing until it bottoms against the seat. Make sure the bearing installer does not contact and damage the speed sensor on ABS equipped vehicles.

12. If the axle shaft seal was removed:

a. Clean and inspect the axle tube housing.

b. Using the GM Axle Shaft Seal Installer tool No. J–33782 or an equivalent driver, seat the new seal into the housing until it is flush with the axle tube. Make sure the seal installer does not contact and damage the speed sensor on ABS equipped vehicles.

c. Using gear oil, lubricate the new seal lips.

13. Slide the axle shaft into the rear axle housing and engage the splines of the axle shaft with the splines of the rear axle side gear, then install the C-lock retainer on the axle shaft button end.

### ✳✳ WARNING

**BE CAREFUL not to damage the wheel bearing seal with the splines on the axle shaft. And, do we even have to mention the SPEED SENSOR again on ABS equipped vehicles!**

14. After the C-lock is installed, pull the axle shaft outward to seat the C-lock retainer in the counterbore of the side gears.

15. Install the pinion shaft through the case and the pinions, then install a NEW pinion shaft lock bolt. Torque the new lock bolt to 25 ft. lbs. (34 Nm) for 1985–93 vehicles or to 27 ft. lbs. (36 Nm) for 1994–96 vehicles.

16. Use a new rear axle cover gasket and install the housing cover.

17. Install the brake drums, followed by the tire and wheel assemblies.

18. Properly refill the housing. For details, please refer to the information in Section 1 of this manual. REMEMBER that the vehicle must be completely level, meaning that if the rear is still raised and supported, the front should also be raised.

19. Remove the jackstands and carefully lower the vehicle.

### Pinion Flange Seal

## REMOVAL & INSTALLATION

➡ See Figures 70, 71 and 72

Because the pinion shaft flange is installed and tightened to achieve a set-preload, the current preload must be measured and matched during installation. The BEST way to achieve this is with a beam type inch lbs. torque wrench with a needle pointer.

➡ In order to perform this procedure you will need a companion flange holding tool and a seal installer.

1. Raise and support the rear of the vehicle safely using jackstands. If possible, lift and support the front of the vehicle as well to keep fluid from draining through the front of the axle housing (when the pinion flange and seal are removed). If this cannot be done, you should remove the rear axle cover in order to drain the fluid.

2. Remove the rear wheels and drums to remove all load from the pinion shaft, except the required pre-load

3. Matchmark and remove the driveshaft from the vehicle. If desired, the driveshaft can be left attached to the transmission (or transfer case, as applicable), but if so, it must be wired up to the body to prevent damage to the slip yoke U-joints. Also, it must be wired out of the way since you'll be working at the pinion flange.

4. Using an inch lbs. torque wrench, measure the force necessary to turn the pinion. This measurement equals the combined pinion bearing, seal, carrier bearing, axle bearing and seal pre-load. IT MUST BE MATCHED UPON INSTALLATION SO MEASURE CAREFULLY.

5. Make accurate matchmarks among the pinion stem, pinion flange and pinion flange nut. Also, count the number of exposed threads on the pinion stem for reference. Again, this will be used to help assure that the proper pre-load is achieved upon installation.

6. Secure the pinion flange using a companion flange holding tool such as J 8614-01, then loosen the flange nut.

7. Remove the pinion flange nut and washer.

➡ If the front of the vehicle is not supported significantly higher than the rear and you have not drained the rear axle, have a drain pan handy to catch any leaking fluid.

8. Remove the pinion flange. The holding tool can provide a useful hand-hold.

9. Remove the old seal using a seal removal tool, but BE CAREFUL not to score or damage the sealing surface in the rear axle housing bore.

10. Check the sealing surface of the pinion flange for tool marks, nicks or damage such as a groove worn by the seal. Replace the flange if necessary. Check the axle housing bore for burrs that might cause leaks around the outside of a new seal.

**To install:**

11. Install the new seal using J 23911, or an equivalent seal driver/installation tool.

12. Coat the outside of the pinion flange and the inside of the sealing lip (on the new seal) with GM seal lubricant No. 1050169, or equivalent.

13. CAREFULLY install the pinion flange to the shaft.

### ✳✳ WARNING

**DO NOT attempt to hammer the flange onto the shaft stem. Damage could occur and the pre-load measurements could be rendered useless.**

14. Install the washer and retaining nut, then tighten the nut as-close-as possible to the reference mark (with the same number of exposed shaft threads as noted during removal) WITHOUT going past the mark. Turn the nut a little at a time, turning the pinion flange several times after each tightening to set the rollers.

➡ If the companion flange holder is used while tightening the nut, make sure it is removed before each pre-load measurement.

15. Using an inch lbs. torque wrench, measure the pre-load (amount of effort necessary to turn the pinion) achieved by this setting. Continue to tighten the nut a little at a time, stopping to measure the pre-load again, until the pre-load measured during removal is matched.

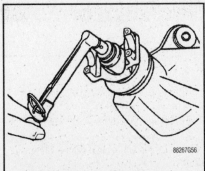

Fig. 70 Measure the pinion flange preload (force necessary to turn the flange) before loosening the retaining nut

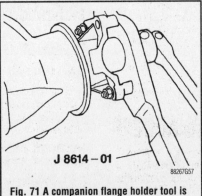

Fig. 71 A companion flange holder tool is necessary to loosen or tighten the nut

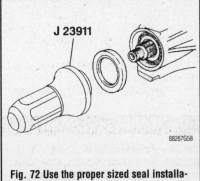

Fig. 72 Use the proper sized seal installation tool or driver to install the replacement pinion seal

➡If the original pre-load measurement was below 3 inch lbs. (0.34 Nm), then set the pre-load to 3–5 inch lbs. (0.34–0.56 Nm) during installation.

## FRONT DRIVE AXLE (ALL WHEEL DRIVE)

### Halfshaft

REMOVAL & INSTALLATION

#### ❊❊ CAUTION

Do not allow the halfshaft to fully extend. The joint may become separated from the axle shaft, resulting in halfshaft failure and vehicle damage.

**1990–93 Vehicles**

◆ See Figure 73

➡In order to loosen the halfshaft retaining nut, you will have to be able to hold the shaft from turning. One acceptable method is to insert a drift into the opening at the top of the brake caliper and through the vanes of the rotor. If you do not have one available, an assistant can apply the brakes while you loosen the nut. BUT, the easiest way, would be to remove the cotter pin and nut locking retainer, then loosen the nut, just slightly, while the vehicle is still on the ground.

1. Disconnect the negative battery cable for safety.
2. Unlock the steering column so the linkage is free to move.
3. Raise the front of the vehicle and support safely using jackstands.
4. Remove the front tire and wheel assemblies.
5. If not done earlier, remove the cotter pin and nut locking retainer.
6. Remove the axle nut and washer.

➡IMPORTANT: Support the lower control arm with a jackstands to release spring tension.

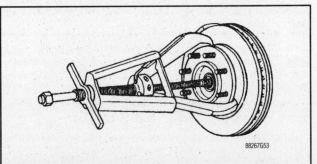

Fig. 73 Separating the halfshaft from the hub—1990–93 vehicles

16. Align and install the driveshaft.
17. Install the brake drums, followed by the tire and wheel assemblies.
18. Remove the jackstands and carefully lower the vehicle.

7. Remove the lower shock absorber nut and bolt.
8. Matchmark the halfshaft flange to the output shaft flange, then remove the halfshaft flange-to-output shaft bolts. Again, you will have to keep the assembly from turning, so insert a drift through the opening in the top of the brake caliper into the vanes of the brake rotor.
9. Use a Posilock® Puller model 110 or equivalent to push the halfshaft through the hub, then remove the halfshaft from the vehicle.
**To install:**
10. Install the halfshaft to the hub, then install the axle washer and nut.
11. Insert a drift through the opening in the top of the brake caliper into the vanes of the brake rotor to keep the halfshaft from turning, then tighten the shaft nut to 160–200 ft. lbs. (220–270 Nm).
12. Install the nut locking retainer and a new cotter pin.
13. Align and install the halfshaft to the output shaft flange, then install the retaining bolts and tighten to 60 ft. lbs. (80 Nm).
14. Install the lower shock bolt and nuts, then tighten to 18 ft. lbs. (25 Nm).
15. Check and refill the front drive axle if any fluid was lost. Remember that the vehicle MUST be level. Refer to Section 1 of this manual for more details.
16. Install the tire and wheel assemblies, then remove the jackstands and carefully lower the vehicle.

#### ❊❊ WARNING

Make sure the ignition switch is in the OFF position before connecting the negative battery cable otherwise the engine control computer could be INSTANTLY destroyed when voltage is applied.

17. Connect the negative battery cable and check for proper operation.

**1994–96 Vehicles**

◆ See Figures 74 thru 79

➡In order to loosen the halfshaft retaining nut, you will have to be able to hold the shaft from turning. One acceptable method is to insert a drift into the opening at the top of the brake caliper and through the vanes of the rotor. If you do not have one available, an assistant can apply the brakes while you loosen the nut. BUT, the easiest way, would be to remove the cotter pin and nut lock, then loosen the nut, just slightly, while the vehicle is still on the ground.

1. Disconnect the negative battery cable for safety.
2. Unlock the steering column so the linkage is free to move.
3. Raise the front of the vehicle and support safely using jackstands.
4. If equipped, remove the front axle skid plate.
5. Remove the front tire and wheel assemblies.
6. If not done earlier, remove the cotter pin and nut locking retainer.

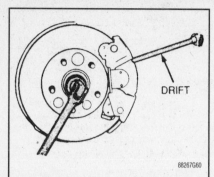

Fig. 74 A drift can be inserted through the top of the caliper and the rotor vanes to keep the shaft from turning

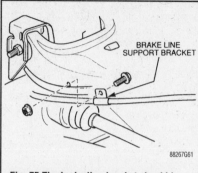

Fig. 75 The brake line bracket should be removed from the upper control arm to provide additional knuckle travel

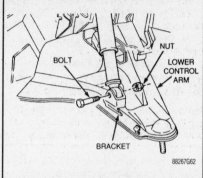

Fig. 76 Disconnect the lower shock fasteners and position the shock out of the way

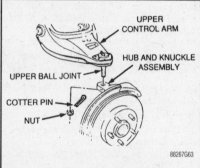

Fig. 77 Disconnect the upper ball joint from the knuckle, so it be repositioned for clearance

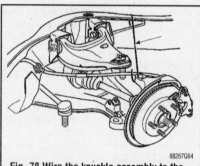

Fig. 78 Wire the knuckle assembly to the upper control arm in order to provide clearance while preventing brake line damage

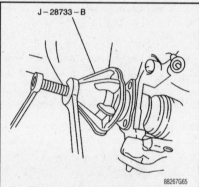

Fig. 79 Use a suitable separator tool to drive the axle shaft from the hub

7. Remove the axle nut and washer. To keep the assembly from turning, insert a drift through the opening in the top of the brake caliper into the vanes of the brake rotor.

8. Matchmark the halfshaft flange to the output shaft flange, then loosen (BUT do not remove at this time) the halfshaft flange-to-output shaft bolts. Again, you will have to keep the assembly from turning.

9. Disconnect the brake hose support bracket from the upper control arm to allow for extra knuckle travel.

10. Disconnect the outer tie rod end from the knuckle. Push the linkage toward the opposite side of the vehicle, then support the outer tie rod up and out of the way to provide necessary clearance.

### ❋❋ WARNING

**DO NOT use a wedge type tool to separate the joint from the knuckle or damage may occur.**

11. Position a floor jack or jackstand to support the lower control arm.

### ❋❋ CAUTION

**The support MUST remain under the control arm for the duration of the procedure to hold the spring in position otherwise serious personal injury could result.**

12. Remove the lower shock absorber nut and bolt. Compress the shock absorber and wire up, out of the way.

13. Remove the cotter pin and stud nut, then separate the upper ball joint from the steering knuckle.

14. Tip the knuckle outward and toward the rear of the vehicle, then wire the knuckle to the upper control arm to prevent stretching and damaging the brake hose.

15. Cover the shock mounting bracket and the ball stud on the lower control arm with a rag to prevent possible damage to the drive axle seal during removal or installation.

16. Drive the splined shaft from the knuckle using J-28733-B or an equivalent shaft removal tool.

17. Remove the halfshaft flange-to-output shaft bolts which were loosened earlier, then carefully lower and remove the halfshaft from the vehicle.

**To install:**

18. Wipe the wheel bearing seal area on the knuckle clean, then check the seal for cuts or tears. If the seal is cut or torn, check the wheel bearings for damage and replace the seal.

19. Lubricate the wheel bearing seal lip.

➡**Make sure the shock bracket and the control arm ball stud are both still covered with rags to help prevent possible damage to the CV-joint boot.**

20. Carefully push the halfshaft into the hub, then install the axle washer and nut, but do not tighten yet.

21. Align the matchmarks made earlier, then loosely install the halfshaft flange to the output shaft flange using the retaining bolts.

22. Install the upper ball joint to the steering knuckle, then tighten the retaining nut and install a new cotter pin. Now is a good time to lube the upper ball joint.

23. Install the shock absorber and secure using the nut and bolt.

24. Install the outer tie rod to the steering knuckle, tighten the retaining nut and install a new cotter pin.

25. Reposition and secure the brake hose bracket to the upper control arm.

26. If not done already, insert a drift through the opening in the top of the brake caliper into the vanes of the brake rotor to keep the halfshaft from turning, then tighten the shaft nut to 160–200 ft. lbs. (220–270 Nm) for 1994–95 vehicles or to 147 ft. lbs. (200 Nm) for 1996 vehicles.

27. Align and install the nut locking retainer, then install a new cotter pin. DO NOT back off the nut or tighten it more than specified in order to align the retainer and install the cotter pin. The retainer should allow sufficient adjustment in order to install a pin.

➡**Be sure to bend the cotter pin so the retainer is held snugly in place to prevent rattling.**

28. Tighten the halfshaft-to-output shaft flange bolts to 60 ft. lbs. (80 Nm).

29. Check and refill the front drive axle if any fluid was lost. Remember that the vehicle MUST be level. Refer to Section 1 of this manual for more details.

30. Install the tire and wheel assemblies, then remove the jackstands and carefully lower the vehicle.

31. If equipped, install the front axle skid plate.

### ✳✳ WARNING

**Make sure the ignition switch is in the OFF position before connecting the negative battery cable otherwise the engine control computer could be INSTANTLY destroyed when voltage is applied.**

32. Connect the negative battery cable and check for proper operation.

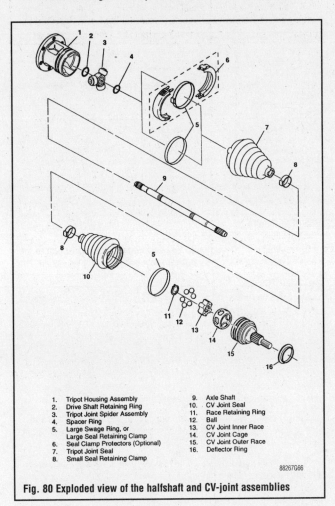

| | | | |
|---|---|---|---|
| 1. | Tripot Housing Assembly | 9. | Axle Shaft |
| 2. | Drive Shaft Retaining Ring | 10. | CV Joint Seal |
| 3. | Tripot Joint Spider Assembly | 11. | Race Retaining Ring |
| 4. | Spacer Ring | 12. | Ball |
| 5. | Large Swage Ring, or | 13. | CV Joint Inner Race |
| | Large Seal Retaining Clamp | 14. | CV Joint Cage |
| 6. | Seal Clamp Protectors (Optional) | 15. | CV Joint Outer Race |
| 7. | Tripot Joint Seal | 16. | Deflector Ring |
| 8. | Small Seal Retaining Clamp | | |

88267G66

**Fig. 80 Exploded view of the halfshaft and CV-joint assemblies**

OVERHAUL

▶ **See Figure 80**

**Outer CV-Joint**

▶ **See Figures 81, 82, 83 and 84**

➡Because of the difficulty and special tools involved, try to get an overhaul kit with replacement clamps as opposed to a swage ring. If you must install a swage ring to retain the boot, follow the kit instructions CLOSELY and borrow or rent the necessary tools. If this is not possible, take the halfshaft to a reputable service facility for overhaul or boot replacement.

1. Remove the drive axle (halfshaft) assembly from the vehicle.

2. Place the axle in a vise using a protective covering on the vise jaws to prevent axle damage.

### ✳✳ CAUTION

**Because the retaining clamps are under tension, use care when cutting and removing them. Wear gloves and safety goggles to protect you should the clamp spring loose upon releasing the tension.**

3. Cut and remove the CV-boot retaining clamps. If the boot is not being replaced, use care not to cut or damage the boot.

➡Some late-model vehicles are equipped with a swage ring. In order to remove the ring, use a hand grinder to cut through the ring. Take care not to damage the outer race while cutting the swage ring free.

4. Once the clamp (or swage ring) is removed, reposition the boot and wipe the grease away in order to locate the snapring.

5. Release the snapring using a suitable pair of snapring pliers, such as J-8059 or equivalent.

6. Remove the CV-joint assembly from the axle shaft.

➡If ONLY THE BOOT is being replaced, stop disassembly here. Only proceed further if component wear or damage is suspected and you wish to perform a complete overhaul of the joint.

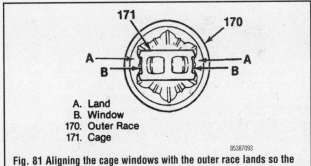

A. Land
B. Window
170. Outer Race
171. Cage

85387093

**Fig. 81 Aligning the cage windows with the outer race lands so the cage (and inner race) may be removed**

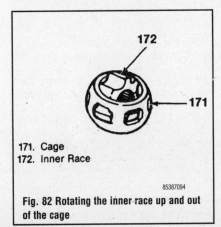

171. Cage
172. Inner Race

85387094

**Fig. 82 Rotating the inner race up and out of the cage**

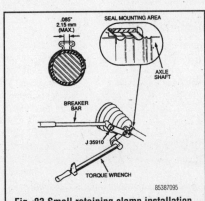

85387095

**Fig. 83 Small retaining clamp installation and ear dimension**

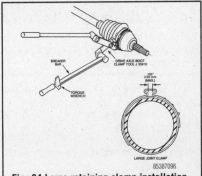

85387096

**Fig. 84 Large retaining clamp installation and ear dimension—outer joint shown (inner joint uses same dimension)**

7. Using a brass drift and hammer, tap the cage until it tilts sufficiently to remove the first ball, remove the remaining balls in the same manner.

8. Pivot the cage so the inner race is 90 degrees to the centerline of the outer race, then align the cage windows with the outer race lands and lift the cage (along with the inner race) from the outer race. Please refer to the illustration for clarification.

9. Rotate the inner race up and out of the cage.

10. Thoroughly clean all parts in an approved solvent, then check for wear or damage and replace, as necessary.

**To install:**

11. Apply a suitable high-temperature grease to the ball grooves of the inner and outer races.

12. Install the inner race to the cage by inserting and rotating.

13. Align the cage windows with the outer race lands, then install the cage (along with the inner race) to the outer race. Make sure the retaining ring side of the inner race faces outward.

14. Use the brass drift to tap the cage to a tilted position, then install the balls.

15. Pack the joint and boot using a suitable high-temperature grease.

16. Position the small boot clamp onto the outboard boot, then install the boot the axle shaft. Tighten the small clamp securely using a suitable clamp tool such as J-35910 or equivalent. If the tool has a torque wrench fitting, secure the clamp using 100 ft. lbs. (136 Nm) of torque.

17. Check the clamp ear gap dimension (distance that the inner bends of the crimp should be from each other), it should be a maximum of 0.085 in. (2.15mm). Please refer to the illustration for clarification.

18. Install the joint assembly to the shaft and secure using the snapring.

Pack the boot and outer joint assembly with the premeasured amount of the grease supplied with the service kit, then snap the boot onto the outer joint assembly and manipulate it to remove excess air.

19. Install the large retaining clamp using the clamp tool and torque wrench. Secure the clamp using 130 ft. lbs. (176 Nm) of torque. Again, check the clamp ear dimension, it should be a maximum of 0.102 in. (2.60mm).

20. Install the drive axle to the vehicle.

## Inner CV-Joint

**♦ See Figures 83, 84, 85 thru 91**

1. Remove the drive axle from the vehicle.

2. Place the axle in a vise using a protective covering on the vise jaws to prevent axle damage.

3. If equipped, remove the seal clamp protectors from the joint assembly.

### ❖ CAUTION

**Because the retaining clamps are under tension, use care when cutting and removing them. Wear gloves and safety goggles to protect you should the clamp spring loose upon releasing the tension.**

4. Cut and remove the CV-boot retaining clamps. If the boot is not being replaced, use care not to cut or damage the boot.

➡ **Some late-model vehicles are equipped with a swage ring. In order to remove the ring, use a hand grinder to cut through the ring. Take care not to damage the outer race while cutting the swage ring free.**

5. Remove the axle shaft with spider assembly from the companion flange housing.

➡ **Handle the spider assembly with care. The tripot balls and needle rollers may separate from the spider trunnions.**

6. Grasp the space ring using J-8059, or an equivalent pair of snapring pliers, then slide the ring back on the axle shaft in order to provide clearance to move the spider assembly.

7. Move the spider assembly back on the shaft in order to expose the retaining snapring.

8. Remove the snapring using a suitable pair of snapring pliers, such as J-8059 or equivalent.

9. Remove the spider assembly.

10. Thoroughly clean all grease from the housing. Check for rust at the boot mounting grooves. If found, remove with a wire brush.

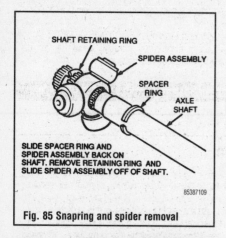

Fig. 85 Snapring and spider removal

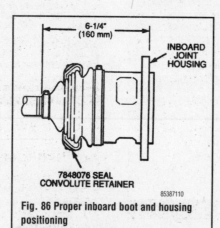

Fig. 86 Proper inboard boot and housing positioning

Fig. 87 Remove the CV-joint housing and check for wear or damage

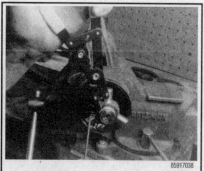

Fig. 88 With the spacer and spider pushed back, grasp the snapring using a pair of snapring pliers

Fig. 89 Remove the snapring from the shaft so the spider assembly may be removed

Fig. 90 With the snapring removed, the spider is free to be pulled from the shaft

**Fig. 91 If necessary, remove the spacer ring from the shaft**

**To install:**

11. Install the small boot clamp and inboard boot to the axle shaft.

12. If the spacer ring was removed, make sure it is positioned up on the shaft leaving room for spider and snapring installation.

13. Install the spider assembly to the axle shaft, making sure the snapring counterbore faces the housing end of the axle.

14. Install the snapring to the shaft, then properly position the spider and spacer ring.

15. Position the small boot clamp and tighten securely using a suitable clamp tool such as J-35910 or equivalent. If the tool has a torque wrench fitting, secure the clamp using 100 ft. lbs. (136 Nm) of torque.

16. Check the clamp ear gap dimension (distance that the inner bends of the crimp should be from each other), it should be a maximum of 0.085 in. (2.15mm). Please refer to the illustration for clarification.

17. Repack the housing using about half of the premeasured grease supplied with the service kit, then place the remainder of the grease in the boot. Coat the inside of the boot sealing lips with grease.

18. Make sure the joint/boot are assembled to the proper dimension of 6¼ in. (160mm) between the clamps. Please refer to the illustration for clarification.

19. Install the large retaining clamp using the clamp tool and torque wrench. Secure the clamp using 130 ft. lbs. (176 Nm) of torque. Again, check the clamp ear dimension, it should be a maximum of 0.102 in. (2.60mm).

20. If used, install the clamp protectors over the large eared clamp.

21. Install the drive axle to the vehicle.

## Shaft and Tube Assembly

### REMOVAL & INSTALLATION

#### 1990–92 Vehicles

1. Disconnect the negative battery cable for safety.

2. Unlock the steering column, then raise and support the vehicle safely using jackstands.

3. Remove the right front wheel.

4. Remove the halfshaft nut and washer.

➡️**IMPORTANT: Support the lower control arm with a jackstand to unload the spring pressure.**

5. Remove the lower shock absorber bolt and nut.

6. Remove the output shaft bolts. Insert a drift through the opening in the top of the brake caliper into the vanes of the brake rotor.

7. Keep the shaft from turning and use a Posilock Puller Model 110 or equivalent to push the halfshaft through the hub.

8. Remove the right halfshaft.

9. Remove the tube support bracket nuts, carrier bolts, shaft and tube assembly.

**To install:**

10. Clean the sealing surfaces of the tube and carrier assembly with solvent.

11. Apply a bead of RTV sealer to the carrier sealing surface.

12. Install the shaft, tube and bolts. Torque the bolts to 36 ft. lbs. (48 Nm).

13. Install the support bracket nuts and torque to 55 ft. lbs. (75 Nm).

14. Install the halfshaft, output shaft-to-halfshaft bolts and torque to 60 ft. lbs. (80 Nm).

15. Install the lower shock bolt and nut.

16. Check the differential lubricant and add if necessary. Remember that the vehicle must be level or you will get an incorrect reading.

17. Install the front tire.

18. Remove the jackstands and carefully lower the vehicle.

### ✳✳ WARNING

**Make sure the ignition switch is in the OFF position before connecting the negative battery cable otherwise the engine control computer could be INSTANTLY destroyed when voltage is applied.**

#### 1993–96 Vehicles

1. Remove the right drive axle (halfshaft) from the vehicle. For details, please refer to the procedure located earlier in this section.

2. Remove the support bracket nuts and washers.

3. Remove the tube-to-carrier bolts.

4. Position a drain pan to catch any leaking fluid, then remove the tube and shaft assembly from the vehicle.

**To install:**

5. Thoroughly clean the sealing surfaces of the tube and carrier using a chlorinated solvent.

6. Apply a bead of sealant such as GM no. 12345739 or equivalent to the carrier sealing surface.

7. Install the shaft and tube assembly, then tighten the retaining bolts to 36 ft. lbs. (48 Nm).

8. Install the support bracket nuts and washers, then tighten to 54 ft. lbs. (73 Nm).

9. Install the right drive axle to the vehicle.

10. Check the differential lubricant and add if necessary. Remember that the vehicle must be level or you will get an incorrect reading.

## Output Shaft Seal and Bearing

### REMOVAL & INSTALLATION

▶ **See Figures 92 and 93**

Tools needed: slide hammer J–29307, countershaft roller bearing remover J–29369-2, axle tube bearing installer J–33844 and output shaft seal installer J–33893.

1. Remove the shaft and tube assembly as outlined in this section.

2. Remove the shaft with deflector and retaining ring by striking the inside of the shaft flange with a brass hammer to dislodge it from the tube. Pull the shaft out of the seal housing.

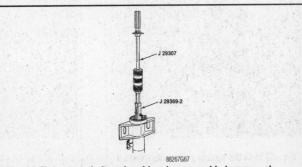

**Fig. 92 The output shaft seal and bearing assembly is removed using a slide hammer and bearing puller**

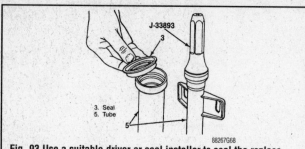

**Fig. 93 Use a suitable driver or seal installer to seal the replacement seal**

3. Remove the shaft seal and bearing by using the slide hammer and bearing puller.

**To install:**

4. Lubricate the seal lips, bearings and friction surfaces with axle lubricant before assembly.

5. Install the bearing. On some applications, the bearing installer will be necessary.

6. Install the seal using a suitable driver or seal installer tool.

7. Insert the shaft to the tube assembly, taking GREAT CARE not to damage the seal with the shaft splines.

8. Install the shaft and tube assembly as outlined in this section.

## Pinion Oil Seal

### REMOVAL & INSTALLATION

▶ See Figures 94, 95 and 96

1. Disconnect the negative battery cable for safety.
2. Raise and support the vehicle safely using jackstands.
3. Matchmark and remove the front driveshaft from the vehicle.
4. Mark the nut, washer and flange so during installation the same amount of torque can be provided for the correct amount of bearing pre-load.
5. Using an inch lbs. torque wrench (beam type with a needle gauge is usually easiest for this), measure the current pinion pre-load (the amount of force necessary to rotate the pinion).
6. Remove the pinion flange nut and washer using a companion flange holder J–8614–01 or equivalent to keep the assembly from spinning.
7. Place a container under the flange to catch any fluid which may leak, then remove the flange.
8. Remove the oil seal by driving it out of the carrier with a blunt chisel.

### ✳✳ WARNING

**Be careful when removing the seal not to damage the sealing surface of the bore.**

**To install:**

9. Clean all seal surfaces and remove burrs.
10. Install the new seal using a suitable driver or an oil seal installer such as J–33782.
11. Lubricate the seal lip and outside of the pinion flange with differential fluid or, if available, GM seal lubricant no. 1050169.

12. Install the pinion flange, washer and nut, aligning all of the marks made earlier. The pinion flange must be installed with the SAME spline relationship marked during removal.

13. Tighten the nut to previously marked position, then check the pre-load.

14. If necessary, tighten the nut additionally to match the pre-load recorded earlier. Remember that the flange holding tool should be removed each time before re-checking the pre-load.

15. For 1990–95 vehicles, tighten the nut until an additional 3–5 inch lbs. (0.3–0.6 Nm) of pre-load is achieved. If no torque wrench is available, tighten the nut approximately 1/16 in. (1.5mm) past the alignment mark.

16. Align and install the front driveshaft.

17. Check and add fluid to the front differential, as necessary. Remember that the vehicle must be level or you will not obtain the proper reading.

18. Remove the jackstands and carefully lower the vehicle.

19. Connect the negative battery cable.

## Differential Assembly

### REMOVAL & INSTALLATION

1. Disconnect the negative battery cable for safety.
2. Unlock the steering.
3. Raise the vehicle and support it with jackstands.
4. Remove the front wheels.
5. Matchmark the positions of the driveshaft and halfshafts to their flanges.
6. Insert a drift through the opening in the top of the brake caliper into the vanes in the brake rotor to keep the axle from turning.
7. Disconnect the front driveshaft from the differential and secure out of the way.
8. Disconnect the vent hose.
9. Remove the halfshaft-to-output shaft bolts.
10. Remove the tube-to-carrier bolts.
11. Unbolt the halfshafts from the front axle (leaving them attached to the hub and knuckle assembly) and support out of the way with wire. Be careful not to damage the joint boots or CV-joints.
12. Remove the axle tube support bracket-to-frame nuts and washers.
13. Remove the upper and lower mounting nuts and bolts.
14. Remove the differential assembly from the vehicle by sliding the entire unit to the right, dropping the tube end and twisting the carrier to clear the mounting brackets, oil pan and steering linkage.
15. Installation is the reverse of the removal procedure. Tighten the following:
   a. mounting bolts: 65 ft. lbs. (90 Nm)
   b. 1990–95 frame nuts: 55 ft. lbs. (75 Nm)
   c. 1996 frame nuts: 63 ft. lbs. (85 Nm)
   d. halfshaft bolts to 60 ft. lbs. (80 Nm)
16. Check and refill the differential fluid, as necessary. Remember that the vehicle must be level or an incorrect level will occur.
17. Remove the jackstands and carefully lower the vehicle.

### ✳✳ WARNING

**Make sure the ignition switch is in the OFF position before connecting the negative battery cable otherwise the engine control computer could be INSTANTLY destroyed when voltage is applied.**

18. Connect the negative battery cable and check for proper operation.

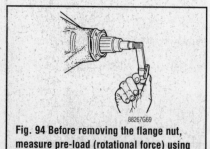

**Fig. 94 Before removing the flange nut, measure pre-load (rotational force) using an inch lbs. torque wrench**

**Fig. 95 A flange holding tool will be necessary to loosen or tighten the pinion nut**

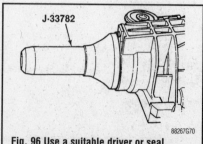

**Fig. 96 Use a suitable driver or seal installer to seat the replacement seal**

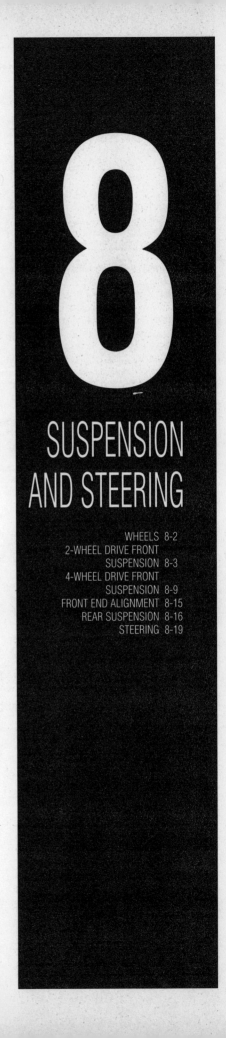

# 8

# SUSPENSION AND STEERING

## WHEELS

### Tire and Wheel Assembly

#### REMOVAL & INSTALLATION

**♦ See Figure 1**

1. Apply the parking brake and block the opposite wheel.
2. If equipped with an automatic transmission, place the selector lever in **P**; with a manual transmission/transaxle, place the shifter in gear.
3. If equipped, remove the wheel cover or hub cap.
4. Break loose the lug nuts. If a nut is stuck, never use heat to loosen it or damage to the wheel and bearings may occur. If the nuts are seized, 1 or 2 heavy hammer blows directly on the end of the bolt head usually loosens the rust. Be careful as continued pounding will likely damage the brake drum or rotor.
5. Raise the vehicle until the tire is clear of the ground. Support the vehicle safely using jackstands.
6. Remove the lug nuts, then remove the tire and wheel assembly.

**To install:**

7. Make sure the wheel and hub mating surfaces, as well as the wheel lug studs, are clean and free of all foreign material. Always remove rust from the wheel mounting surfaces and the brake rotors/drums. Failure to do so may cause the lug nuts to loosen in service.
8. Position the wheel on the hub or drum and hand-tighten the lug nuts. Make sure the coned ends face inward.
9. Tighten all the lug nuts, in a crisscross pattern, until they are snug.

➡**Wheel lug nut torque is especially important on disc brake vehicles where the wheel studs are attached to the hub and bearing assembly. Improper tightening could lead to disc warpage on these vehicle.**

10. Remove the jackstands and carefully lower the vehicle. Tighten the lug nuts, in a crisscross pattern. Always use a torque wrench to achieve the proper lug nut torque and to prevent stretching the wheel studs. For 1985–92 vehicles, tighten the lug nuts to 90 ft. lbs. (120 Nm). For 1993–96 vehicles, tighten the nuts to 100 ft. lbs. (140 Nm).
11. Repeat the torque pattern to assure proper wheel tightening.
12. If equipped, install the hub cab or wheel cover.

#### INSPECTION

Check the wheels for any damage. They must be replaced if they are bent, dented, heavily rusted, have elongated bolt holes, or have excessive lateral or radial runout. Wheels with excessive runout may cause a high-speed vehicle vibration.

Replacement wheels must be of the same load capacity, diameter, width, offset and mounting configuration as the original wheels. Using the wrong wheels may affect wheel bearing life, ground and tire clearance, or speedometer and odometer calibrations.

### Wheel Lug Studs

#### REMOVAL & INSTALLATION

**Front Wheels on 2wd Vehicles**

**♦ See Figure 2**

1. Raise and support the front of the vehicle safely using jackstands, then remove the wheel.
2. Remove the brake pads and caliper. Support the caliper aside using wire or a coat hanger. For details, please refer to Section 9 of this manual.
3. Remove the outer wheel bearing and lift the rotor off the axle. For details on wheel bearing removal, installation and adjustment, please refer to Section 1 of this manual.
4. Properly support the rotor using press bars, then drive the stud out using an arbor press.

➡**If a press is not available, CAREFULLY drive the old stud out using a blunt drift. MAKE SURE the disc is properly and evenly supported or it may be damaged.**

**To install:**

5. Clean the stud hole with a wire brush and start the new stud with a hammer and drift pin. Do not use any lubricant or thread sealer.
6. Finish installing the stud with the press.

➡**If a press is not available, start the lug stud through the bore in the hub, then position about 4 flat washers over the stud and thread the lug nut. Hold the disc, while tightening the lug nut and the stud should be drawn into position. MAKE SURE THE STUD IS FULLY SEATED, then remove the lug nut and washers.**

7. Install the rotor and adjust the wheel bearings.
8. Install the brake caliper and pads.
9. Install the wheel, then remove the jackstands and carefully lower the vehicle.

**Rear Wheels and Front Wheels on 4wd Vehicles**

**♦ See Figure 3**

1. Raise and support the vehicle safely using jackstands, then remove the wheel.
2. On front wheels, remove the brake caliper and rotor. Support the caliper from the suspension using wire or a coat hanger. For details, please refer to Section 9 of this manual.
3. On rear wheels, remove the brake drum.

➡**When replacing the front hub bolts on vehicles with 4 wheel anti-lock brakes, remove and replace only 1 wheel lug stud at a time to avoid misaligning the speed sensor exciter ring.**

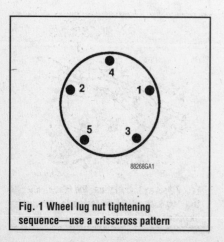

**Fig. 1 Wheel lug nut tightening sequence—use a crisscross pattern**

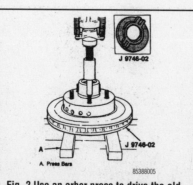

**Fig. 2 Use an arbor press to drive the old stud from the rotor—front wheel of 2wd vehicles**

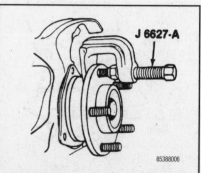

**Fig. 3 On many vehicles a stud press tool may be used with the hub still installed on the vehicle**

4. DO NOT hammer the wheel stud to remove it. This will ruin the wheel bearing. Use the stud press tool such as J-6627A or equivalent to press the stud out of the hub. If sufficient clearance is not available with the hub or shaft installed, the components must be removed.

**To install:**

5. Clean the hole with a wire brush and start the new stud into the hole. Do not use any lubricant or thread sealer.

6. Stack 4 or 5 washers onto the stud and then put the nut on. Tighten the nut to draw the stud into place. It should be easy to feel when the stud is seated.

7. Install the rotor and caliper or drum, as applicable.

8. Install the wheel, then remove the jackstands and carefully lower the vehicle.

## 2-WHEEL DRIVE FRONT SUSPENSION

♦ See Figure 4

### Coil Springs

➥In order to maintain proper suspension balance and vehicle handling, coil springs should only be replaced in axle sets.

REMOVAL & INSTALLATION

♦ See Figures 5, 6 and 7

➥The following procedure requires the use of the GM Spring Remover tool No. J–23028 or equivalent.

1. Raise and support the front of the vehicle on jackstands so the lower control arms hang free.

2. Disconnect the shock absorber-to-lower control arm nuts, then push the shock absorber up into the coil spring.

3. Secure the GM Spring Remover tool No. J–23028 or equivalent, to a floor jack, then position the assembly under the lower control arm so it cradles the inner bushings.

4. Disconnect the stabilizer bar from the lower control arm.

5. Install a chain around the coil spring and through the lower control arm for safety, then remove the lower control arm nuts and bolts.

### ❊❊❊ CAUTION

**The coil springs are under a considerable amount of tension. Be extremely careful when removing or installing them; they can exert enough force to cause serious injury!**

6. Raise the floor jack (with the spring remover tool) to take the tension off the lower control arm-to-chassis bolts/nuts.

➥When removing the lower control arm-to-chassis fasteners, be sure to remove the rear set first, then the front set.

7. Slowly and carefully, lower the floor jack (USING THE SPRING REMOVER TOOL) until the tension is released from the coil spring.

➥When removing the coil spring, DO NOT apply force to the lower control arm or the lower ball joint. Proper maneuvering of the spring will provide easy removal.

8. Remove the safety chain from the coil spring and control arm ONLY AFTER ALL SPRING TENSION has been released. Remove the coil spring from the control arm.

**To install:**

9. Before installing the coil spring, position it in the following order:

a. For 1985–92 vehicles, visually identify the top and bottom of the coil spring. The spring top has a coiled, flat shape with a gripper notch at the end of the coil; the bottom has a coiled, helical shape.

b. On all models, the coil spring should be positioned so the tape (on the coil) is at the bottom.

c. Position the lower end of the coil spring so it covers part or all of the inspection drain hole. The other drain hole MUST BE partially or completely uncovered.

d. Place the insulator at the top of the coil spring, and on 1993–96 vehicles, make sure the lower insulator is positioned onto the control arm.

10. Secure the spring remover tool to the floor jack assembly, then raise the lower control arm/coil spring assembly using the floor jack and install the lower

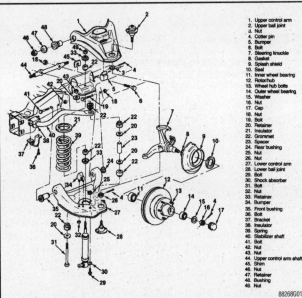

**Fig. 4 Two wheel drive front suspension—Note that ABS equipped vehicles use a different splash shield (with a speed sensor)**

Parts list:
1. Upper control arm
2. Upper ball joint
3. Nut
4. Cotter pin
5. Bumper
6. Bolt
7. Steering knuckle
8. Gasket
9. Splash shield
10. Seal
11. Inner wheel bearing
12. Rotor/hub
13. Wheel hub bolts
14. Outer wheel bearing
15. Washer
16. Nut
17. Cap
18. Nut
19. Bolt
20. Retainer
21. Insulator
22. Grommet
23. Spacer
24. Rear bushing
25. Nut
26. Nut
27. Lower control arm
28. Lower ball joint
29. Bolt
30. Shock absorber
31. Nut
32. Nut
33. Retainer
34. Bumper
35. Front bushing
36. Bolt
37. Bracket
38. Insulator
39. Spring
40. Stabilizer shaft
41. Bolt
42. Nut
43. Nut
44. Upper control arm shaft
45. Shim
46. Nut
47. Retainer
48. Bushing
49. Nut

88268G01

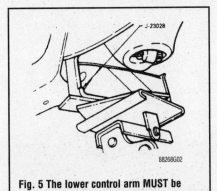

**Fig. 5 The lower control arm MUST be supported using a spring remover tool and suitable jack**

SPRING TO BE INSTALLED WITH TAPE AT LOWEST POSITION. BOTTOM OF SPRING IS COILED HELICAL, AND THE TOP IS COILED FLAT WITH A GRIPPER NOTCH NEAR END OF SPRING COIL.

AFTER ASSEMBLY, END OF SPRING COIL MUST COVER ALL OR PART OF ONE IN-SPECTION DRAIN HOLE. THE OTHER HOLE MUST BE PARTLY EXPOSED OR COM-PLETELY UNCOVERED. ROTATE SPRING AS NECESSARY.

88268G03

**Fig. 6 Positioning the coil spring**

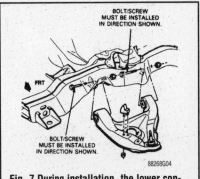

**Fig. 7 During installation, the lower control arm bolts MUST be facing the proper direction**

control arm-to-chassis nuts/bolts. The bolts must be installed facing the proper direction, please refer to the illustration for details. DO NOT fully tighten the nuts and bolts at this time.

### ✳✳ CAUTION

**Failure to properly secure the spring remover tool to the floor jack could result in a sudden movement of the suspension or tool that would allow the spring to leap free. This could cause SERIOUS personal injury.**

11. Secure the stabilizer shaft to the lower control arm.
12. Pull the shock absorber down, then install the shock absorber-to-lower control arm nuts/bolts. Torque the nuts and bolts to 18 ft. lbs. (25 Nm).
13. Remove the jackstands and carefully lower the front of the vehicle, so it is resting on its own weight.
14. With the suspension at normal height, tighten the lower control arm-to-chassis nuts/bolts (starting with the front nut, then the rear) to 96 ft. lbs. (128 Nm) for 1985–92 vehicles, to 92 ft. lbs. (125 Nm) for 1993–95 vehicles or to 66 ft. lbs. (90 Nm) for 1996 vehicles.
15. Check and/or adjust the front end alignment, as necessary.

## Shock Absorbers

➡In order to maintain proper suspension balance and vehicle handling, shock absorbers should only be replaced in axle sets.

### REMOVAL & INSTALLATION

▶ **See Figures 8, 9, 10 and 11**

1. Raise and support the front of the vehicle on jackstands. Remove the wheels.
2. While holding the upper end of the shock absorber (to keep it from turning), remove the shock absorber nut, retainer and grommet. A hex is normally provided in the shock absorber stem to make this possible. If no hex is provided, look for an accessible flat.

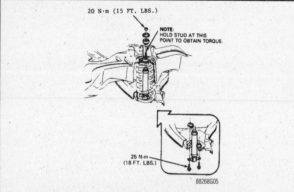

**Fig. 8 Exploded view of the front shock absorber retainers**

3. Remove the shock absorber-to-lower control arm bolts (on most applications the nuts remain attached to the control arm), then slide the shock absorber from the bottom of the lower control arm.
4. Test the shock absorber and replace it, if necessary.
**To install:**
5. Fully extend the shock absorber, insert it through the coil spring and the upper control arm, then loosely install the retainers.
6. While holding the stem from turning, tighten the shock absorber upper retaining nut to 15 ft. lbs. (20 Nm).
7. Tighten the shock absorber-to-lower control arm bolts to 18 ft. lbs. (25 Nm).

### TESTING

Visually inspect the shock absorber. If there is evidence of leakage and the shock absorber is covered with oil, the shock is defective and should be replaced.

If there is no sign of excessive leakage (a small amount of weeping is normal) bounce the van at one corner by pressing down on the bumper and releasing it. When you have the van bouncing as much as you can, release the bumper. The van should stop bouncing after the first rebound. If the bouncing continues past the center point of the bounce more than once, the shock absorbers are worn and should be replaced.

## Upper Ball Joint

### INSPECTION

▶ **See Figures 12 and 13**

➡Before performing this inspection, make sure the wheel bearings are adjusted correctly and that the control arm bushings are in good condition.

1. Raise and support the front of the vehicle by placing jackstands under each lower control arm as close as possible to each lower ball joint.

➡Before performing the upper ball joint inspection, be sure the vehicle is stable and the lower control arm bumpers are not contacting the frame.

2. Wipe the ball joints clean and check the seals for cuts or tears. If a seal is damaged the ball joint MUST be replaced.
3. Position a dial indicator so it contacts the wheel rim.
4. To measure the horizontal deflection, perform the following procedures:
   a. Grasp the tire (top and bottom), then pull outward on the top and push inward on the bottom; record the reading on the dial indicator.
   b. Grasp the tire (top and bottom), then pull outward on the bottom and push inward on the top; record the reading on the dial indicator.
   c. If the difference in the dial indicator reading is more than 0.125 in. (3.18mm), or if the ball joint can be twisted in its socket (with finger pressure) once it is disconnected from the knuckle, it must be replaced.

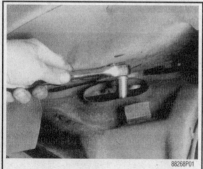

**Fig. 9 DON'T loosen the retainer without holding the shaft (a box wrench is usually better than a socket)**

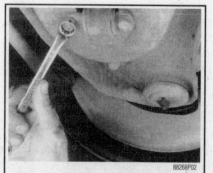

**Fig. 10 Once the upper shock retainer is removed, loosen the lower retaining bolts . . .**

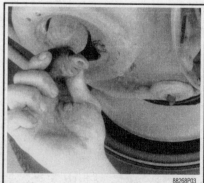

**Fig. 11 . . . and carefully lower the shock from the control arm**

## REMOVAL & INSTALLATION

◆ **See Figures 14, 15, 16 and 17**

➡ **The following procedure requires the use of the GM Ball Joint Remover tool No. J–23742 or equivalent.**

1. Raise and support the front of the vehicle by placing jackstands under the lower control arms, between the spring seat and the lower ball joint. If jackstands are placed anywhere else, a floor jack MUST be used between the spring seat and the lower ball joint.

➡ **Allow the jackstand or jack to remain under the lower control arm seat, to retain the spring and the lower control arm position.**

2. Remove the tire and wheel assembly.
3. From the upper ball joint, remove the cotter pin, the nut and the grease fitting.
4. Using the GM Ball Joint Remover tool No. J–23742 or equivalent, separate the upper ball joint from the steering knuckle. Pull the steering knuckle free of the ball joint after removal and wire it to the body.

➡ **After separating the steering knuckle from the upper ball joint, be sure to support steering knuckle/hub assembly to prevent damaging the brake hose.**

5. Remove the upper ball joint from the upper control arm:
   a. Using a ⅛ in. (3mm) bit, drill a ¼ in. (6mm) deep hole into each rivet.
   b. Using a ½ in. (13mm) bit, drill off the rivet heads.
   c. Using a pin punch and the hammer, drive the rivets from the upper ball joint-to-upper control arm assembly and remove the upper ball joint.

**To install:**

6. Clean and inspect the steering knuckle hole. Replace the steering knuckle, if any out of roundness is noted.
7. Install a service replacement upper ball joint, positioning the ball joint-to-upper control arm bolts facing upward.

8. Tighten the upper ball joint-to-upper control arm bolts to the specification provided with the replacement joint. If no specification was provided, tighten the bolt to 96 inch lbs. (11 Nm) for 1985–89 vehicles or to 22 ft. lbs. (30 Nm) for 1990–96 vehicles.
9. Remove the steering knuckle support, then seat the upper ball joint into the steering knuckle and install the nut. Make sure the ball joint is FULLY SEATED into the steering knuckle, then tighten the upper ball joint-to-steering knuckle nut to 52 ft. lbs. (70 Nm) for 1985–87 vehicles, or to 65 ft. lbs. (85 Nm) on 1988–96 vehicles.
10. Install a new cotter pin to the lower ball joint stud.

➡ **When installing the cotter pin through the upper ball joint-to-steering knuckle nut, if the hole is not clear, always tighten the castle nut additionally to expose the cotter pin hole. NEVER loosen the nut for alignment.**

11. Install the grease fitting, then lubricate the upper ball joint using a grease gun.
12. Install the tire and wheel assembly.
13. Inspect and/or adjust the wheel bearing and the front end alignment.
14. Remove the jackstands and carefully lower the vehicle.

## Lower Ball Joint

### INSPECTION

◆ **See Figure 18**

➡ **Remember that mis-adjusted wheel bearings or worn control arm bushings can also produce symptoms similar to that of worn ball joints. If visual inspection shows the lower ball joints to be good, check these items next.**

Wipe the joint clean of old grease and road crud, then check the seal to make sure it is not torn or cut. Visually check the wear indicator (the shoulder which

Fig. 12 To check the ball joint, first wipe the grease and road crud off the it for a visual inspection

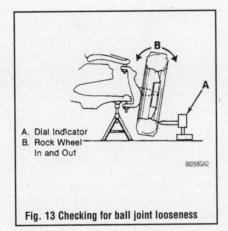

A. Dial Indicator
B. Rock Wheel In and Out

Fig. 13 Checking for ball joint looseness

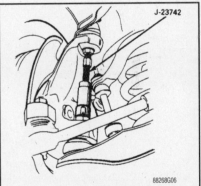

Fig. 14 Use a separator tool to free the upper ball joint from the steering knuckle

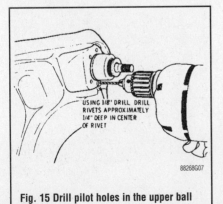

USING 1/8" DRILL DRILL RIVETS APPROXIMATELY 1/4" DEEP IN CENTER OF RIVET

Fig. 15 Drill pilot holes in the upper ball joint rivets . . .

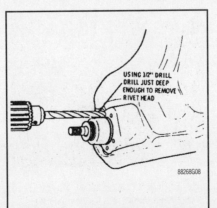

USING 1/2" DRILL DRILL JUST DEEP ENOUGH TO REMOVE RIVET HEAD

Fig. 16 . . . then drill off the rivet heads

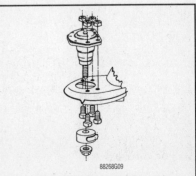

Fig. 17 When installing a service replacement upper ball joint, be sure the bolts are positioned on the bottom (nuts on top)

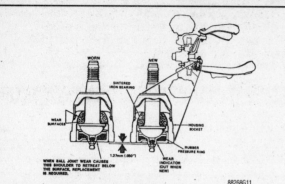

Fig. 18 The lower ball joint can be inspected for wear visually using the built-in indicator (the grease fitting)

the grease fitting is threaded into); if it is flush or inside the ball joint cover surface, replace the ball joint. If the indicator protrudes from the housing and the seal is intact, the joint is considered good. The joint must be replaced if the seal is damaged or if the indicator shows it to be worn past serviceability.

## REMOVAL & INSTALLATION

▶ See Figures 19 thru 26

➡The following procedure requires the use of the GM Ball Joint Remover (separator) tool No. J–23742 or equivalent, and the GM Ball Joint Remover and Installer Set tool No. J–9519–E. The set includes a C-clamp like pressing tool and various fixture and driver adapters.

1. Raise and support the front of the vehicle on jackstands.
2. Remove the tire and wheel assembly.
3. Place a floor jack under the spring seat of the lower control arm, then raise the jack to support the arm.

➡The floor jack MUST remain under the lower control arm, during the removal and installation procedures, to retain the arm and spring positions.

### ❋❋ CAUTION

Improper placement or sudden release of the jack during this procedure could dislodge the coil spring causing serious personal injury.

4. Remove and discard the cotter pin from the lower ball joint stud, then remove the ball joint nut.
5. Using the GM Ball Joint Remover tool No. J–23742 or equivalent, disconnect the lower ball joint from the steering knuckle.
6. Pull the steering knuckle away from the lower control arm, place a block of wood between the frame and the upper control arm in order to hold the knuckle and hub assembly out of the way; make sure the brake hose is free of tension.
7. Remove the rubber grease seal and the grease fitting from the lower ball joint.
8. Remove the lower ball joint from the lower control arm using the ball joint remover set.

**To install:**
9. Position the new lower ball joint into the lower control arm, then use the ball joint installer set to press the joint into the lower control arm.
10. Install the grease fitting and the grease seal onto the lower ball joint; the grease seal MUST BE fully seated on the ball joint and the grease purge hole MUST face inboard.
11. Remove the wooden block, then press the steering knuckle assembly onto the lower ball joint until is fully seated.
12. Install the ball joint-to-steering knuckle nut and tighten to 81 ft. lbs. (110 Nm) for 1985–92 vehicles, or to 90 ft. lbs. (125 Nm) on 1993–96 vehicles.
13. Install a new cotter pin to the lower ball joint stud.

➡When installing the cotter pin through the lower ball joint-to-steering knuckle nut, if the hole is not clear, always tighten the castle nut additionally to expose the cotter pin hole. NEVER loosen the nut for alignment.

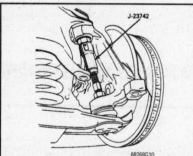

Fig. 19 The proper ball joint separator tool MUST be used if the joint is not being replaced, otherwise the joint may be damaged requiring replacement

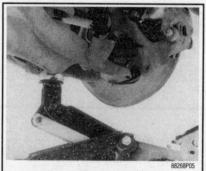

Fig. 20 Support the lower control arm using a floor jack—this will keep the coil spring and arm in position

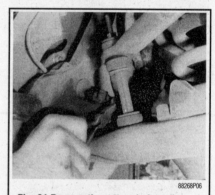

Fig. 21 Remove the cotter pin from the lower ball joint stud . . .

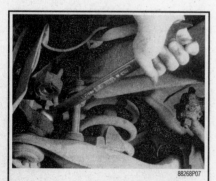

Fig. 22 . . . then loosen the stud nut—note that the tie rod end was removed earlier for illustration purposes

Fig. 23 Remove the ball joint nut then install a separator tool to free the joint . . .

Fig. 24 . . . use this tool ONLY if the joint is being replaced as the seal will likely be destroyed by the tool

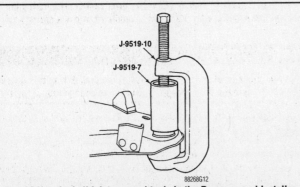

**Fig. 25 Use the ball joint removal tools in the Remover and Installer Set to press the old joint from the lower control arm**

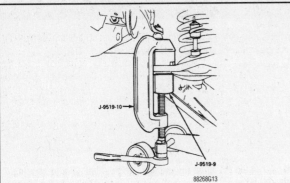

**Fig. 26 The new ball joint should also be pressed into position using the tool set**

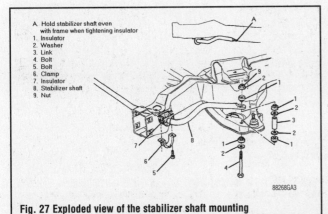

A. Hold stabilizer shaft even with frame when tightening insulator
1. Insulator
2. Washer
3. Link
4. Bolt
5. Bolt
6. Clamp
7. Insulator
8. Stabilizer shaft
9. Nut

**Fig. 27 Exploded view of the stabilizer shaft mounting**

14. Remove the floor jack.
15. Using a grease gun, lubricate the lower ball joint.
16. Check and adjust the wheel bearings and the front end alignment, as necessary.
17. Remove the jackstands and carefully lower the vehicle.

## Stabilizer (Sway) Bar

### REMOVAL & INSTALLATION

▶ **See Figures 27, 28, 29 and 30**

1. Raise and support the front of the vehicle on jackstands.
2. Remove the wheels to provide access (and light).
3. Disconnect the stabilizer bar link nuts, then slowly pull the bolts down, from underneath the lower control arms. As the bolts are removed, the retainers, insulators and link spacer will be freed from the bolt. BE SURE to note the locations for each of these components and keep them in order. It is probably best to install them in order over the bolt and put the nut on the end to keep any part from being lost.
4. Remove the stabilizer bar-to-frame clamps.
5. Remove the stabilizer bar from the vehicle. If necessary, remove the insulators from the shaft.

**To install:**

6. If removed, install the insulators on the shaft. The slit on the insulator should be positioned toward the front of the vehicle.
7. Install the stabilizer shaft and brackets to the van, making sure the shaft is mounted with the identification on the right side of the vehicle. Install the shaft offset in the downward position and make sure the insulators are positioned squarely in the clamps.
8. Loosely install the stabilizer bar-to-frame clamps in order to hold the bar.
9. Install the stabilizer links through the control arms, positioning the necessary components (insulators, washers, retainers and the link spacer) as it is inserted. Connect the links to the ends of the bar, installing the washer and nut.
10. Tighten the stabilizer bar link-to-lower control arm bolts to 13 ft. lbs. (18 Nm) and the stabilizer retainer-to-frame bolts to 22 ft. lbs. (29 Nm) for 1985–87 vehicles or to 27 ft. lbs. (36 Nm) for 1988–96 vehicles.

## Upper Control Arm

### REMOVAL & INSTALLATION

▶ **See Figures 31, 32 and 33**

➡ **The following procedure requires the use of the GM Ball Joint Remover tool No. J–23742 or equivalent.**

Before starting the procedure, identify and note the location of the alignment shims. They must be installed in their original locations in order to preserve current vehicle wheel alignment.

**Fig. 28 Loosen the stabilizer bar link nut, while using a wrench to hold the bolt from turning . . .**

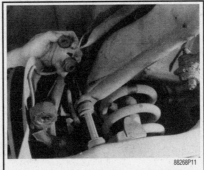

**Fig. 29 . . . then remove the bolt, gathering each of the link components and keeping them in order**

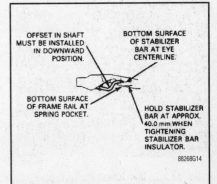

OFFSET IN SHAFT MUST BE INSTALLED IN DOWNWARD POSITION.

BOTTOM SURFACE OF STABILIZER BAR AT EYE CENTERLINE.

BOTTOM SURFACE OF FRAME RAIL AT SPRING POCKET.

HOLD STABILIZER BAR AT APPROX. 40.0 mm WHEN TIGHTENING STABILIZER BAR INSULATOR.

**Fig. 30 Make sure the offset on the bar is aligned properly during installation**

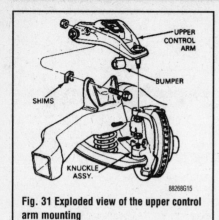

**Fig. 31 Exploded view of the upper control arm mounting**

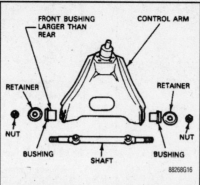

**Fig. 32 Exploded view of the upper control arm, pivot shaft and bushings**

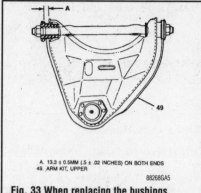

A. 13.3 ± 0.5MM (.5 ± .02 INCHES) ON BOTH ENDS
49. ARM KIT, UPPER

**Fig. 33 When replacing the bushings, make sure they are positioned as shown**

1. Raise and support the front of the vehicle by placing jackstands under the lower control arms, between the spring seat and the lower ball joint. If the jackstands are placed in a different location, then a floor jack MUST be used under the lower control arm.

➡**Allow the jackstand or floor jack to remain under the lower control arm seat, to retain the spring and the lower control arm position.**

2. Remove the tire and wheel assembly.
3. Remove the cotter pin and nut from the upper ball joint.
4. Using the GM Ball Joint Remover tool No. J–23742 or equivalent, separate the upper ball joint from the steering knuckle/hub assembly. Pull the steering knuckle free of the ball joint after removal.

➡**After separating the steering knuckle from the upper ball joint, be sure to support steering knuckle/hub assembly to prevent damaging the brake hose.**

5. Remove the upper control arm-to-frame nuts and bolts, then lift and remove the upper control arm from the vehicle.

➡**Tape the alignment shims together and identify them so they can be installed in the proper positions from which they were removed.**

6. Clean and inspect the steering knuckle hole. Replace the steering knuckle, if any out of roundness is noted.
7. If replacement is necessary, mount the control arm in a vise, then remove the pivot shaft nuts and washers. Use a control arm bushing fixture (C-clamp like tool) along with a slotted washer and a piece of pipe (slightly larger than the bushing) to remove the old bushings.

**To install**

8. If removed, position the pivot shaft to the control arm and install the bushing using the fixture tool, washer and a length of pipe with the same outer diameter as the bushing. Tighten the tool until the bushing is positioned on the shaft as shown in the illustration. Install the bushing retaining nuts and washers, then tighten them to 85 ft. lbs. (115 Nm).
9. Attach the upper control arm to the frame aligning the holes in the shaft with the holes in the frame. Insert the shims in their proper positions (as noted during removal). You may have to lift the upper control arm to gain access for shim installation.
10. Tighten the upper control arm-to-frame bolts to 66 ft. lbs. (90 Nm) for 1985–87 vehicles, to 75 ft. lbs. (100 Nm) for 1988–95 vehicles, or to 81 ft. lbs. (110 Nm) for 1996 vehicles.
11. Seat the upper ball joint into the steering knuckle and install the nut.
12. Tighten the upper ball joint-to-steering knuckle nut to 52 ft. lbs. (69 Nm) for 1985–87 vehicles, or to 65 ft. lbs. (85 Nm) for 1988–96 vehicles.
13. Install a new cotter pin to the upper ball joint stud.

➡**When installing the cotter pin through the upper ball joint-to-steering knuckle nut, if the hole is not clear, always tighten the castle nut additionally to expose the cotter pin hole. NEVER loosen the nut for alignment.**

14. Install the tire and wheel assembly.
15. Remove the jackstands and carefully lower the vehicle.
16. Check and adjust the wheel alignment, as necessary.

## Lower Control Arm

### REMOVAL & INSTALLATION

◆ **See Figure 34**

➡**The following procedure requires the use of the GM Ball Joint Remover tool No. J–23742 or equivalent.**

1. Refer to the Coil Spring, Removal and Installation procedures in this section and remove the coil spring.
2. Remove and discard the cotter pin, then remove the lower ball joint nut.
3. Using the GM Ball Joint Remover tool No. J–23742 or equivalent, disconnect the lower ball joint from the steering knuckle and the lower control arm from the vehicle.

➡**Place a block of wood between the frame and the upper control arm; make sure the brake hose is free of tension.**

4. If the bushings are being replaced, use a suitable bushing service set to remove the bushings from the control arm. The front bushing is normally flared and the flare must be driven down flush with the rubber using a blunt chisel before attempting removal.

**To install:**

5. If the bushings were removed, use the bushing service set to install them to the control arms. If the front bushing is the flared type, use a flaring tool to produce an approximate flare of 45 degrees.
6. Position the lower ball joint stud into the steering knuckle.
7. Install the ball joint-to-steering knuckle nut and tighten to 81 ft. lbs. (110 Nm) for 1985–92 vehicles, or to 90 ft. lbs. (125 Nm) on 1993–96 vehicles.
8. Install a new cotter pin to the lower ball joint stud.

➡**When installing the cotter pin through the lower ball joint-to-steering knuckle nut, if the hole is not clear, always tighten the castle nut addi-**

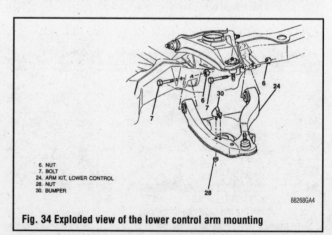

6. NUT
7. BOLT
24. ARM KIT, LOWER CONTROL
28. NUT
30. BUMPER

**Fig. 34 Exploded view of the lower control arm mounting**

tionally to expose the cotter pin hole. NEVER loosen the nut for alignment.

9. Install the coil spring as detailed earlier in this section.

## Knuckle and Spindle

### REMOVAL & INSTALLATION

▶ See Figures 35 and 36

➡The following procedure requires the use of the GM Tie Rod End Puller tool J–6627 or equivalent, and the GM Ball Joint Remover tool No. J–23742 or equivalent.

1. Raise and support the front of the vehicle on jackstands.
2. Remove the wheels.

➡When supporting the vehicle on jackstands, DO NOT place the jackstands directly under the lower control arms for the vehicle may slip off the jackstands during the steering knuckle removal.

3. Remove the brake caliper from the steering knuckle and support it on a wire.
4. Remove the grease cup, the cotter pin, the castle nut and the hub assembly.
5. Remove the splash shield-to-steering knuckle bolts and the shield.

➡When removing the splash shield on late-model vehicles equipped with ABS, be sure to disconnect the speed sensor wiring and to treat the shield like an electrical component (Don't submerge it in solvent or anything which could damage the speed sensor assembly.

6. At the tie rod end-to-steering knuckle stud, remove the cotter pin and the nut. Using the GM Tie Rod End Puller tool J–6627 or equivalent, separate the tie rod end from the steering knuckle.
7. From the upper and lower ball joint studs, remove the cotter pins and the nuts.
8. Place a floor jack under the spring seat of the lower control arm and support the arm.
9. Using the GM Ball Joint Remover tool No. J–23742 or equivalent, separate the upper ball joint from the steering knuckle.
10. Carefully raise the upper control arm just sufficiently to separate it from the steering knuckle.
11. Using the GM Ball Joint Remover tool No. J–23742 or equivalent, separate the lower ball joint from the steering knuckle, then lift the steering knuckle from the lower control arm.
12. Clean and inspect the steering knuckle and spindle for signs of wear or damage; if necessary, replace the steering knuckle.
13. Installation is the reverse of the removal procedure. Tighten the following components:
   • 1985–87 upper ball joint-to-steering knuckle nut: 52 ft. lbs. (70 Nm)

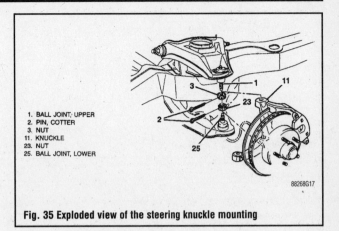

1. BALL JOINT, UPPER
2. PIN, COTTER
3. NUT
11. KNUCKLE
23. NUT
25. BALL JOINT, LOWER

88268G17

**Fig. 35 Exploded view of the steering knuckle mounting**

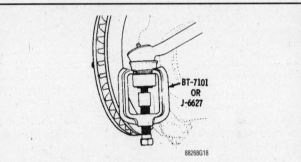

BT-7101
OR
J-6627

88268G18

**Fig. 36 Use a suitable steering linkage puller to disconnect the tie rod end from the knuckle**

   • 1988–96 upper ball joint-to-steering knuckle nut: 65 ft. lbs. (85 Nm)
   • 1985–92 lower ball joint-to-steering knuckle nut: 81 ft. lbs. (110 Nm)
   • 1993–96 lower ball joint-to-steering knuckle nut: 90 ft. lbs. (125 Nm)
   • Splash shield-to-steering knuckle bolts: 10 ft. lbs. (14 Nm)
14. Before attempting to move the vehicle, pump the brake pedal slowly until a firm pedal is felt (this will seat the brake pads). Check and adjust the front end alignment, as necessary.

## Front Wheel Bearings

Because the front wheel bearings on 2-wheel drive vehicles must be periodically removed, inspected, repacked and installed, the necessary procedures have been included with the maintenance information found in Section 1 of this manual. Please refer to this information for front wheel bearing/race removal and installation.

## 4-WHEEL DRIVE FRONT SUSPENSION

▶ See Figure 37

## Torsion Bars and Support

Certain procedures in this manual, including torsion bar removal and installation require that you first UNLOAD the torsion bar. This is accomplished using a special unloading tool such as J–36202 or equivalent. If you are performing service on another part of the vehicle, that first requires the torsion bars to be unloaded, refer to that portion of the torsion bar removal and installation procedure in this section and perform the necessary steps as outlined.

### REMOVAL & INSTALLATION

▶ See Figures 38, 39 and 40

1. Disconnect the negative battery cable for safety.
2. Raise and support the front of the vehicle safely using jackstands.
3. Mark and unload the torsion bars:

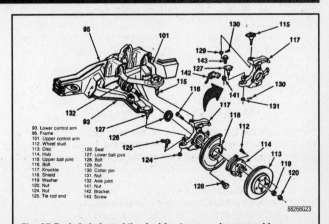

93. Lower control arm
95. Frame
101. Upper control arm
112. Wheel stud
113. Disc
114. Hub
115. Upper ball joint
116. Bolt
117. Knuckle
118. Shield
119. Washer
120. Nut
124. Nut
125. Tie rod end
126. Seal
127. Lower ball joint
128. Bolt
129. Nut
130. Cotter pin
131. Nut
132. Axle joint
141. Nut
142. Bracket
143. Screw

88268G23

**Fig. 37 Exploded view of the 4wd front suspension assembly**

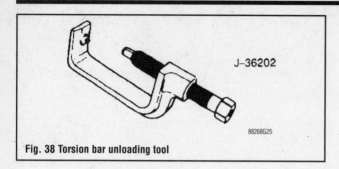

**Fig. 38 Torsion bar unloading tool**

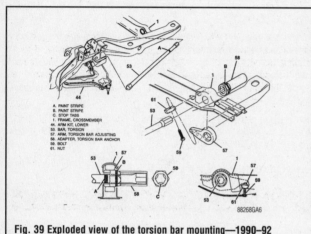

A. PAINT STRIPE
B. PAINT STRIPE
C. STOP TABS
1. FRAME, CROSSMEMBER
44. ARM KIT, LOWER
53. BAR, TORSION
57. ARM, TORSION BAR ADJUSTING
58. ADAPTER, TORSION BAR ANCHOR
59. BOLT
61. NUT

**Fig. 39 Exploded view of the torsion bar mounting—1990–92**

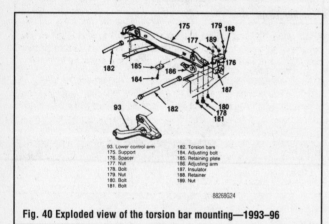

93. Lower control arm
175. Support
176. Spacer
177. Nut
178. Bolt
179. Nut
180. Bolt
181. Bolt
182. Torsion bars
184. Adjusting bolt
185. Retaining plate
186. Adjusting arm
187. Insulator
188. Retainer
189. Nut

**Fig. 40 Exploded view of the torsion bar mounting—1993–96**

a. Mark the adjustment bolt setting on the bolt adjusters.

b. Increase tension on the adjustment arm using the unloader tool J–36202, or equivalent.

c. Remove the adjusting bolt and retainer plate.

d. Move the tool aside.

4. For 1990–92 vehicles:

a. Slide the torsion bar forward and remove the adjustment arm.

b. Remove the nuts and bolts from the torsion bar support-to-crossmember. Slide the crossmember rearward.

c. Mark the location of the front and rear ends. Mark either left or right because the bars are different.

d. Remove the support crossmember, retainer, spacer and insulator from the crossmember.

5. For 1993–96 vehicles:

a. Remove the torsion bar anchor adapter by sliding the adapter out toward the rear, then removing the adjustment arm.

b. Note the location of the tape or painted stripe at the rear ends of the torsion bar (since there are different bars for the right and left sides), then remove the torsion bar from the vehicle.

**To install:**

6. For 1993–96 vehicles:

a. Note the location of the tape or painted stripe at the rear ends of the torsion bar and position the bar to the vehicle. Remember that there are different bars for different sides of the vehicle and the tape or paint should be located to the rear.

b. Install the bar anchor adapter, by positioning the adjustment arm, then sliding the adapter tube over the torsion bar and adjustment arm.

c. Make sure the adapter tube is properly seated into the front face of the crossmember. Make sure the torsion bar is properly seated into the rear of the adapter tube against the stop tabs.

7. For 1990–92 vehicles:

a. Install the insulator, spacer and retainer onto the support crossmember.

b. Install the crossmember onto the frame, rearward of the mounting holes.

c. Make sure the bars are on their respective sides. Slide the crossmember forward until the bars are supported.

d. Install the adjustment arms, crossmember bolts and nuts. Torque the center nut to 18 ft. lbs. (24 Nm) and the edge nuts to 46 ft. lbs. (62 Nm).

8. Properly tension and adjust (as necessary) the torsion bar:

a. Increase the tension on the torsion bar using the unloader tool.

b. Install the adjustment retainer plates and bolt.

c. Set the adjuster to the position marked during removal.

d. Release the tension on the bar until the load is taken up by the adjustment bolt, then remove the unloader tool.

9. Remove the jackstands and carefully lower the vehicle.

10. Check and adjust the "Z" height as outlined in the alignment information later in this section.

## Shock Absorbers

➡ **In order to maintain proper suspension balance and vehicle handling, shock absorbers should only be replaced in axle sets.**

### REMOVAL & INSTALLATION

▸ **See Figures 41 and 42**

1. Raise the front of the vehicle and support safely using jackstands.
2. Remove the front tire and wheel assemblies.
3. For 1992 and later vehicles, remove the inner wheel well splash shields.
4. Remove the lower nut, washer and bolt.

➡ **Note the direction which the bolts are facing before removal. The bolts must be installed in the same direction as noted to assure there is not interference with suspension components during vehicle operation.**

5. Remove the upper nut, washer and bolt, then collapse and remove the shock absorber.

**To install:**

6. Install the shock absorber to the brackets using the nuts and bolts. Be sure the bolts are facing the proper direction as noted during removal.

7. Tighten the nuts to 66 ft. lbs. (90 Nm) for 1990–95 vehicles or to 46 ft. lbs. (62 Nm) for 1996 vehicles.

8. If applicable, install the inner wheel well splash shields.

9. Install the front tire and wheel assemblies.

10. Remove the jackstands and carefully lower the vehicle.

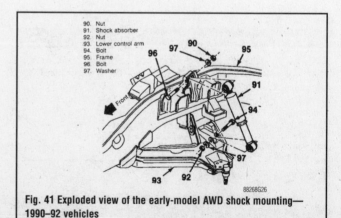

90. Nut
91. Shock absorber
92. Nut
93. Lower control arm
94. Bolt
95. Frame
96. Bolt
97. Washer

**Fig. 41 Exploded view of the early-model AWD shock mounting—1990–92 vehicles**

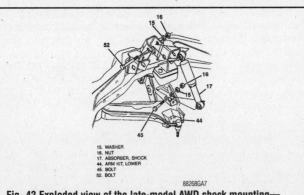

15. WASHER
16. NUT
17. ABSORBER, SHOCK
44. ARM KIT, LOWER
45. BOLT
52. BOLT

88268GA7

**Fig. 42 Exploded view of the late-model AWD shock mounting— 1993–96 vehicles**

## Upper Ball Joint

### INSPECTION

◊ **See Figure 43**

➡**Before performing this inspection, make sure the wheel bearings and control arm bushings are in good condition.**

1. Raise and support the front of the vehicle by placing jackstands under each lower control arm as close as possible to each lower ball joint.

➡**Before performing the upper ball joint inspection, be sure the vehicle is stable and the lower control arm bumpers are not contacting the frame.**

2. Wipe the ball joints clean and check the seals for cuts or tears. If a seal is damaged the ball joint MUST be replaced.
3. Position a dial indicator so it contacts the wheel rim.
4. To measure the horizontal deflection, perform the following procedures:
   a. Grasp the tire (top and bottom), then pull outward on the top and push inward on the bottom; record the reading on the dial indicator.
   b. Grasp the tire (top and bottom), then pull outward on the bottom and push inward on the top; record the reading on the dial indicator.
   c. If the difference in the dial indicator reading is more than 0.125 in. (3.18mm), or if the ball joint can be twisted in its socket (with finger pressure) once it is disconnected from the knuckle, it must be replaced.

### REMOVAL & INSTALLATION

◊ **See Figures 44 and 45**

1. Raise the front of the vehicle and support safely using jackstands.
2. Remove the front tire and wheel assembly.
3. Remove the brake hose and bracket from the upper control arm.
4. Loosen the riveted ball joint from the control arm:
   a. Drill a ⅛ in. (3mm) hole, about ¼ in. (6mm) deep into each rivet.

b. Then use a ½ in. (13mm) drill bit, to drill off the rivet heads.
   c. Using a pin punch and the hammer, drive out the rivets in order to free the ball joint from the control arm assembly.
5. Remove the cotter pin and nut.
6. Remove the ball joint from the knuckle using a ball joint separator tool such as J–36607.
   **To install:**
7. Position the new ball joint to the control arm.
8. Install the nuts and bolts supplied with the new ball joint. The bolt should be inserted from the top with the nut on the bottom. Tighten the nuts to 22 ft. lbs. (30 Nm).
9. Install the ball joint to the steering knuckle then secure using the nut. Tighten the nut to 95 ft. lbs. (128 Nm) for 1990–95 vehicles or to 66 ft. lbs. (90 Nm) for 1996 vehicles.

➡**The upper ball joint retaining nut MUST be tightened with the vehicle suspension at normal ride height. This can either be accomplished by installing the wheels and lowering the vehicle, or by moving jackstands under the ends of the lower control arms and resting the vehicle on them. If the latter solution is tried, make sure the FULL WEIGHT of the vehicle front end is on the suspension.**

10. Install a new cotter pin to the castellated nut. Tighten the nut (but no more than an additional ⅛ turn) in order to align the cotter pin. DO NOT loosen the nut from the specified torque.
11. The remainder of installation is the reverse of the removal procedure. Check and adjust the front end alignment, as necessary.

## Lower Ball Joint

### INSPECTION

◊ **See Figure 46**

➡**Remember that worn wheel bearings or control arm bushings can also produce symptoms similar to that of worn ball joints. If visual inspection shows the lower ball joints to be good, check these items next.**

Wipe the joint clean of old grease and road crud, then check the seal to make sure it is not torn or cut. Visually check the wear indicator (the shoulder which the grease fitting is threaded into); if it is flush or inside the ball joint cover surface, replace the ball joint. If the indicator protrudes from the housing and the seal is intact, the joint is considered good. The joint must be replaced if the seal is damaged or if the indicator shows it to be worn past serviceability.

### REMOVAL & INSTALLATION

◊ **See Figure 47**

#### 1990–92 Vehicles

1. Raise the front of the vehicle and support safely using jackstands.
2. Remove the front wheels.

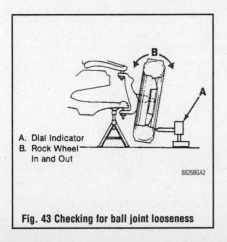

A. Dial Indicator
B. Rock Wheel In and Out

88268GA2

**Fig. 43 Checking for ball joint looseness**

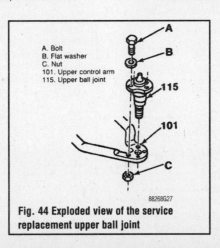

A. Bolt
B. Flat washer
C. Nut
101. Upper control arm
115. Upper ball joint

88268G27

**Fig. 44 Exploded view of the service replacement upper ball joint**

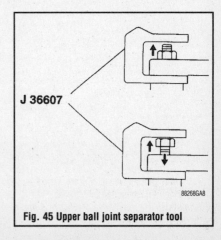

J 36607

88268GA8

**Fig. 45 Upper ball joint separator tool**

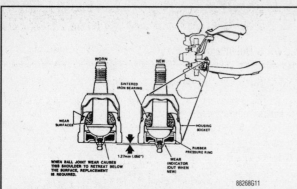

**Fig. 46 The lower ball joint can be inspected for wear visually using the built-in indicator (the grease fitting)**

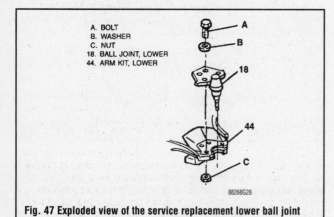

A. BOLT
B. WASHER
C. NUT
18. BALL JOINT, LOWER
44. ARM KIT, LOWER

**Fig. 47 Exploded view of the service replacement lower ball joint**

3. Remove 2 bolts from the front splash shield and pivot it in order to gain access to the tie rod.

4. Remove the inner tie rod end from the relay using a suitable steering linkage puller tool.

5. Remove the halfshaft nut and washer from the hub assembly. In order to accomplish this you will have to keep the halfshaft from turning. A drift can be inserted through the top of the caliper into the brake rotor vanes.

6. Remove the halfshaft assembly as outlined in Section 7 of this manual.

7. Loosen the riveted ball joint from the control arm:
    a. Center punch the bottom of the rivets.
    b. Drill a ⅛ in. (3mm) hole, about ¼ in. (6mm) deep into each rivet.
    c. Then use a ½ in. (13mm) drill bit, to drill off the rivet heads.
    d. Using a pin punch and the hammer, drive out the rivets in order to free the ball joint from the control arm assembly.

8. Remove the ball joint cotter pin.

9. Support the lower control arm with a floor jack.

10. Remove the ball joint nut.

11. Mark the adjustment bolt, then unload the torsion bar using a suitable unloader tool. For details, please refer to the Torsion Bar removal and installation procedure found earlier in this section.

12. Free the ball joint from the knuckle using a ball joint separator tool, such as J–29193 or equivalent, then remove the ball joint.

**To install:**

13. Install the ball joint to the control arm using the bolts, washers and nuts in the service kit. The bolts should be installed from the top, facing downward and the nuts should be placed from underneath the arm. Tighten the nuts to 22 ft. lbs. (30 Nm).

14. Raise or lower the control arm (as necessary) using the floor jack and position the ball joint stud in the knuckle.

➡The lower ball joint retaining nut MUST be tightened with the vehicle suspension at normal ride height. This can either be accomplished by starting the nut now, then installing the remaining components along with the wheels and lowering the vehicle, or by moving jackstands under the ends of the lower control arms and resting the vehicle on them. If the latter solution is tried, make sure the FULL WEIGHT of the vehicle front end is on the suspension.

15. Install the joint-to-control arm nut, then tighten the nut to 92 ft. lbs. (125 Nm) with the suspension at normal ride height and compression.

16. Install a new cotter pin to the castellated nut. Tighten the nut (but no more than an additional ⅙ turn) in order to align the cotter pin. DO NOT loosen the nut from the specified torque.

17. Load the torsion bar using the loading tool J–36202 and by setting the adjustment bolt to the mark made during removal. For details, please refer to the Torsion Bar procedures found earlier in this section.

18. Install the halfshaft assembly as outlined in Section 7.

19. Install the inner tie rod end, tighten the nut to 35 ft. lbs. (47 Nm) and install a new cotter pin, if so equipped.

20. Install the splash shield.

21. If not done already, install the tire and wheel assembly, then remove the jackstands and carefully lower the vehicle.

22. Check and adjust the front end alignment, as necessary.

### 1993–96 Vehicles

1. Raise the front of the vehicle and support safely using jackstands.

2. Remove the front wheels.

3. Remove 2 bolts from the front splash shield and pivot it in order to gain access to the tie rod.

4. Remove the inner tie rod end from the relay using a suitable steering linkage puller tool.

5. Remove the halfshaft nut and washer from the hub assembly. In order to accomplish this you will have to keep the halfshaft from turning. A drift can be inserted through the top of the caliper into the brake rotor vanes.

6. Remove the bolts retaining the hub and bearing assembly.

7. Remove the ball joint cotter pin.

8. Remove the ball joint nut.

9. Support the lower control arm with a floor jack.

10. Mark the adjustment bolt, then unload the torsion bar using a suitable unloader tool. For details, please refer to the Torsion Bar removal and installation procedure found earlier in this section.

11. Free the ball joint from the knuckle using a ball joint separator tool, such as J–35917 or equivalent, then remove the ball joint.

12. Loosen the riveted ball joint from the control arm:
    a. Center punch the bottom of the rivets.
    b. Drill a ⅛ in. (3mm) hole, about ¼ in. (6mm) deep into each rivet.
    c. Then use a ½ in. (13mm) drill bit, to drill off the rivet heads.
    d. Using a pin punch and the hammer, drive out the rivets in order to free the ball joint from the control arm assembly.

13. Remove and discard the worn ball joint.

**To install:**

14. Install the ball joint to the control arm using the bolts, washers and nuts in the service kit. The bolts should be installed from the top, facing downward and the nuts should be placed from underneath the arm. Tighten the nuts to 22 ft. lbs. (30 Nm).

15. Raise or lower the control arm (as necessary) using the floor jack and position the ball joint stud in the knuckle.

➡The lower ball joint retaining nut MUST be tightened with the vehicle suspension at normal ride height. This can either be accomplished by starting the nut now, then installing the remaining components along with the wheels and lowering the vehicle, or by moving jackstands under the ends of the lower control arms and resting the vehicle on them. If the latter solution is tried, make sure the FULL WEIGHT of the vehicle front end is on the suspension.

16. Install the joint-to-control arm nut, then tighten the nut to 95 ft. lbs. (128 Nm) with the suspension at normal ride height and compression.

17. Install a new cotter pin to the castellated nut. Tighten the nut (but no more than an additional ⅙ turn) in order to align the cotter pin. DO NOT loosen the nut from the specified torque.

18. Load the torsion bar using the loading tool J–36202 and by setting the adjustment bolt to the mark made during removal. For details, please refer to the Torsion Bar procedures found earlier in this section.

19. Secure the hub and bearing assembly to the steering knuckle, then tighten the retaining bolts to 66 ft. lbs. (90 Nm).

20. Install the drive axle to the hub and bearing assembly, using the washer and nut. Tighten the nut to 160–200 ft. lbs. (220–270 Nm) for 1993–95 vehicles or to 147 ft. lbs. (200 Nm) for 1996 vehicles.
21. Install the inner tie rod end to the relay rod.
22. Reposition and secure the splash shield.
23. If not done already, install the tire and wheel assembly, then remove the jackstands and carefully lower the vehicle.
24. Check and adjust the front end alignment, as necessary.

## Stabilizer (Sway) Bar

### REMOVAL & INSTALLATION

▶ **See Figure 48**

➡**Keep the right or left suspension components separated and do not interchange.**

1. Raise and support the front of the vehicle on jackstands.
2. If necessary, remove the wheels to provide access (and light).
3. Disconnect the stabilizer bar link spacer nuts, then slowly pull the bolts up, from above the control arms and shaft. As the bolts are removed, the nut, insulators and link spacer will be freed from the bolt. BE SURE to note the locations for each of these components and keep them in order. It is probably best to install them in order over the bolt and put the nut on the end to keep any part from being lost.
4. Remove the stabilizer bar-to-frame clamps. On some models the clamps are retained by bolts only, while other models may use both nuts (studs) and bolts.
5. Remove the stabilizer bar from the vehicle. If necessary, remove the insulators from the shaft.

**To install:**

6. If removed, install the insulators on the bar. The slit on the insulator should be positioned toward the front of the vehicle.
7. Install the stabilizer bar and brackets to the van. Loosely install the clamps to the frame in order to hold the bar in position. In order to align the holes in the control arm and stabilizer bar, it may be necessary to unload the torsion bars. For details, please refer to the Torsion Bar removal and installation procedure found earlier in this section.
8. Tighten the clamp bolts to 12 ft. lbs. (17 Nm) for 1990–92 vehicles or tighten the clamp bolts and nuts (as applicable) to 41 ft. lbs. (55 Nm) for 1993–96 vehicles.
9. Install the spacers, link bolts and nuts. Tighten the nuts to 22 ft. lbs. (30 Nm) for 1990–92 vehicles or to 13 ft. lbs. (150 inch lbs. / 17 Nm) for 1993–96 vehicles.
10. Load the torsion bars, following the Torsion Bar installation procedure earlier in this section.
11. If removed, install the front wheels.
12. Remove the jackstands and carefully lower the vehicle.
13. Check and adjust the "Z" height as outlined in the alignment information later in this section.

## Upper Control Arm

### REMOVAL & INSTALLATION

▶ **See Figure 49**

➡**This procedure requires the use of a ball joint separator tool and NEW upper control arm retaining nuts.**

1. Disconnect the negative battery cable for safety.
2. Raise the vehicle and support with jackstands.
3. Remove the front wheels.
4. If necessary, remove the air cleaner extension.
5. Remove the brake hose from the control arm and tie out of the way.
6. Remove the upper ball joint cotter pin and nut.
7. Disconnect the control arm from the knuckle using a ball joint separator.
8. For 1990–91 vehicles, remove the control arm nuts, bolts and washers.
9. For 1992–96 vehicles, remove the control arm cam hardware (nuts, cams and bolts).
10. Remove the control arm from the vehicle. If replacement is necessary, remove the bushings.

**To install:**

11. If removed, install the new bushings.
12. Install the upper control arm to the frame.
13. Install the upper control arm mounting hardware (bolts and cams or washers, as applicable, along with the NEW nuts). Make sure the bolt threads are opposed inside the bracket. On 1992–96 vehicles, make sure the cam lobes are pointing downward.

➡**The control arm retainers MUST be tightened with the vehicle suspension at normal ride height. This can either be accomplished by starting the nuts now, then installing the remaining components along with the wheels and lowering the vehicle, or by moving jackstands under the ends of the lower control arms and resting the vehicle on them. If the latter solution is tried, make sure the FULL WEIGHT of the vehicle front end is on the suspension.**

14. Tighten the control arm nuts to 88 ft. lbs. (120 Nm) for 1990–92 vehicles, to 105 ft. lbs. (145 Nm) for 1993–95 vehicles or to 91 ft. lbs. (123 Nm) for 1996 vehicles, all with the suspension at normal ride height and compression.

➡**When tightening the control arm nuts, start with the FRONT NUT FIRST.**

15. Install the upper ball joint to the steering knuckle then secure using the nut. Tighten the nut to 95 ft. lbs. (128 Nm) for 1990–95 vehicles or to 66 ft. lbs. (90 Nm) for 1996 vehicles.

➡**The upper ball joint retaining nut MUST be tightened with the vehicle suspension at normal ride height. This can either be accomplished by installing the wheels and lowering the vehicle, or by moving jackstands under the ends of the lower control arms and resting the vehicle on them. If the latter solution is tried, make sure the FULL WEIGHT of the vehicle front end is on the suspension.**

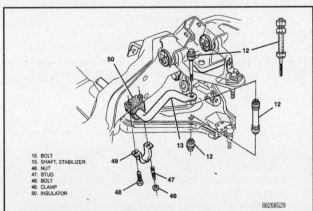

12. BOLT
13. SHAFT, STABILIZER
46. NUT
47. STUD
48. BOLT
49. CLAMP
50. INSULATOR

88268G29

**Fig. 48 Exploded view of the stabilizer bar mounting—1993–96 vehicles (early-models similar)**

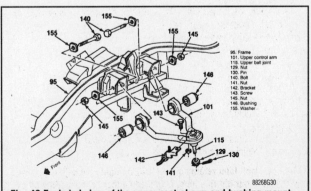

95. Frame
101. Upper control arm
115. Upper ball joint
129. Nut
130. Pin
140. Bolt
141. Nut
142. Bracket
143. Screw
145. Nut
146. Bushing
155. Washer

88268G30

**Fig. 49 Exploded view of the upper control arm and bushing mounting—1990–96 vehicles**

16. Install a new cotter pin to the castellated nut. Tighten the nut (but no more than an additional ⅙ turn) in order to align the cotter pin. DO NOT loosen the nut from the specified torque.

17. Connect the brake hose and bracket to the control arm.

18. If removed, install the air cleaner extension.

19. If not done already, install the tire and wheel assembly, then remove the jackstands and carefully lower the vehicle.

20. Connect the negative battery cable.

## Lower Control Arm

### REMOVAL & INSTALLATION

▶ See Figure 50

➡ **Tools Needed: universal tie rod separator J–24319–01, torsion bar unloader J–36202, lower control arm bushing service kit J–36618 (if the control arm bushing are being replaced) and ball joint C-clamp J–9519–23. Parts Needed: whether or not the control arm or bushing are being replaced, NEW control arm retaining nut should be used once the old ones have been loosened and removed.**

1. Disconnect the negative battery cable for safety.

2. Raise and support the vehicle safely using jackstands.

3. Remove the front wheels.

4. Remove 2 bolts from the front splash shield and pivot it in order to gain access to the tie rod.

5. Disconnect the stabilizer bar from the control arm (keeping all of the link hardware sorted for proper installation). If necessary, completely remove the bar from the vehicle for access.

6. Remove the shock absorber as outlined in this section.

7. Disconnect the inner tie rod from the relay rod using a tie rod separator.

8. Remove the outer halfshaft nut and washer.

9. For 1990–92 vehicles, remove the halfshaft from the hub as outlined in Section 7.

10. For 1993–96 vehicles, remove the bolts from the hub and bearing kit.

11. Unload the torsion bar using the unloading tool J–36202. First, mark the adjuster for installation. For details, please refer to the Torsion Bar removal and installation procedures found earlier in this section.

12. Support the lower control arm with a jackstand, then remove the adjustment arm. Slide the bar forward and the adapter out of the rear to remove the adjusting arm.

13. Remove the lower ball joint cotter pin, nut and ball joint from the control arm using a ball joint separator.

14. Remove the nuts and bolts and lower control arm with the torsion bar assembly. Note the direction which the control arm retaining bolts are facing for installation purposes.

15. If replacing bushings: unbend the crimps (usually front bushing only) using a punch, then remove the bushings using a bushing service kit J–36618–2, J–9519–23, J–36618–4 and J–36618–1.

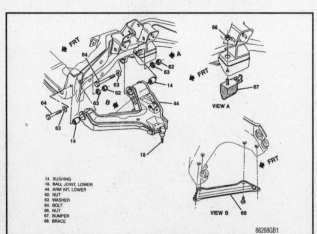

**14.** BUSHING
**18.** BALL JOINT, LOWER
**44.** ARM KIT, LOWER
**62.** NUT
**63.** WASHER
**64.** BOLT
**66.** NUT
**67.** BUMPER
**68.** BRACE

88268GB1

**Fig. 50 Exploded view of the lower control arm assembly mounting—1992–96 vehicles shown, earlier models similar**

**To install:**

16. Install the front bushing using tools J–36618 and J–9519–23. Crimp the bushing in place after installation.

17. Install the rear bushing using J–36618 and J–9519–23.

18. Install the torsion bar to the lower control arm and install the assembly into the vehicle. Position the front leg of the lower control arm into the crossmember before installing the rear leg into the frame bracket.

19. Install the control arm bolts (facing in the direction as noted during removal or shown in the accompanying illustration) with NEW nuts.

➡ **The control arm retainers MUST be tightened with the vehicle suspension at normal ride height. This can either be accomplished by starting the nuts now, then installing the remaining components along with the wheels and lowering the vehicle, or by moving jackstands under the ends of the lower control arms and resting the vehicle on them. If the latter solution is tried, make sure front suspension is at actual ride height compression. If you are unsure, it is best to start the nuts now and tighten them to specification once the vehicle is lowered.**

20. Position the ball joint stud in the knuckle.

21. With the suspension at the correct height, tighten the control arm retaining nuts to 135 ft. lbs. (185 Nm) for 1990–92 vehicles, 125 ft. lbs. (170 Nm) for 1993–95 vehicles or to 98 ft. lbs. (133 Nm) for 1996 vehicles.

➡ **The lower ball joint retaining nut MUST be tightened with the vehicle suspension at normal ride height. This can either be accomplished by starting the nut now, then installing the remaining components along with the wheels and lowering the vehicle, or by moving jackstands under the ends of the lower control arms and resting the vehicle on them. If the latter solution is tried, make sure the FULL WEIGHT of the vehicle front end is on the suspension.**

22. Install the joint-to-control arm nut, then tighten the nut to 92 ft. lbs. (125 Nm) with the suspension at normal ride height and compression.

23. Install a new cotter pin to the castellated nut. Tighten the nut (but no more than an additional ⅙ turn) in order to align the cotter pin. DO NOT loosen the nut from the specified torque.

24. Install the adjuster arm by sliding the adapter forward, over the torsion bar to install the sides of the nut. Load the torsion bar and install the adjuster bolt aligning the installation mark. For more details, please refer to the Torsion Bar procedure found earlier in this section.

25. For 1993–96 vehicles, insert the drive axle through the hub and bearing assembly, then install and tighten the hub and bearing assembly retaining bolts. Install and tighten the drive axle shaft nut and washer. For details, please refer to Section 7 of this manual.

26. For 1990–92 vehicles, install the halfshaft assembly, as outlined in Section 7 of this manual.

27. Install the inner tie rod end to the relay rod.

28. Install the shock absorber.

29. Install the stabilizer bar (if removed completely) and the stabilizer link(s) to the control arm(s).

30. Reposition and secure the splash shield.

31. Install the front wheels and lower the vehicle.

32. Recheck all fasteners for proper torque and installation before road testing.

33. Refill the differential if any fluid was lost.

34. Check and adjust the front end alignment, as necessary.

## Knuckle, Hub and Bearings

### REMOVAL & INSTALLATION

➡ **You will need an approved ball joint separator (NOT A PICKLE FORK), along with any tools which are required for halfshaft removal (as covered in Section 7 of this manual).**

1. Remove ⅔ of the fluid from the brake reservoir.

2. Raise the vehicle and support with jackstands.

3. Remove the front wheels. Place a protective cover over the halfshaft boots.

### ✳✳ CAUTION

**Some brake pads contain asbestos, which has been determined to be a cancer causing agent. Never clean the brake surfaces with compressed air! Avoid inhaling any dust from any brake surface! When cleaning brake surfaces, use a commercially available brake cleaning fluid.**

4. Remove the brake caliper as outlined in Section 9. Support the caliper (with the brake line still attached) aside with a piece of wire.

5. Remove the brake disc, halfshaft nut and washer.

6. Remove the retaining nut, then disconnect the tie rod end from the knuckle using a tie rod separator.

7. Remove the hub and bearing assembly. Most AWD vehicles use a sealed hub and bearing assembly that is bolted to the knuckle. Loose and remove the mounting bolts, then if necessary, use a puller to separate the assembly from the halfshaft.

8. Remove the halfshaft as outlined in Section 7 of this manual.

9. If necessary, remove the splash shield from the knuckle.

10. Support the lower control arm with jackstands.

11. Remove the upper ball joint nut and disconnect the joint from the knuckle using a ball joint separator.

12. Remove the lower ball joint nut and disconnect the joint from the knuckle using a ball joint separator.

13. Remove the knuckle from the vehicle. Check and, if necessary, remove the old seal from the knuckle.

➡The front wheel bearings are a sealed unit that requires no periodic maintenance or repacking. The hub and bearing has to be replaced as a unit if defective.

**To install:**

14. If removed, install a new seal into the knuckle using a seal installer J–36605.

15. Install the knuckle to the upper and lower ball joints. Install and tighten the nuts, but do not tighten fully at this time, they must be tightened with the suspension at normal compression and ride height.

16. If removed, install the splash shield.

17. Install the halfshaft assembly.

➡Obviously, you cannot install the shaft washer and nut until after the hub and bearing assembly has been installed, but it will be easier to keep the shaft from turning if you wait until the brake caliper is installed as well.

18. Install the hub and bearing assembly. Torque the bolts to 66 ft. lbs. (90 Nm).

19. Install the tie rod end to the steering knuckle. Tighten the nut and install a new cotter pin.

20. Install the brake disc and caliper

21. If not done earlier, install the halfshaft washer and nut, then tighten to specification. For details, please refer to Section 7 of this manual.

22. Install the front wheels.

23. Remove the jackstands and carefully lower the vehicle.

24. Properly refill the brake master cylinder. Pump the brake pedal a few times to seat the brake pads before moving the vehicle. DO NOT attempt to move the van until a firm pedal is obtained.

25. If not done earlier, tighten the upper and lower ball joint nuts to specification and install new cotter pins. For details, please refer to the ball joint procedures found earlier in this section.

26. Recheck all fasteners for proper torque and assembly.

27. Check and adjust the front end alignment, as necessary.

## FRONT END ALIGNMENT

### Wheel Alignment

If the tires are worn unevenly, if the vehicle is not stable on the highway or if the handling seems uneven in spirited driving, the wheel alignment should be checked. If an alignment problem is suspected, first check for improper tire inflation and other possible causes. These can be worn suspension or steering components, accident damage or even unmatched tires. If any worn or damaged components are found, they must be replaced before the wheels can be properly aligned. Wheel alignment requires very expensive equipment and involves minute adjustments which must be accurate; it should only be performed by a trained technician. Take your vehicle to a properly equipped shop.

Following is a description of the alignment angles which are adjustable on most vehicles and how they affect vehicle handling. Although these angles can apply to both the front and rear wheels, usually only the front suspension is adjustable.

### CASTER

◆ **See Figure 51**

Looking at a vehicle from the side, caster angle describes the steering axis rather than a wheel angle. The steering knuckle is attached to a control arm or strut at the top and a control arm at the bottom. The wheel pivots around the line between these points to steer the vehicle. When the upper point is tilted back, this is described as positive caster. Having a positive caster tends to make the wheels self-centering, increasing directional stability. Excessive positive caster makes the wheels hard to steer, while an uneven caster will cause a pull to one side. Overloading the vehicle or sagging rear springs will affect caster, as will raising the rear of the vehicle. If the rear of the vehicle is lower than normal, the caster becomes more positive.

### CAMBER

◆ **See Figure 52**

Looking from the front of the vehicle, camber is the inward or outward tilt of the top of wheels. When the tops of the wheels are tilted in, this is negative

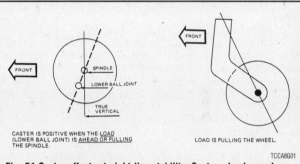

CASTER IS POSITIVE WHEN THE LOAD (LOWER BALL JOINT) IS AHEAD OR PULLING THE SPINDLE.

LOAD IS PULLING THE WHEEL.

TCCA8G01

**Fig. 51 Caster affects straight-line stability. Caster wheels used on shopping carts, for example, employ positive caster**

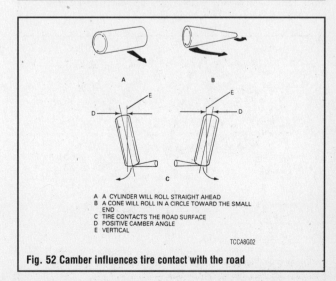

A  A CYLINDER WILL ROLL STRAIGHT AHEAD
B  A CONE WILL ROLL IN A CIRCLE TOWARD THE SMALL END
C  TIRE CONTACTS THE ROAD SURFACE
D  POSITIVE CAMBER ANGLE
E  VERTICAL

TCCA8G02

**Fig. 52 Camber influences tire contact with the road**

camber; if they are tilted out, it is positive. In a turn, a slight amount of negative camber helps maximize contact of the tire with the road. However, too much negative camber compromises straight-line stability, increases bump steer and torque steer.

## TOE

**◗ See Figure 53**

Looking down at the wheels from above the vehicle, toe angle is the distance between the front of the wheels, relative to the distance between the back of the wheels. If the wheels are closer at the front, they are said to be toed-in or to have negative toe. A small amount of negative toe enhances directional stability and provides a smoother ride on the highway.

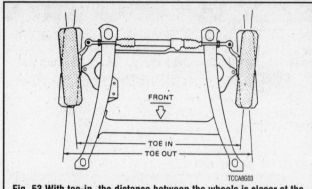

Fig. 53 With toe-in, the distance between the wheels is closer at the front than at the rear

## REAR SUSPENSION

**◗ See Figures 54 and 55**

### Leaf Spring

➡ **In order to maintain proper suspension balance and vehicle handling, leaf springs should be replaced only in axle sets.**

REMOVAL & INSTALLATION

**1985–94 Vehicles**

**◗ See Figures 56 and 57**

➡ **The following procedure requires the use of 2 jackstands and 2 floor jacks.**

1. Raise and support the rear of the vehicle safely using jackstands.

➡ **When supporting the rear of the vehicle, support the axle and the body separately to relieve the load on the rear spring. Because the axle**

Fig. 55 These rear suspension parts are shared by all these vans (springs, shocks and floating rear axle)

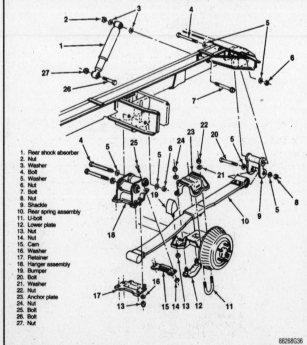

1. Rear shock absorber
2. Nut
3. Washer
4. Bolt
5. Washer
6. Nut
7. Bolt
8. Nut
9. Shackle
10. Rear spring assembly
11. U-bolt
12. Lower plate
13. Nut
14. Nut
15. Cam
16. Washer
17. Retainer
18. Hanger assembly
19. Bumper
20. Bolt
21. Washer
22. Nut
23. Anchor plate
24. Nut
25. Bolt
26. Bolt
27. Nut

Fig. 54 Exploded view of the rear suspension assembly—1985–94 models shown (late-model similar)

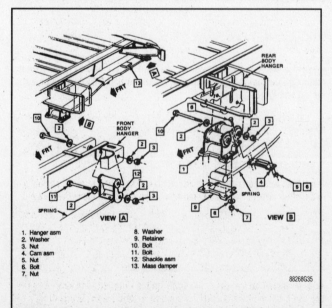

1. Hanger asm
2. Washer
3. Nut
4. Cam asm
5. Nut
6. Bolt
7. Nut
8. Washer
9. Retainer
10. Bolt
11. Bolt
12. Shackle asm
13. Mass damper

Fig. 56 Exploded view of the leaf spring mounting—1985–94 vehicles

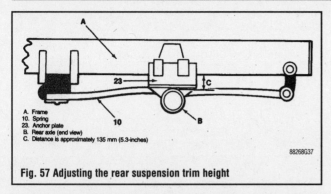

A. Frame
10. Spring
23. Anchor plate
B. Rear axle (end view)
C. Distance is approximately 135 mm (5.3-inches)

88268G37

**Fig. 57 Adjusting the rear suspension trim height**

may need to be raised or lowered, you probably want to support the van using the jackstands and secure the rear axle to the floor jacks.

2. Remove the rear wheel and tire assemblies.
3. Remove the shock absorber.
4. Remove the nuts from the U-bolt and lower plate (attaching the spring to the axle at the center of the spring). If the vehicle is equipped with a stabilizer bar it will be necessary to remove the lower nuts, washers and clamps. If necessary, swing the stabilizer bar down to obtain clearance when lowering the axle assembly.

➡The U-bolts, nuts and washers should be discarded when removed and replaced with new parts upon installation.

5. Remove the U-bolt, lower plate and anchor plate, then CAREFULLY lower the axle away from the spring.

### ✳✳ WARNING

**DO NOT let the axle hang by the brake hose at any point during the procedure or the hose may be severely damaged.**

6. At the rear of the fiberglass spring, loosen (but DO NOT remove) the shackle-to-frame and the shackle-to-spring nuts and bolts.
7. At the front of the fiberglass spring, remove the retainer-to-hanger assembly nuts, washers and the retainer(s).
8. At the rear of the fiberglass spring, remove the spring-to-shackle nut, washer and bolt.
9. Remove the fiberglass spring from the vehicle.
**To install:**
10. Attach the spring to the shackle (DO NOT tighten the nuts/bolts), rotate the shackle forward to clear the rear bumper bracket, position the spring into the slot on the hanger and attach the retainer-to-hanger fasteners.
11. Using the axle supports, raise and position the axle housing under the fiberglass spring. Using NEW U-bolts, nuts and washers, along with the lower plates, connect the axle housing to the spring.

➡When installing the axle housing, be sure the full weight of the axle is resting on the supports; the fiberglass spring MUST NOT support any of the axle weight.

12. Torque the axle U-bolt-to-spring nuts to 48 ft. lbs. (65 Nm) and the axle lower plate-to-spring nuts to 41 ft. lbs. (55 Nm).
13. To adjust the rear suspension trim height, perform the following:
   a. Raise the axle/spring assembly until the clearance between the top of the axle and the bottom of the frame is 5.3–6.1 in. (135–155mm).

➡If the axle supports are not in complete contact with the axle housing and resting firmly on the floor, damage to the spring and axle could result.

   b. Tighten the shackle retainers to 81 ft. lbs. (110 Nm) for 1985–89 vehicles. For 1990–94 vehicles tighten the shackle-to-frame bolt to 81 ft. lbs. (110 Nm) and the shackle-to-spring bolt to 103 ft. lbs. (140 Nm).
   c. Tighten the retainer-to-hanger assembly nuts to 28 ft. lbs. (38 Nm).
14. Install the shock absorber to the axle housing.

➡When installing the shock absorber on the right side, be sure to position the parking brake bracket on the bolt before the nut is installed.

15. Install the wheel assemblies, then remove the jackstands and carefully lower the vehicle.

### 1995–96 Vehicles

♦ See Figures 58 and 59

➡The following procedure requires the use of 2 jackstands and 2 floor jacks.

1. Raise and support the rear of the vehicle safely using jackstands.

➡When supporting the rear of the vehicle, support the axle and the body separately to relieve the load on the rear spring. Because the axle may need to be raised or lowered, you probably want to support the van using the jackstands and secure the rear axle to the floor jacks.

2. Remove the rear wheel and tire assemblies.
3. For 1995 vehicles, remove the shock absorber.
4. On 1996 vehicles, if necessary for access to the lower spring plate front nut, remove the axle bumper and retainer.
5. Remove the nuts securing the U-bolt and lower plate (attaching the spring to the axle at the center of the spring). If the vehicle is equipped with a stabilizer bar it will be necessary to remove the lower nuts, washers and clamps, then swing the stabilizer bar down to obtain clearance when lowering the axle assembly.
6. Remove the U-bolt, lower plate and anchor plate, then CAREFULLY lower the axle away from the spring.

### ✳✳ WARNING

**DO NOT let the axle hang by the brake hose at any point during the procedure or the hose may be severely damaged.**

7. At the rear of the fiberglass spring, remove the shackle nut and bolt, then disengage the spring from the shackle.
8. At the front of the fiberglass spring, remove the hanger nut and bolt, then remove the spring from the hanger and from the vehicle.

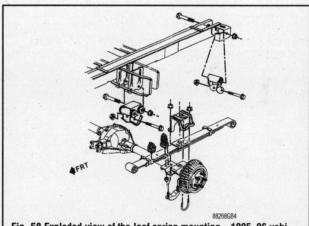

88268GB4

**Fig. 58 Exploded view of the leaf spring mounting—1995–96 vehicles**

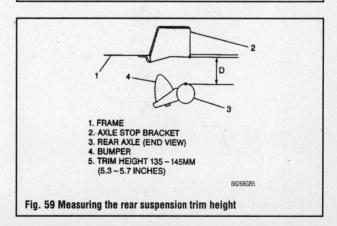

1. FRAME
2. AXLE STOP BRACKET
3. REAR AXLE (END VIEW)
4. BUMPER
5. TRIM HEIGHT 135 – 145MM
   (5.3 – 5.7 INCHES)

88268GB5

**Fig. 59 Measuring the rear suspension trim height**

**To install:**

➡**To assure proper seating and attachment of the anchor plate over the spring end and the axle, the installation procedure must be followed closely.**

9. Position the spring to the hanger, then loosely install the retaining nut and bolt.

10. Position the spring to the shackle, then loosely install the retaining nut and bolt.

11. CAREFULLY raise the axle until it contacts the spring.

12. Apply rubber lubricant to the isolator on the spring in order to aid installation of the anchor plate, then install the anchor plate to the top of the spring.

13. Install the lower plate and U-bolt around the axle and through the anchor plate. If your van is equipped with a stabilizer bar it will be necessary to install the clamps, washers and nuts.

14. Install the nuts to the lower plate and U-bolts. Starting with the inner (lower plate side) nuts, gradually tighten the 4 nuts so the anchor plate moves uniformly, side-to-side, over the spring. Tighten the nuts to 52 ft. lbs. (70 Nm) for 1995 vehicles or to 41 ft. lbs. (56 Nm) for 1996 vehicles.

➡**After tightening the fasteners to specification, there should be no gap between the anchor plate, axle tube bracket and the lower plate. A metal-to-metal contact should exist.**

15. Raise the axle so the vehicle's weight is supported by the spring. The rear suspension height should be approximately 5.3–5.7 in. (135–145mm). With the suspension at normal ride height, tighten the shackle and hanger retainers to 81 ft. lbs. (110 Nm) for 1995 vehicles or to 74 ft. lbs. (100 Nm) for 1996 vehicles.

16. If removed on 1996 vehicles, install the axle bumper and tighten the nut to 33 ft. lbs. (45 Nm).

17. For 1995 vehicles, install the shock absorber.

18. Install the tire and wheel assemblies.

19. Remove the jackstands and carefully lower the vehicle.

## Shock Absorbers

### TESTING

Visually inspect the shock absorber. If there is evidence of leakage and the shock absorber is covered with oil, the shock is defective and should be replaced.

If there is no sign of excessive leakage (a small amount of weeping is normal) bounce the van at one corner by pressing down on the bumper and releasing it. When you have the van bouncing as much as you can, release the bumper. The van should stop bouncing after the first rebound. If the bouncing continues past the center point of the bounce more than once, the shock absorbers are worn and should be replaced.

### REMOVAL & INSTALLATION

◆ **See Figures 60 thru 65**

➡**In order to maintain proper suspension balance and vehicle handling, shock absorbers should only be replaced in axle sets.**

The following procedure requires the use of a lifting device and 2 jackstands.

1. Raise and support the rear of the vehicle using jackstands. Installation may be easier if you position the jackstands under the frame and support the axle housing independently using a floor jack. The jack can then be raised or lowered to help align the shock absorber with the mounts.

2. Remove the shock absorber-to-frame retainers at the top of the shock assembly.

3. Remove the shock absorber-to-axle housing retainers at the bottom of the assembly, then remove the shock absorber from the vehicle.

➡**When removing the shock absorber-to-axle housing bolt on the right shock, the parking brake bracket must be removed after the nut.**

4. Inspect and test the shock absorber, then replace as necessary.

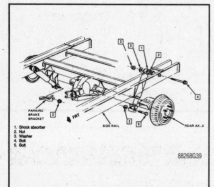
Fig. 60 Exploded view of the rear shock mounting

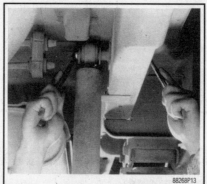
Fig. 61 Loosen and remove the shock absorber upper retaining nut . . .

Fig. 62 . . . then remove the lower retainers

Fig. 63 On the right shock, the parking brake cable bracket must be removed and repositioned

Fig. 64 Lift the shock out of the lower mounting bracket, then . . .

Fig. 65 . . . remove it from the upper mounting stud and remove it from the vehicle

**To install:**

5. Connect the shock absorber-to-frame nut/bolt (DO NOT tighten) and the shock absorber-to-axle nut/bolt.

➡**If installing the shock absorber onto the right side, be sure to install the parking brake bracket.**

6. Tighten the upper and lower shock absorber retainers to 75 ft. lbs. (102 Nm).
7. Remove the jackstands and carefully lower the vehicle.

## Stabilizer (Sway) Bar

### REMOVAL & INSTALLATION

#### 1985–93 Vehicles

▶ **See Figure 66**

1. Raise the vehicle and support with jackstands.
2. Remove the bolts and washers from the link brackets.
3. Remove the nuts, washers and clamps from the anchor block studs.
4. Remove the insulator from the stabilizer bar.
5. Remove the upper link nuts, washers and bolts from the link assembly.
6. Remove the link bracket.
7. Remove the link nuts, washers and bolts. Pry open the lower link to obtain clearance from the link insulator.
8. Remove the link insulator from the stabilizer bar.

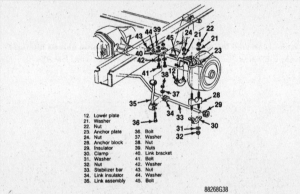

| | | | |
|---|---|---|---|
| 12. | Lower plate | 36. | Bolt |
| 21. | Washer | 37. | Washer |
| 22. | Nut | 38. | Nut |
| 23. | Anchor plate | 39. | Nuts |
| 24. | Nut | 40. | Link bracket |
| 28. | Anchor block | 41. | Bolt |
| 29. | Insulator | 42. | Washer |
| 30. | Clamp | 43. | Nut |
| 31. | Washer | 44. | Washer |
| 32. | Nut | 45. | Bolt |
| 33. | Stabilizer bar | | |
| 34. | Link insulator | | |
| 35. | Link assembly | | |

88268G38

**Fig. 66 Exploded view of the rear stabilizer bar mounting—1985–93 vehicles**

9. Installation is the reverse of the removal procedure. Tighten the retainers to the following specifications:
   - Link bracket bolts: 25 ft. lbs. (35 Nm)
   - Lower link bolts: 12 ft. lbs. (17 Nm)
   - Upper link bolts: 33 ft. lbs. (45 Nm)
   - Cap nuts: 38 ft. lbs. (52 Nm)
10. Remove the jackstands, then carefully lower and road test the vehicle.

#### 1994–96 Vehicles

▶ **See Figure 67**

1. Raise and support the rear of the vehicle safely using jackstands.
2. Remove the top bolts from the stabilizer links.
3. Remove the stabilizer links from the frame brackets.
4. Remove the nuts from the stabilizer clamps, then remove the clamps. The stabilizer bar assembly will be free from the vehicle at this point.
5. If necessary for component replacement:
   a. Remove the insulator from the stabilizer bar.
   b. Remove the lower link nuts, washers and bolts from the link assembly.
   c. Pry open the lower link to obtain clearance from the link insulator, then remove the link from the insulator and stabilizer assembly.
   d. Remove the link insulator from the stabilizer bar.
6. Installation is the reverse of the removal procedure. Tighten the retainers to the following specifications:
   - Lower link bolts: 14 ft. lbs. (18 Nm)
   - Upper link bolts: 33 ft. lbs. (45 Nm)
   - Clamp nuts (1994–95): 52 ft. lbs. (70 Nm)
   - Clamp nuts (1996): 44 ft. lbs. (60 Nm)
7. Remove the jackstands, then carefully lower and road test the vehicle.

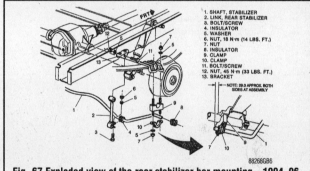

1. SHAFT, STABILIZER
2. LINK, REAR STABILIZER
3. BOLT/SCREW
4. INSULATOR
5. WASHER
6. NUT, 18 N·m (14 LBS. FT.)
7. NUT
8. INSULATOR
9. CLAMP
10. CLAMP
11. BOLT/SCREW
12. NUT, 45 N·m (33 LBS. FT.)
13. BRACKET

NOTE: 29.0 APPROX. BOTH SIDES AT ASSEMBLY

88268GB6

**Fig. 67 Exploded view of the rear stabilizer bar mounting—1994–96 vehicles**

## STEERING

On late-model vehicles equipped with a driver's side Supplemental Inflatable Restraint (SIR) or Air Bag system it is EXTREMELY IMPORTANT that you follow correct servicing procedures in order to prevent serious personal injury that could result from an accidental deployment, or worse that could result if a repair prevents the system from operating properly. The air bag system should be properly disarmed BEFORE ANY PROCEDURE ON OR NEAR THE STEERING COLUMN. Also, after repairs are performed, the system should be properly armed and the system trouble indicator light should go out, indicating proper system operation. IF THE LIGHT REMAINS ON, HAVE THE VEHICLE TOWED TO A REPUTABLE REPAIR FACILITY.

## Steering Wheel

### REMOVAL & INSTALLATION

#### Steering Column Without Air Bag

▶ **See Figure 68**

➡**The following procedure requires the use of the GM Steering Wheel Puller tool No. J–1859–03 or equivalent.**

1. Disconnect the negative battery cable.
2. Rotate the steering wheel so it is in the horizontal position.
3. If equipped with a horn cap, pry the cap from the center of the steering wheel. If equipped with a steering wheel shroud, remove the screw(s) from the rear of the steering wheel and remove the shroud.

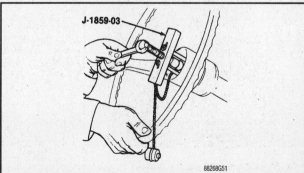

J-1859-03

88268G51

**Fig. 68 Remove the steering wheel from the column using a suitable threaded puller**

➡If the horn cap or shroud is equipped with an electrical connector, disengage it.

4. Remove the steering wheel-to-steering shaft retainer (snapring) and nut.

➡Since the steering column is designed to collapse upon impact, it is recommended NEVER to hammer on it.

5. Matchmark the relationship of the steering wheel to the steering shaft in order to assure proper alignment upon installation.

6. Using the GM Steering Wheel Puller tool No. J–1859–03 or equivalent, press the steering wheel from the steering column.

➡Before installing the steering wheel, be sure the combination control switch is in the Neutral position. DO NOT misalign the steering wheel more than 1 in. (25mm) from the vertical centerline.

**To install:**

7. Install the steering wheel by aligning the matchmarks and carefully pushing it onto the steering shaft splines.

8. Install the steering wheel-to-steering shaft nut and tighten to 30 ft. lbs. (41 Nm).

9. Connect the horn wire, then install the horn pad or shroud, as applicable.

10. Connect the negative battery cable and check operation.

### Steering Column With Air Bag

#### EXCEPT 1996 MODELS

▶ **See Figure 69**

1. Properly disable the SIR (air bag) system, then disconnect the negative battery cable. For details on disabling the air bag system, please refer to Section 6 of this manual.

2. Remove the SIR inflator module from the steering wheel:

a. Remove the screws from the back of the steering wheel.

b. Carefully lift the module away from the wheel, then push down and twist the horn contact lead to the right in order to remove it from the cam tower.

c. Remove the Connector Position Assurance (CPA) retainer, then disengage the SIR wiring connector from the inflator module.

d. Carefully remove the inflator module and position it aside in a safe place. MAKE SURE THE MODULE IS FACING UPWARD to leave space for air bag inflation should the unlikely event of an accidental deployment occur.

➡ALWAYS be very cautious when handling a live (undeployed) SIR module. Always leave room for air bag expansion should a deployment occur. This means it should always be placed face up, without ANYTHING on top of it. You should also carry it facing away from you for the same reason.

3. Loosen and remove the steering wheel retaining nut.

4. If applicable, disengage the horn lead assembly.

5. Matchmark the relationship of the wheel to the steering shaft. This is necessary to assure proper alignment upon installation.

6. Remove the wheel from the shaft using a suitable threaded steering wheel puller such as J–1859–03 or equivalent.

**To install:**

7. Make sure the turn signal lever is in the neutral (no signal) position before attempting to install the steering wheel.

8. Slide the wheel onto the shaft splines while aligning the matchmarks made earlier. DO NOT misalign the wheel more than 1 in. (25mm) from the horizontal centerline.

9. If applicable, engage the horn lead assembly.

10. Install the steering wheel retaining nut and tighten to 30 ft. lbs. (40 Nm).

11. Install the SIR inflator module

a. Position the module at the steering wheel, then engage the SIR connector and install the CPA retainer.

b. Position the SIR wires into the channel in the lower right portion of the steering wheel.

c. Route the horn contact lead through the wheel and into the cam tower. Press the lead into the tower and twist to the right (to the locked position).

d. Install the module to the steering wheel (starting with the top) while making sure NONE of the wires are pinched.

e. Install the retaining screws through the back of the module assembly and tighten to 70 inch lbs. (8 Nm).

12. Make sure the ignition is **OFF**, then connect the negative battery cable.

13. Properly enable the SIR system.

#### 1996 MODELS

▶ **See Figures 70 and 71**

1. Properly disable the SIR (air bag) system, then disconnect the negative battery cable. For details on disabling the air bag system, please refer to Section 6 of this manual.

2. Remove the SIR inflator module from the steering wheel:

a. Turn the steering wheel 90 degrees to access the rear shroud hole for the inflator module.

b. Carefully insert a screwdriver and push the leaf spring to release the pin.

c. Turn the wheel 180 degrees to access the remaining rear shroud holes.

d. Again, insert the screwdriver and push the leaf spring to release the pin.

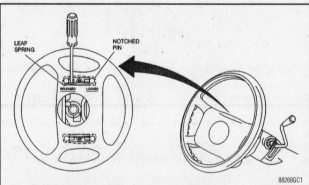

**Fig. 70 The inflator module is secured to the steering wheel using leaf springs and notched pins—1996 models**

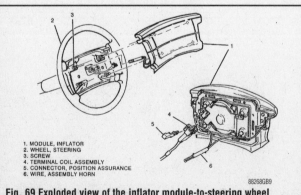

1. MODULE, INFLATOR
2. WHEEL, STEERING
3. SCREW
4. TERMINAL COIL ASSEMBLY
5. CONNECTOR, POSITION ASSURANCE
6. WIRE, ASSEMBLY HORN

**Fig. 69 Exploded view of the inflator module-to-steering wheel mounting—except 1996 models**

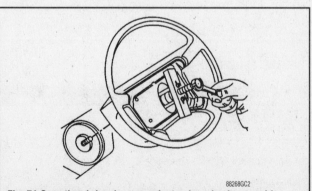

**Fig. 71 Once the air bag is removed, steering wheel removal is much the same as it is for non-air bag models**

e. Tilt the module rearward from the top in order to access the wiring.

f. Disconnect the lead wire from the clip on the inflator module and from the clip on the steering wheel.

g. Remove the Connector Position Assurance (CPA) retainer from the module connector, then disengage the wiring.

h. Carefully remove the inflator module and position it aside in a safe place. MAKE SURE THE MODULE IS FACING UPWARD to leave space for air bag inflation should the unlikely event of an accidental deployment occur.

➠**ALWAYS be very cautious when handling a live (undeployed) SIR module. Always leave room for air bag expansion should a deployment occur. This means it should always be placed face up, without ANY-THING on top of it. You should also carry it facing away from you for the same reason.**

3. Loosen and remove the steering wheel retaining nut.

4. If applicable, remove the horn plunger contact.

5. Matchmark the relationship of the wheel to the steering shaft. This is necessary to assure proper alignment upon installation.

6. Remove the wheel from the shaft using a suitable threaded steering wheel puller such as J–1859–A or equivalent.

**To install:**

7. Slide the wheel onto the shaft splines while aligning the matchmarks made earlier. DO NOT misalign the wheel more than 1 in. (25mm) from the horizontal centerline.

8. If applicable, install the horn plunger contact.

9. Install the steering wheel retaining nut and tighten to 30 ft. lbs. (40 Nm).

10. Install the SIR inflator module

a. Position the module at the steering wheel, then engage the SIR connector and install the CPA retainer.

b. Secure the SIR lead wire to the clips on the steering wheel and the module.

c. Install the module to the steering wheel by pressing it firmly into the wheel until all 4 notched pins are engaged in the leaf springs. DO NOT pinch the wires during this.

11. Make sure the ignition is **OFF**, then connect the negative battery cable.

12. Properly enable the SIR system.

## Turn Signal Switch

➠**When servicing any components on the steering column, should any fasteners require replacement, be sure to use only nuts and bolts of the same size and grade as the original fasteners. Using screws that are too long could prevent the column from collapsing during a collision.**

### REMOVAL & INSTALLATION

#### Steering Column Without Air Bag

◆ **See Figures 72, 73 and 74**

➠**The following procedure requires the use of the GM Lock Plate Compressor tool No. J–23653 or equivalent.**

1. Disconnect the negative battery cable.

2. Refer to the Steering Wheel, Removal and Installation procedures in this section and remove the steering wheel.

3. If necessary, remove the steering column-to-lower instrument panel cover. Disengage the electrical harness connector from the steering column jacket (under the dash).

4. Using a small prytool, insert into the slots between the steering shaft lock plate cover and the steering column housing, then pry upward to remove the cover from the lock plate.

5. Using the GM Lock Plate Compressor tool No. J–23653–A or equivalent, screw the center shaft onto the steering shaft (as far as it will go), then screw the center post nut clockwise until the lock plate is compressed.

6. Using a small prybar, carefully pry the snapring from the steering shaft slot.

➠**If the steering column is being disassembled on a bench, the steering shaft will slide out of the mast jacket when the snapring is removed.**

7. Remove the GM Lock Plate Compressor tool No. J–23653 or equivalent, and the lock plate.

8. Remove the multi-function lever-to-switch screw and the lever.

9. To remove the hazard warning switch, press the knob inward and unscrew it.

10. Remove the turn signal switch assembly-to-steering column screws.

11. Lift the turn signal switch assembly from the steering column, then slide the electrical connector through the column housing and the protector.

➠**If the steering column is the tilting type, position the steering housing into the Low position.**

12. To remove the harness cover, pull it toward the lower end of the column; be careful not to damage the wires.

13. To remove the wire protector, grab the protector's tab with a pair of pliers, then pull the protector downward, out of the steering column.

➠**When assembling the steering column, use only fasteners of the correct length; overlength fasteners could prevent a portion of the assembly from compressing under impact.**

**To install:**

14. Install the turn signal switch electrical connector:

a. On the non-tilt columns, be sure the electrical connector is on the protector, then feed it and the cover down through the housing and under the mounting bracket.

b. On the tilt columns, feed the electrical connector down through the housing and under the mounting bracket, then install the cover onto the housing.

15. Install the electrical connector to the clip on the jacket, the turn signal switch-to-steering column mounting screws, the lower instrument trim panel, the turn signal lever/screws and the hazard warning knob.

➠**With the multi-function lever installed, place it into the Neutral position. With the hazard warning knob installed, pull it Outward.**

16. Onto the upper end of the steering shaft, install the washer, the upper bearing preload spring, the canceling cam, the lock plate and a new retaining ring (snapring). Using the GM Lock Plate Compressor tool No. J–23653 or

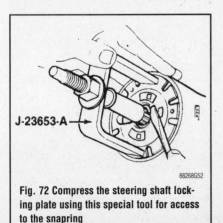

**Fig. 72 Compress the steering shaft locking plate using this special tool for access to the snapring**

**Fig. 73 Removing the turn signal wiring harness protective cover from the column**

**Fig. 74 Removing the turn signal switch from the column**

equivalent, compress the lock plate and slide the new retaining ring into the steering shaft groove.

17. Torque the multi-function switch-to-steering column screws to 35 inch lbs. (4 Nm) and the steering wheel nut to 30 ft. lbs. (41 Nm).

18. Connect the negative battery cable and check operation.

### Steering Column With Air Bag

#### EXCEPT 1996 MODELS

♦ See Figures 75, 76, 77 and 78

1. Properly disable the SIR (air bag) system, then disconnect the negative battery cable. For details on disabling the air bag system, please refer to Section 6 of this manual.

2. Matchmark and remove the steering wheel.

3. Remove the SIR coil assembly retaining ring, then remove the coil assembly and allow it to hang freely from the wiring. Remove the wave washer.

4. Push downward on the shaft lock assembly until the snapring is exposed using the shaft lock compressor tool.

5. Remove the shaft lock retaining snapring, then carefully release the tool and remove the shaft lock from the column.

6. Remove the turn signal canceling cam assembly.

7. Remove the upper bearing spring, inner race seat and inner race.

8. Move the turn signal lever upward to the "Right Turn" position.

9. Remove the access cap and disengage the multi-function lever harness connector, then grasp the lever and pull it from the column.

10. Loosen and remove the hazard knob retaining screw, then remove the screw, button, spring and knob.

11. Remove the screw and the switch actuator arm.

12. Remove the turn signal switch retaining screws, then pull the switch forward and allow it to hang from the wires. If the switch is only being removed for access to other components, this may be sufficient.

13. If the switch is to be replaced, cut the wires near the top of the switch and discard the switch. Before cutting the wires, verify that the wire color codes are the same. Secure the connector of the new switch to the old wires, and pull the new harness down through the steering column while removing the old switch.

14. If the original switch is to be reused, attach a piece of wire or string around the connector and pull the harness up through the column, while pulling the string up through the column and leaving the string or wire in position to help with reinstallation later.

15. After freeing the switch wiring protector from its mounting, pull the turn signal switch straight up and remove the switch, switch harness, and the connector from the column.

➡On some vehicles access to the connector may be difficult. If necessary, remove the column support bracket assembly and properly support the column, and/or remove the wiring protectors.

#### To install:

16. Install the switch and wiring harness to the vehicle. If the switch was completely removed, use the length of mechanic's wire or string to pull the switch harness through the column, then engage the connector.

➡If the column support bracket or wiring protectors were removed, install them before proceeding.

17. Position the switch in the column and secure using the retaining screws.

18. Install the switch actuator arm and retaining screw.

19. Install the hazard knob assembly, then install the multi-function lever.

20. Install the inner race, upper bearing race seat and upper bearing spring.

21. Lubricate the turn signal canceling cam using a suitable synthetic grease (usually included in the service kit), then install the cam assembly.

22. Position the shaft lock and a new snapring, then use the lock compressor to hold the lock down while seating the new snapring. Make sure the ring is firmly seated in the groove, then carefully release the tool.

➡The coil assembly will become uncentered if the steering column is separated from the steering gear and allowed to rotate or if the centering spring is pushed down, letting the hub rotate while the coils assembly is removed from the steering column.

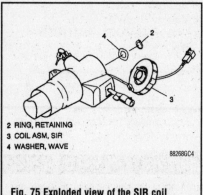

2 RING, RETAINING
3 COIL ASM, SIR
4 WASHER, WAVE

88268GC4

**Fig. 75 Exploded view of the SIR coil mounting in the upper steering column**

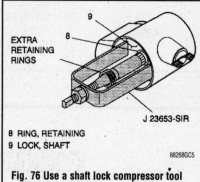

EXTRA RETAINING RINGS

J 23653-SIR

8 RING, RETAINING
9 LOCK, SHAFT

88268GC5

**Fig. 76 Use a shaft lock compressor tool to expose the shaft lock snapring (retaining ring)**

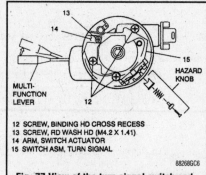

MULTI-FUNCTION LEVER

HAZARD KNOB

12 SCREW, BINDING HD CROSS RECESS
13 SCREW, RD WASH HD (M4.2 X 1.41)
14 ARM, SWITCH ACTUATOR
15 SWITCH ASM, TURN SIGNAL

88268GC6

**Fig. 77 View of the turn signal switch and related component mounting in the upper steering column**

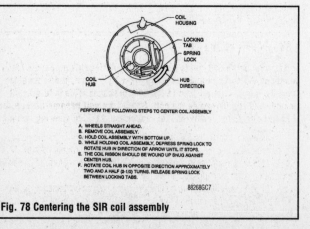

COIL HOUSING

LOCKING TAB
SPRING LOCK

COIL HUB

HUB DIRECTION

PERFORM THE FOLLOWING STEPS TO CENTER COIL ASSEMBLY

A. WHEELS STRAIGHT AHEAD.
B. REMOVE COIL ASSEMBLY.
C. HOLD COIL ASSEMBLY WITH BOTTOM UP.
D. WHILE HOLDING COIL ASSEMBLY, DEPRESS SPRING LOCK TO ROTATE HUB IN DIRECTION OF ARROW UNTIL IT STOPS.
E. THE COIL RIBBON SHOULD BE WOUND UP SNUG AGAINST CENTER HUB.
F. ROTATE COIL HUB IN OPPOSITE DIRECTION APPROXIMATELY TWO AND A HALF (2-1/2) TURNS. RELEASE SPRING LOCK BETWEEN LOCKING TABS.

88268GC7

**Fig. 78 Centering the SIR coil assembly**

23. Make sure the coil is centered, then install the wave washer, followed by the coil and the retaining ring. The coil ring must be firmly seated in the shaft groove.

24. Align and install the steering wheel.

25. Make sure the ignition is **OFF**, then connect the negative battery cable.

26. Properly enable the SIR system.

#### 1996 MODELS

Instead of the long time used steering column found on most older GM vehicles the 1996 Astro and Safari vans are equipped with a new column that uses a multi-function combination switch mounted at the head of the column (below the steering wheel) and an upper/lower shroud assembly. The combination switch performs such functions as the wiper switch and the turn signal switch along with any other duties of the multi-function lever. For removal or installation of the multi-function switch assembly, please refer to the Combination Switch procedure found in this section.

## Windshield Wiper Switch

➡When servicing any components on the steering column, should any fasteners require replacement, be sure to use only nuts and bolts of the same size and grade as the original fasteners. Using screws that are too long could prevent the column from collapsing during a collision.

### REMOVAL & INSTALLATION

#### Steering Column Without Air Bag

1. Disconnect the negative battery cable.
2. Matchmark and remove the steering wheel.
3. If necessary for access, remove the steering column.

➡Although in some cases the components necessary to remove the wiper switch may be removed with the steering column installed in the vehicle, it is usually necessary to at least unbolt, lower and support the column.

4. Remove the turn signal switch.
5. Remove the lock cylinder assembly.
6. Remove the lock housing cover screws.
7. If applicable, remove the tilt lever.
8. Remove the lock housing cover assembly.
9. Except for vehicles with a floor shift, remove the column housing cover end cap (in some cases, this should be done along with the switch rod actuator), then remove the switch actuator pivot pin.
10. If necessary, unbolt the steering column support bracket from the column.
11. Disengage the wiper switch (pivot and pulse switch) connector from the wiring harness, then remove the wiring protector.
12. Attach a length of mechanic's wire to the switch connector, then carefully pull the harness through the column (from the top), leaving the wire in the column for assembly.
13. Remove the switch.

**To install:**

14. Install the switch to the lock housing cover assembly, then install the pivot pin.
15. Except for vehicles equipped with floor shift:
    a. Carefully pull the switch harness through the steering column using the mechanic's wire, then engage the connector to the harness.
    b. If applicable, install the column support bracket.
    c. Lubricate the dimmer switch rod actuator using lithium grease, then if removed, install the actuator to the column housing cover end cap.
    d. Install the end cap to the lock housing cover assembly. Make sure the bottom edge of the dimmer switch rod actuator is resting on the bend in the dimmer switch rod.
    e. Install the lock housing cover assembly, then secure using the retaining screws. Tighten the screw in the 12 o'clock position first, then the 8 o'clock position next and finally the screw in the 3 o'clock position.
16. On vehicles equipped with a floor shift:
    a. Install the gearshift bowl shroud to the floor shift lever bowl.
    b. Install the bowl with shroud to the steering column assembly, then secure using the 3 cross recess screws.
    c. Using the mechanic's wire, gently pull the wiper and turn signal switch wiring through the column.
    d. Install the upper bearing retainer, then install the lock housing cover assembly to the jacket. Finger-tighten the cover screws in a clockwise pattern, then tighten the screws to 47 inch lbs. (5.3 Nm).
    e. Install the wiring protectors and the support bracket.
17. Install the lock cylinder assembly.
18. Install the turn signal switch.
19. If removed or lowered, position and secure the steering column.
20. Align and install the steering wheel.
21. Connect the negative battery cable.

#### Steering Column With Air Bag

##### EXCEPT 1996 MODELS

1. Properly disable the SIR (air bag) system, then disconnect the negative battery cable. For details on disabling the air bag system, please refer to Section 6 of this manual.

2. Matchmark and remove the steering wheel.

➡Although in some cases the components necessary to remove the wiper switch may be removed with the steering column installed in the vehicle, it is usually necessary to at least unbolt, lower and support the column.

3. Remove the turn signal switch.
4. Remove the lock cylinder assembly.
5. Remove the lock housing cover screws.
6. If applicable, remove the tilt lever.
7. Remove the lock housing cover assembly.
8. Remove the column housing cover end cap (in some cases, this should be done along with the switch rod actuator), then remove the switch actuator pivot pin.
9. If necessary, unbolt the steering column support bracket from the column.
10. Disengage the wiper switch (pivot and pulse switch) connector from the wiring harness, then remove the wiring protector.
11. Attach a length of mechanic's wire to the switch connector, then carefully pull the harness through the column (from the top), leaving the wire in the column for assembly.
12. Remove the switch.

**To install:**

13. Install the switch to the lock housing cover assembly, then install the pivot pin.
14. Carefully pull the switch harness through the steering column using the mechanic's wire, then engage the connector to the harness.
15. If applicable, install the column support bracket.
16. Lubricate the dimmer switch rod actuator using lithium grease, then if removed, install the actuator to the column housing cover end cap.
17. Install the end cap to the lock housing cover assembly. Make sure the bottom edge of the dimmer switch rod actuator is resting on the bend in the dimmer switch rod.
18. Install the lock housing cover assembly, then secure using the retaining screws. Tighten the screw in the 12 o'clock position first, then the 8 o'clock position next and finally the screw in the 3 o'clock position.
19. Install the lock cylinder assembly.
20. Install the turn signal switch.
21. If removed or lowered, position and secure the steering column.
22. Align and install the steering wheel.
23. Make sure the ignition is **OFF**, then connect the negative battery cable.
24. Properly enable the SIR system.

##### 1996 MODELS

These vehicles use a combination switch assembly instead of a separate switch mounted in the column. For more details, please refer to the Combination Switch procedure found later in this section.

## Combination Switch

➡When servicing any components on the steering column, should any fasteners require replacement, be sure to use only nuts and bolts of the same size and grade as the original fasteners. Using screws that are too long could prevent the column from collapsing during a collision.

### REMOVAL & INSTALLATION

◆ See Figures 79 and 80

➡Removal of the SIR coil is not necessary during this procedure. Avoid removing the coil and make sure the steering column, if disconnected from the gear, is not allowed to rotate excessively. This is to prevent uncentering and damaging the coil. Should the coil become uncentered, it must be removed, centered and repositioned on the steering column.

1. Properly disable the SIR (air bag) system, then disconnect the negative battery cable. For details on disabling the air bag system, please refer to
2. Matchmark and remove the steering wheel from the column. For details, please refer to the procedure earlier in this section.
3. Either lower the steering column from the instrument panel for access or unbolt and remove the column. If the column is removed, prevent it from rotating so the SIR coil does not become uncentered.

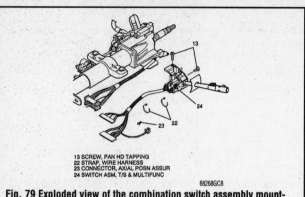

13 SCREW, PAN HD TAPPING
22 STRAP, WIRE HARNESS
23 CONNECTOR, AXIAL POSN ASSUR
24 SWITCH ASM, T/S & MULTIFUNC

88268GC8

**Fig. 79 Exploded view of the combination switch assembly mounting—1996 vehicles only**

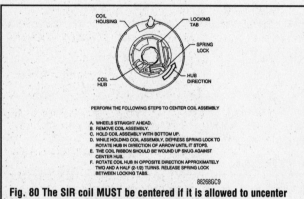

PERFORM THE FOLLOWING STEPS TO CENTER COIL ASSEMBLY

A. WHEELS STRAIGHT AHEAD.
B. REMOVE COIL ASSEMBLY.
C. HOLD COIL ASSEMBLY WITH BOTTOM UP.
D. WHILE HOLDING COIL ASSEMBLY, DEPRESS SPRING LOCK TO ROTATE HUB IN DIRECTION OF ARROW UNTIL IT STOPS.
E. THE COIL RIBBON SHOULD BE WOUND UP SNUG AGAINST CENTER HUB.
F. ROTATE COIL HUB IN OPPOSITE DIRECTION APPROXIMATELY TWO AND A HALF (2-1/2) TURNS. RELEASE SPRING LOCK BETWEEN LOCKING TABS.

88268GC9

**Fig. 80 The SIR coil MUST be centered if it is allowed to uncenter (unwind) during steering column service**

4. If applicable, remove the tilt lever by pulling outward.

5. Remove the 2 Torx screws or pan head tapping screws (as applicable) from the lower column shroud, then tilt the shroud down and slide it back to disengage the locking tabs. Remove the lower shroud.

6. Remove the 2 Torx head screws from the upper shroud.

7. Lift the upper shroud for access to the lock cylinder hole. Hold the key in the **START** position and use a 1/16 in. Allen wrench to push on the lock cylinder retaining pin.

8. Release the key to the **RUN** position and pull the steering column lock cylinder set from the lock module assembly. Remove the upper shroud.

9. If necessary, remove the shift lever clevis, then remove the lever.

10. Remove the wiring harness straps (noting the positioning for installation purposes), then disengage the steering column bulkhead connector from the vehicle wiring harness.

11. Disengage the grey and black connectors for the multi-function combination switch from the column bulkhead connector.

12. Remove the 2 Torx switch retaining screws, then remove the switch from the steering column.

**To install:**

13. Position the multi-function switch assembly, then use a suitable small bladed tool to compress the electrical contact while moving the switch into position. Make sure the electrical contact rests on the canceling cam assembly.

14. Install the switch retaining screws and tighten to 53 inch lbs. (6.0 Nm).

15. Engage the grey and black multi-function switch connectors to the column bulkhead connector.

16. Install the wiring harness straps as noted during removal.

17. If removed, install the shift lever and secure the clevis.

18. Position the shift lever and multi-function lever seals to ease installation of the upper and lower shrouds.

19. Install the upper shroud and lock cylinder. With the key installed to the lock cylinder and turned to the **RUN** position, make sure the sector in the lock module is also in this position.

20. Install the lock cylinder to the upper shroud, then align the locking tab and positioning tab with the slots in the lock module assembly. With the tabs aligned, carefully push the cylinder into position.

21. Install the upper shroud Torx head retaining screws and tighten to 12 inch lbs. (1.4 Nm).

22. Install the lower shroud, making sure the slots on the shroud engage with the upper shroud tabs. Tilt the lower shroud upward and snap the shrouds together.

23. Install the 2 lower shroud pan head or Torx head retaining screws and tighten to 53 inch lbs. (6.0 Nm).

24. Move the shift and multi-function lever seals into position.

25. If removed, install the tilt lever by aligning and pushing inward.

26. Position and secure the steering column.

27. Align and install the steering wheel.

28. Make sure the ignition is **OFF**, then connect the negative battery cable.

29. Properly enable the SIR system.

## Ignition Switch

For anti-theft reasons, on all models in this manual, the ignition switch is located where access is difficult. On all except 1996 vehicles, the switch is located inside the channel section of the brake pedal support and is completely inaccessible without first lowering the steering column. The switch is actuated by a rod and rack assembly. A gear on the end of the lock cylinder engages the toothed upper end of the actuator rod.

For 1996, the redesigned steering column relocated the ignition switch up the column, under the upper shroud and attached to the lock cylinder housing assembly. Although access is arguably easier here than in the channel of earlier columns, it still requires some effort.

➡**When servicing any components on the steering column, should any fasteners require replacement, be sure to use only nuts and bolts of the same size and grade as the original fasteners. Using screws that are too long could prevent the column from collapsing during a collision.**

### REMOVAL & INSTALLATION

#### Steering Column Without Air Bag

▶ **See Figures 81 and 82**

1. Disconnect the negative battery cable. Remove the lower instrument panel-to-steering column cover. Remove the steering column-to-dash bolts and lower the steering column; be sure to properly support it.

2. Place the ignition switch in the **Locked** position.

➡**If the lock cylinder was removed, the actuating rod should be pulled up until it stops, then moved down 1 detent; the switch is now in the Lock position.**

3. Remove the 2 ignition switch-to-steering column screws and the switch assembly.

**To install:**

4. Before installing the ignition switch, place it in the **Locked** position, then make sure the lock cylinder and actuating rod are in the **Locked** position (1st detent from the top).

➡**When installing the ignition switch, use only the specified screws since overlength screws could impair the collapsibility of the column.**

5. The remainder of installation is the reverse of the removal procedure. Tighten the ignition switch-to-steering column screws to 35 inch lbs. (4 Nm) and the steering column-to-instrument bolts to 22 ft. lbs. (30 Nm).

#### Steering Column With Air Bag

***EXCEPT 1996 MODELS***

▶ **See Figure 83**

1. Properly disable the SIR (air bag) system, then disconnect the negative battery cable. For details on disabling the air bag system, please refer to Section 6 of this manual.

2. Remove the lower column trim panel, then remove the steering column-to-instrument panel fasteners and carefully lower the column for access to the switch.

3. On some vehicles, the dimmer switch must be removed in order to remove the ignition switch. If necessary, remove the dimmer switch.

4. Place the ignition switch in the **OFF-LOCK** position.

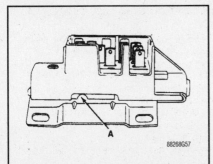

**Fig. 81 Common early-model style ignition switch—NOTE proper switch position for installation**

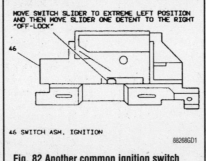

**Fig. 82 Another common ignition switch found on GM steering columns—again finding the LOCK position is critical to assure proper adjustment during installation**

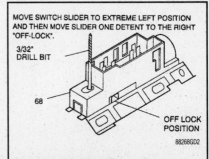

**Fig. 83 Before installation, make sure the switch is in the OFF-LOCK position—a drill bit can be used to hold the switch in this position during installation**

➥If the lock cylinder was removed, the switch slider should be moved to the extreme left position, then 1 detent to the right.

5. Remove the ignition switch-to-steering column retainers and disengage the switch wiring, then remove the assembly.

**To install:**

6. Before installing the ignition switch, place it in the **OFF-LOCK** position, then make sure the lock cylinder and actuating rod are in the **Locked** position (1st detent from the top or 1st detent to the right of far left detent travel).

➥Most replacement switches are pinned in the OFF-LOCK position for installation purposes. If so, the pins must be removed after installation or damage may occur. You can make your own pin by insert a ³⁄₃₂ in. drill bit into the adjustment hole provided in the switch in order to limit switch travel. Just remember to remove the bit before attempting to place the switch in service.

7. Install the activating rod into the ignition switch and assemble the switch onto the steering column. Once the switch is properly positioned, tighten the ignition switch-to-steering column retainers to 35 inch lbs. (4.0 Nm).

➥When installing the ignition switch, use only the specified screws since over length screws could impair the collapsibility of the column.

8. If removed, install the dimmer switch.
9. Raise the column into position and secure, then install any necessary trim plates.
10. Make sure the ignition is **OFF**, then connect the negative battery cable.
11. Properly enable the SIR system.

### 1996 MODELS

▶ **See Figures 84 and 85**

1. Properly disable the SIR (air bag) system, then disconnect the negative battery cable. For details on disabling the air bag system, please refer to Section 6 of this manual.
2. Either lower the steering column from the instrument panel for access or unbolt and remove the column. If the column is removed, prevent it from rotating so the SIR coil does not become uncentered.

3. Remove the combination switch from the steering column.
4. If equipped, remove the alarm switch from the lock module assembly by gently prying the retaining clip on the alarm switch using a small blade prytool. Then, rotate the alarm switch ¼ turn and remove
5. Remove the 2 ignition switch self-tapping retaining screws.
6. Disengage the connector, then remove the wiring harness from the slot in the steering column. Remove the ignition and key alarm switch.

**To install:**

7. Position the switch to the column. Route the wire harness through the slot in the column housing assembly. Secure the harness using a wire strap through the hole located in the bottom of the housing assembly.
8. Install the switch retaining screws and tighten to 12 inch lbs. (1.4 Nm) in order to secure the switch.
9. If applicable, install the alarm switch to the lock module assembly by aligning the switch (with the retaining clip) parallel to the lock cylinder, then rotating the switch ¼ turn until locked in place.
10. Install the combination switch to the steering column.
11. Position and secure the steering column.
12. Make sure the ignition is **OFF**, then connect the negative battery cable.
13. Properly enable the SIR system.

## Dimmer Switch

➥When servicing any components on the steering column, should any fasteners require replacement, be sure to use only nuts and bolts of the same size and grade as the original fasteners. Using screws that are too long could prevent the column from collapsing during a collision.

### REMOVAL & INSTALLATION

#### Except 1996 Models

▶ **See Figure 86**

1. If equipped, properly disable the SIR (air bag) system. For details on disabling the air bag system, please refer to Section 6 of this manual.

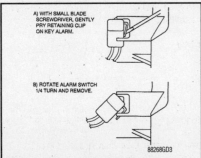

**Fig. 84 Use a small bladed prytool or screwdriver to gently release the retaining clip on the key alarm**

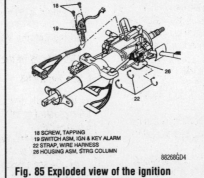

**Fig. 85 Exploded view of the ignition switch and key alarm assembly**

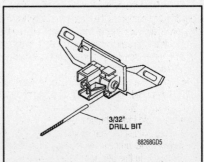

**Fig. 86 A drill bit should be used to limit switch travel and aid in dimmer switch adjustment**

2. Disconnect the negative battery cable.

3. If equipped, remove the lower column trim panel.

4. Remove the steering column-to-instrument panel fasteners and lower the column for access to the switch. Extreme care is necessary to prevent damage to the collapsible column.

5. On some vehicles it may be necessary to remove the steering wheel in order to fully lower the column. If equipped with a tilt column, position the column in the upper most position for additional lowering clearance.

➡ **If the ignition switch shares fasteners with the dimmer switch it may be necessary to remove it first.**

6. Remove the dimmer switch-to-steering column retainers, then remove the switch from the column. Disengage the switch wiring and remove it.

**To install:**

7. Position the switch to the column and loosely install the retainers.

8. Insert a 3/32 in. drill bit into the adjustment hole provided in the switch in order to limit switch travel, then push the switch up against the actuator rod in order to remove lash.

9. Tighten the switch retainers, then remove the drill bit.

10. The remainder of installation is the reverse of the removal procedure.

11. Make sure the ignition is **OFF**, then connect the negative battery cable.

12. If equipped, properly enable the SIR system.

### 1996 Models

Instead of the long time used steering column found on most older GM vehicles the 1996 Astro and Safari vans are equipped with a new column that uses a multi-function combination switch mounted at the head of the column (below the steering wheel) and an upper/lower shroud assembly. The combination switch performs such functions as the wiper switch and the turn signal switch along with any other duties of the multi-function lever. For removal or installation of the multi-function switch assembly, please refer to the Combination Switch procedure found in this section.

## Ignition Lock Cylinder

➡ **When servicing any components on the steering column, should any fasteners require replacement, be sure to use only nuts and bolts of the same size and grade as the original fasteners. Using screws that are too long could prevent the column from collapsing during a collision.**

### REMOVAL & INSTALLATION

#### Steering Columns Without Air Bag

▶ **See Figure 87**

1. Disconnect the negative battery cable.

2. Refer to the Turn Signal Switch, Removal and Installation procedures in this section and remove the turn signal switch.

3. Place the lock cylinder in the **RUN** position.

4. Remove the buzzer switch, the lock cylinder screw and the lock cylinder.

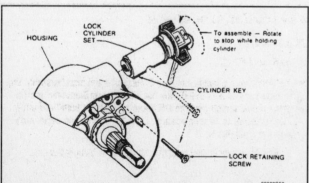

**Fig. 87 Exploded view of the lock cylinder mounting—early-model shown (late-model, except 1996, similar)**

88268G58

---

**If the screw is dropped upon removal, it could fall into the steering column, requiring complete disassembly to retrieve the screw.**

**To install:**

5. Rotate the lock cylinder clockwise to align the cylinder key with the keyway in the housing.

6. Push the lock cylinder all the way in.

7. Install the cylinder lock-to-housing screw. Tighten the screw to 14 inch lbs. (1.6 Nm).

8. Connect the negative battery cable and check operation.

#### Steering Column With Air Bag

##### EXCEPT 1996 MODELS

▶ **See Figure 87**

1. Properly disable the SIR (air bag) system, then disconnect the negative battery cable. For details on disabling the air bag system, please refer to Section 6 of this manual.

2. Matchmark and remove the steering wheel.

3. Remove the SIR coil assembly retaining ring, then remove the coil assembly and allow it to hang freely from the wiring. Remove the wave washer.

➡ **On some SIR equipped vehicles, it may be necessary to completely remove the coil and wiring from the steering column before removing the lock cylinder assembly. If so, attach a length of mechanic's wire to the coil connector at the base of the column, then carefully pull the harness and wire through the steering column towards the top. Leave the wire in position inside the column in order to pull the harness back down into position during installation.**

4. Remove the turn signal switch from the column and allow it to hang from the wires (leaving them connected).

5. Remove the buzzer switch assembly. On some vehicles it may be necessary to temporarily remove the key from the lock cylinder in order to remove the buzzer. If so, the key should be reinserted before the next step.

6. Carefully remove the lock cylinder screw and the lock cylinder. If possible, use a magnetic tipped screwdriver on the screw in order to help prevent the possibility of dropping it.

**If the screw is dropped upon removal, it could fall into the steering column, requiring complete disassembly in order to retrieve the screw and prevent damage.**

**To install:**

7. Align and install the lock cylinder set.

8. Push the lock cylinder all the way in, then carefully install the retaining screw. Tighten the screw to 22 inch lbs. (2.5 Nm) on tilt columns or to 40 inch lbs. (4.5 Nm) on standard non-tilt columns.

9. If necessary, install the buzzer switch assembly.

10. Reposition and secure the turn signal switch assembly

➡ **The coil assembly will become uncentered if the steering column is separated from the steering gear and allowed to rotate or if the centering spring is pushed down, letting the hub rotate while the coils assembly is removed from the steering column.**

11. Make sure the coil is centered, then install the wave washer, followed by the coil and the retaining ring. The coil ring must be firmly seated in the shaft groove.

12. Align and install the steering wheel.

13. Make sure the ignition is **OFF**, then connect the negative battery cable.

14. Properly enable the SIR system.

##### 1996 MODELS

▶ **See Figures 88 and 89**

1. Properly disable the SIR (air bag) system, then disconnect the negative battery cable. For details on disabling the air bag system, please refer to Section 6 of this manual.

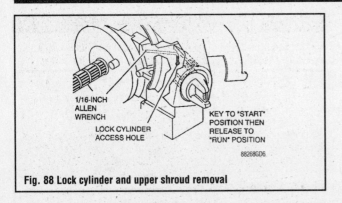

**Fig. 88 Lock cylinder and upper shroud removal**

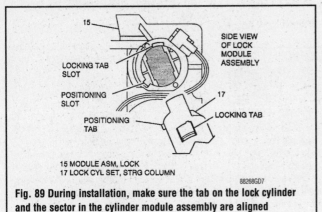

**Fig. 89 During installation, make sure the tab on the lock cylinder and the sector in the cylinder module assembly are aligned**

2. Either lower the steering column from the instrument panel for access or unbolt and remove the column. If the column is removed, prevent it from rotating so the SIR coil does not become uncentered.

3. If applicable, remove the tilt lever by pulling outward.

4. Remove the 2 pan head tapping screws from the lower column shroud, then tilt the shroud down and slide it back to disengage the locking tabs. Remove the lower shroud.

5. Remove the 2 Torx head screws from the upper shroud.

6. Lift the upper shroud for access to the lock cylinder hole. Hold the key in the **START** position and use a 1⁄16 in. Allen wrench to push on the lock cylinder retaining pin.

7. Release the key to the **RUN** position and pull the steering column lock cylinder set from the lock module assembly. Remove the upper shroud.

**To install:**

8. Install the upper shroud and lock cylinder. With the key installed to the lock cylinder and turned to the **RUN** position, make sure the sector in the lock module is also in this position.

9. Install the lock cylinder to the upper shroud, then align the locking tab and positioning tab with the slots in the lock module assembly. With the tabs aligned, carefully push the cylinder into position.

10. Install the upper shroud Torx head retaining screws and tighten to 12 inch lbs. (1.4 Nm).

11. Install the lower shroud, making sure the slots on the shroud engage with the upper shroud tabs. Tilt the lower shroud upward and snap the shrouds together.

12. Install the 2 lower shroud pan head retaining screws and tighten to 53 inch lbs. (6.0 Nm).

13. Move the shift and multi-function lever seals into position.

14. If applicable, install the tilt lever by aligning and pushing inward.

15. Position and secure the steering column.

16. Make sure the ignition is **OFF**, then connect the negative battery cable.

17. Properly enable the SIR system.

## Steering Linkage

♦ **See Figures 90 and 91**

The steering linkage consists of: a forward mounted linkage (parallelogram type), crimp (or torque prevailing) nuts at the inner pivots, castellated nuts at the steering knuckle arm, a second idler arm and steering gear pitman arm-to-relay rod connecting rod to maintain proper geometry, and a steering damper (some manual steering models). Each joint is equipped with a grease fitting, for durability.

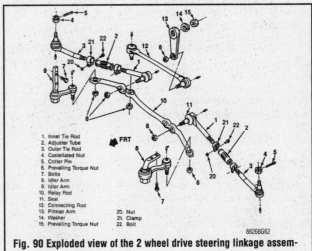

**Fig. 90 Exploded view of the 2 wheel drive steering linkage assembly**

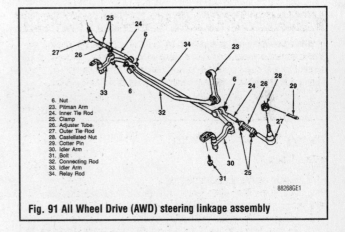

**Fig. 91 All Wheel Drive (AWD) steering linkage assembly**

## REMOVAL & INSTALLATION

♦ **See Figures 92, 93, 94, 95 and 96**

**Pitman Arm**

♦ **See Figure 97**

➡ **The following procedure requires the use of a universal steering linkage puller such as J–24319–B, the GM Pitman Arm Remover tool No. J–29107 or equivalent, and the GM Steering Linkage Installer tool No. J–29193 (12mm) for most models or J–29194 (14mm) for some early models (or equivalent).**

1. Raise and support the front of the vehicle safely using jackstands.

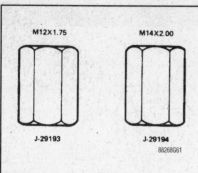

Fig. 92 These special tools are used to seat linkage shaft tapers during installation

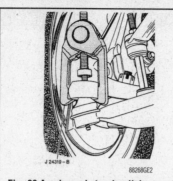

Fig. 93 A universal steering linkage puller is necessary for almost all linkage replacement procedures

Fig. 94 Most steering linkage components are removed by first loosening and removing the nut . . .

Fig. 95 . . . then using a universal steering linkage puller to loosen the stud

Fig. 96 Once the stud is freed, separate the linkage

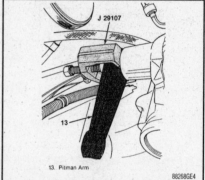

Fig. 97 Pitman arm removal requires the use of this special tool

2. Disconnect the nut from the pitman arm ball joint stud.

3. Using a universal steering linkage puller (such as J–24319–B or equivalent), separate the connecting rod from the pitman arm. Pull down on the connecting rod and separate it from the stud.

4. Remove the pitman arm-to-pitman shaft nut and washer, then matchmark the relationship of the arm to the shaft (this will permit proper alignment during assembly).

5. Separate the pitman arm from the pitman shaft using J–29107, or an equivalent pitman arm removal tool.

➡When separating the pitman arm from the shaft, DO NOT use a hammer or apply heat to the arm.

**To install:**

6. Align the pitman arm-to-pitman shaft matchmark, then install the washer along with a prevailing torque nut. Tighten the pitman arm-to-pitman shaft nut to 185 ft. lbs. (250 Nm).

7. Connect the pitman arm to the connecting rod ball stud (make sure the seal is on the stud). Position a steering linkage installer tool such as J–29193 (12mm) for most models or J–29194 (14mm) for some early models, onto the ball stud. Tighten the installer tool to 40 ft. lbs. (54 Nm) to seat the tapers; after seating, remove the tool.

8. Install the pitman arm-to-connecting rod ball joint nut, then tighten the ball joint nut to 35 ft. lbs. (47 Nm).

9. Remove the jackstands, then carefully lower the vehicle.

**Idler Arm**

♦ See Figures 98, 99, 100 and 101

➡The following procedure requires the use of a universal steering linkage puller such as J–24319–B, and the GM Steering Linkage Installer tool No. J–29193 (12mm) for most models or J–29194 (14mm) for some early models (or equivalent).

1. Raise and support the front of the vehicle safely using jackstands.

➡Jerking the right wheel assembly back and forth is not an acceptable testing procedure; there is no control on the amount of force being applied to the idler arm. Before suspecting idler arm shimmying complaints, check the wheels for imbalance, runout, force variation and/or road surface irregularities.

2. To inspect for a defective idler arm, perform the following procedures:

a. Position the wheels in the straight-ahead position.

b. Position a spring scale near the relay rod end of the idler arm and exert 25 lbs. (110 N) of force upward, then downward.

c. Measure the distance between the upward and downward directions that the idler arm moves. The allowable deflection is 1/8 in. (3.2mm) for each direction; a total difference of 1/4 in. (6.4mm). If the idler arm deflection is beyond the allowable limits, replace it.

3. Remove the idler arm-to-frame bolts.

4. Remove the idler arm-to-relay rod ball joint nut.

5. Using a universal steering linkage puller tool (such as J–24319–B or equivalent), separate the relay rod from the ball joint stud.

6. Inspect and/or replace (if necessary) the idler arm.

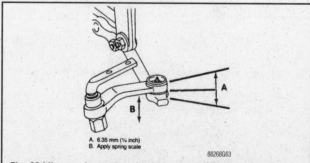

Fig. 98 Idler arm inspection should be conducted using a spring scale

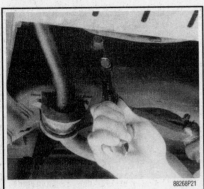

**Fig. 99 Loosen and remove the idler arm-to-frame mounting bolts . . .**

**Fig. 100 . . . then separate the idler ball stud from the relay rod . . .**

**Fig. 101 . . . and remove the idler arm from the vehicle**

**To install:**

7. Install the idler arm-to-frame bolts and tighten to 52 ft. lbs. (70 Nm) for all 1985–91 vehicles, 78 ft. lbs. (105 Nm) for 1992–95 vehicles (except 1992–93 AWD vehicles which should be tightened to 102 ft. lbs. using Loctite® on the threads) or to 102 ft. lbs. (138 Nm) for 1996 vehicles.

8. Connect the relay rod to the idler arm ball joint stud. Using the proper sized GM Steering Linkage Installer tool (either No. J–29193/12mm for most models or J–29194/14mm for some early models), seat the relay rod-to-idler arm ball joint stud. Tighten the tool to 40 ft. lbs. (54 Nm) in order to fully seat the taper, then remove the tool.

9. Install the idler arm-to-relay rod stud nut and torque it to 35 ft. lbs. (47 Nm).

10. Remove the jackstands and carefully lower the vehicle.

11. Check and adjust the front end toe-in, as necessary.

### Relay Rod

➡The following procedure requires the use of a universal steering linkage puller such as J–24319-B, and the GM Steering Linkage Installer tool No. J–29193 (12mm) for most models or J–29194 (14mm) for some early models (or equivalent).

1. Raise and support the front of the vehicle safely using jackstands.

2. Refer to the Tie Rod, Removal and Installation procedures in this section and disconnect the inner tie rod ends from the relay rod.

3. Remove the connecting rod stud-to-relay rod nut and the idler arm stud-to-relay rod nuts.

4. Using the universal steering linkage puller, disconnect the connecting rod from the relay rod.

5. Using the universal steering linkage puller, disconnect the relay rod from the idler arms, then remove the relay rod from the vehicle.

**To install:**

6. Clean and inspect the threads on the tie rod, the tie rod ends and the ball joints for damage, then replace them (if necessary). Inspect the ball joint seals for excessive wear, then replace them (if necessary).

7. Position the relay rod onto the idler arms (no mounting nuts). Thread the GM Steering Linkage Installer tool No. J–29193 (12mm) or J–29194 (14mm) or equivalent, onto the idler arm studs. Tighten the tool to 40 ft. lbs. (54 Nm) in order to seat the tapers. Remove the installer tool, then install the mounting nuts and torque the idler arm-to-relay arm stud nuts to 35 ft. lbs. (47 Nm).

8. Position the connecting rod onto the relay rod (no mounting nut). Thread the proper steering linkage Installer tool onto the connecting rod stud, then tighten to 40 ft. lbs. (54 Nm) to seat the taper. Remove the installer tool, then install the mounting nuts and torque the connecting rod-to-relay rod stud nuts to 35 ft. lbs. (47 Nm).

9. Position the inner tie rod ball joints onto the relay rod (no mounting nuts). Thread the proper steering linkage installer tool onto the tie rod studs and tighten to 40 ft. lbs. (54 Nm) to seat the tapers. Remove the installer tool, then install the mounting nuts and torque the tie rod-to-relay rod stud nuts to 35 ft. lbs. (47 Nm).

10. Remove the jackstands and carefully lower the vehicle. Check the steering linkage performance.

11. Check and adjust the front end toe-in, as necessary.

### Connecting Rod

➡The following procedure requires the use of a universal steering linkage puller such as J–24319-B, and the GM Steering Linkage Installer tool No. J–29193 (12mm) for most models or J–29194 (14mm) for some early models (or equivalent).

1. Raise and support the front of the vehicle safely using jackstands.

2. Remove the connecting rod stud-to-relay rod nut and the connecting rod stud-to-pitman arm nut.

3. Using the universal steering linkage puller, separate the connecting rod from the relay rod and the pitman arm, then remove the connecting rod from the vehicle.

4. Clean and inspect the ball joint threads for damage, then replace the rod (if necessary). Inspect the ball joint seals for excessive wear, then replace them (if necessary).

**To install:**

5. Position the connecting rod onto the relay rod and the pitman arm (no mounting nuts). Thread the steering linkage installer tool onto the connecting rod studs, then tighten to 40 ft. lbs. (54 Nm) to seat the tapers. Remove the installer tools, then install the mounting nuts and torque them to 35 ft. lbs. (47 Nm).

6. Remove the jackstands and carefully lower the vehicle. Check the steering linkage performance.

7. Check and adjust the front end toe-in, as necessary.

### Tie Rod

♦ **See Figures 102 thru 110**

➡The following procedure requires the use of a universal steering linkage puller such as J–24319-B, the GM Wheel Stud and Tie Rod Remover tool No. J–6627-A or equivalent, and the GM Steering Linkage Installer tool No. J–29193 (12mm) for most models or J–29194 (14mm) for some early models (or equivalent).

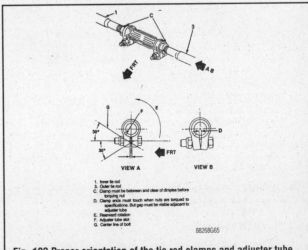

**Fig. 102 Proper orientation of the tie rod clamps and adjuster tube**

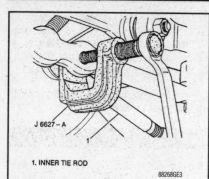

**Fig. 103 Inner tie rod and relay rod connections require the use of a press-type linkage/wheel stud remover**

**Fig. 104 To separate the tie rod end from the steering knuckle, first straighten the cotter pin . . .**

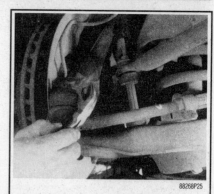

**Fig. 105 . . . then remove and discard the old cotter pin**

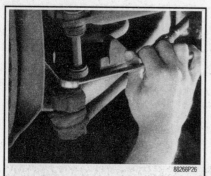

**Fig. 106 Using a wrench (shown) or a deep socket, loosen the tie rod stud retaining nut**

**Fig. 107 Unthread the nut from the stud . . .**

**Fig. 108 . . . then use a universal steering linkage puller to free the stud from the knuckle**

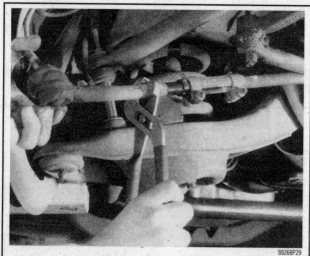

**Fig. 109 If only the rod end is being removed, matchmark the threads (to preserve toe adjustment) . . .**

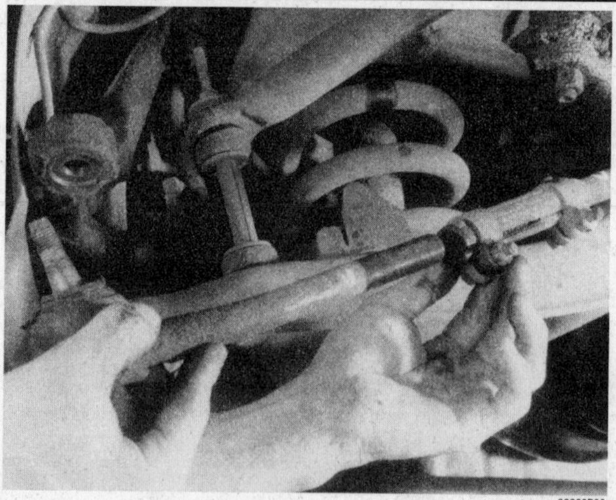

**Fig. 110 . . . then loosen the adjuster clamp bolt and unthread the end from the adjuster tube**

1. Raise and support the front of the vehicle safely using jackstands.
2. Remove the cotter pin from the tie rod-to-steering knuckle stud.
3. Remove the tie rod-to-relay rod stud nut and the tie rod-to-steering knuckle stud nut.

➡**DO NOT attempt to separate the tie rod-to-steering knuckle joint using a wedge type tool for seal damage could result.**

4. Using the GM Wheel Stud Remover tool No. J–6627–A or equivalent, separate the outer tie rod stud from the steering knuckle and the inner tie rod stud from the relay rod. Remove the tie rod from the vehicle.

5. If removing ONLY the tie rod end, perform the following procedures:
   a. Disconnect the defective ball joint end of the tie rod.
   b. Loosen the adjuster tube clamp bolt.
   c. Unscrew the tie rod end from the adjuster tube; count the number of turns necessary to remove the tie rod end.
   d. Clean, inspect and lubricate the adjuster tube threads.
   e. To install a new tie rod end, screw it into the adjuster tube using the same number of turns necessary to remove it.
   f. Position the clamp bolts between the adjuster tube dimples (located at each end) and in the proper location (see illustration). Torque the adjuster tube clamp bolt 13 ft. lbs. (17 Nm).

### To install:

6. Position the tie rod onto the steering knuckle and the relay rod. Thread the proper sized steering linkage installer tool onto the studs and tighten to 40 ft. lbs. (54 Nm) to seat the tapers. After seating the tapers, remove the tools, install the mounting nuts and torque mounting nuts to 35 ft. lbs. (47 Nm).

7. At the tie rod-to-steering knuckle stud, tighten the nut until a castle nut slot aligns with the hole in the stud, then install a new cotter pin.

8. Remove the jackstands and carefully lower the vehicle. Check the steering linkage performance.

9. Check and adjust the front end toe-in, as necessary.

### Damper Assembly

The damper assembly is used to the remove steering wheel vibration and vehicle wander; not all vehicles are equipped with it.

1. Raise and support the front of the vehicle safely using jackstands.
2. Remove the damper assembly-to-connecting rod cotter pin and nut.
3. Remove the damper assembly-to-bracket nut/bolt and remove the damper assembly from the vehicle.
4. Installation is the reverse of the removal procedure. Tighten the damper assembly-to-bracket nut/bolt to 22 ft. lbs. (29 Nm) and the damper assembly-to-connecting rod nut to 41 ft. lbs. (56 Nm).

## Power Steering Gear

The recirculating ball type power steering gear used on these vehicles is basically the same as the manual steering gear, except that it uses a hydraulic assist on the rack piston.

The power steering gear control valve directs the power steering fluid to either side of the rack piston, which rides up and down the worm shaft. The steering rack converts the hydraulic pressure into mechanical force. Should the vehicle loose the hydraulic pressure, it can still be controlled mechanically.

### REMOVAL & INSTALLATION

#### ▶ See Figure 111

1. Disconnect the negative battery cable for safety.
2. Raise and support the front of the vehicle safely using jackstands.
3. Position a fluid catch pan under the power steering gear.
4. At the power steering gear, disconnect and plug the pressure hoses; any excess fluid will be caught by the catch pan.

➡Be sure to cap or plug the hoses and the openings of the power steering pump to keep dirt out of the system.

5. Remove the intermediate shaft-to-steering gear bolt. Matchmark the intermediate shaft-to-power steering gear and separate the shaft from the gear.

6. Remove the pitman arm-to-pitman shaft nut and washer, then matchmark the relationship of the arm to the shaft (this will permit proper alignment during assembly).

7. Separate the pitman arm from the pitman shaft using J–29107, or an equivalent pitman arm removal tool.

➡When separating the pitman arm from the shaft, DO NOT use a hammer or apply heat to the arm.

8. Remove the power steering gear-to-frame bolts and washers, then carefully lower and remove the steering gear from the vehicle.

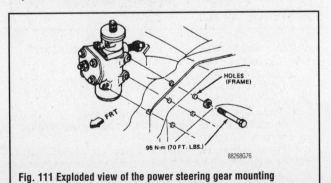

**Fig. 111 Exploded view of the power steering gear mounting**

9. Installation is the reverse of the removal procedure. Tighten the gear-to-frame bolts to 55 ft. lbs. (75 Nm) for 1985–93 vehicles and 1994–96 2 wheel drive vehicles, or tighten the bolts to 100 ft. lbs. (135 Nm) for 1994–96 AWD vehicles.

10. Tighten the intermediate shaft-to-power steering gear bolt to 30 ft. lbs. (41 Nm) and tighten the pitman arm-to-pitman shaft nut and washer to 185 ft. lbs. (250 Nm).

11. Refill the power steering reservoir and bleed the power steering system. Road test the vehicle, then check and top-off the power steering fluid.

## Power Steering Pump

### REMOVAL & INSTALLATION

#### ▶ See Figures 112 thru 118

➡The following procedure requires the use of the GM Puller tool No. J–29785–A (1985–92), Puller J–25034–B (1993–96) or equivalent, and the GM Pulley Installer tool No. J–25033–B or equivalent.

1. Disconnect the negative battery cable for safety.
2. For 1996 vehicles, remove the air cleaner assembly for access.
3. For 1993–96 vehicles, remove the hood latch and the upper fan shroud.
4. Release tension and remove the drive belt. For details, please refer to Section 1 of this manual.
5. Remove the power steering pump pulley using a suitable puller tool.
6. Remove the power steering pump retaining bolts, then reposition the pump as necessary for access to the hoses.
7. Position a fluid catch pan under the power steering pump.
8. Remove the hoses from the power steering pump and drain the excess fluid into the catch pan.

### ✳✳ WARNING

Be sure to cap all openings in the pump hydraulic system to prevent excessive fluid spillage and the possibility of system contamination.

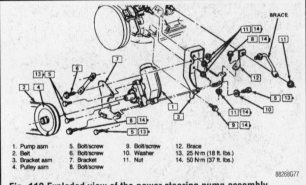

| | | | |
|---|---|---|---|
| 1. Pump asm | 5. Bolt/screw | 9. Bolt/screw | 12. Brace |
| 2. Belt | 6. Bolt/screw | 10. Washer | 13. 25 N·m (18 ft. lbs.) |
| 3. Bracket asm | 7. Bracket | 11. Nut | 14. 50 N·m (37 ft. lbs.) |
| 4. Pulley asm | 8. Bolt/screw | | |

**Fig. 112 Exploded view of the power steering pump assembly mounting—2.5L engine**

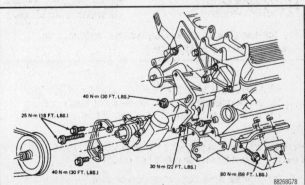

**Fig. 113 Exploded view of the power steering pump assembly mounting—early-model 4.3L engine**

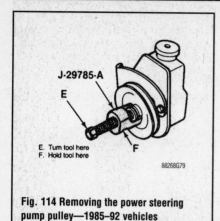

Fig. 114 Removing the power steering pump pulley—1985–92 vehicles

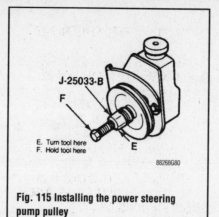

Fig. 115 Installing the power steering pump pulley

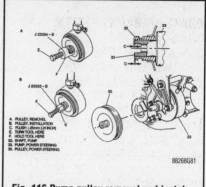

Fig. 116 Pump pulley removal and installation—1993–96 vehicles

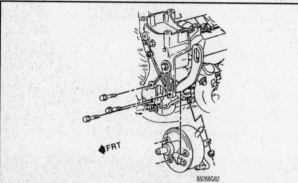

Fig. 117 Exploded view of the power steering pump mounting—late-model 4.3L engines (1993–96 shown)

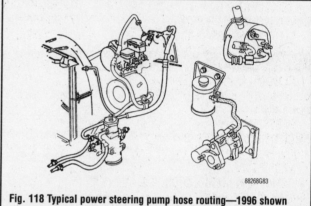

Fig. 118 Typical power steering pump hose routing—1996 shown

9. Remove the power steering pump from the vehicle.
**To install:**
10. Position the pump to the vehicle, then uncap and connect the pump hoses.
11. Install the steering pump to the retaining bracket, then secure using the retaining bolts. Tighten the power steering pump-to-bracket bolts to 37 ft. lbs. (50 Nm). For 1996 vehicles, tighten the nut to 30 ft. lbs. (41 Nm).

➡**On early-model vehicles where the drive belt is tensioned by pivoting the power steering pump assembly, do NOT fully tighten the mounting bolts at this time, since you will just have to loosen them again for belt installation and adjustment.**

12. Install the pump pulley using the GM Pulley Installer tool No. J–25033–B or equivalent. Press the drive pulley onto the power steering pump.
13. Hand-tighten the pivot bolt, the adjusting bolt and the washer.
14. Install the drive belt. On early-model vehicles so equipped, properly adjust the belt tension. For details on belt installation and tension adjustment, please refer to Section 1 of this manual.
15. For 1993–96 vehicles install the upper fan shroud and the hood latch assembly.
16. For 1996 vehicles, install the air cleaner assembly.
17. Connect the negative battery cable.
18. Refill the power steering reservoir and bleed the power steering system.
19. Remove the jackstands and carefully lower the vehicle.
20. Road test the vehicle, then check and top-off the power steering fluid.

## SYSTEM BLEEDING

The power steering system should be bled after any component has been replaced, after any fluid line has been disconnected or air is suspected as the cause of a noise in the system. The system must be properly bled to help prevent possible pump damage, and to ensure proper, trouble and noise-free operation.

➡**Bleeding will take significantly longer on a system that has been completely emptied and/or on systems that contain long fluid lines and multiple components (such as a fluid cooler in addition to the pump, gear and reservoir).**

1. Begin the bleeding procedure with the engine and fluid COLD.
2. FIRMLY set the parking brake and block the rear wheels.
3. Raise and support the front of the vehicle safely using jackstands.
4. Turn the steering wheel to the full left position, then check and top off the fluid reservoir to the FULL COLD mark.
5. Turn the steering wheel from lock-to-lock at least 20 times, while an assistant checks the fluid level and condition in the reservoir. Add fluid as necessary to keep the level at or near the FULL COLD mark.

➡**Remember that if only the front wheels are raised, the fluid level on the dipstick will not be completely accurate. Keep the level a little below the mark, until the vehicle is lowered, then check and top it off as necessary.**

6. Remove the jackstands and carefully lower the vehicle. If not done earlier, install the filler cap to the reservoir.
7. Start the engine and allow it to idle. Run the engine for approximately 2 minutes in order to allow the fluid to warm-up.
8. With the engine idling, turn the wheels in both directions (to the stops) several times.
9. Stop the engine, then check the fluid level and condition. Add power steering fluid to the level indicated on the reservoir.

➡**Fluid with air in it will have a light tan or milky appearance. This air must be eliminated from the fluid before normal steering action can be obtained.**

10. Road test the vehicle to make sure the steering functions normally and is free from noise.
11. Allow the vehicle to stand for 2–3 hours, then recheck the power steering fluid.

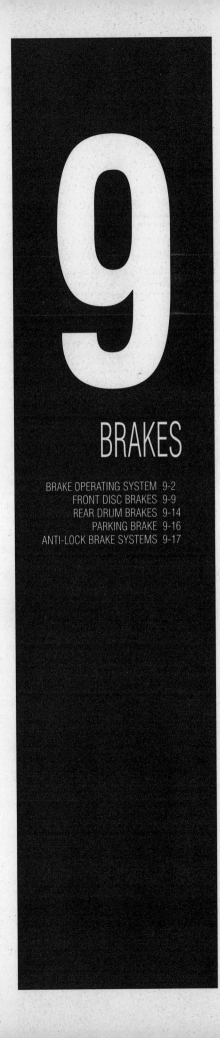

# 9

## BRAKES

## BRAKE OPERATING SYSTEM

### ✳✳ WARNING

**Clean, high quality brake fluid is essential to the safe and proper operation of the brake system. You should always buy the highest quality brake fluid that is available. If the brake fluid becomes contaminated, drain and flush the system, then refill the master cylinder with new fluid. Never reuse any brake fluid. Any brake fluid that is removed from the system should be discarded.**

### Adjustments

#### REAR DRUM BRAKES

▶ **See Figures 1, 2, 3 and 4**

Normal adjustments of the rear drum brakes are automatic and are made during the reverse applications of the brakes. ONLY, if the lining has been renewed or if the self adjusters haven't worked properly, should the following procedure be performed.

➡ **The following procedure requires the use of the GM Brake Adjustment tool No. J–4735 or equivalent.**

1. Raise and support the rear of the vehicle on jackstands.
2. Using a punch and a hammer, at the rear of the backing plate, knock out the lanced metal area near the star wheel assembly.

➡ **When knocking out the lanced metal area from the backing plate, the wheels must be removed and all of the metal pieces discarded.**

3. Using the GM Brake Adjustment tool No. J–4735 or equivalent, insert it into the slot and engage the lowest possible tooth on the star wheel. Move the end of the brake tool downward to move the star wheel upward and expand the adjusting screw. Repeat this operation until the brakes lock the wheel.

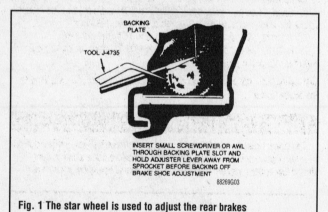

**Fig. 1 The star wheel is used to adjust the rear brakes**

4. Insert a small screwdriver or piece of firm wire (coat hanger wire) into the adjusting slot and push the automatic adjuster lever out and free of the star wheel on the adjusting screw.
5. While holding the adjusting lever out of the way, engage the topmost tooth possible on the star wheel (with the brake tool). Move the end of the adjusting tool upward to move the adjusting screw star wheel downward and contact the adjusting screw. Back off the adjusting screw star wheel until the wheel spins freely with a minimum of drag. Keep track of the number of turns the star wheel is backed off.
6. Repeat this operation for the other side. When backing off the brakes on the other side, the adjusting lever must be backed off the same number of turns to prevent side-to-side brake pull.

➡ **Backing off the star wheel 12 notches (clicks) is usually enough to eliminate brake drag.**

7. Repeat this operation on the other side of the rear brake system.
8. After the brakes are adjusted, install a rubber hole cover into the backing plate slot. To complete the brake adjustment operation, make several stops while backing the vehicle to equalize the wheels.
9. Road test the vehicle.

#### BRAKE PEDAL TRAVEL

▶ **See Figure 5**

The brake pedal travel is the distance the pedal moves toward the floor from the fully released position. Inspection should be made with 90 lbs. pressure on the brake pedal, when the brake system is cold. The brake pedal travel should be 4½ in. (114mm) for manual, or 3½ in. (89mm) for power.

➡ **If equipped with power brakes, be sure to pump the brake pedal at least 3 times with the engine OFF, before making the brake pedal check.**

1. From under the dash, remove the pushrod-to-pedal clevis pin and separate the pushrod from the brake pedal.
2. Loosen the pushrod adjuster lock nut, then adjust the pushrod.
3. After the correct travel is established, reverse the removal procedure.

## Brake Light Switch

▶ **See Figures 6 and 7**

#### REMOVAL & INSTALLATION

#### Plunger Type

1. Disconnect the negative battery terminal from the battery.
2. Disconnect the electrical connector from the brake light switch.
3. Turn the brake light switch retainer (to align the key with the bracket slot), then remove the switch with the retainer.
4. To install, reverse the removal procedures. Adjust the brake light switch.

**Fig. 2 Use a punch to pop out the adjuster knockouts if it hasn't already been done**

**Fig. 3 Remove the metal tab from the backing plate. DO NOT allow it to fall into the drum**

**Fig. 4 Use a brake adjusting spoon to turn the starwheel. A screwdriver just won't work that well**

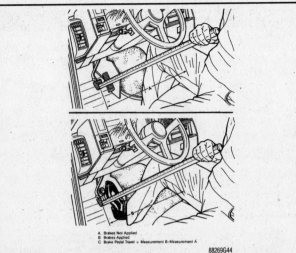

**Fig. 5 The use of a pedal force gauge will make testing the pedal travel more accurate**

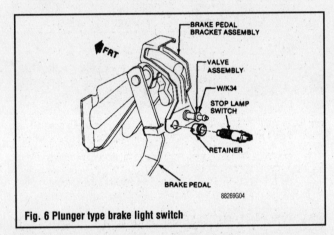

**Fig. 6 Plunger type brake light switch**

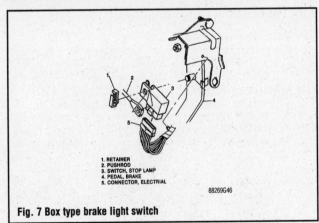

1. RETAINER
2. PUSHROD
3. SWITCH, STOP LAMP
4. PEDAL, BRAKE
5. CONNECTOR, ELECTRIAL

**Fig. 7 Box type brake light switch**

### Box Type

1. Disconnect the negative battery terminal from the battery.
2. Disconnect the electrical connector from the brake light switch.
3. Release the brake pushrod retainer, then remove the switch with the retainer.
4. To install, reverse the removal procedures.

## ADJUSTMENT

Only the plunger type of brake light switch needs to be adjusted. The box type is self adjusting.

1. Depress the brake pedal and press the brake light switch inward until it seats firmly against the clip.

➡ **As the switch is being pushed into the clip, audible clicks can be heard.**

2. Release the brake pedal, then pull it back against the pedal stop until the audible click can no longer be heard.
3. The brake light switch will operate when the pedal is depressed 13mm (0.53 in.) from the fully released position.

## Master Cylinder

### REMOVAL & INSTALLATION

◗ **See Figures 8 thru 14**

➡ **The master cylinder removal and installation procedures are basically the same for all brake systems. Always use flare nut wrenches to remove the hydraulic brake line. Damage to the fitting nut may occur if this procedure is not followed.**

1. Disconnect the negative battery cable. Apply the parking brakes or block the wheels.
2. Using a siphon, remove and discard some of the brake fluid from the master cylinder reservoirs.
3. Disconnect and plug the hydraulic lines from the master cylinder using flare nut wrenches only.
4. If equipped with a manual brake system, disconnect the pushrod from the brake pedal.
5. Remove the master cylinder-to-bracket (manual) or vacuum booster (power) nuts, then separate the combination valve/bracket from the master cylinder.
6. Remove the master cylinder, the gasket and the rubber boot from the vehicle.

**To install:**

7. Bench bleed the master cylinder and install the cylinder onto the vehicle. Torque the master cylinder mounting nuts to 28 ft. lbs. (38 Nm).
8. Connect the hydraulic lines and torque to 15 ft. lbs. (20 Nm).
9. Refill the master cylinder with clean brake fluid, bleed the brake system and check the brake pedal travel.

➡ **If equipped with manual brakes, be sure to reconnect the pushrod to the brake pedal.**

## Vacuum Power Brake Booster

The power brake booster is a tandem vacuum suspended unit, equipped with a single or dual function vacuum switch that activates a brake warning light should low booster vacuum be present. Under normal operation, vacuum is

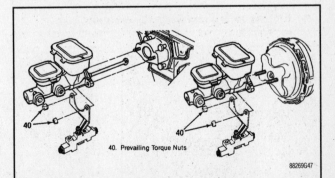

40. Prevailing Torque Nuts

**Fig. 8 All master cylinders are held with two nuts, regardless of the booster type**

Fig. 9 Remove as much of the used fluid as possible from the reservoirs

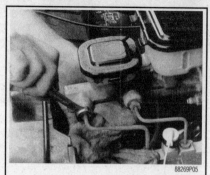

Fig. 10 Use only flare wrenches on the line fittings or the fitting might get damaged

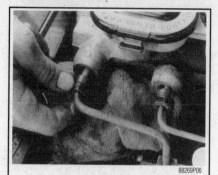

Fig. 11 Use a rag to catch any brake fluid that spills, otherwise the fluid could cause paint damage

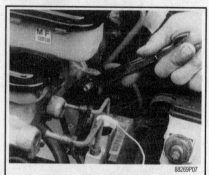

Fig. 12 Be careful when removing the master cylinder nuts, they are close to the positive battery terminal

Fig. 13 Remove the master cylinder and check for fluid in the booster

Fig. 14 Use fresh fluid when reinstalling the master cylinder

present on both sides of the diaphragms. When the brakes are applied, atmospheric air is admitted to one side of the diaphragms to provide power assistance.

## REMOVAL & INSTALLATION

♦ See Figures 15 and 16

1. Disconnect the negative battery cable. Apply the parking brake or block the wheels.
2. Remove the master cylinder-to-power brake booster nuts and move the master cylinder out of the way; if necessary, support the master cylinder on a wire.

➡When removing the master cylinder from the power brake booster, it is not necessary to disconnect the hydraulic lines.

3. Disconnect the vacuum hose from the power brake booster.
4. From under the dash, disconnect the pushrod from the brake pedal.
5. From under the dash, remove the power brake booster-to-cowl nuts.

6. From the engine compartment, remove the power brake booster and the gasket from the vehicle.

➡If equipped with anti-lock brakes, support the control valves out of the way while removing the brake booster.

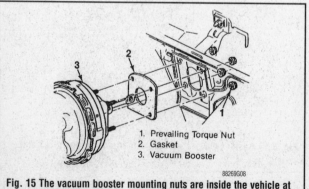

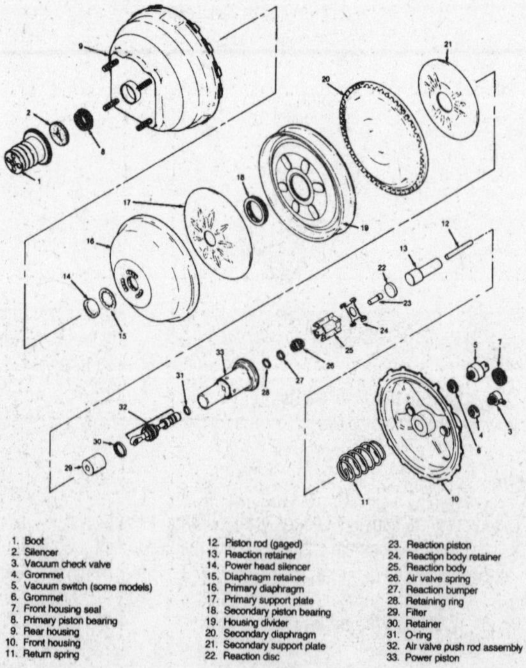

1. Prevailing Torque Nut
2. Gasket
3. Vacuum Booster

Fig. 15 The vacuum booster mounting nuts are inside the vehicle at the pedal assembly

1. Boot
2. Silencer
3. Vacuum check valve
4. Grommet
5. Vacuum switch (some models)
6. Grommet
7. Front housing seal
8. Primary piston bearing
9. Rear housing
10. Front housing
11. Return spring
12. Piston rod (gaged)
13. Reaction retainer
14. Power head silencer
15. Diaphragm retainer
16. Primary diaphragm
17. Primary support plate
18. Secondary piston bearing
19. Housing divider
20. Secondary diaphragm
21. Secondary support plate
22. Reaction disc
23. Reaction piston
24. Reaction body retainer
25. Reaction body
26. Air valve spring
27. Reaction bumper
28. Retaining ring
29. Filter
30. Retainer
31. O-ring
32. Air valve push rod assembly
33. Power piston

Fig. 16 Exploded view of the vacuum booster assembly

**To install:**

7.  Use a new gaskets and install the brake booster onto the firewall. Torque the power brake booster-to-cowl nuts to 21 ft. lbs. (29 Nm) and the master cylinder-to-power brake booster nuts to 28 ft. lbs. (38 Nm).

8.  Connect the pushrod and the vacuum hose.

9.  Start the engine and check the brake system operation.

## Hydro-Boost

### TESTING

1.  A defective Hydro-Boost cannot cause any of the following conditions:
    a.  Noisy brakes
    b.  Fading pedal
    c.  Pulling brakes
    If any of these occur, check elsewhere in the brake system.

2.  Check the fluid level in the master cylinder. It should be within ¼ in. (6mm) of the top. If is isn't add only DOT-3 or DOT-4 brake fluid until the correct level is reached.

3.  Check the fluid level in the power steering pump. The engine should be at normal running temperature and stopped. The level should register on the pump dipstick. Add power steering fluid to bring the reservoir level up to the correct level. Low fluid level will result in both poor steering and stopping ability.

### ✳✳ CAUTION

**The brake hydraulic system uses brake fluid only, while the power steering and Hydro-Boost systems use power steering fluid only. Don't mix the two!**

4.  Check the power steering pump belt tension, and inspect all the power steering/Hydro-Boost hoses for kinks or leaks.

5.  Check and adjust the engine idle speed, as necessary.

6.  Check the power steering pump fluid for bubbles. If air bubbles are present in the fluid, bleed the system:

a.  Fill the power steering pump reservoir to specifications with the engine at normal operating temperature.

b.  With the engine running, rotate the steering wheel through its normal travel 3 or 4 times, without holding the wheel against the stops.

c.  Check the fluid level again.

### REMOVAL & INSTALLATION

▸ **See Figures 17 thru 25**

### ✳✳ CAUTION

**Power steering fluid and brake fluid cannot be mixed. If brake seals contact the steering fluid or steering seals contact the brake fluid, damage will result!**

1.  Turn the engine off and pump the brake pedal 4 or 5 times to deplete the accumulator inside the unit.

2.  Remove the two nuts from the master cylinder, and remove the cylinder keeping the brake lines attached. Secure the master cylinder out of the way.

3.  Remove the hydraulic lines from the booster.

4.  Remove the booster unit from the firewall.

5.  To install, reverse the removal procedure. Tighten the nuts to booster mounting nuts to 22 ft. lbs. (30 Nm); the master cylinder mounting nuts to 20 ft. lbs. (27 Nm). Bleed the Hydro-Boost system.

### HYDRO-BOOST SYSTEM BLEEDING

The system should be bled whenever the booster is removed and installed.

1.  Fill the power steering pump until the fluid level is at the base of the pump reservoir neck. Disconnect the battery lead from the distributor.

➡**Remove the electrical lead to the fuel solenoid terminal on the injection pump before cranking the engine.**

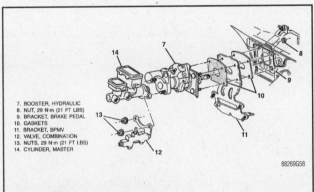

7.  BOOSTER, HYDRAULIC
8.  NUT, 29 N·m (21 FT LBS)
9.  BRACKET, BRAKE PEDAL
10.  GASKETS
11.  BRACKET, BPMV
12.  VALVE, COMBINATION
13.  NUTS, 29 N·m (21 FT LBS)
14.  CYLINDER, MASTER

88269G58

**Fig. 17 Hydro-boost mounting order**

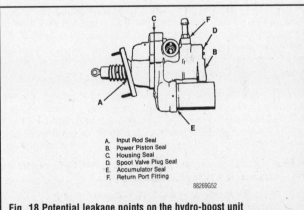

A.  Input Rod Seal
B.  Power Piston Seal
C.  Housing Seal
D.  Spool Valve Plug Seal
E.  Accumulator Seal
F.  Return Port Fitting

88269G52

**Fig. 18 Potential leakage points on the hydro-boost unit**

88269P10

**Fig. 19 Use a rag to catch the fluid when disconnecting the pressure hoses**

88269P11

**Fig. 20 Always use a flare wrench on the fittings**

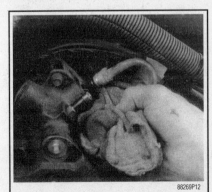

88269P12

**Fig. 21 Note the O-ring on the end of the fitting. Use a new one when reconnecting**

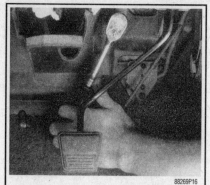

Fig. 22 Loosen and remove the booster mounting nuts from inside the vehicle

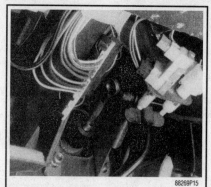

Fig. 23 Disconnect the pushrod from the pedal

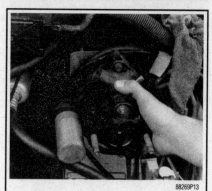

Fig. 24 Withdraw the booster assembly by pulling straight out

Fig. 25 Once the booster is out far enough to clear the pushrod, it can be removed from the vehicle

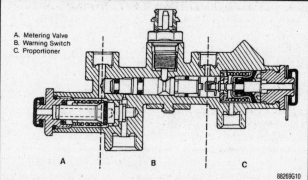

A. Metering Valve
B. Warning Switch
C. Proportioner

Fig. 26 Cut away view of a combination valve. The style of valve can vary

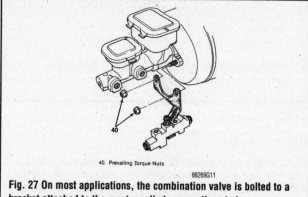

40. Prevailing Torque Nuts

Fig. 27 On most applications, the combination valve is bolted to a bracket attached to the master cylinder mounting studs

2. Jack up the front of the car, turn the wheels all the way to the left, and crank the engine for a few seconds.

3. Check steering pump fluid level. If necessary, add fluid to the "ADD" mark on the dipstick.

4. Lower the car, connect the battery lead, and start the engine. Check fluid level and add fluid to the "ADD" mark, as necessary. With the engine running, turn the wheels from side to side to bleed air from the system. Make sure that the fluid level stays above the internal pump casting.

5. The Hydro-Boost system should now be fully bled. If the fluid is foaming after bleeding, stop the engine, let the system set for one hour, then repeat the second part of Step 4.

The preceding procedures should be effective in removing the excess air from the system, however sometimes air may still remain trapped. When this happens the booster may make a gulping noise when the brake is applied. Lightly pumping the brake pedal with the engine running should cause this noise to disappear. After the noise stops, check the pump fluid level and add as necessary.

## Combination Valve

The standard combination valve is located in the engine compartment, directly under the master cylinder. It consists of 3 sections: the metering valve, the warning switch and the proportioning valve.

### REMOVAL & INSTALLATION

▶ **See Figures 26 and 27**

1. Disconnect and plug the hydraulic lines from the combination valve to prevent the loss of brake fluid or dirt from entering the system.

2. Disconnect the electrical connector from the combination valve.

3. Remove the combination valve-to-bracket nuts and the combination valve from the vehicle.

➡**The combination valve is not repairable and must be replaced as a complete assembly.**

4. Installation is the reverse of the removal procedure. Tighten the combination valve-to-bracket nuts to 37 ft. lbs. (49 Nm).

5. After installation is complete, bleed the brake system.

### SWITCH CENTERING

Whenever work on the brake system is done, it is possible that the brake warning light will come on and refuse to go off when the work is finished. In this event, the switch must be centered.

1. Raise and support the truck.

2. Attach a bleeder hose to the rear brake bleed screw and immerse the other end of the hose in a jar of clean brake fluid.

3. Be sure that the master cylinder is full.

4. When bleeding the brakes, the pin in the end of the metering portion of the combination valve must be held in the open position (with the tool described in the brake bleeding section installed under the pin mounting bolt). Be sure to tighten the bolt after removing the tool.

5. Turn the ignition key **ON**. Open the bleed screw while an assistant applies heavy pressure on the brake pedal. The warning lamp should light. Close the bleed screw before the helper releases the pedal.

6. To reset the switch, apply heavy pressure to the pedal. This will apply hydraulic pressure to the switch which will re-center it.

7. Repeat Step 5 for the front bleed screw.

8. Turn the ignition **OFF** and lower the truck.

➡**If the warning lamp does not light during Step 5, the switch is defective and must be replaced.**

## Brake Hoses and Lines

Metal lines and rubber brake hoses should be checked frequently for leaks and external damage. Metal lines are particularly prone to crushing and kinking under the vehicle. Any such deformation can restrict the proper flow of fluid and therefore impair braking at the wheels. Rubber hoses should be checked for cracking or scraping; such damage can create a weak spot in the hose and it could fail under pressure.

Any time the lines are removed or disconnected, extreme cleanliness must be observed. Clean all joints and connections before disassembly (use a stiff bristle brush and clean brake fluid); be sure to plug the lines and ports as soon as they are opened. New lines and hoses should be flushed clean with brake fluid before installation to remove any contamination.

### REMOVAL & INSTALLATION

▶ **See Figures 28, 29 and 30**

1. Disconnect the negative battery cable.

2. Raise and safely support the vehicle on jackstands.

3. Remove any wheel and tire assemblies necessary for access to the particular line you are removing.

4. Thoroughly clean the surrounding area at the joints to be disconnected.

5. Place a suitable catch pan under the joint to be disconnected.

6. Using two wrenches (one to hold the joint and one to turn the fitting), disconnect the hose or line to be replaced.

7. Disconnect the other end of the line or hose, moving the drain pan if necessary. Always use a back-up wrench to avoid damaging the fitting.

8. Disconnect any retaining clips or brackets holding the line and remove the line from the vehicle.

➡**If the brake system is to remain open for more time than it takes to swap lines, tape or plug each remaining clip and port to keep contaminants out and fluid in.**

**To install:**

9. Install the new line or hose, starting with the end farthest from the master cylinder. Connect the other end, then confirm that both fittings are correctly threaded and turn smoothly using finger pressure. Make sure the new line will not rub against any other part. Brake lines must be at least 1/2 in. (13mm) from the steering column and other moving parts. Any protective shielding or insulators must be reinstalled in the original location.

**Make sure the hose is NOT kinked or touching any part of the frame or suspension after installation. These conditions may cause the hose to fail prematurely.**

10. Using two wrenches as before, tighten each fitting.

11. Install any retaining clips or brackets on the lines.

12. If removed, install the wheel and tire assemblies, then carefully lower the vehicle to the ground.

13. Refill the brake master cylinder reservoir with clean, fresh brake fluid, meeting DOT 3 specifications. Properly bleed the brake system.

14. Connect the negative battery cable.

## Bleeding the Brake System

The hydraulic brake system must be bled any time one of the lines is disconnected or any time air enters the system. If the brake pedal feels spongy upon application, and goes almost to the floor but regains height when pumped, air has entered the system. It must be bled out. Check for leaks that would have allowed the entry of air and repair them before bleeding the system. The correct bleeding sequence is; right rear, left rear, right front and left front.

### MANUAL

▶ **See Figures 31, 32 and 33**

This method of bleeding requires 2 people, one to depress the brake pedal and the other to open the bleeder screws.

➡**The following procedure requires the use of a clear vinyl hose, a glass jar and clean brake fluid.**

1. Clean the top of the master cylinder, remove the cover and fill the reservoirs with clean fluid. To prevent squirting fluid, replace the cover.

➡**On vehicles equipped with front disc brakes, it will be necessary to hold in the metering valve pin during the bleeding procedure. The metering valve is located beneath the master cylinder and the pin is situated under the rubber boot on the end of the valve housing. This may be tapped in or held by an assistant.**

2. Fill the master cylinder with brake fluid.

3. Install a box end wrench onto the bleeder screw on the right rear wheel.

4. Attach a length of small diameter, clear vinyl tubing to the bleeder screw. Submerge the other end of the tubing in a glass jar partially filled with clean

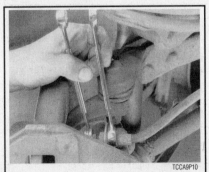

**Fig. 28 Use two wrenches to loosen the fitting. If available, use flare nut type wrenches**

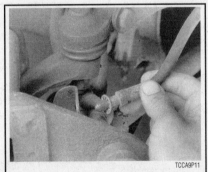

**Fig. 29 Any gaskets/crush washers should be replaced with new ones during installation**

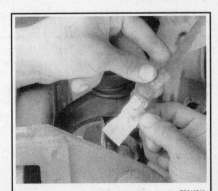

**Fig. 30 Tape or plug the line to prevent contamination**

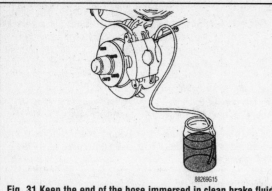

Fig. 31 Keep the end of the hose immersed in clean brake fluid to prevent air from being drawn back into the system

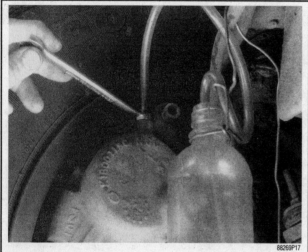

Fig. 32 Make sure that the end of the bleeder hose is below the level of the bleeder screw

Fig. 33 The use of a long handled wrench makes bleeding the rear wheel cylinder easier

brake fluid. Make sure the tube fits on the bleeder screw snugly or you may be squirted with brake fluid when the bleeder screw is opened.

5. Have your assistant slowly depress the brake pedal. As this is done, open the bleeder screw ½ turn and allow the fluid to run through the tube. Close the bleeder screw, then return the brake pedal to its fully released position.

6. Repeat this procedure until no bubbles appear in the jar. Refill the master cylinder.

7. Repeat this procedure on the left rear, right front and the left front wheels, in that order. Periodically, refill the master cylinder so that it does not run dry.

8. If the brake warning light is ON, depress the brake pedal firmly. If there is no air in the system, the light will go OFF.

## PRESSURE

▶ See Figures 34 and 35

➡The following procedure requires the use of the GM Brake Bleeder Adapter tool No. J–29567 or equivalent, and the GM Combination Valve Depressor tool No. J–35856 or equivalent.

1. Using the GM Brake Bleeder Adapter tool No. J–29567 or equivalent, fill the pressure tank to at least ⅓ full of brake fluid. Using compressed air, charge the pressure tank to 20–25 psi. (138–172 kPa), then install it onto the master cylinder.

2. Using the GM Combination Valve Depressor tool No. J–35856 or equivalent, install it onto the combination valve to hold the valve open during the bleeding operation.

3. Bleed each wheel cylinder or caliper in the following sequence: right rear, left rear, right front and left front.

4. Connect a hose from the bleeder tank to the adapter at the master cylinder, then open the tank valve.

5. Attach a clear vinyl hose to the brake bleeder screw, then immerse the opposite end into a container partially filled with clean brake fluid.

6. Open the bleeder screw ¾ turn and allow the fluid to flow until no air bubbles are seen in the fluid, then close the bleeder screw.

7. Repeat the bleeding process to each wheel.

8. Inspect the brake pedal for sponginess and if necessary, repeat the entire bleeding procedure.

9. Remove the depressor tool from the combination valve and the bleeder adapter from the master cylinder.

10. Refill the master cylinder to the proper level with brake fluid.

### Anti-Lock Brakes EHCU Valve

▶ See Figure 36

➡The rear wheel and 4-wheel anti-lock brakes are bled the same way as the standard brakes, pertaining to the master cylinder and each wheel cylinder. The difference is in the 4-wheel anti-lock system. The Electro-hydraulic Control Unit (EHCU) valve has to be bled after replacement only.

Use the 2 bleed screws on the EHCU valve for bleeding. There are also 2 bleeders on the front of the unit that look like normal brake bleeders. These are NOT the correct bleeders for bleeding the valve and they should not be turned.

1. Bleed the calipers and wheel cylinder first.

2. Install a valve depressor tool J–35856 onto the left high pressure accumulator bleed stem of the EHCU valve.

3. Slowly depress the brake pedal one time and hold. Loosen the left bleeder screw ¼ turn to purge the air from the EHCU valve.

4. Tighten the bleeder screw to 60 inch lbs. (7 Nm) and slowly release the pedal.

5. Wait 15 seconds, then repeat the sequence, purging the EHCU valve.

6. Repeat steps 2–5 at the right side of the EHCU valve.

7. Remove the valve depressor tool.

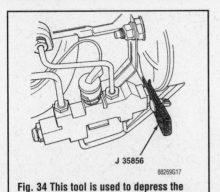

Fig. 34 This tool is used to depress the combination valve plunger to allow proper flow of brake fluid during bleeding

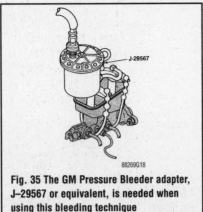

Fig. 35 The GM Pressure Bleeder adapter, J–29567 or equivalent, is needed when using this bleeding technique

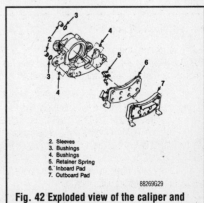

A. Internal bleed screw
B. EHCU valve-to-bracket bolts
C. Depress during bleeding

Fig. 36 The EHCU should need to be bled ONLY after replacement

## FRONT DISC BRAKES

### ❋❋ CAUTION

**Brake shoes contain asbestos, which has been determined to be a cancer causing agent. Never clean the brake surfaces with compressed air! Avoid inhaling any dust from any brake surface! When cleaning brake surfaces, use a commercially available brake cleaning fluid.**

### Brake Pads

#### INSPECTION

▶ **See Figures 37, 38, 39 and 40**

Brake pads should be inspected once a year or at 7500 miles (12,000 km), which ever occurs first. Check both ends of the outboard shoe, looking in at each end of the caliper; then check the lining thickness on the inboard shoe, looking down through the inspection hole. The lining should be more than $\frac{1}{32}$ in. (0.8mm) thick above the rivet (so that the lining is thicker than the metal backing). Keep in mind that any applicable state inspection standards that are more stringent, take precedence. All 4 pads must be replaced if one shows excessive wear.

➡ All models have a wear indicator that makes a noise when the linings wear to a degree where replacement is necessary. The spring clip is an integral part of the inboard shoe and lining. When the brake pad reaches a certain degree of wear, the clip will contact the rotor and produce a warning noise.

#### REMOVAL & INSTALLATION

▶ **See Figures 41 thru 54**

➡ The following procedure requires the use of a C-clamp and slip-joint lock pliers.

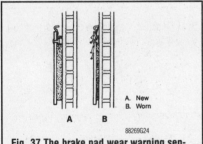

A. New
B. Worn

Fig. 37 The brake pad wear warning sensor will squeal once the pad is thin enough that the tab touches the rotor

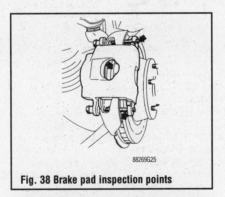

Fig. 38 Brake pad inspection points

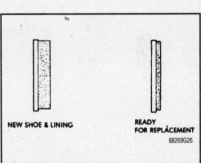

NEW SHOE & LINING    READY FOR REPLACEMENT

Fig. 39 Get to know what a worn pad looks like versus a new pad

Fig. 40 Measure the thickness of the friction material, not the backing plate

Fig. 41 The standard GM front disc brake

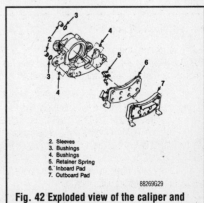

2. Sleeves
3. Bushings
4. Bushings
5. Retainer Spring
6. Inboard Pad
7. Outboard Pad

Fig. 42 Exploded view of the caliper and pad components—Two wheel drive

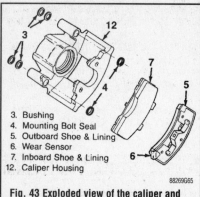

3. Bushing
4. Mounting Bolt Seal
5. Outboard Shoe & Lining
6. Wear Sensor
7. Inboard Shoe & Lining
12. Caliper Housing

Fig. 43 Exploded view of the caliper and pad components—All wheel drive

Fig. 44 A prybar can be used to press the pads into the caliper enough to remove the caliper . . .

Fig. 45 . . . or a C-clamp applied to the outboard pad will press the piston in the bore without cocking

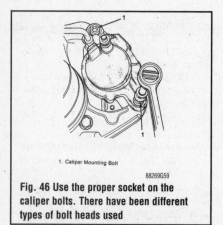

1. Caliper Mounting Bolt

Fig. 46 Use the proper socket on the caliper bolts. There have been different types of bolt heads used

Fig. 47 The pins are the only thing that hold the caliper to the mount

Fig. 48 Check the pins for corrosion and damage

Fig. 49 Pull the caliper straight off the rotor to remove otherwise it could bind

Fig. 50 Support the caliper so the weight does not pull on the brake line

Fig. 51 Separate the outer pad from the caliper. You may need a small prybar to do this if the fit is tight

Fig. 52 The inner pad is held by this spring. Make sure it is in place before installing the new pad

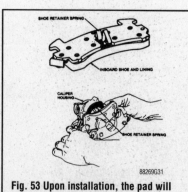

Fig. 53 Upon installation, the pad will click into place if the retainer spring is installed properly

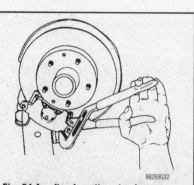

Fig. 54 An often forgotten step is compressing the brake pad ears. If it isn't done, the pads can rattle

1. Siphon off about ⅔ of the brake fluid from the master cylinder reservoirs.

### ❊❊ CAUTION

**The insertion of thicker replacement pads will push the piston back into its bore and will cause a full master cylinder reservoir to overflow, possibly causing paint damage. In addition to siphoning off fluid, it would be wise to keep the reservoir cover on during pad replacement.**

2. Raise and support the front of the vehicle on jackstands. Remove the wheels.

➡**When replacing the pads on just one wheel, uneven braking will result; always replace the pads on both wheels.**

3. Install a C-clamp on the caliper so that the frame side of the clamp rests against the back of the caliper and so the screw end rests against the metal part (shoe) of the outboard pad.

4. Tighten the clamp until the caliper moves enough to bottom the piston in its bore. Remove the clamp.

5. Remove the 2 Allen head caliper mounting bolts enough to allow the caliper to be pulled off the disc.

6. Remove the inboard pad and loosen the outboard pad. Place the caliper where it will not strain the brake hose; it would be best to wire it out of the way.

7. Remove the pad support spring clip from the piston.

8. Remove the 2 bolt ear sleeves and the 4 rubber bushings from the ears.

9. Riveted-style brake pads should be replaced when they are worn to within ⅟₃₂ in. (0.8mm) of the rivet heads; bonded style pads should be replaced when they are worn to no less than ⅟₃₂ in. (0.8mm) of the backing plate.

10. Check the inside of the caliper for leakage and the condition of the piston dust boot.

**To install:**

11. Lubricate the 2 new sleeves and 4 bushings with a silicone spray.

12. Install the bushings in each caliper ear. Install the 2 sleeves in the 2 inboard ears.

13. Install the pad support spring clip and the old pad into the center of the piston. You will then push this pad down to get the piston flat against the caliper. This part of the job is a hassle and requires an assistant. While the assistant holds the caliper and loosens the bleeder valve to relieve the pressure, obtain a medium pry bar and try to force the old pad inward, making the piston flush with the caliper surface. When it is flush, close the bleeder valve so that no air gets into the system.

➡**Make sure that the wear sensor is facing toward the rear of the caliper.**

14. Place the outboard pad in the caliper with its top ears over the caliper ears and the bottom tab engaged in the caliper cutout.

15. After both pads are installed, lift the caliper and place the bottom edge of the outboard pad on the outer edge of the disc to make sure that there is no clearance between the tab on the bottom of the shoes and the caliper abutment.

16. Place the caliper over the disc, lining up the hole in the caliper ears with the hole in the mounting bracket. Make sure that the brake hose is not kinked.

17. Start the caliper-to-mounting bracket bolts through the sleeves in the inboard caliper ears and through the mounting bracket, making sure that the ends of the bolts pass under the retaining ears of the inboard shoe.

18. Push the mounting bolts through to engage the holes in the outboard shoes and the outboard caliper ears and then threading them into the mounting bracket.

19. Torque the mounting bolts to 37 ft. lbs. (50 Nm). Pump the brake pedal to seat the linings against the rotors.

20. Using a pair of slip-joint locking pliers, place them on the notch on the caliper housing, bend the caliper upper ears until no clearance exists between the shoe and the caliper housing.

21. Install the wheels, lower the vehicle and refill the master cylinder reservoirs with brake fluid. Pump the brake pedal to make sure that it is firm. If it is not, bleed the brakes.

### Brake Caliper

REMOVAL & INSTALLATION

▶ **See Figures 55, 56 and 57**

1. Remove the brake caliper from the steering knuckle.

2. Disconnect the flexible brake hose-to-caliper bolt, discard the pressure fitting washers, then remove the brake caliper from the vehicle and place it on a work bench.

3. To inspect the caliper assembly, perform the following procedures:

   a. Check the inside of the caliper assembly for signs of leakage; if necessary, replace or rebuild the caliper.

   b. Check the mounting bolts and sleeves for signs of corrosion; if necessary, replace the bolts.

➡**If the mounting bolts have signs of corrosion, DO NOT attempt to polish away the corrosion.**

**To install:**

4. Use new caliper bushings and sleeves, use Delco® Silicone Lube or equivalent to lubricate the mounting bolts and new brake pads (if necessary).

5. After both pads are installed, lift the caliper and place the bottom edge of the outboard pad on the outer edge of the disc to make sure that there is no clearance between the tab on the bottom of the shoes and the caliper abutment.

6. Place the caliper over the disc, lining up the hole in the caliper ears with the hole in the mounting bracket.

7. Start the caliper-to-mounting bracket bolts through the sleeves in the inboard caliper ears and through the mounting bracket, making sure that the ends of the bolts pass under the retaining ears of the inboard shoe.

8. Push the mounting bolts through to engage the holes in the outboard shoes and the outboard caliper ears, then thread them into the mounting bracket.

9. To complete the installation, use new flexible brake hose-to-caliper washers. Torque the caliper-to-steering knuckle bolts to 30–45 ft. lbs. (41–61 Nm) and the flexible brake hose-to-caliper bolt to 18–30 ft. lbs. (25–41 Nm). Refill the master cylinder reservoirs and bleed the brake system. Pump the brake pedal to seat the linings against the rotors.

10. Using a pair of slip-joint locking pliers, place them on the caliper housing notch, bend the caliper upper ears until no clearance exists between the shoe and the caliper housing.

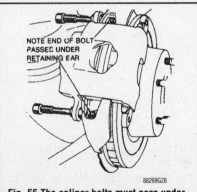

Fig. 55 The caliper bolts must pass under the pad retaining ears

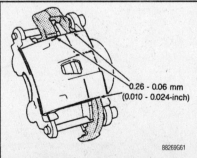

Fig. 56 Check the clearance between the caliper and caliper mount. The numbers shown are total clearance, not individual sides—Two wheel drive

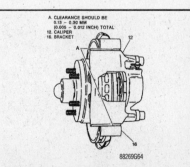

Fig. 57 Check the clearance between the caliper and caliper mount. The numbers shown are total clearance, not individual sides—All wheel drive

11. Install the wheels, lower the vehicle. Pump the brake pedal to make sure that it is firm. Road test the vehicle.

## OVERHAUL

♦ **See Figures 58 thru 67**

1. Remove the brake caliper from the vehicle.
2. Remove the inlet fitting from the brake caliper. Cap all openings to prevent system contamination or excessive fluid leakage.
3. Position the caliper on a work bench and place clean shop cloths in the caliper opening. Using compressed air, force the piston from its bore.

### ✳✳ CAUTION

**DO NOT apply too much air pressure to the bore, for the piston may jump out, causing damage to the piston and/or the operator.**

4. Remove and discard the piston boot and seal (with a plastic or wooden tool).
5. Clean all of the parts with non-mineral based solvent and blow dry with compressed air. Replace the rubber parts with those in the brake service kit.
6. Inspect the piston and the caliper bore for damage or corrosion. Replace the caliper and/or the piston (if necessary).
7. Remove the bleeder screw and its rubber cap.
8. Inspect the guide pins for corrosion, replace them (if necessary). When installing the guide pins, coat them with silicone grease.
9. To install, perform the following procedures:
   a. Maintain the proper tolerances.
   b. Lubricate the piston, caliper and seal with clean brake fluid and install those parts.

➡ **When positioning the piston dust boot on the piston, it goes in the groove nearest the piston's flat end with the lap facing the largest end. If placement is correct, the seal lips will be in the groove and not extend over the groove's step.**

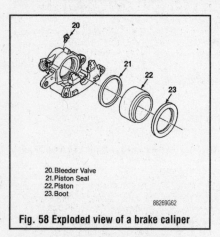

20. Bleeder Valve
21. Piston Seal
22. Piston
23. Boot

88269G62

**Fig. 58 Exploded view of a brake caliper**

88269P31

**Fig. 59 Apply a small amount of compressed air to remove the piston, but pad the opposite side of the caliper with a piece of wood to prevent the piston from flying out**

88269P32

**Fig. 60 Pull the piston out and away from the dust boot**

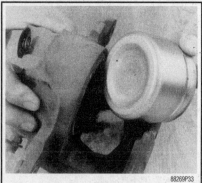

88269P33

**Fig. 61 Check the surface of the piston for damage and corrosion**

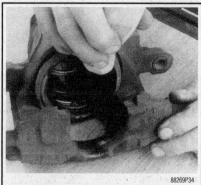

88269P34

**Fig. 62 Inspect the caliper for obvious defects before continuing the rebuild**

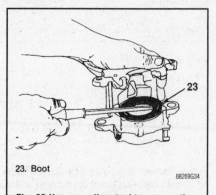

23. Boot

88269G34

**Fig. 63 Use a small prytool to remove the dust boot**

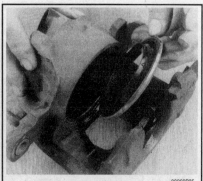

88269P35

**Fig. 64 The dust seal needs to be replaced every time it is removed**

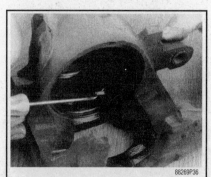

88269P36

**Fig. 65 Be careful when removing the piston seal not to nick or scratch the bore and seal seating area**

88269P37

**Fig. 66 Using the appropriate dust boot installation tool will help make sure the boot is properly seated**

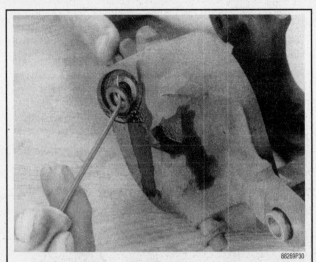

**Fig. 67 Before installation, check that the old crush gasket isn't stuck at the inlet port**

c. Replace the mounting bolts and torque to 22–25 ft. lbs. (30–34 Nm).
10. Bleed the brake system after installation and pump the pedal before moving the vehicle.

## Brake Disc (Rotor)

The 2-wheel drive brake disc rotor and the wheel bearing hub assembly are designed as one piece; therefore, to remove the brake disc, remove the wheel bearing assembly.

The 4-wheel drive brake disc rotor is separate from the hub assembly and can be removed without removing the hub and bearings assembly. The hub and bearing assembly is non-serviceable and has to be replaced as a unit.

### REMOVAL & INSTALLATION

#### 2WD Model

▶ See Figure 68

1. Raise and support the front of the vehicle safely using jackstands.
2. Remove the tire and wheel assembly.
3. Remove the brake caliper mounting bolts and carefully remove the caliper (along with the brake pads) from the rotor. Do not disconnect the brake line; instead wire the caliper out of the way with the line still connected.

➡**Once the rotor is removed from the vehicle the wheel bearings may be cleaned and repacked or the bearings and races may be replaced. For more information, please refer to the wheel bearing procedures in Section 1 of this manual.**

4. Carefully pry out the grease cap, then remove the cotter pin, spindle nut, and washer. Remove the hub, being careful not to drop the outer wheel bearings. As the hub is pulled forward, the outer wheel bearings will often fall forward and they may easily be removed at this time.

**To install:**
5. Carefully install the wheel hub over the spindle.
6. Using your hands, firmly press the outer bearing into the hub.
7. Loosely install the spindle washer and nut, but do not install the cotter pin or dust cap at this time.
8. Install the brake caliper.
9. Install the tire and wheel assembly.
10. Properly adjust the wheel bearings:
    a. Spin the wheel forward by hand and tighten the nut to 12 ft. lbs. (16 Nm) in order to fully seat the bearings and remove any burrs from the threads.
    b. Back off the nut until it is just loose, then finger-tighten the nut.
    c. Loosen the nut ¼-½ turn until either hole in the spindle lines up with a slot in the nut, then install a new cotter pin. This may appear to be too loose, but it is the correct adjustment.
    d. Proper adjustment creates 0.001–0.005 in. (0.025–0.127mm) end-play.
11. Install the dust cap.
12. Install the wheel/hub cover, then remove the supports and carefully lower the vehicle.

#### 4WD Model

▶ See Figure 69

1. Raise and support the front of the truck safely using jackstands under the frame.
2. Remove the tire and wheel assembly.
3. Remove the brake caliper mounting bolts and carefully remove the caliper (along with the brake pads) from the rotor. Do not disconnect the brake line; instead wire the caliper out of the way with the line still connected.
4. If equipped, remove the lockwashers from the hub studs in order to free the rotor.
5. Remove the brake disc (rotor) from the wheel hub.
6. Inspect the disc for nicks, scores and/or damage, then replace if necessary.
7. Installation is the reverse of the removal. DO NOT attempt to move the vehicle unless a firm brake pedal is felt.

### INSPECTION

▶ See Figure 70

1. Raise and support the front of the vehicle on jackstands. Remove the wheels.
2. To check the disc runout, perform the following procedures:
    a. Using a dial indicator, secure and position it so that the button contacts the disc about 1 in. (25mm) from the outer edge.
    b. Rotate the disc. The lateral reading should not exceed 0.004 in. (0.1mm). If the reading is excessive, recondition or replace the disc.

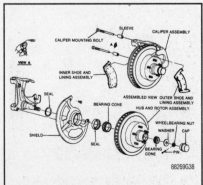

**Fig. 68 Exploded view of brake assembly—Two wheel drive**

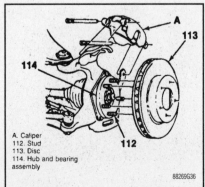

A. Caliper
112. Stud
113. Disc
114. Hub and bearing assembly

**Fig. 69 Rotor, hub and bearing assembly—All wheel drive**

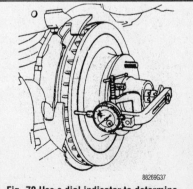

**Fig. 70 Use a dial indicator to determine brake disc runout**

3. To check the disc parallelism, perform the following procedures:

a. Using a micrometer, check the disc thickness at 4 locations around the disc, at the same distance from the edge.

b. The thickness should not vary more than 0.0005 in. (0.013mm). If the readings are excessive, recondition or replace the disc.

## REAR DRUM BRAKES

### ✳✳ CAUTION

**Brake shoes contain asbestos, which has been determined to be a cancer causing agent. Never clean the brake surfaces with compressed air! Avoid inhaling any dust from any brake surface! When cleaning brake surfaces, use a commercially available brake cleaning fluid.**

### Brake Drums

#### REMOVAL & INSTALLATION

1. Raise and support the rear of the vehicle on jackstands.
2. Remove the wheel and tire assemblies.
3. Pull the brake drum off. It may by necessary to gently tap the rear edges of the drum to start it off the studs.
4. If extreme resistance to removal is encountered, it will be necessary to retract the adjusting screw. Remove the access hole cover from the backing plate and turn the adjuster to retract the linings away from the drum.
5. Install a replacement hole cover before reinstalling the drum.
6. Install the drums in the same position on the hub as removed.

➡**The rear wheel bearings are not adjustable, they are serviced by replacement ONLY.**

#### INSPECTION

1. Check the drums for any cracks, scores, grooves or an out-of-round condition; if it is cracked, replace it. Slight scores can be removed with fine emery cloth while extensive scoring requires turning the drum on a lathe.
2. Never have a drum turned more than 0.060 in. (1.5mm).

### Brake Shoes

#### INSPECTION

Remove the drum and inspect the lining thickness of both brake shoes. The rear brake shoes should be replaced if the lining is less than 1/16 in. (1.5mm) at the lowest point (bonded linings) or above the rivet heads (riveted linings) on the brake shoe. However, these lining thickness measurements may disagree with your state inspections laws.

➡**Brake shoes should always be replaced in sets.**

4. The surface finish must be relatively smooth to avoid pulling and erratic performance, also, to extend the lining life. Light rotor surface scoring of up to 0.015 in. (0.38mm) in depth, can be tolerated. If the scoring depths are excessive, refinish or replace the rotor.

### REMOVAL & INSTALLATION

➧ **See Figures 71 thru 83**

➡**The following procedure requires the use of the GM Brake Spring Pliers tool No. J–8057 or equivalent.**

1. Raise and support the rear of the vehicle on jackstands.
2. Slacken the parking brake cable.
3. Remove the rear wheels and the brake drum.
4. Using the GM Brake Spring Pliers tool No. J–8057 or equivalent, disconnect the brake shoe return springs, the actuator pullback spring, the hold-down pins/springs and the actuator assembly.

➡**Special brake spring tools are available from the auto supply stores, which will ease the replacement of the spring and anchor pin, but the job may still be performed with common hand tools.**

5. Disconnect the adjusting mechanism and spring, then remove the primary shoe. The primary shoe has a shorter lining than the secondary and is mounted at the front of the wheel.
6. Disconnect the parking brake lever from the secondary shoe and remove the shoe.

**To install:**

7. Clean and inspect all of the brake parts.
8. Check the wheel cylinders for seal condition and leaking.
9. If necessary, repack the wheel bearings and replace the oil seals.
10. Inspect the replacement shoes for nicks or burrs, lubricate the backing plate contact points, the brake cable, the levers and adjusting screws, then reassemble them.

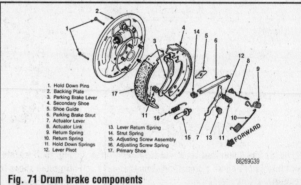

1. Hold Down Pins
2. Backing Plate
3. Parking Brake Lever
4. Secondary Shoe
5. Shoe Guide
6. Parking Brake Strut
7. Actuator Lever
8. Actuator Link
9. Return Spring
10. Return Spring
11. Hold Down Springs
12. Lever Pivot
13. Lever Return Spring
14. Strut Spring
15. Adjusting Screw Assembly
16. Adjusting Screw Spring
17. Primary Shoe

**Fig. 71 Drum brake components**

**Fig. 72 The standard GM drum brake**

**Fig. 73 Use proper brake tools when removing parts like the return springs**

**Fig. 74 Note the direction in which each spring and component is installed for ease during installation**

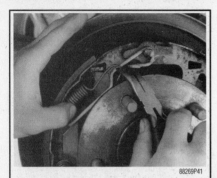

Fig. 75 Sometimes tools such as needle nosed pliers allow you additionally needed flexibility

Fig. 76 Use this tool by placing the socket over the pin and rotating until the tang lifts the spring or linkage off

Fig. 77 Do not lose this plate. Nothing holds it in place once the springs are removed

Fig. 78 A brake shoe retention pin removal tool makes the job much easier

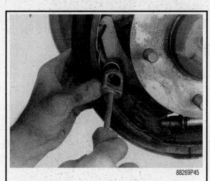

Fig. 79 Press on the back side of the pin while using the tool to allow the pin to be released from the lock

Fig. 80 Try to remove most of the parts as entire assemblies. This will ease installation

Fig. 81 The shoes can come out together at this point and be disassembled on the bench

Fig. 82 Separate the parking brake lever from the shoes to free the shoes from the brake assembly

Fig. 83 After the shoes have been removed, this link will be one part left behind

11. Make sure that the right and left hand adjusting screws are not mixed. You can prevent this by working on one side at a time. This will also provide you with a reference for reassembly. The star wheel should be nearest to the secondary shoe when correctly installed.

12. Using lithium grease or equivalent, lubricate the shoe pads (on the backing plate) and the adjusting screw threads.

13. Install the springs and adjusters. When completed, make an initial adjustment as previously described.

## Wheel Cylinders

### REMOVAL & INSTALLATION

▶ **See Figures 84, 85 and 86**

1. Remove the brake shoe assembly from the backing plate.

2. Clean away all of the dirt, crud and foreign material from around the wheel cylinder. It is important that dirt be kept away from the brake line when the cylinder is disconnected.

3. Disconnect and plug the inlet tube at the wheel cylinder.

4. Remove the wheel cylinder-to-backing plate bolts and the wheel cylinder from the backing plate.

➡**If the wheel cylinder is sticking, use a hammer and a punch to drive the wheel cylinder from the backing plate.**

**To install:**

5. Install the wheel cylinder and bolts. Tighten the wheel cylinder-to-backing plate bolts to 13 ft. lbs. (18 Nm).

6. Install the rear brake shoes and hardware as outlined earlier in this Section.

7. Bleed the rear brake system. Adjust the rear brake assembly.

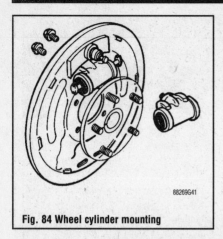

**Fig. 84 Wheel cylinder mounting**

**Fig. 85 Only 2 bolts hold the wheel cylinder in place (Plug the line to prevent system contamination)**

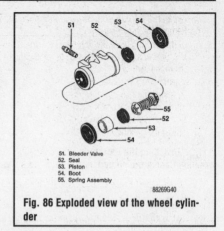

51. Bleeder Valve
52. Seal
53. Piston
54. Boot
55. Spring Assembly

**Fig. 86 Exploded view of the wheel cylinder**

## PARKING BRAKE

### Front Cable

#### REMOVAL & INSTALLATION

▶ **See Figures 87 and 88**

1. Raise and support the front of the vehicle on jackstands.
2. Under the left center of the vehicle, loosen the cable equalizer assembly.
3. Separate the front cable connector from the equalizer cable.
4. Remove the front cable retaining bolts and clips, then bend the retaining fingers.
5. Disconnect the front cable from the parking pedal assembly and the cable from the vehicle.

**To install:**

6. To install the front cable, attach a piece of wire to the cable, fish it through the cowl and connect it to the equalizer cable. Adjust the parking brake.
7. Lower the vehicle and check the parking brake operation.

### Rear Cable

#### REMOVAL & INSTALLATION

▶ **See Figures 89, 90, 91 and 92**

1. Raise and support the rear of the vehicle on jackstands.
2. Under the left center of the vehicle, loosen the cable equalizer assembly.

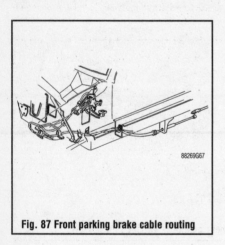

**Fig. 87 Front parking brake cable routing**

**Fig. 88 Front parking brake cable bracket**

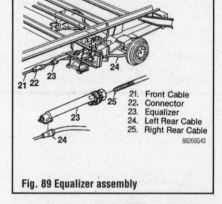

21. Front Cable
22. Connector
23. Equalizer
24. Left Rear Cable
25. Right Rear Cable

**Fig. 89 Equalizer assembly**

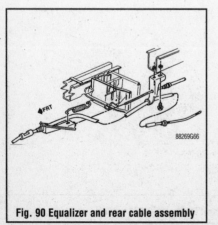

**Fig. 90 Equalizer and rear cable assembly**

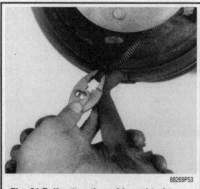

**Fig. 91 Pull out on the cable end to free the lever from the cable**

**Fig. 92 Use a box end wrench to press in the clips to free the cable from the backing plate**

3. Separate the front cable connector from the equalizer cable.

4. Remove the brake shoes.

5. At the backing plate, bend the cable retaining fingers.

6. Disconnect the rear cable(s) from the secondary brake shoe(s) and the cable(s) from the vehicle.

**To install:**

7. To install the rear cable(s), insert the cable through the backing plate and engage it with the secondary brake shoe.

8. Connect the cable to the equalizer cable.

9. Adjust the parking brake.

➡**When installing the rear parking brake cables, make sure that the retaining fingers are completely through the backing plate.**

10. Lower the vehicle and check the parking brake operation.

### ADJUSTMENT

◆ **See Figure 93**

➡**Before adjusting the parking brakes, check the condition of the service brakes; replace any necessary parts.**

1. Block the front wheels.

2. Raise and support the rear of the vehicle on jackstands.

3. Under the left center of the vehicle, loosen the equalizer.

4. Position the parking brake pedal on the second click (2 ratchet clicks).

5. Turn the cable equalizer until the rear wheel drags (when turned by hand).

**Fig. 93 Adjusting the parking brake at the equalizer**

6. Tighten the equalizer lock nut.

7. Release the parking brake pedal, then test it; the correct adjustment should be 9–16 clicks.

## ANTI-LOCK BRAKE SYSTEMS

### General Information

◆ **See Figures 94, 95, 96, 97 and 98**

There are two basic types of anti-lock systems available for this vehicle; a Rear Wheel Anti-Lock (RWAL) brake system and 4 Wheel Anti-Lock (4WAL) brake system. The 4WAL system has two variations; a 3 sensor system and a 4 sensor system. The 2WD vehicles will be equipped with the 3 sensor system, but the AWD vehicles can be equipped with either. The systems are easily identified by looking at the rear wheels for a sensor harness. If there is a sensor harness and thus, rear wheel sensors, it is the 4 sensor system. If the vehicle is not equipped with a harness, it is the 3 sensor system. The 4 sensor system takes it speed references from each of the wheels. The 3 sensor system takes its speed references from each of the front wheels and the vehicle speed sensor located in the transmission (2WD) or the transfer case (AWD).

The RWAL system components consist of the Vehicle Speed Sensor (VSS), the Electronic Control Unit (ECU), the isolation/dump valve and the Vehicle Speed Sensor Buffer (also known as the Digital Ratio Adapter). The ECU also receives signals from various brake switches.

The 4WAL system components consist of the Electro-Hydraulic Control Unit (ECHU) valve (also known as the Brake Pressure Modulator Valve or BPMV), the wheel speed sensors, Vehicle Speed Sensor (VSS) on 3 sensor systems and the VSS Buffer.

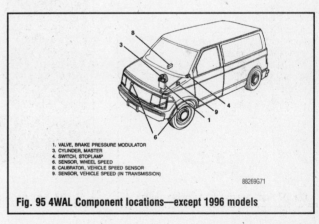

1. VALVE, BRAKE PRESSURE MODULATOR
3. CYLINDER, MASTER
4. SWITCH, STOPLAMP
5. SENSOR, WHEEL SPEED
8. CALIBRATOR, VEHICLE SPEED SENSOR
9. SENSOR, VEHICLE SPEED (IN TRANSMISSION)

**Fig. 95 4WAL Component locations—except 1996 models**

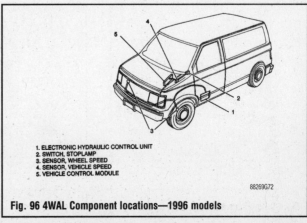

1. ELECTRONIC HYDRAULIC CONTROL UNIT
2. SWITCH, STOPLAMP
3. SENSOR, WHEEL SPEED
4. SENSOR, VEHICLE SPEED
5. VEHICLE CONTROL MODULE

**Fig. 96 4WAL Component locations—1996 models**

- - - - ELECTRIC
——— HYDRAULIC

A. To Front Brakes
1. Master Cylinder
2. Brake Light Switch
3. Instrument Cluster
4. Digital Ratio Adapter
   (Part of Instrument Cluster)
5. Speed Sensor
6. Transmission
7. Isolation/Dump Valve
8. RWAL Control Module
9. Brake Warning Light
10. Combination Valve

**Fig. 94 RWAL brake system diagram**

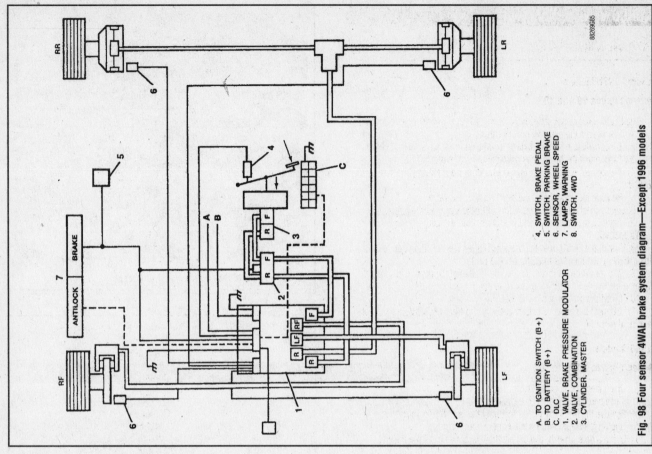

A. TO IGNITION SWITCH (B+)
B. TO BATTERY (B+)
C. DLC
1. VALVE, BRAKE PRESSURE MODULATOR
2. VALVE, COMBINATION
3. CYLINDER, MASTER

4. SWITCH, BRAKE PEDAL
5. SWITCH, PARKING BRAKE
6. SENSOR, WHEEL SPEED
7. LAMPS, WARNING
8. SWITCH, 4WD

Fig. 98 Four sensor 4WAL brake system diagram—Except 1996 models

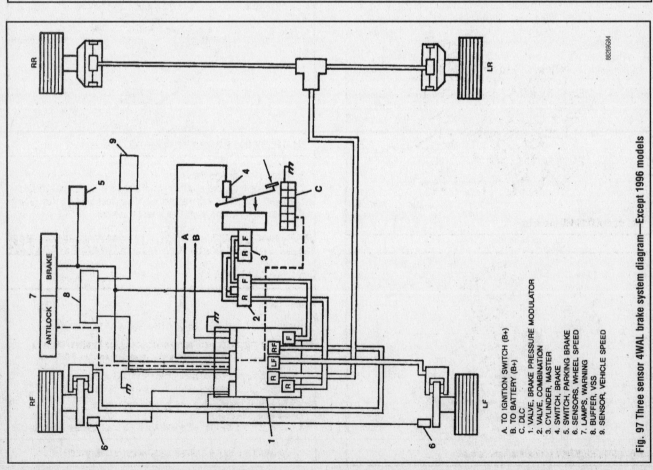

A. TO IGNITION SWITCH (B+)
B. TO BATTERY (B+)
C. DLC
1. VALVE, BRAKE PRESSURE MODULATOR
2. VALVE, COMBINATION
3. CYLINDER, MASTER
4. SWITCH, BRAKE
5. SWITCH, PARKING BRAKE
6. SENSORS, WHEEL SPEED
7. LAMPS, WARNING
8. BUFFER, VSS
9. SENSOR, VEHICLE SPEED

Fig. 97 Three sensor 4WAL brake system diagram—Except 1996 models

## EHCU Valve/BPMV (4WAL)

### REMOVAL & INSTALLATION

#### Except 1996 Models

**♦ See Figures 99 and 100**

The EHCU valve is not serviceable. Replace the valve only when defective.
1. Disconnect the negative battery cable.
2. Disconnect the intermediate steering shaft from the steering column.
3. Disconnect the brake lines from the bottom of the combination valve.
4. Disconnect the electrical connectors from the master cylinder and EHCU.
5. Remove the master cylinder and combination valve.
6. Disconnect the brake lines from the EHCU using a flare nut wrench.
7. Remove the bolts, nuts and EHCU from the vehicle.

**To install:**

8. Install the EHCU onto the bracket. Tighten the mounting bolt to 33 ft. lbs. (45 Nm) and the nuts to 20 ft. lbs. (27 Nm).
9. The remainder of installation is the reverse of the remove procedure. Tighten the hydraulic line fittings to 16 ft. lbs. (25 Nm).
10. Bleed the system and the EHCU.
11. Connect the negative battery cable, pump the brakes before road test and road test

#### 1996 Models

**♦ See Figures 101 and 102**

1. Disconnect the negative battery cable.
2. Raise and safely support the vehicle.
3. Remove the two 13mm bolts that hold the unit to the bracket.
4. Unplug the electrical connectors from the unit.
5. Using a flare wrench, disconnect the hydraulic lines from the unit.

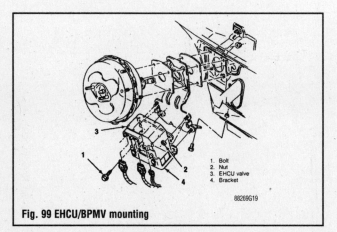

**Fig. 99 EHCU/BPMV mounting**

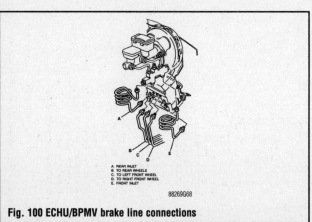

**Fig. 100 ECHU/BPMV brake line connections**

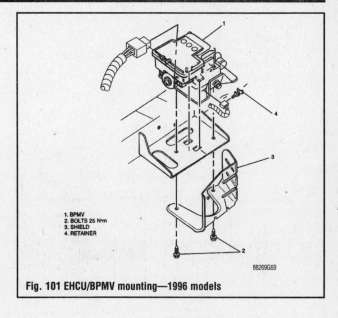

**Fig. 101 EHCU/BPMV mounting—1996 models**

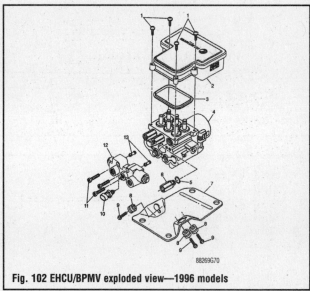

**Fig. 102 EHCU/BPMV exploded view—1996 models**

6. Remove the unit from the vehicle.
7. Installation is the reverse of the removal procedure. Tighten the hydraulic lines fittings to 18 ft. lbs. (24 Nm) and the two 13mm bolts to 84 inch lbs. (9 Nm).
8. Bleed the hydraulic system, then lower the vehicle.

## Electronic Control Unit (RWAL)

### REMOVAL & INSTALLATION

**♦ See Figure 103**

The ECU is not serviceable. Replace the unit only when defective.

➥**Do not touch the electrical connections and pins or allow them to come in contact with brake fluid as this may damage the ECU.**

1. Disconnect the negative battery cable and ECU connectors.
2. Remove the ECU by prying the tab at the rear of the ECU and pulling it toward the front of the vehicle.

**To install:**

3. Install the ECU by sliding the unit into the bracket until the tab locks into the hole.
4. Connect the electrical connectors and negative battery cable.

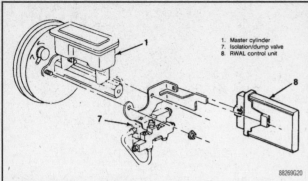

1. Master cylinder
7. Isolation/dump valve
8. RWAL control unit

88269G20

**Fig. 103 Electronic control unit and isolation/dump valve mounting location—RWAL**

## Isolation/Dump Valve

### TESTING

1. Disconnect the negative battery cable.
2. Disconnect the isolation/dump valve harness from the ECU.
3. Check the dump valve coil resistance between terminals B and D. If the resistance is greater than 3.0 ohms, replace the assembly. The resistance should be between 1.0 and 3.0 ohms.
4. Check the isolation valve coil resistance between terminals A and D. The resistance should be between 3.0 and 6.0 ohms. Replace the assembly if the resistance is above 6.0 ohms.
5. Check the resistance of the anti-lock valve switch between terminals C and D and then check it between C and the assembly body. If the resistance is less than 50,000 ohms in either test, replace the assembly.

### REMOVAL & INSTALLATION

▶ **See Figure 103**

The isolation/dump valve is not serviceable. Replace the unit only when defective.
1. Disconnect the negative battery cable.
2. Disconnect the brake line fittings using a flare nut wrench.
3. Disconnect the bottom electrical connector from the ECU. Do not allow the isolation/dump valve to hang by the pigtail.
4. Remove the valve from the vehicle.
5. Installation is the reverse of the removal procedure. Tighten the valve bolts to 21 ft. lbs. (29 Nm) and the brake line fittings to 18 ft. lbs. (24 Nm).
6. Connect the negative battery cable and bleed the system.

## Front Wheel Speed Sensor

### TESTING

▶ **See Figures 104 and 105**

1. Disconnect the negative battery cable.
2. Raise the vehicle and support with jackstands. Remove the wheel and tire assembly.

| WHEEL SPEED SENSOR TEMPERATURE VS. SENSOR RESISTANCE (APPROXIMATE) | | |
|---|---|---|
| TEMP. (°C) | TEMP. (°F) | RESISTANCE (OHMS) |
| -40 TO 4 | -40 TO 40 | 920 TO 1387 |
| 5 TO 43 | 41 TO 110 | 1125 TO 1620 |
| 44 TO 93 | 111 TO 200 | 1305 TO 1900 |
| 94 TO 150 | 201 TO 302 | 1530 TO 2200 |

88269G76

**Fig. 104 Front wheel speed sensor resistance chart—Non-integral sensors**

| WHEEL SPEED SENSOR TEMPERATURE VS. SENSOR RESISTANCE (APPROXIMATE) | | |
|---|---|---|
| TEMP. (°C) | TEMP. (°F) | RESISTANCE (OHMS) |
| -40 TO 4 | -40 TO 40 | 1900 TO 2950 |
| 5 TO 43 | 41 TO 110 | 2420 TO 3450 |
| 44 TO 93 | 111 TO 200 | 2810 TO 4100 |
| 94 TO 150 | 201 TO 302 | 3320 TO 4760 |

88269G77

**Fig. 105 Front wheel speed sensor resistance chart—Integral sensors**

3. Disconnect the front wheel speed sensor.
4. Measure the resistance of the sensor and compare to the chart.
5. Replace the sensor if the resistance does not meet specification.

### REMOVAL & INSTALLATION

**2-Wheel Drive**

▶ **See Figures 106, 107, 108, 109 and 110**

1. Disconnect the negative battery cable.
2. Raise the vehicle and support with jackstands. Remove the wheel and tire assembly.

### ※※ CAUTION

**Some brake pads contain asbestos, which has been determined to be a cancer causing agent. Never clean the brake surfaces with compressed air! Avoid inhaling any dust from any brake surface! When cleaning brake surfaces, use a commercially available brake cleaning fluid.**

3. Remove the brake caliper, hub and rotor.
4. Disconnect the sensor electrical connector.
5. Remove the splash shield with the sensor from the steering knuckle.
6. Installation is the reverse of the removal procedure. Tighten the splash shield and sensor bolts to 11 ft. lbs. (15 Nm).
7. Connect the negative battery cable and check operation.

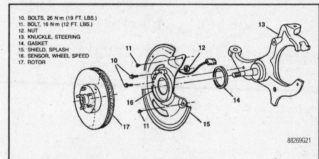

10. BOLTS, 26 N·m (19 FT. LBS.)
11. BOLT, 16 N·m (12 FT. LBS.)
12. NUT
13. KNUCKLE, STEERING
14. GASKET
15. SHIELD, SPLASH
16. SENSOR, WHEEL SPEED
17. ROTOR

88269G21

**Fig. 106 Front wheel speed sensor—2WD**

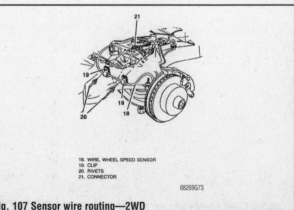

18. WIRE, WHEEL SPEED SENSOR
19. CLIP
20. RIVETS
21. CONNECTOR

88269G73

**Fig. 107 Sensor wire routing—2WD**

**Fig. 108 The front wheel speed sensor is accessible after removing the hub and rotor**

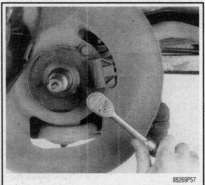

**Fig. 109 Simply remove the two mounting bolts to replace the sensor**

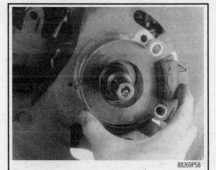

**Fig. 110 Pull the sensor off the backing plate and route the wires through the opening**

### 4-Wheel Drive

There are two basic styles of front wheel sensor, integral and non-integral. The integral sensor is mounted in the hub bearing assembly, while the non-integral is mounted on the backing plate.

#### INTEGRAL SENSORS

▶ See Figures 111 and 112

1. Disconnect the negative battery cable.
2. Raise the vehicle and support with jackstands. Remove the wheel and tire assembly.

#### ✳✳ CAUTION

**Some brake pads contain asbestos, which has been determined to be a cancer causing agent. Never clean the brake surfaces with compressed air! Avoid inhaling any dust from any brake surface!**

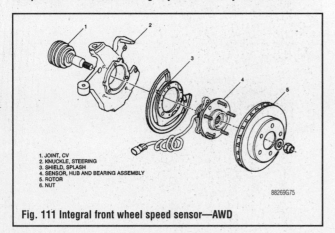

1. JOINT, CV
2. KNUCKLE, STEERING
3. SHIELD, SPLASH
4. SENSOR, HUB AND BEARING ASSEMBLY
5. ROTOR
6. NUT

**Fig. 111 Integral front wheel speed sensor—AWD**

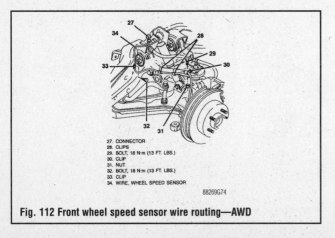

27. CONNECTOR
28. CLIPS
29. BOLT, 18 N·m (13 FT. LBS.)
30. CLIP
31. NUT
32. BOLT, 18 N·m (13 FT. LBS.)
33. CLIP
34. WIRE, WHEEL SPEED SENSOR

**Fig. 112 Front wheel speed sensor wire routing—AWD**

**When cleaning brake surfaces, use a commercially available brake cleaning fluid.**

3. Remove the brake caliper and rotor.
4. Remove the sensor wire clips from the frame and the control arm.
5. Disconnect the sensor electrical connector.
6. Remove the sensor from the bearing assembly.

**To install:**

7. Install a new O-ring on the sensor. Do not contaminate the lubricant in the sealed bearing.
8. Install the sensor into the bearing assembly and torque the bolts to 13 ft. lbs. (18 Nm).
9. The remainder of installation is the reverse of the removal procedure.
10. Connect the negative battery cable and check operation.

#### NON-INTEGRAL SENSORS

▶ See Figures 112 and 113

1. Disconnect the negative battery cable.
2. Raise the vehicle and support with jackstands. Remove the wheel and tire assembly.

#### ✳✳ CAUTION

**Some brake pads contain asbestos, which has been determined to be a cancer causing agent. Never clean the brake surfaces with compressed air! Avoid inhaling any dust from any brake surface! When cleaning brake surfaces, use a commercially available brake cleaning fluid.**

3. Remove the brake caliper and rotor.
4. Remove the hub and bearing assembly.
5. Disconnect the sensor electrical connector.
6. Remove the splash shield with the sensor from the steering knuckle.
7. Installation is the reverse of the removal procedure. Tighten the splash shield and sensor bolts to 11 ft. lbs. (15 Nm).
8. Connect the negative battery cable and check operation.

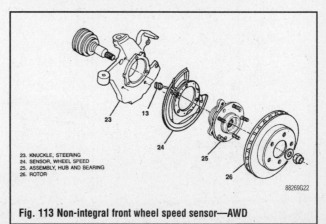

23. KNUCKLE, STEERING
24. SENSOR, WHEEL SPEED
25. ASSEMBLY, HUB AND BEARING
26. ROTOR

**Fig. 113 Non-integral front wheel speed sensor—AWD**

## Rear Wheel Speed Sensor

### TESTING

▶ **See Figure 114**

1. Disconnect the negative battery cable.
2. Raise the vehicle and support with jackstands. Remove the wheel and tire assembly.
3. Disconnect the rear wheel speed sensor.
4. Measure the resistance of the sensor and compare to the chart.
5. Replace the sensor if the resistance does not meet specification.

| WHEEL SPEED SENSOR TEMPERATURE VS. SENSOR RESISTANCE (APPROXIMATE) | | |
|---|---|---|
| TEMP. ('C) | TEMP. ('F) | RESISTANCE (OHMS) |
| -40 TO 4 | -40 TO 40 | 920 TO 1387 |
| 5 TO 43 | 41 TO 110 | 1125 TO 1620 |
| 44 TO 93 | 111 TO 200 | 1305 TO 1900 |
| 94 TO 150 | 201 TO 302 | 1530 TO 2200 |

88269G76

**Fig. 114 Rear wheel speed sensor and vehicle speed sensor resistance chart**

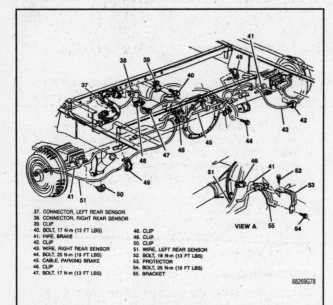

37. CONNECTOR, LEFT REAR SENSOR
38. CONNECTOR, RIGHT REAR SENSOR
39. CLIP
40. BOLT, 17 N·m (13 FT LBS)
41. PIPE, BRAKE
42. CLIP
43. WIRE, RIGHT REAR SENSOR
44. BOLT, 25 N·m (19 FT LBS)
45. CABLE, PARKING BRAKE
46. CLIP
47. BOLT, 17 N·m (13 FT LBS)
48. CLIP
49. CLIP
50. CLIP
51. WIRE, LEFT REAR SENSOR
52. BOLT, 18 N·m (13 FT LBS)
53. PROTECTOR
54. BOLT, 25 N·m (19 FT LBS)
55. BRACKET

88269G78

**Fig. 115 Rear wheel speed sensor wiring harness routing**

### REMOVAL & INSTALLATION

▶ **See Figures 115, 116, 117 and 118**

1. Disconnect the negative battery cable.
2. Raise the vehicle and support with jackstands.
3. Remove the rear wheels.

**✳✳ CAUTION**

**Some brake pads contain asbestos, which has been determined to be a cancer causing agent. Never clean the brake surfaces with compressed air! Avoid inhaling any dust from any brake surface! When cleaning brake surfaces, use a commercially available brake cleaning fluid.**

4. Remove the brake drum and primary brake show.
5. Disconnect the sensor connector.
6. Remove the 2 bolts and sensor by pulling the wire through the hole in the backing plate.
7. Installation is the reverse of the removal procedure. Tighten the sensor bolts to 26 ft. lbs. (35 Nm).
8. Connect the negative battery cable and check operation.

## Vehicle Speed Sensor

The vehicle speed sensor is mounted in the transmission tail housing on 2WD vehicles and in the transfer case on 4WD vehicles.

### TESTING

▶ **See Figure 114**

1. Disconnect the negative battery cable.
2. Raise the vehicle and support with jackstands.
3. Disconnect the vehicle speed sensor wiring.
4. Measure the resistance of the sensor and compare to the chart.
5. Replace the sensor if the resistance does not meet specification.

### REMOVAL & INSTALLATION

▶ **See Figures 119, 120, 121, 122 and 123**

1. Disconnect the negative battery cable.
2. Raise the vehicle and support with jackstands.
3. Disconnect the sensor connector.
4. Remove the bolt and sensor by pulling the sensor from the transmission or transaxle housing. Fluid will drip out of the opening, so be ready to catch the spillage.
   **To install:**
5. Install a new O-ring on the vehicle speed sensor and coat with transmission fluid.
6. Install the sensor, bolts and torque to 97 inch lbs. (11 Nm).
7. Connect the electrical connector.
8. Connect the negative battery cable and check transaxle or transmission fluid level.

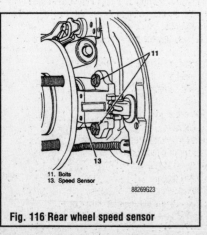

11. Bolts
13. Speed Sensor

88269G23

**Fig. 116 Rear wheel speed sensor**

88269P59

**Fig. 117 The tone ring splines need to be clean to work properly**

88269P60

**Fig. 118 Rear wheel speed sensor mounting. Axle is removed for clarity**

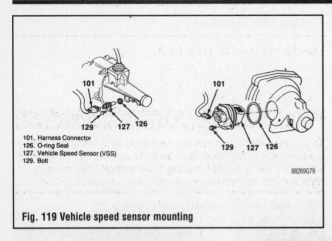

**Fig. 119 Vehicle speed sensor mounting**

101. Harness Connector
126. O-ring Seal
127. Vehicle Speed Sensor (VSS)
129. Bolt

**Fig. 120 Unplug the weatherpak connector from the VSS**

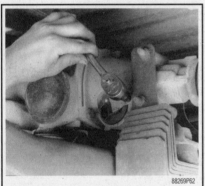

**Fig. 121 The VSS is held by the one bolt and clamp**

**Fig. 122 Withdraw the VSS from the transmission or transaxle**

**Fig. 123 Fluid will come out of the VSS opening so be ready to catch the spillage**

## Self Diagnostics

### READING TROUBLE CODES

◆ See Figure 124

**Rear Wheel Anti-lock Brakes**

The trouble codes are read by jumping terminal **A** and terminal **H** of the ALDL (assembly line diagnostic link) with a jumper wire. Observe the flashing of the brake warning light. The terminals must be jumped for about 20 seconds before the code will begin to flash.

Count the number of short flashes starting from the long flash. Include the long flash as a count. Sometimes the first count sequence will be short, however, following counts will be accurate.

If there is more than one failure, only the first recognized code will be retained and flashed.

- Code 1—ECU malfunction
- Code 2—Open isolation valve or faulty ECU
- Code 3—Open dump valve or faulty ECU
- Code 4—Grounded anti-lock valve switch
- Code 5—Excessive dump valve activity during stop
- Code 6—Erratic speed system
- Code 7—Shorted isolation valve or faulty ECU
- Code 8—Shorted dump valve or faulty ECU
- Code 9—Open speed signal circuit
- Code 10—Brake lamp switch circuit
- Code 11—Faulty ECU
- Code 12—Faulty ECU
- Code 13—Faulty ECU
- Code 14—Faulty ECU
- Code 15—Faulty ECU

**4-Wheel Anti-lock Brakes**

#### EXCEPT 1996 MODELS

The trouble codes are read by jumping terminal **A** and terminal **H** of the ALDL (assembly line diagnostic link) with a jumper wire. Observe the flashing of the ANTI-LOCK warning light. The terminals must be jumped for about 20 seconds before the code will begin to flash.

Count the number of short flashes starting from the long flash. Include the long flash as a count. Sometimes the first count sequence will be short, however, following counts will be accurate.

If there is more than one failure, only the first recognized code will be retained and flashed.

- Code 21—RF speed sensor or circuit open
- Code 22—Missing RF speed signal
- Code 23—Erratic RF speed sensor
- Code 25—LF speed sensor or circuit open
- Code 26—Missing LF speed signal
- Code 27—Erratic LF speed sensor
- Code 29—Simultaneous drop out of front speed sensors
- Code 31—RR speed sensor or circuit open
- Code 32—Missing RR speed signal
- Code 33—Erratic RR speed signal
- Code 35—VSS or LR speed sensor or circuit open
- Code 36—Missing VSS or LR speed sensor or circuit open
- Code 37—Erratic VSS or LR speed sensor signal

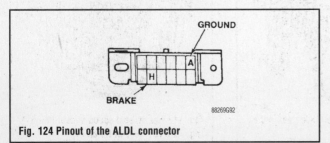

**Fig. 124 Pinout of the ALDL connector**

- Code 38—Wheel speed error
- Code 41–54—Control valves
- Code 61–63—Reset switches
- Code 65–66—Open or shorted pump motor relay
- Code 67—Open motor circuit or shorted BPMV output
- Code 68—Locked motor or shorted motor circuit
- Code 71–74—Memory errors
- Code 81—Brake switch circuit shorted or open
- Code 86—Shorted anti-lock indicator lamp
- Code 88—Shorted brake warning lamp

### 1996 MODELS

Trouble codes on the 1996 vehicles can only be read using a scan tool. It is not possible to read the trouble codes by the flashing light method. The trouble codes are the same as the earlier year vehicles.

### CLEARING TROUBLE CODES

On 1985–95 vehicles the trouble codes may be cleared using a Tech I scan tool or by performing the following procedures. On 1996 vehicles, the trouble codes can only be cleared by the Tech 1 scan tool.

1. Turn the ignition switch to the **RUN** position.
2. Use a jumper wire to ground the ALDL terminal **A** to **H** for 2 seconds.
3. Remove the jumper wire for 2 seconds.
4. Repeat the grounding and ungrounding 2 more times.
5. Check that the memory is cleared by making a diagnostic request.
6. Turn the ignition switch **OFF**.

## BRAKE SPECIFICATIONS

All measurements in inches unless noted

| Year | Model | Master Cylinder Bore | Brake Disc | | | Brake Drum Diameter | | | Minimum Lining Thickness | |
| | | | Original Thickness | Minimum Thickness | Maximum Runout | Original Inside Diameter | Max. Wear Limit | Maximum Machine Diameter | Front | Rear |
|---|---|---|---|---|---|---|---|---|---|---|
| 1985 | Astro/Safari | NA | 1.040 | 0.980 | 0.004 | 9.50 | 9.59 | 9.56 | 0.030 | 0.030 |
| 1986 | Astro/Safari | NA | 1.040 | 0.980 | 0.004 | 9.50 | 9.59 | 9.56 | 0.030 | 0.030 |
| 1987 | Astro/Safari | NA | 1.040 | 0.980 | 0.004 | 9.50 | 9.59 | 9.56 | 0.030 | 0.030 |
| 1988 | Astro/Safari | NA | 1.040 | 0.980 | 0.004 | 9.50 | 9.59 | 9.56 | 0.030 | 0.030 |
| 1989 | Astro/Safari | NA | 1.040 | 0.980 | 0.004 | 9.50 | 9.59 | 9.56 | 0.030 | 0.030 |
| 1990 | Astro/Safari | NA | 1.040 | 0.980 | 0.004 | 9.50 | 9.59 | 9.56 | 0.030 | 0.030 |
| 1991 | Astro/Safari | NA | 1 | 2 | 0.004 | 9.50 | 9.59 | 9.56 | 0.030 | 0.030 |
| 1992 | Astro/Safari | NA | 1 | 2 | 0.004 | 9.50 | 9.59 | 9.56 | 0.030 | 0.030 |
| 1993 | Astro/Safari | NA | 1 | 2 | 0.004 | 9.50 | 9.59 | 9.56 | 0.030 | 0.030 |
| 1994 | Astro/Safari | NA | 1 | 2 | 0.004 | 9.50 | 9.59 | 9.56 | 0.030 | 0.030 |
| 1995 | Astro/Safari | NA | 1 | 2 | 0.004 | 9.50 | 9.59 | 9.56 | 0.030 | 0.030 |
| 1996 | Astro/Safari | NA | 1 | 2 | 0.004 | 9.50 | 9.59 | 9.56 | 0.030 | 0.030 |

NA - Not Available
1  Available with 1.040" and 1.250" rotors
2  1.040" rotors: 0.980
   1.250" rotors: 1.230

88269C06

## Troubleshooting the Brake System (cont.)

| Problem | Cause | Solution |
|---|---|---|
| Fading brake pedal (pedal height decreases with steady pressure applied.) | · Fluid leak in hydraulic system | · Fill master cylinder reservoirs to fill mark, have helper apply brakes, check calipers, wheel cylinders, differential valve, tubes, hoses, and fittings for fluid leaks. Repair or replace parts as necessary. |
| | · Master cylinder piston seals worn, or master cylinder bore is scored, worn or corroded | · Repair or replace master cylinder |
| Decreasing brake pedal travel (pedal travel required for braking action decreases and may be accompanied by a hard pedal.) | · Caliper or wheel cylinder pistons sticking or seized | · Repair or replace the calipers, or wheel cylinders |
| | · Master cylinder compensator ports blocked (preventing fluid return to reservoirs) or pistons sticking or seized in master cylinder bore | · Repair or replace the master cylinder |
| | · Power brake unit binding internally | · Test unit according to the following procedure:<br>(a) Shift transmission into neutral and start engine<br>(b) Increase engine speed to 1500 rpm, close throttle and fully depress brake pedal<br>(c) Slow release brake pedal and stop engine<br>(d) Have helper remove vacuum check valve and hose from power unit. Observe for backward movement of brake pedal.<br>(e) If the pedal moves backward, the power unit has an internal bind—replace power unit |
| Grabbing brakes (severe reaction to brake pedal pressure.) | · Brakelining(s) contaminated by grease or brake fluid | · Determine and correct cause of contamination and replace brakeshoes in axle sets |
| | · Parking brake cables incorrectly adjusted or seized | · Adjust cables. Replace seized cables. |
| | · Incorrect brakelining or lining loose on brakeshoes | · Replace brakeshoes in axle sets |
| | · Caliper anchor plate bolts loose | · Tighten bolts |
| | · Rear brakeshoes binding on support plate ledges | · Clean and lubricate ledges. Replace support plate(s) if ledges are deeply grooved. Do not attempt to smooth ledges by grinding. |
| | · Incorrect or missing power brake reaction disc | · Install correct disc |
| | · Rear brake support plates loose | · Tighten mounting bolts |

88269C02

## Troubleshooting the Brake System

| Problem | Cause | Solution |
|---|---|---|
| Low brake pedal (excessive pedal travel required for braking action.) | · Excessive clearance between rear linings and drums caused by inoperative automatic adjusters | · Make 10 to 15 alternate forward and reverse brake stops to adjust brakes. If brake pedal does not come up, repair or replace adjuster parts as necessary. |
| | · Worn rear brakelining | · Inspect and replace lining if worn beyond minimum thickness specification |
| | · Bent, distorted brakeshoes, front or rear | · Replace brakeshoes in axle sets |
| | · Air in hydraulic system | · Remove air from system. Refer to Brake Bleeding. |
| Low brake pedal (pedal may go to floor with steady pressure applied.) | · Fluid leak in hydraulic system | · Fill master cylinder to fill line; have helper apply brakes and check calipers, wheel cylinders, differential valve tubes, hoses and fittings for leaks. Repair or replace as necessary. |
| | · Air in hydraulic system | · Remove air from system. Refer to Brake Bleeding. |
| | · Incorrect or non-recommended brake fluid (fluid evaporates at below normal temp). | · Flush hydraulic system with clean brake fluid. Refill with correct-type fluid. |
| | · Master cylinder piston seals worn, or master cylinder bore is scored, worn or corroded | · Repair or replace master cylinder |
| Low brake pedal (pedal goes to floor on first application—o.k. on subsequent applications.) | · Disc brake pads sticking on abutment surfaces of anchor plate. Caused by a build-up of dirt, rust, or corrosion on abutment surfaces | · Clean abutment surfaces |

88269C01

## Troubleshooting the Brake System (cont.)

| Problem | Cause | Solution |
|---|---|---|
| Spongy brake pedal (pedal has abnormally soft, springy, spongy feel when depressed.) | · Air in hydraulic system<br>· Brakeshoes bent or distorted<br>· Brakelining not yet seated with drums and rotors<br>· Rear drum brakes not properly adjusted | · Remove air from system. Refer to Brake Bleeding.<br>· Replace brakeshoes<br>· Burnish brakes<br>· Adjust brakes |
| Hard brake pedal (excessive pedal pressure required to stop vehicle. May be accompanied by brake fade.) | · Loose or leaking power brake unit vacuum hose<br>· Incorrect or poor quality brakelining<br>· Bent, broken, distorted brakeshoes<br>· Calipers binding or dragging on mounting pins. Rear brakeshoes dragging on support plate.<br><br>· Caliper, wheel cylinder, or master cylinder pistons sticking or seized<br>· Power brake unit vacuum check valve malfunction<br><br>· Power brake unit has internal bind | · Tighten connections or replace leaking hose<br>· Replace with lining in axle sets<br>· Replace brakeshoes<br>· Replace brake mounting pins and bushings. Clean rust or burrs from rear brake support plate ledges and lubricate ledges with molydisulfide grease.<br>NOTE: If ledges are deeply grooved or scored, do not attempt to sand or grind them smooth—replace support plate.<br>· Repair or replace parts as necessary<br>· Test valve according to the following procedure:<br>(a) Start engine, increase engine speed to 1500 rpm, close throttle and immediately stop engine<br>(b) Wait at least 90 seconds then depress brake pedal<br>(c) If brakes are not vacuum assisted for 2 or more applications, check valve is faulty<br>· Test unit according to the following procedure:<br>(a) With engine stopped, apply brakes several times to exhaust all vacuum in system<br>(b) Shift transmission into neutral, depress brake pedal and start engine<br>(c) If pedal height decreases with foot pressure and less pressure is required to hold pedal in applied position, power unit vacuum system is operating normally. Test power unit. If power unit exhibits a bind condition, replace the power unit. |

88269C03

## Troubleshooting the Brake System (cont.)

| Problem | Cause | Solution |
|---|---|---|
| Hard brake pedal (excessive pedal pressure required to stop vehicle. May be accompanied by brake fade.) | · Master cylinder compensator ports (at bottom of reservoirs) blocked by dirt, scale, rust, or have small burrs (blocked ports prevent fluid return to reservoirs).<br>· Brake hoses, tubes, fittings clogged or restricted | · Repair or replace master cylinder CAUTION: Do not attempt to clean blocked ports with wire, pencils, or similar implements. Use compressed air only.<br>· Use compressed air to check or unclog parts. Replace any damaged parts. |
| Dragging brakes (slow or incomplete release of brakes) | · Brake fluid contaminated with improper brake fluids (motor oil, transmission fluid, causing rubber components to swell and stick in bores<br>· Low engine vacuum<br>· Brake pedal binding at pivot<br>· Power brake unit has internal bind<br>· Parking brake cables incorrectly adjusted or seized<br>· Rear brakeshoe return springs weak or broken<br>· Automatic adjusters malfunctioning<br>· Caliper, wheel cylinder or master cylinder pistons sticking or seized<br>· Master cylinder compensating ports blocked (fluid does not return to reservoirs). | · Replace all rubber components, combination valve and hoses. Flush entire brake system with DOT 3 brake fluid or equivalent.<br><br><br>· Adjust or repair engine<br>· Loosen and lubricate<br>· Inspect for internal bind. Replace unit if internal bind exists.<br>· Adjust cables. Replace seized cables.<br>· Replace return springs. Replace brakeshoe if necessary in axle sets.<br>· Repair or replace adjuster parts as required<br>· Repair or replace parts as necessary<br>· Use compressed air to clear ports. Do not use wire, pencils, or similar objects to open blocked ports. |
| Vehicle moves to one side when brakes are applied | · Incorrect front tire pressure<br>· Worn or damaged wheel bearings<br>· Brakelining on one side contaminated<br>· Brakeshoes on one side bent, distorted, or lining loose on shoe<br>· Support plate bent or loose on one side<br>· Brakelining not yet seated with drums or rotors<br>· Caliper anchor plate loose on one side<br>· Caliper piston sticking or seized<br>· Brakelinings water soaked<br>· Loose suspension component attaching or mounting bolts<br>· Brake combination valve failure | · Inflate to recommended cold (reduced load) inflation pressure<br>· Replace worn or damaged bearings<br>· Determine and correct cause of contamination and replace brakelining in axle sets<br>· Replace brakeshoes in axle sets<br>· Tighten or replace support plate<br>· Burnish brakelining<br>· Tighten anchor plate bolts<br>· Repair or replace caliper<br>· Drive vehicle with brakes lightly applied to dry linings<br>· Tighten suspension bolts. Replace worn suspension components.<br>· Replace combination valve |

88269C04

## Troubleshooting the Brake System (cont.)

| Problem | Cause | Solution |
|---|---|---|
| Chatter or shudder when brakes are applied (pedal pulsation and roughness may also occur.) | • Brakeshoes distorted, bent, contaminated, or worn<br>• Caliper anchor plate or support plate loose<br>• Excessive thickness variation of rotor(s) | • Replace brakeshoes in axle sets<br>• Tighten mounting bolts<br>• Refinish or replace rotors in axle sets |
| Noisy brakes (squealing, clicking, scraping sound when brakes are applied.) | • Bent, broken, distorted brakeshoes<br>• Excessive rust on outer edge of rotor braking surface | • Replace brakeshoes in axle sets<br>• Remove rust |
| Noisy brakes (squealing, clicking, scraping sound when brakes are applied.) (cont.) | • Brakelining worn out—shoes contacting drum of rotor<br><br>• Broken or loose holdown or return springs<br>• Rough or dry drum brake support plate ledges<br>• Cracked, grooved, or scored rotor(s) or drum(s)<br><br>• Incorrect brakelining and/or shoes (front or rear). | • Replace brakeshoes and lining in axle sets. Refinish or replace drums or rotors.<br>• Replace parts as necessary<br><br>• Lubricate support plate ledges<br><br>• Replace rotor(s) or drum(s). Replace brakeshoes and lining in axle sets if necessary.<br>• Install specified shoe and lining assemblies |
| Pulsating brake pedal | • Out of round drums or excessive lateral runout in disc brake rotor(s) | • Refinish or replace drums, re-index rotors or replace |

88269C05

# DIAGNOSIS OF THE HYDRAULIC BOOSTER SYSTEM

| PROBLEM | POSSIBLE CAUSE | CORRECTION |
|---|---|---|
| **Slow Brake Pedal Return** | 1. Excessive seal friction in booster.<br>2. Faulty spool action.<br><br>3. Restriction in return hose from booster to pump reservoir.<br>4. Damaged input rod end. | 1. Overhaul with new seal kit.<br>2. Flush steering system while pumping brake pedal.<br>3. Replace hose.<br><br>4. Replace input rod and piston assembly. |
| **Grabby Brakes-Booster Chatters - Pedal Vibrates** | 1. Faulty spool action caused by contamination in system.<br>2. Power steering pump belt slips.<br>3. Low fluid level in power steering pump. | 1. Flush steering system while pumping brake pedal.<br>2. Fill reservoir and check for external leaks. |
| **Accumulator Leak-Down System Does Not Hold Charge** | 1. Contamination in steering or booster system.<br>2. Internal leakage in accumulator system. | 1. Flush steering system while pumping brake pedal.<br>2. Overhaul unit using accumulator rebuild kit and seal kit. |
| **Brakes Self-Apply When Steering Wheel Turned** | 1. Contamination in steering or booster system.<br>2. Restriction in return hose from booster to pump reservoir. | 1. Replace hydraulic booster. Flush complete system.<br>2. Replace hose. |

88269C54

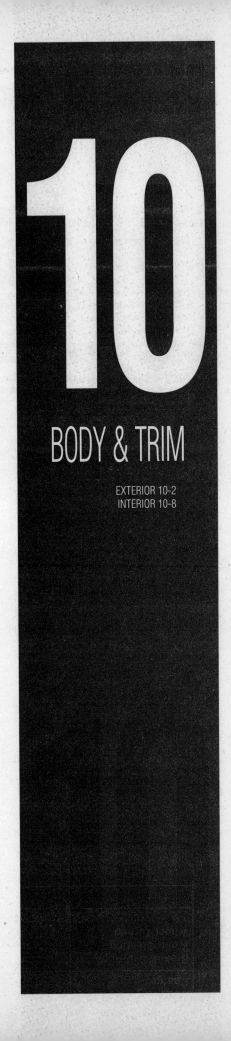

# 10

# BODY & TRIM

## EXTERIOR

### Front Doors

#### REMOVAL & INSTALLATION

◆ **See Figure 1**

➡ **The following procedure requires the use of the GM Door Hinge Spring Compressor tool No. J–28625–A or equivalent.**

1. If equipped with power door components, perform the following procedures:

a. Disconnect the negative battery cable from the battery.

b. Refer to the Door Panel, Removal and Installation procedures in this section and remove the door panel.

c. Disconnect the electrical harness connector from the power door lock motor and/or the power window regulator.

d. Remove the electrical harness from the door.

#### ✳✳ CAUTION

**Before removing the hinge spring from the door, be sure to cover it (to keep it from flying); it could cause personal injury.**

2. Using the GM Door Hinge Spring Compressor tool No. J–28625–A or equivalent, compress the door hinge spring and remove it.

3. To remove the door hinge pin clips, spread the clips and move them above the recess on the pin; when the pin is removed, the clip will ride on the pin and fall free of it.

4. Using a soft-head hammer and a pair of locking pliers, remove the lower pin from the door hinge; then, install a bolt (in the lower pin hole) to hold the door in place until the upper hinge pin is removed.

5. Remove the upper door hinge pin and support the door, then remove the bolt from the lower hinge pin hole and the door from the vehicle.

**To install:**

6. Position the door onto the hinges and insert a bolt through the lower hinge pin hole.

7. Using a new hinge pin clip, install the upper hinge pin.

8. Remove the bolt from the lower hinge pin hole. Using a new hinge pin, install it into the lower hinge pin holes.

9. Using the GM Door Hinge Spring Compressor tool No. J–28625–A or equivalent, compress the door hinge spring and install it into the door hinge.

10. If equipped with power door components, reconnect the electrical harness connector(s), install the door panel and the reconnect the negative battery cable.

#### ADJUSTMENTS

Factory installed hinges are welded in place, so no adjustment of the system is necessary or recommended.

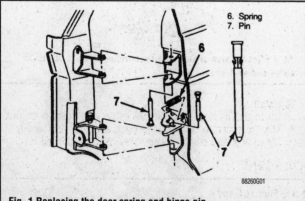

6. Spring
7. Pin

88260G01

**Fig. 1 Replacing the door spring and hinge pin**

### Front Door Hinges

➡ **The following procedure requires the use of an ⅛ in. (3mm) drill bit, ½ in. (13mm) drill bit, a center punch, a cold chisel, a portable body grinder, a putty knife, and a scribing tool.**

#### REMOVAL & INSTALLATION

1. Remove door(s) and place on a padded workbench.

2. Using a putty knife, remove the sealant from the around the edge of the hinge.

3. Using a scribing tool, outline the position of the hinge(s) on the door and the body pillar.

4. Using a center punch, mark the center position of the hinge-to-door and the hinge-to-body pillar welds.

5. Using a ⅛ in. (3mm) bit, drill a pilot hole completely through each weld.

➡ **When drilling the holes through the hinge welds, DO NOT drill through the door or the body pillar.**

6. Using a ½ in. (13mm) bit, drill a hole through the hinge base, following the ⅛ in. (3mm) pilot hole.

7. Using a cold chisel and a hammer, separate the hinge from the door and/or the body pillar. Using a portable grinder, clean off any welds remaining on the door or the body pillar.

**To install:**

8. To fasten the replacement hinge(s) to the door and/or body pillar, perform the following procedures:

a. Align the replacement hinge, with the scribe lines, previously made.

b. Using a center punch and the new hinge as a template, mark the location of each bolt hole.

c. Using a ½ in. (13mm) bit, drill holes (using the center marks) through the door and body pillar.

d. If the upper body side hinge is to be replaced, remove the instrument panel fasteners, pull the panel outwards and support it.

9. Use medium body sealant (apply it to the hinge-to-door or body pillar surface), the hinge-to-door/body pillar bolts and tapped anchor plate.

10. Tighten the hinge-to-door/body pillar bolts to 20 ft. lbs. (27 Nm).

11. Apply paint to the hinge and the surrounding area.

#### ADJUSTMENT

◆ **See Figures 2, 3 and 4**

➡ **The ½ in. (13mm) drill hinge holes provide for some adjustment.**

1. Loosen, adjust, then tighten the hinge-to-door/body pillar bolts; close the door, then check the door gap, it should be 4–6mm between the door and the door frame.

2. With the door closed, it should be flush, plus or minus 1.0mm, with the body; if not, enlarge the striker hole.

### Rear Doors

#### REMOVAL & INSTALLATION

◆ **See Figures 5 and 6**

1. Disconnect the negative battery cable.

2. Remove the door trim panel on the right door only.

3. Disconnect the wiring harness from the license plate lamp and power door lock, if so equipped. Remove the harness from the door.

4. Disconnect the check strap from the door frame.

5. Drive out the hinge pins while an assistant holds the door in place.

6. Remove the door from the vehicle.

7. With an assistant, install the door onto the vehicle. The remainder of installation is the reverse of the removal procedure.

Fig. 2 Exploded view of the front door striker mounting

25. Striker
26. Spacer
27. Insulator
28. Nut

Fig. 3 If the striker must be removed, first scribe an alignment mark . . .

Fig. 4 . . . then loosen the striker using a suitable driver (usually a Torx®)

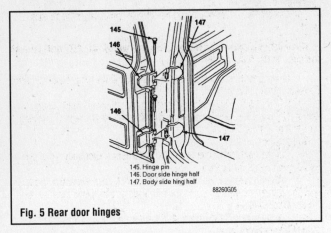

145. Hinge pin
146. Door side hinge half
147. Body side hing half

Fig. 5 Rear door hinges

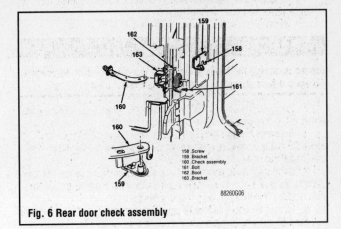

158. Screw
159. Bracket
160. Check assembly
161. Bolt
162. Boot
163. Bracket

Fig. 6 Rear door check assembly

## ADJUSTMENT

The original door hinges are welded in place, and adjustment is not recommended. However, with service bolt-on hinges, adjustment is possible.

1. Loosen the door striker.
2. Adjust the left door first and then the right.
3. Adjust the left door so that there is a 5.0mm gap between the door and the door frame at the top, bottom and side of the door.
4. Adjust the right door so that there is a 5.0mm gap between the door and the door frame at the top, bottom and side of the door.

## Rear Door Check

### REMOVAL & INSTALLATION

1. Open the door and disconnect the check assembly from the bracket.
2. Remove the mounting bracket screws, bracket and door trim panel.
3. Remove the boot-to-bracket bolts and boot.
4. Remove the bracket and check assembly from the inside of the door.
5. To install, reverse the removal procedure.

## Sliding Door

### REMOVAL & INSTALLATION

▶ See Figure 7

1. Remove the track cover.
2. Matchmark the alignment of the lower roller bracket-to-door position.
3. Remove the upper roller bracket-to-door screws, then the lower roller bracket-to-sliding door bolts.
4. Using an assistant, to support the sliding door, open the door and roll the center roller bracket off the end of the track.

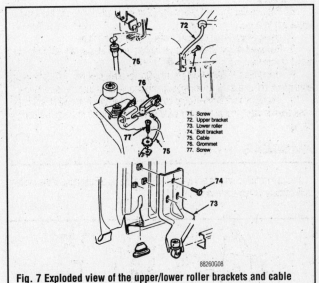

71. Screw
72. Upper bracket
73. Lower roller
74. Bolt bracket
75. Cable
76. Grommet
77. Screw

Fig. 7 Exploded view of the upper/lower roller brackets and cable latch—sliding door assembly

To install,
5. Use an assistant to roll the center roller bracket onto the end of the track.
6. Align the lower roller bracket-to-door marks and install the mounting bolts. Tighten all of the door roller bracket bolts to 20 ft. lbs. (27 Nm).

## ADJUSTMENT

▶ See Figures 8 and 9

Although the sliding door is designed without any adjustment provisions, it is possible to rework certain portions of the system.

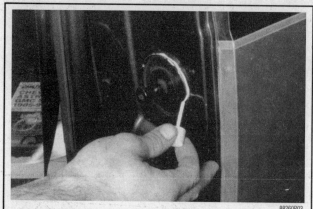

**Fig. 8 If the sliding door striker must be removed, first make alignment marks . . .**

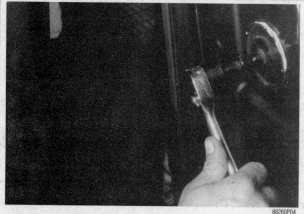

**Fig. 9 . . . then loosen and remove the striker bolt using a suitable driver (usually a Torx®)**

• Using the rear striker, at the center rear of the door, adjust the height and flushness.

• Using the lower roller bracket, adjust the parallel gap at the base of the door.

• To obtain flushness and vertical support, at the front of the door, adjust the door locator pins and sockets.

• To obtain proper gap and a level swing-in, at the rear of the door, adjust the center roller track fore and aft.

• Using Lubriplate® or equivalent, lubricate the roller track contact surfaces.

1. To obtain the height (up/down) and the flushness (in/out) movements, between the door and the rear quarter panel, enlarge the rear striker hole.

➡ **When making the rear striker adjustments, DO NOT bend the striker to obtain the adjustment.**

2. To obtain a parallel gap between the base of the door and the rocker panel, loosen the lower roller bracket bolts. Check and/or adjust the gap between the quarter panel and the door; the gap should be parallel from the window area down to the rocker panel. Tighten the lower bracket mounting bolts to 20 ft. lbs. (27 Nm).

➡ **To obtain the parallel adjustment, the upper bracket hole may have to be enlarged; enlarging the hole may mean that the feature alignment of the door may have to be compromised.**

3. To obtain flushness between the door and the rocker panel, adjust the lower locating pin so that its surface is in contact with the outer edges of the locator guide. If you are having trouble obtaining the flushness, perform the following procedures:

a. Using a rubber hammer, strike the locator pin (while in position) to bend the sheet metal slightly.

b. Using a portable grinder, remove some of the material from the top or bottom of the locator guide; DO NOT remove too much material that a hole is ground through the guide.

c. Readjust the door height at the lower roller bracket.

4. Adjust the upper locator pin until it is flush with the locator guide; the locator should rub the outer edge of the locator guide. If you are having trouble obtaining the adjustment, perform the following procedures:

a. Using a rubber hammer, strike the locator pin (while in position) to bend the sheet metal slightly.

b. Using a portable grinder, remove some of the material from the top or bottom of the locator guide; DO NOT remove too much material that a hole is ground through the guide.

5. To obtain equal gaps between the door, the quarter panel and the door pillar, perform the following procedures:

a. For access to the center roller track, remove the right rear tail light bezel, the interior trim from around the track and the track cover.

b. Inspect the track rollers; the bottom rollers should ride on the track base and the side roller should ride on the outer flange of the track.

c. Loosen the track fasteners and slide the track rearward until it comes in contact the center rollers, then center the door in the opening. Tighten the track fasteners by starting with the one closest to the rear door striker.

d. Loosen the forward track fastener, then push the track up or down until the rear latch rolls onto the striker in a level position; if necessary, elongate the hole.

e. Install the track cover, the interior trim and the rear tail light bezel.

6. Adjust the upper roller bracket so that the roller runs in the middle of the track; it must not touch the upper or lower edge of the track. If necessary physically adjust it, remove it from the bracket and bend it at its base.

## Grille

### REMOVAL & INSTALLATION

▶ **See Figures 10 and 11**

1. Remove the headlight bezel and front end panel-to-grille bolts.

➡ **On some late-model vehicles it will be necessary to remove the entire combination lamp assembly in order to remove the grille.**

2. Remove the grille-to-radiator support screws and the grille.

3. Installation is the reverse of the removal procedure.

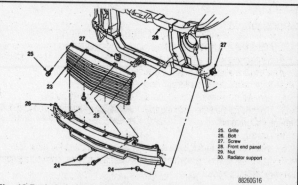

25. Grille
26. Bolt
27. Screw
28. Front end panel
29. Nut
30. Radiator support

**Fig. 10 Exploded view of a typical early-model Astro and Safari grille and front end panel mounting**

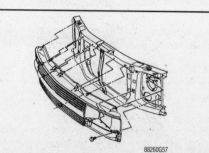

**Fig. 11 Exploded view of a typical late-model Astro and Safari grille mounting**

## Outside Mirrors

### REMOVAL & INSTALLATION

#### ♦ See Figure 12

1. Disconnect the negative battery cable.
2. Remove the door trim panel as outlined in this section.
3. Disconnect the electrical connector, if so equipped.
4. Remove the retaining nuts and mirror assembly from the door.
5. To install, reverse the removal procedure. Check mirror operation before installing the door trim panels.

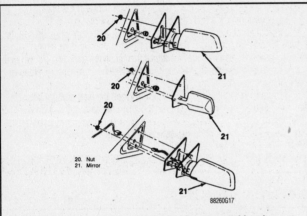

20. Nut
21. Mirror

88260G17

**Fig. 12 Exploded view of the standard and power outside mirrors**

## Radio Antenna

### REMOVAL & INSTALLATION

#### Outer

#### ♦ See Figure 13

1. Disconnect the negative battery cable.
2. Remove the wiper arms and antenna mast from the base. The mast will unscrew using a pliers and rag to protect the mast finish.
3. Remove the cowl screws and cowl screen.
4. Remove the antenna base screws and lower dash extension.
5. Disconnect the outer antenna lead from the inner antenna lead and pull through the grommet.

**To install:**

6. Install the lead through the grommet and connect it to the inner lead.
7. Install the lower dash extension, antenna base screws, cowl screen and screen retaining screws.

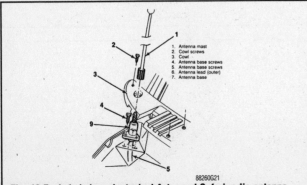

1. Antenna mast
2. Cowl screws
3. Cowl
4. Antenna base screws
5. Antenna base screws
6. Antenna lead (outer)
7. Antenna base

88260G21

**Fig. 13 Exploded view of a typical Astro and Safari radio antenna mounting**

8. Install the antenna mast, wiper arms and connect the negative battery cable.

#### Inner

#### ♦ See Figure 14

1. Remove the dash panel speaker by prying up the grille and remove the retaining screws.
2. Remove the lower dash extension and inner antenna lead mounting screws.
3. Disconnect the antenna lead from the routing clips and radio receiver.
4. Installation is the reverse of the removal procedure.

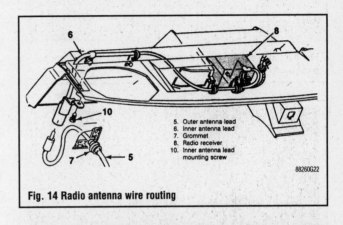

5. Outer antenna lead
6. Inner antenna lead
7. Grommet
8. Radio receiver
10. Inner antenna lead mounting screw

88260G22

**Fig. 14 Radio antenna wire routing**

## Door Locks

### REMOVAL & INSTALLATION

#### Front Door Manual Locks

#### *OUTSIDE HANDLE AND LOCK CYLINDER*

#### ♦ See Figure 15

1. Refer to the Door Panel, Removal and Installation procedures in this section and remove the door panel.
2. Remove the outside handle-to-door nuts.

➡**Removing the soft plug at the edge of the door may provide additional room to access the bottom door handle nut.**

3. Remove the outside handle-to-lock rod and the handle from the door.
4. Remove the lock rod from the lock cylinder, then the lock cylinder retainer, the gasket and the lock cylinder from the door.
5. To install, reverse the removal procedure.

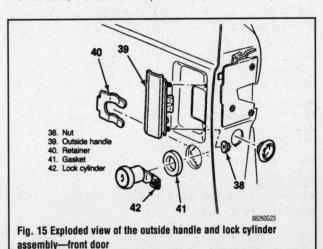

38. Nut
39. Outside handle
40. Retainer
41. Gasket
42. Lock cylinder

88260G23

**Fig. 15 Exploded view of the outside handle and lock cylinder assembly—front door**

## LOCK ASSEMBLY

▶ See Figure 16

1. Refer to the Door Panel, Removal and Installation procedures in this section and remove the door panel.
2. Remove the outside handle-to-lock assembly rod.
3. Remove the lock cylinder-to-lock assembly rod.
4. Remove the inside handle-to-lock assembly rod.
5. Remove the inside lock-to-lock assembly rod.
6. Remove the lock assembly-to-door screws and the lock assembly from door.
7. Installation is the reverse of the removal.

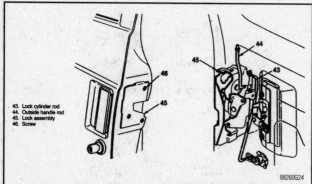

43. Lock cylinder rod
44. Outside handle rod
45. Lock assembly
46. Screw

Fig. 16 Lock cylinder assembly mounting and related components—front door

## INSIDE HANDLE

▶ See Figure 17

➡ The following procedure requires the use of a ³⁄₁₆ in. (5mm) drill bit, ¼ in. x ½ in. (6mm x 13mm) pop rivets and a pop rivet gun.

1. Refer to the Door Panel, Removal and Installation procedures in this section and remove the door panel.
2. Remove the inside handle-to-lock rod.
3. Using a ³⁄₁₆ in. (5mm) bit, drill out the inside handle-to-door rivets, the remove the inside handle from the door.

**To install**

4. Use ¼ in. x ½ in. (6mm x 13mm) pop rivets and a pop rivet gun to install the inside handle to the door. Install the trim panel and check operation.

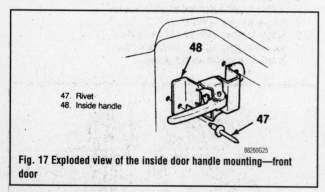

47. Rivet
48. Inside handle

Fig. 17 Exploded view of the inside door handle mounting—front door

## Front Door With Power Locks

▶ See Figure 18

## REMOTE LOCK LEVER

➡ The following procedure requires the use of a ³⁄₁₆ in. (5mm) drill bit, ¼ in. x ½ in. (6mm x 13mm) pop rivets and a pop rivet gun.

1. Refer to the Door Panel, Removal and Installation procedures in this section and remove the door panel.

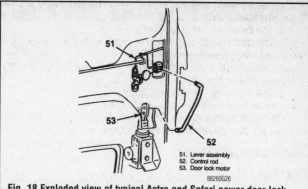

51. Lever assembly
52. Control rod
53. Door lock motor

Fig. 18 Exploded view of typical Astro and Safari power door lock components

2. Remove the power door lock motor to remove the lever rod.
3. Remove the remote lever-to-lock assembly rod.
4. Remove the remote lever-to-inside lock lever rod.
5. Using a ³⁄₁₆ in. (5mm) bit, drill out the inside handle-to-door rivets, the remove the handle from the door.

**To install**

6. Use ¼ in. x ½ in. (6mm x 13mm) pop rivets and a pop rivet gun to install the inside handle to the door.
7. Connect the remote lever-to-lock lever rod.

## POWER DOOR LOCK MOTOR

1. Refer to the Door Panel, Removal and Installation procedures in this section and remove the door panel.
2. Remove the power door lock motor to remove the lever rod.
3. Disconnect the electrical connector from the power door lock motor.
4. Remove the motor-to-door bolts and the motor from the door.
5. **To install**, position the motor to the door and install the mounting bolts. Reconnect the electrical connector and install the door trim panel.

## Sliding Door

## LOCK ASSEMBLY

▶ See Figure 19

1. Refer to the Sliding Door Panel, Removal and Installation procedures in this section and remove the door panel.
2. To remove the upper control-to-lock rods, perform the following procedures:

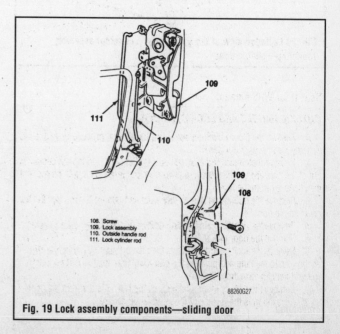

108. Screw
109. Lock assembly
110. Outside handle rod
111. Lock cylinder rod

Fig. 19 Lock assembly components—sliding door

a. Using a small prybar, pry the anchor clip out of the hole and push the clip away from the lever.

b. Pull the rod and clip away from the lever.

3. To remove the remote control-to-locks rods from the remote control, perform the following procedures:

a. Using a small prybar, pry the anchor clip out of the hole and push the clip away from the lever.

b. Pull the rod and clip away from the lever.

4. Remove the lock screws and the lock from the door.

5. **To install**, position the lock and screws to the door. Connect the clips to the levers and check operation. Install the door trim panel.

### POWER DOOR LOCK MOTOR

▶ **See Figure 20**

➡**The following procedure requires the use of ¼ in. x ½ in. (6mm x 13mm) pop rivets and a pop rivet gun.**

1. Refer to the Door Panel, Removal and Installation procedures in this section and remove the door panel.

2. Disconnect the negative battery cable from the battery.

3. Refer to the Sliding Door Panel, Removal and Installation procedures in this section and remove the door panel.

4. Disconnect the electrical wiring harness from the power door lock motor.

5. Using a ³⁄₁₆ in. (5mm) bit, drill out the door lock motor-to-door rivets, then remove the motor from the door.

#### To install

6. Use ¼ in. x ½ in. (6mm x 13mm) pop rivets and a pop rivet gun to install the inside handle to the door.

7. Install new rivets or bolts to the power door lock motor-to-door.

8. Connect the electrical wiring harness.

9. Refer to the Sliding Door Panel, Removal and Installation procedures in this section and install the door panel.

10. Connect the negative battery cable to the battery and check operation.

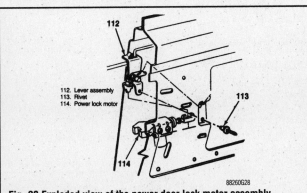

**112.** Lever assembly
**113.** Rivet
**114.** Power lock motor

**Fig. 20 Exploded view of the power door lock motor assembly mounting—sliding door**

### Rear Door With Manual Locks

### OUTSIDE HANDLE AND LOCK CYLINDER

1. Refer to the Door Panel, Removal and Installation procedures in this section and remove the door panel.

2. Remove the control rod from the outside handle by prying the clip anchor out of the hole and pushing the clip away from the lever. Then pull the rod and the clip away from the lever.

3. Remove the outside handle-to-lock nuts and remove the rod and the handle from the door.

4. Remove the license plate housing bolts, and the license plate housing.

5. Remove the door lock shield.

6. Remove the lock control rod from the lock cylinder by prying the clip anchor out of the hole and pushing the clip away from the lever. Then pull the rod and the clip away from the lever.

7. Remove the lock cylinder retainer, and the lock cylinder from the door.

8. Installation is the reverse of the removal procedure.

### LOCK ASSEMBLY

▶ **See Figure 21**

1. Refer to the Door Panel, Removal and Installation procedures in this section and remove the door panel.

2. Remove the outside handle-to-lock assembly rod.

3. Remove the lock cylinder-to-lock assembly rod.

4. Remove the inside handle-to-lock assembly rod.

5. Remove the inside lock-to-lock assembly rod.

6. Remove the lock assembly-to-door screws and the lock assembly from door.

7. Installation is the reverse of the removal.

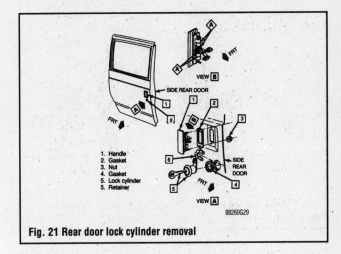

**1.** Handle
**2.** Gasket
**3.** Nut
**4.** Gasket
**5.** Lock cylinder
**5.** Retainer

**Fig. 21 Rear door lock cylinder removal**

### UPPER AND LOWER LATCH REPLACEMENT

▶ **See Figure 22**

1. Refer to the Door Panel, Removal and Installation procedures in this section and remove the door panel.

2. Remove the control rods from the remote control by prying the clip anchor out of the hole and pushing the clip away from the lever. Then pull the rod and the clip away from the lever.

3. Remove the upper latch screws.

4. Remove the upper latch insulator cover.

5. Pry the plastic nails holding the weatherstrip away from the door and remove the weatherstrip from around the latch area.

6. Remove the door latch insulator.

7. Remove the upper latch and rod from the door.

8. Remove the lower latch screws.

9. Remove the lower latch reinforcement plate.

10. Remove the lower latch and rod from the door.

11. To install, reverse the removal procedure.

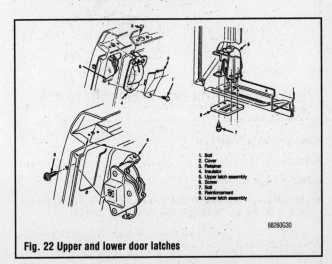

**1.** Bolt
**2.** Cover
**3.** Retainer
**4.** Insulator
**5.** Upper latch assembly
**6.** Screw
**7.** Bolt
**8.** Reinforcement
**9.** Lower latch assembly

**Fig. 22 Upper and lower door latches**

**Rear Door With Power Locks**

### REMOTE LOCK LEVER

1. Refer to the Door Panel, Removal and Installation procedures in this section and remove the door panel.
2. Disconnect the negative battery cable and remove the actuator to lever rod.
3. Using a ³⁄₁₆ in. (5mm) bit, drill out the head of the actuator-to-door rivets.
4. Remove the actuator from the door.
5. **To install**, use ¼ in. diameter bolt (½ in. long) with a spring washer and nut to attach the actuator to the door. Connect the lever rod to the actuator. Check operation, then install the door trim panel.

### POWER LOCK ACTUATOR

▶ See Figure 23

1. Refer to the Door Panel, Removal and Installation procedures in this section and remove the door panel.
2. Remove the power door lock actuator to remove the lever rod.
3. Disconnect the electrical connector from the power door lock actuator.
4. Remove the actuator-to-door bolts and the actuator from the door.
5. **To install** position the actuator to the door and install the bolts. Connect the electrical connector and lever rod. Check operation, then install the door trim panel.

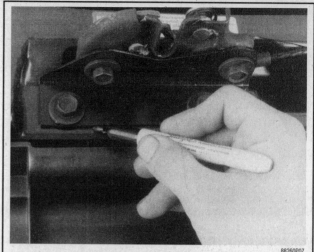

Fig. 24 Before loosening ANY fasteners, ALWAYS scribe matchmarks as points of reference

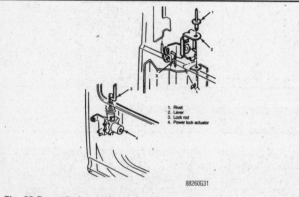

Fig. 23 Power lock actuator and related components

1. Rivet
2. Lever
3. Lock rod
4. Power lock actuator

Fig. 25 Loosen the bolts and reposition the latch, as necessary for adjustment

## Hood

### REMOVAL & INSTALLATION

▶ See Figures 24 and 25

1. Disconnect the negative battery cable. Mark the area around the hinges to make installation easier. Tape or cover the painted areas around the hood for finish protection.
2. With an assistant, support the hood and remove the hinge to hood frame bolts.
3. Remove the hood from the van.
4. **To install**, position the hood onto the van, with an assistant, and install the retaining bolts. Adjust the hood to the original position and tighten the

bolts to 20 ft. lbs. (27 Nm). Check alignment before slamming the hood. If adjustment is necessary, some adjustment is provided by the hinges, while other can usually be found at the striker on the hood or the latch on the radiator support.

➡Before loosening fasteners to make an adjustment, always scribe a matchmark as a point of reference.

## INTERIOR

## Door Trim Panels

Special tool J–9886–01 or an equivalent door handle clip remover, is required to perform the following procedure.

### REMOVAL & INSTALLATION

▶ See Figures 26 thru 35

1. Remove the retaining screws and remove the armrest. Once the screws are removed on most models, the armrest can be removed by sliding

towards the rear. On other models, the armrest should be CAREFULLY pried free.
2. Unless equipped with power windows, remove the window regulator handle using tool J–9886–01 or equivalent. If necessary, remove the window regulator handle bezel.
3. Remove the door handle trim cover by carefully prying it from the clips using J–9886–01 or equivalent. On models equipped with power locks and windows, pull the cover away from the door carefully, then disengage the wiring.
4. Remove any door trim panel retaining screws.

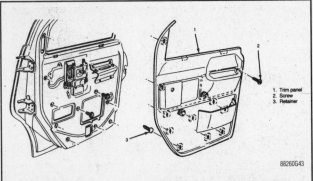

Fig. 26 Exploded view of a typical Astro and Safari door trim panel mounting

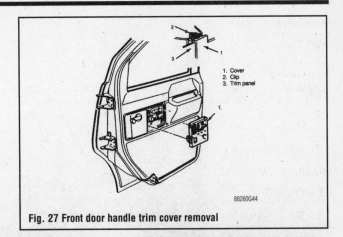

1. Cover
2. Clip
3. Trim panel

Fig. 27 Front door handle trim cover removal

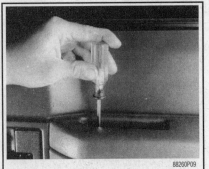

Fig. 28 Remove the armrest screws and slide it back off the trim panel (on early-model vehicles) . . .

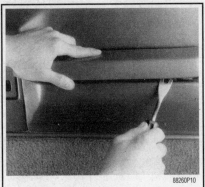

Fig. 29 . . . or carefully pry the armrest free (on late-model vehicles)

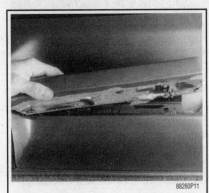

Fig. 30 Remove the armrest from the trim panel for access

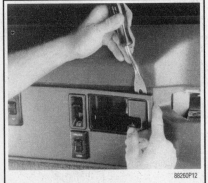

Fig. 31 CAREFULLY pry the door handle trim cover free and pull outward . . .

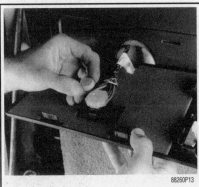

Fig. 32 If equipped, remove the wiring retainer by twisting . . .

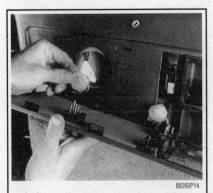

Fig. 33 . . . then disengage the wiring from the power lock and window switches

Fig. 34 Remove any trim panel retaining screws (like this one normally found under the armrest) . . .

➡There is usually at least one door trim panel retaining screw, located behind the armrest pad.

5. CAREFULLY pry the door trim panel plastic fasteners free using a trim panel removal tool. The door handle clip remover can also usually be used for this.

6. Remove the trim panel from the door.

7. Position the door trim panel to the door. On most models you will have to place the window seal portion of the panel OVER the door frame.

8. The remainder of installation is the reverse of removal.

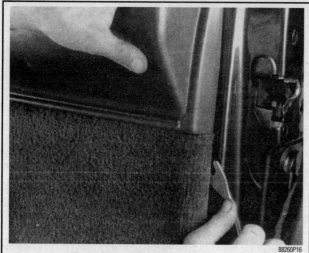

88260P16

**Fig. 35 . . . then remove the trim panel by CAREFULLY prying the plastic snap-fasteners free from the door**

## Door Glass and Regulator

REMOVAL & INSTALLATION

♦ **See Figure 36**

### ❊❊ CAUTION

**Always wear heavy gloves when handling glass to minimize the risk of injury!**

### Door Glass

1. Lower the glass to the bottom of the door and remove the door trim panel.
2. Remove the door channel run assembly.

➡**Mask or cover any sharp edges that could scratch the glass.**

3. Slide the glass forward until the front roller is in line with the notch in the sash channel.
4. Disengage the roller from the channel.
5. Push the window forward, then tilt it up until the rear roller is disengaged.

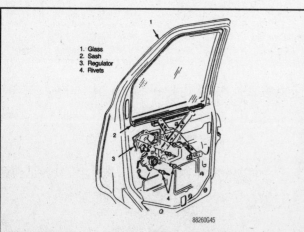

1. Glass
2. Sash
3. Regulator
4. Rivets

88260G45

**Fig. 36 Window regulator components and mounting**

6. Place the window in a level position, and raise it straight up and out of the door.
7. Installation is the reverse of the removal procedure.

### Regulator

1. Raise the window and tape the glass in the full up position using cloth body tape.
2. Remove the door trim panel and the door panel, then, using a ³⁄₁₆ in. (5mm) bit, drill the head from the rivet.
3. Slide the regulator forward and then rearward to disengage the rear roller from the sash channel. Then disengage the lower roller from the regulator rail.
4. Disengage the forward roller from the sash channel at the notch in the sash channel.
5. Collapse the regulator and remove it through the access hole in the door.
6. Lubricate the regulator and the sash channel and regulator rails with Lubriplate® or its equivalent.
7. Collapse the regulator and install it through the access hole in the door.
8. The remainder of installation is the reverse of the removal procedure.

### Power Window Regulator

1. Remove the negative battery cable.
2. Remove the door trim panel.
3. Remove the armrest bracket and water deflector.
4. Raise the window and tape the glass in the full up position using cloth body tape.
5. Remove the wiring harness from the regulator motor.
6. Remove the regulator to door rivets, using a ³⁄₁₆ in. (5mm) bit to drill the heads from the rivets.
7. Slide the regulator forward and then rearward to disengage the rear roller from the sash channel. Then disengage the lower roller from the regulator rail.
8. Disengage the forward roller from the sash channel at the notch in the sash channel.
9. Collapse the regulator and remove it through the access hole in the door.

**To install:**

10. Lubricate the regulator and install through the access hole in the door.
11. Engage the forward roller to the sash channel at the notch in the sash channel.
12. Slide the regulator forward and then rearward to engage the rear roller to the sash channel. Then engage the lower roller to the regulator rail.
13. Install the regulator to door rivets, using ³⁄₁₆ in. (5mm) rivets.
14. Install the remaining components in the reverse order of removal.
15. Connect the negative battery cable and check operation.

## Electric Window Motor

REMOVAL & INSTALLATION

♦ **See Figure 37**

1. Remove the power window regulator as described above.

### ❊❊ CAUTION

**Step 2 MUST be performed if the regulator motor is to be removed from the regulator. The regulator lift arms are under pressure from the counterbalance spring and can cause serious injury if the motor is removed without locking the sector gear in position.**

2. Install a pan head sheet metal tapping screw through the sector gear and the backing plate at the hole provided to lock the sector gear into position. Then drill out the motor to regulator attaching rivets.
3. Remove the motor from the regulator.
4. **To install,** lubricate the motor drive gear and the regulator sector teeth. Install the motor to the regulator and check the mesh of the motor to the regulator.
5. The remainder of installation is the reverse of removal.

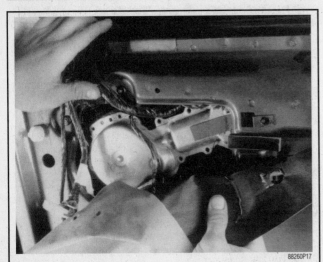

Fig. 37 To access the window motor, remove the door panel, then pull back the inner liner (water deflector)

## Inside Rearview Mirror

### REMOVAL & INSTALLATION

▶ **See Figure 38**

The rearview mirror is attached to a support which is secured to the windshield glass. A service replacement windshield glass has the support bonded to the glass assembly. To install a detached mirror support or install a new part, use the following procedures to complete the service.

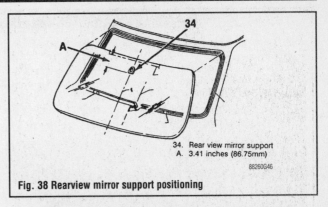

34. Rear view mirror support
A. 3.41 inches (86.75mm)

Fig. 38 Rearview mirror support positioning

1. Locate the support position at the center of the glass 86.75mm from the top of the glass to the top of the support.
2. Circle the location on the outside of the glass with a wax pencil or crayon. Draw a large circle around the support circle.
3. Clean the area within the circle with household cleaner and dry with a clean towel. Repeat the procedures using rubbing alcohol.
4. Sand the bonding surface of the support with fine grit (320–360) emery cloth or sandpaper. If the original support is being used, remove the old adhesive with rubbing alcohol and a clean towel.
5. Apply the adhesive as outlined in the kit instructions.
6. Position the support to the marked location with the rounded end UP.
7. Press the support to the glass for 30–60 seconds. Excessive adhesive can be removed after five minutes with rubbing alcohol.

**✳✳ CAUTION**

**Do NOT apply excessive pressure to the windshield glass. The glass may break, causing personal injury!**

## GLOSSARY

**AIR/FUEL RATIO:** The ratio of air-to-gasoline by weight in the fuel mixture drawn into the engine.

**AIR INJECTION:** One method of reducing harmful exhaust emissions by injecting air into each of the exhaust ports of an engine. The fresh air entering the hot exhaust manifold causes any remaining fuel to be burned before it can exit the tailpipe.

**ALTERNATOR:** A device used for converting mechanical energy into electrical energy.

**AMMETER:** An instrument, calibrated in amperes, used to measure the flow of an electrical current in a circuit. Ammeters are always connected in series with the circuit being tested.

**AMPERE:** The rate of flow of electrical current present when one volt of electrical pressure is applied against one ohm of electrical resistance.

**ANALOG COMPUTER:** Any microprocessor that uses similar (analogous) electrical signals to make its calculations.

**ARMATURE:** A laminated, soft iron core wrapped by a wire that converts electrical energy to mechanical energy as in a motor or relay. When rotated in a magnetic field, it changes mechanical energy into electrical energy as in a generator.

**ATMOSPHERIC PRESSURE:** The pressure on the Earth's surface caused by the weight of the air in the atmosphere. At sea level, this pressure is 14.7 psi at 32°F (101 kPa at 0°C).

**ATOMIZATION:** The breaking down of a liquid into a fine mist that can be suspended in air.

**AXIAL PLAY:** Movement parallel to a shaft or bearing bore.

**BACKFIRE:** The sudden combustion of gases in the intake or exhaust system that results in a loud explosion.

**BACKLASH:** The clearance or play between two parts, such as meshed gears.

**BACKPRESSURE:** Restrictions in the exhaust system that slow the exit of exhaust gases from the combustion chamber.

**BAKELITE:** A heat resistant, plastic insulator material commonly used in printed circuit boards and transistorized components.

**BALL BEARING:** A bearing made up of hardened inner and outer races between which hardened steel balls roll.

**BALLAST RESISTOR:** A resistor in the primary ignition circuit that lowers voltage after the engine is started to reduce wear on ignition components.

**BEARING:** A friction reducing, supportive device usually located between a stationary part and a moving part.

**BIMETAL TEMPERATURE SENSOR:** Any sensor or switch made of two dissimilar types of metal that bend when heated or cooled due to the different expansion rates of the alloys. These types of sensors usually function as an on/off switch.

**BLOWBY:** Combustion gases, composed of water vapor and unburned fuel, that leak past the piston rings into the crankcase during normal engine operation. These gases are removed by the PCV system to prevent the buildup of harmful acids in the crankcase.

**BRAKE PAD:** A brake shoe and lining assembly used with disc brakes.

**BRAKE SHOE:** The backing for the brake lining. The term is, however, usually applied to the assembly of the brake backing and lining.

**BUSHING:** A liner, usually removable, for a bearing; an anti-friction liner used in place of a bearing.

**CALIPER:** A hydraulically activated device in a disc brake system, which is mounted straddling the brake rotor (disc). The caliper contains at least one piston and two brake pads. Hydraulic pressure on the piston(s) forces the pads against the rotor.

**CAMSHAFT:** A shaft in the engine on which are the lobes (cams) which operate the valves. The camshaft is driven by the crankshaft, via a belt, chain or gears, at one half the crankshaft speed.

**CAPACITOR:** A device which stores an electrical charge.

**CARBON MONOXIDE (CO):** A colorless, odorless gas given off as a normal byproduct of combustion. It is poisonous and extremely dangerous in confined areas, building up slowly to toxic levels without warning if adequate ventilation is not available.

**CARBURETOR:** A device, usually mounted on the intake manifold of an engine, which mixes the air and fuel in the proper proportion to allow even combustion.

**CATALYTIC CONVERTER:** A device installed in the exhaust system, like a muffler, that converts harmful byproducts of combustion into carbon dioxide and water vapor by means of a heat-producing chemical reaction.

**CENTRIFUGAL ADVANCE:** A mechanical method of advancing the spark timing by using flyweights in the distributor that react to centrifugal force generated by the distributor shaft rotation.

**CHECK VALVE:** Any one-way valve installed to permit the flow of air, fuel or vacuum in one direction only.

**CHOKE:** A device, usually a moveable valve, placed in the intake path of a carburetor to restrict the flow of air.

**CIRCUIT:** Any unbroken path through which an electrical current can flow. Also used to describe fuel flow in some instances.

**CIRCUIT BREAKER:** A switch which protects an electrical circuit from overload by opening the circuit when the current flow exceeds a predetermined level. Some circuit breakers must be reset manually, while most reset automatically.

**COIL (IGNITION):** A transformer in the ignition circuit which steps up the voltage provided to the spark plugs.

**COMBINATION MANIFOLD:** An assembly which includes both the intake and exhaust manifolds in one casting.

**COMBINATION VALVE:** A device used in some fuel systems that routes fuel vapors to a charcoal storage canister instead of venting them into the atmosphere. The valve relieves fuel tank pressure and allows fresh air into the tank as the fuel level drops to prevent a vapor lock situation.

**COMPRESSION RATIO:** The comparison of the total volume of the cylinder and combustion chamber with the piston at BDC and the piston at TDC.

**CONDENSER:** 1. An electrical device which acts to store an electrical charge, preventing voltage surges. 2. A radiator-like device in the air conditioning system in which refrigerant gas condenses into a liquid, giving off heat.

**CONDUCTOR:** Any material through which an electrical current can be transmitted easily.

**CONTINUITY:** Continuous or complete circuit. Can be checked with an ohmmeter.

**COUNTERSHAFT:** An intermediate shaft which is rotated by a mainshaft and transmits, in turn, that rotation to a working part.

**CRANKCASE:** The lower part of an engine in which the crankshaft and related parts operate.

**CRANKSHAFT:** The main driving shaft of an engine which receives reciprocating motion from the pistons and converts it to rotary motion.

**CYLINDER:** In an engine, the round hole in the engine block in which the piston(s) ride.

**CYLINDER BLOCK:** The main structural member of an engine in which is found the cylinders, crankshaft and other principal parts.

**CYLINDER HEAD:** The detachable portion of the engine, usually fastened to the top of the cylinder block and containing all or most of the combustion chambers. On overhead valve engines, it contains the valves and their operating parts. On overhead cam engines, it contains the camshaft as well.

**DEAD CENTER:** The extreme top or bottom of the piston stroke.

**DETONATION:** An unwanted explosion of the air/fuel mixture in the combustion chamber caused by excess heat and compression, advanced timing, or an overly lean mixture. Also referred to as "ping".

**DIAPHRAGM:** A thin, flexible wall separating two cavities, such as in a vacuum advance unit.

**DIESELING:** A condition in which hot spots in the combustion chamber cause the engine to run on after the key is turned off.

**DIFFERENTIAL:** A geared assembly which allows the transmission of motion between drive axles, giving one axle the ability to turn faster than the other.

**DIODE:** An electrical device that will allow current to flow in one direction only.

**DISC BRAKE:** A hydraulic braking assembly consisting of a brake disc, or rotor, mounted on an axle, and a caliper assembly containing, usually two brake pads which are activated by hydraulic pressure. The pads are forced against the sides of the disc, creating friction which slows the vehicle.

**DISTRIBUTOR:** A mechanically driven device on an engine which is responsible for electrically firing the spark plug at a predetermined point of the piston stroke.

**DOWEL PIN:** A pin, inserted in mating holes in two different parts allowing those parts to maintain a fixed relationship.

**DRUM BRAKE:** A braking system which consists of two brake shoes and one or two wheel cylinders, mounted on a fixed backing plate, and a brake drum, mounted on an axle, which revolves around the assembly.

**DWELL:** The rate, measured in degrees of shaft rotation, at which an electrical circuit cycles on and off.

**ELECTRONIC CONTROL UNIT (ECU):** Ignition module, module, amplifier or igniter. See Module for definition.

**ELECTRONIC IGNITION:** A system in which the timing and firing of the spark plugs is controlled by an electronic control unit, usually called a module. These systems have no points or condenser.

**END-PLAY:** The measured amount of axial movement in a shaft.

**ENGINE:** A device that converts heat into mechanical energy.

**EXHAUST MANIFOLD:** A set of cast passages or pipes which conduct exhaust gases from the engine.

**FEELER GAUGE:** A blade, usually metal, or precisely predetermined thickness, used to measure the clearance between two parts.

**FIRING ORDER:** The order in which combustion occurs in the cylinders of an engine. Also the order in which spark is distributed to the plugs by the distributor.

**FLOODING:** The presence of too much fuel in the intake manifold and combustion chamber which prevents the air/fuel mixture from firing, thereby causing a no-start situation.

**FLYWHEEL:** A disc shaped part bolted to the rear end of the crankshaft. Around the outer perimeter is affixed the ring gear. The starter drive engages the ring gear, turning the flywheel, which rotates the crankshaft, imparting the initial starting motion to the engine.

**FOOT POUND (ft. lbs. or sometimes, ft.lb.):** The amount of energy or work needed to raise an item weighing one pound, a distance of one foot.

**FUSE:** A protective device in a circuit which prevents circuit overload by breaking the circuit when a specific amperage is present. The device is constructed around a strip or wire of a lower amperage rating than the circuit it is designed to protect. When an amperage higher than that stamped on the fuse is present in the circuit, the strip or wire melts, opening the circuit.

**GEAR RATIO:** The ratio between the number of teeth on meshing gears.

**GENERATOR:** A device which converts mechanical energy into electrical energy.

**HEAT RANGE:** The measure of a spark plug's ability to dissipate heat from its firing end. The higher the heat range, the hotter the plug fires.

**HUB:** The center part of a wheel or gear.

**HYDROCARBON (HC):** Any chemical compound made up of hydrogen and carbon. A major pollutant formed by the engine as a byproduct of combustion.

**HYDROMETER:** An instrument used to measure the specific gravity of a solution.

**INCH POUND (inch lbs.; sometimes in.lb. or in. lbs.):** One twelfth of a foot pound.

**INDUCTION:** A means of transferring electrical energy in the form of a magnetic field. Principle used in the ignition coil to increase voltage.

**INJECTOR:** A device which receives metered fuel under relatively low pressure and is activated to inject the fuel into the engine under relatively high pressure at a predetermined time.

**INPUT SHAFT:** The shaft to which torque is applied, usually carrying the driving gear or gears.

**INTAKE MANIFOLD:** A casting of passages or pipes used to conduct air or a fuel/air mixture to the cylinders.

**JOURNAL:** The bearing surface within which a shaft operates.

**KEY:** A small block usually fitted in a notch between a shaft and a hub to prevent slippage of the two parts.

**MANIFOLD:** A casting of passages or set of pipes which connect the cylinders to an inlet or outlet source.

**MANIFOLD VACUUM:** Low pressure in an engine intake manifold formed just below the throttle plates. Manifold vacuum is highest at idle and drops under acceleration.

**MASTER CYLINDER:** The primary fluid pressurizing device in a hydraulic system. In automotive use, it is found in brake and hydraulic clutch systems and is pedal activated, either directly or, in a power brake system, through the power booster.

**MODULE:** Electronic control unit, amplifier or igniter of solid state or integrated design which controls the current flow in the ignition primary circuit based on input from the pick-up coil. When the module opens the primary circuit, high secondary voltage is induced in the coil.

**NEEDLE BEARING:** A bearing which consists of a number (usually a large number) of long, thin rollers.

**OHM:** ($\Omega$) The unit used to measure the resistance of conductor-to-electrical flow. One ohm is the amount of resistance that limits current flow to one ampere in a circuit with one volt of pressure.

**OHMMETER:** An instrument used for measuring the resistance, in ohms, in an electrical circuit.

**OUTPUT SHAFT:** The shaft which transmits torque from a device, such as a transmission.

**OVERDRIVE:** A gear assembly which produces more shaft revolutions than that transmitted to it.

**OVERHEAD CAMSHAFT (OHC):** An engine configuration in which the camshaft is mounted on top of the cylinder head and operates the valve either directly or by means of rocker arms.

**OVERHEAD VALVE (OHV):** An engine configuration in which all of the valves are located in the cylinder head and the camshaft is located in the cylinder block. The camshaft operates the valves via lifters and pushrods.

**OXIDES OF NITROGEN (NOx):** Chemical compounds of nitrogen produced as a byproduct of combustion. They combine with hydrocarbons to produce smog.

**OXYGEN SENSOR:** Use with the feedback system to sense the presence of oxygen in the exhaust gas and signal the computer which can reference the voltage signal to an air/fuel ratio.

**PINION:** The smaller of two meshing gears.

**PISTON RING:** An open-ended ring with fits into a groove on the outer diameter of the piston. Its chief function is to form a seal between the piston and cylinder wall. Most automotive pistons have three rings: two for compression sealing; one for oil sealing.

**PRELOAD:** A predetermined load placed on a bearing during assembly or by adjustment.

**PRIMARY CIRCUIT:** the low voltage side of the ignition system which consists of the ignition switch, ballast resistor or resistance wire, bypass, coil, electronic control unit and pick-up coil as well as the connecting wires and harnesses.

**PRESS FIT:** The mating of two parts under pressure, due to the inner diameter of one being smaller than the outer diameter of the other, or vice versa; an interference fit.

**RACE:** The surface on the inner or outer ring of a bearing on which the balls, needles or rollers move.

**REGULATOR:** A device which maintains the amperage and/or voltage levels of a circuit at predetermined values.

**RELAY:** A switch which automatically opens and/or closes a circuit.

**RESISTANCE:** The opposition to the flow of current through a circuit or electrical device, and is measured in ohms. Resistance is equal to the voltage divided by the amperage.

**RESISTOR:** A device, usually made of wire, which offers a preset amount of resistance in an electrical circuit.

**RING GEAR:** The name given to a ring-shaped gear attached to a differential case, or affixed to a flywheel or as part of a planetary gear set.

**ROLLER BEARING:** A bearing made up of hardened inner and outer races between which hardened steel rollers move.

**ROTOR:** 1. The disc-shaped part of a disc brake assembly, upon which the brake pads bear; also called, brake disc. 2. The device mounted atop the distributor shaft, which passes current to the distributor cap tower contacts.

**SECONDARY CIRCUIT:** The high voltage side of the ignition system, usually above 20,000 volts. The secondary includes the ignition coil, coil wire, distributor cap and rotor, spark plug wires and spark plugs.

**SENDING UNIT:** A mechanical, electrical, hydraulic or electro-magnetic device which transmits information to a gauge.

**SENSOR:** Any device designed to measure engine operating conditions or ambient pressures and temperatures. Usually electronic in nature and designed to send a voltage signal to an on-board computer, some sensors may operate as a simple on/off switch or they may provide a variable voltage signal (like a potentiometer) as conditions or measured parameters change.

**SHIM:** Spacers of precise, predetermined thickness used between parts to establish a proper working relationship.

**SLAVE CYLINDER:** In automotive use, a device in the hydraulic clutch system which is activated by hydraulic force, disengaging the clutch.

**SOLENOID:** A coil used to produce a magnetic field, the effect of which is to produce work.

**SPARK PLUG:** A device screwed into the combustion chamber of a spark ignition engine. The basic construction is a conductive core inside of a ceramic insulator, mounted in an outer conductive base. An electrical charge from the spark plug wire travels along the conductive core and jumps a preset air gap to a grounding point or points at the end of the conductive base. The resultant spark ignites the fuel/air mixture in the combustion chamber.

**SPLINES:** Ridges machined or cast onto the outer diameter of a shaft or inner diameter of a bore to enable parts to mate without rotation.

**TACHOMETER:** A device used to measure the rotary speed of an engine, shaft, gear, etc., usually in rotations per minute.

**THERMOSTAT:** A valve, located in the cooling system of an engine, which is closed when cold and opens gradually in response to engine heating, controlling the temperature of the coolant and rate of coolant flow.

**TOP DEAD CENTER (TDC):** The point at which the piston reaches the top of its travel on the compression stroke.

**TORQUE:** The twisting force applied to an object.

**TORQUE CONVERTER:** A turbine used to transmit power from a driving member to a driven member via hydraulic action, providing changes in drive ratio and torque. In automotive use, it links the driveplate at the rear of the engine to the automatic transmission.

**TRANSDUCER:** A device used to change a force into an electrical signal.

**TRANSISTOR:** A semi-conductor component which can be actuated by a small voltage to perform an electrical switching function.

**TUNE-UP:** A regular maintenance function, usually associated with the replacement and adjustment of parts and components in the electrical and fuel systems of a vehicle for the purpose of attaining optimum performance.

**TURBOCHARGER:** An exhaust driven pump which compresses intake air and forces it into the combustion chambers at higher than atmospheric pressures. The increased air pressure allows more fuel to be burned and results in increased horsepower being produced.

**VACUUM ADVANCE:** A device which advances the ignition timing in response to increased engine vacuum.

**VACUUM GAUGE:** An instrument used to measure the presence of vacuum in a chamber.

**VALVE:** A device which control the pressure, direction of flow or rate of flow of a liquid or gas.

**VALVE CLEARANCE:** The measured gap between the end of the valve stem and the rocker arm, cam lobe or follower that activates the valve.

**VISCOSITY:** The rating of a liquid's internal resistance to flow.

**VOLTMETER:** An instrument used for measuring electrical force in units called volts. Voltmeters are always connected parallel with the circuit being tested.

**WHEEL CYLINDER:** Found in the automotive drum brake assembly, it is a device, actuated by hydraulic pressure, which, through internal pistons, pushes the brake shoes outward against the drums.

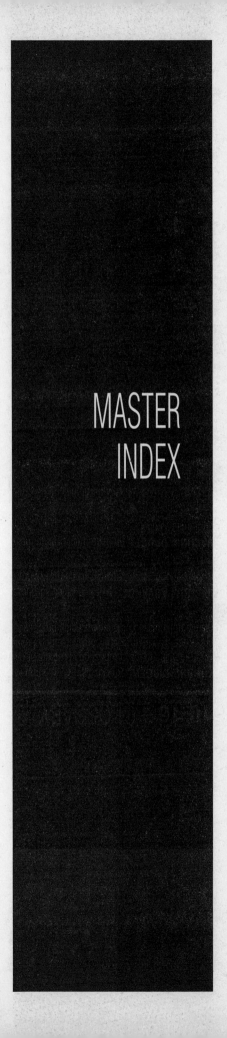

MASTER
INDEX